Words

This volume has emerged from a collaboration among:

The NWO Research Council for the Humanities (GW),
The NWO Research Council for Social Sciences (MaGW), and
The Netherlands Foundation for the Advancement of Tropical Research (WOTRO).

International Advisory Board

Veena Das, Chair
Christoph Auffarth
Peter Clarke
Galit Hasan-Rokem
Michael Lambek
Regina M. Schwartz

Netherlands Organisation for Scientific Research

THE FUTURE OF THE RELIGIOUS PAST

Hent de Vries, General Editor

In what sense are the legacies of religion–its powers, words, things, and gestures–disarticulating and reconstellating themselves as the elementary forms of life in the twenty-first century? This sequence of five volumes publishes work drawn from an international research project that seeks to answer this question.

Editorial Board

Meerten ter Borg
Jan Bremmer
Martin van Bruinessen
Jan Willem van Henten
Dick Houtman
Anne-Marie Korte
Birgit Meyer

Words

RELIGIOUS LANGUAGE MATTERS

ERNST VAN DEN HEMEL

and   ASJA SZAFRANIEC

Editors

FORDHAM UNIVERSITY PRESS   NEW YORK   2016

Copyright © 2016 Fordham University Press

All rights reserved. No part of this publication may be reproduced, stored in a retrieval system, or transmitted in any form or by any means—electronic, mechanical, photocopy, recording, or any other—except for brief quotations in printed reviews, without the prior permission of the publisher.

Fordham University Press has no responsibility for the persistence or accuracy of URLs for external or third-party Internet websites referred to in this publication and does not guarantee that any content on such websites is, or will remain, accurate or appropriate.

Fordham University Press also publishes its books in a variety of electronic formats. Some content that appears in print may not be available in electronic books.

Visit us online at www.fordhampress.com.

Library of Congress Control Number: 2015938860

Printed in the United States of America

18 17 16   5 4 3 2 1
First edition

in memory of
Helen Tartar

Contents

ix

Acknowledgments

This book is first and foremost indebted and dedicated to the late Helen Tartar. The start of our engagement with this publication, the conference "Words" in Groningen, unrolled itself against the backdrop of the sound of Helen's knitting needles. Far from being a deterrent, the thought of engaging relatively junior scholars as editors for this volume excited her. Helen had been a famous and infamous figure in our circle—famous for editing some of the most exciting volumes in our fields and infamous for starting to knit when she was less interested in the lecture that was given. Having the chance to work with her was a thrilling opportunity. During the construction of this book, she was a sagacious and humorous guide whose professionalism and degree of involvement exceeded by far that of the average academic editor. Her suggestions for enriching and broadening the scope of the volume combined with her impressive knowledge and network ensured that our shared wish to make this book more than a selection of conference proceedings was firmly entrenched since the beginning.

The tragic passing of Helen was a shock to us all. As our inbox and the Internet were buzzing with utterances of disbelief and testimonials to Helen's work, the true impact of Helen on the world of academic publishing became apparent also to those who did not know her.

We were now faced with the task of finishing a book that was two-thirds finished yet fully indebted to Helen. As many of the testimonials mentioned, Helen stated that her books were like her children. We hope to have continued this orphaned book with the energy, enthusiasm, and professionalism that characterized Helen's personality and approach to academic publishing.

The fact that a finished project lies in front of you now is thanks to a number of people who helped complete it. Next to Helen Tartar, this book is indebted to Hent de Vries, who conceptualized and made happen the very idea of having a series of volumes addressing the future of the religious past, each focusing on particular type of expression: Concepts, Things, Words, Gestures. Hent kept watch over the progress of the "futures" project from the very beginning, and when in the wake of

Helen's passing away the publication process seemed to be threatened, he was the first to make sure that Helen's and our work would not be lost.

Many people at Fordham University Press contributed to finish this project. We thank especially Tom Lay, Eric Newman, and Teresa Jesionowski for doing all in their power to pick up the project, with contributions at various stages of editing, searching for the most recent versions saved on Helen's computer. Bud Bynack, Helen's widower, was so generous to continue Helen's editing work, insisting on staying faithful to Helen's spirit. With his help, the final remaining parts of the book were also edited. But the contributors to this volume, whose patience was already tested by such a large multiauthor project, also showed their patience and understanding in the long process of publishing this book. We also acknowledge the staff at the Press for the professional manner with which they continued work after having lost such an important cornerstone of their publishing house.

A large number of people were instrumental in earlier phases of this book. First of all Jan Bremmer, organizer and original architect of the conference "Words," for his help at the initial stages of this publication. Michael Lambek, whose role was not limited to providing the opening essay of this book; his programmatic lecture at the Groningen conference also provided important inspiration for the book in general. We would like to acknowledge Birgit Meyer, whose wonderful predecessor of this volume, *Things*, raised the bar for our volume, for her insightful and productive comments on an early draft of the introduction. Burcht Pranger, director of the subproject "The Pastness of the Religious Past," for his sagacious support for us during the "Future of the Religious Past" project. We also thank the team of Religion, Secularism, and Political Belonging at the Centre for the Humanities of Utrecht University for their support during the final stages of this project. The funding of Netherlands Organisation for Scientific Research (NWO) was of course essential for the entire "Future of the Religious Past" project.

To conclude with Helen's own words, in a 2004 interview with *Fordham Magazine*, she described her attitude toward academic publishing, which formulates clearly the open spirit with which she worked with us on this volume: "[In academic publishing] you're a perpetual student. . . . You're constantly learning, even if [the authors] are much younger than you are." We hope to take this as a guide for our own future projects.

Words

Introduction

Any More Deathless Questions?

Asja Szafraniec and Ernst van den Hemel

So, any other deathless questions?

—Robert Creeley

It is something miraculous that words can mean at all, that such things can
be said, that there are words.

—Stanley Cavell

It is sometimes said that words are like people in that one can encounter
them daily and yet not come to know their true selves. In any case, the
meaning of words tends to involve more than can be grasped by resort-
ing to a dictionary. This definitely seems to be the case for the word
"religion," as well as for the many words that it draws to itself. Despite its
ubiquity today, merely encountering the word in everyday discourse
does not necessarily lead to a better understanding of it. Sometimes the
familiarity of a word actually occludes its sense or its multiple senses,
which will be revealed only after the word is examined in contrasting
contexts and under competing angles of approach. And debates since at
least the 1970s have shown that the understanding of the word "religion"
is continuously shifting. Just as the boundaries between religion and
other spaces in society, such as politics, law, or science, are not as clear
cut and as stable as they were once perceived to be, there is no stable
definition of the word "religion" itself. For a long time, since the Reformation and certainly since the Enlightenment, the assumption prevailed
that secularization produced a growing dichotomy between the public
sphere and an increasingly private religious sphere, implying a sort of
stability in the meaning of both terms, even as their relations shifted.
However, the impression of the progressive triumph of secularization

over religion has been countered by more nuanced scholarly appraisals of secularism, as well as by contemporary political events.

At the beginning of the twenty-first century, global debates about fundamentalisms and about the way in which religion intersects with the problematic fields of secularism, power, violence, modernity, political liberalism, democracy, and individual freedom and debates about the nature and the future of religion itself have given rise to a new scholarly challenge: how to address religion without embracing unwarranted grand histories that tend to be invoked by certain connotations of the word. At the same time, it became clear that the very notion of religion itself and the desire to grasp it conceptually can themselves be part and parcel of a grand history, placing religion squarely in opposition to its classical counterparts, politics, law, or science.[1]

What is in question here is how we can speak of religion. This question is not just limited to the status of language in religious practices but also involves the implicit and explicit conceptualizations of language that is used to make sense of religion, both inside academic practice and in societies. This volume does not seek to supply the last word about the word "religion" or about the many words that are associated with it. Instead, it restages the question, gauging not only in what ways religion has been spoken about in the past, but also how it is possible to speak about religion anew. Instead of trying to establish once and for all the notoriously unstable boundaries of the notion of religion, it embraces the ongoing evolution of the term as a necessary part of speaking about religion, recognizing that, as Hent de Vries has put it, "'religion' is nothing outside or independent of the series of its metamorphoses, its metastases."[2] Its manifestations are not the instantiation of a common concept, but phenomena exhibiting at most a set of family resemblances at different historical moments and in different geographical locations. It is thus impossible to do justice to the phenomena of religion without conceding that the "analytic coherence, discreteness, and universality of the category of religion are problematic."[3] The series to which the present volume is a contribution consequently approaches religion via the study of the singular or the particular—things, gestures, powers,[4] or, in this case, words—rather than starting out from some purported universal, such as the concept of religion.[5] Following upon earlier volumes, the contributions presented here assess the present and the future of religion by examining the status of words, expressions, and vocabularies associated either with religious contexts (ritual speech, prophecy, divination, magic, myth, and more) or with discourse(s) about religion.

And the focus here is indeed on words, not on the putatively universal category of language. It is true that our views of religion are influenced by how we understand the nature and origins of language, and beginning with the so-called "linguistic turn" in the 1970s, the way in which language is understood has dominated many approaches to the several domains of the humanities and the human sciences for the past several decades. But conceptions of the nature and origins of language have themselves been so various and varied that the coherence, discreteness, and universality of that category is

2

problematic and in flux, as well. While the category of "language" may be advanced as universal, how it is conceptualized dissolves into a variety of particular preconceptions about the nature of language—as simply referring to things, as a system of signs and associated concepts, or as performative of actions in the world, among others.

Our views of religion are most directly manifest in our attachments to particular words—our penchant to privilege certain senses or aspects of certain words above others. But our views of religion are also concerned with an understanding of what words in general are. The famous biblical phrase from John 1:1 "In the beginning was the Word," taken up in a collection of books known as the Word of God, a word whose meaning is to be deciphered, is just one example around which a particular conceptualization of and interaction with words takes central stage. But of course, there are many more. This volume discusses religious words in practices ranging from tantric repetitions of words void of meaning (Karmen MacKendrick) to ritual repetition of the word "God" in Sufi prayers (Michael Lambek), from Irish magic spells (Jacqueline Borsje) to the transformation of flesh into word in medieval Kabbalah (Elliot Wolfson). But this volume not only offers analyses of words in religious practice. The sheer variety of practices into which religious words are taken up calls for a revisiting of the various dominant "semiotic ideologies" that determine our relationship with words. Originally coined by Webb Keane and discussed by Michael Lambek in the introductory essay in this volume, the concept of semiotic ideology functions as a way to discuss "basic assumptions about what signs are and how they function in the world." It is semiotic ideology that determines "what people will consider the role that intentions play in signification to be, what kinds of possible agent (humans only? Animals? Spirits?) exist to which acts of signification might be imputed, whether signs are arbitrary or necessarily linked to their objects, and so forth."[6]

Semiotic ideology determines different approaches to religious words, for instance. Whereas in some contexts correct repetition is seen as a central element of religious practice, in others, sincerity and authenticity are seen as more important. Between many of these instances, what a word means or does differs radically. "Faith," "materiality," "sincerity," "agency"—all these terms are dependent on semiotic ideology. Keane highlights how certain dominant modes of thinking about how words and things interrelate can be traced back to Protestant Christian origins. The prevalence of the spiritual over the material is an example of a mode of thinking that resonates with a Protestant sensitivity, to the detriment of other practices. The emphasis on spirituality over materiality and of inwardness over exteriority has also influenced the scientific approach to religious words. This influence can bee seen in the obviously pejorative characterizations of "nonrational" "fetish" religions that characterized scientific approaches to religion well into the twentieth century, but it can also be seen to steer more recent approaches to religious words. In a reading of the theory of Ferdinand de Saussure, which was highly influential during the "linguistic turn," Keane emphasizes how deeply engrained the dematerialization of signifying practices has become. By highlighting how the separation of signifier and signified

3

is part of a distinction between "signs and the world," "what Saussure called *semiology* concerned only virtual types, never concrete tokens."[7] This, according to Keane (and others), has been part of a "dematerialization" and a skewed and biased outlook on religious practices.

Keane's critical stance toward this dematerialization of signifying practices, his criticism of the approach to religion during the "linguistic turn," and his emphasis on the problematic boundaries between word and thing, meaning and form, has been highly influential in the reevaluation of materiality. One of the things that has been less extensively discussed, however, is what this critical reevaluation means when we return to that vestige of internal, spiritual meaning, the word. What is the effect of trying to do away with unwarranted Protestant forms of approaching language for the analysis of words in religion?

We would like to highlight two principal productive perspectives on the relationship between religion and words. The first is informed by the turn to materiality, the second by the performative dimensions of language. Both developments help in thinking beyond the opposition between the spiritual and the material, between any inner and outer dimensions of language. These debates have generated a lot of new work concerning the material aspects of religion and the material effects of language. Yet they also generate new questions. What about inwardness? Sincerity? Discursivity? Informed by these approaches, how can we revisit the topic of words?

As this volume will argue, these debates are much helped by a discussion of the "turn to the ordinary" as described in the work of J. L. Austin and Stanley Cavell. This perspective, without renouncing the idea of materiality or performativity, acknowledges the fundamental discursivity of words, calling for interpretation and explanations: "Every sign *by itself* seems dead."[8] But let us begin with one of the principal critical responses to Protestant-inspired modes of conceptualizing language and the "linguistic turn": the turn to materiality.[9] For it is the "material turn" that has given an impetus to the study of religion, taking its distance from the semiotic ideology that has guided approaches to religion, meaning, and words.

Materiality, Performativity, and the "Material Turn" in Religion

According to Dick Houtman and Birgit Meyer in another volume in this series, *Things: Religion and the Question of Materiality*, words need to be "rematerialized," that is, we should revaluate them as forms of outward behavior.[10] This call for the rematerialization of words follows a more general shift in religious studies away from approaches that understand religion in terms of personal experience, immediate encounters with the divine, inward belief, and, more generally, in terms of meaning and content, a shift toward interest in "media, form and outward behavior,"[11] part of a broader call for a revaluation of the "magical, orgiastic, ecstatic, and ritual elements of religiosity."[12] Thus, for example, in this volume, Jacqueline Borsje describes the context of magic spells in medieval Ireland, where tracing words with a finger on an object or bringing a sacred manuscript in contact with it was taken to have healing or protective effects.

What are the consequences of this turn to the materiality for words? One possible reaction would be to focus on the "flesh" of words, whether vocal or graphic, as opposed to their psychological status as signs of concepts—to treat them as that from which the mental is subtracted. In "Words and Word-Bodies: Writing the Religious Body" in this volume, Loriliai Biernacki thus proposes a notion of language that is "divorced from its semantic function," emphasizing "free-floating meaningless syllables," rather than "meaning-bearing components," and claiming that the purely material language of the mantra "points to a quality of language that is mostly neglected in the West."

While this way of looking at language is possible from within some traditions, as Biernacki demonstrates, she always warns against turning the mental or the spiritual into a mere epiphenomenon of the material practices. This would amount to reproducing the much-criticized binary logic according to which the material is excluded from the spiritual, simply reversing the hierarchy. In this context, it is also important to remember that one of the most powerful critics of the view according to which we use words merely to represent meaning, Maurice Merleau-Ponty, was also just as critical of what he called the "mechanistic" understanding of language, where all that is at stake is the reproduction of the word or a syllable and where uttering a word becomes primarily a physiological phenomenon.[13] When the meaning of a word is disregarded, Locke's old charge that this is like talking like a parrot, without understanding, still needs to be refuted.[14] Are such utterances even words? Jean-Luc Nancy, who identifies words with concepts, argues in "The Name *God* in Blanchot" in this volume that terms such as "being" or "neutral" "are words (concepts), whereas God is a name (without concept)," so even names (such as the name of God) cannot, strictly speaking, be called words.[15] The challenge is analogous to what Webb Keane saw as the main challenge in thinking about things: "The goal is to open up social analysis to the historicity and social power of material things without reducing them either to being only vehicles of meaning, on the one hand, or ultimate determinants, on the other"[16]

The rematerialization that is called for, in short, does not involve a simple repudiation of all meaning, but rather only a repudiation of meaning that pretends to emancipate itself from its material basis, presenting itself as independent and radically distinct from the material medium that carries it. The material quality of words, which is frequently mistaken as merely the "medium" of an independent mental message, its cloak or garb, and hence as something that potentially could efface itself or become wholly transparent, must instead be understood as what is simultaneously, to borrow Marshall McLuhan's phrase, the medium *and* the message.[17] To rematerialize words is to acknowledge this inseparability, so that the word's incarnate form does not alienate what it allows to be thought. Adapting the call for the revaluation of the role of media in religion to the problem field of words, we might say with Birgit Meyer that to rematerialize words is to "vest the mediation in which [they] take part with some sense of immediacy."[18]

This focus on the materiality of words is part of a movement that aims to offer an antidote to the Western-centered, post-Enlightenment Protestant perspective in which meaning has a central place and religion becomes a matter of (unfathomable) individual belief. For example, the tendency attributed to post-Enlightenment liberal Protestantism to seek a sense of immediacy (say, of God) beyond the medium of words, an immediacy merely transmitted by words, rather than in them (the claim, for example, that it is not the form of the prayer that is important, but its sincerity), should be countered by acknowledging the immediacy of the media itself—that what counts is the ritual of pronouncing certain particular words and phrases.[19] But to the extent that this antidote involves a focus on the flesh of words—the desire to see words in the flesh again, the flesh invested with spiritual power—it is good to remember that this antidote is in itself hardly religiously and culturally neutral, brought up as it is from a tradition in which the materialization of the religious has a particular heritage and pedigree—in which the word indeed supposedly has become flesh.[20] Emphasizing materiality, focusing on the surface of the ritual, generates questions concerning the inward experience of it. The distinction between surface and inwardness, while considered questionable by some advocates of the material turn, cannot be abandoned, if only in view of the problems that skepticism raises about the impossibility of fathoming individual belief—of knowing other minds.

A similar challenge is offered by the second materialist perspective that we want to highlight, which is the performative aspect of words.[21] If words say something meaningful to us, it is because the words themselves, as material objects, often come to us infused with significance, spiritualized or otherwise credited with an emphatic sense of presentness, force, or monumentality. They have effects. The use of and response to words in religious contexts might thus be conceived of as primarily a matter of seeking performative felicity, which suggests that words are like gestures. Our use of language, as Merleau-Ponty puts it, is a form of "verbal 'gesticulation.'"[22] Beyond the familiar use of words as symbols, words are extensions of our bodies: means of intervention, of poking or prodding at the world, occasionally with the power to heal and to produce injury. Religious words are treated as things autonomously incarnating meaning and exuding this meaning. But if they do have this causal link to reality, it is not on their own account (as things, or even as signifiers), but on account of us, the gesticulating bodies who use, hear, or read them. Whether they are spoken or written, they are invested with a feature of "holiness," with a supernatural power of seduction (as Karmen MacKendrick argues in "Prayer: Addressing the Name" in this volume) or with the "sensual presence of the greatest imaginable intensity."[23] Such words are then conceived not as "merely" mediating vehicles for some mental content but as the *source* of the mental content.

Thinking about words as performative, as in prayer or in rituals, generates questions concerning the status and importance of inwardness of meaning, shifting the burden of performative felicity from the speaker's true intention or commitment to the cause to the presence of a certain context, audience, and in case the latter is conceived very broadly, eventually to nature or divine powers. (If the rain ritual does not work, it is nature that is at fault.) Performative felicity remains an important topic, if only because not all our word uses are felicitous. Every religion faces the possibility that the prayer may not be answered or the magic spell may not work, which in turn might lead to skepticism regarding the question whether the conditions of the performance have been fulfilled.[24] Has the inner attitude been right? Have the holy words been pronounced with appropriate dignity? Has the prayer been sufficiently engaging? As Jan Assmann notes in his contribution to this volume, "Inscriptional Violence and the Art of Cursing: A Study of Performative Writing," fundamental uncertainty about the felicity of performatives is a problem of "every . . . writing that makes claims to eternity."[25] Using words (in prayer and otherwise) thus is not a matter of mechanistic causality, but indeed a form "verbal 'gesticulation.'" In short, an approach that de-emphasizes or seeks to sublate inwardness in the name of the focus on performativity generates questions concerning the status of lived experience that safeguards the ritual.

We cannot but conclude that while words are not merely the garb of meaning, they are not merely material objects, either (such as calligraphic ornaments or articulate sounds), nor are they merely forms of outward behavior. An experience of words that does not include conveying a meaning, whether intended or not, or signifying, and of doing so always in context, is no longer an experience of words, but an acoustic or visual experience—which does not preclude its being spiritual, as in case of glossolalia or ritual calligraphy.

The performativity of religious words (their having efficacy) can be seen in a vitalist context. The words are vibrant with life and produce their effects on their own account or ascribe their results to the working of ideology, self-induced or not: "Move your lips in prayer and you will believe," to speak with Pascal. But in this volume, we argue that something more is needed. Phenomena such as the "absentheist" versions of the discourse on God (see Nancy's reading of Blanchot in this volume) or the discourses of negative or mystical theology (as discussed below by Jean-Luc Marion), or such elusive ways of speaking of religion as Cavell's, point to another vantage point. In religion, the words said or written also need to be seen as part of a discourse involving questioning the significance of what is said, as involving persuasion—a discourse requiring interpretation, or, in Austin's language, involving questions concerning the inherent discursivity of perlocutionary utterances.

Unlike in an illocutionary act that does what it says (for example, "I do" in marriage) and that is designed to fit neatly in the ready-made context of its ritual, a perlocutionary act does something else *by* what it says (it can move me, scare me off, influence me) *and* is improvised (there is no conventional procedure, which is to be executed "correctly and completely" by people "having certain thoughts and feelings" who "must in the future so behave"). Cavell called Austin's privileging of the illocutionary act (and the consequent privileging of it in scholarly work on performativity) "a catastrophe in his theory."[26] What Cavell wants by emphasizing the perlocutionary type of utterances is to take "Austin's picture beyond performance as ritual." To do so, he not only needs to go beyond the illocutionary acts, but also needs to focus on a certain group of perlocutionary acts that Cavell calls "passionate utterances" that is, "judgments directed by one person to another," such as "I am bored" or "I love you." It is typical of passionate utterances that they require interpretation.[27] To say that interpretation is characteristic part of those utterances—that they hence frequently need explanation—is to say that they are fundamentally discursive, involving questioning of their significance, explanation, and persuasion, and hence inferential in the sense that they participate in our activity of "giving and asking for reasons." (This is true for Cavell, if not for negative theology.)

In one of his lectures, Robert Brandom observed that some of Wittgenstein's language games are not, properly speaking, *language* games, because they are not inferential, that is, they do not involve giving and asking for reasons. Would Brandom consider religion such a game? Or perhaps only some manifestations of it? Do we need to choose between religion as a form of inferential discourse or religion as extralinguistic? Cavell's work in any case offers a possibility of—no, calls for—including religion in discourse. Cavell considers doing so necessary because while a "performative utterance is an offer of participation in the order of law," "a passionate utterance is an invitation to improvisation in the disorders of desire."[28] In other words, the illocutionary utterance (the ritual) symbolizes the degree to which we are determined, but the perlocutionary utterance signifies the degree to which we are free. To give up the discursive dimension of religious words is to give up freedom. It is because of this that, instead of distancing itself from belief, Cavell's thought remains critically open to it, on the assumption that religion is not a set of unchangeable dogmas, but a body of thought with which one can quarrel.

The change in thinking about language—emphasizing the ongoing use of words and often addressed as a critique of the referential character of language—influences the very core of the debate about religion, bearing its imprint on our thinking about religion as a unified phenomenon. Emphasizing the ongoing use of words in religion puts in question the purported specificity of its language or the assumptions about the common ground or source of its phenomena. (Sometimes it is held that religion has its common ground in subjective experience, sometimes, on the contrary, in participation in a set of practices.) While what religion is consequently becomes problematic—whether there is a religious language, whether there is a universal source of religion—other questions become more prominent. These are questions not so much about the essence of a phenomenon arrested in time and captured by concepts, but about the continuation of (to use Wittgenstein's formulation) the "understanding of a game as we go on." Emphasizing the ongoing use of words in religion involves understanding its in-depth entwinements with other games, its hidden sources of life. The central problematic is then changed: from questions about religion and secularism as if these were stable domains to a questioning of what it means to inherit religion as a ongoing possibility, or at least to inherit a culture that is infused with religion, and what ways there are of responding to it.

The words of the everyday are in a lot of respects unlike philosophical or scientific concepts. Their use does not presuppose the clear-cut application of a definition, or an exhaustive set of rules for their application, or a metaphysical reality. When their use is felicitous, they convey to their addressee only as much as is needed for that instant and for that particular use. Moreover, their conceptual boundaries may change from one language game to another and are never established once and for all, since, as Veena Das points out, this language is never a totality and is "mastered only in fragments."

This is also visible in Talal Asad's interest in the movement of concepts in history. (Asad has repeatedly acknowledged his debt to Wittgenstein.) In his account, the development of a new doctrine, leads to the coming into being of a new concept and presupposes an often implicit change in other concepts—for example, "secularism" presupposes a new concept of "religion." In this sense, much of Asad's work is essentially a study of the constant movement and evolution of concepts with respect to one another—of the changing distribution of meaning between them, as well as of the evolution of the hidden dividing lines within what looks like a single conceptual category ("secular" and "secularism," for example).[29]

If constitutive insecurity in language is indeed part and parcel of the life of religious words, the approach to religious words should perhaps likewise take this sense of indeterminacy and insecurity into account. A core characteristic of Keane's notion of semiotic ideology is "openness." It is this openness that "perpetually threatens to destabilize semiotic ideologies."[30] Instead of contributing once more to the heap of definitions, it might be more productive to see the religious words as perpetually challenging academic frameworks. In a blog named after Charles Taylor's concept of the "immanent frame"—the context that frames our reality to such a degree that we do not even notice its implications—there is a section titled "Deathless Questions."[31] This section is named after the question that American poet Robert Creeley used to ask his students during a lull in class discussions: "So, any other deathless questions?" Speaking of religion may amount to asking deathless questions within immanent frames.

Perspectives

The present volume offers a spectrum of perspectives on these matters. It pays attention to how linguists, philosophers, and anthropologists conceive what words are and what they do; it considers the implications of the focus on the material appearance of words and on words as they are chanted, recited, calligraphed, or chiseled in stone; finally, it addresses the preconceptions connected to the everyday dimension of language. The volume also focuses on the effect that the prevalence of these perspectives may have had on the academic study of religion and on the understanding of the meaning of religious practices by religious subjects themselves. In doing so, it seeks to offer a vantage point that might take into account the problems posed by speaking about religion without falling into entrenched disciplinary positions or simply repeating unquestioned presuppositions, whether these involve the focus on the exclusively material qualities of words or on their intended meaning. The volume thus seeks to provide a specific point of focus for rethinking how to speak about religion by addressing our conceptions of the nature of speaking itself—the act, its objectives, its material ingredients, and more.

Part I, "What Are Words?" opens with two papers directly exploring the common ground of the majority of approaches to the relation between religion and language—that is, the various dimensions of performativity. The three papers that follow examine other traditions. In "Word as Act: Varieties of Semiotic Ideology in the Interpretation of Religion," Michael Lambek, drawing on the work of Roy A. Rappaport, provides background for the ensuing discussions by examining three widely held presuppositions about the nature of language, showing in what way each of them determines our understanding of religious phenomena. In particular, Lambek shows how investment in the performative force of words (whether illocutionary or perlocutionary) influences our understanding of religion. In the chapter that follows, Jacqueline Borsje similarly addresses the field of performativity. In "Medieval Irish Spells: 'Words of Power' as Performance," she focuses on examples of magic spells recorded in medieval Irish manuscripts so as to reconstruct the working of a performative mode of language use specifically requiring (or mobilizing) belief in its (magic) power (whether in the intrinsic power of words themselves or in the power conferred on them by intervention of a divine being), making it a form of speech act characteristic of religion and ritual. The subsequent two chapters offer different perspectives on the role of words in religious discourse, emphasizing their material aspects or their relation to matter. In "Inscriptional Violence and the Art of Cursing: A Study of Performative Writing," Jan Assmann emphasizes not only the performative dimension of curses, but also its ties to the inherent insecurity of words as expressed in any practice of writing that claims a connection to eternity. Loriliai Biernacki, in "Words and Word-Bodies: Writing the Religious Body," focuses on tantric practice to analyze the intense bond between words and the bodies that can be said to be construed in them. Finally, in "Flesh Become Word: Textual Embodiment and Poetic Incarnation," Elliot Wolfson addresses the textual nature of bodiliness: Taking inspiration from Merleau-Ponty's ontology of the "flesh" of things, understood as a dimension shared by subject and object, he juxtaposes the Christian idea of the incarnation of word (in the person of Jesus) with the transfiguration of flesh into word in medieval Kabbalah, where the body of words of the Torah is the poetic incarnation of what exists in the world, the "hypertext" revealing the "semantic character of nature."

From the field of words conceptualized as immanent events, Part II, "Religious Vocabularies," addresses significant words associated with the context of religion, either vocabularies drawn from religious texts and rituals or vocabularies mobilized on the account of examining religious phenomena, linking them to their historical, social, and cultural contexts.

In "Semantic Differences, or 'Judaism'/'Christianity,'" Daniel Boyarin discusses the evolution of some of the most potent terms in the history of religious vocabularies—"Judaism" and "Christianity." His "inquiry into how language produces social 'facts' and how social facts produce language," deals with "Christianity" and "Judaism" as the "names for a difference that we call 'religions.'" In the short piece that follows, "The Name *God* in Blanchot," Jean-Luc Nancy derives from Blanchot's work a seminal insight that will prove an important factor in Nancy's subsequent thought on Christianity: In the work of the atheist Blanchot, the name *God* (which, according to Nancy, is not a word, but a name whose role is to address the infinite "absenting of sense"), although it does not signify, retains its function as a nonsignifier: "It never stops not making sense." The relevance retained by the name *God* for Blanchot, despite his overt investment in atheism, with which Blanchot explicitly connects the practice of writing, opens up a new way of thinking about religion for Nancy, "absentheism," a mode of religion "beyond all positing of an object of belief or disbelief," which informs much of his thought about Christianity. This short text by Nancy is framed and situated by a more extensive contribution titled "Humanism's Cry: On Infinity in Religion and Absence in Atheism—A Conversation with Blanchot and Nancy" by Laurens ten Kate in which he explores the Blanchotian roots of Nancy's project (and the Hegelian roots of Blanchot's own), devoting particular attention to Nancy's conceptualization of infinity as inseparable from finitude. Ten Kate subsequently applies the consequences of this line of thinking to the old binary opposition between humanism and religion while questioning whether the two are really that far apart in this theoretical framework. In the fourth contribution to this part, "Intuition, Interpellation, Insight: Elements of a Theory of Conversion," Nils Schott argues for a renewed philosophical approach to and conceptualization of conversion. Schott points to the similarities between the philosopher's task in giving duration to intuition, according to Bergson, and the task of the convert to give duration to his conversion, and he suggests seeing Louis Althusser's notion of interpellation as way of conceptualizing conversion. In a reading of Augustine's *Confessions*, Schott provides a way of conceptualizing the conversion narrative, "in which nothing has really changed, nothing will ever be the same," without giving up the philosophical importance of conversion.

So far, Part II has addressed specific words, names, or concepts, but Christoph Auffarth offers a more general vantage point from which to consider the very idea of concept or conceptualization. In "Allowed and Forbidden Words: Canon and Censorship in *Grundbegriffe*, Critical Terms, Encyclopedias," he discusses the recent transition from an "age of lexicons" to "an age of companions." He argues that the *Grundbegriffe* of religion, the terms used in lexicons and encyclopedias to define and limit the field of study, have shown themselves to be inescapably fluid and dynamic. By tracing interactions between practices of religion and their lexical definitions, Auffarth, influenced by Wittgenstein, argues for a study of religion that departs from using "normative terms" and that is geared toward a dynamic notion of religion as a belonging to a constellation of "family resemblances." The study of religion, a phenomenon whose terms are in constant flux, he argues, should focus on the history of its problems, instead of on definitions.

Part III of this volume, "Transmitting and Translating the Implicit," moves the focus from vocabularies to the space between performative felicity and the ungraspable dimensions of religious language: the transmission and translation of the implicit dimension in religious traditions. In "God Lisped: Divine Accommodation and Cracks in Calvin's Scriptural Voice," Ernst van den Hemel proposes a new interpretation of the notion of accommodation in the work of John Calvin. Following the work of James Simpson and Brian Cummings, van den Hemel focuses on the notion of "divine accommodation," described by John Calvin as God "lisping" to humanity. The continuously expanding scope of accommodation problematizes both interior meaning and performative felicity and sheds new light on the tension between doubt and affirmation that lies at the heart of Protestant textuality. Focusing on the Jewish tradition, Sergey Dolgopolski, in "Rethinking the Implicit: Fragments of the Project on Aggada and Halakhah in Walter Benjamin," addresses the question of how we should understand the notion of the implicit as a topos for the transmission of Talmudic tradition: The function of "the machinery of mistake" in the interpretation of the Talmud is to keep implicit what always was implicit and cannot be articulated—what articulation cannot articulate. In a response to speech-act theory, Jean-Luc Marion, in "What Cannot Be Said: Apophasis and the Discourse of Love," revisits the debate around negative theology in order to assess its problematics with the conceptual apparatus of ordinary-language philosophy. By discussing the language game connected to the utterance "I love you," he identifies a new field (not limited to the religious experience alone) in the form of a language game that can dispense with affirmation and negation, truth and falsity, and still remain meaningful to those who engage in it. Tarek Dika's "Givenness and the Basic Problems of Phenomenology" then closes this part, addressing the transmission of the theological into philosophy. Focusing on Jean-Luc Marion's philosophical project, Dika employs "revelation" as a way to test the possibility of phenomenology as a philosophy capable of accounting for "the theological." Dika raises the question whether Marion's phenomenology can account for revelation, which Marion says is "the theological phenomenon par excellence."

Part IV, titled "Situating Oneself via Language," leaves the problems of transmission and examines the way in which certain unacknowledged historical modalities of language have influenced the formation of religious traditions. In "Prayer: Addressing the Name," Karmen MacKendrick discusses the possibility of situating oneself in a particular modality of language use that brings its subject into a singular relation with the divine (even if it is a relation with "a certain absence"): prayer. She offers an analysis of this modality and of the nature of the relation it makes possible, emphasizing its desirous, even erotic or seductive quality. Drawing on the work of Jean-Luc Nancy and Maurice Blanchot, among others, MacKendrick directs particular attention to such aspects of prayer as the nonreferentiality of the name to which the prayer addresses itself (which also dislocates the position of the speaker), to prayerful genres (praise, repetition, lamentation), and to the corporeality of prayer (the prayer is a prayer of a body, and it is incorporated in a particular use of language, attentive for example, to sound). In "A Quarrel with God: Cavell on Wittgenstein and Hegel," Asja Szafraniec argues that the sense of "religion" or of whatever may come to take its place spells itself out in the ordinary language, the environment of our "fight for recognition or 'quarrel' with God." Szafraniec examines the nature of the project that Cavell calls the "rescue of language" by superposing Wittgenstein's reflection on seeing aspects (we cannot see both the rabbit and the duck in Joseph Jastrow's famous drawing) on the traditional reading of Hegelian "fight for recognition." In her reading, Hegelian enslavement is understood in terms of a failure of an aspect (of meaning) to dawn. In "Thinking about the Secular Body, Pain, and Liberal Politics," Talal Asad offers a different vantage point on the relation between language and our conceptions of religion, inquiring what the language of the body, in particular, the experience of pain, tells us about the distinction between the religious and the secular. Asad suggests that the distinction between the secular roots of representative democracy and the religious roots of the democratic ethos can be elucidated in terms of the knowledge we gain from understanding human attitudes toward pain (sadism, hypochondria, masochism). In "The Rise of Literal-Mindedness," Peter Burke then examines the complex ways in which human investment in the metaphorical or literal aspects of language can influence the development of religions. Burke proposes a new "master narrative" in which the rise of literal-mindedness is seen as less linear than it is represented in many current master narratives and in which multiplying the connections between microhistory and macrohistory becomes a part of writing the history of literal-mindedness. In "From *Star Wars* to Jediism: The Emergence of Fiction-based Religion," Markus Altena Davidsen presents an analysis of a form of religion, "Jediism," that has its roots in the fictional universe of the *Star Wars* movies. Focusing on the boundaries between fiction and reality in literature, Davidsen shows how words can conjure up a space in which the lines between the two are blurred. Part IV ends with "The Words of the Martyr: Media, Martyrdom, and the Construction of a Community," in which Pieter Nanninga analyzes suicide attacks as "messages." In tuning his ear to what these "performances" have to say and in what ways they are staged, Nanninga aims to expand traditional views of communication to include the use of violence as a way to communicate. Seen in this light, suicide attacks are shown to be intimately tied to issues surrounding the grounding of communities. Furthermore, close readings of the highly mediatized messages surrounding these attacks shed light on the complex interweavings of identity, religion, and violence in an increasingly mediatized world.

The volume closes with Part V, "Religious Language and Nationalism," examining ways in which religious language use founds national communities. Part V examines the ways words shape interpretative communities and provides a new vantage point on the way in which communities revolve around the use of language. In "Militant Religiopolitical Rhetoric: How Abraham Kuyper Mobilized His Constituency," Arie Molendijk analyzes the rhetorical strategies of what has been called the Netherlands' first mass politician, Abraham Kuyper. Kuyper was well known for his militant and invective rhetoric. Molendijk charts the strategic use of Kuyper's lectures. ("His rhetoric was not only 'rhetoric,' but determined his politics to a great extent.") Words continually shape Kuyper's adversaries, as well as his allies, and Molendijk uncovers a tendency in Kuyper to refer to the effects of his own words as telltale signs of his own capacities as an absolute leader of his movement. Finally, in "Thinking through Religious Nationalism," Roger Friedland and Kenneth Moss argue, against Talal Asad (who has claimed that nationalism "requires the concept of the secular to make sense"), that at least in certain historical contexts, such as Polish Catholicism or Zionism, it is instead the concept of religion that has proven to be indispensable for the concept of nationalism. According to Friedland and Moss, the problem of nationalism should not be conceived in isolation from the problem of religion. Thus, the volume ends with a polemical discussion of the associations between words, religion, and nation, and the final last words of Friedland and Moss's contribution underline the concerns of this book in multiple ways. Resisting any idea of purification, they promote the understanding that "religion and nation-state can be co-implicated in a multiplicity of ways." Any attempt to purify this into abstract oppositions is risky: "Purification protects our political imaginations; it does not promote our understanding of the world that has been shaking beneath our feet."

PART I

What Are Words?

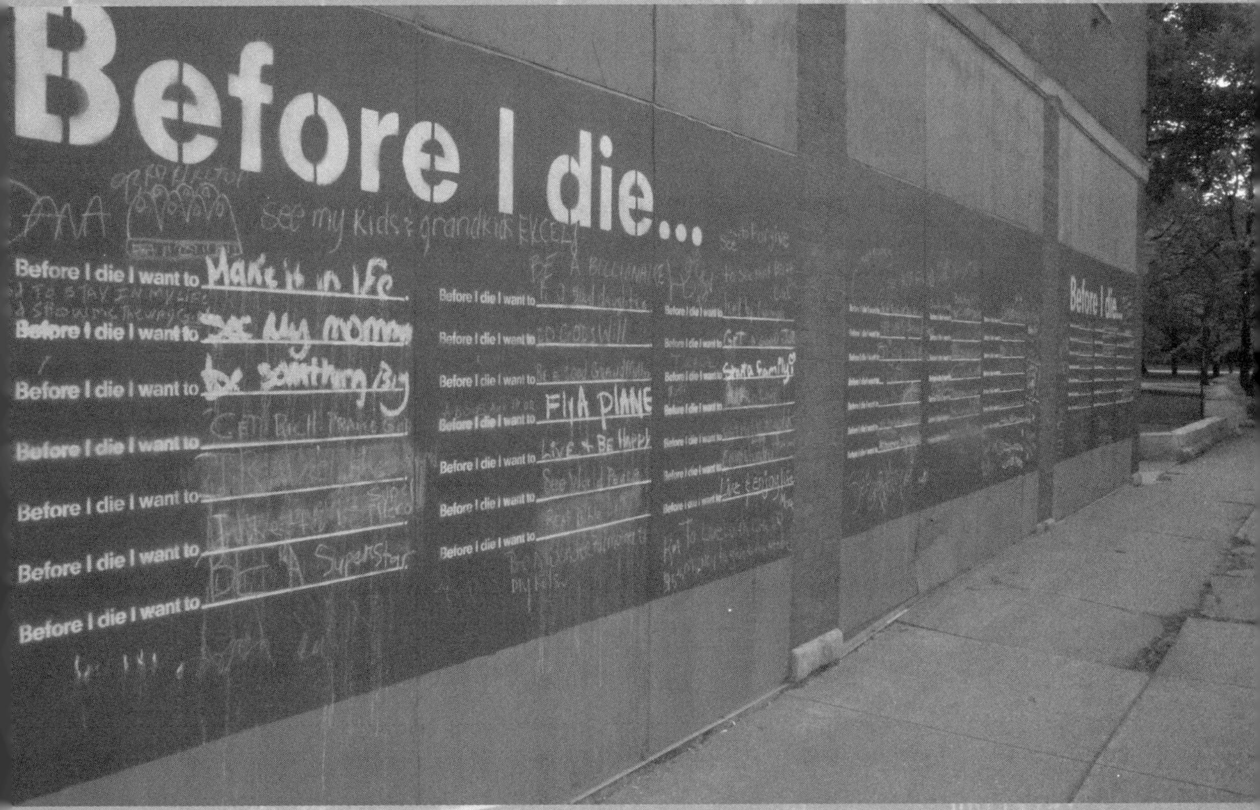

Word as Act

Varieties of Semiotic Ideology in the Interpretation of Religion

Michael Lambek

It is a privilege but also a risk and challenge to write about words to readers who make their living using words to study words. We are all textual scholars and text makers, professional interpreters of varying kinds. Yet it is an occupational hazard or dispensation of the scholar to see words as discrete and abstract phenomena. They sit, resonating on the page, and we struggle to translate or interpret them in and for themselves. In fact, though, words are uttered. An utterance is an act, not an abstraction, and acts take place in specific social contexts and have entailments and consequences. Every utterance invites response; hence I am confident mine will not be the last word.[1]

Semiotic Ideologies

Consider the following questions:

> Why and how do words matter to religion?
> Is "religious" language different from "ordinary" language, and in what ways?
> Is the specificity of its language a criterion of religion, a way of distinguishing it from other phenomena?
> Do these questions and their answers apply universally or only to some specific set of historical formations?

These questions have provoked the present essay but will not be fully answered in it. Thinking about them in my capacity as an anthropologist led inevitably to consideration of some of the things anthropologists who study religion have already had to say about words, the observation that their approaches have been diverse, and eventually the conclusion that the answers to the initial questions cannot be absolute. I draw on the concept of semiotic ideology to clarify the picture. How one sees the place of "word" or "words" in religion depends not only on which semiotic ideologies we discern at play within religion or among religious practitioners but also on those that inform the anthropologist's (or other scholar's) own thought.

Semiotic ideology is a concept developed by Webb Keane, who drew in turn on Michael Silverstein's concept of language ideology and cultural beliefs about language structure and its use in contexts of social difference.[2] The concept of language ideology helps address such questions as the formation of national language policies and debates about what makes "good English." By semiotic ideology Keane means "basic assumptions about what signs are and how they function in the world."[3] In a brilliant and wide-ranging discussion to which I cannot possibly do justice, Keane describes semiotic ideologies as offering reflexive accounts of the relations of signs and language to what is outside them, hence to materiality, to intentionality, and to agency. He contrasts religious contexts in which it is correct to repeat ritual formulas with those, especially in certain forms of Protestantism, in which one should speak sincerely, individually, and from the heart. The role and function of words and speaking are conceptualized very differently in the two cases. To answer Stanley Cavell's famous question *Must We Mean What We Say?*, the ritual formalist would claim, in effect, that we can mean only what we have said (and what others have said before us), whereas the Protestant semiotic ideology would urge that we must say only what we mean (and what is uniquely ours).[4] In other words, the respective semiotic ideologies differ on whether "saying" or "meaning" is prior and critical. This implies further that the meaning of "meaning something" itself differs in the two cases. My tentative conclusion, and answer to the big questions posed above, is that what we or our interlocutors distinguish as specifically *religious* language marks the salience and consequentiality of the particular semiotic ideology in play, such that saying something and meaning it are brought together as closely as they can be under the semiotic ideology in question. This is a fancy way of saying that religious utterances are ones whose truth value and ethical force are marked relative to ordinary utterances. Specific words and actions are often brought into play to enhance such marking and force, as when we begin, but not under every semiotic ideology, "In the name of God" or place our hands on a Bible.

If the concept of semiotic ideology can differentiate among alternative kinds of speech communities or religious congregations, formations, and practices, surely we can distinguish among both philosophical and anthropological arguments according to their respective semiotic ideologies as well. To take a well-known illustration from philosophy, consider the positions of Austin and Wittgenstein. To summarize so severely that I risk caricature, where Austin sees answers in the ways in which we ordinarily use words, Wittgenstein sees problems in the way we use words, as though language "lets us down." Not only are words to be purged of metaphysical excess, but as Simon Blackburn, quoting

Fritz Mauthner (interpreting a famous Wittgenstein aphorism), puts it, "as soon as we really have something to say, we are forced to be silent."[5] Both Wittgenstein and Austin are concerned less with the definitions of specific words than with what they perceive to be an incorrect understanding of their functions and especially with a misplaced emphasis on the function of reference itself. However, whereas Austin shows the incredible precision and fineness of distinction in "ordinary language," its ability unselfconsciously to get things right, Cavell, after Wittgenstein, attends to the danger of getting them wrong. Cavell points to the huge risks that ordinary speaking entails, the enormous consequentiality of being taken to mean what we say and of acknowledging having said it. It is precisely to the difficulty and consequentiality of meaning what one says that anthropologist Roy Rappaport suggests that ritual, and hence religion, offers some assistance.[6]

Conceptualizing "Religion" and "Words"

In this essay I explore how anthropology has explicitly addressed my original questions or implicitly assumed answers to them by means of its own diverse semiotic ideologies. One thing that anthropologists have certainly not agreed upon is a definition of the word *religion* itself, or even whether religion is the sort of thing of or for which a definition is possible. This is not the place to rehearse those debates, although we ought to be clear about one matter: Namely, that in both most nonmodern and non-Western societies, once the staple of anthropological investigation, religion is not disembedded as a discrete institution in the way we have taken it, rightly or wrongly, to be the case in contemporary ("secular") Western societies. As such, religion may not always be conceptually distinguished by members of such societies as a discrete domain or phenomenon—that is to say, in such societies there is generally neither a single, homogeneous phenomenon to be labeled "religion," nor are there distinctions made between different, discrete, or mutually exclusive "religions"—"ours" versus "theirs," for example. That does not imply, however, that analytic concepts of "religion" are completely inadequate for framing, discerning, and investigating a series of roughly comparable dimensions of human thought, cultural constructions, and social practices across a range of times and places or that they cannot be made sharper or fuzzier.[7] My point is that any general definition of religion, including the very possibility of such definition, is going to be shaped, in part, by the underlying semiotic ideology of the particular theorist.[8]

I do not think it useful or possible to make an absolute distinction between religious words or utterances and nonreligious ones, but there may be certain things about language uttered in ritual contexts or with religious intention or consequence that render them relatively distinct from other usages that one could by comparison call ordinary, unmarked, or belonging to other language games. I take it that such distinctions will be relative and that there are no stable or firm boundaries between the domain of religion and what is outside it in any sense other than that marked by legal decree on the part of the state. Certainly, the functions of anthropology do not include drawing or policing the borders.

By comparison to "religion," anthropologists and linguists have had a somewhat easier time agreeing about the concept of "words." Although the issues here cannot be resolved either and remain the subjects of lively debate, I will mention some features of words about which we do, more or less, agree. Words never appear alone but are located within fields of other words. We may speak here of syntactic and paradigmatic axes or chains. Syntactically, words are grammatically linked in phrases, sentences, conversations, and texts of various kinds—speeches, prayers, poems, and so on. Paradigmatically, each word substitutes for a chain of possible other words: its dictionary definition in the first instance, but also green instead of red or blue; God instead of man, woman, humankind, power, spirits, ancestors, prophets, and so on. Each word exists within a specific language, although languages are neither stable nor discrete; their boundaries are always open, and words are easily borrowed between languages. The point is, however, that each word is, or was, reasonably comprehensible to, or usable by, a collectivity of speakers or readers in a universe of other words syntactically and paradigmatically related to one another.[9] As Geertz notes, the universal human facility and need for language nevertheless implies and requires that we speak in one particular language at a time.[10] Neither polyphony nor code switching refutes this point.[11] Indeed, language is inherently social, not only spoken, but spoken to and with other speakers and perhaps auditors, and is thereby always context-sensitive. If we do not generally speak with the parsimony and unambiguousness advocated by logical positivists, we nevertheless usually speak in order to communicate, to make ourselves understood, to make our words available for interpretation and response by certain others who share sufficient features of our code and practice to be able to do so. We may also speak in such a manner as to be deliberately ambiguous or incomprehensible to those who stand outside our immediate speech community. It is clear from the facts of linguistic diversity that both concealment and word play have been as important functions of language as direct communication.

Another point about words is that—with the exception of many native speakers of English—most people are competent in more than one language. In any context, the play between languages and the diverse values accorded to each are relevant: the mother tongue, the father tongue, the conqueror's tongue, the tongue of exile, of bureaucracy, of refuge, of the academy, or of God, sometimes spoken directly and sometimes in quotation or degrees of dequotation.[12] Romanian or German, Yiddish or Hebrew: The jostling or struggle of languages with one other can produce great poetry, like that of Paul Celan. While proper names might appear to cross such divides, both Celan and Cavell changed their last names, essentially from one language to another. More mundanely, code switching, as sociolinguists call it, is widely prevalent, as conversations slide, let us say, between Frisian and Dutch or Dutch and English. There are shifts not only of language, but also of dialect, register, tone, and so on. This reminds us again that, outside the exercises of professional linguists, words are never abstract or neutral,[13] but utterances invested with the intentions and histories of interlocutors and audiences as they respond to, but also transform, the immediate social context. To summarize, words are not simply abstractions but both intrinsically related to other words and deployed in specific speech acts and language games. What distinguishes speech acts and language games from one another surely entails their respective semiotic ideologies.

A Tripartite Framework

I distinguish, in very broad strokes, three semiotic ideologies that have been applied, implicitly or explicitly, by anthropologists in thinking about religion. These have appeared successively, but they are not mutually exclusive, and one mode does not definitively displace the previous ones. They fit roughly with some other tripartite distinctions developed by philosophers.

Aristotle describes three kinds of human activity as thinking, making, and doing. Words can be examined with respect to each of these, thus not only with respect to thought, reflection, or disinterested contemplation—by contrast to experience, passion, interest, creativity, action, or ethics. Words offer a means or mode of making, creating, or bringing into being, in the voice of the prophet or poet no less than the coolly rational philosopher. And, as certain coolly rational philosophers have proposed, words carry force and are also a matter of doing. Of course, there is often a doing entailed in making or thinking, a making in thinking or doing, and a thinking in doing or making, such that each could be considered a matter of emphasis, as a frame through which to understand something larger rather than as a discrete form of activity. But at times it is important to distinguish that something is thought without making, done without thinking, and so on. Moreover, each form of activity has inspired particular modes of study; linguistics itself has moved from abstract analysis of syntax and semantics to include poetics and also pragmatics.

C. S. Peirce developed a roughly parallel set of distinctions among kinds or functions of signs, of which words are perhaps the most prominent examples. Although his classificatory scheme gets quite elaborate, at base the system is tripartite, distinguishing among symbol, icon, and index. I apply the syllogism that symbol : icon : index :: thinking : making : doing. I propose further that this syllogism can be extended to include Austin's distinction among the locutionary, perlocutionary, and illocutionary functions of utterances, as shown in the table.

Thinking	: Making	: Doing
Symbol	: Icon	: Index
Locutionary	: Perlocutionary	: Illocutionary

I suggest that one can discern among anthropological approaches to religion three semiotic ideologies along these lines. The first is that language serves primarily as an instrument of predication, reason, and argument. Emphasis is on thinking, on words as arbitrary symbols carrying meaning, and on utterances as primarily locutionary. The second semiotic ideology is that language is creative of texts and ultimately constitutive of lived worlds. The emphasis is on making—what Aristotle called *poiesis*—and on the iconic dimension and mimetic faculty of language. Words depict, but depictions have a persuasive, or perlocutionary, function or effect, shaping experience and intention. Finally, the third position begins neither with words as toolkit nor with words as related within a system or structure—*langue*—but with speech—*parole*. That is, it begins with utterances as acts. Here the focus is on Aristotelian *praxis*, or doing, on the indexical, immediate properties of spoken words and on the illocutionary function of utterances. Just as the second approach only comes to fruition with the concepts of sign and symbol as developed variously in Peircean semiotics and European structuralism, so the third approach develops from Austin's account in *How to Do Things with Words*.[14] Before going further, I want to emphasize that in practice the three approaches have been neither mutually exclusive nor internally homogeneous; I am conducting an exercise in broad ideal types.

I am suggesting that the anthropological investigation of words in religion has emphasized their function either as reference, resemblance, or act. These are roughly equivalent to Peirce's symbolic, iconic, and indexical, respectively, and to Austin's locutionary, perlocutionary, and illocutionary functions. There is a match between the line of investigation or mode of analysis and the semiotic ideology. In offering translations, explanations, or rationalizations of and for religious ideas and practices, the referential and rational function is primary; in interpreting performance, poetry, myth, and religious symbols, and in elucidating the constructions and classificatory schemes that Lévi-Strauss attributes more generally to the *pensée sauvage*,[15] the resemblance and creative function is highlighted. In the study of ritual, ethical practice, and religious agency, it is word as utterance or act that is most salient, even when the illocutionary force is mystified to members of the relevant speech community.

Many debates about religion depend on which semiotic ideology is dominant. Rationalists emphasize the referential function of individual words and the predicative quality of sentences and sometimes like to point to the falsity of other peoples' referents and predications. Nietzsche saw the importance of the iconic dimension and elegantly if acidly summarized the mistake of both the rationalists and the religious by declaring religion the worship of dead metaphors. From this perspective the general question of the research program "The Future of the Religious Past" could be rephrased as the future life of dead metaphors. Are dead metaphors to be revived, repeated, or replaced, taken literally or deconstructed, and with what consequences?

The history of anthropological thinking about religion can be divided into roughly three phases, or waves, in which each of these attributes or functions of language has held prominence in turn.

First Semiotic Ideology: Words as Vehicles of Thought

From Edward Tylor through E. E. Evans-Pritchard, there is attention to language as a vehicle for reasoning, and words are assumed to have primarily referential qualities. The focus is on individual words, and they are understood to be names for things— whether understood as natural objects, concepts, or supernatural beings. Thus for Tylor, "spirits" refers to beings in the worlds of those who mistakenly believe in them. For Evans-Pritchard, Azande witchcraft and oracles are also to be understood with respect to reason and reference. Despite his strong and salutary critique of Tylor, Evans-Pritchard remains concerned with the same general question: namely, the rationality of religion. He shows that the language of Zande witchcraft is not unreasonable once it is understood in context.[16] Context refers both to the large body of ideas and practices of which witchcraft is a part and, to anticipate the turn to utterances, to the ways in which specific causal attributions and accusations appear in social interaction. Evans-Pritchard works to give the best possible translation into English for Zande words, and in his later book on Nuer religion he addresses not only the specific words, ostensibly nouns, for various beings, but also the question of the copula—what it means when Nuer say, for example, "twins are birds."[17] In this conception of anthropology the central task is one of translation, and much hangs on the subtlety with which key words and phrases are rendered.

One of the central questions that is raised in this work is whether it is correct to describe the relationship between speakers or practitioners and their words and concepts as one of "belief." Rodney Needham explores problems with grasping the subjective beliefs of others, while Jean Pouillon and Malcolm Ruel raise aspects of the translation problem.[18] Pouillon shows the divergent entailments of believing, believing in, and believing that (or rather, *croire, croire en*, and *croire que*), whereas Ruel documents shifts in the meaning of the word *belief* over the course of the history of Christianity. The point here is both that the concept of "belief" is central to this semiotic ideology ("belief" in spirits, God, or witchcraft) and that the rationalist program was able to generate an auto-critique concerning its own key words and central concepts. However, insofar as "belief" remains central both to Protestant Christianity and to our broader folk theory or definition of religion and its contrast with science, it remains prevalent in the introductory textbooks.[19] Religion stubbornly and provincially remains something one "believes in," attesting to what one might call a semiotic hegemony.

The questioning of the very concept of "belief," which has its roots in Evans-Pritchard's critique of what he called the intellectualist position of Tylor, found parallels in Franz Steiner's questioning of taboo and Lévi-Strauss's of totemism.[20] It could be added that these works epitomize the larger dialectical process characteristic of, and possibly intrinsic to, anthropological thought, in which words are developed for cross-cultural comparison and subsequently taken apart.[21] This could be expanded to say that anthropology progresses by discovering the limits of its own semiotic ideologies. Insofar as anthropology is inherently auto-critical, the frequent assertions I hear among colleagues that they (alone) are carrying out a thorough "critique of anthropology" are oxymoronic. In fact, one cannot help noting that the rhetoric of reform in anthropology smacks of both Protestant Christianity and the semiotic ideology that underpins it. (Perhaps that is also to observe that the concept of semiotic ideology itself stems from a particular semiotic ideology.)

Questions concerning the reasonableness of religion continue to be posed today, by anthropologists no less than by practitioners of religion and their critics. Thus anthropologist Eva Keller follows her informants, Seventh Day Adventists in a poor region of Madagascar, when they assert that their Bible study is a form of science.[22] And cognitive anthropologists attempt to distinguish concepts from words and to examine the emergence and reproduction of what they call nonintuitive concepts that are compelling on other grounds. It is evident that the rationalist program inevitably must respond to the question of relativism, whether by accepting it in some form, as Evans-Pritchard did, or by actively rejecting it, as the cognitivists do. Put another way, this semiotic ideology inevitably produces polemics.

While in some respects the deconstructionist and genealogical programs are in direct opposition to the rationalist and cognitivist ones and should be added as distinct semiotic ideologies to my list, they all share the potential, if not the expression of, or claims for, radical skepticism. However, insofar as anthropologists must respect the practical wisdom of their subjects as fellow humans, I submit that they cannot rest in either fully rationalist or fully genealogical skeptical waters, but must seek positions that are more ethnographically grounded—that are located, as it were, several degrees closer to the practices of our subjects. That is to say, they must seek a position from which to see from within rather than from outside, from earth rather than from an Archimedean point beyond it (heaven?), from commitment no less than skepticism, from making and doing no less than thinking.

Second Semiotic Ideology: Words as Vehicles of Creation

Keller's restatement of the Malagasy (northern Betsimisaraka) remark that Bible study is science is not unlike Evans-Pritchard's quotation from Nuer that twins are birds or the phrase of the Bororo that circulates within anthropology, "my brother, the parrot." It can be argued that such phrases are easier to grasp from the second semiotic ideology. In this view, words have a poietic function: They draw things into presence or being by concretizing abstractions and making images or tropes. Rather than referring to the world, they depict or represent it and become part of it, transforming ideas iconically into new media. Language here has both a poietic and a mimetic quality or function: that of realizing the world. Words, as signs, are deployed in complex analogies and iterations. They are not autonomous abstractions or constituted in relation to specific external referents, but formed in relation to one another. It is their relations to each other within larger structures that count more than their relations to an external world. As Lévi-Strauss shows, here the paradigmatic dimension of language trumps the syntagmatic.

This semiotic ideology, which by no means gives rise to a single, homogeneous approach, draws on a variety of sources. From Durkheim comes the idea that religion is ultimately expressive of the transcendent power of society, hence that it is metaphorical at heart, its words and images not to be taken literally. From Weber and German *Kultur* theory comes the idea that we live suspended in webs of meaning of our own inherited tradition and making, subject to interpretation. And from structural poetics come theories of tropes and of poetic composition.

Anthropologists from different traditions have given different weight to different elements. British Durkheimians emphasize the representation of the social, a thread that emerges also in the Marxist notion of ideology. This is a partial approach, not only because the social need not be the only subject of representation, but more importantly because *representation* is only a subform of the larger process that is at issue: namely, *presentation*, bringing into presence. Geertz emphasizes the relative autonomy and distinctiveness of meaningful worlds and sees the religious portions of those worlds as anchoring the rest, asserting ultimate meaningfulness in the face of considerable evidence to the contrary.[23] He also emphasizes that our access to the meaningful worlds of others is similar to their own: namely, through the interpretation of the compositions—what he calls texts—inherited, created, performed, and observed by members of a given society or adherents of a given religion.[24] Like many American anthropologists, Geertz here conceptualizes culture by analogy to language, but the texts he has in mind are composed in multiple media, not only, or even predominantly, words—his illustrations include the Balinese dance of Rangda and Barong and the Javanese cockfight[25]—and they do not have the fixity and boundedness that in the heyday of print culture, now past, we attributed to texts in the literal sense. Critics of the text metaphor have too often taken it literally, or assumed mistakenly that Geertz did, thereby committing the same sin that anthropologists of religion who hold this semiotic ideology have ascribed to those holding the ideology of reference—that is, of taking the statements of their subjects too literally. Moreover, it would follow from a Geertzian position that one should explore both the underlying semiotic ideologies and the way these get played out in social life.

Ultimately, Geertz's position leads him away from the means and modes by which texts are constructed and toward their interpretation. Hence he gives voice to the hermeneutic strain in anthropology that approaches the goal of translation in Evans-Pritchard. The object is to appreciate and understand the cultural works and worlds of others rather than to locate their building blocks or mechanisms and hence to take them apart, to dissolve culture, as he remarks critically of Lévi-Strauss.[26] It is the art of reading, not composing, that Geertz is after. Hence, too, his is not primarily a hermeneutics of suspicion.

The best exemplar of the second semiotic ideology (or an alternate variant), the person who takes it to its logical extreme or most fully develops its potential, is not Geertz but Lévi-Strauss. For Lévi-Strauss, at the end of the day, human poiesis, creatively produced form, is just that. The referential, predicative, situational, and meaningful qualities of creative practice are successively worn away under his gaze, which is one not of interpretation but of analysis. Although he acknowledges the acute observational powers of human beings in small-scale societies and hence the specific referential qualities of individual words for plants and animals, he is more interested in such words as elements in a second order of construction, in analogical thought.[27] Metaphors are taken to refer not to the world but to one another, until ultimately the constructions that emerge are just the play of form itself as spontaneously generated by the mind. By the four-volume *Mythologiques*,[28] the filaments and nebulae of mythemes, like the molecules of matter or astral configurations, in some respects find their closest counterpart and most successful analogy in music   that is, in musical composition—to be judged as beautiful with respect to internal ordering rather than as accurate or believable in the conformity of representation to an external reality. In music, reference is reduced to pattern; moreover, music is aesthetic and sensory, filling a room rather than saying something about something, and especially not predicating in a rational way such that the claim could be countered with an alternative argument. It is relatively pure presentation rather than representation. In his interest in music Lévi-Strauss perhaps draws close to Wittgenstein, who "felt that philosophy aspires to the condition of music."[29] A different analogy, less used by Lévi-Strauss, would be to liken mythical constructions to abstract mathematics, not the practical arithmetic of counting but the playful world of number theory. One might go so far as to say that this impulse to free oneself from all worldly reference could itself be viewed as a kind of hyperintellectualized religious aspiration.

Today the legacy of structuralism has been renewed by restoring elements of meaning and cultural distinctiveness. The best exemplifications are the work of Eduardo Viveiros de Castro on cosmological deixis, which clarifies the richly developed relationship of nature to culture that prevails in Amerindian culture, in contrast to that of Europe, and Philippe Descola's exploration of the logical possibilities humans have for conceptualizing themselves in relation to who they are not.[30]

One of the omissions of structuralism is that it does not consider whether there are words that are protected from being drawn into analogical reasoning, that stand apart or remain sealed within their radical incommensurability with respect both to ordinary reference and to structure. I refer to words that fall outside specific semantic domains, words that are not constructed in relation to other words, as parts of paradigm sets (like pronouns) or typologies (like plant terms). Structuralism operates as though all words were commensurable with one another, articulated along binary distinctions; major binary oppositions, like life and death, are mediated by lesser ones. I suggest there are many words that are not commensurable in this sense. Consider, for example, the triad found in German-speaking Switzerland and elsewhere among *Körper, Geist*, and *Seele*. My interlocutors have a difficult time discriminating consistently among them or indicating precisely what corresponds to each. Surely the point of Cartesian dualism, often misunderstood by Descartes's successors, though well explicated by Gilbert Ryle, is that mind and body are incommensurable with one another. That means you cannot draw a line between them. To try to do so is not to mediate between them but to commit a category error. The possibility for category errors marks the limits of structuralism.

I suggest that many words that carry considerable religious weight are incommensurable with other words; this may be because of their extreme comprehensiveness, their complex multivalence, or conversely, because they are informationless. An example of an almost excessively comprehensive word is *sila* in the language of the Greenlandic Inuit as described by Mark Nuttall. This word comprehends "weather, the outside, intelligence, consciousness, [and] the universal breath soul."[31] Or consider the Dinka of Southern Sudan, whose concept of divinity Godfrey Lienhardt carefully tries to translate not as spirits on the order of human beings but as powers. Moreover, Lienhardt begins to grasp a distinctive semiotic ideology. "Flesh," said a Christian Dinka to Lienhardt, "was the divinity of all masters of the fishing-spear. . . . Flesh is one word," he said. "The Dinka expression *one word* [*wet tok*] means the word that is superior to many words, the decisive word, beyond argument and addition, and hence the true word. . . . Many words conceal the truth while 'one word' proclaims it." Flesh makes the thighs quiver during the invocation at a sacrifice, and Lienhardt tells us that what a man says when inspired by Flesh is true.[32]

Third Semiotic Ideology: Words as Vehicles of Action

The words that Rappaport considers to lie at the heart of religion, what he calls ultimate sacred postulates, are essentially incommensurable. Such words can be virtually informationless, in his terms, and hence not constituted by means of either reference or binary relations with other words. An additional feature of such words is that they are the most resistant to translation into other languages, again for lack of commensurability. Yet they can be deeply meaningful. To see this we have to turn to the third semiotic ideology and the third wave of anthropological thought on religion.

If, in the first semiotic ideology, meaning is contained in abstract, individual words and in the arguments made from them, according largely to the way they approximate something outside of themselves, already in the world, and if, in the second perspective, meaning emerges from the fruitful conjunction and juxtaposition of words, in the third perspective meaning emerges from the force of specific utterances. Words are conceived primarily as utterances rather than as referents or icons, and it is what they do rather than what they refer to or how they are composed that is highlighted. Utterances are understood, in the first instance, as acts. This approach draws from Austin's seminal work on the performative or illocutionary function of words, but has earlier appearances in Malinowski and Lienhardt, among others. The citation from Lienhardt makes the point: Flesh "proclaims" the truth rather than depicts, argues, refers to, or symbolizes it, and it does so in the performance of the invocation at a sacrifice. The thighs quiver and the word is manifestly embodied; in fact, of course, the voice is always embodied.

Austin turns linguistic philosophy from sentence to utterance and shows that reference is only one of the kinds of acts that words can perform. Illocutionary utterances bring states of being into effect, as in naming a ship, bestowing a knighthood, issuing a legal judgment, or pronouncing a marriage, but also in greeting a friend, making a promise, offering an apology, casting a blessing or a curse, deferring to a superior, and so forth. Every utterance achieves such acts as asserting something, inviting, or offering a response. To achieve these ends certain conditions have to be met—in the more formal cases, drawing on people with the right to conduct the performance, at the right time and place, and so forth.[33] Highly formulated conventions of performance produce what we call "ritual," and the most formalized rituals are often what we call "religious"; conversely, much of what is accomplished in ritual and religion can be understood as illocutionary (albeit not exclusively).

This has a number of entailments that Rappaport elucidates. First, a focus on words as acts not only avoids the problems with the concept of belief mentioned earlier, but it leads to the insight that ritual is effective irrespective of individual belief. For Rappaport, participation in the enactment of a part of the liturgical order entails acceptance of its terms irrespective of the psychological state of the performers. I can be married against my will or with due ambivalence; that need not affect the consequentiality of the act, including the utterances "I do" and "I now pronounce you husband and wife." Public saying trumps private thinking. It replaces indecision and uncertainty with established fact and also insulates social order from psychic variability.[34] This situation corresponds to the semiotic ideology of the nonmissionized Indonesians described by Keane, and it may be the case even among those Protestants who explicitly hold the converse, although in that case sincerity or conviction may serve as a felicity condition for effective enactment.

Second, the very act of participating in the ritual, whether by officiating or submitting to it, is a sign—an index—of commitment to both the particular act accomplished and to the order of which the ritual is part. Performers become accountable for what they have said and done and to the world of which such acts are a part—that is, the world in which they fall under a particular kind of description produced by such acts or that obliges or encourages them to perform acts of this kind. Performers, says Rappaport, are the first addressees of the messages uttered in rituals, and their actions are reinforced by witnesses. In other words, ritual performance has ethical entailments. We become certain kinds of people through having undergone certain rituals, and we must acknowledge our subsequent actions in their light. This can be understood politically as a kind of subjection to power or authority, but more generally performance establishes the criteria by which subsequent practice is judged, hence producing ritual actors as ethical subjects. From another direction, Cavell has illuminated the great difficulty of speaking and of being accountable for and to one's words.[35] In the context of ritual, the weightiness of ordinary speaking that he so acutely discerns is somewhat redistributed; ritual speech absolves us in some respects and deepens our commitment in others.[36] Speakers are deeply implicated in, and even constituted through, their words. We take one path rather than another and henceforth must acknowledge this is who we are and where we stand.

Third, related to the ethical dimension of ritual utterances are important consequences for the concept of truth. In the first semiotic ideology I described, truth is a matter of correspondence and also of logic. In the second, truth is poetic, disclosed in aesthetic experience or, as Heidegger puts it, unconcealed. Where words are understood as utterances and their illocutionary function is highlighted, the matter is somewhat different. Austin argues that truth is simply not a question that can be put to performative statements. Rappaport, however, argues that the relation of truth to utterance is reversed between locutionary and illocutionary utterances. In the case of the former, an utterance is discerned as true or false according to its conformity to the facts, which have precedence. I am lying or mistaken if I tell you it is raining when it is not. In the second case, however, the state of affairs is judged true or false according to its conformity to the utterance. Once the rain magic has been performed, it is the weather that is at fault if it doesn't rain. If I do not keep my promise, it is my subsequent action (or inaction) that is faulty, not my original utterance. Here again Lienhardt anticipates Rappaport when he writes, "The [Dinka] sacrifice is its own end. It has already created a moral reality, to which physical facts are hoped eventually to conform." As he elaborates, "Human symbolic action moves with the rhythm of the natural world around, re-creating that rhythm in moral terms and not merely attempting to *coerce* it to conformity with human desires." [37] Rappaport distinguishes the truths of nature from the "fabricated truths peculiar to humanity." The latter are true only so long as they are accepted, as indicated in their reiteration in ritual. "They are, in essence, moral. They declare the truth of 'should' against which actions and actual states of affairs are judged and often found to be wanting, immoral, or wrong. . . . They are the truths upon which social systems have always been built."[38] In this depiction of ethical truth, Rappaport reaches on analytic grounds the point that Lienhardt discovers through ethnographic interpretation when he writes, "The word *yic*, which is translated as 'truth,' has in fact a somewhat wider range of meanings than our word *now* has. It implies uprightness, 'righteousness,' and 'justice.' "[39]

Finally, Rappaport argues that the most powerful illocutionary utterances are often couched in reiterated words and phrases that he refers to as ultimate sacred postulates. These are performatively realized claims that are unfalsifiable on either empirical or logical grounds, yet are taken to be unquestionable. In fact, Rappaport defines "sanctity *as the quality of unquestionableness imputed by congregations to postulates in their nature objectively unverifiable and absolutely unfalsifiable.*"[40] This unquestionableness derives from the formal properties of ritual enactment, not from reason or persuasion. Ultimate sacred postulates carry no information but strengthen the illocutionary force of utterances with specific content, rendering them, as it were, extra-felicitous. Thus one does not merely swear to a particular fact but swears on the Bible, or in the name of God, in words that are given to the oath taker and repeated by her. The canonical, reiterated quality of these words is marked, as is the indexical quality of the utterance, as unique individual event.

The questions with which I began included why language matters for religion and what is distinctive about religious language. Part of Rappaport's originality is to turn this around, to ask instead: Why does ritual or religion matter to or for language? He argues that ritual is needed as a kind of control over two of the capacities of human language: namely, its enabling of lying and of imagining alternatives. Rappaport argues that ritual and language coevolved, as it were, with ritual offering order to language's code. The potential to say new things every time, which, if left unchecked, would produce radical uncertainty and an absence of commitment to specific goals, hence both social disorder and anomie, is offset by the properties of ritual that enable the production of certainty and truth. In ritual, certain phrases are reiterated, time after time and generation after generation; such unquestionable words come to exemplify and produce certainty. Yet insofar as each utterance, each repetition and application, is a new and unique event, it affords a reestablishment of orientation, commitment, and truth.

Sacred postulates can be invalidated only by being ignored or rejected;[41] conversely, what is striking is their perdurance and invariance. The historical perdurance of certain phrases in the Abrahamic religions informs Rappaport's argument. Islam, in particular, is a religion that highlights invariant sacred utterances. The Qur'an is received by Mohammed and passed on through a chain of recitation. Pious Muslims learn to recite the Qur'an and utter its phrases throughout life, to open and close activities of all kinds and to mark life transitions. Prayers are uttered five times daily, and the call to prayer reverberates across urban and village spaces. Words are put to music and sung in Sufi hymns and poetry, and the rapid repetition of the word of God is used to bring on states of ecstasy. One could say that sacred words permeate the lives of Muslims; that Muslims are bathed in words. Islam has developed elaborate models for both recitation and audition. As Saba

Mahmood and Charles Hirschkind have respectively shown, these have deep ethical entailments.[42] In Mayotte, where I have worked, the commemoration ceremony held for deceased relatives entails inviting large numbers of men into the mosque, where together they recite a key phrase (the *tahlil*) some seventy thousand times in order to ease the burden of the deceased in the afterlife. This is a blessing of their parents sponsored by the adult offspring, as mediated by the Muslim community. Indeed, in Muslim communities, the continuous circulation of words could be said to exemplify the gift in Mauss's analysis; here the primary vehicle is not material objects, money, or even food, which are also significant, but sacred words. Yet what is critical is not the words in themselves, available anonymously or abstractly in the form of print or electronic media, but specific acts of utterance and reception.

A common Muslim phrase like "In the name of God, the compassionate, the merciful" includes elements of reference and poetic depiction, but most salient is the utterance and its effects. Pronounced at the onset of any activity, it sanctifies the act, places the activity under a description, and establishes criteria according to which what follows is to be judged. It makes a meal, a journey, or a sexual act into a specifically Muslim and sanctified one. It neither reports nor argues, depicts nor persuades, but proclaims and establishes. It is both indexical in Peirce's sense and illocutionary in Austin's. An even stronger utterance in Islam is the *shahada*; to utter the *shahada*, the profession of faith, is not only to assert that one is a Muslim, but also to demonstrate that fact and to commit oneself to it; to utter it is to *be* Muslim or to *become* Muslim. To utter it casually is to take Islam in vain. Sacred words uttered in the wrong contexts become the strongest profanities. Whereas the abstract sentence that there is no God but God is something of a logical tautology, with no clear referent, as an utterance, an act of witness, it has tremendous force and meaning.

Here is an illustration of the significance of illocutionary utterance and the clash of semiotic ideologies in contemporary Christianity, as taken from the BBC website of Saturday, March 14, 2009. It is entitled "Atheists call for 'debaptism.'"[43] British atheists claim that it is not sufficient to merely ignore or withdraw from the church but that they need a performative act to undo the original act that placed them within it as infants.

> However, baptism is proving a difficult thing to undo. The local Anglican diocese . . . refused to amend the baptismal roll as Mr Hunt had wanted, on the grounds that it was a historical record. "You can't remove from the record something that actually happened," said the Bishop of Croydon, the Right Reverend Nick Baines. . . . In the face of resistance from the church, the [National Secular] Society has come up with a document of its own. . . . Sitting on a bench in the grounds of St. Jude's Church, John Hunt intoned the opening lines. "I, John Geoffrey Hunt, having been subjected to the rite of Christian baptism in infancy . . . hereby publicly revoke any implications of

that rite. I reject all its creeds and other such superstitions in particular the perfidious belief that any baby needs to be cleansed of original sin."

The certificate has apparently been downloaded more than sixty thousand times.

Insofar as words not only carry or convey meanings, the very meaning (sense, intention, reference, effect) of the word *word* itself can shift and may not be directly translatable or commensurable from language to language or language game to language game within a given language. Among the language games that could be distinguished are: Protestant-ism in its various denominations, Roman Catholicism, and charismatic Christianity; Muslim daily prayers, supernumerary prayers, odes, and theology; and anthropological, philosophical, and religious studies approaches to religion. The meaning of the word *word* can even shift within a given language game, as I have indicated with respect to successive waves of anthropological thought on religion.

I have suggested that religious discourse includes radically incommensurable words and elementary utterances of sacred postulates that may be radically difficult, if not impossible, to translate. But translation needs to take function as well as meaning into effect. My father records that when as an adolescent he moved from Germany to England in 1939, he was perplexed by the graffiti he saw there. He thought he knew what the English word *fuck* meant and so could not imagine why anyone other than the most devoted Nazi would write "Fuck Hitler."

Depending on one's semiotic ideology—or one's theory of language—one takes one or another approach to words in religion and hence to religion itself. I have suggested that when we attend not only to words in the abstract or in textual compositions but to words as utterances, new kinds of questions are opened up and new answers made available. Utterances lead us to a theory of action. This is not to attend exclusively to the spoken word or to abandon the concept of the text. We should include acts of writing, reading, interpretation, and, most saliently, of recitation and reiteration. Conversely, it is not to take all utterances equally. To speak is to intervene in the course of social interaction and is always of consequence. But some moments of speaking, and some utterances, are more portentous or decisive than others. Ultimate sacred postulates add to the illocutionary force.

Every utterance is an original act, but most utterances draw on previously entextual-ized phrases—good morning, thank you, what a beautiful day, thank God—and so on. At the least, we draw on words whose previously encoded signification, if we are speaking the same language, we share. Rappaport describes ritual as the conjunction of the indexical and the canonical. In contexts we describe as religious, the canonical reiterated dimen-sion is prominent. Utterances are framed and set apart from ongoing discourse; they contain ultimate sacred postulates; and it may be requisite to repeat them exactly. Conversely, one could add that in prophetic utterance the weight may be placed on the indexical dimension, the unexpectedness of the occasion, or the originality of the utterance. And from the perspective of participants, the indexical dimension—the event, the experience, and the personal and possibly momentous transformation—is salient.

In Lienhardt's account of Dinka religion, acts from the relatively trivial, like tying a knot in the grass, to the profound, like the entombment of the live master of the fishing spear, are meaningful. It is a short move to realize the converse—that meaningful utterances, like giving thanks, are acts; powerful acts include words, gestures, and often material objects. Stanley Tambiah shows that the composition of such acts often follows the logic of poetic composition and analogical reasoning discerned by Malinowski and Lévi-Strauss.[44] Rappaport identifies several additional important aspects of formal acts, which he refers to as rituals, including the fact that their consequences lie primarily in the ethical field, that they change the relationship between words and world, such that truth is ascertained according to whether the world now corresponds to the word rather than vice versa, and that speakers are deeply implicated in their utterances. Illocutionary utterances, I argue, are inherently ethical—in the sense of being ethically consequential rather than inherently good or right. Illocutionary acts place persons and contexts under a description, establish criteria and commitments, and thus provide the basis and means for judgment. Ethical life depends on speech acts, and acts of speaking entail ethics.[45]

Religion has been the sphere in which the consequentiality of utterances has been recognized most explicitly; conversely, when we have observed highly consequential utterances in other societies, we have tended to call them religion, ritual, or magic.

Although I have been operating throughout by means of triads, I do not mean to imply that speech as action will be the last semiotic ideology to appear historically or that my survey has been comprehensive and up to date. Nor are these ideologies mutually exclusive in practice. A given religious phrase may be simultaneously beautiful, persuasive, logical, accurate, and effective—and appreciated by practitioners for each of these qualities. Likewise, a given scholarly analysis can bridge the three positions, as does Tambiah's wonderful essay on magic.[46] Thus each stage ideally does not replace the previous one but adds a new dimension to it; from the perspective of speech act theory, reference itself becomes a kind of act. It is noteworthy, however, that most scholarly presentations aspire to operate by means of a semiotic ideology of reason and reference. I myself have been primarily speaking about something, constructing an argument, rather than explicitly drawing a portrait in words or effecting a change of state.

Austin has insight into the subtlety of ordinary language, the richness of what it offers, its power to discriminate. But is religious language "ordinary" in Austin's sense, or is it different and perhaps even problematic, needing the therapy that Wittgenstein sought to provide? I would say there is no single answer to these questions. On the one hand, skeptical anthropologists like Lienhardt and Ruel have applied Wittgensteinian therapy, reducing the metaphysical load that certain words like *spirit* or *sacrifice* have been supposed to carry.[47] On the other hand, the core of much religious language may not be either ordinary or metaphysical in the first place. And besides, who are anthropologists to criticize rather than to attempt to understand the metaphysicians we encounter in the field? We could offer criticism only from within a specific semiotic ideology of our own. Rappaport is interesting in part because the concept of sanctity he offers sits at an angle to the ordinary different from that offered by metaphysics. He argues that sanctity is a property of discourse; words are sacred rather than ordinary not because of what they portend but because of their perdurance and self-closedness.

It is true that I have been speaking somewhat as a disciple of the prophet Rappaport. But I would also like to see a return to grammar in the sense in which it has been studied by linguists interested in cultural difference, in the tradition from Edward Sapir and Benjamin Whorf to Alton Becker, a kind of poetics of syntax.[48] Grammar is often ignored because it is difficult to grasp, and those who specialize in its study too often cannot or do not speak to broader audiences. However, it is my impression that distinctive semiotic ideologies probably lie embedded, or find their roots, in different grammars. To paraphrase Nietzsche, semiotic ideologies may be the rationalizations of dead (or live) grammars.

If language "matters to philosophers" differently at different times, so too it matters differently for different communities of religious practitioners. As practitioners and theologians argue about the nature of language, perhaps what anthropologists ought to do is stand apart and merely listen, record the varieties of relations they see, and explore the semiotic ideologies that underlie them or are explicitly debated among practitioners. In so doing they may be able to generalize about the ways in which words are constitutive of religion and the limits to those ways, about how and why words matter to and for religion. And yet they cannot do so without semiotic ideologies of their own.

The complexity of the intersection of semiotic ideologies in actual life may be illustrated by events in Groningen (where this paper was first delivered). I close with a quote from the BBC website of March 7, 2009, that will also reassure you about the future of the religious past:

> An art exhibition opening in the Netherlands will allow people to call a telephone number designated for God—but they will have to leave a message. Dubbed God's Hotline, it aims to focus attention on changes to the ways Dutch people perceive religion. Dutch artist Johan van der Dong chose a mobile phone number to show that God was available anywhere and anytime, Radio Netherlands reported. Critics say the project mocks those with religious beliefs. Forming part of an art installation in the town of Groningen, the voicemail message says: "This is the voice of God, I am not able to speak to you at the moment, but please leave a message."[49]

CHAPTER 2

Medieval Irish Spells

"Words of Power" as Performance

Jacqueline Borsje

On March 11, 2010, a Roman Catholic priest descended deep into the earth below the city of Amsterdam.[1] He traveled to this "underworld" in order to bless the start of the breaking of ground for a tunnel for the new metro line. He performed this religious act by blessing water, a statue of Saint Barbara (the patron saint of miners and tunnel builders), two enormous drills, and the builders. This is a modern example of the belief in the power of words, which is a belief that words can influence reality in a supernatural way,[2] in a material sense although not by empirically verifiable methods. Certain words are believed to have the power to transform reality through some intrinsic power or through their instrumentality in invoking the agency of a supernatural entity.[3] In this way, human beings use blessings, curses, spells, charms, incantations, and prayers for good or for evil: to protect, to harm, to exert power, to heal, and to inflict disease.

The blessing of the priest did not consist only of audible words (the final blessing was sung, the first three spoken); it was also a perceptible act involving a tangible substance (the sprinkling of blessed or holy water). Other elements of the ritual performance in this cold, damp, underground space were: the statue, which was to be blessed and left underground; those about to begin building the tunnel and their implements, which were both to be blessed; the Roman Catholic dean who was to perform the blessing, in his liturgical garb, assisted by a verger; and the public (prominent citizens, schoolchildren, scholars, the press—through the media, the event had an even wider public). All these visible, invisible, audible, olfactory, and tangible elements together constituted the performance.

In such a contemporary context, we are able to study empirically all these elements of the performance, and we can interview people to find out what they believe is happening and what the blessing is supposed to do.[4] Moreover, we can study the historical roots of the performance, because blessings are a well-known phenomenon in the history of Judaism and Christianity. When we turn to examples of blessings in the distant past, however, our sources are often fragmentary. While we may use information from the past to explain contemporary beliefs, we must be careful when we reverse this method to study rituals in the past.[5] The past is a foreign country, so we need to build our reconstructions with care. Past performative contexts are alien to us; we have only textual remnants of complex, multidimensional ritual performances.[6] Historians must work with static texts and images instead of contemporary, dynamic recordings of rituals.

In this essay I will examine the performative context of "words of power" in medieval Irish manuscripts. Words of power fall into the category of speech acts: By uttering words one performs an act.[7] If we compare a speech act (such as the passing of a death sentence) with a speech act performed by uttering words of power (such as a curse) we note a difference. When a judge condemns a person to death, a complete judicial-administrative human apparatus exists to take care that these words come true. In the case of a curse, it is believed that the words themselves and/or supernatural entities (whether or not explicitly mentioned) as invisible agents cause the words to come true. Words of power are a form of religious, ritual performative language.[8]

The medieval Irish tradition is a rich treasure, comprising numerous texts in Latin and Irish. The oldest Irish Latin (or Hiberno-Latin) texts were written in the fifth century. Texts in the vernacular language (Irish) are extant from the seventh century onward, which is very early for northern Europe. We can divide this language into three early periods: Old Irish (ca. 600 to ca. 900), Middle Irish (ca. 900 to ca. 1200), and Early Modern Irish (ca. 1200 to ca. 1650). Words of power often occur as complicated, ambiguous expressions that are difficult to translate, and the context is sometimes only hinted at. My exploration of the performative context of verbal power can therefore be only tentative and preliminary: There is a lot that we do not know, and often we must refrain from attempting definitive conclusions.

As a first step toward mapping this unknown territory, I will propose a model for describing performance of words of power as a communication process: The performers send a message (i.e., the words of power) to an addressee (i.e., the reality to be influenced or transformed). I will then give a preliminary survey of structural elements that comprise words of power. Finally, I will investigate the performance of verbal power in a medieval Irish context: How were static, written words actualized in a dynamic performance?

To accomplish that, we must first contextualize the people involved, the actors in the ritual communication process. We must trace the roles of the scribe, the performer, and the patient or client, as well as their possible verbal contributions to the performance, whether as monologue, dialogue, or a conversation among more than two actors. The next step will be to sketch the use of proper names and personal pronouns in the texts and the prescribed rituals. But how were these texts actualized in time and place? Where and how were they to be uttered, or were they used in a different way? In particular, what was done with written words? In what way were the human senses involved when these visible, written words became part of a multidimensional ritual? The words would have been tangible as part of a piece of manuscript and could thereby touch other objects, too. Alternatively, words could touch objects by being written on them with a finger instead of with ink. Words reached ears as sounds. The breath that carried the words touched objects, as well. When words were believed to transform butter, water, oil, and other substances to be consumed, they may even have been tasted. In conclusion, I will explore these dimensions of verbal power.

Words of Power as Messages

Medieval Irish words of power are found mostly in manuscripts. They play a role in narratives, yet they are also extant outside a narrative context. They were sung, spoken, chanted, whispered, or murmured, either by a narrative character or by a historical person who used the text in order to influence reality in a supernatural way. Such deeds are commonly referred to as "miracles" or "magic," depending on the identity of the performer. I prefer the use of "neutral" or umbrella terms, such as *supernatural art*, given that the terms *miracles* and *magic* have acquired an ideological content in the course of their semantic history.[9] My key concept "words of power" is another attempt to introduce neutral terminology: This umbrella term aims at encompassing the words uttered by the performers in a more inclusive way.[10]

Such terminological efforts are part of a larger paradigm shift that seeks to accommodate a new, more neutral perspective on religion.[11] "Words of power" have often been identified as *magic*, a term generally evaluated negatively. On the one hand, this is due to the emic view of (especially monotheistic) religious texts; on the other, it is part of the semantic history of the term and concept *magic*, and as such is part of Europe's intellectual heritage.[12] As a concept, magic has been contrasted with religion, which, especially when the religion involved was Christianity, was given a positive evaluation. Numerous examples, however, show that the dividing line between the two concepts is not altogether clear.[13]

The aim of the performer of verbal power is to influence or transform reality. Before the current paradigm shift, it was common to describe spells and prayers as distinct from and even opposed to each other. In this dichotomy, a "spell" is expected to be either evil, pre-Christian, or a form of popular religion, and a "prayer" is expected to be good, Christian, and a recognizable part of an official religion. A believer supposedly prays piously in order to supplicate a deity to grant a wish, whereas a sorcerer utters a spell and thereby constrains a demon to comply with the command, or the sorcerer's words would "automatically" or "mechanically" have a supernatural effect. We need, however, a neutral model that could accommodate all types of performer and all types of verbal power without building in a priori points of view or stereotypes. Moreover, this model should also incorporate ritual processes in which the supernatural power is intrinsic to the words themselves. In an attempt to devise such a model, I have kept the common way of describing the act of the performer as the sending of a message but changed the description of the ultimate receiver of the message. This change is based on a comparison of descriptions of the process of changing reality by verbal power with descriptions of the process of changing reality by casting the evil eye.[14] The eye is believed to radiate its influence directly into a reality that is thereby transformed.

Thus the performer sends a message (words of power) to an addressee (the reality to be transformed).[15] Schematically, we can envisage this as shown in Diagram 1.

performer/sender → words of power/message → reality to be transformed/addressee

The arrows indicate the direction of the process. We can specify this structure further by inserting the entities who are supposed to possess the power to transform reality (Diagram 2).

performer → message + supernatural power → addressee
                                ↑
                                ↓
                        a. supernatural entity
                        b. intrinsic power of the words

Furthermore, we can distinguish between a human and a nonhuman addressee (the part of reality to be transformed). If the addressee is nonhuman, I refer to it as the *designated object*. Moreover, we observe the use of names in words of power. We call names of supernatural entities or sacral human interveners *background names*. The term *subject names* refers to proper names. These are the names of human beings who are to benefit or suffer from the words of power; they are the human addressees of the verbal power.[16] Thus, we get the schematic reflection of the purported communication process as shown in Diagram 3.

performer → message + background name → a. subject name (human addressee)
                       intrinsic wordpower   b. designated object (nonhuman addressee)

Although it is more common to view supernatural entities, such as demons and gods, as the addressees of words of power, the model I propose has the advantage of accommodating the power intrinsic to words on the same level as power attributed to supernatural entities. The model may thereby help us to study the process of communication and/or transformation in a more neutral way.

Let us now see how this basic model allows us to analyze the structural elements of a healing text from medieval Ireland.[17] By structural elements I mean characteristic components that are the building blocks of words of power. Words of power constitute a literary genre that is creatively constructed in a *bricolage*-like manner with the aid of these structural elements.

Structural Elements of the Verbal Message

The first of the three "spells" from the Stowe Missal will serve as our example.[18] This manuscript, probably the private service-book of a traveling priest, may have been written in the monastery of Tallaght in the period between 792 and 815, with a revision soon after.[19] On its last page (fol. 67b) are written three texts for healing ailments.[20]

The first of these texts deals with the healing of an eye:

arond d . . . suil[21]

ADmunniur[22] epscop nibar iccas . . . arrar roicca do ṡúil sen de ecc (*or* dee et c)[23] . . . gi crist[24] conderc[25] lais sid conasellais . . . rosc slán[26] do sulo.

    Hæc cum dixisset ex[s]puit in terram et fecit lutum ex [s]puto et linuit lu[tum] super oculos eius 7 dixit ei uade et laua in natatoria siloe quod interpretatur misus abiit *ergo* et lauit *et* uenit uidens.[27]

Against the[28] . . . eye

I invoke Bishop Íbar who heals . . . in order that the blessing of God and (?) the . . . of Christ may heal your eye[29] . . . the healthy sight/vision of your eye (?).

When he had said these things, he spat on the ground, and made clay of the spittle, and spread the clay on his eyes and said to him: "Go, and wash in the pool of Siloe" (which is interpreted "Sent"). He went therefore and washed, and he came seeing.[30]

The person who wrote this short text did not call it a spell, but the editors did.

The text as it stands can be divided into three parts: a heading in Irish, the invocation in Irish, and a Latin *historiola*, "a small (hi)story," also called "narrative charm."[31] The sender of these words of power is the "I"; the addressee is a designated object in the form of an ailing eye, specified as "your eye." The use of the personal pronoun "I" and the possessive pronoun "your" signifies that we cannot connect the text to a concrete, historical person. This would make it possible for the healing text to be applied numerous times. Each time the "I" may be embodied by a new healer, and the "you" with the ailing eye may be a new patient. The supernatural power invoked is represented both by background names and by intrinsic word power. Even though the text is short and incomplete, we can detect several elements that appear to be structurally part of words of power.

First, a heading consisting of a preposition (here *ar*, "against") followed by an ailment describes the aim of the text. Such a heading is a common characteristic of words of power, especially healing texts. The two accompanying texts are also preceded by such headings. The second text is intended to work "against a thorn" (*ar delc*), and the third "against a urinary disease" (*ar galar fuel*). In this book, the missal's owner, who may have been an itinerant priest, could easily have found what he needed even without the heading, because the prescriptions for diseases are all on the last leaf of the manuscript and there are only three of them. In larger collections of healing texts, such headings aided performers in finding what they needed.

A second element is the invocation, an adjuration or other way to address someone or something whose power is needed. Our text indicates this by the verb *ad-muinethar*, which is elsewhere used to invoke the aid of saints, (possibly pre-Christian) supernatural entities, and objects. There are, for instance, invocations of Saint Brigit, the name of Saint Columba or Columcille, the seven daughters of the sea, the three daughters of Flidais, and the healing salve of Dian Cécht.[32] In these instances, the verb is given in the first person singular or plural. In our text it is singular, which is common not only in spells or incantations but also in liturgical formulas, which are found in the Stowe Missal as well.[33]

There are three background names in the Irish part: Bishop Íbar, God, and Christ.[34] Bishop Íbar (d. 500?), who is also a saint (i.e., a human being with supernatural qualities), is invoked as a sacral intervener. God and Christ are examples of supernatural entities. God's blessing is requested as aid in the healing process. Christ's help seems also to be invoked in the Irish part, but because of the illegibility of the manuscript we do not know in what way this is done. The Latin part implicitly refers to the healing power of Jesus. While these background names represent a saint and supernatural entities from Christianity, Irish invocations of this kind moreover mention well-known names from Irish mythology (Flidais, Dian Cécht), designations unfamiliar to us (the seven daughters of the sea), and abstract entities, such as personified forces of nature.[35] Such names serve as signals to evoke a larger narrative tradition of Irish sagas and biblical narratives. They are clues allowing the participants in the ritual to complete the brief signals with traditional knowledge, whether in Irish or Latin (depending on the knowledge level of the participant).[36]

This text draws upon the power of a saint and supernatural entities—the former by invocation, the latter by the expression of the wish that God and Jesus Christ influence the healing positively. This is accomplished not only by verbal forms of *íccaid*, "heals, cures, mends; saves, redeems," but also by mentioning a blessing of God. Blessings are commonly believed to have a positive effect, and they have a negative parallel in curses.[37] Both verbal forms are words of power, but they may also be incorporated in other genres of verbal power, as in this instance. Because of a stain in the manuscript, it is uncertain what exactly is requested from Christ. Heinrich Zimmer suggests reading *ro(n)icca do s̄uil sen dee* et *c[roi]gi crist*, "May the blessing of God and of the cross of Christ heal your eye for us (*n* in *ro(n)icca* means 'for us')."[38] Whitley Stokes and John Strachan also transcribe *et* and *ronicca*.[39] John Carey tentatively suggests reconstructing *et commairge crist*, "and the protection of Christ."[40] Looking at the page in Irish Script on screen,[41] I could not make out whether the manuscript reads *ecc* or *et c*, nor did I see the abbreviation stroke for the *n* (the basis for "for us" in Zimmer's translation).

Another important structural feature is repetition, often of words that refer to the desired effect. This text repeats Irish words for "eye" (*súil* three times; *rosc* once), with another repetition in Latin in a plural form (*oculi*). This bilingual verbal and thematic repetition is further reinforced by Latin *videns*, "seeing," to which we might tentatively add a few words in Irish that are difficult to translate: *conderc* (*derc* means "eye," and *dercaid*, "looks at, gazes, beholds") and *conasellais* (*sellaid*, "sees, perceives"; *sell*, "the iris of an eye; an eye, a glance"). I cannot make sense of these phrases, but if we were to segment the words as follows: *co n-derc lais sid* (read *side*?) // *co n-a sel lais* (cf. the phrase *fer maeldub co n-oens̄úil lais*, "a man with black, cropped hair, with one eye"),[42] the text gives a formulaic repetition as well. Another important verbal and thematic repetition is present in the references to healing and health: There are two forms (*iccas*, *roícca*) of the verb *iccaid*, "heals, cures, mends," and a word for "eye" is combined with *slán*, "whole, sound, unimpaired, healthy, safe," again reinforced (or specified) by the Latin text, which implies the healing of a blind person. Words of power frequently involve repeated sounds, not only as a matter of stylistic features such as assonance and alliteration, but also in the repetition of enigmatic sounds.[43] Sometimes words of power are prescribed to be repeated a number of times. This is true not only of magical texts but also of prayers; constant repetition of words of power belongs to "the very oldest stratum of Celtic Christianity."[44]

The fact that more than one language is used in this text can be accounted a structural element, given the frequency with which it occurs in words of power. In this case, despite the fragmentary state of the Irish part (due to stains in the manuscript), both languages can to a certain extent be understood. This is not always the case: Words of power may contain cryptic letters, words, numbers, and signs. These may represent coded language, foreign language that we cannot identify (yet), or language that is mysterious on purpose.[45] We should also bear in mind the medieval Irish love of obscure and difficult words, sometimes stemming from Greek and Hebrew. The Irish enjoyed using such words to show off their erudition, and they also delighted in creatively exploiting their etymological wordplay.[46]

The Latin part of our example represents another characteristic. It is a quotation from the Gospel of John (9:6–7), which appears to function as a paradigmatic narrative, also termed *historiola*, "a little (hi)story."[47] Such a narrative may be identical with words of power as a "narrative charm" or may be *part* of words of power, as in the present case.[48] A narrative charm consists of a *historiola*, "usually relating a successful act . . . in the past, and an application of the past act to the present situation."[49] Here, the biblical quotation is added and appears to reinforce the preceding Irish part; no explicit formulation of its application is given. The healing of a blind man by Jesus forms the paradigm that the person using the spell may want to follow in healing an eye. Thus this text not only draws upon the supernatural power of Christ in the Irish part (perhaps his blessing, cross, or protection) but also in the Latin part refers to Jesus as healer as a model to follow. Reciting a successful healing by Jesus Christ may also be seen as an implicit invocation of him as supernatural entity.[50] It should be noted, though, that the absence of Jesus's name in the *historiola* enables the reading of the line "When he had said these things" as referring to the preceding Irish text. If the performer imitates the acts of Jesus while pronouncing the text, his role merges ritually with that of Jesus, while invoking and representing Jesus at the same time.[51]

If we focus on the Latin part of our healing text, two further characteristics become apparent. First, the *historiola* gives an example of words with intrinsic supernatural power. Jesus's words "Go and wash in the pool of Siloe" are the words with which the blind man is healed: The words appear to be powerful, although this does not overshadow the fact that they are spoken by a supernatural entity. Interestingly, given that bi- or multilingualism and the use of mysterious language seem to characterize words of power, in the gospels the healing words of Jesus are sometimes given in Aramaic and are thus different from the main language of the text—namely, Greek.[52] Second, the words of Jesus are accompanied by acts: the making of a "salve" from saliva and sand/earth. This act performed by the supernatural model may have been seen as a ritual prescription for the whole healing text. Thus we can discern further structural elements: the use of body parts (here, the healing hands, making and applying the salve) and of bodily matter (here, bodily fluid in the form of saliva). Finally, other substances are used. Earth or sand is mentioned here; elsewhere we find herbs, plants, water, butter, oil, and so on.

If we are to reconstruct the heading as *arind dercsuil*, 'against the red eye,' or—less likely—*arind drochsúil*, 'against the evil eye,'[53] then this text may be not only a healing text but also a counterspell. An evil eye is an eye that people believe can cause harm by looking at someone or something. Casting the evil eye was believed to be done by looking in a certain manner (e.g., gazing, looking angrily or enviously) at someone or something. Defective eyes or eyes with an anomaly—such as blindness, squinting, or having two eyes of different colors—were sometimes believed to be evil eyes as well, therefore, a "stare" from such eyes was seen as potentially harmful. In other words: A harmed eye could do harm. Thus people with such eyes may have been seen as possessing the evil eye and capable of causing harm, even though they may have had no intention to do so. Healing (the effect of) such eyes would be the same as exorcising the influence of the evil eye. Saliva is a well-known instrument against the evil eye, not only in Ireland but also outside this culture.[54] Moreover, blessings (sometimes combined with the application of saliva) were believed to counteract the workings of the evil eye.[55] In view of the state of the manuscript, however, the interpretation of this text as both healing and countering evil remains, of course, tentative.

The performer or sender of this healing text or message is represented by the "I," who invokes supernatural aid and who uses Jesus the healer as a model. The background names whose supernatural power is invoked are those of a saint, God, and Christ. The command uttered by Jesus in the *historiola* represents intrinsic word power. The message is formed by words pertaining to the healing of an eye; the addressee or designated object is an eye, which is made personal by the preceding "your."

The Performative Context of Verbal Power

We can better grasp the performance of verbal power by subdividing the phenomenon into three areas. First, I will focus on words of power as a communicative performance. Then, I will look at how the communication it seeks to deliver is actualized in time and place. Finally, I will address the implications of the fact that the text is not only a script for a verbal performance but also an object.

When a powerful text is voiced in order to communicate words of power, it can be actualized by (1) inserting a subject name; (2) being pronounced by one or more actors in the ritual process; and (3) embodying the "I" mentioned in the text. To actualize a text using subject names, there are two options. First, a specific proper name is part of the written text and will be uttered during the ritual performance. Second, a general mark, such as *N.* for Latin *nomen*, "name," is written in the text and a specific proper name then inserted upon utterance during the ritual performance. If the written subject name is the proper name of a specific individual, this might mean that the performance was enacted only once or only on behalf of this specific person.[56] This may be true of specimens that are part of a literary narrative and perhaps have never been performed in reality.

Let us take, for example, the example of the satire uttered against King Caíar.[57] Medieval Irish satire was a powerful literary genre associated with poets, and ranging from base invective to complex poetry; this artful ridiculing purportedly worked like a curse or a destructive spell, verbally wounding or even killing its target. Satire in early Ireland was thus thought to be dangerous: If someone was satirized, this meant loss of face, both literally and figuratively.[58] Important targets of satire are human cheeks, which will redden or pale with the shame aroused by the harmful words. Specific blemishes on the face attributed to satire are blisters. Significantly, the word for face (*enech, ainech*) also means "honor, repute, good name." Loss of face led to loss of status, one's rights and one's position in society.[59] Being satirized could diminish one's honor. The narrative literature even claims that satire could result in death from shame. In the tale about King Caíar, such blisters and shame become fatal: He loses first his kingship and later his life. The satire that is said to cause these tragic events goes as follows:

Maile, baire, gaire Caíar,
cot-mbéotar celtrai catha Caíar,
Caíar di-bá, Caíar di-rá—Caíar!
fo ró, fo mara, fo chara Caíar!

Evil, death, short life to Caíar,
Spears of battle will have killed Caíar,
May Caíar die, may Caíar depart—Caíar!
Caíar under earth, under embankments, under stones![60]

Interestingly, this text is literally said to be "a satire through a spell" (áer tri bricht).[61] This destructive text, here equated with a spell, does not really ridicule Caíar but verbally attacks him and functions as a satire in that his cheeks become blistered as an immediate result, and, after a year, he dies from shame. Repetition obviously plays an important part in this satirical performance. The subject name is not simply inserted into a frame text, but the whole satire seems to have been woven around the name Caíar, which is repeated no fewer than six times.[62] We have seen how power is supposedly drawn from background names; here, we see how a subject name is used as an instrument to victimize the target. Naming the victim, either by proper name or by nickname, was important in certain types of satire.[63] The narrative literature supplies several examples of how knowledge of a name gives the performer power over its owner and how ignorance of names equals lack of power.[64] The motif of knowing names is also used creatively: for instance, when a poet is not able to make a satire on a long name and when a supernatural female seer with a grotesque appearance threatens a king with satire by chanting the long list of her names.[65] This use of names is not limited to satire or to Ireland; we find it also in other sorts of verbal power and in a wider cultural context. For instance, the use of either the mark *N.* or specific proper names is an important characteristic of late-antique curse tablets and binding spells; several Fathers of the Church discuss the intrinsic power of holy names and untranslatable foreign terms.[66]

On the other hand, we note that if we remove the name Caíar from the satire, the short text still shows assonance, alliteration, rhyme and repetition. We should, therefore, keep open the possibility that this text had an existence outside the literary context in historical reality, and that our extant text could have been an example of a proper name being inserted into a preexistent spell that indicated its victim with the common mark *N*.[67] Words of power that were intended for multiple use consist of formulas into which the performer could insert a proper name as subject in place of the letter *N*.[68] Both the mark *N*. and the personal pronouns "I" and "we" are tools that enable repetitive use, and are to be found in liturgical as well as magical texts. The following spell, extant in two manuscripts, shows the use of background names as the mediators of power (four saints and a supernatural entity) and a subject name indicated by *N*. as the one to benefit from the performance directed at healing an eye:[69]

Obaid ar galur sul annso[70]

A Coll*uim* Cill*e* a Brigid a Pad*r*aicc
A Muiri a ri na ndula
dingaibh in gal*ar* n-inglan
fuil ac inn*r*ad do sula. N.
A cantain fo t*r*i ꝛ p*aidi*r *r*oime ꝛ na d*iaig*.

A Spell against Eye-Disease

O Colum Cille, O Brigit, O Patrick,
O Mary, O King of the elements,
remove the putrid disease
that is attacking your eye, *N*.
Sing it thrice with a *Pater*[*noster*] before and after it.[71]

This text thus needs to be repeated three times in its entirety, accompanied by the "Our Father" prayer repeated six times. The variant version in MS 24 B 3 has a different order of the saints (Colum Cille, Patrick, Mary, and Brigit), and the penultimate line reads, "that is damaging my eye, *N*."[72] The text in MS G 11 is to be voiced by the healer, who supplies the name of the patient for *N*. In MS 24 B 3, however, the text appears to be used for the healing of one's own eye, and presumably one's own name needs to be inserted for *N*., because the first-person-singular possessive pronoun precedes the noun for eye. The heading and the ritual prescription in the last sentence appear to stem from the scribe of the manuscript. It looks as if according to the former manuscript the healer should pray the Paternoster, and the patient should do so according to the latter manuscript.

Other healing texts seem to have been voiced by more than one person in a dialogue or ritual in which more than one person utters words. Our first spell against eye disease is preceded in MS 24 B 3 by another that seems to reflect more than one voice in the performance. It may therefore be an example of the message being uttered as a form of "conversation":

Obaid ar brod bis fo shuil

.i. focerd obaid *frit* suil. N.

ar gac nduil bis[73] fot shuil ar brod ar bir ar colg *frit* rosc ar rosc ar amrosc[74] dorala
   *con*a fergaib fai

gu[75] roib ar mo dernai*n*d in brod ita mo tshuil

ꝛ *p*ai*di*r rompi ꝛ na diaig ꝛ bolgum us*ce* at bel.

A Spell against a Splinter / a Piece of Dirt in an Eye[76]

That is: he/she casts[77] a spell on your eye, *N.*,

Against each thing[78] that is in your eye,

against a splinter / a piece of dirt, against a spike, against a prickle in [lit. against]
   your eye,[79] against eye/vision, against blindness / defective vision that came
   with its irritants in it [or: that set in with disastrous inflammation].

May the splinter / piece of dirt that is in my eye be on my palm.

And a *Pater* before and after it with a sip of water in your mouth.[80]

We note the repetitive use of the preposition *ar*, explaining the multiple use of the
text. The text seems to portray various roles for different actors, such as the scribe of the
manuscript, the performer/healer, and the patient. It is not totally clear how the roles are
divided, but it seems probable that the first and last lines belong to the scribe, who
explains why and how to use this spell. The second line seems to be an explanation of the
preceding heading because of the common abbreviated explicative *.i.: id est*, "that is." If
this is correct, the general heading is personalized by the introduction of a person
addressed by the possessive pronoun *your*, whose name is to be inserted for *N*. If I interpret this correctly, the person indicated by the third person singular would be the per-
former/healer and the addressed party the patient with the ailing eye. The fact that
someone is addressed makes it likely that the phrase is uttered in the performance, but if
so, who speaks this line? Would the performer refer to him- or herself by the personal
pronoun in the third person singular? Or is there a third party who explains what is
going on? Alternatively, the second line might be a diagnosis of the problem: The eye is a
victim of bewitchment by an enemy, for which the present spell serves as counterspell.
This last interpretation is, however, difficult to harmonize with the present tense of
fo-ceird, "he/she casts."

The last line gives rise to further questions concerning interpretation. If this line
stems from the scribe, which seems likely, because such prescriptions concerning ritual
performance are common in Irish healing texts, then who is the scribe addressing? Is it
the healer or the patient who should pray the Paternoster with a sip of water in the mouth?
The penultimate line referring to "my eye" seems to be a line uttered by the afflicted one.
"My eye" is contrasted with "your eye" (mentioned three times) and "your mouth." Is this

spell a dialogue, with the healer speaking the lines with "your eye" (and perhaps "your mouth") and the patient uttering the line with "my eye"?

A third way of actualizing the written text focuses on what happens with the central performer, who is indicated by the personal pronoun in the first person singular. Each time the written text is voiced, the written "I" becomes embodied, receiving the personality of the performer. Moreover, because this utterance takes place in a ritual context, the identity of the "I" transcends the historical individual who utters the words. The performer draws supernatural power into him- or herself by embodying this empty textual "I" in uttering powerful words or by invoking the power of a supernatural entity.[81] The performer and the supernatural entity may even merge in the ritual process through the use of ambiguous expressions.

A good example may be the following spell from the Stowe Missal:[82]

Ar delc

Macc[83] saele án tofasci delc nip hon nip ani*m* nip at[t][84] nip galar nip crú cruach nip loch liach mo[85] aupaith líi grene frisben att benith galar.[86]

Against a Thorn

The splendid son of spittle
Who/that squeezes out a thorn.
Let it not be a blemish.
Let it not be a disfigurement.
Let it not be a swelling.
Let it not be a disease.
Let it not be bloody gore.
Let it not be a grievous hole.
The brightness/glory of the sun [is] my charm [*epaid*].
It heals [or: strikes against] a swelling.
It strikes a disease.[87]

Strictly speaking, only the possessive pronoun "my" in "my charm" refers to the first person singular in this text. I think, however, that we also find a reference to the performer in the first line. The editors of the text, Stokes and Strachan, translate this line as "A splendid salve which binds a thorn."[88] I would suggest that "the splendid son of spittle," a more literal translation, may refer to the healer.[89] A similar way of speaking is found in the gospels, where Jesus often refers to himself in the third person singular as "the son of man."[90] "The splendid son of spittle" may therefore also refer to the Son, Jesus Christ, who is represented as using saliva when healing people in the *historiola* of the preceding spell. The healer may, therefore, identify both Jesus and himself as splendid sons of spittle, merging the identity of Jesus as a model and a supernatural entity with that of the performer in the ritual process. Other spells against thorns also supposedly employ the supernatural power of Jesus.[91] Again, there is a *historiola* in the background: the crown of thorns in the Passion narrative.[92] *Delg* may also mean "spike, nail, pointed implement," and could thus also allude to the nails that pierced Jesus's hands and feet. Moreover, Jesus was not only associated with saliva as instrument for healing but he was also spat upon in the Passion tales.[93] The saliva being designated is perhaps that of the healer, which may have been used in the healing performance when the thorn was removed.

Once more, repetition is an important structural element: Not only are sounds repeated through alliteration and assonance, but in a list of evils, each item is preceded by *nip*, "let it not be." Such lists create a cadence or rhythm in oral performance. Their content is also important, as we know from similar enumerative procedures in exorcisms, ritual binding formulas in legal texts, and the genre of protective texts known as *lorica*, "breastplate."[94] It is as if the text needs to be as elaborate as possible: All risks should be verbally expressed and thus exorcised. The list form also enables contextual improvisation, expansion, and adaptation during the performance.

The *lorica* genre is a good example of how words of power were actualized in time and place. These texts enumerate body parts to be protected, dangers from which to protect them, and supernatural entities whose protection is invoked. The reciter believed he or she would be protected by voicing these written breastplates. Maartje Draak has connected this genre with medieval Irish spells that were supposed to work for a night and a day.[95] She argues that, similarly, these breastplates were believed to protect the reciter for a night and a day.

The following incantation presents a similar enumerative procedure in which body parts, virtues, and bodily matter are connected with background names:

Caput Christi Oculus Isaie Frons Helie Nassus Noe Labia Iob Linga Salamonis Collum Mathei Mens Beniamin Pectus Pauli Gratia Iohandis Fides Abrathe Sangis Abel. Sanctus, sanctus, sanctus, Dominus Deus Sabaoth. Amen.

Neam ⁊ saegul ⁊ ana donti gebus fo lige ⁊ erge.[96]

The head of Christ
The eye of Isaiah
The forehead of Elijah
The nose of Noah
The lip of Job
The tongue of Solomon
The neck of Matthew
The mind of Benjamin

The breast of Paul
The grace of John
The faith of Abraham
The blood of Abel.
Holy, holy, holy, Lord God Sabaoth.
Amen.

Heaven and long life and riches to him who will sing/chant/recite it, lying down and rising up.[97]

The Irish ending promises a blessed, long life on earth and heaven to those who utter this Latin text at night and at the start of the day. The line "Holy, holy, holy, Lord God Sabaoth" stems from the Bible and is used in the liturgy of the Eucharist. Because the line was uttered during Mass, it would have been very familiar to those who understood Latin. The biblical connotations may have played a role for the composer(s) of the text. In the Book of Isaiah, seraphim sing this line around the throne of God; they also say that the earth is full of God's glory.[98] The Apocalypse of John describes "living creatures" who are covered with eyes and rest neither by day nor by night. They utter this phrase, combined with the statement that God was, is, and is to come.[99] The reference to these supernatural guardians seems to function in this context to underline the desired omnipresent and eternal protection.[100] The prescription in Irish indicates the proper time and place for the utterance of this text: just before one falls asleep and just after one wakes up. The text supposedly works for either a day or a night, because it needs to be uttered twice every twenty-four-hours.

A famous specimen of the *lorica* genre is the Old Irish "Deer's Cry," from the eighth century.[101] The Middle Irish preface to the text ascribes it to Saint Patrick and advises that it be recited every day as a protection against all sorts of danger.[102] The text consists of eight stanzas in Irish; the first and the last are identical. The conclusion is an adaptation of the last verse of Psalm 3 in Latin. Each stanza covers a certain meta-empirical or empirical field whose perceived powers are called forth for the sake of protection: Stanza 1 refers to the Trinity; stanza 2 to events from the life of Christ; stanza 3 to angelic and human orders; stanza 4 to forces of nature; stanza 5 to God; stanza 7 to Christ; and stanza 8 to the Trinity again, rounding off with the Latin prayer to Christ. The ending of stanza 5, the whole of stanza 6, and the beginning of stanza 7 enumerate the evils from which one wants to be protected.

It is as if the speaker dresses him- or herself in the morning with the virtues listed in order to be protected. Six stanzas begin with *Atomriug indiu*, "Today I girt [or I bind] myself," followed by lists of virtues or powers. A biblical paradigm for this idea exists in the Pauline descriptions of spiritual armor.[103] The preface, moreover, demands a certain inner attitude of the reciter: One should recite the "Deer's Cry" every day with one's mind fixed wholly upon God.

The metaphor of dressing oneself in spiritual armor by reciting a text hints at another important issue: the idea of a text as a powerful object. Michael Herren has argued that the *lorica* genre may have originated as counterspells, used by missionaries as protection against native sorcery. He adds that the *loricae* were perhaps not only voiced but also literally worn as a kind of protective charm.[104]

We know that objects related to supernatural arts were carried on one's person: For instance, Old Irish laws forbid people to carry (love) charms or spells.[105] The so-called Heavenly Letter from Jesus on Sunday observance is a good example of a powerful text that gives information, demands certain things from people, and is treated as a powerful object. This letter claims to have been written by Jesus in heaven (e.g., with his blood, or in golden letters) and to have been sent to an altar on earth (in, e.g., Jerusalem or Rome), and it demands that people abstain from work on Sundays and other holy days. There are numerous specimens of this letter, of which its first trace goes back to sixth-century Spain. They were used as textual amulets: For instance, men wore it when they went into battle, and women put it on their bellies during childbirth.[106] The Old Irish version of the Letter of Jesus demands to be read aloud, copied, and obeyed.[107] The supernatural power of texts is evident not only in their use as talismans or amulets but also in the role they played in ritual as material objects. This falls into three categories. In the first, something is done with the piece of manuscript on which the words of power are written, as in the instances mentioned above and in the following example from the manuscript containing the *Caput Christi* text:

> † In nomine patris *et reliqua* † salauan*tur* † alibria † trifon † *et* troferia
> †a†g†l†a
> Ar echb*ad* i n-etan eich i scribenn ⏉ tri p*atera* ⏉ tri haue ⏉ creda na lorg ⏉ ni fogain gan aifrenn don spirut naem.

> † In the name of the father etc. † *salauantur* † *alibria* † *trifon* † and *troferia*
> † *'attah* † *gibbor* † *le'olam* † *Adonai*, "You are mighty forever, O Lord."[108]
> Against horse plague.

> [Put it] on the forehead of a horse in a script, and [recite] three *Paters* and three *Aves* and a *Credo* after it, and it avails not without a mass to the Holy Spirit.[109]

The first line is in Latin and contains four enigmatic words that look like Latin, followed by the Hebrew AGLA formula. Nine crosses adorn these words of power, but in this context they do not seem to be prescriptions to make the sign of the cross, for the Irish part specifies that the words are to be attached in written form to the head of a horse. An alternative explanation is also possible, however: *i scríbenn*, "in writing," might mean that the signs and letters are to be written with one's finger on the horse's head. The familiar

Latin prayers, the *credo*, and a Mass dedicated to the Holy Spirit are the words to be voiced. The aim of this procedure is also given in Irish: Its goal is to heal a sick horse and/or protect the horse against disease.

Several examples fall into a second, ambiguous class. The Irish language causes the ambiguity. Verbs used in the prescriptions often have more than one meaning. Thus *fo-ceird* means both "places, puts" and also "casts."[110] The verb *gabaid* signifies not only "puts, applies" but also "sings, chants, recites, declares." Even *do-beir*, which usually means "gives, places; brings, gets," may sometimes be translated as "utters, pronounces." Hence, we have examples in which a text should be laid in butter, oil, wool, or water—but we do not know whether this means putting a piece of manuscript there or reciting the spell over these objects. We do know, by the way, that a love charm should not be cast on or put in salt.[111]

The third category is unambiguous again: Words are treated as objects that should be applied to the addressee to be affected by them. Thus, an ailing head is to be treated as follows, according to the variant version of the *Caput Christi* text from the Saint Gall leaf.[112] This text should be sung every day around the patient's head against a disease of the head. Then the patient should put saliva on his or her palm and apply it to the two temples and the back of the head. After singing the Paternoster thrice, the patient needs to make the sign of the cross five times on the crown of the head with saliva.

Objects may similarly be treated with words. An example is the incantation that Saint Patrick is said to have sung in order to make a poisonous drink, offered by a druid, harmless.[113] The legal version of this tale describes Patrick's performance as follows:

> dorinde pat*raic* na briathra-sa isan lind: iubu fis friibu fis ibu anfis frisbru uatha ibu lithu xp̄i iħcu [*christi iēsu*].[114]

Patrick composed these words into the liquid:
I drink knowledge
I drink against/with/towards (?)[115] knowledge
I drink ignorance[116]
I smash terrors[117]
I drink the feasts of Christ Jesus.[118]

A statement follows that whoever pronounces these words over poison or liquid will not be harmed by it. Then a more orthodox alternative is given:

> no comad e inoīe dei p̄ris doneth and ꝛ rochanad isin li*n*d.[119]

> or it was the poem/hymn *In nomine Dei Patris*, "In the name of God the Father," that he made then, and he sang it into the liquid.[120]

These examples are expressions of the belief that the human breath carries the words with their power into the object. The words touch the object and transform it in consequence.

Conclusions

I have discussed the performative dimension of "words of power," namely, verbal utterances with which people believed they could influence or transform reality. The term *words of power* is a neutral umbrella term for various genres of text, such as prayers and spells, protective and healing texts, satires, curses, and blessings. I approach these words of power as being part of a communicative process in which the words of power form the message, the performer functions as sender, and the addressee is the reality to be influenced by the message. The source of power that is supposed to bring about such influence may be represented by background names, referring to supernatural entities and human sacral interveners, and/or by the intrinsic power of the words themselves.

I have named several elements contributing to a basic structure for words of power: headings, invocations, conjurations or adjurations, background names pertaining to sacral interveners and/or supernatural entities, the intrinsic power of words, blessings, curses, repetition (of sounds, words, and partial or whole texts), bi- or multilingualism, mysterious language and/or cryptic signs and letters, *historiolae* or paradigmatic narratives, the use of the first person singular or (less often) plural, and ritual prescriptions that refer to gestures, the use of body parts, bodily matter, and other substances, such as butter, oil, (holy) water, earth, plants, herbs, and so on.

When the addressee of the message of words of power is human, a specific individual proper name may mean that the performance is unique, whereas the abbreviation *N.*, for which proper names can be inserted, makes the words of power suitable for repeated performances. In the latter case, each concrete human addressee embodies the abstract reference of *N.*, while the performer embodies the empty "I" of the text or other references to the performer, which may be in the third person singular. Reference to the performer is metaphorical via indication of a supernatural or sacral entity (such as a background name, an epithet, or any other mode of reference); the historical performer transcends his or her human personality to a certain extent through merging with the supernatural/sacral beings.

Sometimes more than one voice appears to be present in the manuscript as witnesses of words of power. These may have represented the performer and the human target, though some sayings may be attributable to the scribe.

A specific form of repetition is the occurrence of lists: of dangers to be averted, of sacral/supernatural entities to be invoked, and of body parts to be protected. Such a listing or enumerative process is found especially in protective texts, which are to a certain extent comparable with exorcism formulas. Speaking these lists aloud was believed to activate the protection, but texts containing the lists may also have been worn or carried on the person. In this usage, we see the importance of a text as object, when a piece of manuscript with letters or words on it is carried, attached to ailing body parts, or put into substances that are part of a ritual. Contact between such a piece of manuscript and the reality to be influenced by it has a parallel in the belief that words are carried on the breath of the performer and in this way reach and touch their addressee, thus transforming this addressee. Writing words of power with one's finger on the object to be transformed is another way of tangible verbal influence.

In these ways, words of power function in a performative context in which written, static words are used in a new, dynamic context and are thus actualized as part of a new (or renewed) process of communication, even though they may acquire an objectlike status within it.

CHAPTER 3

Inscriptional Violence and the Art of Cursing

A Study of Performative Writing

Jan Assmann

When Justice Fails: Legislation versus Imprecation

Deuteronomy

In the book of Deuteronomy, we read near the end that after the crossing of the Jordan and the conquest of the Promised Land stones should be set up on Mt. Ebal, covered with plaster and bearing as an inscription the whole text of the Torah "in very plain characters" (27:7). Then six leaders should stand on Mt. Garizim and six others on Mt. Ebal. Those on Mt. Garizim should shout blessings (27:11–13), and those on Mt. Ebal should shout curses. The ensuing text gives twelve verses of curses (15–26). The next chapter (28) starts with fourteen verses of blessings, for diligent obedience to the voice of God (3–13), but again there follow no fewer than fifty-three verses containing a seemingly endless enumeration of elaborate and painful punishments (16–68) for disobedience. Apparently, those standing on Mt. Ebal have a task four times heavier than those on Mt. Garizim. But a closer analysis reveals that the curses to be shouted from Mt. Ebal are to be distinguished from those of Deuteronomy 28. The former constitute a fact of structural orality, the latter a fact of structural literacy or, to be more precise, of "inscriptionality." The former are a fact of *voice*, the latter a fact *of stone*. They belong to the stones to be erected on Mt. Ebal, the mountain of cursing, and to be inscribed with the Torah.

Let us look at the structure and content of these curses. The first set (27:11–13) begins with "cursed be he who [*arûr*]," followed by a specific crime. These curses are to be shouted before all the people, and the people are to confirm every one of them by responding "Amen." Therefore, they are actually self-imprecations, and the repeated "cursed be he" must be understood as "cursed shall I be if I . . . ." This is a purely oral performance. The second set of (blessings and) curses shows an inverse structure. Here, the curse is specified, and the crime consists invariably in not hearkening to the voice of God. These curses are not self-imprecations; they say "cursed be you if you . . . ," and it is Moses himself who curses the people, referring to THE LORD THY GOD as the agent or executor of punishment. The list begins with an outline of the range of the curses, which pertain not only to the person himself, his soul and body, his destiny and affairs, but also to his belongings, his social and material sphere of interest and identity:

> But it shall come to pass, if thou wilt not hearken unto the voice of THE LORD THY GOD, to observe to do all his commandments and his statutes which I command thee this day;[1] that all these curses shall come upon thee, and overtake thee: Cursed shalt thou be in the city, and cursed shalt thou be in the field. Cursed shall be thy basket and thy store. Cursed shall be the fruit of thy body, and the fruit of thy land, the increase of thy kine, and the flocks of thy sheep, Cursed shalt thou be when thou comest in, and cursed shalt thou be when thou goest out. (28:15–19)

Then follow specific misfortunes. First come maladies: pestilence, consumption, fever, inflammation, extreme burning, the sword, blasting, and mildew (28:21–22). Then comes sterility of heaven and earth (28:23–24). In the third place, we find defeat and political disaster: "The LORD shall cause thee to be smitten before thine enemies: thou shalt go out one way against them, and seven ways before them: and shalt be removed into all the kingdoms of the earth" (28:25). Then there are dreadful diseases: the botch of Egypt, the emerods, the scab, the itch, "whereof thou canst not be healed" (28:27). Then follow madness, blindness, and "astonishment of heart" (28:28). Afterward come failures of all sorts: a wife with whom another will sleep, a house in which one never will dwell, a vineyard where one will never gather grapes, an ox one will never eat, sheep, sons, and daughters given away, and, what is worst, all this is to happen before the eyes of the person concerned: "And thine eyes shall look," "from before thy face," "so that thou shalt be mad for the sight of thine eyes which thou shalt see" (28:29–34).[2] Another set of diseases (28:35) and political misfortunes ensue, among them deportation "unto a nation which neither thou nor thy fathers have known; and there shalt thou serve other gods, wood and stone" (28:36), followed by failures in harvesting and housing (28:38–42). Social revolutions are threatened: "The stranger that is within thee shall get up above thee very high; and thou shalt come down very low" (28:43). To this, oppression by enemies is added: "He shall put a yoke of iron upon thy neck, until he have destroyed thee" (28:48). The political theme prevails again. God will bring a nation from afar, from the end of the world, "whose tongue thou shalt not understand; a nation of fierce countenance, which shall not regard the person of the old, nor shew favor to the young," such a one as "shall not leave thee either corn, wine, or oil, or the issue of thy kine, or flocks of thy sheep," who "shall besiege thee in all thy gates" throughout the land (28:49–52). Now a siege is depicted in the most gruesome colors: "And thou shalt eat the fruit of thine own body, the flesh of thy sons and of thy daughters . . . the man that is tender among you, and very delicate, his eye shall be evil toward his brother, and toward the wife of his bosom, and toward the remnant of his children which he shall leave," a scene dwelt upon in several more verses (28:53–57). There follow plagues, like the plagues of Egypt and plagues as yet unheard of, and expulsion from the land and dispersion among the peoples (28:59–61).

> And among these nations shalt thou find no ease, neither shall the sole of thy foot have rest: but the LORD shall give thee there a trembling heart, and failing of eyes, and sorrow of mind: and thy life shall hang in doubt before thee; and thou shalt fear day and night, and shalt have none assurance of thy life: in the morning thou shalt say, Would God it were even! and at even thou shalt say, Would God it were morning! for the fear of thine heart . . . and for the sight of thine eyes. (28:65–67)

Curses upon curses, a grandiose tableau of despair and desolation, of misery and confusion, of destruction and annihilation, a masterpiece in the art of cursing and in imagination (a real *Todesfuge*, already saturated with experience after centuries of Assyrian and Babylonian oppression, and only to become even more true in centuries to come). There can be no doubt that we are dealing here with a genre that one could perhaps call the "imprecatory catalogue" (*Fluchkatalog*), and even with the apex in the history of this genre. The point of catalogue cursing seems to be to give an exhaustive enumeration of all the constituent parts of the entity one wants to curse and to curse every one of them. In the following essay I would like to follow up some lines in this history and to do a very small and sketchy investigation into its forms and functions.

Deuteronomy is a book of law, *sefer ha-torah*. The curses concern those who break the law, and the blessings for those who keep it. But we must not confound legislation and imprecation. Legislation establishes a nexus between norm and sanction, on the one hand, and action and consequence, on the other. If an action implies violation of a law, then as a consequence there will be a penalty. (There is, of course, no question of any blessings for those who do *not* violate the law.) The nexus between crime and penalty is to be defined by legislation and to be enacted by judiciary and executive institutions—that is, by society and the state. This is what I call "connective justice." Connective justice provides and protects the link between action and consequence, doing and faring (see Figure 1).

But there are two cases in which connective justice is bound to fail: (1) if the crime is committed secretly and there is no accuser, and (2) if the law as a whole is not properly enacted, is altered, or even is completely done away with by society and/or the state. In these cases, other agencies must take care of the nexus between action and consequence, agencies that I shall call, for want of a better term, "metaphysical" (see Figure 2).[3]

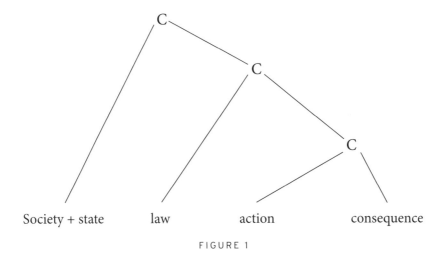

FIGURE 1

This is the formal structure of a curse or imprecation. A curse triggers "metaphysical agents" to bring about the consequence of a given action. It establishes a link between crime and penalty that is independent of sociopolitical institutions and therefore quasi-automatic.[4] Disbelief in metaphysical agents will cause a decline in the art of cursing;[5] disbelief in the functioning of sociopolitical institutions will have the opposite effect. Hidden criminality and the breakdown of connective justice provide the two cases where legislation stops and imprecation takes over. The first set of curses, to be shouted from Mt. Ebal, refers to the first case. These curses concern undetected or undetectable crimes.[6] Because of their dialogical structure (curse and "Amen") they constitute, as we have seen, a purely oral performance. The second set of curses refers to the second case: when the law as a whole ceases to be valid among the people. These curses are not to be shouted from Mt. Ebal and not to be confirmed by "Amen." They form a purely literal or "inscriptional" performance. Their status as a "literal" event, a fact of writing, has three closely interrelated aspects, which I shall refer to as (a) contractual, (b) testamentary, and

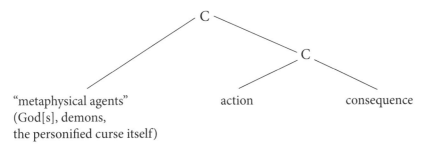

FIGURE 2

57

(c) monumental. The contractual character is what the text itself says. The long series of curses is closed by the remark, "These are the words of the covenant [eläh divrê ha-b'rît], which the LORD commanded Moses to make with the children of Israel in the land of Moab" (28:69; 29:1 in the King James version), and the curses are later in the text referred to as "the curses of the covenant which are written in the book of the Torah" (29:20). This points both to their literal and to their contractual character.[7]

The genre of elaborate cursing or "imprecative catalogues" is an integral part of ancient treaties.[8] A covenant, or treaty of alliance, is made, or rather sealed, by swearing an oath.[9] This conforms to very ancient oriental practice. The oath automatically subjects the parties to the powers who watch over the observance of the treaty. Breaking a treaty means breaking an oath and becoming exposed to the curses that are included in and released by swearing an oath. You can break a given stipulation of a treaty and still remain within the frame of alliance and connective justice. You will then be subject to a penalty, and this penalty is part of the treaty. But you can also break the alliance as a whole by changing sides, etc. Then you no longer place yourself inside, but outside, the treaty, and you will not be subject to any of the internal punishments, but to the external curses whose function is to protect the treaty as a whole and to prevent partners from breaking it.

The idea of a treaty also differs from that of a law in that it implies not only penalties but also rewards. Thus we find in many ancient treaties a section containing the typical combination of blessings and cursings.[10] After an enumeration of the deities by whom the treaty is to be sworn, who are invoked to act as metaphysical agents watching over its observance, follows a list of blessings for whoever keeps the treaty and a list of curses for whoever breaks it.[11] A treaty, therefore, is a very special and ambivalent kind of text, a text with great consequences. It entails, again to quote Deuteronomy, "life and luck, death and disaster" (30:15). As a treaty, in its "contractual" aspect Deuteronomy places the reader in a dilemma, a "bivious" position. He must choose between two ways that the text opens before him: "I have set before you life and death, blessing and cursing: therefore choose life, that both thou and thy seed may live" (30:19). A treaty is a text that structures reality in a bivious form. This is the *contractual* aspect.

The other two aspects I have termed "testamentary" and "monumental." All three are, as I said before, closely interrelated, the testament being a kind of contract and the monument a kind of testament. All three seem to me to have some bearing on the question of "Writing, Ecriture, Schrift."[12] Deuteronomy presents itself as a record of Moses's last speech or sermon, which he delivered before the people of Israel on the eve of crossing the Jordan and entering the Promised Land. Moses will not go with them, but will stay and die in Moab. His speech is a speech of farewell and has an unmistakably *testamentary* character. The speech is recorded in a book that constitutes a fact of literature: legal literature. It is, as we have seen, a book of law, *sefer ha-torah,* and a book of alliance or "covenant," *sefer ha-b'rît.* But it also implies and prescribes a fact of monumentality and inscriptionality. This is represented by the stones on Mt. Ebal: "And it shall be on the day when ye shall pass over Jordan unto the land which the LORD thyGOD giveth thee, that thou shalt set thee up great stones, and plaister them with plaister: and thou shalt write upon them all the words of this law" (27:2–3).[13]

From the fact that these stones or stelae are to be placed on Mt. Ebal, of all places, the mountain of cursing, it is to be deduced that there is an intrinsic relationship between cursing and inscriptional erection and exhibition—that is, *monumentality*. This relationship is to be seen in the institution of the witness. Curses and blessings, which usually appear in the context of treaties, are elements of an oath, which is to be sworn by both parties. The stone that the parties set up as a visual sign of the binding force of the contract is explicitly described as fulfilling the function of witness. This *testimonial* function is made explicit in the book of Joshua, where the same covenant ceremony as in Deuteronomy is related:

> So Joshua made a covenant with the people that day, and set them a statute and an ordinance in Shechem. And Joshua wrote these words in the book of the law of God, and took a great stone, and set it up there under an oak, which was by the sanctuary of the LORD. And Joshua said unto all the people, Behold, this stone shall be a witness unto us; for it hath heard all the words of the LORD which he spake unto us: it shall be therefore a witness unto you, lest ye deny your GOD. (Joshua 24:25–27)

The stones act as witnesses of the oath by which the treaty is sealed. They materialize, visualize, and eternalize the oath.

There is a second dimension of monumentality, however, that I would like to call the *commemorative* function; witnessing, testifying, and memorializing are, of course, closely related functions. The monument functions as *lieu de mémoire*. In exactly this function, the erection of stones occurs over and over again in the book of Joshua—the narrative of the conquest—and accompanies the various steps of the invasion. Stones are set up by the Jordan River in order to commemorate its miraculous parting, which allowed the Israelites to cross over on dry ground. Twelve stones are picked out of the Jordan and set up in Gilgal.[14] We are dealing here with what could be called "prospective memoria," the foundation of memory for future generations.

In a third dimension of monumentality, these stones seem to be connected with a *limitative* or *demarcative* function. They could be compared to boundary stones, which occur in the ancient Near East as a primary *Sitz im Leben*, or function of inscriptionality. Again, the marking and remembering of boundaries are closely related, and boundaries have a very strong contractual character. Contracts and treaties typically concern boundaries.[15] Thus stones commemorate the treaty and the boundary. An affinity seems to exist between inscriptionality and territoriality. The inscription serves to make the spoken word of the oath sedentary, *ortsfest*, immobile. We may thus subsume the "functions of monuments and inscriptionality" in the three notions of witness, memory, and boundary.

Hammurabi

Apart from treaties, blessings and curses in the form of a catalogue occur in still another genre of ancient Near Eastern literature: Mesopotamian law codes.[16] Here, too, the blessings and curses do not belong within the main body of laws and sanctions but are set apart in the form of an epilogue, with a clear predominance of curses. But among the many Mesopotamian law books, only two texts with such an epilogue have been preserved: that of Lipit-Ishtar and that of Hammurabi. What they have in common, by contrast to the other law codes, is that both involve a stela. The Lipit-Ishtar code is preserved on clay tablets pretending to be a copy of a stela, and the epilogue refers to that stela.[17] The code of Hammurabi is preserved on a stela, which today is the pride of the Louvre.[18] All the other Mesopotamian codes, which are preserved only on clay tablets and do not mention any monumental form of recording, do not contain any epilogue or imprecatory catalogue. This shows beyond a doubt that the blessings and imprecations belong not to the act of law giving but to that of stela erecting. It is the stela, not the law, that embodies the three aspects of contract, testament, and monument.

The imprecatory section of Hammurabi's epilogue not only far outweighs its few blessings (three lines of blessings, a hundred lines of curses), but parallels Deuteronomy in imprecatory emphasis. It proves beyond a doubt that cursing must be considered an art and an important literary genre. In this section ten particular gods, then the totality of the gods, are invoked to take care of the culprit

> who did not heed my words that I wrote on my stela,
> and disregarded my curses,
> and did not fear the curses of the gods,
> but has abolished the law that I enacted,
> has distorted my words,
> has altered my statutes,
> effaced my name inscribed thereon
> and has written his own name.

Enlil, the supreme god, is invoked to incite revolts, bring misfortune, shorten his days, destroy his city, abolish his name and memory from the land. Ninlil, "the mighty mother," shall induce Enlil to decree "the destruction of his people, the pouring out of his life like water." Enki, the god of wisdom, shall "deprive him of knowledge and understanding, and constantly lead him astray, dam up his rivers at the source, take away grain, the life of his people." Shamash, the sun god and supreme judge, shall "cause the foundations of his nation to crumble," give evil omens, cut him off from among the living; even "below, in the underworld, may he cause his shade to thirst for water." Sin, the moon god and lord of destiny, shall "lay upon him heavy guilt"; "may he determine as the fate for him a life that is constantly wrestling with death." Adad, the lord of abundance, shall bring famine and destructive floods. Zababa and Ishtar, the deities of war, shall "let his enemy trample upon him" and "deliver him into the hands of his enemies." Nergal, the lord of the underworld, shall "break his body in pieces like an earthen image." Nintu, the goddess of birth, shall "deny him an heir." Ninkarrak, the goddess of maladies, shall "inflict upon him a serious injury that never heals, whose nature no physician knows." Finally, all the gods, and again Enlil, are invoked to "curse him with these curses."

I would like to stress four aspects of this text that illustrate the difference between legislation and imprecation:

1. *The person of the addressee.* In the case of Hammurabi, the person involved is specifically a ruler. This shows beyond a doubt that the addressee of the curses is not identical to the addressee of the laws. The legal penalty threatens whoever transgresses a law, the curses whoever alters it. The laws address and concern everybody, but the curses address and concern only the person who is responsible for their functioning. In this point Deuteronomy and Hammurabi differ. In Deuteronomy, both laws and curses address the same collective person, who is called Israel and addressed now as "thou" and now as "you." In the Israelite world the mediating position of a ruler, who takes upon himself responsibility for the functioning of the law, is abolished, and every individual member of the new community becomes responsible both for keeping the individual law and for respecting "the law" in its everlasting totality. In Deuteronomy the curses are directed against (a) the individual person and (b) the collective, political person of "Israel." In the Hammurabi inscription they are directed against (a) the individual person of the ruler and (b) his political person as representative of his country.

2. *Concepts of person and annihilation.* Penalties aim at restoring the damage that has been done by transgressing a particular rule or law. They are devised to meet and to match a particular crime. Curses, on the other hand, aim at total destruction and annihilation. They do not know any measure and limitation in drawing on the imaginary of destruction. They aim at the total dissolution and decomposition of a person in all his aspects, in this world and in the hereafter. In so doing, they provide important insights into the concepts of person involved in these images of destruction. The art of cursing consists in knowing how to undo a person. It presupposes a concept of person, a knowledge of what constitutes and belongs to a person and how these different elements and constituents are most effectively disintegrated and annihilated. Thus a comparative study of the art and genre of cursing should lead to a much more detailed knowledge about ancient anthropological conceptions. But this is not our present concern.

3. *The role of the gods.* In Hammurabi several gods take the place of the "metaphysical agent," who in Deuteronomy and Joshua is called THE LORD THY GOD (*IHWH 'elohekha*). The gods are invoked to protect the law, not against a simple trespasser, a protection provided for by institutionalized "connective justice," but against a future ruler of Babylon who might change or neglect the law and thereby weaken connective justice. The ruler's

task is to watch over the application of the law, and the god's task is to watch over the ruler. They point to both the contractual and the monumental aspects of cursing. Contracts and treaties are sealed by a solemn oath, binding both parties and invoking deities to watch over the strict observance of the terms.

4. *Prescriptive versus performative sentences.* The Codex Hammurabi makes the difference between legislation and imprecation absolutely clear. Legislative sentences are prescriptive. They acquire a performative function only when applied by a judge to a given case and transformed into a judgment/verdict/sentence. Curses, by contrast, are performative. They do not describe or refer to a fact, but create it. But what they create is a "potential fact," not an actual one, because they are aimed at a person who is (negatively) specified but not identified. In Deuteronomy we are dealing with a similar situation, but there the person ("you") is identified, and the negative specification is only potential. This is the defining difference between treaties and monuments. Curses in treaties concern persons who are identified, but not (yet) negatively specified. Curses in monuments refer to persons who are negatively specified, but not yet identified. In both cases, curses function as *potential performatives.* My thesis is that potential performatives show an intrinsic affinity to monumental writing, writing on monuments—that is, inscriptionality. The stela of Hammurabi is an excellent illustration of this intrinsic relationship between curse and monument, imprecation and inscription. It is very probable that in a clay-tablet form of recording, the imprecatory epilogue would be absent. It belongs not to the code but to the monument, not to the message but to the medium. The Hammurabi stela demonstrates what is meant by the stones to be set up on Mt. Ebal. It not only codifies the law but represents and eternalizes its ambivalent charisma of blessing and cursing, luck and disaster, life and death.

Curses and Monuments

Treaty and Property

One objection imposes itself. Both Deuteronomy and the Codex Hammurabi are law books. Would it not be much more plausible to see in their common genre the reason for the occurrence of blessings and curses in both texts than to claim a common category like "potential performatives"? The answer is simple. The parallels for the epilogues in the codes of Lipit-Ishtar and Hammurabi are to be found not in law books but on statues and in tombs. Thus we read on a statue of Gudea of Lagasch, several centuries earlier, "Whosoever will bring it [the statue] out from E-ninnu or will efface its inscription, . . . Anu, Enlil . . . etc. shall change his destiny, they shall break his days like an ox, they shall cast on the ground his strength like a wild bull, they shall cast to the ground the throne that he has built."[19] This is the tradition to which the law codes of Lipit-Ishtar and Hammurabi are linked, not in their quality as law codes but in their quality as monuments.

There is even a verbatim parallel to Deuteronomy among the large corpus of imprecatory monumental inscriptions. It comes from Chalcis in Euboia. It is an inscription, erected by a certain Amphicles, in order to protect a statue and a place, a public bath, where it was situated. Among the many threats this inscription directs against a potential violator of the statue or area, we read the following: "God shall smite him with consumption, fever, inflammation, extreme burning, destructive storm, madness, blindness, mental confusion."[20]

This is a verbatim quotation of two verses of Deuteronomy. Amphicles must have been a Jew who knew his Torah and who adapted some of its curses for his private purposes. This fact is interesting enough, but what concerns us here is the parallelism between treaty and property, so that a person could apply to protecting his own foundations and monuments against violation the same imprecation formulas he knew to be directed by his god against apostates from his covenant. At first sight, the two cases seem very different. On the one hand, we have a treaty between god and his people, implying a set of laws and stipulations to be observed and confirmed by strong oaths that will turn into curses against whoever breaks the alliance. On the other hand, we have a statue, erected in a public place and protected by the very same curses, directed against whoever removes or damages the statue. Where is the parallel?

Both cases have a "contractual character." In the case of the treaty, this is self-evident and needs no further commentary. In the case of the statue, the contractual character is not so clear. But let us consider for a moment what erecting a monument means. A monument is meant to outlast its founder; it has, therefore, an unmistakably testamentary character. Erecting a monument means bequeathing a legacy to posterity and thereby forming a kind of contract. It is not easy to convince posterity of the advantage in accepting this legacy. The imprecation formulas compensate for this deficiency. They strengthen the contractual character of the relationship with the dedicator of the monument into which every reader is supposed to enter. The dedicator, in erecting a statue, exposes himself to the good will and respect of unknown visitors for an unlimited future. This future depends totally on the "reception" of the monument by posterity. The imprecation formulas are meant to direct and to determine this reception. They are "metamonumental," in the same sense as the curses in Deuteronomy are metatextual.

Egyptian Tombs

The most ancient and common kind of monuments are tombs. It is in this context that the earliest imprecatory inscriptions occur. I would like to give a very brief outline of this history, limiting myself to Egypt.[21] The interest of this genre lies in the insights it gives not only into the concept of the person of the addressee, whose personality they are meant to destroy, but also into the concept of the addresser. Who is entitled to curse and bless?

The earliest imprecation formulas occur in tombs of the fourth dynasty, around 2600 B.C.E. They are brief and violent. The gods are not yet involved in the persecution of the trespasser; beasts appear in the role of "metaphysical agents":

the crocodile against him in the water,
the snake against him on earth,
who will do anything against "this.[22]

A little later, the imprecations become more elaborate. Now, the monument is to be protected not only from material damage but also from profanation by impurity: "As for any person who will enter this my tomb in his state of impurity after having eaten what a spirit abominates." For the persecution of the trespasser, neither crocodile nor snake is invoked, but the deceased presents himself as a source of terror and violence. "I shall grab his neck like a bird's, I will spread in him the terror that I inspire, in order that the living on earth may see, so that they will fear a potent spirit who has passed on to the West."[23] Some texts go even further: "I shall exterminate their offspring, I shall prevent their farmsteads from being inhabited."[24] But these texts would not correspond to Egyptian convictions if the deceased were to act on his own arbitrary decision. Before using violence he must get the authority for revenge by a formal verdict. Therefore, the imprecations start with the menace of accusing the criminal before the "tribunal of the Great God": "There will be judgment against him in the West in the tribunal of the Great God" or "he will be judged on account of it by the Great God."[25] If the verdict is in his favor, the deceased himself will be turned into a metaphysical agent of justice (what in Egyptian is called *ma'a-kheru,* "justified").

During the First Intermediate Period and the Early Middle Kingdom, the art of cursing flourished, and imprecations developed into texts of considerable length. They even increased in violence and cruelty, though the deceased himself appears less often as an active agent of revenge:

Further, as regards the one who commits unjust acts against this stela, he is judged, and his neck is cut off like a bird's.[26]

As for any governor, any wab-priest, any ka-priest, any scribe or any nobleman, who takes it [the offering] away from my statue, his arm will be cut off like an ox and his neck will be severed like a bird; his position will no longer exist; the position of his son will no longer exist; his house in the Nubian nome will no longer exist; his tomb in the necropolis will no longer exist; and his god will not accept his white bread. He is destined to the fire, and his children to the flame, his corpse being destined to "smelling the earth." I shall be against him as a crocodile in the water, as a snake on the earth, and as an enemy in the necropolis.[27]

As regards any nome governor, any son of a man, any nobleman, or any civilian who fails to protect this tomb and its contents, his god will not accept his white bread, he will not be buried in the West, and his flesh will burn together with that of the criminals, having been turned into one who does not exist.[28]

As for any rebel who rebels and who plans in his heart to commit blasphemy against this tomb and what it contains, who destroys the inscriptions and damages the statues in the tombs of the ancestors in the necropolis of Siut and the temple of the lord of Raqert without being afraid of the tribunal which is therein, he shall not be glorified in the necropolis, the seat of the glorified spirits, his property shall not exist in the necropolis, his children shall be expelled from their tombs, he shall be an enemy of the glorified spirits, whom the lord of the necropolis does not know, his name shall not be called among the spirits, his memory shall not be among those living on earth, water shall not be poured in libation for him, offerings shall not be given to him, on the Wag feast and any other beautiful feast of the necropolis.

He shall be delivered to the tribunal,
his city-god shall abominate him,
his relatives shall abominate him,
his farm shall fall to fire,
his house to the devouring flame.
Everything that comes forth from his mouth
the gods of the necropolis shall pervert.[29]
As for any rebel and any adversary
who commits destruction in spite of what he has heard,
his name shall not exist,
he shall not be buried in the desert
he shall be cooked together with the criminals,
whom god has cursed;
his city-god shall abominate him,
his fellow-citizen shall abominate him.[30]
As for anybody who will not recite this,
he shall fall to the anger of his city-god,
and to the slaughter of the king.
He shall not be remembered among the spirits
and nevermore shall his name be mentioned on earth,
he shall not be buried in the West,
he shall be burned together with the criminals,
since Thoth has condemned him;
his face shall be spat at.[31]

As for anybody who displaces this stela from the tomb that I have built,
he will not stand before Thoth and Ma'at shall not judge him.[32]

In Egypt also, cursing is not an act of legislation. It seems to me mistaken to assume
that what these texts depict as the consequences of an act of profanation or violation
corresponded to legal penalties.[33] The execution of legal punishments belongs to the state
and its juridical institutions. The execution of curses, however, belongs to deities and
demons in the hereafter, and—this is typically Egyptian—to that world's juridical institutions. Many spells of what Egyptologists call "funerary literature" deal with these lawsuits
and executions and enjoy to the full all kinds of destructive fantasies (especially CT'spell
149).[34] Along with the idea of a prolongation of connective justice into the other world,
there appears the concept of hell. The so-called "Books of the Netherworld" depict the
infernal punishments.[35] All this pertains to the history of hell, not that of jurisdiction.

During the New Kingdom, imprecation formulas seem almost to disappear from
tombs. Perhaps this period was a safer and more civilized, and perhaps also a more
enlightened, age. Perhaps the necropolis police were strong enough to protect the tombs,
and the juridical institutions were strong enough to do without metaphysical agents. Or
is it possible that, on the other hand, belief in metaphysical agency was on the decline?
That this was not the case is shown by strong imprecations that now appear in other
contexts, above all in inscriptions documenting royal and private donations. Very typical
is this curse, in which divine vengeance is apportioned to a triad of gods: "As for anyone
who is deaf to this decree, Osiris shall be after him, Isis after his wife, and Horus after his
children, and the great ones, the lords of the holy land, will make their reckoning with
him."[36] "As for anyone who speaks against it, Amon-Re, king of the gods, shall be after
him to destroy him, Mut shall be after his wife, and Khonsu after his child, so that he shall
hunger, he shall thirst, he shall become weak, and he shall suffer."[37]

With the multiplication of donations in the Third Intermediate Period, curses become
very common. I limit myself to quoting only one example: an inscription pretending to be
the copy of a foundation document of the funerary temple of the sage Amenhotep, son of
Hapu.

As for the general or military scribe who follows after me and who finds the ka-chapel
falling into ruin together with its male and female servants who are cultivating the
fields for my endowment, and takes away a man therefrom in order to put him to any
business of Pharaoh or any commission on his own behalf, or if another trespasses on
them and does not answer on their behalf: he shall be exposed to the destruction of
Amun, . . . he shall not let them enjoy their office of royal scribe of the army, which
they got on my behalf. He shall deliver them to the fire of the king on the day of his
anger. His Uraeus shall spit fire on their heads, annihilating their bodies and devouring their flesh, they becoming like Apopis on the morning of New Year. They shall

capsize in the ocean that it may hide their corpses—They shall not receive the dignity of the righteous; they shall not eat the offering cakes of the "cavern-dwellers" [the deceased in their tombs]; one shall not pour for them libations of water from the river; their sons shall not be installed in their place; their wives shall be raped while their eyes watch; the superiors shall not set foot [ts] in their houses as long as they are upon earth; the leaders of the two aides shall not introduce them, nor shall they hear the words of the king in the hour of gladness. They shall belong to the sword on the day of destruction; they shall be called enemies; their bodies shall be consumed; they shall hunger without bread; and their bodies shall die. If the vizier, overseer of the treasury, chief overseer of the estate, superintendent of the granary, high priests, divine fathers, and priests of Amun, to whom has been read this edict, issued for the ka-chapel of . . . Amenhotep, do not show solicitude for his ka-chapel, the edict shall touch them, and them especially. But if they shall show solicitude for the ka-chapel, with the male and female servants who are cultivating the fields for my endowment, then all favor shall be shown them. Amon-Re, king of gods, shall reward them with prosperous life. The king of your day shall reward you as he rewards. . . . There shall be doubled for you office upon office, ye shall receive from son to son and heir to heir. They shall be sent on as messengers, and the king of their day will reward them. Their bodies shall rest in the West after 110 years, doubled to you shall be the mortuary oblations likewise.[38]

Near the end of the New Kingdom, obscene curses appear among these formulas. In the decree for Amenhotep occurs the idea that the trespasser will see his wife raped before his eyes. Even more common in this genre of literature (especially in donation stelae) is the strange idea that the trespasser himself, together with his wife, will be sexually abused by a donkey, which must have been considered a particularly destructive blow against the personality of the culprit:

As for whoever makes this endure, his sons shall endure in his place, one after the other, his name shall not perish in eternity. But as for whoever removes it, the power of Neith will be against him in all eternity, his son shall not remain in his place, the donkey shall abuse him, his wife, and his children.[39] He shall go to the fire from the mouth of Sakhmet and to the . . . of the lord of all and all the gods; whoever destroys this donation for Neith, his property will be destroyed, his tomb will burn and not receive his children. Beware of Neith.[40]

Let us resume. Our theme is cursing as a genre of Writing, Ecriture, Schrift. Cursing, both oral and literate, refers to the future. It institutes consequences that will befall future generations.[41] Curses are long-range weapons. In this far-reaching prospective intentionality, I see the affinity of cursing to a specific kind of writing: namely, monumental writing, inscriptions on monuments. Monuments are meant to address posterity; they lay claims to the future. They cannot expect to be respected and their inscriptions to be read without exerting a certain amount of coercion and persuasion. This is what the curses and the blessings are meant for. Monuments are ambivalent: They mean a blessing for those who respect and read them and a curse for those who neglect and destroy them. In this ambivalence resides their contractual character. Monuments pretend to form a contract with posterity, a treaty of alliance, promising the reader certain blessings and threatening him with utmost destruction. They not only address the reader but shape him. The less they can be sure of being properly received and respected, the stronger must be the shaping force and coercion they exert on the reader.

Plato, in a famous passage in the *Phaedrus,* depicts in lively colors the miserable destiny of a written speech: "Once a thing is put in writing, it rolls about all over the place, falling into the hands of those who have no concern with it just as easily as under the notice of those who comprehend; it has no notion of whom to address or whom to avoid. And when it is ill-treated or abused as illegitimate, it always needs its father to help it, being quite unable to protect or help itself."[42] All writing faces this problem. Certain kinds of texts, however, traditionally do not resign themselves to this state of affairs, among them treaties, boundary stelae, foundation stelae, and tombs. They try to influence, to train and shape the reader, to force him into the way of reception and reaction they want. They entangle him, by the very act of reading, in a kind of contract, where he will automatically be exposed to a bivious situation and to the consequences as specified by the blessings and curses. This is what I call inscriptional violence. Inscriptional violence is a compensation or substitute for what Plato calls paternal support. It occurs only where the intervention of the "father" or "author" of the text is categorically excluded—that is, where the father is emphatically absent. This is the case with monuments, which always stand for something or somebody dead, abstract, or at any rate belonging to another world. Monuments are alone, solitary, exposed because they are put into a realm of eternal duration, where their mortal father cannot accompany them. Never, as a rule, does the author of an inscription threaten to intervene in person on behalf of his monument. Where in some early Egyptian inscriptions the deceased speaks of "grabbing his [the trespasser's] neck like a bird's," he always makes sure he is entitled to this activity by a divine law court. Regularly, the author or "father" of the text must leave persecution of the trespasser to metaphysical agency. This invocation of metaphysical agency, together with the violence that it is bound to use against the trespasser, makes up for and points to the inherent weakness of writing.

In closing, I would like to venture a rather bold guess: Could it not be possible that this particular speech act, or rather, writing act—the written curse as a potential performative—shows us like a magnifying glass some elements of ambivalence and coercive violence that are intrinsic, albeit in a very attenuated form, to every use of writing that makes similar claims to eternity? Seen in this light, both treaty and monument, with their accompanying curses, can be interpreted as an "allegory of reading." A first step in this direction of generalization was already taken by Mesopotamian scribes when they inserted blessings and curses into the colophons of literary texts in order to prevent not only material damage of the tablet but also willful alteration of the text: "Neither add nor subtract!"[43] This custom survives well into the Hellenistic age. "Then, following their custom, he ordered a solemn curse laid on whoever might mistreat the text by adding something to what was written, or altering it, or subtracting from it," we read in the *Letter of Aristeas* about the translation of the Hebrew Bible into Greek. Not reading and misreading, perhaps, but in any event copying and miscopying—that is, tradition and transmission— are here treated in contractual categories. If writing is meant to establish not only a contact but a *contract* between author and reader, it will try to put the reader in an ambivalent situation, where reading means bliss and ignoring means loss. Thus, for example, the *Instruction of Ptahhotep*, the most ancient and important of Egyptian wisdom texts, presents itself as "beneficent for him who will hear, but woe to him who would neglect it."[44] I would classify this form of addressing a reader as "inscriptional violence," extending the contractual character of monuments, testaments, and treaties into the sphere of literary discourse. Treaty and contract function as "allegories of reading," oath and curse as protection against misreading, Thus we read, toward the end of one of the Nag Hammadi texts, the Hermetical treatise "The Ogdoad Reveals the Ennead," dating from the fourth or fifth century c.e., when the divine teacher Hermes bids his disciple Tat to write the dialogue down "in hieroglyphic characters on stelae of turquoise for the temple at Diospolis": "Write an oath in the book, lest those who read the book bring the language into abuse, or oppose the acts of fate."[45]

CHAPTER 4

Words and Word-Bodies

Writing the Religious Body

Loriliai Biernacki

Cartesian Transgressions

When theorizing historical understandings of the body in religious contexts, we see familiar and related images of the body: the religious body as martyred body, the religious body as submissive body, the religious body as that which must be veiled. When one contemplates all the things done to the body, done *for* the body, from fasting to ascetic mortification to hook piercings to motionless sitting to veils to habits, all in the quest of religion, it is hard not to see this past as a history of flight from the body, even as the body is the very mechanism for this flight.

Much of this imagery of the religious body is founded on an axiomatic dualism separating spirit and body as two poles of an antithesis that ultimately favors only one of these poles. Apart from the social and political effects of this dualism, it would be not unfair to suggest that one key piece of the self-understanding of many if not all religious traditions has been this message: both the possibility of and the techniques for transcending that flawed, permeable, and impermanent lump of matter we call the body.

We might add that the turn away from religion heralded by the humanism of the Enlightenment and modernity did little to undo the dominant model that privileges the transcendence of the body, with its intrinsic antithesis of body and spirit. Instead, the Cartesian split between mind and body reinvested this split with a scientific authority. It embedded this antithesis in the very heart of our modern understanding of rationality. Rethinking the religious body, then, requires a shift of this central metaphor in mapping the body's place in relation to spirit.

Of course, religion has not been only about escaping the body. The point of the Christian concept of the resurrection is precisely the preservation of the body, in its physical, most corporeal sense, even as this notion necessarily arises out of the overwhelming impulse to flee the body. And yet the very point of the resurrection is that it only happens once; the new body that will rise on Judgment Day will not have to be exchanged or made whole again. It is a body one can keep, a body guaranteed to be free from the body's customary pains and permeability, susceptibility to disease, and uncontrollable desires. It is the antithesis of what *we* know as body.

Similarly, one can consider as a counter to the religious desire to flee the body the idea of incarnation, which emerges in a variety of religious traditions. In Christianity, for instance, Jesus is the Word made flesh. One can read this message of Christianity, understood as God incarnating (which is radical, I think, in light of its Jewish roots), in psychological terms so as to turn the flight from the body into an embrace of bodies. Yet here as well, theologically Jesus dies a rather brutal death precisely so that we do not have to—though only in our essence, only metaphorically, not in our bodies. Christians still are subject to bodily death, even as we all are. The divine body of Christ is mutilated precisely so that the *spirit* in all these other bodies can be free. Indeed one can read the incarnation as conveying precisely the opposite import: a displacement of the sufferings of *spirit*, of souls condemned in the afterlife, by the idea that God acts in a body to reconcile the terrible fate of mortality that hounds this human condition of being embodied.

Yet this Christian conceptualization alerts us to something essential in the formulation of the relationship between body and spirit. The idea of spirit is inflected in a particular way where language—the Word, *logos*—becomes the marker for spirit. Indeed, a number of contemporary thinkers—including especially Judith Butler, but also others, from Jacques Lacan to Jacques Derrida, have articulated this Cartesian binary as founded particularly on language. In a series of influential studies, Butler has focused on this marker of language as the fundamental mooring for identity, as that which shapes the very life of the body.[1] The articulation of this binary and the deconstruction of the political and social givens it implicates have spawned an intellectual industry, one that seeks to unravel the political agendas imbricated in the ways language constrains, defines, and even boldly creates the body.[2]

In this essay, I will not address this discourse or attempt to nuance this theme. I mention it to highlight its obverse, which has largely been neglected: I want to explore how language itself might be understood to be constrained, even created by the idea of the body. In other words, what if we were to try to think the resolution of the problem of the body from the other end? What if we rethink the Word? What if word itself might be understood as always already flesh? What if the word in its essence never was anything other than body?

I focus on a specific example, that of *nyāsa*, a Tantric practice that transforms the human body into a divine body by ritually inserting magical words, by writing language on the body. I will suggest that this practice of writing the body allows us to rethink the religious body from the other side of the equation—that is, by allowing us to rethink what language is and how it functions in relation to the idea of body. The cosmology implicated in this practice not only provides a new understanding of body (i.e., body made divine), it also affords an even more daring philosophical transgression—a corporealizing of spirit. This practice rearticulates the essence of language to configure it as a body, doing what bodies do. In other words, here the model of *body* infuses what *language* is—in its deepest core, as its essence.

Tantra as a practice is infamous for transgressions against social norms. I will suggest that the transgressions that Tantra proposes are so potent at least in part because they are philosophical and cosmological transgressions. They run counter to the way we think and the way we order the universe. I will propose that the transgression Tantra enacts works to undo the Cartesian chasm, the ubiquitous binary opposition between body and spirit: It works by reconfiguring language itself in its most powerful essence as a body.

I have argued elsewhere that some forms of Tantric practice operate precisely to refuse the Cartesian paradigm, the hierarchical split between body and spirit, which turns out also to be a prevalent model in much Indian philosophical thought.[3] That is, in some instances, the heart of the transgression that the sex rite presents is a reversal of the terms body and spirit. So we see the God Śiva revealing the secret of the sex rite by saying, "O Goddess I am the body [*deha*] and you are the spirit within the body [*dehin*],"[4] reversing the standard trope of female as body and male as spirit. In this context, as I have argued, rewriting cosmology is the real secret, the transgression; sex merely operates to distract from this deeper philosophical move.

The case of *nyāsa* also rewrites cosmology by rewriting the Cartesian binary, fusing the very categories *body* and *word*. In what follows, I will first discuss *nyāsa*, inserting language on the body in its general instance and in a particular case that also involves actually writing with sandalwood paste on a woman's body. I will thereby show that the Tantric practice of *nyāsa* offers a cosmological articulation of language that understands language first and foremost as a body. Language in this context is performative; it is a body. The practice of *nyāsa* transforms the physical body by fusing these two bodies, the word-body and the body made of matter. After discussing the practice of *nyāsa*, I will briefly relate this conception of language to the idea of an alternate, performative language in the West as the language of the dream, nonsense, the gibberish of the mental patient. By way of conclusion, I will suggest that we ought to pay attention to this Tantric notion of language because in fact this reconceptualization of language and the body is already taking hold in popular imagination in the West. I will suggest that popular scientific conceptions of the body look very much like a Tantric notion of the body, in the images of superhero mutants and terminators. The mutant body and the terminator body both reflect a parallel of writing the body like the one we see in the case of *nyāsa*. In these cases, like the Tantric instance of *nyāsa*, the body is written with a language that is performative, not semantically driven, and then transformed by this writing into a powerful, divinelike body.

Nyāsa: Language and the Body

Nyāsa is a Hindu Tantric technique that uses language to transform the ordinary body into a divine body. The practitioner ritually places words and syllables of words on the different limbs of the body. These syllables and words make up a *mantra*, a magical verbal formula, which through the power of these words transforms the subtle essence of the physical body into a more powerful body, indeed, a body capable of superhuman feats, *siddhis* such as flying, becoming massively heavy, controlling the elements water and fire, becoming invisible, and so on. The *mantra* used for *nyāsa* in most cases is a simple formula that includes the name of the deity one is worshipping. I will give a widespread and popular example. A well-known *mahāmantra*, that is, a "great" *mantra* or *mantra* that works even if one has not been properly initiated in it, is the *mantra* "*Om namaḥ Śivāya*" for the god Śiva. The *mantra* literally translates as "*Om*, honor to Śiva." The first syllable, "*om*," is a word that carries no semantic content but performatively evokes a creative subtle energy that imbues the space where it is recited with imperceptible yet potent efficacies for prosperity and spiritual potency.

In the *nyāsa* performed with this *mantra*, the practitioner recites the first syllable, "*om*," either aloud or mentally, places the fingers of both hands on the heart, and then mentally imagines the sound being inserted into his or her heart. The practitioner recites, "*om hṛdayāya namaḥ*," "*om* to the heart, honor." With this, the practitioner's heart changes its subtle substance, becomes imbued with the inherent potency of the sound "*om*." He or she then recites the syllable "*na*" while placing the first three fingers of both hands on the top of the head. The practitioner recites, "*na śirase swāhā*," "*na* the offering to the top of the head." Again, the practitioner imagines the subtle essence of the first part of this word, *namaḥ*, meaning to honor, to enter into the head and transform it via the subtle power of the word. The word "*swāhā*," like "*om*," is used ritually at the end of an offering into a sacrificial fire, but it does not carry semantic meaning. Next the practitioner places the back of the fists with thumbs outstretched to the back of the head and completes the word with the syllable "*maḥ*," with the same mental insertion of the word and its subtle energy into the back of the head. With this, the practitioner recites, "*maḥ śikhayai vaṣat*," "*maḥ* to the crest of the back of the head, *vaṣat*." Again, *vaṣat* is a word that is used ritually and that does not carry semantic meaning. Then the practitioner crosses the arms across the torso, placing each hand on the opposite arm, reciting the first syllable of the name Śiva, "*śi kavacāya huṁ*," "*śi* to the protective armor, *huṁ*." He or she then touches the eyes with the next syllable, "*vā*," and completes the word *Śivāya* with its final syllable," "*ya*," while rolling the palms on top of one another

73

ritually to create an *astra*, a subtle weapon for protecting this newly imbued divine body.

With this, the original *mantra* is atomically broken down into its syllabic components, and each of the syllables is inserted on a different part of the body. In this way the whole mantra, which is normally spoken and thus temporally located, becomes spatially located, mapped onto the physical body.

There are a number of variations on this technique, including *nyāsas* that involve placing *mantras* on the feet, the sex organ, and the thighs, others that include the stomach, the sex organ, and the *ajña cakra*, which is the place of the third eye in the forehead, and the base of the spine. Moreover, in most cases, *nyāsa* is also performed on the hands as an initial supplement to the performance of *nyāsa* on the body. In a *nyāsa* taken from the Śrī Vidyā tradition, one mentally imagines offering substances such as incense, a flame lamp, flowers—standard items offered in a *pūjā*, a worship ceremony, to the deity residing in the various parts of the body, including the base of the spine, the throat, the heart, the stomach, and the sexual organ. For this, one recites a *mantra* in Sanskrit that notes the substance offered, for instance, "*Om ram vahnitattvātmikāyai Lalitāmbikāyai dīpaṃ parikalpayāmi*" "*Om ram* to the goddess Lalitā, who is the essence of the element of fire I offer a lamp." Here the syllable "*ram*" is an esoteric encoding of the body part, the stomach, signified by the syllable "*ram*'s" association with the energy center called the "jewel" (*maṇi cakra*), located in the stomach. One can ascertain this esoteric association by cross-referencing textual sources; however, it is usually passed down as part of an oral tradition.

Nyāsa is so common that often ritual texts do not describe how to perform *nyāsa*, but simply tell the practitioner to do it. Thus we find in the *Bṛhannīla Tantra*, when the Goddess asks for a secret rite related to awakening the energy at the base of the spine, the God Bhairava responds with a mere stipulation that *nyāsa* first be performed, after which he explains the rest of the rite. We see, "Bhairava said: After having thoroughly performed the *mantra nyāsa*, he performs the *ṛṣi nyāsa*, etc. First, having given a seat, he should worship the highest deity."[5] Details of the rite and its results follow. In this case, the author of the text assumes the reader already knows how to do the *nyāsa* and promptly proceeds to detail the rest of the rite. Likewise, in the text of the three hundred names of Lalitā, the *Lalitā Trīśati*, an important text for the Śrī Vidyā tradition, after the opening verses and a detailed statement of intention for the ritual recitation known as the *saṅkalpa*, a mere textual nod, not even a complete sentence, indicates that following this the practitioner should do the *nyāsa*. "With the root [syllables], the *nyāsa* of the six limbs."[6] The six limbs here are the heart, the top of the head, the back of the head, the two arms, the eyes, and the palms of the hands.

As part of the basic ritual template, *nyāsa* is incorporated as an essential element of nearly every Tantric ritual. Tantric praxis is multiple, with a wide variety of deities, a wide range of practices, and a multiplicity of motives for the practices undertaken, yet *nyāsa* is performed across the board, regardless of the deity and the lineage of the practice.

Why is *nyāsa* so essential to the Tantric ritual?—that is, what exactly does *nyāsa* do? I have pointed out that the practitioner understands *nyāsa* as a means of transforming the ordinary body into a more powerful, divine body. The subtext is that language is the link to the divine. The gods, like humans, have bodies, but their bodies are different from our physical bodies because they are fundamentally bodies made of language. Thus we see in a popular hymn to the Goddess Lakṣmī , "O Goddess, whose body is always the *mantra*, honor to you O Great Lakṣmī."[7] By a kind of contagion, in the practice of *nyāsa* one's own body modulates itself to the higher body of the deity, whose body is made of language. Abhinavagupta, an eleventh-century Tantric philosopher, articulates how this idea operates philosophically. He says:

> "This-ness" [the state of being an object rather than subject] in fact is predominant in the physical body, in the intellect and in the vital air, and so on. These [the physical body and so on] are not at all like the form which a word [*śabda*][8] takes when it is perceived. The [physical body and so on] cause consciousness to contract, become limited; they cover and obscure consciousness very tightly indeed! In this way the body that language takes—and this is what *mantra* is—this language-body continually reverberates in the sky of the heart as the form of pure awareness, with its innate capacity to act as active awareness [*vimarśa*]. For this reason *mantra* is called the unstruck sound constantly arising.[9]

Thus, language takes a kind of body, but a kind of body different from the physical body. The physical body causes our awareness to contract. Moreover, in Abhinava's scheme, even the intellect and the breath operate to limit our awareness. One might expect the opposite with the intellect, since in our worldview it stands akin to the transcendent life of the mind. Yet in Abhinavagupta's system it functions in the same way as do bones and flesh—to contract consciousness. In contrast, the body that language takes is a sound continually echoing in the heart. This language is pure awareness, *vimarśa*, which for Abhinava's system is one of two forms of the highest reality of the cosmos.

Language offers a special facility in this movement toward greater freedom and awareness. The body that language takes generates awareness. The practice of *nyāsa* then, by merging the physical body with the language body of *mantra*, causes the physical to become lightened, we may say "enlightened," less burdened by its weight as object and more closely aligned with the freedom and awareness of subject that the *vimarśa* entails.

Again Abhinavagupta tells us:

> "*Vācakaḥ*" is "the Word, i.e., what signifies,"[10] this "Word" is the heart of supreme awareness, deliberate awareness, but not only in particular words which are heard [and spoken]. Rather it also pertains to the Word which is more profound than *Māyā*,

the phenomenal world, which does not belong to *Māyā*, but instead enlivens and makes the phonemes which exist on the level of *Māyā* alive.[11]

Language exists both on the level of the word that is spoken and as a subtle reality that gives life to language as phoneme, as word on the phenomenal level of existence. Language lies at the very heart of awareness, and words have a power beyond the life of the body. It is this idea of language, the Word, that causes the words that one hears spoken to have life. Indeed, language operates performatively.

In the cosmology of this Tantric system, life is bound up on a great chain of being. One's place within this great chain depends upon the mode of one's perspective. There are in this cosmological blueprint two modes; everything exists on a continuum between them. These two modes are the place of the subject, on one end of the spectrum, and the place of the object, on the other. It is no accident that these two fundamental perspectives derive from a linguistic appreciation of phenomena.

The subjective and the objective each divide into three "pathways," "*adhvans*." The pathways of subjectivity divide into letters (*varṇa*), *mantras*, and words (*pāda*), while the three pathways of objectivity divide into *kalā*, the smallest elements of the material world, *tattva*, archetypes of the cosmos, and *bhuvana*, the various worlds. In other words, the pole of subjectivity is understood fundamentally to be language. The letters (*varṇa*), being the atomic particles of language (*śabda*), represent subjectivity at its most primordial, most powerful, and most inarticulate. Cosmologically the world expands first out of letters. Following out of them secondarily in the expansion (*prapañca*) of subjective being come *mantras*, magical performative language, and then finally words (*pāda*). The *varṇas* do not indicate meaning. Rather, they indicate essence, the essence of being and subjectivity. As the most subtle form they are also the most powerful.[12]

In contrast to the pole of language and subject, the more one identifies with the idea of object, the less powerful, more bound one becomes. The object is a thing, the "it" as opposed to the "I," which is the subject. By moving to the pole of subjectivity, one moves toward divinity and the greater freedom, awareness, and power that it brings. This cosmological great chain of being moves through objects from gross matter—stones and clay—through plant and animal life and up higher on the scale into human life. As one moves higher up the scale, one aligns more with subjectivity; one's body becomes more subtle and powerful. Higher than the human are those beings, *mantreśvaras* and *vidyeśvaras*, whose bodies consist of *mantra*, powerful magical language.

On the lower levels, purely physical matter occurs in the hierarchy of the five elements: earth, water, fire, air, and space. These five have five more subtle analogues: odor, taste, form, feeling, and sound. Sound here occupies a curious position, since it functions as both a material phenomenon in physical sound and as language, words. The Sanskrit word *śabda*, which Abhinavagupta uses, incorporates both these meanings. Language as sound naturally forms a bridge from gross body to the subtle world. Abhinavagupta explains this:[13]

That [*vācakaḥ*, Word] is the Self, and partakes of I-consciousness. The beings who exist as rulers of words [*vidyeśvaras*] become limited because of the mutual interaction of the word-body and the class of objects. Language and sound [*śabda*] have limitless light because they lack a dense covering over them [unlike form, taste, touch etc.]. . . . Thus, this [language] is the Subject and so on, wrapped around and made limited and precise by a particular handle as particular word [*graha*- not *śabda* here] and by a particular material basis [the actual object].[14]

This quote takes us into an aspect of cosmology that I do not have the space to address in depth here: namely, that in Abhinava's system beings who, like gods, are higher than humans have bodies that are made of words. We saw this briefly above in the quote from the hymn to the Goddess Lakṣmī, whose body is the *mantra*. This, of course, is radically different from our own view of language. In this system, words and sound are akin to the realm of the physical, insofar as they also consist of bodies, literally word-bodies (*śabdaśarīratva*). A word-body is less dense than a body made of bones and blood. Language exists as limitless light, yet language can also be wrapped around by materiality and a particular word—here, literally, something that grasps it (*graha*).

What this entails is a continuity of body and language. In Abhinava's monistic Tantric view, matter at base is fundamentally not different from pure consciousness. Language is an especially subtle, less dense form of the elements, and as such it acts as a kind of alchemical rod, transforming the human physical body into the subtle sound body of the deity. Body and language, rather than being polar antipodes, are obverse sides of each other. Language is in fact simply a subtle transformation of the physical materiality of human bodies.

We see *nyāsa* everywhere performed in Tantra precisely because it taps into the morphability of bodies—into a body's capacity to move up the chain from the space of body as physical object to a body of words, functioning in the mode of subject rather than object. Language is a body, and it is body extended to its most refined condition.

The cosmology in which *nyāsa* figures offers a kind of literal twist on some contemporary ideas of self as constructed by language, such as Judith Butler's, in which the self is interpolated and constructed by the linguistic world, with its limiting parameters into which we are born and socialized. That is, one can read this cosmology as subscribing to a deconstructivist notion of identity, whose very possibilities are determined by the language we have available to talk of them. It does so, however, in a very literal and profound way, a way that extends the very idea of language to language as bodied—even as it retains as language's most superficial level our Western models of language as conceptual and semantic. Thus, when performing *nyāsa*, the practitioner not only acknowledges that our identities are constructed by the parameters of the language we inherit, he or she actively works to construct identity out of language. Here, however, the most effective way to construct an identity, to build a body out of language, is to use the more powerful form of language that is *mantra*, performative language, rather than *pāda*, language as semantic concept.

This brings us to a telling element of *nyāsa* that deserves close attention. *Nyāsa* breaks up the *mantra*, without regard for its semantic content. When the practitioner inserts the words onto the body, the words are split apart and dispersed over the various limbs. In the example given, the sentence "*om namaḥ Śivāya*" has a meaning, "honor to Śiva," yet the meaningful units—the words in the sentence—are not kept intact. They are, rather, free-floating, meaningless syllables, "*na*" on the top of the head, "*śi*" on the arms, and so on. The physical mapping of these phonemes proposes a notion of language divorced from its semantic function. Rather than meaning-bearing components, these phonemes are treated iconically, the sonic form as itself full of power, a deity. These phonemes function as bodies themselves.

Indeed, elsewhere we find that *mantras* are treated in just this way, not as meaning-bearing sentences or even names, but rather more like bodies. In a discussion of how the practitioner might remedy the effects of his laziness or delusions that might arise along the Tantric path, the *Bṛhannīla Tantra* offers a number of procedures designed to restore the strength (*vīrya*) of the practitioner's *mantra*.[15] The text enjoins, for instance: "by separating the consonants from the vowels, that is called 'causing life' [*jīvanam*] for that [*mantra*]."[16] Similarly, we find, "having written all together the letters of the *mantra*, he should strike each letter one by one with sandalwood water [reciting] the syllable of the wind, *yam*. That is called striking it."[17] Interestingly, here, the word for striking (*tāḍanam*) is the same word that this text uses to denote the act of sex. In another example, we see, "he should sprinkle each individual letter of the *mantra* with the water of the *kuśa* plant, saying mentally the *mantra*. This procedure is known as 'nourishing' [*āpyāyana*]."[18]

Each of these procedures treats this language as a body—to be hit, made love to, nourished, or sprinkled with water. This especially powerful language, the magical language of the *mantra*, is not semantically driven; rather, it is itself corporeal. It does not exist in an abstracted dimension of meaning. It exists rather as bodies; one interacts physically with these words. Indeed, language in its essence and at its most powerful is not a semantic enterprise. It is not, as Saussure proposed, fundamentally a communication of meaning in which signs, the words chosen for this communication, are arbitrarily set by social, cultural conventions. Rather, the essence of language is a subtle body, a kind of matter that lacks the limitations of bodies and matter made of clay and flesh.

Moreover, the use of *mantra* in ritual context emphasizes the lack of semantic content. One receives a *mantra* through initiation and then recites that *mantra* in a practice called *japa*, over and over and over, whether ten thousand or one hundred thousand times, to an extent long past the point where semantic content might be conveyed. Like the compulsive repetition of the Freudian symptom, the *mantra* functions performatively rather than semantically. I would suggest that the repetition of the *mantra*, like the Freudian symptom, is a repetition writ large that functions via repetition to connect the body to the word. One recites the *mantra* over and over in order to effect a kind of fusion of the physical body with the word-body that is the *mantra*. One could argue that the symptom of the neurotic operates on this template as well, to bring the repressed meaning that the patient cannot bring himself to name into the performative functioning of the body, the handwashing that is obsessively performed again and again, and so on.

I noted above that the word used for "striking" the *mantra* is the same word used to describe the act of sex. In other words, the male practitioner engages with these words in the same way as he engages with a woman in the sex rite. Elsewhere I have argued that this is not an accident. There is a homology between women and the magical language of *mantras*; moreover, women have a special facility with *mantras*. Along with this, I have argued that the *mantra* as performative speech is gendered, and that women's speech has been understood to be performative.[19] I will not rehash this here, except to note that the magical language of *mantra*—which in Tantra is generally considered more powerful than ordinary, semantically driven language—points to a quality of language that is mostly neglected in the West. This performative magical language linked to women—who are, in the history of the West and in India, linked with the body—echoes a logic of association whereby women/body/performative language stand in contrast to male/spirit/word as logical or semantically cohesive language. It makes sense that this particular type of performative language, which is already more akin to bodies, would be the lynchpin tying the physical body together with the abstract element of mind that is language. Inchoately seething through the inarticulate gestures of the body is a philosophical transgression; in this Tantric magical technology, *nyāsa* is a engineered to break and bridge the boundary between word and body, spirit and flesh.

Writing the Feminine Body

One more uncannily suggestive element of the ritual inflects this association of woman/body/magical language and the body's transformation into language by means of *nyāsa*. In a worship, or *pūjā*, involving a woman, *nyāsa* is performed with a variation in which the practitioner ritually writes the letters of the *mantra* onto the body of a woman seated on the dais, the *maṇḍala*, using red sandalwood paste.[20] "He should write all of these with devotion, according to the rules, with the stalk of the Acacia plant."[21] We find, "on her two breasts, the syllable of Rāmā, on each side of her jaw, the two syllables of Bhaga. Below her armpits, O supreme Goddess, he should write the two syllables of the one who holds the Ganges river,"[22] and so on. These rites are secret, illicit; they are performed in the dead of night at an abandoned house or a lonely spot in a forest. Moreover, the writer disguises the actual syllables scripted on the body in a secret code, that is, as "the one who holds the Ganges river." The key to decode these veiled clues is handed down orally from teacher to disciple.

Now, one wonders, why write the letters on the body of the woman, rather than insert them mentally as is done in all other performances of *nyāsa*?[23] Why does a woman's body necessitate this more tangible articulation of language through writing? Apart from the ritually powerful rhetorical flourish gained in this externalized act, the implications of this gesture are multiple and profound. Is it, as Lévi-Strauss suggests, that writing carries an originary violence, where it functions as a sociological rather than an intellectual enterprise, as a tool of domination?[24] In this scenario, writing on the body of the woman might be read as a literalization of the hierarchy of the genders.

However, the force of Lévi-Strauss's critique is no doubt tainted by a Rousseauian nostalgia for nature, the natural in opposition to the civilized, as Derrida has pointed out.[25] In any case, the theme of nature in contrast to culture is also not alien to the Indian context. One can reconstruct the dilemma of nature and culture in the Brahminical rites of *saṃskāra*, the *upanāyana*, for instance, which frees the twice-born boy from the ill-favored idiocy of being without culture—even though we see that in the Brahminical context the terms are reversed. That is, in the Indian context, culture, *Saṃskṛti*, perennially trumps nature, *Prakṛti*. In this case nature, *Prakṛti*, is not the sentimental figure of the lost mother; she is the treacherous feminine deceiver, the multiform of *Māyā*, whose wiles keep the sincere seeker from enlightenment. One, of course, may also read this opposition between nature and culture as a recapitulation of the opposition between body and mind, or flesh and spirit. Here we might also extend it to the dichotomy we noted earlier—women / body / performative language standing in contrast to male / spirit / word as logical or semantically cohesive language.

It is, of course, not an accident that the Tantric worldview we address here reverses this pervasive orthodox devaluation of *Māyā*. Just as we saw earlier, as Abhinava's monistic Tantra works to bridge the boundary between the body and spirit and does so via the magical language of *mantra*, so too Abhinavagupta reinvests *Māyā* in a strategic Tantric move to embrace the multiplicity and messiness of the world. Critiquing the more orthodox Vedantin and Sāṃkhya views, he tells us, "*Māyā* is in fact the form of the Energy of God."[26] This reversal extends to the understanding of the chain of associations that links body to woman to performative speech. *Māyā* as nature stands as the woman's body, upon which are scripted the powerful phonemes evocative in the Tantric context of the Goddess's own self-revelation as *mālinī*, the letters of the alphabet, which create the cosmos. With this, the opposition between nature and culture in effect collapses—as it must in a truly monist philosophical system. In other words, writing the letters on the body of the woman is an invocation of language and a refusal of the opposition between language and body; it refuses any notion of language as identity that transcends and opposes the presence of body. It is a concentrated, deliberate fusing of physical body with language as subtle body, fusing the two via language.

The writing on the body is not of the order of the logos, the word carving and mapping a meaning into the territory of the body. Rather, as we saw earlier, the practitioner scripts onto the body simple, meaningless syllables, *bīja,* "seed" letters, that have no semantic content. As letters (*varṇa*), the basic constituents that make up the *mantra*, these letters reach down to a primordial, inchoate essence just beginning to blossom into life.

To script the letters, the *varṇas*, onto the body of a woman is at once a recognition of a primordial subjectivity—the pathway of letters, *varṇa adhvan*— appropriately replicated on the body of the female and also a secret sharing, a re-membering, an articulation of each limb as its subtle counterpart as word-body. That which is body and "other," namely, object, is made into subject by the writing of letters. *Nyāsa* is a preparatory rite in seeing the woman as goddess; this writing effects the fusion of body with Goddess as *mantra.*

The Underside of Language

The writing on the body that the Tantric practice of *nyāsa* entails offers a way to rethink the relationship between language and the body by rethinking what language does *to* the body. Moreover, this rethinking of the relationship between language and the body generates and derives from a broader model of the function of language itself, namely, what it is that language does. That is, rather than constructing the body through discourse, as mere object of language, in a discourse that pits mute body against transcendent mind or spirit, spirit aligned with language, this Tantric practice hints at transforming our ideas of language instead. The word becomes akin to the body, becomes itself a body.

One of Foucault's most productive insights was his postulation that the seventeenth century marked the birth of an epoch, a transformation in ideologies governing the body, insofar as it produced a wealth of discursive attention to the body in numerous discourses, medical treatises, and the institutions of psychiatry and pedagogy. He tells us that what marks off modernity is a profusion of writing about the body, and a new kind of writing about the body.[27] The writing of the body that he discusses represents the triumph of a rationality, a use of language to master its other, the corporeal, amorphous collection of pains and desires that is the body.

This profusion, however, brought in its wake attention to another kind of language in relation to the body. The advent of psychoanalysis attempted to map out this other kind of language, the underside of language, the gibberish of the patient, language as nonsense, the obscure automatic writing that Myers, Janet, and James saw as a doorway to other selves,[28] language as performative embodiment of the symptom and the incoherence of metaphors in dreams. Since I have elsewhere in much greater detail discussed the correspondences between the magical language of *mantra* and this other performative language, language as the symptom of the patient,[29] I will here only reiterate that both *mantra* and language as symptom operate primarily as performative language, as language divorced from semantic impart. The nonsensical language of the *mantra* is the

81

underside of language as rationality. In contrast, the Tantric view reverses the hierarchy of rational to irrational, semantic to performative that Freud assumes, instead transposing the pathology Freud imputes to it onto divinity, superior power. This language, atomically split in a destruction of its semantic element, this language as body, transforms both language and body as it fuses with body as matter. The *mantra* is semantically dismantled and the body becomes a super-body. Technical mastery over the subtle body of words gives way to the magical *siddhis*, the magical powers that Tantra offers; it enables the practitioner to attain physically a super-body.

Rethinking the religious body in such a way that reincorporates language in the body and invests the body with language and *as* language, as we see in the practice of *nyāsa*, operates as a metaphor for a psychological restructuring of the relationship between body and mind, between matter and spirit. This performative, unsemantic language that defies the rational strictures of language offers a way of rethinking the religious body; it is homologous with the body and represents a transformation of the body.

Writing the Religious Body, Writing the Mutant Body

In 2009 *Newsweek* ran an article by Lisa Miller proclaiming that Americans are conceptually and ideologically becoming Hindus.[30] The emphasis on a plurality of religious horizons and an increasing acceptance of reincarnation are two of the beliefs she cites as signaling this ecclesiastical sea change. Perhaps, however, it may be more apropos to suggest that in fact we may be becoming Tantrics. Specifically, our understanding of the body as it participates in cosmos and the religious construction of cosmos is transforming. As we leave the twentieth century and venture into the next millennium, one of the most striking conceptual transformations centers on the idea of the religious body. Indeed, one could argue that the dominant political challenge of our first decade, terrorism, pivots around a conflict between older and newer conceptions of the religious body.[31] I would suggest that science, and the idea of science, have changed the way we view our cosmos. They have especially changed the way we view the human body in the cosmos, inadvertently moving us in the direction of a Tantric notion of the body.

By a Tantric notion of the body, I mean an ideology that reincorporates the body, literally. Tantric practice in general—and *nyāsa* is an instance of this—works to transform and replace the ordinary physical body with a divine, more powerful body. One other well-known practice of Tantra, though not as ubiquitous as *nyāsa*, is the practice of *bhūta śuddhi*, the purification of the elements. Like the practice of *nyāsa*, this practice also transforms the body, in this case by mentally destroying the five constituent elements of the body—earth, air, water, fire, and space, and rebuilding the body again out of these elements in a more powerful way with *mantras*. Thus, rather than a flight from the body, through the invocation of a transcendence from the body into spirit, one might understand a Tantric perspective toward the body as one that instead reinvests and embraces the body.

As I pointed out at the outset, one could suggest that historically, within a traditional religious framework, the religious body has stood as something of an oxymoron. That is, religions have in the main sought to erase the body in favor of a transcendence of the body, particularly as a response to mortality, the fact that the body dies. By contrast, Tantric practices generally operate instead to reclaim the body through the transformation of the body into a divine body and a super-body. I would suggest that we find a similar transformation of the body creeping into contemporary popular culture via a scientific displacement of Darwin's body, as the mutant body, the body of the X-men, and more recently in the body of the cyborg. This twenty-first-century body of our popular fantasies, in fact, looks very much like a Tantric body. These mutant bodies and terminators, like the transformed Tantric body, display all sorts of *siddhis*, magical powers: the power to fly, to command the elements, to bring storms and attract iron, the power to become invisible.

What is more interesting is the mechanism constituting this new, powerful mutant body. These new bodies are being reconfigured by a code—that is to say, by a language. It is not a language that is semantically driven; rather, like the Tantric use of *mantra*, it is a performative language. In other words, I suggest that DNA is a code, a language, yet it is a performative language, not semantically driven.[32] The transformation into the mutant body is a transformation that occurs through a kind of writing on the body with a primordial language, the DNA, the mystical language written deep into the cells of our bodies, fusing physical body and language. Like the *varṇa*s, the letters that the Tantric uses to script the body, the code of DNA is a primordial and creative power, which does not "mean" something but instead "does" something, transforming the very fabric of the body into a super-body with special powers. And like the *varṇa*s, the powerful writing of DNA can be dismantled into its component pieces, atomically dispersed in the formation of new body-transfiguring effects. Similarly, the terminator body is also a body made powerful by a kind of writing, in this case, writing computer code, a fusing of body and language in order to effect a new and technically superior super-body, capable of fantastic feats. In this case, this writing on the body affords the terminator body an imperviousness to the usual frailty of the body, its susceptibility to death.

Thus the monism of science, which finds its apogee in a scientific reductionism that seeks to erase any traces of transcendent spirit, a spirit free from the body, inevitably leads us to a kind of language writing the body via the codes of DNA. The imaginary of this performative language is itself a kind of virtual body, DNA strands as a more subtle body writing of the external physical body, in a fusing of language as body with the physical.

CHAPTER 5

Flesh Become Word

Textual Embodiment and Poetic Incarnation

Elliot R. Wolfson

Principle 1: That the Poetic Genius is the true Man, and that the body or outward form of Man is derived from the Poetic Genius.
—William Blake, "All Religions Are One"

For kabbalists in the late Middle Ages, in consonance with contemporaneous patterns of Christian and Islamic piety but especially the former, the body was a site of tension, the locus of sensual and erotic pleasure on the one hand, and the earthly pattern of God's image, the representation of what lies beyond representation, the mirror that renders visible the invisible, on the other. Given the intractable state of human consciousness as embodied—not to be understood, as I will elaborate below, along the lines of Cartesian dualism of mind/body but rather in Merleau-Ponty's phenomenological sense of the embodied mind/mindful body— it should come as no surprise that in spite of the negative portrayal of the body and repeated demands of preachers and homilists to escape from the clasp of carnality, in great measure due to the impact of Platonic psychology and metaphysics on the spiritual formation of the intellectual elite, the flesh continued to serve as the *prima materia* out of which ritual gestures, devotional symbols, and theological doctrines were fashioned.[1] There is, however, a critical difference that distinguishes Christianity from the various forms of mystical devotion that evolved historically in Judaism and Islam.

In the domain of the theological, which cannot be surgically extracted from other facets of medieval Christian societies, the dual role of body as "stigma of the fall" and "instrument of redemption" was mediated by the Eucharist, the central priestly rite that celebrated the mystery of transub-

84

stantiation through the miraculous consecration of bread and wine into body and blood, the sacrament believed to occasion liturgically the presence of Christ, a prolepsis of the Second Coming, advent of the appointed time, fostering the "paradoxical union of the body with the evanescence of the sacred."[2] As one might expect, Jews and Muslims provided alternative narratives to account for the commingling of the corporeal and transcendent, the visible and invisible, the literal and spiritual. Focusing on sources composed within rabbinic circles in places as diverse as Palestine, Provence, Catalonia, Castile, the Rhineland, Italy, northern France, and England, just to name some of the geographic spots Jewish occultism can be detected in the twelfth and thirteenth centuries, we can identify a hermeneutic principle that explains the theomorphic representation of the human as divine and the anthropomorphic representation of the divine as human, the transfiguration of flesh into word, which I will pose alongside—not in binary opposition to—the more readily known Christological incarnation of the word into flesh.

To be sure, I think it artificial to distinguish these positions too sharply, for the hypothetical tenability of the word becoming flesh rests on the assumption that flesh is, in some sense, word, but flesh can be entertained as word only if and when word, in some form, becomes flesh. As it happens, in the history of medieval Latin Christendom, there is evidence of scribal inscriptions (including the words *Verbum caro factum est*) on the hearts of male and female saints—a hyperliteral reading of the figurative "book of the heart"—a gesture that effected the transformation of the written word into flesh and, conversely, the transformation of flesh into the written word.[3] Notwithstanding the compelling logic of this reversal and the empirical evidence to substantiate it, the distinction should still be upheld in an effort to account for the difference in the narratological framework of the two traditions, a difference that ensues from, though at the same time gives way to, an underlying sameness, sameness in the Heideggerian sense of belonging-together.[4]

If I were to translate my thinking into contemporary academic discourse, I would put it this way: Pitched in the heartland of Christian faith, one encounters the logocentric belief in the incarnation of the word in the flesh of the person Jesus, whereas in the textual panorama of medieval kabbalah, the site of the incarnational insight is the ontographic inscripting of flesh into word and the consequent conversion of the carnal body into the ethereal, luminous body, finally transposed into the literal body, the body that is the letter, hyperliterally, the name that is the Torah. Both narratives, therefore, presume a correlation of body and book but in an inverse manner: For Christians, the literal body is embodied in the book of the body; for Jews, the literal body is embodied in the body of the book.[5]

In the first chapter of *Language, Eros, Being* I mentioned briefly Maurice Merleau-Ponty's signature notion of the "flesh" expressed in the latter stages of his thinking. At this juncture, I shall revisit the transition from "phenomenology of body" to "ontology of flesh" that ensues from his thought in greater length,[6] as it provides a valuable theoretical introduction to the analysis of the phenomenon of textual embodiment and poetic incarnation in the religious philosophy cultivated by kabbalists.[7]

Intertext/Fleshword

As part of the effort to get beyond the epistemological and ontological binaries that have pervaded Western philosophy, Merleau-Ponty identifies "flesh" as the common dimension shared by subject and object: "It is already the flesh of things that speaks to us of our own flesh, and that speaks to us of the flesh of the other."[8] Merleau-Ponty begins from the standpoint that the "perceptual presence of the world" rests not on positive or negative judgments about the veracity of what is perceived in/by consciousness but on "our experience, prior to every opinion, of inhabiting the world by our body, of inhabiting the truth by our whole selves, without there being need to choose nor even to distinguish between the assurance of seeing and the assurance of seeing the true, because in principle they are one and the same thing—faith, therefore, and not knowledge, since the world is here not separated from our hold on it, since, rather than affirmed, it is taken for granted, rather than disclosed, it is non-dissimulated, non-refuted."[9]

The dichotomy between exterior and interior, largely informed by grammatical habit, is to be transcended in this faith, not in objectivity, not in subjectivity, but in that which is not disclosed, the nondissimulated, and hence the irrefutable, the present absence that haunts the visible as the desire for invisibility.[10] The philosophical effort to establish "intramundane" or "interobjective" relations linking body and world is misplaced, as it is given—the very opening that allows for the question—as the faith of being-in-the world.[11] Being (*l'Être*) or reality (*la réalité*)—terms that Merleau-Ponty uses as substitutes for the "in-itself" (*l'en soi*)—constitute the "common inner framework" (*membrure commune*) of the "macrophenomenon" and the "microphenomenon,"[12] two foci, or folds, of the perceptual field. Hence, as Merleau-Ponty remarks elsewhere, if we are to speak of the "meaning of being *In Itself*," "distance, divergence, transcendence, the flesh" will determine it.[13]

The "incarnate subjectivity"[14] of human perception can be described in optical terms as the double openness of body to world and world to body,[15] embodied consciousness of conscious embodiment, the reciprocity of "proximal vision" based on the presumed synergy between bodies. The "hard core" of this intercorporeality, therefore, the "thickness of flesh," is constituted by a "symbiotic interpenetration and interdependency" whereby "individual beings continuously mirror and reflect one another, setting in motion a process of reversibility in which sameness and difference turn into one another: the seer is seen; the seer sees herself being seen; the seer sees herself as seeing, as a seeing being. . . . It is in the medium of this reversibility, this interplay, that rudimentary forms of reciprocity first emerge."[16] Reflecting accurately the philosophic discourse of his time, Merleau-Ponty observed that philosophy had flattened the curve by moving to one or the other end of the spectrum, the "sole plane of ideality" or the "sole plane of existence." Avoiding the lure of the extremes of absolute objectivity and pure consciousness, one should seek a midpoint between "in-itself" and "for-itself," the midpoint of double vision—turning one way in turning the other—that looms in the center of the perceptual faith that Merleau-Ponty refers to as "the presence of the world" (*la présence du monde*): "The presence of its flesh to my flesh, that I 'am of the world,' and that I am not it, this is what is no sooner said than forgotten: metaphysics remains coincidence."[17] Expanding an insight of Husserlian phenomenology, Merleau-Ponty identifies the essence of corporeity as intentionality: Human bodiliness thus is not determined by quantifiable extension or measurable sensoriality, the "objective body," but by kinesthetic sensations, hyletic materiality, impressionality, *Empfindnisse*, the "lived body," a complex field of intentional forms, physiological and psychological.[18]

In the imaginal domain here labeled "metaphysical," there is no difference to overcome, no opposites to coincide, but the coincidence of coincidence, the correlation by which the other without is perceived within the other without and the other within without the other within.[19] To be attuned to this coincidence/correlation is to comprehend something Merleau-Ponty designates as "primordial definition of sensibility," the "return of the visible upon itself, a carnal adherence of the sentient to the sensed and of the sensed to the sentient. For, as overlapping and fission, identity and difference, it brings to birth a ray of natural light that illuminates all flesh and not only my own."[20] Interflesh, correlation of body, subject, and word, the enfolding of flesh in the fold-between. Of this fold we can say it is not "an ontological void, a non-being," but the "hiatus . . . spanned by the total being of my body, and by that of the world; it is the zero of pressure between two solids that makes them adhere to one another."[21] Embodied consciousness of human subjectivity—a cumbersome but accurate formulation—is referred to as the "perceiving-perceived *Einfühlung*," for the "reflexivity of body" (*la réflexivité du corps*) is constituted by the twofold intuition that presumes that

> we are already in the being thus described, that we are of it, that between it and us there is *Einfühlung*. That means that my body is made of the same flesh as the world, . . . and moreover that this flesh of my body is shared by the world, the world *reflects* it, encroaches upon it and it encroaches upon the world. . . . They are in a relation of transgression or of overlapping—This also means: my body is not only one perceived among others, it is the measurant [*mesurant*] of all, *Nullpunkt* of all the dimensions of the world.[22]

It will be evident to the discerning ear that Merleau-Ponty aligns himself with an archaic perspective expressed in the history of early Greek philosophy—an idea, I might add in passing, for which there are impressive analogies in a number of ancient Eastern philosophical schools—regarding our inability to conceive being without language. For Merleau-Ponty, of course, the focus is cast on perception as the principal modality of experience, though in some manner the very contrast between perception and conception is rendered insignificant. What is novel is his relegating to language a secondary status vis-à-vis a more primary groping toward speech that (be)(speaks) the reciprocity of language and being:

> As my body, which is one of the visibles, sees itself also and thereby makes itself the natural light opening its own interior to the visible, in order for the visible there to become my own landscape, realizing (as it is said) the miraculous promotion of Being to "consciousness," or (as we prefer to say) the segregation of the "within" and the "without"; so also speech [la parole]—which is sustained by the thousands of ideal relations of the particular language [le langage], and which, therefore, in the eyes of science, is, as a constituted language, a certain region in the universe of significations—is also the organ and the resonator of all the other regions of signification and consequently coextensive with the thinkable. Like the flesh of the visible, speech is a total part of the significations, like it, speech is a relation to Being through a being, and, like it, it is narcissistic, eroticized, endowed with a natural magic that attracts the other significations into its web, as the body feels the world in feeling itself.[23]

The relationship between being and speech (la parole), openly distinguished from language (le langage), is one of "solidarity" and "intertwining," rather than "parallel" or "analogy." If the function of language is to demarcate indifferent difference, speech is to intone different indifference, the "belongingness of the body to being and the corporeal relevance of every being." Reversing the Platonic legacy, Merleau-Ponty insists that we can no longer presume the existence of essences "above us, like positive objects, offered to a spiritual eye," but there is an essence "beneath us, a common nervure of the signifying and the signified, adherence in and reversibility of one another—as the visible things are the secret folds of our flesh, and yet our body is one of the visible things."[24] There is something beneath us, the invisible supposition of visible presence, the "nervure" (the word used in the original) that "bears the leaf from within, from the depths of its flesh, the ideas are the texture of experience, its style, first mute, then uttered."[25] Silence bears the speech as the "flesh" that demarcates and eradicates boundary in the joining-separating—"*that without which* there would be neither world nor language nor anything at all," the "essence" that "makes the world be a world," the "imperative grammar of Being," the "indecomposable nuclei of meaning, systems of inseparable properties."[26] The visible is thus "pregnant with the invisible," for the visible is always the other, but the other as such cannot be wholly visible and persist as other. The visible is the "flesh" in proximity that "ceases to be inaccessible" but nevertheless is subject to "infinite analysis."[27]

The word "flesh" does not denote facticity, whether material or spiritual, but a "*general thing*, midway between object and subject, a sort of incarnate principle that brings a style of being wherever there is a fragment of being."[28] "Fragments of being" are fleshed, as it were, from within the intertext of body and world, the "two circles," "two vortexes," "two concentric spheres,"[29] wheels within wheels, interweaving, crisscrossing, embodying language through/in language embodied, the word made flesh, the flesh made word. Merleau-Ponty demonstrates the circularity by appeal to the texture of sight and touch; both senses manifest, disclose, a "reflective redoubling"—to know what it is, one must be what one is yet to come to know; no touch without touching what is to be touched, no sight without seeing what is to be seen.[30] "Flesh," therefore, refers not to an empirical datum or "fact"; it is rather the basic "element" of being that nonetheless can be thought of as adhering to place and time, "to *location* and to the *now*."[31] Merleau-Ponty is emphatic on this point: "We must not think the flesh starting from substances, from body and spirit—for then it would be the union of contradictories—but we must think it, as we said, as an element, as the concrete emblem of a general manner of being."[32]

Merleau-Ponty's ontology, in some ways typically Cartesian, differs in one crucial respect from the rationalist psychology inspired by the meditations of Descartes on the nature of material being and mindfulness: No division between *cogito* and *cogitatum* has to be bridged, as the two never were and never can be separate; their opposition is the *raison d'être* of their being opposite. If we grasp the texture of flesh as the "coiling over of the visible upon the seeing body, of the tangible upon the touching body,"[33] then we would understand that there is no ontological difference to be made up, no epistemological need to explain what Pascal referred to as the inconceivable intermingling of matter and spirit.[34] The fleshliness of being, according to Merleau-Ponty, is not to be construed ontically as either material or mental substance, but as the *Horizonthaftigkeit*, the fold "surrounding the thin pellicle of the strict visible between two horizons,"[35] the "invisible," which is contrasted with the "non-visible." The latter refers to that which is visible but is not now in view, an absent presence, and the former to the "absence" that is "'behind' the visible, imminent or eminent visibility," the "*Urpräsentiert* precisely as *Nichturpräsentierbar*, as another dimension," the "primeval(ly)-offered" that re/presents itself, doubling,[36] as the "non-primevally presentable,"[37] the focal point where secrecy and exposure exchange glances, the "lacuna that marks its place in one of the points of passage of the 'world.' It is this negative that makes possible the vertical world, the union of incompossibles, the being in transcendence, and the topological space and the time in joints and members, in dis-junction and dis-membering."[38]

In response to Kant's critique and, curiously, closer in spirit to the apophatic tradition, Merleau-Ponty was willing to continue to speak of metaphysics, but for him, the latter deals with the invisible, which is not "another visible," that is, a "positive" presence that is presently absent, but the negative absence as such that can only be absent as absently present:

Verborgenheit by principle, i.e., invisible *of the visible*, *Offenheit* of the *Umwelt* and *Unendlichkeit*—*Unendlichkeit* is at bottom the *in itself*, the *ob-ject*—For me the infinity of Being that one can speak of is *operative*, militant finitude: the openness of the *Umwelt*—I am against finitude in the empirical sense, a factual existence that *has limits*, and this is why I am for metaphysics. But it lies no more in infinity than in the factual finitude.[39]

There is no metaphysical object, no metaphysical subject; if there is a thematized metaphysical topos, it is *Vergorbenheit*, "concealment," by definition nonthematizable, demarcated, paradoxically, as the invisible of the visible, that is, the invisibility that makes visibility possible, nay, is the very sense of possibility, openness to being, the "environment." This openness is contrasted with the quality of *Unendlichkeit*, "limitlessness," the very property that makes feasible the "factual existence of that which has limits," and hence associated semantically with "in itself" and "ob-ject," the polarity of subjectivity withheld and objectivity projected, concealment of the one in disclosure of the other. Thus, in the continuation of the richly poetic meditation on the invisible, Merleau-Ponty associates it with "the possible as a claimant of existence (of which 'past' and 'future' are but partial expressions)—and the male-female relation (the two pieces of wood that children see fitting together of themselves, irresistibly, because each is the *possible of the other*)— and the 'divergence,' and the totality above the divergencies—and the thought-unthought relation (Heidegger)—and the relation of *Kopulation* where two intentions have one sole *Erfüllung*."[40]

The parallels to traditional kabbalistic symbolism are striking. The path winds its way to the unthought of thought, that is, the thought that is thought as unthought, an invisibility that renders visible the invisible presence by rendering invisible the visible absence, seeing within and without the metaphysical breach, open enclosure, divergence converging, convergence diverging, toward transcendence, difference in, identity indifferent, subject-object, gendered male female, duplicity singularly duplicitous.[41] Interestingly, Merleau-Ponty turns to the image of copulation to illumine the truth of duplicity; copulation—or at least of the sort the French philosophic poet generalized—presumes two intentions aiming at one target, the moment/place, here-now, of realization, fulfillment of will, *Erfüllung*.

Merleau-Ponty thus provides the contemporary ear a rhetoric to articulate anew the ancient kabbalistic hermeneutic of secrecy: The invisible is not an object of metaphysics— the transcendental other, ideal form, immaterial substance, or even astral body—nor is it to be identified as a metaphysical subject—the eye of mind/heart presumed to see what is beneath the veneer of appearance; it is, rather, the chasm between subject and object, the mark of divergence, noncoincidence, ontological in-difference, "a sort of straits between exterior horizons and interior horizons ever gaping open . . . a certain differentiation, an ephemeral modulation of this world."[42] For speech to capture this, it must come to and as silence:

Speech does indeed have to enter the child as silence—break through to him through silence and as silence. . . . Silence = absence of the word due. It is this fecund negative that is instituted by the flesh, by its dehiscence—the negative, nothingness, is the doubled-up, the two leaves of my body, the inside and the outside articulated over one another—Nothingness is rather the difference between the identicals—.[43]

In the ensuing portrait of God's incorporate body elicited from select but sufficiently representative kabbalistic texts, I draw inspiration from Merleau-Ponty's notion of flesh as the "fecund negative," "dehiscence," the nothingness "doubled-up" as nothingness. In this "difference between identicals," the enfolded fold, inside is out and outside in, a place in thinking reminiscent of the account on the part of some kabbalists of the third *sefirah*, *Binah*, emblematic of the mother, the womb that bears the seed-thought of *Ḥokhmah*, the father, composed of the twenty-two letters of the Hebrew alphabet, which are comprised in YHWH; in the matrix of the womb, the letters take the form of *qol gadol*, the great voice that re/sounds as silence in the speaking forth of the seminal name. The voice/womb is inscripted with—circumscribed by—the second *ehyeh* in the name revealed to Moses, *ehyeh asher ehyeh*, "I will be as I will be" (Exod. 3:14), the name that signifies the temporal opening of ontological closure, the gesture mimicked in the prophetic expanse of interpretative constriction.

To apprehend the point, one must have in mind that the other occurrence of *ehyeh* is assigned to *Keter*, which is identified by some kabbalists as will and by others as thought, though proponents of both views agree that it is coterminous with infinity. The primary *sefirah*, the origin, signified by *alef*, paradoxically, cannot be the beginning, for the beginning bears the mystery of *beit*, the dyad, the second that is first.[44] The second is encoded semiotically—though decoded interpretatively—in *asher*, the word that links the two occurrences of *ehyeh*. A sign for this, a textual anchor, is implicit in the consonants of *asher*, for when rearranged they spell *ro'sh*, the "head," the beginning, *Ḥokhmah*, the bridge that connects *Keter* and *Binah*; inception and termination are both signified by *ehyeh*, "I will be," the resolute mark of time's curve, swerving from determinate indeterminacy at the inception to indeterminate determinacy at the termination. The temporal bend, so to speak, impels us to think the correlation of the unity of the three uppermost *sefirot* as the replication of nothing (*Keter*) (un)becoming everything (*Binah*) from the seed-word (*Ḥokhmah*) that comprises everything as nothing. From this spot we can begin to ponder the image-symbol of poetic incarnation in the mystical orchard of medieval kabbalah.

Hebrew and the Semiotics of Creation

A current that runs through the landscape of Jewish esotericism presumes that the microbe of being, the genome, as it were, is constituted by the letters that make up its name; in that respect, Hebrew, the sacred tongue, may be viewed as the cosmic language or, in the telling phrase of Böhme, *Natursprache*,[45] the single Adamic language that is purportedly the source to which all other languages may be traced.[46] The principle is enunciated in the following passage in *Sefer ha-Bahir*: "It is said that with regard to everything that the holy One, blessed be he, created in his world, he placed its name according to its matter, as it is written, 'and whatever Adam called each living creature, that would be its name' (Gen. 2:19), that is, its essence [*gufo*] was in this manner."[47]

The assertion that the name (*shem*) of an entity is its essence (*guf*)—when cast in the terminology of Western philosophy, the realist as opposed to the nominalist orientation—presupposes an intrinsic connection between language and being[48] that rests in turn on the assumed correlation of letter and matter, a correlation likely springing from the mythopoeic sensibility expressed in detail in the second part of *Sefer Yeṣirah*,[49] where the line between religion, magic, and mysticism is not so easily drawn.[50] In the words of Jacob ben Sheshet, "The matter of the letters comprises the forms of all created beings, and you will not find a form that does not have an image in the letters or in the combination of two, three, or more of them. This is a principle alluded to in the order of the alphabet, and the matters are ancient, deep waters that have no limit."[51]

What exists in the world, examined subphenomenally, are the manifold permutations of the twenty-two Hebrew letters, themselves enfolded in the four-letter name YHWH; yet what is/appears phenomenally cannot be experienced but through the prismatic mosaic of "bodily language," the "corporeal intentionality," of the ecstatic and enstatic body,[52] that is, the body that stands without and is contiguous within an external world, the body that projects upon and receives from other projecting bodies;[53] whatever exists, ultimately, is nameable, even, or especially, the unnameable, the nameless that is un(named) in every (un)naming, the other of speech, the event—though in being so unnamed, it, too, slips from the abandon of namelessness—that is impossible to say, the unsaying that is heard repeatedly in the infinite speaking, speaking of the infinite, discourse—literally, that which "runs about" (*dis/currere*)—always extending beyond the grip of language.[54]

The kataphatic paradox is articulated in a brief observation in *Baddei ha-Aron u-Migdal Ḥananel*, an important but relatively neglected compendium of kabbalistic secrets on the nature of language composed in the fourteenth century by Shem Tov Ibn Gaon, disciple of Solomon Ibn Adret and Isaac ben Todros, disciples of Moses ben Naḥman, better known as Ramban or Naḥmanides, the thirteenth-century panoramic personality—halakhic authority, talmudic scholar, communal leader, biblical exegete, liturgical poet, and kabbalist. According to a passage in Shem Tov's treatise, the word *otiyyot* denotes that "letters" are "signposts" (*otot*) whose task it is to point the way leading from what is revealed to the concealed (*lirmoz al ha-nistarot min ha-niglot*).[55] Letters may be viewed as planks on a bridge connecting matters open and hidden. In medieval kabbalistic parlance, typified in the aforecited comment by Shem Tov, the terms *nistarot* and *niglot*, derived from Deuteronomy 29:28, refer respectively to the concealed world of emanation, the fullness of the divine potencies, and the revealed world of creation, the plethora of the material cosmos.

In the minds of kabbalists, the ontic division between upper and lower realms of existence, the world of unity (*olam ha-yiḥud*) and the world of separation (*olam ha-perud*), corresponds to the hermeneutical distinction between inner and outer layers of meaning in Scripture, an approach enhanced by the philosophically inspired reshaping of rabbinic exegesis in the Middle Ages, especially in the writings of Maimonides, which profoundly influenced kabbalists in the thirteenth century and beyond.[56] From the manifest we learn of the latent; letters, words, names, the name, language as such, serve as overt signs through which the in/significant is signified, signposts that allow us to imagine[57] a way across the chasm. As Azriel of Gerona put it succinctly, explaining the anthropomorphic language used to describe the *sefirot* in *Sefer Yeṣirah* (1:3): "Thus you must contemplate the hidden from the revealed" (*yesh lekha lehitbonen min ha-galuy al ha-nistar*).[58]

In a second passage, commenting on the characterization of the measure (*middah*) of the *sefirot* in the first part of *Sefer Yeṣirah* as *eser she-ein lahem sof*, "ten that are without limit" (1:6), Azriel elaborated the paradox of the merging of finitude and infinity in the sefirotic emanations presented as four links in an ontological chain—perhaps meant to convey the Neoplatonic hypostases leading invertedly from nature to the One[59]—disseminating from and leading back (through the contemplative gaze and practice of the enlightened kabbalist) to Ein Sof, *mehawweh*, the source of all being:[60]

> Everything is from the infinite [*ein sof*], and even though the matters [*devarim*] have a dimension [*shi'ur*] and measure [*middah*], and they are ten, the very measure that they have has no limit [*ein lah sof*], for the natural [*muṭba*] is from the sensible [*murgash*], and the sensible is from the intelligible [*muskal*], which is from the concealed height [*rom ha-ne'lam*], and the concealed is from the infinite. It follows that even the sensible, intelligible, and natural have no limit, and hence these attributes came to be, to contemplate the infinite through them [*lehitbonen bahem be-ein sof*].[61]

The world of ten emanations—divided into four quarters, from bottom to top, the natural, sensible, intelligible, and the concealed height—occupies a median position between the boundlessness of Ein Sof and the boundedness of the material cosmos, a theme that Azriel captures in the seventh of the twelve hypothetical questions—presented in the form of a catechism[62]—with the evocative phrase *koaḥ bi-gevul mi-beli gevul* ("finite power that is unlimited").[63] The starting point for comprehending the paradox is to ponder philosophically that the infinite must produce that which is limited to illustrate that the limitlessness of its power must perforce include the capacity to produce a limit to that power:

> The infinite [*ein sof*] is perfection without deficiency [*sheleimut beli ḥissaron*] and it has finite power that is unlimited [*koaḥ bi-gevul mi-beli gevul*], and the boundary [*ha-gevul*] that emanates from him, which endows boundary on every existent

[*ha-magbil le-khol maṣuy*], consists of the *sefirot,* for they have the capacity to act perfectly or deficiently [*koaḥ lif ʿol be-hashlamah u-ve-ḥissaron*]. And if he did not create for them a boundary, we would not discern that he has the capacity to produce a boundary. Thus, to substantiate that there is nothing outside him [*ein ḥus mim-menu*], he produces a boundary by which things bounded are discerned in their boundedness [*ha-mugbalim nikkarim be-hagbalatam*]. Even though there is no boundary above, there is an allusion to the musing that comes from the infinite [*remez ha-hirhur me-ein sof*], which ascends and eludes extending in a boundary [*mitʿaleh u-mitʿalem me-hitpasheṭ bi-gevul*]. There is a boundary for everything grasped in the rumination of the heart and the allusion of thought [*yesh bi-gevul le-khol ha-nitpas be-hirhur ha-lev u-ve-remez ha-maḥashavah*] that extends below to be found in the word and to be seen by action [*ha-mitpasheṭ lemaṭah lehimaṣṣei be-dibbur u-le-harʾot lemaʿaseh*]. All that which comes under boundary has a mea-surement [*shiʿur*] and it has corporeality [*gashmut*], for every being that is grasped through rumination of the heart is called "body" [*guf*] even the spirit [*ha-ruaḥ*], and since the *sefirot* are the principle for everything bounded [*kelal le-khol mugbal*] they are the root [*shoresh*]. The philosophers [*ḥakhmei ha-meḥqar*] say that human intel-lect [*sekhel ha-adam*] has a limit, and from the way of custom [*mi-derekh ha-minhag*] we see that every thing has a boundary [*gevul*], measure [*shiʿur*], and dimension [*middah*].[64]

In his typical manner, Azriel offers a razor-sharp philosophical account (particularly indebted to Neoplatonic speculation) of Ein Sof assuming the form of the *sefirot*, which are ten in number. The paradox was alluded to in a cautionary manner by Azriel's master, Isaac the Blind, in his epistle to Naḥmanides and Jonah Gerondi in an attempt to respond to the charge that some "sages [*ḥakhamim*], wise men [*nevonim*], and pious individuals [*ḥasidim*]" in Spain were expounding kabbalistic secrets openly both in writing and orally and that they were guilty of the heresy of "cutting the shoots," that is, creating a division in the unity of God by positing a plurality of divine potencies: "The entities[65] are unified [*meyuḥadim*] 'like a flame bound to the coal, for the Lord is unique and there is no sec-ond, and before one what can you count?'[66] That is, 'before one' is the great name unified in all ten [*ha-shem ha-gadol ha-meyuḥad be-khol eser*], but I cannot elaborate in writing concerning what you asked."[67] Though Isaac was clearly alarmed at the public exposition of esoteric teaching on the part of kabbalists, perhaps his own disciples,[68] he could not allow the allegation concerning heresy to go unanswered. The response centers on the paradox of the one in ten, but Isaac holds back from elaborating in detail in writing, given the sensitive nature of the matter.

Azriel seeks to explicate the paradox by delineating the progression from the form-less source, divested of all form, even the form of formlessness, to the finite form that is unlimited, the sefirotic potencies, which are the principle of everything that has a measure. Inasmuch as all things measurable are considered corporeal, it is possible, indeed necessary, to speak of the *sefirot* as the spiritual body that embodies the immeasurable infinite beyond all representation. Traversing the threshold of the imaginal to the image-less refocuses one's vision on the ultimate metaphysical puzzle, the mystery of the garment, in kabbalistic parlance, the nameless donning the garb of the name that is not spoken as written nor written as spoken, the delimiting of the limitless in the infinitely complex tenfold unicity, that is, one manifest in ten, configured as four letters of the name, which assume in the imagination the form of the primal anthropos, Israel, the firstborn son of the father.

Curiously but by no means uniquely, kabbalistic literature exemplifies an intersecting of two conceptual currents: on the one hand, the disparity between appearance that is truly apparent and truth that is apparently true, a metaphysical enigma that can be traced, at least in the history of Western philosophy, to the dualism of transcendence and corporeality that issues from the formalism of Platonic idealism,[69] and on the other, the creed of archaic Jewish wisdom, for lack of a better term, which views the world as having been created by means of Torah, the Hebrew letters through which vestments of the ineffable name are woven, semiotic ciphers that constitute the plentitude of being. The roots for this esoteric tenet may be sought in the cosmological belief that Hebrew is the "language of creation," according to the formulation of Jubilees 12:26, a treatise composed in all probability in the mid-second century B.C.E., presumably by a Jew in Palestine, perhaps of priestly lineage.[70] It is reasonable to assume that this conception is related to the older wisdom teaching, the contours of which may be culled from sections of Proverbs, Ecclesiastes, Job, Psalms, apocalyptic visions, apocryphal wisdom literature, Qumran fragments, passages in the Philonic corpus, and the dicta of Jesus preserved in canonical and gnostic gospels.[71] We are more concerned with the aftermath than the fore-history of this sapiential tradition, but an initial word, no matter how insufficient, about the latter can open the way to the former.

In one current of ancient Israelite tradition, with roots stretching back to ancient Mesopotamia,[72] wisdom was hypostasized or metaphorically depicted—there seems little sense in distinguishing sharply between these options when assessing the scriptural context—as the first of God's creations, the idealized woman of valor and glory, counterpoint to the degrading image of the whoring woman of sin and temptation. By the later part of the Second Temple period, as is attested in a number of sources (for example, Sirach 24:9–13 and Baruch 3:36–4:4), the image of the fullness of primordial wisdom[73] was identified by some as the Torah of Moses.[74] Philosophically, the symbolic identification must have engendered the thought that if God creates by means of wisdom, which is Torah, then matters (*devarim*) created by the agency of the word (*dibbur*) would constitute and be constituted by the materiality of words (*devarim*).

Didactically, it may be useful to translate the ancient Jewish esoteric precept into contemporary scientific jargon. The letters would be viewed, accordingly, as elementary particles, waves of energy, cosmic strings, described by Paul Davies, a professor of natural philosophy, as "extremely narrow threadlike tubes of concentrated field energy." These tubes were possibly—astronomical searches have so far proved inclusive—produced after the Big Bang, when, it is further presumed, on account of the exceeding heat and density of the universe, the supraliminal, superluminal particles of stellar dust "tied themselves into knots and twists."[75] The undoing of these electromagnetic ripples of light-energy results in the coalescing of bodies, the objects of human scientific inquiry, philosophical wonder, and artistic inspiration, exemplifying motion and mass in an indecipherably linked manner. As we observed in the Prologue to *Language, Eros, Being*, from a theoretical standpoint it is imagined that the gravitational arrangement of spacetime is such that an individual trajectory betrays the characteristic of looping back. Consequently, the past may be as much drawn out of the future as the future is drawn out of the past, a reverting of temporal and spatial coordinates that disrupts the commonly held presumption regarding the linear sequence of cause preceding effect.

Utilizing this symbolic discourse, we might say that Hebrew letters for kabbalists are excitation nodes that generate visual and sonic aftershocks, producing semblance of light and resonance of sound expressive of infinity, looping round metric intervals of the fourth dimension, the space-time continuum, on the one hand, contracting gravity in restricting expansion, and on the other hand, attenuating antigravity in expanding restriction.[76] Matter, on this account, is a cloak, a veil, through which the luminous form-shadows of the Hebrew letters are concomitantly concealed and revealed. Scholem had in mind this foundational principle of kabbalistic cosmology when he wrote that the "worlds are nothing but names inscribed on the paper of the divine reality."[77] In spite of the diversity of opinions that properly characterizes the history of Jewish mysticism, the assumption that Hebrew is the "holy language" (*leshon ha-qodesh*) in the manner that I have just indicated binds together masters of Jewish esoteric lore across generations without any discernible rupture of time or space.[78]

The gnosis of the letters is worked out in intricate detail in the second part of *Sefer Yeṣirah*, although, interestingly enough, no explicit or even implicit reference to wisdom or Torah is discernible therein. As I have had the occasion to comment on this text in several of my previously published studies, I will not subject the work to a close textual scrutiny. In a sense, the particulars of this matter do not impinge on the argument I am advancing here, though, in general, I certainly acknowledge that particulars cannot be ignored if one is to determine the provenance and pedigree of a text. What is noteworthy for my purposes, however, is the principle of cosmic semiotics that one may elicit from the text, a taxonomy of embodiment: The materiality of body is constituted by the underlying letter permutations, subatomic linguistic structures—edifices constructed dynamically from the different combinations and vocalizations of the consonants—invisible to corporeal sight.

Textual confirmation for this idea can be sought in rabbinic literature of the formative period, as we find, for example, in the following dictum attributed to R. Simon: "Just as the

Torah was given in the holy language, so the world was created by means of the holy language."[79] R. Simon's statement presumes an affinity, perhaps synchronicity, betwixt creation and revelation—just as the object of the latter consisted of Hebrew, the "holy tongue," so too the instrument of the former. The sentiment well attested in late antique Judaism that God created the world by gazing into the inscripted text of Torah in its primordial state can be viewed as an exegetical elaboration pieced together from several archaic theologoumena, including the demiurgical representation of divine wisdom, embracing, *inter alia*, the image of God's female playmate, visual figuration of the verbal icon of the will. The idea of a primordial text, the textualization of wisdom, resonates with a still older mythic notion of the heavenly tablets that bear the divine inscription whence the visionary sage learns the secrets of the cosmos, history, and time; the hypothetical green line, as it were, that circumscribes the symbolic tableau of the imagination.[80] If the instrument/blueprint of divine creativity, according to the mythologic of R. Simon or the teaching transmitted in his name, consists of letters, then objects of creation must be analogously constituted.

Book of Nature—Mirroring—Nature of Book

Whatever differences pertain to the rabbinic and occult perspectives, and surely such differences are essential to note, a shared view emerges with regard to the ascription of an ontic status to language and the consequent textual interpretation of reality; indeed, employing terminology that became fashionable in the speculative renaissance of the Latin West in the twelfth century, Torah can be identified as the "book of nature."[81] In the Jewish context, the metaphor is not to be understood metaphorically but hyperliterally, that is, Torah, the prototype of all books, the *hypertext*, if you will, informs us about the semantic character of nature; alternatively expressed, Torah was thought to impart cosmological and anthropological knowledge because the substance of the world and of the human self consists of the letters that constitute the building blocks of the revealed word. Medieval kabbalistic authors understood the rabbinic idealization of Torah in this manner, and there is at least enough ambiguity in dicta attributed to rabbis of the early period to entertain seriously the possibility that kabbalistic sources open a way to ascertain older forms of a mystical specularity predicated on the promotion of viewing the book as a speculum of nature and nature as a speculum of the book.[82] Franz Rosenzweig, a thinker who is on occasion critical of a mystical approach, correctly perceived that Jewish mysticism bridged the gap between God and Torah on precisely these grounds. Although no specific mention is made of the kabbalah, careful attention to Rosenzweig's words makes it abundantly clear that he is formulating matters in accord with kabbalistic gnosis:

> The plain wording of the law conceals a hidden meaning which expresses nothing so much as the essence of the world. For the Jew, the book of the law can thus, as it were,

replace the book of nature or even the starry heavens from which the men of yore once thought they could interpret terrestrial matters by intelligible omens. That is the basic idea of countless legends with which Judaism expands the apparently constricted world of its law into the whole world, and on the other hand, precisely because it finds this world presaged in its law, already sees the world-to-come in it.[83]

Judah Halevi, the twelfth-century Andalusian poet and religious thinker with a discernible mystical propensity shaped in part by Sufi terminology,[84] provided a theoretical framework for this belief that was readily appropriated by kabbalists, given its resonance with semiotic notions expressed in older esoteric sources. In an extensive section from *Sefer ha-Kuzari* that deals with *Sefer Yeṣirah*, Halevi remarks that Hebrew is the "divine language" (*ha-lashon ha-elohit*) that God taught Adam and by which he assigned a name to every living creature (Gen. 2:19).[85] In an earlier part of the work, Halevi had already noted that according to tradition, Hebrew, the "noblest of languages," was spoken by God to Adam and Eve, as well as by Abraham, even though he came from Ur of the Chaldeans, where the indigenous language was Aramaic, which is the "mundane language" (*leshon ḥol*) in comparison to Hebrew, the "holy language" (*leshon ha-qodesh*).[86] To be sure, in that context Halevi acknowledges the semantic kinship between Hebrew, Aramaic, and Arabic, but he still argues that the former is superior to the others.[87] Hebrew is the "most perfect of all languages" because only in this language is there an intrinsic relationship between letters and the objects they signify. Hebrew is thus the "natural language," the original language spoken by God, angels,[88] and the first human couple, whereas all other languages are considered a matter of contrivance and convention.[89] Strictly speaking, the truth of this claim rests not in rational demonstration but in faith and commitment to tradition.[90] Just as there is, for Halevi, an ontic chasm separating angelic Israel and the rational human being, the special prophetic status of the Jews linked to the metarational divine matter (*amr ilāhī*; *inyan elohi*) that belongs uniquely to them, so there is an unbridgeable and inexplicable linguistic gap distinguishing Hebrew from other languages.

A similar outlook is affirmed by kabbalists in the second half of the thirteenth century (and countless others in the subsequent centuries who have added little substance to the early formulations), including, to name but a few salient examples, Joseph Gikatilla,[91] Joseph ben Shalom Ashkenazi,[92] and even Abraham Abulafia, whose views on language (not to mention many other topics) were largely dependent on Maimonides.[93] While it is true that Abulafia speaks about the containment of all seventy languages in Hebrew,[94] the linguistic assumption that justifies the use of other languages in the meditational practice, it is nonetheless clear from his writings that Hebrew is always singled out as the "natural" language, as opposed to other languages, which are conventional. A particular interesting formulation is offered by Abulafia in *Imrei Shefer*:

The world in its entirety was created by means of our letters and our language, and the rest of the letters, languages, and nations are all of them set images [*dimyonot nisdarot*] to be comparable to us, just as an ape performs actions that he sees in the actions of man, in his desire to be like him, and just as the shadow-image [*ṣel*] of a man appears to a man in a mirror that is in his hand, and he begins to do actions like him, neither adding nor subtracting. But these are without substance and everything is an act of reflection. Thus is the secret of all magic.[95]

I concur with Idel's observation that for Abulafia, the "holy language," which comprises all the other languages, "is not Hebrew in its semantic aspect but rather Hebrew in its more fundamental aspects, namely the consonants and vowels and the principle of the combination of letters, which is one of the major sources for the diversification of languages."[96] I cannot, however, accept the additional contention that "Abulafia emphasizes the natural dimension of human language not to prove that it was revealed by God but to underline that it is an integral part of human nature. It is because it is natural that it is also divine; the two concepts overlap in Abulafia's view." On this basis Idel concludes, "the ecstatic kabbalist is much closer to the Aristotelian naturalistic position, a fact that clearly distinguishes this kind of Kabbalah from the two other kabbalistic models."[97] My own reading of kabbalistic sources renders such a distinction gratuitous. Abulafia and Moses de León, taken respectively as paradigmatic proponents of the two main types of kabbalah, prophetic-ecstatic and theosophic-theurgic,[98] would agree that Hebrew is the essential or natural language, the language by means of which the structure of natural entities may be decoded.[99] For both, moreover, the ontic character of the natural language is not to be sought in its semantic morphemes, that is, particular cultural configurations of the language, but in the phonemic and graphemic potentiality contained in Hebrew as a conceptual grid to chart the character of language more generally. Consider the following zoharic passage elucidating the immediately preceding assertion that Israel is distinguished among the Gentile nations (*goyim*), for only they can lay claim to possessing language that is veritable in its written and oral form (*ketav we-lashon*). "Through each letter they can envision the image [*diyoqna*] and form [*ṣiyyura*] as is appropriate. In the idolatrous nations, however, this mystery is not considered for they do not have a script [*ketav*] or speech [*lashon*]."[100] I propose that this comment can be interpreted in a manner that is perfectly consistent with Abulafia's understanding of Hebrew as the cosmic language.

The semantic essentialism, moreover, affords the Jew a distinctive opportunity to emulate God, for whom there is no schism between word and reality, since the linguistic gesticulation (whether spoken or written) is an actualization of divine volition.[101] Halevi adduces the latter point from the opening paragraph of *Sefer Yeṣirah*, where mention is made of three books, *sefarim*, by which God created the world. The three books, which are delineated as *sefar*, *sippur*, and *sefer*, allude to the congruence of thought, speech, and writing. From the anthropocentric perspective, the three are experienced linearly as an evolution from the idea/image that is thought mentally without verbal expression, to words that are orally inflected, to the grapheme, the letter-marks, that are handwritten; whether thought, spoken, or inscripted, words at best are "signs" or "symbols" that point to the things they name but not to their essence. From a theocentric perspective, words in all three modalities constitute the essence of things they name, whence derives the creative potency of language. Yet Jews are distinguished linguistically from other ethnocultural identities because they possess the "holy language," the cant of prophecy that bestows upon them an angelic status and allows them to be guardians of the cosmic language.[102]

The kabbalistic ethnocentrism notwithstanding, a precise analogue to the perspective I have outlined in this section is found in Islamic mysticism; indeed, with respect to this matter, the notional proximity between Islam and Judaism is far more conspicuous than between Christianity and either Judaism or Islam. As with so much of Islamic occultism, the starting point is an expression in the Qur'ān in a section that delineates various signs (*āyāt*) of the divine in the world, which serve as part of the liturgical glorification of Allah in the evening and morning (30:17–27). The signs consist of the creation of man from dust and the creation of his spouse, the helpmate, with whom man can settle down and live harmoniously (20–22), the creation of the heavens and earth, and the diversity of ethnic and racial identities (22), the creation of patterns of human behavior and natural phenomena (23–24), and, finally, the fact that all things in the heavens and earth arise by the command, or will, of Allah (25). Everything that is in the cosmos, therefore, may be viewed as a sign marking the way to one that is both within and outside the cosmos.

These signs, we learn from another *sūrah*, should not be worshipped, for prayer is to be directed exclusively to Allah, the all-hearing and all-knowing (41:37–38). At the end of the *sūrah*, after a sustained chastisement of the "unbelievers," "Allah's enemies" (26– 28), which unquestionably refers in this context to the Jews, who rejected the claims of the prophet and the authority of the Qur'ān, the new book of revelation, there appears the following remark: "We shall show them our signs in the distant regions and in their own souls, until it becomes clear to them that it is the Truth" (53). The Jews will be shown the signs in the "horizons," that is, the created universe, and in "human souls," until they finally discern the truth. The word "sign," *āya*, denotes the presence of the deity concealed in the manifestations of natural and psychological phenomena, *signa naturalia* and *signa data* in Augustinian terms.[103]

The significance of the sign is that it points beyond itself to the reality for which there is no sign; the plurality of signs reveal the transcendent one by veiling it in the multiplicity of forms by which it is revealed. Each letter of the revealed text is a sign—at once aurally and visually manifest—that comprises an infinity of meaning, inasmuch as the text is the incarnation of the divine form; hermeneutically, the matter of infinity is manifest in the potentially endless explications of the text elicited by countless readers, links in the cumulative chain of interpreters that stretches across the divide of time. Here it would be opportune to recall the contemporary notion of "infinite semiosis," as expressed in Robert Corrington's summation of Umberto Eco:[104] "All semiosis is prospectively infinite, because any given sign will have its own plentitude of dimensions and its own movement outward into uncountable radii of involvement."[105] From the standpoint of medieval Sufis and kabbalists, the innumerable transmutations of meaning stem from the fact that each sign/letter is a component of the textual corpus that constitutes the name of the nameless, the veil that renders the invisible visible and the visible invisible. Moreover, the occult wisdom in both traditions proffered a view of the cosmos in similar terms: Everything is a sign, a discrete indivisible, that guides one to the in/significant beyond the universe, devoid of all forms and images, the oneness of being (*waḥdat al-wujūd*) present in all things by virtue of being absent from all things. The world may accordingly be viewed as the book in which one discerns (de)scripted forms that lead from the visible to invisible or, better, from the visible invisibility to invisible visibility, from faces manifestly hidden to faces hiddenly manifest.[106]

The full implication of the Islamic notion of nature as the book in which the divine will is exposed and the paradoxes that pertain to the presumption that the natural and psychological phenomena are signs by which one discerns the unseen is drawn by the esoteric interpreters of the Qur'ān, the inscripted text of revelation, the "rolled-out parchment," whose words are considered to be signs of divine intention, linked especially to the eschatological day of judgment, comparable to entities in nature such as the mountain and the sea (Q 512:1–8). The esoteric reading elevates the book itself to a supreme position, embellishing the tradition that assigned the qur'ānic expression *umm al-kitāb*, literally, "mother of the book" (Q 3:7, 13:39, 43:4), to the Qur'ān itself, the "well-preserved tablet," *al-lawḥ al-maḥfūz* (Q 85:21–22), the *Urschrift*, fore/script, that comprises the forms of all that exists.

Read esoterically, the Arabic letters—bones, tissue, and sinews of the qur'ānic body—are signs that point to the unseen and thereby reveal the light by concealing it. The attitude of Sufis articulated by Annemarie Schimmel presents a perfect analogue to the perspective affirmed by kabbalists with respect to Hebrew: "Learning the Arabic letters is incumbent upon everybody who embraces Islam, for they are the vessels of revelation; the divine names and attributes can be expressed only by means of these letters—and yet, the letters constitute something different from God; they are a veil of otherness that the mystic must penetrate."[107] The metaphor of the veil is instructive, as the function of the veil is to disclose but at the same time to hide, indeed it discloses by hiding, hides by disclosing. In a similar vein, the letters of the matrix text, Torah for kabbalist, Qur'ān for Sufi, reveal and conceal the divine essence, the *face* beyond all veils, the pre/face, devoid of form, the pre/text, devoid of letter.[108] Kabbalist and Sufi would agree that if one remains bound to the letters of the scriptural text, then one is fettered by an idolatry of the book, mistaking the image for the imageless, the figurative for the prefigurative, but both would also insist that the way beyond letters (scripted and/or voiced) is by way of letters, visual-auditory signs, semiotic ciphers at once visible and audible—seen as heard,

heard as seen—signs that communicate the incommunicable not through an equational model of symbolic logic but through an implicational model of poetic allusion.[109]

The proximity to the kabbalistic orientation becomes even more pronounced when we consider the embellishment of these motifs in the theosophic gnosis of Ibn 'Arabī, a teaching that has many affinities to kabbalistic wisdom. Just as the Qur'ān is the book that manifests the invisible deity through verbal images, so the cosmos is a book that unveils the divine presence through veils of phenomenal existence. In Ibn 'Arabī's own words, "God dictates to the hearts through inspiration everything that the cosmos inscribes in *wujūd*, for the cosmos is a divine book inscribed."[110] Two qur'ānic motifs are combined here: the identification of cosmic phenomena as signs pointing to the unicity of all being, and the idea of the heavenly book, primordial scripture, inscribed by the divine pen, *qalam* (Q 68:1).

In another passage, the hypostatic dimension is foregrounded as Ibn 'Arabī offers the Muslim corrective to the Christological trinity: "The Christians supposed that the Father was the Spirit (*al-Rúḥ*), the Mother Mary, and the Son Jesus; then they said 'God is the Third of Three,' not knowing that 'the Father' signifies the Name Allah, and that 'the Mother' signifies the *Ummu 'l-Kitáb* . . . i.e., the ground of the Essence, and that 'the Son' signifies the Book, which is Absolute Being because it is a derivative and product of the aforesaid ground."[111] The common thread that ties together the triad of potencies is the belief in the ontological reality of the Arabic letters; the first manifestation, envisioned as father, is the most sacred of names, Allah; the second manifestation, envisioned as mother, corresponds to *umm al-kitāb*, the primordial text or the ground of the Essence; and finally, the third manifestation, envisioned as son, is the book, the absolute being that derives from the ground. There is much more to say about Ibn 'Arabī and the different layers of the Islamic esoteric tradition, but what is most critical for our purposes is to underscore the hypostatic personification of the qur'ānic text as the tablet that contains all cosmic forms that serve as the veils through which God is manifest and the concomitant figural representation of the cosmos as the book that comprises all semiotic signs that point to the truth that cannot be signified.

Envisioning YHWH/Eradicating Root Word

The unique contribution of medieval kabbalists—and on this point I do not see any appreciable difference between the two major trends according to the taxonomy that has dominated contemporary scholarship—centers around viewing YHWH, the most sacred of divine names, as comprising all the letters of the Hebrew alphabet, the one language considered natural and not conventional, essential and not contingent.[112] I cite here a representative formulation of this assumption from *Sha'ar ha-Niqqud*, a treatise on the meaning of the vowels composed by Gikatilla. The relevant remark weaves together the rabbinic tradition that the world-to-come and this world were created respectively by *yod* and *he*, the first two letters of the Tetragrammaton,[113] and the system laid out in the second part of *Sefer Yeṣirah* in which the letters are presented both as the means by which all things are created and their substance:

> All the worlds are dependent on the twenty-two letters, and the one who contemplates the secret of the permutation of the alphabet will comprehend the secret of the rotation of all entities in their ascent and descent by means of the secret of the property of the letters. The one who merits comprehending this will understand several mysteries and several levels that are hidden from the eyes of creatures, and he will comprehend and know the greatness of God, blessed be he, and how everything is made from the truth of his great name and how all is dependent on his name.[114]

In *Sha'arei Orah*, a more extensive delineation of the different symbolic names associated with each of the ten emanations progressing from the bottom to the top, Gikatilla offers a succinct account of the linguistic theory that informed the thinking of kabbalists in his time and beyond to the present. The twenty-two letters are depicted as branches stemming from a tree whose trunk is inscribed with YHWH, the root word that is the origin of all language, the mystical essence of Torah.[115] Accordingly, all that exists may be perceived as a garment that both hides and reveals the name. Consider the formulation of this matter in the commentary on *Sefer Yeṣirah*, which records the teachings of Isaac the Blind, on the words "Thus every creature and every word goes forth in one name":[116]

> "In one name"[117]—their root is in one name, for the letters are branches that appear as flickering flames, within which there is movement, that are bound to the coal, and they are like twigs of a tree, its branches, and boughs, whose root is in the tree. Thus the weighing is from the hewing, the permutation from the weighing, and from the permutation is the form. All things [*devarim*] are made into a form, and all forms come forth from one name like a branch that comes forth from the root. It follows that everything is in the root, which is the one name, and thus it says at the end "one name."[118]

The "one name" from which all being comes forth is YHWH, the name that comprises within itself all letters of the Hebrew alphabet. From this vantage point, being is construed semiotically, that is, the letters constitute the nature of what is real, a point that is conveyed philologically by the expression *devarim*, which has the double connotation "things" and "words," though it is likely that in the above passage the term denotes more specifically the sefirotic entities, which are contained in the one name that comprises all the letters.[119] In the words of Azriel of Gerona:

Thus the blessed holy One made everything inscribed [*rashum*], engraved [*ḥaquq*], hewn [*ḥaṣuv*], and sealed [*ḥatum*] in his name and its letters so that there will be in them the power to exist and to carry out their activities in his seal in which they are sealed, for they constantly receive from his well that is prepared to irrigate those in need. He and his name preceded it, and through his name he created everything, as it is written, "all that is called in my name" (Isa. 43:7), and he is the fount of life to sustain all living beings.[120]

That the human being plays a particularly important role in unifying the different realms through language is expressed in another passage from the commentary on *Sefer Yeṣirah* that preserves the teachings of R. Isaac:[121] "Man [*adam*] himself is constructed by the letters, and when that edifice was constructed the supernal spirit that guides him guides everything, and thus everything is joined together in the supernal and lower beings."[122] Just as the anthropomorphic shape above, primal Adam, is composed of the letters comprised in the name, so Adam below is made in the image of the name, the Torah in human garb, and thus the ideal body is composed of letters.[123] The linguistic conception of corporeality taken hyperliterally, that is, the letters constitute the material substance whence the body is constructed, is affirmed by Azriel in his commentary on the depiction of the covenant of the foreskin in *Sefer Yeṣirah*: "It produces an offspring that is formed by means of the twenty-two letters, and therefore one must contemplate from the revealed to the hidden."[124]

In the earliest kabbalistic documents, moreover, which remain the only tenable way for the contemporary scholar to uncover what the tradition may have been, even if it was, as kabbalists themselves insist, in part or whole transmitted orally, it is presumed that the potencies of God are correlated with the limbs of a human body, a theosophical claim linked exegetically to the anthropological assumption that Adam is created in the image and likeness of God (according to the account recorded by a priestly scribe) as well as the prophetic presumption (expressed perhaps most boldly by Ezekiel) that the divine glory appears in the likeness of a human form.[125] In subsequent generations, the anthropomorphism was embellished, or at least articulated more overtly,[126] but from its very inception, kabbalistic ontology rests on the supposition that the anthropos, to be identified more specifically as the circumcised Jewish male,[127] serves as the conduit connecting the divine and mundane realms.

The role of mediating agent is realized primarily through contemplative prayer and Torah study, as these ritual activities are dependent on the utilization and manipulation of the Hebrew alphabet, the constitutive element of all that exists. The goal for the kabbalist—indeed what justifies his being called a kabbalist[128]—is to receive the secret of the name, that is, to cleave to YHWH, the Deuteronomistic injunction interpreted in a manner very close to twelfth-century Neoplatonically influenced philosopher-poets, primarily of an Andalusian cultural background, as conjunction of thought (*devequt ha-maḥshavah*). Isaac and his disciples claim that this conjunction is the true mystical intent (*kawwanah*) of liturgical worship and study, an ideal achieved by few but with ramifications for all.[129]

In another crucial way, the ideal promulgated by kabbalists betrays affinity with the view enunciated in Islamic and Jewish philosophical sources. The kabbalists of the twelfth and thirteenth centuries, not to mention later generations, understood this conjunction, which comprised both an intellective and imaginal component, as an expression of prophecy, though in their case the contemplative ascent is more emphatically a personal experience of *unio mystica*, a more deeply expressed existential awareness that the fragmented soul can attain a sense of wholeness by being reincorporated into the Godhead.[130] Union with the divine name is occasioned by psychic transport—which is consequent to clearing mundane matters from the mind[131]—that in turn facilitates the theurgical unification of the divine potencies signified by letters of the name.

Though I have just spoken of the mystical conjunction facilitating the theurgical task, I think it better to imagine a core experience of ecstasy with two facets: reintegration of the soul in the divine and fusion of the sefirotic potencies into harmonious unity.[132] Applying a linear logic, one might be tempted to treat these as two phases aligned in causal sequence, the former occasioning the latter. While there is cogency and heuristic value to this angle, it is not the only way the geometry of the matter may be diagrammed. When viewed morphologically as opposed to typologically, that is, under the semblance of form rather than type,[133] ecstasy and theurgy can be seen as two manifestations of the same phenomenon. The consonance of these two elements, which have been too sharply bifurcated by the prevailing slant in the critical study of Jewish mysticism, is necessitated by the ontological conviction regarding the divine/angelic status of the Jewish soul, an idea whose roots lie in the belief that the righteous or holy ones of Israel have been endowed with an angelomorphic nature, a conception that evolved in earnest in late–Second Temple Judaism, though likely based on a still older ancient near-Eastern mythological understanding of kingship.[134] In the intellectual milieu inhabited by medieval kabbalists, it is presumed that God and Israel are circumscribed within a monopsychic unity that levels out the ontic difference between cause and effect, and hence mystical union and theurgic unification are concurrent processes that have been artificially separated for extraneous taxonomic concerns by contemporary scholars of kabbalah.

A key text in which the contemplative ideal is laid out is the explanation of the vision of the *sefirot* mentioned in another passage from *Sefer Yeṣirah* 1:8: "Ten intangible *sefirot*: their vision [*ṣefiyyatan*] is like the appearance of lightning [*ke-mar'eh ha-bazaq*], and their limit [*takhlitan*] has no end, his speech is in them like that which flees, and they pursue his utterance like the storm, and before his throne they bow down." The "vision" (*ṣefiyyah*) is construed in the commentary attributed to Isaac as mystical comprehension designated on the basis of rabbinic elocution as "contemplation of one thing from another" (*hitbonenut davar mi-tokh davar*).[135] The phenomenological contours of this state are elucidated by the verse "And I wait to see what he will speak to me," *wa-aṣappeh lir'ot mah yedabber bi* (Hab. 2:1), which Isaac (or the anonymous hand allegedly recording his teaching for posterity) glosses as "for the word appeared to him" (*she-hayah ha-dibbur nir'eh elav*). From this one can deduce that contemplative visualization, which relates to the activity of both the emanations and the kabbalist, is a seeing of the word, an experience of synesthesia wherein image and sound, optic and verbal, coincide, to see what is spoken as the text coming to be written.[136]

But to what does the "word" (*dibbur*) precisely refer? And how is it seen? In the continuation of the commentary, the scope of the matter is further delineated through the image of the chain of being that extends from the lowest demarcation, *middah*, to the highest, *ne'elemet*, from the measurable and thus more fully exposed attribute to what is hidden, the secret beyond spatial demarcation even in the imaginal realm:

The vision relates to the fact that each and every cause [*sibbah*] receives from the cause above it, for the attribute [*middah*] draws forth from the attribute that is hewn [*ḥaṣuvah*], and that which is hewn from the engraved [*ḥaquqah*], and that which is engraved from the marked [*reshumah*], and that which is marked from the hidden [*ha-ne'elemet*], everything is such that this is within that and that within this, everything is bound so that this is in that and that is in this.[137] How do they receive? The way of their receiving—something subtle and an essence [*davar daq we-ha-wayah*]. "Like the appearance" [*ke-mar'eh*], contemplation that has no substance [*hitbonenut she-ein bo mammash*], and "the appearance" is the pure and translucent splendor of the apprehension of one who receives [*zohar daqut zakkut hassagat ha-mitqabbel*]. "The appearance of lightning" [*ke-mar'eh ha-bazaq*], this is the purity and translucency of the apprehension of one who receives [*daqut zakkut hassagat ha-mitqabbel*]. "Their limit" [*takhlitan*] is not like their measure [*middatan*], for the measure [*ha-middah*] is a matter received by differentiated beings [*davar ha-mitqabbel la-nifradim*],[138] for the prophets saw the attributes [*middot*] in accord with their comprehension and by means of receiving their potencies they would expand their minds [*marḥivin maḥashavtan*] more than other human beings, and on account of this they had an expansion of soul to extend infinitely in the details [*raḥav ha-nefesh lehitpasheṭ bi-feratim be-ein sof*]. . . . "For the Lord is one," now the measure [*middah*] in the infinite alludes that it has no limit on any side. "From contemplating" the matters hidden from thought lest one get lost, for from what one comprehends one can discern what one cannot comprehend, and thus the measures [*middot*] arose, for language can comprehend only that which comes out from it, since a man cannot comprehend the measure of speech and the letters [*middat ha-dibbur we-ha-otiyyot*] but only the measure itself [*middatah be-aṣmah*], and there is no measure outside the letters. All the sublime measures are given to be meditated upon [*lehitbonen*], for each measure receives from the measure above it, and they are given to Israel to contemplate from the measure seen in the heart, to contemplate infinitely.[139]

On a previous occasion I had the opportunity to discuss some of the details of this richly nuanced and intricate account of the contemplative praxis. Here I will focus on the contribution this text makes to the theme of textual embodiment and poetic incarnation. The form contemplatively envisioned is the word of God as it is diffused through the chain of being that extends from what is concealed (*ha-ne'elemet*) to the exposed measure (*middah*). The hidden source is revealed in four links on the chain designated in descending order as "marked," "hewn," "engraved," and "measured," terms that relay the delimiting of the limitless light as it passes sequentially through the sefirotic filters. Significantly, the materialization of spirit is portrayed as the concretization of thought into letters whence speech—in both written and oral form[140]—is constructed, the articulation of the inaudible name in the constellation of the invisible image.[141]

The prophets, who are cast typologically as protokabbalists—the reinterpretation of classical prophecy is so basic to the kabbalistic worldview that ancient prophets are portrayed as having access to the secret wisdom of kabbalah and contemporary kabbalists, the "enlightened of Israel" (*maskilei yisra'el*),[142] as having experiences of a prophetic nature—are distinguished by their capacity to expand their thought limitlessly beyond the limit of thought. By thought thinking what lies beyond the parameters of thought to think, the mind of the kabbalist envisions complex infinity from infinite complexity. The visualization is thus expressed as an ascent through various gradations, from the measurable attribute on the bottom to what is hidden on top, from the comprehensible to the incomprehensible. The spiritual elite of Israel are set apart by their capability of contemplating from the measure as it is seen in the heart to the infinite (*lehitbonen mi-tokh ha-middah ha-nir'eit ba-lev lehitbonen ad ein sof*); hence the mystical state is referred to as "contemplation that has no substance" (*hitbonenut she-ein bo mammash*)—what is visualized contemplatively is "all that which the comprehension of thought comprehends to the infinite" (*kol mah she-hassagat ha-maḥashavah masseget ad ein sof*),[143] the trail of thought winding its way not to that which is not thought but to that which is thought as what cannot be thought, the unthought, beyond the polarity of being and not being.

Mystical illumination ensues from "contemplation that has no substance," that is, contemplation of what cannot be reified as an object of knowledge or subject of predication, the one that is lacking substance precisely because of the fullness of its insubstantiality. The "way of contemplation" (*derekh hitbonenut*) is thus compared figuratively to "sucking" (*yeniqah*) as opposed to "knowing" (*yedi'ah*)[144] to convey the idea that meditation yields and is generated by an intimate and direct gnosis of divinity rather than discursive knowledge, a unified intuition of many in one rather than a composite inference of one from many.[145]

Seeing No-Thing: In/Sight Blinding Vision

To appreciate the phenomenological and ontological contours of the contemplative ideal, it would be beneficial to frame the discussion in light of certain assumptions in Neoplatonic literature and especially in Plotinus, who exerted in one way or another a profound influence on medieval philosophical and mystical accounts of psychic conjunction in the three monotheistic faiths. The limitations of space obviously prevent me from treating the Plotinian worldview adequately, let alone developments in Neoplatonic thought subsequent to Plotinus and particularly those that evolved in medieval Islamic centers of speculative learning in the tenth and eleventh centuries.

According to Plotinus, for the human mind to contemplate the first principle, the unknowable, nameless One,[146] a tenet traceable to Plato's description of the Good as that which is "beyond being,"[147] it must become like the One. The logic underlying this assumption rests on the ancient Hellenic wisdom espoused in the adage of Anaxagoras that things of similar nature are attracted to one another, or, in the related formulation of Empedocles, wisdom consists of "like by like," since it is "either identical with or closely akin to perception."[148] Even more pertinent for understanding Plotinus is his utilization of the Aristotelian formula, which is based on the aforementioned pre-Socratic principle, that the knower must be like the thing that is known.[149]

One passage in particular that is worthy of citation is from a relatively early treatise in the Plotinian corpus, indeed the one listed first in Porphyry's chronological order, in which Plotinus sets out to explain the "inner sight" by which one can apprehend the true form of the "inconceivable beauty," a way of seeing that is awakened when the eyes are shut.[150] If the mind is sufficiently purified of corporeal matters, then in turning inward, which is also depicted as an ascent to the intelligible realm[151]—a theme reiterated by many a mystic visionary, as Blake, for instance, put it in his epic poem *Jerusalem: The Emanation of the Great Albion*, "What is Above is Within, for every-thing in Eternity is translucent"[152]—it will see the "true light" that cannot be measured by metric dimensions; in the speculum of inner vision, the mind's eye sees what is without within and what is within without, and hence spectator and spectacle can no longer be differentiated: "For one must come to the sight with a seeing power made akin to and like what is seen. No eye ever saw the sun without becoming sun-like, nor can a soul see beauty without becoming beautiful. You must become first all godlike and all beautiful if you intend to see God and beauty."[153]

In the continuation of the passage, Plotinus distinguishes the vision of the Intellect, the place of forms or ideas, which are characterized as the intelligible beauty, and the vision of the Good, the "primary beauty," the origin that is beyond the "screen" of beauty.[154] If, however, the One is utterly unique, it can be like no other thing; in its absolute simplicity,[155] the One can have no form or substance, and hence the only way to become "like" the One is to be assimilated into the One. However, to be assimilated into what is "beyond being"—a designation, Plotinus reminds us, that makes no positive state-ment about the One but only implies that it is "not this," that is, it is not a particular something and thus cannot be compared to anything[156]—the mind must transcend the specificity of its own being by disposing the filters of intellection.

> [I]t would be absurd to seek to comprehend that boundless nature . . . but just as he who wishes to see the intelligible nature will contemplate what is beyond the percep-tible if he has no mental image of the perceptible, so he who wishes to contemplate what is beyond the intelligible will contemplate it when he has let all the intelligible go. . . . But we in our travail do not know what we ought to say, and are speaking of what cannot be spoken, and give it a name because we want to indicate it to ourselves the best we can.[157]

An iconoclastic breaking of all form occasions contemplative envisioning of the form-less.[158]

For Plotinus, there are three stages to the life of mind that correspond to the three hypostases, a correspondence that is predicated on the correlation of being and experience, the phenomenological and ontological, a critical feature of medieval kabbalah, as I have argued elsewhere:[159] what is real is real as experienced and what is experienced is experi-enced as real.[160] The ascent of mind can be seen as a progressive attempt to apprehend beauty,[161] to rise from discursive knowledge appropriate for the sensible world, that is, reasoning from premise to conclusion and transitioning from one object of thought to another, to an inner vision of intellect and the world of ideal forms wherein the distinction between subject and object is transcended, and finally to seeing the formless, the Good that is the source of ultimate beauty, radiant darkness beyond intellect and description.

Plotinus conceives the ascent in accord with a major impulse in the Platonic under-standing of the philosophical life, as a way to attain knowledge of self, "to face death before we die."[162] But contained herein is a fundamental paradox, for the higher one ascends on the ladder of self-knowledge, climbing from the multiplicity of the sensible to the complexity of the intelligible and beyond to the simplicity of the One, the more one loses awareness of self, the more one gains knowledge of self;[163] at the summit of knowl-edge—the intellect contemplating naught but intellect, a mirror turned inward to mirror the mirror turned outward, the mirror mirroring the mirror mirrored in the mirror—is what Dionysius the Areopagite referred to as the source of all being, which is "before be-ing"[164] and hence neither is nor is not, known "through unknowing" (*agnosia*).[165] The path of contemplation is a process of purification, emptying the mind of images, concepts, and words,[166] but in the final stage, the return of the "alone" to the "Alone," the purging culminates in vision, albeit a seeing where the difference between seer and seen is no longer viable; the eye that sees is the eye that is seen as the eye that sees the eye that is seen.[167] This, Plotinus suggests, occurs when one is "possessed" by a god who brings his contemplation to a point of vision, and presents himself to his own mind and looks at a beautified image of himself; but then he dismisses the image, beautiful though it is, and comes to unity with himself, and, making no more separation, is one and all together with that god silently present, and is with him as much as he wants to be and can be. . . . While he is coming to know the god he must keep to an impression of him and form distinct ideas of him as he seeks him and discern what he is entering into; and when he has learnt with confidence that it is into the highest blessedness, he must give himself up to what is within and become, instead of one who sees, an object of vision to another who contemplates him shining out with thoughts of the kind which come from that world.[168]

In the meditative state—a noetic circle in which boundaries of thinking, thinker, and thought can no longer be discriminated—the mind stretches beyond the limits of mindfulness to be absorbed in the mindless but fully conscious source of all being.[169] Intellect is the most perfect image of the One, but even that image must be transcended if one is to see the imageless light about which we cannot speak adequately.[170] Concerning the One we must say that it is all things "by and in itself," since it contains all things in itself and they exist only by participation in it, but it is also none of them, since its being is in no way dependent on them.[171] Inasmuch as the One "is all things and not a single one of them,"[172] Plotinus insists that when we speak or think about it, we must dispense with every name; at best, we can "make signs [*sēmainein*] to ourselves about it"[173] in the manner of Egyptian hieroglyphs, a nondiscursive language based on ideogrammatic symbols rather than words and propositions:[174]

When you have put away all things and left only himself, do not try to find what you can add, but if there is something you have not yet taken away from him in your mind. For even you can grasp something about which it is not possible any more to say or apprehend anything else; but it is something which has its place high above everything, this which alone is free in truth, because it is not enslaved to itself, but is only itself and really itself, while every other thing is itself and something else.[175]

Paradoxically, that which is known and named to be truly itself and nothing else cannot be known or named—as knowing and naming entail relating a thing to other things—but only experienced in the vision of that which is invisible, a seeing that sees nothing, not even not-seeing, the mind's eye gazing in the darkness of seeing light[176] wherein nothing is seen and nobody sees.[177] Even the term "one" is to be interpreted at best negatively, as denial of multiplicity, for if it were to be taken positively,

it would be less clear than if we did not give it a name at all: for perhaps this name [One] was given it in order that the seeker, beginning from this which is completely indicative of simplicity, may finally negate this as well, because, though it was given as well as possible by its giver, not even this is worthy to manifest that nature; since that nature cannot be heard, nor may it be understood by one who hears, but, if at all, by one who sees. But if the seer tries to look at a form, he will not know even that.[178]

Not-seeing is previewed by abandoning all concepts and images, a seeing through the glass darkly.[179] From this vantage point, apophasis and mystical envisioning go hand in hand.[180]

Inscripting Ineffability / Enfolding Scroll

The Neoplatonic orientation, briefly outlined above, greatly informed the mystical speculation in the three monotheistic faiths and thereby transformed their respective theological sensibilities, based in great measure on the positive representations of the deity elicited from the canonical texts of ancient Israelite prophecy. In terminology used by historians of religion, the mystical element in the three monotheisms ensues from the juxtaposition of the kataphatic and apophatic, that is, a mysticism predicated on the possibility of envisioning the shape of God in conjunction with a mysticism that steadfastly denies the possibility of ascribing any form to the being beyond all configuration, indeed the being to whom we cannot even ascribe the attribute of being without denying the nature of that (non)being.

In mystical accounts gesticulated within the hermeneutical matrix of scriptural religious belief, the most important way the visionary and unitive experiences are mediated is through study of canonical texts. The experiences themselves may surpass the limits of language, but it is only through language that those limits are surpassed. The apophatic tendency to submerge all forms of sentient imaging in the formlessness of pure consciousness cannot be completely severed from the kataphatic insistence on the possibility of being in the presence of the divine. The juxtaposition of the kataphatic and apophatic has fostered the awareness on the part of the ones initiated in the secret gnosis that mystical utterance is an unsaying, which is not the same as the silence of not-speaking, but rather that which remains ineffable in being spoken, that which remains unknown in being known, that which remains unseen in being seen.

An important mystical theologian of the early church in the fourth century who set out to expound the apophatic way was the Cappodocian father, Gregory of Nyssa, a man of letters who studied Scripture and Platonic writings as well as the treatises of Origen and Clement of Alexandria. In spite of Gregory's great admiration for Origen, in one crucial dimension their spiritual outlooks are incongruous.[181] For Origen, the soul pursues a path of light on the way to God, whereas for Gregory, the journey is from light to darkness, a

111

darkness that is, to be sure, more fully light, indeed so luminous that it cannot be apprehended phenomenally except as dark.

In *De vita Moysis*, Gregory distinguishes three levels of vision of the invisible God that we may call the cosmological, anthropological, and theophanic. According to the first, the divine is seen in the contemplation of the potencies that act in the world, that is, vision by way of analogy, from the manifest to the hidden. According to the second, God is seen through the agency of the human being who is created in the divine image, that is, an internal seeing of the mind. The third is exemplified by the epiphany at the burning bush (Exod. 3:1–6): Moses divested himself of the earthly covering—depicted metaphorically by removing the sandals from his feet[182]—and beheld "the ineffable and mysterious illumination."[183] Moses was privileged to be instructed in the theophany (ἐν τῇ θεοφανείᾳ παιδευθείς) because "he came to know that none of those things which are apprehended by sense perception and contemplated by the understanding really subsists, but that the transcendent essence and cause of the universe (ὑπερανεστώσης οὐσίας καὶ αἰτίας τοῦ παντὸς), on which everything depends, alone subsists."[184] Just as Moses attained "knowledge of truth" (τῆς ἀληθείας γνῶσίς) through apprehension of the "truly real Being" (ἀληθῶς τὸ ὄντως ὄν),[185] "so now does everyone who, like him, divests himself of the earthly covering and looks to the light shining from the bramble bush, that is, to the Radiance which shines upon us through this thorny flesh and which is (as the Gospel says) the true light and the truth itself."[186]

The location of the vision in the bush is interpreted typologically by Gregory as a foreshadowing of "the mystery of the Lord's incarnation" (τὸ διὰ σαρχὸς παραδηλοῦσθαι τοῦ Κυρίου μυστήριον) whereby the hidden radiance of the one true being is manifest in the material body.[187] To apprehend the light of the invisible deity in the visible form of the "thorny flesh"—the incarnate body of Christ, the image of the infinite (τῇ εἰχόνι ἀοράτου)[188]—one must, like Moses, divest oneself of one's material corporeality; envisioning the body of what has no form is correlated with diminishing one's own bodiliness.

But what does it mean to see God? Gregory sheds further light on this enigma in a second passage in *De vita Moysis*, expounding the verse "So the people remained at a distance, Moses approached the thick cloud where God was" (Exod. 20:18). At the outset, Gregory remarks that this seems to contradict the theophany at the burning bush, "for then the Divine was beheld in light but now he is seen in Darkness."[189] Gregory is quick to point out, however, that the contradiction is only apparent: "Scripture teaches by this that religious knowledge comes at first to those who receive it as light. . . . But as the mind progresses and, through an ever greater and more perfect diligence, comes to apprehend reality, as it approaches more nearly to contemplation [θεωρία], it sees more clearly what of the divine nature [θείας φυσεως] is uncontemplated [αθεωρητον]."[190] By leaving behind all empirical data and conceptual categories, the mind penetrates deeper into the darkness:

until by the intelligence's yearning for understanding it gains access to the invisible and the incomprehensible, and there it sees God. This is the true knowledge of what is sought: this is the seeing that consists in not seeing [τὸ ἰδεῖν ἐν τῷ μὴ ἰδεῖν], because that which is sought transcends all knowledge, being separated on all sides by incomprehensibility as by a kind of darkness.[191]

Inspired by Philo's interpretation of the scriptural locution of Moses entering into the dark cloud (*arafel*) as an allegorical depiction of his entry into the invisible and incorporeal realm, a view substantiated as well by God's response to Moses that he can behold the back but not the face of the glory (Exod. 33:23),[192] Gregory reads the verse as an expression of the view that contemplation is a progression to what cannot be contemplated; the pinnacle of the mind's ascent consists of beholding the "luminous darkness" (λαμπρῷ γνόφῳ), an oxymoron that resolves the exegetical problem with which Gregory began his exposition, the ostensible conflict between the theophany at the bush where God appears in the light and the later statement that Moses enters the cloud of darkness to encounter God is no clash at all, as the mystic vision is a seeing of *luminous darkness*, a vision of unseeing through the mirror of the infinite, the image of God mysteriously embodied in the person of Christ and to some degree in each human being,[193] that is, a seeing through which one comes to see that one cannot see, the blindness that is true insight.

The interweaving of affirmative and negative theology, anagogy and apophaticism, was expounded in more intricate philosophical detail by Dionysius the Areopagite.[194] Combining the rigor of logical analysis and the passion of poetic sensibility, Dionysius sought to articulate a mystical theology that was true to the kataphasis of scriptural faith and to the apophasis of philosophical contemplation. According to Dionysius's formulation in the *Divine Names* (588A–B):

[W]e must not dare to resort to words or conceptions concerning the hidden divinity which transcends being, apart from what the sacred scriptures have divinely revealed. Since the unknowing of what is beyond is something above and beyond speech, mind, or being itself, one should ascribe to it an understanding beyond being. . . . Indeed the inscrutable One is out of the reach of every rational process. Nor can any words come up to the inexpressible Good, this One, this source of all unity, this supra-existent Being. Mind beyond mind, word beyond speech, it is gathered up by no discourse, by no intuition, by no name.[195]

God is hidden and transcendent and thus technically "surpasses all discourse and all knowledge" (593A);[196] the only positive attributions that are legitimately ascribed to God are the characteristics derived from the language of Scripture.

In this manner, Dionysius established a model employed subsequently by mystical exegetes in Judaism, Christianity, and Islam who sought to combine the apophatic and kataphatic, remaining faithful to the philosophical insight regarding the unknowability and ineffability of the One, on the one hand, and to the revealed word of God predicated on a plethora of affirmative statements about the divine nature, on the other. The juxtaposition of these distinct orientations to the texture of religious experience resulted in a paradox expressed by Dionysius and reiterated in one form or another by numerous mystic visionaries in the three faiths: "God is therefore known in all things and as distinct from all things. He is known through knowledge and through unknowing" (872A).[197] In more conventional terms, God is both transcendent and immanent, "the cause of everything" but not identical to any one thing, "since it transcends all things in a manner beyond being" (593C).[198] Insofar as there can be nothing outside God, God is "all things in all things," and thus it must be the case that God is known in all things. Yet God is "no thing among things (872A),"[199] for the one cannot be delimited or contained in any single entity and remain the one that is boundless, and hence God is apart from everything and is not known.

It is in this *unknowing* that God is most truly known, a matter that is considered to be a secret that should not be divulged to the uninitiated (597C). In his *Mystical Theology*, Dionysius follows Gregory of Nyssa and ascribes to Moses the status of having freed himself from "what sees and is seen," plunging

> into the truly mysterious darkness of unknowing. Here, renouncing all that the mind may conceive, wrapped entirely in the intangible and the invisible, he belongs completely to him who is beyond everything. Here, being neither oneself nor someone else, one is supremely united to the completely unknown by an inactivity of all knowledge, and knows beyond the mind by knowing nothing. (1001A)[200]

For Dionysius, the mystical agnosticism is attained in the last of the three stages of the mystical path: purgation, illumination, and union (*henosis*). The ideal of union is appropriated from Plotinus, but in Dionysius it should be rendered more precisely as divinization (*theosis*). The way that one rises to this state is by unknowing (*agnosia*), that is, by stripping the mind of all positive knowledge related to sense data and rational concepts, one is unified with the "intellectual light" (φῶς νοητὸν) (*Divine Names* 700D), which transcends all being and knowledge: "But again, the most divine knowledge of God, that which comes through unknowing, is achieved in a union far beyond mind, when mind turns away from all things, even from itself, and when it is made one with the dazzling rays, being then and there enlightened by the inscrutable depth of Wisdom" (872A–B).[201] The mandate of the contemplative life is to move beyond all images to the imageless. As Dionysius put it in the first of the letters to Gaius, "Someone beholding God and understanding what he saw has not actually seen God. . . . He is completely unknown and non-existent. He exists beyond being and he is known beyond the mind. And this quite positively complete unknowing is knowledge of him who is above everything that is known." The author leads his reader once again to the mystical paradox: "Complete unknowing is knowledge of him who is above everything that is known" (1065A).[202]

With this ideational background we can better approach the nexus between negative theology and the mystical ideal of conjunction articulated in the history of kabbalah. In another passage from the commentary on *Sefer Yeṣirah* attributed to Isaac, the matter is presented in an appropriately enigmatic manner, centered on the doctrine of ten upper potencies that correspond to the lower ten *sefirot*:[203]

> Even though the word [*dibbur*] is in the infinite, there is nonetheless a subtle cause [*sibbah daqqah*] or subtle essence [*hawayah daqqah*] that thought comprehends through contemplation of the allusion from it [*masseget bah be-hitbonenut remez mimmenah*]; therefore, there is an emanation in thought [*sefirah ba-maḥashavah*], which is the subtle essence in which there is ten. The entities [*devarim*] have a measure and dimension but thought has no dimension, and thus they go ten in ten, from the subtle ones the inscribed [*min ha-daqqot ha-reshumot*], for from ten there are ten, subtle ones from the inwardness of the subtle ones [*daqqot mi-penimiyyut ha-daqqot*]. We discern from the potency of allusion of thought [*remez ha-maḥashavah*] what we can comprehend and what we must leave aside, for there is no comprehension of the thought of allusion [*hassagat maḥashevet ha-remez*] from there and beyond, since there is no power in the created being to comprehend the inwardness of the allusion of thought to comprehend the infinite [*penimiyyut remez ha-maḥashavah lehassig be-ein sof*]. . . . There is no capacity to contemplate the hidden essences that have no demarcation except through the thing that emanates from them. . . . From the demarcated essences there is contemplation of those that are not demarcated, and from the inwardness of the comprehension of their thought is there contemplation of their cause in the infinite [*mi-tokh penimiyyut hassagat maḥashavtam hitbonenut sibbotam be-ein sof*].[204]

The name can be viewed as the absolute language, a "mystical language of unsaying,"[205] lingering betwixt affirmation and negation, apophasis and kataphasis, speaking-away and speaking-with, a language that serves as the index of its own inability to be indexed, the computation of indeterminacy. If truth is truly beyond language, then silence alone is appropriate to truth, but silence is realized not in not-speaking but in unsaying, which is a saying nonetheless. If, however, not-speaking is the articulation of truth, then nothing is spoken, but if nothing is spoken, nothing is unspoken. To express the point more prosaically, images of negation are not the same as negation of images, for if the latter were faithfully heeded, the former would truly not be, as there would be nothing of which to (un)speak and hence there would be no data for either study, critical or devotional. Mystical claims of ineffability—to utter unutterable truths—utilize images that are negative but no less imagistic than the affirmative images they negate.[206]

This is precisely the point underscored in the contemplative mysticism propounded by Isaac and other kabbalists who considered him their master. The ultimate signifier is the Tetragrammaton, ultimate in the sense that it signifies what cannot be signified and thus itself resists signification. The name is a garment that reveals the nameless it conceals by concealing the revealing by which it reveals what it conceals. That the root word is ineffable, the proper name par excellence, indicates that the final (in a teleological and not a chronological sense) avowal of language transcends language, an insight conveyed in the technical designation of the uppermost gradation in the divine pleroma as *remez ha-maḥashavah* ("allusion of thought"), the aspect of thought grasped allusively, that which eludes thought, the "thought of allusion" (*maḥashevet ha-remez*), whence the incomprehensible is measured in the comprehension of the immeasurable.[207] Although not stated explicitly, this measure is the Torah, which is the name, envisioned in the heart of the kabbalist, as the imaginal body of the macroanthropos.

Support for this surmise is found in an interpretation of the aggadic motif that God looked into Torah before creating the world, which Jacob ben Sheshet reports having heard in the name of Isaac the Blind: "This is similar to the explanation of 'he was contemplating Torah,' he saw the essences in himself, for they were essences from wisdom, and from within these essences, which are the essences of wisdom, he discerned that they would in the future be revealed."[208] In the continuation of the passage, Jacob ben Sheshet mentions the account of divine omniscience in the *Mishneh Torah* of Maimonides[209]— God knows all things by knowing himself, since his intellect contains the form of all things—as confirmation of the tradition attributed to Isaac, and he cites another passage from the *Guide* in which Maimonides discusses the mythopoeic theme that God takes counsel with his angelic retinue before acting in conjunction with the idea attributed to Plato that God contemplates the intelligible world.[210]

The attempt to harmonize the rabbinic, kabbalistic, and philosophic modes of discourse is noteworthy and demands fuller analysis, especially as it might shed light on the taxonomic distinctions that have dominated historiographical conceptions of medieval Jewish religious thought,[211] but for the purposes of this discussion I want only to emphasize that Jacob ben Sheshet preserves indisputable evidence that in the kabbalah of Isaac (or at least what is reported in his name), Torah is equated with the essences comprised in divine wisdom whence the sefirotic potencies emanate; to be even more precise, the emanations can be viewed as the disclosure of the hidden wisdom that is the primordial Torah.

An allusion to this may be discerned in the explanation of the expression *takhlitan* ("their limit") applied to the *sefirot* in *Sefer Yeṣirah*: "The limit of their comprehension, for each attribute has a limit and each limit has an end . . . but your commandment even though its beginning has a limit it extends and keeps going to the infinite, and if every thing that perishes has an end, no one can comprehend the limit of comprehension of your commandment, for a man only comprehends the chief attributes [*ro'shei middot*]."[212] The contrast between the limitless commandment and the limited *sefirot* underscores the fact that the former denotes the boundless aspect of the divine that unfurls within the boundary of the name.

Unsaying the Name / Naming the Unsaid

From the kabbalist's standpoint, the name is the paradigmatic symbol, the symbol of the paradigm, for it is expressive of the inexpressible. In the (un)saying of the name—apophasis as speaking-away, which entails not-speaking by speaking rather than speaking by not-speaking—divine potencies are concealed in the disclosure of their concealment. Inasmuch as the name is representative of language more generally, we can deduce from the prior statement that every speech-act (whether oral or written) is inherently analogical, comparing two ostensibly disparate things, a material entity and its spiritual counterpart. From a logical standpoint, however, the ontotheological schema of traditional kabbalah is informed by two ostensibly clashing claims: On the one hand, it is repeatedly emphasized that all language about God or the world of emanation is analogical, since God is inherently incomparable to all other things, but on the other hand, it is presumed that an uninterrupted continuity permeates and connects all levels of existence from top to bottom, and thus there is a basic similarity of all things to the divine.[213]

In a sense, these two claims can be correlated with the description of the One in Plotinus (briefly mentioned above) as transcendent to and immanent in all things, a distinction that derives from Plato's account of the One in the *Parmenides*. If there is no rupture in the "chain of being," to use Lovejoy's memorable phrase—and as far as I can discern, no kabbalist from the late Middle Ages would tolerate such a rupture—why should analogy be the only means available to us to fashion theological discourse? To speak analogically is to use words equivocally as a bridge joining two incongruent things rendered the same by being different. Kabbalists would have surely assented to the view expressed by Ibn ʿArabī that one must concurrently affirm the transcendence of true reality vis-à-vis all beings and the immanence of that reality in all beings, the perspective that Corbin calls "theomonism" in contrast to monotheism, that is, the esoteric belief that the oneness of being (*waḥdat al-wujūd*) is manifest through the multiplicity of epiphanies (*tajalliyāt*) that constitute the different names of the ineffable, unnameable truth (*al-ḥaqq*) beyond all discrimination.[214]

The quintessential paradox of kabbalistic ontotheology can be expressed semiotically in the recognition that signifier discloses the nature of signified, and signified, the nature of signifier, precisely because the two are indifferently identical by being identically indifferent. The matter is expressed with rhetorical artistry in one zoharic passage wherein four different levels of meaning in Scripture are distinguished. The relevant comment occurs in the first part of the homily, where only two levels of meaning are mentioned: narratological and mystical, the garment and what is beneath it:

Come and see: The supernal world and the lower world are balanced on one scale. Israel below and the supernal angels above. Concerning the supernal angels it is written, "He makes his angels into spirits" (Ps. 104:4). When they descend below they are garbed in the garment of this world, and if they were not garbed in the garment that is in the likeness of this world, they could not exist in this world and the world could not endure them. If this is so with respect to angels, how much more so with respect to Torah, which created them and all the worlds, and they exist on account of it, when it descends to this world, if it were not garbed in the garments of this world, the world could not endure. Thus the narrative of Torah is the garment of Torah. The one who thinks that the garment is the Torah itself, and not another matter, let his spirit deflate, and he will have no share in the world-to-come. Therefore, David said, "Open my eyes that I may perceive the wonders of your Torah" (Ps. 119:18), what is beneath the garment of Torah.[215]

In the continuation of the passage, the exegetical layering of Scripture is expanded from two to four levels, to wit, garment, body, soul, and soul of souls, which correspond respectively to the stories, laws, esoteric wisdom, and messianic secrets comprised within the text. In turn, the four levels of meaning are correlated ontically with the heavens and their angelic hosts, *Kenesset Yisra'el*, *Tif'eret Yisra'el*, and *Atiqa Qaddisha*, that is, the tenth, sixth, and first of the sefirotic emanations.[216] What is essential for the present discussion is the initial contrast between the revealed and concealed. It is likely that the author of this unit was operating with the twofold distinction between soul and body, the latter configured as the visible garment that covers the invisible essence of the former, imagery (linked exegetically to Job 10:11) that is attested in zoharic literature and other kabbalistic treatises, including works of de León.[217]

The hermeneutical principle of dual meaning in the text, an orientation fairly widespread in the rabbinic elite from various geographical localities at the time *Zohar* began to crystallize into a discernible textual reality,[218] is based on the ontological parallelism between the supernal and mundane. The image of two worlds "balanced on one scale" (*be-ḥad matqela itqalu*) conveys similitude through difference.[219] Given the virtual identity of thing and word, there is no substantial difference whether we think of this weighing as a metaphysical gesture or a grammatical speech-act; to render dissimilar things equal in their incongruity is a claim about the nature of being as well as a claim about the nature of language.

In typical medieval fashion, kabbalists maintained that the spiritual is discerned through the physical, a cosmological principle that shaped their hermeneutic, as the hidden meaning of the text was thought to be discovered through its literal body, the body that is letter; mystical gnosis thus entails, according to the locution of one zoharic passage, a seeing of the secret "through the garment" (*mi-go levusha*) rather than by removing the garment,[220] a formulation that may be profitably compared to Ibn 'Arabī's insistence, reflecting the stance affirmed by a number of distinguished Sufi masters who preceded him, that the hidden, true reality—the face—cannot be seen except from behind a veil.[221] The veil renders the face spectacular, for in the effacement of the veil, the face is unveiled as that which is inherently not phenomenalizable.[222] In reverse emulation of the dissimilitude of Torah to conceal in the charade of revealing, the master of esoteric gnosis possesses the ability to reveal in the display of concealing. The capacity to divulge secrets, attributed in the zoharic passage to Simeon ben Yoḥai, is traced to the "skilled tongue," *leshon limmudim* (Isa. 50:4), which is identified as the "holy tongue," *leshon ha-qodesh*[223] or the "holy spirit," *ruaḥ ha-qodesh*, that is, the phallic potency of *Shekhinah*,[224] the lower wisdom (*ruaḥ*) that receives the overflow from the upper wisdom (*qodesh*) and is thereby transformed from passive female to active male.[225]

The intent of the aforecited zoharic passage is brought into sharper focus when discussed in conjunction with another text from this literary collage that appears in a dramatic section that chronicles the discourse of the elderly donkey driver focused on the mystery of conversion and the doctrine of metempsychosis.[226] The old man lures other members of the fraternity (and by implication, the reader) into his path by initially uttering three seemingly incomprehensible parables. In time, through the unfolding of the narrative, which is a staging of the hermeneutical dilemma of esotericism marked at each level of disclosure by the tension between the urge to reveal and the need to conceal, the donkey driver, outwardly foolish, discloses himself to be a true master.

It lies beyond the scope of this chapter to do justice to the literary complexity of this unit, but suffice it to note one critical point. The implicit hermeneutic principle in the narrative of the old man—the principle that shapes the mythologic of the story and that incites the exegetical moves of the kabbalist author—is that by plumbing the depths of the mystery of conversion of the Gentile, one shall be led to a mystical understanding of Torah. To grasp this one must bear in mind that the social-historical phenomenon of conversion suggested to the Castilian kabbalists a crossing of ontic boundaries that seemingly challenged the dualistic posture reiterated on numerous occasions in the zoharic text: Israel correlated with divine purity, and the nations of the world, with demonic impurity.

For our purposes it is necessary to ponder the part of the text that articulates the assumption regarding Torah and mystical secrets, an assumption that is at once ontological and hermeneutical—indeed, the two cannot be separated in the thinking of these kabbalists. The explanation of the garbing of a Jewish soul in a non-Jewish body, the key factor in understanding the mechanics of conversion, is interrupted, so it seems, by the observation of the old man that God hides secrets in the garments of Torah. Only the wise who are replete with eyes are capable of apprehending secrets, a vision designated as seeing through rather than discarding the garment, a crucial point to which I have already alluded. Shortly after the reader encounters this principle, the old man offers a parable of the beautiful maiden in a castle that recounts the erotic relationship that pertains between Torah and the "wise one of the heart" (*ḥakkima de-libba*).[227]

As in the zoharic homily that I have previously mentioned, four levels of meaning are delineated: *remiza* or *remizu* ("sign"); *derasha* ("homily"); *ḥiddah* ("allegory") or *haggadah* ("narrative"); and *razin setimin* ("hidden mysteries"). The four levels are presented sequentially as stages of ever-increasing disclosure, the first offered through the barrier of a wall, the second from behind a curtain, the third through a more subtle screen, and finally, the fourth, ostensibly clearing away all obstructions; the reader encounters the text face-to-face, which in zoharic idiom signifies union of the most intimate sort, the epitome of the erotic engagement.[228] When Torah exposes herself fully to her lover, he comes to realize that the secret was already present in the first stage when the initial hint was offered, and at that moment of enlightenment he understands that *peshaṭei di-qera*, the "literal" text—the text in its literal embodiment, the mien of letters—must be as it is, with no word added or subtracted. The linear progression from *peshaṭ* to *sod*, the exoteric to the esoteric, turns out, in fact, to be a circular excursion, as one learns that the mystical meaning disclosed at the end is the same as the literal sense revealed at the beginning.

To discern the mystery of the initial insinuation at the end confirms the hermeneutical point that the secret can be seen only through the garment of letters, the body of the text, unmasking the face in effacing the mask.[229] The uncovering of the innermost meaning at the culmination of the journey is thus a recovery of the overt sense disclosed allusively in the beginning. If it is true that every translation is interpretation, it is equally true that every interpretation is translation, literally "crossing over," by which one gives expression to the inward sense through the outward forms.[230] The somewhat unusual choice of the term *remiza* to denote *peshaṭ* in the initial delineation underscores that the mystical understanding—the illumination of the moment, momentarily momentous—of the revealed word, the light that manifests the name, and by extension of language more generally, rests on the presumption that the literal is metaphorical and the metaphorical literal.[231]

To be sure, on the face of it, the final disclosure—the fourth level—bears the intimacy of the face-to-face encounter, a showing that ostensibly does away with barriers and thus stands in sharp contrast to the intermediaries of the previous revelations: the wall, curtain, and screen; however, when one apprehends the truth that the secret exposed at the end was contained in the hint offered at the beginning, then it becomes apparent that even the "face" is a veil,[232] indeed the greatest of veils, since it can be unveiled only if it remains veiled as that which cannot be unveiled.[233] The polysemous and dissimulating nature of truth is such that when one lifts the veil, one does not uncover truth unveiled but yet another veil reveiling the invisible reality; seen everywhere, it is nowhere seen.

Unveiling the Veil / Veiling the Unveiled

Here it would serve us well to consider the image of the veil a bit more circumspectly, as the veil—distinctively, it seems—manifests qualities typically engendered as feminine and associated with an esoteric hermeneutic, allusive, concealing, masking, beckoning, alluring, tempting one to imagine the face yet to be seen.[234] The preceding discussion illustrated the extent to which this dynamic is at play in the zoharic parable of the maiden without eyes. In chapter 1 of *Language, Eros, Being* I commented briefly on the affinity between kabbalistic esotericism and the symbol of the veil in Sufism. It would be beneficial to expand on that discussion at this juncture as a way to open up further the boundaries of discourse regarding secrecy and its double arc of projecting and withholding in the zoharic text, which I take to be emblematic of a more ubiquitously held kabbalistic hermeneutic related to the duplicity of revealing and concealing, what I shall call analogical exemplarism, the mirror of mirroring.

By exploring this trajectory, moreover, we will be in a position to understand better the complex interface between the three Abrahamic faiths in the symbolic imaginary of the zoharic kabbalists, which had a profound impact on subsequent generations, including the ecumenism that achieves full theoretical flourish in the messianic heresies of Sabbatianism and Frankism of the seventeenth and eighteenth centuries whereby the borderlines separating Judaism, Christianity, and Islam are eradicated even as they are preserved. Uprooting may be the operative word, as it conveys both the sense of uncovering and of ravaging the root. In terms of the specific theme of this discussion, the symbol of the veil seems to have been appropriated from an Islamic cultural orbit but applied in the service of the intricate polemical engagement with the Christological notion of incarnation of the Word.

Given the prominence of the veil in the dress code of Arabs before and after the rise of the prophet Muḥammad and the religion of Islam—originally, it seems, part of the attire for men as a sign of their being desert warriors and eventually transferred to women as an external mark of modesty, subservient social status, or self-effacing complicity through renunciation of sexual embodiment, in order to demarcate the boundary between believers and nonbelievers and thereby maintain the *umma* (the community of Muslims) and its symbolic order[235]—it should come as no surprise that the veil and the acts of veiling (*sitr*) and unveiling (*kashf, mukāshafah*) related to it would come to play a prominent role in Islamic esotericism in general and in Sufi epistemology in particular.[236] Needless to say, in this context, I can hardly do justice to the multifaceted texture of this symbol in the religious imagination of Muslims through the centuries. What I wish to emphasize particularly is the paradoxical nature of the veil as the site of concomitant disclosure and concealment, for it is with respect to this quality that we can discern a precise analogy to the image of the garment (*levush, malbush*) employed in kabbalistic literature to denote the medium that reveals by concealing and conceals by revealing.[237]

From a relatively early period, the image of lifting the veil was utilized by Sufis to convey mystical enlightenment or awakening, based on verses in the Qur'ān (50:22; 53:57–58; 82:1–6) where this activity is associated with the vision that will be manifest on the day of reckoning (*yawm ad-dīn*).[238] In general, it may be said that Sufis removed the image from its eschatological context and applied it to the inner journey of the seeker (*sālik*) to see the truth (*al-ḥaqq*) behind the veil, the visionary formulation of the mystical quest for union with the one. I do not mean to say that there is a categorical rejection of traditional eschatology on the part of Sufis, but only that their spiritual propensity for inwardness opened the way to a mystical interpretation that renders the eschaton more immediately present; in this sense, Sufis can be spoken of as having embraced an eschatology of and in the moment, mystical illumination in the present, the epiphany of the one true reality in the durationless instant (*ān* or *waqt*) that has no before or after, the interval that endures as that which elapses and elapses as that which endures.[239]

Al-Niffarī, active in the tenth century, expressed the matter laconically in words he attributes to God in his *Kitāb al-mawāqif* (*Book of Standings*): "My moment has come / The time has come for me to unveil my face and manifest my splendor."[240] The revelatory experience, the unveiling of the face (*wajh*), results in gnosis (*maʿrifa*), illumination (*ishrāq*), intuition (*dhawq*), knowledge by presence (*al-ʿilm al-ḥudūrī*), the momentous apprehension of the "oneness of existence" (*waḥdat al-wujūd*) in which the particularity of beings is annihilated like water dissolved in water, or like the flame burst into flame.[241]

One of the earliest attestations of the prominence of the symbol of the veil in Sufism is associated with Rābiʿa of Basra (d. 801), the most celebrated woman in Sufi history. What is especially noteworthy is the manner in which Rābiʿa eroticized the image of the veil by describing the goal of the path as an unveiling of the beloved by the lover.[242] The gender implications of this representation are profound—the usual hierarchy on the face of it overturned by the image of the unveiling of the face of the beloved. The image of the veil in Islamic tradition, as I have already noted, is associated with the female, as the Muslim custom demands that women cover their faces in a display of sexual modesty. Recall the beginning of the account of Rābiʿa offered by the thirteenth-century Persian poet ʿAṭṭār: "Veiled with a special veil, veiled with the veil of sincerity, burned up in love and longing, enamored of proximity and immolation, lost in love-union, deputy of Maryam the pure, accepted among men."[243] Instead of the veil of modesty that one would expect to be associated with a Muslim woman, Rābiʿa is veiled in the "special veil," which is the "veil of sincerity." I assume this garb signifies her celibate renunciation, presented in Muslim hagiography as the prerequisite for her passionate and unmitigated yearning to unite with the one.[244] This would explain the designation of her as the "deputy of Maryam the pure," that is, the Virgin Mary.[245] Smith's rendering of the expression is even more striking, the "one accepted by men as a second spotless Mary."[246]

The veneration of Mary, mother of Jesus,[247] as the paragon of a chaste woman is anchored in several critical verses from both the Meccan (609–622 C.E.) and Medinan (622–632 C.E.) periods that uphold the Christological belief in the virginal conception (Q 3:35–47, 21:91; 66:12).[248] The acceptance of this tenet of orthodox Christianity is all the more striking given the unequivocal rejection of ascribing divine status to either Jesus (Q 4:171; 5:17, 75–76; 19:35–36; 43:57–59)[249] or Mary (Q 5:72–75, 116–20);[250] from the qurʾānic perspective, the conception of Jesus without a father is not taken as a proof of the incarnation but only as a mark of his unique prophetic status, his having come into being as an expression of God's direct creative fiat (Q 3:45, 4:171, 19:21), which places Jesus on a par with Adam (Q 3:59).[251]

Especially important for our discussion is the depiction of Mary in *Sūrat Maryam* (the only extended narrative from the Meccan period that deals with Jesus) as "screening herself away" from her people, the withdrawal that preceded the appearance of an angel (identified by later interpreters as Gabriel) in the form of a "well-shaped human being" (19:17). The scriptural linkage of the occlusion of Mary behind the curtain (*ḥijāb*) and the virginal conception (19:20–22) fostered a metaphorical interpretation on the part of Sufi exegetes focused on the ascetic renunciation required to traverse the spiritual path.[252] I suggest that *ḥijāb* in particular became a symbol of Mary's virginity, the denotation of the term as "curtain" giving way to the "veil." The adoration of Rābi'a as a "second spotless Mary" is doubtless related to her own virginity and celibate lifestyle.[253] The "special veil" or the "veil of sincerity," it seems to me, may function as a symbolic denotation of Rābi'a's celibacy, the overt sign of the gender transformation that facilitated her being accepted "among men," the "friends of God," on the way to unveiling the beloved.

Another critical dimension of the image of the veil is revealed in the following passage cited anonymously in the compendium of principles of Sufi piety, *Risāla al-qushayriyya*, by al-Qushayrī (d. 1074): "Certainty is unveiling, and unveiling takes place in three ways: by means of informing, by means of disclosure of the power [of God], and by means of the truths of faith." Explaining this dictum, al-Qushayrī advises the reader: "Know that in their way of speaking, unveiling consists of the revelation of something to the heart when it is possessed by remembrance of Him with no doubt remaining. Sometimes by unveiling they mean something similar to what is seen between waking and sleep. Many times they designate this state as steadfastness."[254]

By means of unveiling (*kashf*), the truth is manifest in the heart (*qalb*), the site that is repeatedly marked as the locus of spiritual vision in Sufi teaching, a manifestation that is all-encompassing, a point related in the above passage by another technical Sufi term, *dhikr*, the repetitive utterance of divine names that occasions the remembrance or recollection of the real, that is, the singular, meditative focus on the divine occasioned by repetition of divine epithets or qur'ānic phrases.[255] The unveiling designates a state of consciousness between wakefulness and sleep. We are not told more about this state, but I would surmise that al-Qushayrī chose this image to convey the idea that this mode of awareness is pure mobility, a state of wavering designated paradoxically as "steadfastness" (*baqā'*), the Sufi expression that denotes persisting in the real.

To grasp the paradoxical identification of absolute motion and absolute stability implied in this depiction of unveiling, one must bear in mind that in technical Sufi terminology, which may be traced to al-Junayd (d. 910), *baqā'* is dialectically tangled up with annihilation of *nafs*, the lower soul of the base instincts, the differentiated ego-self.[256] If one were to lay out the mystical path sequentially, *baqā'* would be preceded by *fanā'* ("passing away"), but from the enlightened perspective the two occur concurrently—the annihilation is the abiding and the abiding the annihilation,[257] an idea that is captured in the seemingly contradictory claim ascribed to al-Junayd in his account of the passing away of oneself from one's ecstasies (*mawājīd*) when one is overpowered by the real: "At that moment you both pass away and abide, and are found truly existent in your passing away; through the found existence (*wujūd*) of your other; upon the abiding of your trace in the disappearance of your name."[258]

True abiding, therefore, as al-Bisṭāmī, al-Junayd, and other Sufi masters put it, consists in the passing away of passing away (*fanā' al-fanā'*), the double negation that yields a positive predication.[259] Following the teaching of al-Junayd, al-Qushayrī spoke of the first passing away as the "passing away of the self and its attributes to endure through the attributes of the real," the second passing away as the "passing away from the attributes of the real through witnessing of the real," and the third and final passing away as "a person's passing away from witnessing his own passing away through his perishing in the ecstatic existentiality (*wujūd*) of the real."[260] When one takes hold of this insight, then one can appreciate al-Qushayrī's account of the unveiling as a state betwixt sleep and dream, a place of nonduality where to subsist one must subside and to subside one must subsist, the fullness of the moment (*waqt*) that abides in its passing and passes in its abiding.[261]

The essential point to draw from this text for the immediate concern of this discussion is that unveiling denotes the mystical awakening of the heart to the one true reality, a gnosis that is intricately connected to the secret of union. In one of the oldest and most celebrated Persian treatises on Sufism, *Kashf al-maḥjūb* (*The Unveiling of the Veiled*), al-Hujwīrī contrasts "absence" and "presence" by stating that the former "involves the sorrow of being veiled" and the latter "involves the joy of revelation."[262] In a second passage, he notes that the veils that obstruct one's knowledge of God are a result of ignorance; when ignorance is annihilated, veils vanish.[263] Apparently, this is the meaning of al-Hujwīrī's comment that "revelation [*mukāshafat*] implies the possibility of a veil [*ḥijāb*],"[264] that is, we can speak meaningfully of the revelation of truth only if it were previously veiled. Explicating a dictum of Abu 'l-'Abbās al-Āmulī, al-Hujwīrī notes, "natural dispositions are the instruments and organs of the sensual part (*nafs*), which is the centre of 'veiling' (*ḥijāb*), whereas the spiritual part (*ḥaqīqat*) is the centre of revelation."[265]

In another passage, al-Hujwīrī uses a slightly different nomenclature to mark the two states of being, the inseparable manifestations of the ontological and psychological: "*Qabd* denotes the contraction of the heart in the state of being veiled (*ḥijāb*), and *basṭ* denotes the expansion of the heart in the state of revelation (*kashf*)."[266] Contraction of the heart is synonymous with the agitation of longing in a state of occultation (*ḥijāb*); expansion is the calm of contemplation in a state of revelation (*kashf*).[267] The master of esoteric gnosis, accordingly, is one who peers beyond the veil of the veil-keepers in the quest for a vision of the face.[268] By contrast, *maḥjūb* ("veiled") assumes the negative connotation of one who is not spiritually illumined and therefore does not perceive the divine light without the veils of sentient and rational forms.[269]

Veiling (*sitr*) and concealment (*istitār*) connote ignorance, whereas removing the veil (*kashf*) results in divine self-revelation (*tajallī*). The Sufi ideal is captured by the masterful pen of the Persian poet Rūmī (1207–1273) in his *Mathnawī*: "Beauty is from God, but the corporealist does not feel (the charm of) beauty without the veil (medium) of the garden. When the bodily medium is removed, (then) he (who is disembodied) perceives without (any) screen, like Moses,[270] the light of the Moon (shining) from (his own) bosom."[271] The depiction of Moses seeing the divine without any barrier is based, of course, on the biblical precedent that Moses was distinguished vis-à-vis all the other prophets insofar as he spoke directly with God ("mouth to mouth") and beheld the image of the Lord (Num. 12:8) and the later rabbinic notion that Moses saw the glory through a speculum that shines whereas the other prophets saw through a speculum that does not shine.[272]

Rūmī's exaltation of Moses along these lines is especially noteworthy in light of the exegesis of Exodus 33:18–23 in Sūra 7:143–44. According to the narrative in Exodus, the request of Moses to see the glory resulted in his seeing the back, not the front. In the qur'ānic reworking, Moses did not see God at all, for when the glory appeared on the mountain, the mountain turned into dust, thereby indicating that God's response to Moses that he should look upon the mountain and if it abides his demand would be answered positively was, in effect, a way of saying that seeing the unseen consists of (not)-seeing. Consider the commentary of Ja'far al-Ṣādiq: "You are not able to see me because you pass away. How can that which passes away find a way to that which abides? . . . The lord's face-to-face vision in respect to the servant is the annihilation of the servant. The servant's face-to-face vision of the lord and in the lord is enduring."[273]

In this text, we are introduced to the two key technical terms utilized in Sufi teaching to express the goal of mystical union, *fanā'* and *baqā'*, passing away and enduring. The scriptural foundation for these terms is Sūra 55:26, "All that dwells upon the earth is perishing [*fanin*], yet still abides [*fa-yabqa*], the face of your Lord, majestic, splendid." According to the mystical interpretation, by undoing the bonds that tie the soul to matters of the body, passing away from the impermanent self, the higher self abides with the beloved; significantly, persisting in that which abides is expressed as seeing the unseen, beholding the face that has no visible form to behold.

In spite of the unequivocal denial of the possibility of seeing God in Muslim faith, based firmly on the qur'ānic precedent of associating the word "unseen" (*ghayb*) with Allah (Q 11:31, 123; 13:9; 16:77; 35:18; 53:35), it is precisely the Sufi mandate, following the teaching of Muḥammad, to worship God "as if you see him."[274] This stands in contrast to Sūra 2:3, where belief in the unseen (*ghayb*) precedes the establishment of prayer (*ṣalāt*), one of the five fundamental pillars of Islam. On the other hand, the nexus between seeking God's face and prayer is attested in several verses (Q 6:52, 13:22, 18:28). Also relevant is the polemic in Sūra 4:153 against the children of Israel, referred to as the "people of the book,"[275] which, closely following the unfolding of the narrative plot in Exodus, links idolatry, exemplified in the worship of the golden calf,[276] to the desire to see God—in the qur'ānic version, the request is attributed to the Israelites as a whole, thus misreading the account in the Torah, where the petition to see the glory frontally (Exod. 33:12–16) is attributed to Moses alone, though, to be sure, the petition is intricately connected to the fate of the national collectivity. With respect to the emphasis placed on seeing the divine in a liturgical context, there is an important phenomenological affinity between Sufism and various forms of medieval Jewish mystical piety, revolving about the claim that prayer in a theistic tradition requires iconic representation of the divine within the imagination.[277]

In a second passage, Rūmī utilizes the erotic implication of unveiling to convey the difference between passing state (*ḥāl*) and permanent station (*maqām*): The former is compared to the "unveiling of that beauteous bride" and the latter to the king's "being alone with the bride." The bride "unveils before commons and nobles (alike)," but "in the bridal chamber the king is (alone) with the bride."[278] The unveiling is a state of attainment enjoyed by Sufis, but for the privileged among them it is followed by the more intimate rank of being exclusively with the bride, a unitive experience that is consequent to disrobing and unmasking. To attain visionary union, unitive vision, the heart of the seer must be purged of all images so that it may behold the invisible in its own reflection. "He whose clear breast has become devoid of (any) image (impression) has become a mirror for the impressions of the Invisible."[279]

The objective for one who walks the path is to rend the veil, to behold truth in its naked form. However, inasmuch as rending the veil reveals that which has no image, the unknowable essence that cannot be essentialized, the inaccessible presence that cannot be represented, it must be said that the veil conceals the face it reveals by revealing the face it conceals. Language is decidedly inadequate to mark the middle ground wherein concealing and revealing are identical in virtue of being different and different in virtue of being identical. Epistemologically the matter may be expressed in the following terms utilized by Ibn 'Arabī: The veil conveys both the incomparability (*tanzīh*) of the face and the image seen through the veil, for the image that is seen is an image and not the face, and the similarity (*tashbīh*) of the face and the image, for in the absence of an image the face could not be perceived.[280] In *Fuṣūṣ al-ḥikam*, Ibn 'Arabī notes that to become an imām and master of spiritual sciences, one must maintain both the incomparability and similarity of the ultimate reality in relation to all other existents in the chain of being, for to insist exclusively on either transcendence or immanence is to restrict that reality inappropriately.[281]

The mandate to lift the veils, therefore, does not result in discarding all possible veils; indeed, there can be no "final" veil to lift, as there must always be another veil through which the nonmanifest will be made manifest. In this respect, Sufi sensibility remained faithful to the qur'ānic declaration that it is not fitting for God to speak to a human "except by inspiration, from behind a veil, or by the sending of a messenger" (Q 42:51), that is, by way of an intermediary that renders the unseen (*ghayb*) visible. What is unveiled in the unveiling is not the face behind the veil but the veil before the face; that is, unveiling is the metaphorical depiction of removing the shells of ignorance that blind one from seeing the truth of the veil in the veil of the truth: God and world are identical in their difference.[282] The transcendence of God, the unity of the indiscriminate one (*aḥadiyyat al-aḥad*), renders all theological discourse at best analogical, since there is no way to speak directly about that which transcends all being, yet the divine is immanent in all things—indeed, mystically conceived, there is nothing but the single true reality that is all things, the unity of multiplicity (*aḥadiyyat al-kathra*).[283]

The Sufi accordingly knows that the light is too bright to be uncovered except through a covering.[284] In the last chapter of *Mishkāt al-anwār* (*The Niche of Lights*), which deals with the qur'ānic passage known in the tradition as the verse of light (Q 24:25), the eleventh-century Iranian mystic, al-Ghazālī, comments on the *ḥadīth* of the prophet: "God has seventy veils of light and darkness; were he to lift them, the august glories of his face would burn up everyone whose eyesight perceived him": "God discloses himself to his essence in his essence. Without doubt, the 'veil' is understood in relation to the thing that is veiled. The veiled among the creatures are of three kinds: those who are veiled by darkness alone, those who are veiled by sheer light, and those who are veiled by light along with darkness."[285] At the conclusion of these classifications there is a further specification of several subgroups of the ones "veiled by sheer lights," the highest being "those who have arrived":

> To them it has been disclosed that the one who is obeyed is described by an attribute that contradicts sheer oneness and utmost perfection. This belongs to the mystery which is beyond the capacity of this book to unveil . . . the relationship of this one who is obeyed is that of the sun among the lights. Therefore, they have turned their faces from the one who moves the heavens. . . . They have arrived at an existent thing that is incomparable with everything their sight has perceived. Hence, the august glories of his face—the first, the highest—burn up everything perceived by the sights and insights of the observers.[286]

Even at this level, where vision is blindness, and blindness, vision, there are different stages of attainment. For some the objects of vision alone are effaced, but for the "elect of the elect," perceived and perceiver are effaced in the supreme mystical state of *fanā'*, passing away, the annihilation of self as an entity ontically distinct from the One; the mimetic figuration gives way to the ecstatic vision in which the self vanishes; there is naught but vision, a seeing without seer or seen: "They become extinct from themselves, so that they cease observing themselves. Nothing remains save the One, the Real. . . . This is the ultimate end of those who have arrived."[287] For al-Ghazālī, the removal of the veil, the symbolic act that signifies the declaration of unity (*tawḥīd*), is the inner meaning of the qur'ānic verse "There is no god but he. Everything will perish except his own face"

(Q 28:88). In the end, when the seventy veils of light and darkness are removed, there is pure light, the face without veil, the veil without face, invisibly visible, visibly invisible.

The self-manifestation of God, therefore, must be through the multitude of veils that make up the cosmos. The paradoxical nature of the veil to disclose what is occluded by way of occluding what is disclosed is evident in the tradition concerning the response of the archangel Gabriel to Muḥammad's query whether he had ever seen the Lord: "As it is, between me and Him there are seventy veils of light. If I ever came close to the one nearest to me I would get burnt."[288] If the highest of angels cannot approach the lowest of the veils separating him from the divine, how much more so must it apply to beings of the natural world. All that we consider real is veritably a veil; truth comes forth as unveiling the unveiling of the veil so that the unveiled is seen in the veil of the unveiled; disposing of the veil would result, by contrast, in veiling the veil and the consequent effacing of the face.

From a relatively early period al-Niffarī discerned that rending the veil—the ostensible goal of the mystical path—would result in an overpowering of light that would baffle the mind of created beings. "Knowings of the veil / cannot bear what appears / when the veil is torn."[289] To see the face behind the veil, one must be veiled from the unveiling; indeed, the one adroit in lifting the veils knows full well that throwing off the veil is itself a form of donning the veil. The paradox is articulated by al-Niffarī in a series of gnomic pronouncements:

Once you have seen Me, unveiling and the veil will be equal.

You will not stand in vision until you see My veil as vision and My vision as veil.

There is a veil that is not unveiled, and an unveiling that is not veiled. The veil that is not unveiled is knowledge through me, and the unveiling that is not veiled is knowledge through me.

No veil remains: Then I saw all the eyes gazing at his face, staring. They see him in everything through which he veils himself. He said to me: They see me, and I veil them through their vision of Me from Me.[290]

Several centuries later—precisely in the period when kabbalah began to flourish in southern France and northern Spain—Ibn ʿArabī elaborated the paradoxical mystery of the veil and its unveiling in a somewhat more technical philosophic tone commensurate with his speculative gnosis: "There is nothing in existence but veils hung down. Acts of perception attach themselves only to veils, which leave traces in the owner of the eye that perceives them."[291] Ephemeral contingencies are but veils hiding the eternal being, the necessary of existence, but it is through the concealment of these veils that the invisible is rendered visible: "Thus the Real becomes manifest by being veiled, so He is the Manifest / the Veiled. He is the Nonmanifest because of the veil, not because of you, and He is the Manifest because of you and the veil."[292] In another passage, Ibn 'Arabī expresses the matter as a commentary on the aforementioned *ḥadīth* that God possesses seventy veils of light and darkness:

> The dark and luminous veils through which the Real is veiled from the cosmos are only the light and the darkness by which the possible thing becomes qualified in its reality because it is a middle. . . . Were the veils to be lifted from the possible thing, possibility would be lifted, and the Necessary and the impossible would be lifted through the lifting of possibility. So the veils will remain forever hung down and nothing else is possible. . . . The veils will not be lifted when there is vision of God. Hence vision is through the veil, and inescapably so.[293]

The veil came to signify the hermeneutic of secrecy basic to the esoteric gnosis of Sufism, envisioning the hidden secret revealed in the concealment of its revelation and concealed in the revelation of its concealment. Accordingly, the task is to discard the veils to reveal the truth, but if the veils were all discarded, there truly would be no truth to see. This is the import of the statement that the "veils will not be lifted when there is vision of God." If the unseen is to be seen, the vision manifestly must be "through the veil."[294] From that vantage point, all that exists is divine. Thus, commenting on the qur'ānic verse (mentioned above), "Everything will perish except his own face" (Q 28:88), in *Kitāb al-aḥadiyyah* (*A Treatise on the One Alone*), Ibn 'Arabī writes, "That which exists and is visible is He. There is nothing but He, so how could nothing cease to be?"[295] In this state of attainment, there is nothing but the One, and hence there is a cessation of cessation, the passing away of passing away (*fanā' al-fanā'*), which is the persistence (*baqā'*) of the manifold in the oneness of being: "Therefore, do not think anymore that you need to become nothing, that you need to annihilate yourself in Him. If you thought so, then you would be His veil, while a veil over Allah is other than He. How could you be a veil that hides Him? What hides Him is His being the One Alone."[296]

In accord with the longstanding Sufi tradition, Ibn 'Arabī affirms that when one passes away from passing away, all veils are abolished. It follows that if one could discard all need, even the need to discard all need, the desire not to desire the desire to desire not, then the last veil—the veil of thinking there is a last veil—would be removed. In the end of the passage, the reader is taken somewhat by surprise by the assertion "What hides Him is His being the One Alone." How can the attribute of oneness (*aḥadiyyah*) be a veil hiding the One? It can only be so if we grasp that veil and face are identical in their difference; to unveil the face, the veil must be faced, but the veil cannot be faced unless all veils are lifted and the very distinction between face and veil is eradicated; in discerning this truth, however, the visionary detects that he is the mirror/veil through which the face is seen as veil and the veil as face. In this unveiling, identity is realized through (not as) difference, and difference through (not as) identity. In *Futūḥāt al-makkiyya*, Ibn ʿArabī enunciates this very point:

> He who sees the Real plainly and openly
> sees Him only from behind a veil. . . .
> The form of the Seer has disclosed itself to him
> while he is the Seer—no, he is the veil.[297]

The mystical path is to train the mind so that one removes the veils in order to see truth unveiled, but the greatest of veils to remove is the belief that one can see truth without a veil. To unveil the veil, therefore, is to veil the unveiling, to see the unseeing as the manifestation of the concealment in the concealment of the manifestation, to behold the face of the veil veiling the veiling of the veil of the face.[298] The veil thus exhibits the structure of the esoteric hermeneutic basic to Sufism, the paradox that the visibility of the medium consists of its invisibility,[299] a supposition that fostered on the part of the adept an envisioning of the secret revealed in the concealment of its revelation and concealed in the revelation of its concealment.

At the peak of the visionary experience, the seer discerns, to paraphrase another celebrated Persian bard, Ḥāfiz (c. 1320–1389), that the only barrier (ḥāyil) separating the lover and the beloved is the selfhood of the lover;[300] the lover's heart is the site of the "synchronic coincidence of planes of vision" marked by a "continual flow back and forth between the heart of the poet and the primeval source from which he draws inspiration," the "perpetual oscillation between self-revelation of the Divine in its self-concealment, and the concealment of the Divine in its self-revelation; between a Beauty that attracts as it repels and a majesty that repels as it attracts."[301] To see the beauty reflected in the heart, the cup of cosmic vision,[302] the mirror of the invisible world, the heart must reveal the veil, an unveiling that imparts to the poet the epithet *lisān al-ghayb* (literally, "tongue of the unseen"), for his task consists of uttering the unutterable and thereby facilitating envisioning the invisible.[303] As the poet himself puts it, "I have made the journey into Nothing. / I have lit the lamp that / Needs no oil. . . . I have become the flame that needs / No fuel."[304] The visionary journey may thus be compared to crossing a bridge that is discerned not to be a bridge once crossed, that is, crossing the very bridge of crossing to the point that one can no longer speak of either bridge or crossing.

Rising Within: Dis/Placing Place in the Topography of the Imaginal

The blurring of the ontological distinction that ensues from crossing the bridge that in the end turns out not to have been a bridge, entering a gate that is no gate,[305] is the task of

poetic metaphor. According to the enigmatic comment from a section in zoharic literature marked as belonging to the *Tosefta* stratum, "The bond of the pure bond [*quṭra
de-quṭra dakhya*] ascends within and within [*saliq le-go le-go*] until the place [*atar*], the
house of dwelling [*beit motva*], is not found. This place is no place [*ha-hu atar law atar*], it
is not found above or below. It is negated with respect to everything, a state of annihilation [*mi-kola itʿ avid avaddon hawwei*]."[306]

It is likely, as a number of traditional commentaries have noted, that there is an allusion in these words to the emanative process by means of which the hidden becomes
manifest, the highest point being point/less, that is the point to which none can point,
extending beyond extension, limitlessness delimiting limit delimiting limitlessness, in
the language of the text, the "place that is no place" (*atar law atar*), the site where being is
nothing and nothing is being, where concealed is revealed and revealed is concealed. I
would add, however, that the dis/placement of place can also be read from an anthropocentric perspective, that is, the soul/mind is the "bond of the pure bond" that ascends
within (*saliq le-go le-go*) until it reaches the highest of the emanations, *ayin*, no/thing, the
threshold to infinity (*ein sof*), the place that is no-place. Yet it must be remembered that
on the mystical path, contemplative ascent is at the same time turning inward.

This critical point is conveyed in the zoharic text by the equivocality of the term *saliq*,
which can mean ascend, enter, and disappear; hence *saliq le-go* can be rendered as "rising
within," an internal ascent, ascending to the chamber of the throne by entering the garden of the heart, entering the garden of the heart by ascending to the chamber of the
throne,[307] to the point of the pointless, the no/thing that is everything, the state of annihilation (*avaddon*), wherein the heart/mind is stripped of all specificity so that it may
behold everything in/as nothing, a state reminiscent of the Sufi *fanāʾ al-fanāʾ* (passing
away of passing away), which constitutes *baqāʾ* (endurance, persistence). From this spot
the poetic word ushers forth, enfolded in silence, disclosing being-as-mystery on the horizon where the imaginal representation of the nonrepresentable is made possible through
disclosing the disclosure of what is openly hidden.

The paradoxical collapse of opposites—indeed the collapse of the collapse that still
presupposes opposites to be collapsed—well captures the affair of language that has
enchanted the poetic imagination of kabbalists in their effort to depict the mystery of the
garment as the mirror that effectuates the overcoming of the inside/outside dichotomy.
An affinity with Sufic terminology is especially evident in the author of *Shaʿarei Ṣedeq*.
The final stages of the meditational practice of *derekh ha-shemot* ("way of the names")
that leads to prophetic experience, which the author equates, following the appropriation
of the Maimonidean ideal on the part of his teacher, Abraham Abulafia, with the disembodied state of intellectual conjunction (*devequt*), identified as well as worship of the
heart (*avodah she-ba-lev*), which is predicated on knowledge of the name (*yediʿat ha-shem*),
is described as follows:

By drawing forth words from thought [*maḥashavah*] he will force himself to come out from under the rule of his natural intellect [*sikhlo ha-ṭivʿi*], for if he wants not to think he cannot, and he should be lead initially in the phases of writing [*ketav*] and speaking [*lashon*], and also through the mouth, which is the form [*ṣiyyur*]. When he is to come out from under its rule, another effort is necessary, which consists of drawing thought gradually forth from its source until reaching the level that will compel him not to speak and concerning which he has no ability to overcome. And if he has it in his power to prevail and to continue drawing forth, then he will go out from his inwardness, and it will take shape in his purified imaginative faculty [*koaḥ ha-dimyoni ha-zakh*] in the form of the translucent mirror [*marʾah zakkah*], and this is "the flame of the encircling sword" (Gen. 3:24), the back rotating and becoming the front. He discerns his inmost being [*mahut penimiyyuto*] as something outside himself. . . . For when a form is not perfect, it is detached from its essence until it is nullified and garbed in a purified imaginal form [*ṣurah dimyonit zakkah*] through which the letters are combined in a perfect, orderly, and adequate combination. It seems to me that this form is called by kabbalists "garment" [*malbush*].[308]

After having documented in graphic detail the arduous phases of the meditational practice of letter combination and the peculiar experiences ensuing therefrom, the author discloses the culminating state of contemplation whereby one passes beyond the threshold of thought and speech. The state of mindfulness devoid of concepts, images, and words leads experientially to the breakdown of the perceptual distinction between inside and outside, as the external form beheld by the adept is the radiance of the internal light, which in turn is a reflection of the external form.[309] The following description by Heinrich Zimmer of the Hindu form of Yoga known as *pūjā*, the veneration of the divine in one of its manifold aspects in the outer form of daily worship that calls forth through an inner image in the devotee, provides an interesting analogue:

The actual goal is that the inner image of the deity and he who has conceived it should emerge from their duality and interpenetrate one another, that they should fuse into One (*samādhi*). The believer experiences the fact that the deity is not something different from himself—it does not dwell somewhere out in the world, it has not just come to visit him; it does not sit on a throne in some heaven beyond the heavens: out of his own formless inwardness he has built up every detail, and at the end of his devotions he lets it dissolve again in his formless inwardness, in the primordial waters of the unconscious, just as the Indian god unfolds the world and then, when it is ripe for dissolution, melts it down again into himself, the universal night, the primordial flood.[310]

To express the matter in a more contemporary phenomenological idiom, influenced particularly by Kantian epistemology, the noematic presence in consciousness inhering in some "objective" substance or substratum, the representation of an outer sense, is given to consciousness as an image of the noetic manifold of an inner sense projected outward as an object that stands over and against the mind (the German word *Gegenstand* is instructive), but that projection is itself predicated on the presumption that the noematic presence is a "subjective" projection of the noetic manifold.[311] At the moment of vision, through the force of the imagination that has been purified by ascetic practice and the purging of all discriminate forms, the heart of the mystic becomes a translucent mirror, the screen/veil through which the internal is externalized and the external internalized, the seeing of one's inward form projected outward as the outward image propelled inward, the vision in which the difference of identity between seer and seen is overcome in the identity of their difference[312]—the mind sees itself as the mirror reflecting the mind that mirrors, embracing thereby the paradox of visible invisibility of which we spoke above— and hence the imagination is referred to by the scriptural image of the "flame of the encircling sword," that is, the sword that revolves in such a way that the back becomes the front in confronting the front becoming the back.

In the polished mirror of imagination, the form detached from its essence, that is, the form that has no form, not even the form of formlessness, clothes itself in an "imaginal form." We are told, moreover, that through this form, "the letters are combined in a perfect, orderly, and adequate combination," which is identified with the kabbalistic notion of the garment (*malbush*).[313] I would suggest that the author is alluding here to the permutation of the Hebrew letters that constitute the Torah.[314] If this conjecture is correct, then the point of the passage is that Torah is the imaginal form through which the formless is envisioned.

It seems to me that Abulafia himself alludes to this secret in his treatises. For our purposes I shall cite and exegete a passage from *Oṣar Eden Ganuz*:

> How can a man comprehend the divine attribute [*middah elohit*] in his imagination [*be-dimyono*]? It is comprehended by him and not by us, for it cannot be comprehended. But we can comprehend what is appropriate for us to do in the ways of our attributes according to the narratives of the Torah and according to the commandments. The Torah was given to man and it speaks in the language of man.[315]

Abulafia begins by affirming an apophatic orientation well attested in philosophical and theological treatises composed by practitioners of the three monotheistic religions.[316] More specifically, it is related in his case (though the epistemological assumption he harbors is hardly unique) to the fact that human cognition is intractably dependent on the imaginative faculty (*koaḥ ha-medammeh*), and hence one cannot access the divine attribute (*middah elohit*) in and of itself, since it has no image. What we can apprehend positively are the stories and laws of Torah, which, according to the medieval philosophic interpretation of a talmudic dictum attributed to the school of R. Ishmael, adopted by

Abulafia, most likely from Maimonides, are spoken in language comprehensible to a human being (*dibberah torah ke-lashon benei adam*). Even more significantly, according to the Maimonidean interpretation of this hermeneutical principle, the "human language," which is the rhetorical idiom of the revealed Scripture, is equated explicitly with the imaginative faculty of the multitude.[317]

That Abulafia speaks affirmatively of an inherently unknowable *middah elohit* is significant, for it underscores that the relation between the ontic and epistemic is asymmetrical; there is something that logically and metaphysically must be presumed to exist—indeed the ultimate being, designated by Abulafia by another technical philosophical term he borrowed from Maimonides, *meḥuyav ha-meṣi'ut* ("the necessary of existence"), that is, the being for whom existence and essence are not distinguishable insofar as the existence of this being is unconditionally necessary—that we cannot know. Abulafia is emphatic on this point for both the masses and the elite. Surely, in the case of the former, God's existence is not adduced on the basis of rational discernment (*hassagah*) but on tradition (*qabbalah*), but even in the case of the latter, Abulafia insists that the enlightened one (*ba'al sekhel*) whose "mind is essentially clear" (*eṣem moḥo zakh*) must receive this gnosis from a master who is accredited with being part of an unbroken chain of tradition.[318]

Wisdom about the name—referred to by various traditional idioms, to wit, "explicit name" (*shem ha-meforash*), "unique name" (*shem ha-meyuḥad*), and "glorious name" (*shem ha-nikhbad*), and also designated by the technical philosophical expression "essential name" (*shem ha-eṣem*)—culminates in a unitive experience attained by way of the meditational practice, which involves the ostensibly transgressive act of vocalization of the name, but even this knowledge is negative. In *Or ha-Sekhel*, Abulafia makes this point with reference to the divine name composed of *alef, he, waw, yod*, identified in medieval sources as "letters of concealment" (*otiyyot ha-ha'alamah*). To clarify the meaning of concealment, Abulafia cites the verse "This shall be my name forever, and this is my appellation from generation to generation," *zeh shemi le-olam we-zeh zikhri le-dor dor* (Exod. 3:15), and offers the following interpretation:

> It says in the tradition that it is written *le'alem*, that is to say, it is appropriate to conceal, and thus its letters are the letters of concealment. This is what is understood by the masses, but the esoteric [*ha-ne'lam*] is not this, for *le'alem* is an equivocal term [*dibbur meshutaf*], the first of its meanings is the matter of concealment [*ha-he'lem*] and the second is the matter of elevation [*ha-ma'alah*]. It is appropriate to conceal [*le'alem*] the letters of the name, that is, to elevate [*la'aleh*] them . . . and proof for this is what is said immediately "this is my appellation" [*zeh zikhri*], which instructs that a man is obligated to mention it [*lehazkiro*]. And the secret of "from generation to generation" [*le-dor dor*] indicates that each generation and generation evolves through a name [*mitgalgel be-shem*].[319]

Abulafia's comment is a subtle subversion of a rabbinic tradition regarding the ineffability of YHWH sanctioned on the basis of the verse *zeh shemi le-olam we-zeh zikhri le-dor dor*. According to a reading of this verse preserved in two contexts in the Babylonian Talmud (Pesaḥim 50a, Qiddushin 71a), *zeh shemi le-olam* ("this is my name forever") is rendered (based on the Masoretic orthography) as *zeh shemi leʿalem* ("this is my name to conceal"). Thus, in a dictum transmitted in the name of R. Avina, the verse is interpreted as the scriptural basis for the custom not to pronounce the Tetragrammaton as it is written. Abulafia links the designation of the letters of the name, *otiyyot ha-haʿalamah* ("letters of concealment"), to the midrashic reading of *zeh shemi le-olam* as *zeh shemi leʿalem*, but he maintains that *leʿalem* is an equivocal term (*dibbur meshutaf*), one of its meanings being concealment (*heʿlem*) and the other, elevation (*ha-maʿalah*). The rabbinic gloss, *leʿalem otam*, to hide the letters of the name, is the reading appropriate for the masses, but for the select few the proper reading is *laʿaleh otam*, that is, to uplift the letters, which entails uttering the name in the manner that is apposite for each generation.

To grasp the full implication of this comment, one must bear in mind that Abulafia accepts the older esoteric equation of the name with Torah, and the further identification of the latter with *sekhel ha-poʿel*, the Active Intellect.[320] This equation fostered an audacious mystical application of the contemplative ideal of *devequt*. Alongside the language of philosophical thinkers, which, *pace* Scholem, I do not consider merely as "rationalizations" obscuring the true mystical intent of his teaching but rather as the speculative framework within which the latter was enveloped,[321] Abulafia construes intellectual conjunction as union with Torah.[322] Insofar as the latter is equated with the Tetragrammaton, the experience of conjunction thereto may be described as incorporation into the name, which, as Abulafia himself asserts in an evidently apophatic nod, denotes the essence that exceeds rational comprehension (*hassagat ha-sekhel*).[323] For Abulafia, as for Maimonides, the imaginative faculty is a vital component of the prophetic vision.

In *Ḥayyei ha-Olam ha-Ba*, Abulafia frames the matter in a standard philosophical manner, beginning with an affirmation of the epistemological basis (traceable to the Platonic tradition) for the *via negativa* embraced by Maimonides as well: "His unity is too strong to be imagined by us in any image, for none of his creatures above or below can comprehend the truth of his unity, and *a fortiori* man cannot know the quiddity of his essence [*mahut aṣmo*], blessed be his name." Abulafia goes on to say that the limit of comprehension for prophets, sages, and philosophers alike is to remove all physical attributes from God, which arise on account of the imagination and thus obstruct one from attaining true knowledge. Abulafia concedes, in a manner that is consonant with Maimonides:

It is not possible to imagine [*leṣayyer*] anything of the intelligible matters [*ha-devarim ha-muskalim*] except by means of participation with comprehension of corporeal forms [*hassagat ṣurot gashmut*].[324] Thus even the prophet, in the moment that he comprehends the prophetic word [*ha-dibbur ha-nevuʾi*] that emanates from God, blessed be he and blessed be his name, through the intermediary of the Active Intellect in man by means of the permutation of letters contemplated in the heart, it is not possible that he will not imagine [*yeṣayyer*] what he has comprehended in a corporeal form from one thing to another thing.[325]

In a critical way, however, Abulafia departs from his philosophical guide and reverts to an explanation of prophecy affirmed in Jewish Neoplatonic sources:[326]

The prophet knows in truth that the body that he imagines in the moment of prophecy has no corporeal existence at all, but it is an intelligible entity that is entirely spiritual [*davar sikhli kullo ruḥani*], and it materializes [*hitgashshem*] in relation to him in the moment of his comprehension on account of the fact that the prophet is a body that envisions the truth in his spiritual intellect [*guf ha-maskil ha-emet be-sikhlo ha-ruḥani*] actualized in that moment.

The corporeal image of the incorporeal substance is configured in the imagination of the enlightened visionary (*maskil*), and it is identified further as the angel (*mal'akh*), a multivalent term that denotes in this context the imaginal form of the Active Intellect, an incarnational presence that assumes the shape of an anthropos (the idealized Israel) in the imaginative faculty.[327]

Abulafia reiterates this mystery in slightly different terms in his discussion in *Sitrei Torah* of the Maimonidean conception of the name of the attribute of action (*shem ha-to'ar*), which is contrasted with the essential name (*shem ha-eṣem*), an "honorable secret that is appropriate for the select few" (*zeh ha-sod ha-nikhbad hu ra'uy la-yeḥidim*):

Concerning this secret it is said "and in the hands of the prophets I will be imaged" [*u-ve-yad ha-nevi'im adammeh*] (Hos. 12:11), and when [the word *adammeh*] is transposed it spells *ha-adam*. And the secret of [the word] *u-ve-yad* refers to the holy name YHWA, the secret of the name of the wise prophets [*sod shem ha-nevi'im ḥakhamim*], and they are the throne of glory [*kisse ha-kavod*], and this is the secret of the high priest [*kohen gadol*] who speaks to the prophets in the form of the prophetic anthropos [*ha-adam ha-navi*].[328]

Displaying his typically brilliant hermeneutical prowess, Abulafia employs linguistic and numerical exegetical devices to adduce the mystery of the prophetic experience from the biblical verse, which in turn is meant to illumine the mystery of the *shem ha-to'ar*, the name derived from God's providential action in the world. The expression *adammeh*, "I will be imaged," is composed of the same consonants as *ha-adam*, a transposition that alludes to Abulafia's contention that the form imagined in the prophetic vision is that of an anthropos. The imaginal form is related, moreover, to the divine name YHWA, the letters *yod he waw alef,* which are the "letters of concealment," *otiyyot ha-ha'alamah,* that I mentioned above; Abulafia deduces the name from the word *u-ve-yad,* for the latter is numerically equal to twenty-two (6 + 2 + 10 + 4), which is the same numerological value of YHWA (10 + 5 + 6 + 1).[329] It is reasonable to assume that this name is a cipher for the Torah, which is the Active Intellect, the objective correlate of the prophetic experience, inasmuch as the Torah is made up of the twenty-two letters. Confirmation of my explication is forthcoming from the final sequence of ideas that Abulafia threads together on the basis of numerical equivalencies, that is, each of the following equals 118: The prophets (*nevi'im*) are the sages (*ḥakhamim*), and they are the throne of glory (*kisse ha-kavod*), as they receive the word from the high priest (*kohen gadol*), that is, Metatron, who speaks to them in the image of the prophetic anthropos (*ha-adam ha-nav'i*).

I note in passing that the view espoused by Abulafia, which is affirmed by other kabbalists in the twelfth and thirteenth centuries who branded *Shekhinah,* the angel of the presence (*mal' akh ha-panim*), the object of conjunction, bears a striking similarity to the Shī'ite belief in a revelatory encounter with the angel identified as the holy spirit (*rūḥ al-quds*) and Active Intellect (*'aql fa'āl*),[330] a theme that is especially prominent in the wisdom of illumination (*ḥikmat al-ishrāq*), the Oriental philosophy, cultivated by Avicenna, Suhrawardī, and Ibn 'Arabī, to name a few central figures. This wisdom entails, in the memorable formulation of Corbin, an "essential *theophanism,*" which implies that "every theophany has the form of an angelophany, because it is determined by this correlation; and precisely in this essential determination, without which the divine being would remain unknown and inaccessible, lies the significance of the *Angel.*"[331] The following account of the angelic epiphany proffered by Corbin could without distortion be applied to Abulafia's depiction of prophetic experience:[332]

> The figure of the Active Intelligence, which dominated all philosophy, reveals its proximity, its solicitude. The Angel *individuates himself* under the features of a definite person, whose annunciation corresponds to the degree of experience of the soul to which he announces himself: it is through the integration of all its powers that the soul opens itself to the transconscious and anticipates its own totality.[333]

The soul on the "way of return," which is the "way of gnosis" that leads one beyond the bondage of the physical cosmos, requires an angelic guide. Insofar as the "archetypal figure" is a mirror image of the soul, it follows that there will be "synchronism between the soul's awakening to itself and its visualization of the Guide."[334]

For Abulafia, the imaginal form of the *angelus interpres* is composed of the letters of Torah, which are comprised within the Tetragrammaton. The imagination thus serves not only as the prism through which the invisible is rendered visible and the ineffable declaimed as the name, but as the vehicle by which the soul merges with Torah in its mystical essence. To be conjoined to the name, therefore, is to be incorporated into the textual embodiment of the name, that is, the imaginal body constituted by the letters YHWH, which comprise all the letters of the Hebrew alphabet, the hylomorphic substance, as it were, of Torah, and, by extension, given the identification of Torah and *sekhel ha-po'el*, of all that exists in the cosmos (the Active Intellect, according to the widespread cosmological view adopted by philosophical sages in each of the three monotheistic faiths in the High Middle Ages, contained the forms of all existents in the sublunar sphere).

In the introduction to *Ḥayyei Olam ha-Ba*, Abulafia assigns to the seventy-two-letter name—that is, the name of seventy-two triplets derived exegetically from or anchored in the account of the angel of God (*mal'akh ha-elohim*) in Exodus 14:19–21, of which each verse contains seventy-two letters—the title *shem ha-divri*, the "name that is spoken," which comprises *divrei ha-shem*, the "words of the name," one of the standard rabbinic epithets for the divine presence. The secret is further unfurled when we recall that Abulafia adduces this name from the verse *mosheh yedabber we-ha-elohim ya'anennu ve-qol*, "Moses spoke and God answered in a voice" (Exod. 19:19); the consonants of *mosheh yedabber* can be transposed into *shem ha-divri* and *divrei ha-shem*.[335] The key to understanding this comment is to bear in mind that in Abulafia's thinking, Moses alludes figuratively to Metatron—an identification related mnemonically to the fact that the letters of *mosheh*—*mem, shin, he*—can be decoded as an acrostic for *meṭaṭron sar ha-panim*—the anthropomorphic personification of the Active Intellect beheld by the visionary at the pinnacle of prophetic experience.[336]

Abulafia derives the designation of the Active Intellect as Metatron from Maimonides, but it takes on a special significance in his thinking. In the visionary encounter, occasioned by the technique of letter combination (*ḥokhmat ha-ṣeruf*), the holy spirit (*ruaḥ ha-qodesh*)—another traditional idiom adopted by Abulafia to speak of *sekhel ha-po'el*—overflows onto the soul, "and it seems as if his entire body is anointed with the anointing oil, from his head to this feet, and he becomes the anointed one of the Lord and his messenger, and he is called angel of God, and his name will be called as the name of his master, which is Shaddai, by which Metatron, the angel of the face [*sar ha-panim*], is called."[337] The soul, unfettered from the knots of corporeality, is united with the Active Intellect and is thereby transposed into the body that is made up of the letters of Torah. The separation of the soul from the body, a form of simulated death that is true life, occasions the transposition of the body that restores the corporeal to its elemental form composed of the Hebrew letters. In *Sitrei Torah*, Abulafia formulates the matter succinctly:

> It is imagined [*meṣuyyar*] in your heart that through this form [*ṣurah*] is the separation of the soul [*peridat ha-nefesh*], which is a portion of the Lord that has 231 gates, and she is called "Assembly of Israel" [*kenesset yisra'el*], "there are 231" [*yesh r'al*], for she collects and gathers every speech beneath her intellective faculty [*koaḥ ha-sikhli*], which is called the "supernal Assembly of Israel" [*kenesset yisra'el ha-elyonah*], which

is the mother of governance [*em ha-hashgaḥah*], that is, the cause of the governance [*sibbat ha-hashgaḥah*], and she is the intermediary between us and the Lord, and she is the Torah that emanates from the twenty-two holy letters. Know that all the limbs of your body are made of combinations of the form of the letters, this one with that one and that one with this one. And know, moreover, that just as you combine them all together and you divide the form of one letter from the form of another letter even though their matter is one, that is, the ink, and in one instant you may erase all of them from the tablet, so this angel will act with respect to all your moisture and to each and every one of your limbs until all of them will be restored to their first matter.[338]

The ecstatic experience is an encounter of the prophet with the Active Intellect, the form (*ṣurah*) that occasions the separation of the soul (*peridat ha-nefesh*) from its somatic confinement. The soul itself is ontically part of the Active Intellect, which is called the "supernal Assembly of Israel" (*kenesset yisra'el ha-elyonah*), a designation that signifies the linguistic nature of the intellect—the consonants of the term *yisra'el* are decoded as *yesh r'al*, "there are 231," a reference to the 231 gates, a cipher for all the possible letter permutations according to a passage in *Sefer Yeṣirah*.[339] The Active Intellect, moreover, is identified as Torah, for the body of the latter is constructed from the prime matter of the twenty-two Hebrew letters.

Utilizing another principle widespread in kabbalistic literature of his time, Abulafia affirms that the human body, that is, the corporeality stripped of its coarse materiality, is constituted by these very letters.[340] Just as all the letters can be reduced to the ink by means of which they were inscripted on a tablet, so the angelic presence of the Active Intellect, the intermediary between divine and human, the matrix of providence in the sublunar world, can decompose the corporeal body of the visionary and restore it to its "first matter." Inasmuch as Abulafia affirms the belief that angels are ontically composed of the twenty-two Hebrew letters, which are comprised within the Tetragrammaton,[341] the process of incorporation into Torah described in the above passage can also be referred to as "angelification." The mystical adept who follows the meditational path to its limit is transformed into the "anointed one of the Lord" (*meshiaḥ yhwh*),[342] the "angel of God" (*mal'akh ha-elohim*),[343] the "angel of the face" (*sar ha-panim*)[344]—all names of Metatron, the highest and most distinguished of the angelic figures, the one whose name is numerically equal to Shaddai, a numerical equivalence used by Abulafia and others before and after him to explain an older esoteric teaching applied to Metatron:[345] "His name is like the name of his master," *she-shemo ke-shem rabbo*, based on the scriptural characterization of the angel sent by God before the people of Israel, "My name is in him," *shemi be-qirbo* (Exod. 23:21).[346]

Metatron assumes the figure of Torah incarnate in the Active Intellect, the body that occupies an intermediary position between matter and form, the senses and reason. The meditational practice leads one to this state of mindfulness, conjunction with the Active Intellect, which translates into cleaving to the name, and being incorporated into the body of the text. I will cite another passage from *Oṣar Eden Ganuz* wherein the secret of prophecy as a progression from image (*ṣiyyur*) to speech (*dibbur*) to intellect (*sekhel*) is disclosed,[347] a sequence that articulates in another pitch the transformative experience implied in Abulafia's mystical ideal of intellectual conjunction and visionary ecstasy:

> Now I will disclose to you the wondrous secret that is hidden from the eyes of most of the sages of our generation, and I can almost say from the eyes of all of them . . . and it is that the imaginative faculty [*koaḥ ha-medammeh*] is the instrument for prophetic comprehension [*hassagat ha-nevu'ah*], and all of its comprehensions are images [*dimyonot*], parables [*meshalim*], and riddles [*ḥiddot*]. And it is one faculty found in most living beings [*ba'alei ḥayyim*] and everyone living that possesses a heart [*ba'al lev*], and its existence in man is as the existence of prophecy in a mirror [*mar'ah*] or in water [*mayim*], and it is an imaginal form [*ṣiyyur dimmuy*]. As its name, so it is,[348] *dimyon medammeh*, and its secret is *daemon*, and he is the evil spirit and Satan. Yet, he is the *mediyun*, that is, the intermediary.[349] . . . The faculty of speech [*koaḥ ha divri*] is the natural, human form [*ha-ṣurah ha-ṭiv'it ha-enoshit*] by which man is distinguished from the rest of the living beings. This faculty is wholly the natural speech that is in man [*kullo dibbur muṭba ba-adam*] in the seventy languages through the permutation [*ṣeruf*] of the twenty-two letters, and this is the faculty found potentially in every word [*dibbur*] and it emerges in its form [*ṣiyyuro*] from potentiality to actuality, moment after moment [*et aḥar et*]. This is what is alluded to in *Sefer Yeṣirah* when it says,[350] "Every word [*dibbur*] is found and every creation [*yiṣṣur*] comes forth from them, and thus every creation comes forth from one name [*shem eḥad*]." . . . It is thus revealed that the word [*dibbur*] instructs about the faculty of speech [*koaḥ ha-divri*], creation [*yiṣṣur*] instructs about the imaginative faculty, and the "one name" [*shem eḥad*], in which everything is, instructs about the rational faculty, and this rational faculty, the third, is superior to the other two, and it is the aim of the intention [*takhlit ha-kawwanah*].[351]

In this passage, Abulafia adduces from *Sefer Yeṣirah* a hierarchy of three potencies, *yiṣṣur* ("creation") refers to *koaḥ ha-medammeh* (the imaginative faculty), *dibbur* to *koaḥ ha-divri* (the faculty of speech), and *shem eḥad* ("one name") to *koaḥ ha-sikhli* (the rational faculty). Although not stated explicitly, it is reasonable to surmise that the latter is affixed to the Tetragrammaton, which is the Torah, the locus of the imaginary forms in and through which the imageless God is made accessible to the imagination of the prophet/mystic who envisions the invisible through the textual prism of narrative and law. In a manner consonant with the zoharic author, the prophetic kabbalist advocates a liberation of vision by means of vision—in beholding the veil of the text, the sage takes hold of the text of the veil and thereby discerns that the veil is neither real nor not-real.[352] In the garment-mirror, the name that is Torah, spirit is embodied and the embodied spiritualized.[353]

Poetic Incarnation and the Embodied Text of Textual Embodiment

What is revealed in the final hermeneutical disclosure is the veil of presuming there is an unveiling that results in a vision of the divine without the veil of the text, to apprehend the essence of God without the shibboleth of the name.[354] As the matter is expressed in another zoharic context, "The letters are inscribed in the supernal mysteries, for they all emerge from the mystery of the supernal Wisdom by way of the thirty-two paths that come forth from Wisdom. . . . All the letters are inscribed in a mystery and they are the bodies of Torah [*gufei torah*] for they exist to instruct and to notify about the supernal mysteries."[355] The author of this comment appropriates the rabbinic expression *gufei torah*, which denotes in the older sources the rudiments of law,[356] to formulate the idea of a mystical body of God, a body that is composed of letters that are at one and the same time linguistic signs and numeric ciphers of divine wisdom.[357]

From a literary standpoint, the hermeneutical maxim of God concealing esoteric matters in Scripture is contextualized in the middle of the discourse about the entrapment of the Jewish soul in a body of a Gentile—the "daughter of the priest," *bat kohen*, married to a "layman," *ish zar* (Lev. 22:12). As I remarked above, the full implication of this thematic juxtaposition is dependent on understanding that the sociohistorical phenomenon of conversion suggested to the Castilian kabbalists entailed a crossing of ontic boundaries that ostensibly contradicted the dualistic posture affirmed on numerous occasions in the zoharic text, Israel aligned with the holy right side of mercy, and the nations of the world, with the unholy left side of judgment.[358] Just as the existential situation of the convert necessitates a disjuncture between the non-Jewish body and the Jewish soul, the former demonic and the latter divine, so in the case of Torah there is a necessary difference that wedges a divide, a barrier, a veil, between the secret, the name that is the light, and the garb of letters. An analogous transgression of boundary, we are to presume, is realized by the enlightened exegete who can discern the absent presence of the present absence in the Torah. The identification of God and Torah has to be understood, at least according to the author of this homily, as a form of incarnation predicated on an ontic estrangement akin to the existential condition that makes conversion possible.

The surmise that the zoharic passage presents a counterincarnational doctrine to the standard Christian conviction that Jesus is the incarnation of the Word is enhanced by the description of the layman in whose body the priestly daughter is found. The author of the zoharic homily interprets the biblical expression *ish zar* as "alien man," that is, the one who comes from a foreign land, the other side, the place of false worship, *avodah zarah*. Following the widespread belief in medieval rabbinic circles,[359] kabbalists in general, and those responsible for the *Zohar* in particular, maintained halakhically that Christianity was idolatry, and hence we are justified in decoding the old man's discussion about conversion in more specific terms as the Christian entering into the covenant of Abraham. When viewed against this background one can appreciate better the import of the image of God hiding secrets in the body of Torah, that is, in the letters of the text that collectively constitute the material of the divine name YHWH. For zoharic kabbalists, it is appropriate to speak of a doctrine of incarnation—understood docetically—inasmuch as this name assumes the textual form of Torah, which is configured imaginally as the ideal anthropos or Israel.[360] Joseph of Hamadan, a somewhat enigmatic figure who may have been part of the fraternity responsible for the zoharic anthology, formulates the incarnational element of kabbalistic symbolism with daring precision:[361]

> Therefore the Torah is called as such for it instructs [*morah*] about the pattern of the holy One, blessed be he . . . the Torah, as it were, is the shadow of the holy One, blessed be he. . . . Praiseworthy is the portion of one who knows how to align limb corresponding to limb and form corresponding to form in the pure and holy chain, blessed be his name. Since the Torah is his form, blessed be he, he commanded us to study Torah so that we may know his pattern of the supernal form as some of the kabbalists[362] have said [with respect to the verse] "Cursed be the one who does not uphold the words of this Torah" (Deut. 27:26), "Is there a Torah that falls?" Rather this is a warning to the cantor to show the letters of the Torah scroll to the congregation so that they might see the pattern of the supernal form. How much more so [is it necessary] to study Torah so that he will see the supernal secrets and he will verily see the glory of the holy One, blessed be he, the whole time he studies Torah and he sits verily in the shade of the blessed One.[363]

In language that is quite bold, Torah is identified as the embodiment of the divine glory, the letters constituting the pattern of the supernal form, and thus the ritual of lifting the scroll affords the community of worshippers the opportunity to gaze upon the iconic manifestation of God.[364] The underlying anthropomorphic nature of this form is alluded to in the remark concerning the ability of the laudable person to align the limbs below and the limbs above. That is, the Torah, which is the name, is the divine form that assumes the shape of an anthropos.

Here it is of interest to recall an important but neglected suggestion made by Jeremy Zwelling in the introduction to his critical edition of *Sefer Tashaq*, one of the major treatises composed by Joseph of Hamadan. Contrary to Alexander Altmann, who proposed that the title should be decoded as an abbreviation for *terumah*, *shir ha-shirim*, and *yeḥezqel*, the three parts of Scripture interpreted in the composition, Zwelling submitted that *tashaq* is an acrostic for *temunat shem qodesh*, "image of the holy name." Zwelling supports his surmise by noting that a central theme in the work is an explication of the seventy-two names of God, but even more important, for Joseph of Hamadan, following the view expressed by kabbalists in the generations previous to him, each of the twenty-two Hebrew letters is to be considered the form and name of divinity. "These letters are images of the Divinity as he is expressed in the likeness of the human body. . . . Indeed the book presents us with numerous pictures of the Divine name, reflecting God's crystallization as a Chariot, the human body, the letters of the alphabet, the tetragrammaton, and the tabernacle, which is described as a body in which the soul of God dwells."[365]

I am inclined to agree with Zwelling's interpretation, though he leaves out the best proof for his position: The central locus of divine embodiment is the Torah, which is the name that comprises all the letters of the Hebrew alphabet, the "holy supernal chariot" (*merkavah elyonah qedoshah*) in whose pattern the tabernacle below was constructed. It is not coincidental that in one passage, immediately after affirming the depiction of Torah as the "pattern of an edifice" (*dugmat binyan*), Joseph of Hamadan describes the tabernacle (*mishkan*) as the body in which the soul of God's will is made tangible, that is, really imagined as imaginally real. Accordingly, Joseph of Hamadan renders the verse obligating every male Israelite to set aside an offering to God, *we-yiqhu li terumah* (Exod. 25:2), as *ya'aseh guf we-ya'asu neshamah wa-ani etgashshem bo* ("make a body and soul and I will materialize therein"):[366]

> By way of wisdom you already know what I have alluded to that the entire Torah is wholly in the pattern of the holy and pure chain [*she-kol ha-torah hi kullah dugmat shalshelet ha-qedushshah we-ha-tehorah*], and therefore there is an open section and a closed section to allude to the pattern of the edifice [*dugmat ha-binyan*]. Everything was in heaven and afterward it materialized [*nitgashshem*] on earth.[367]

As I have already intimated, in the kabbalistic tradition, the anthropomorphic shape of God refers not to humanity in general but specifically to the Jew, a point often expressed in the relevant texts in terms of the rabbinic dictum (linked exegetically to Ezek. 34:31) that the title *adam* applies to Israel and not to the nations of the world.[368] In particular, the ethnocentric dimension of the incarnational myth, which has informed the kabbalistic orientation, is captured in the symbolic identification of God, Torah, and Israel implied in the zoharic comment "there are three gradations bound one to the other, the holy One, blessed be he, Torah, and Israel,"[369] an early formulation of the belief in a threefold unity that became axiomatic in later kabbalistic ontology and anthropology.[370] The full implication of this symbolism is brought to the surface in another passage from Joseph of Hamadan wherein he explicates the obligation incumbent upon every male Jew to write his own Torah scroll:[371]

The reason for this commandment by way of kabbalah alludes to the fact that the Torah scroll is the holy of holies . . . for the entire Torah is the name of the holy One, blessed be he . . . and his Torah is within the holy One, blessed be he, and within him is his Torah, and this is what the kabbalists say the holy One, blessed be he, is in his name and his name is in him. "His name" is his Torah and the Torah is made through the pure and holy chain in the supernal image, and it is verily the shade of the holy One, blessed be he. . . . Therefore he commanded that each man should make a Torah scroll for himself to discern and to know that he cherishes the Torah and to allude to the unity and to demonstrate the pattern of the Creator, blessed be he. When the holy One, blessed be he, sees that each and every one in Israel has a Torah scroll that is precisely in the likeness of his pattern, blessed be he, the holy One, blessed be he, immediately causes his presence to dwell upon Israel, verily in his pattern, in the Torah scroll. Therefore God, blessed be he, commanded each and every man from Israel to make a Torah scroll for himself . . . this alludes to the fact that all of Israel is one form, as the sages, blessed be their memory, said all Israel is one body. . . . Since all of Israel is one supernal pattern, and each and every one from Israel is a limb of the chariot, each and every man from Israel must take a Torah scroll for himself so that the limb will cleave to the limb in the pure and holy chain.[372]

The incarnational theology that informs the kabbalistic standpoint is predicated on a distinctive understanding of corporeality. "Body" does not denote physical mass that is quantifiable and measurable but the phenomenological sense of the corporeal as lived presence. Medieval kabbalists, due to the influence of philosophical thinking that had informed the general cultural trends of European societies in the High Middle Ages, adopted a negative view toward the corporeal body (indeed, according to some passages in zoharic literature, the physicality of the human is linked to the demonic other side)[373] and thus considered the contemplative life as a way to escape the bonds of carnality. This explains the adoption of ascetic forms of piety on the part of kabbalists, with special emphasis placed on sexual abstinence.[374]

The positive valence accorded the body in kabbalistic symbolism, reflected in the repeated use of anthropomorphic images to depict God, images that on occasion embrace an intense erotic tone, is related to the textual nature of bodiliness, which, in turn, rests on an assumption regarding the bodily nature of textuality. The linguistic comportment of embodiment accounts as well for the theurgical underpinnings of the kabbalistic under-standing of ritual epitomized in the saying "limb strengthens limb," that is, the performance of ceremonial acts by human limbs fortifies the divine attributes, which are imaginally envisioned as bodily limbs.[375] Alternatively expressed, insofar as Torah is the name YHWH, and the latter takes the form of an anthropos (an idea buttressed by the numerical equiva-lence of the four letters of the name written out in full and the word *adam*), it follows that each commandment can be represented as a limb of the divine body.[376]

Such a perspective reverses the generally assumed allegorical approach to scriptural anthropomorphisms promoted by medieval rabbinic exegetes, for instead of explaining anthropomorphic characterizations of God as a figurative way to accommodate human understanding,[377] the attribution of corporeal images to an incorporeal God indicates that the real body, the body in its most abstract tangibility, is the letter,[378] a premise that I shall call the principle of poetic incarnation.[379] When examined from the kabbalistic perspective, anthropomorphism in the canonical texts of Scripture indicates that human and divine corporeality are entwined in a mesh of double imaging through the mirror of the text that renders the divine body human and the human body divine.[380] Phenomenologically speaking, the lifeworld of kabbalists revolves about the axis of the embodied text of textual embodiment.

Embodying Ritual and Mystical Transfiguration

Beyond providing a radically different hermeneutical key to interpret Scripture, not to mention later rabbinic legends that ascribe corporeality to God, the understanding of textual embodiment advanced by kabbalists had practical implications in the mystical approach to ritual, which, in the final analysis, cannot be severed from the theurgical element described previously.[381] A hallmark of medieval kabbalists, both influenced by and reacting to philosophical explications of the commandments, was to view sacramental behavior as an instrument through which the physical body is conjoined to and transformed in light of the imaginal body of God manifest in the inscripted body of Torah. An early formulation of this theme can be found in Ezra of Gerona:

> The Torah and commandments, positive and negative, have been given to accustom man and to guide him in the good attributes, and so that the evil inclination will be drawn after the good inclination and it will be nullified in relation to it .... For this purpose are the commandments, devotional acts, prayers, and fasting, to subdue the evil inclination so that it will be compliant to the good inclination, and so that the body, whose foundation is dust and whose nature is evil and descends below, will be drawn after the soul whose foundation is life and whose nature is entirely good and ascends above.[382]

The performance of a ritual act requires a blessing that specifies the holiness with which God has sanctified the Jewish people:

> [F]ulfillment of a commandment is the light of life, and the one who accomplishes it below establishes and sustains its power ... and in the separation of the soul from the body this light is like a magnet for the soul ... for this light draws it ... that is, the

splendor of the soul is uplifted and stands in the place of the supernal beings and inwardly in the glory of the holy One, blessed be he.[383] . . . The intention in all of this is that man is comprised of all the spiritual matters [*devarim ruḥaniyyim*], and when a man walks in the good path the attribute of goodness, which is called the good angel, emanates on him, but when he walks in an evil path the attribute of evil, which is called the angel of death, emanates on him.[384]

The experience of being assimilated into the light as a consequence of fulfilling the ritual is predicated on the assumption that the action below stimulates the light above; since the commandments are part of Torah, and Torah is identical with God, ritualized gestures serve as the means by which the soul separates from the body and ascends to the light, augmenting the overflow of the divine efflux.[385] To cite a parallel passage from Ezra's commentary on talmudic aggadot:

> You must know that the commandment is light and the one who performs it below establishes and does something above. Therefore when a man is occupied with a commandment, the commandment itself is light, and thus it says, "for the commandment is a lamp and the teaching is a light" (Prov. 6:23), and he walks in the ways of light and he does not depart from it and it dwells in his midst. When the soul is separated from the body, this light is like a magnet for the soul, and[386] this is "his righteousness lasts forever" (Ps. 112:9), for this attribute[387] draws him. Thus, in the doing of the commandment, he takes the reward, for there is no reward above this . . . and concerning this the rabbis, blessed be their memory, said "the reward of a commandment is the commandment,"[388] that is, the speculum that shines.[389] And this is what Antigonus said to his disciples, "Do not be like servants who serve their master for the sake of receiving a reward."[390] Do not think that the performance of the commandment and the recompense are two things, it is not so.[391]

Utilizing earlier rabbinic dicta that affirm a deontological deportment based on recognizing the intrinsic value of fulfilling the law without any concern for reward, Ezra qualifies his own instrumentalist posture by positing that the rituals themselves are construed as textual instantiations of the divine essence: "The commandments are the attributes."[392] To equate the commandments and attributes implies that Torah, mystically conceived, is the name, whence it follows that ritual performance is the means by which the corporeal body is textualized and the textual body corporealized:

> The 248 positive commandments are to guide the limbs of man, which equal 248,[393] in a straight and good path, to purify him, to sanctify him, to cleanse him, to bless him, so that he may imitate his creator. The 365 negative commandments are to guide the sinews of man, which are 365, in a straight and good path and to protect him from

an evil path and from a despicable quality. By means of this the soul and the body will be on one path and in harmony [*yihyu ha-guf we-ha-neshamah be-derekh eḥad u-ve-haskamah aḥat*].[394] You must know that the pure Torah in its entirety was spoken from the mouth of God and there is no letter or dot in it that is not necessary for it is entirely a divine structure [*binyan elohim*][395] hewn from the name of the holy One, blessed be he.[396] . . . Since the commandments are the holy and pure body [*guf ha-ṭehorah we-ha-qedoshah*] the one engaged [in them] will be purified and sanctified.[397]

According to the perspective enunciated by Ezra, which is widely attested in kabbalistic literature, rituals not only purify the practitioner's body of its physicality but they transmute it into the luminous body composed of the letters comprised within the name, which is the Torah—at work here is the convergence of light and letter symbolism, a recurrent phenomenon in kabbalistic sources, as scholars have duly noted.[398] That ritual acts may be considered limbs out of which the divine structure, *binyan elohi*, is assembled is predicated on this transformative mechanism. One should recall here that in a short treatise on the secret of the Tree of Knowledge, *Sod Eṣ ha-Da'at*, Ezra comments that Adam, prior to his having eaten the forbidden fruit, was "completely spiritual" (*kullo ruḥani*) and "garbed angelically" (*lovesh mal'akhut*) like Enoch and Elijah. Hence he was permitted to eat of all the fruits of the Garden of Eden, which, Ezra is quick to point out, are "fruits of the soul," that is, just as in the corporeal realm food nourishes the body, in this antediluvian state these fruits were to sustain the life of the soul.[399]

The force of the expression *lovesh mal'akhut* is to convey the view that Adam's original body was angelic, that is, he wore—a locution that in medieval Hebrew texts denotes embodiment, since the soul was typically portrayed as being enclothed in the body—the angelic nature, a spiritual body (*guf ruḥani*)[400] that is sustained by the fruits of Eden, an idea doubtless influenced by the earlier rabbinic tradition that as a consequence of their transgression, the "garments of light" originally invested in Adam and Eve were changed into "garments of skin."[401] What is crucial for us to emphasize is that in Ezra's religious philosophy, the means by which the Jew, who is in the image of Adam and hence composed of the spiritual entities (*devarim ruḥaniyyim*), can be restored in part to this autochthonous state through observing the commandments.

Implicit in the approach articulated by Ezra is an inextricable link between the referential and performative aspects of kabbalistic symbolism,[402] that is, insofar as rituals are ontologized as divine attributes and the latter are configured as limbs of an imaginal body correlated through ritual with the idealized body of the Jewish male, the envisioning of God on the part of the medieval kabbalist affords him an opportunity to act upon the reality to which he is ecstatically bound and within which he is ontically reincorporated. Moreover, given the semiological nature of that reality, the somatic performance may be viewed as a form of symbolic utterance. Just as the ontic identification of Torah and God effectively effaces the difference between commander and command and thus challenges a basic presupposition of biblical and rabbinic theism—an implication of the kabbalistic doctrine that has yet to be appreciated by critical scholarship—so the ontic identification of the Jewish soul and God effectively effaces the difference between commander and commanded.

The matter is made more explicit by Azriel of Gerona, who wrote that the "Torah is called 'name' [*shem*] . . . and God is his name and his name is he [*she-ha-shem hu shemo u-shemo hu*][403] . . . and by placing dust on [the scroll][404] the bodies of the sages trembled on account of the fear of the bodies of Torah [*gufei torah*], which is called 'name,' for they restore the soul[405] in the body, and since the Torah restores the soul in the body the bodies of the sages trembled."[406] What is especially noteworthy for our purposes is Azriel's appropriation of the idiom *gufei torah*, which, as I have already noted, is employed in the zoharic corpus as well in a hyperliteral sense to denote the textual body of God, which is the name. In the case of the Catalan kabbalist, however, *gufei torah* refer to the commandments, so-called because they restore the soul in the body of one who fulfills them.[407] A more mystical nuance intended by this expression, closer to the aforecited zoharic text, is offered in the continuation of the passage:

> Since the Torah is called "name" and it restores the soul, it has sections, chapters, and paragraphs, which are the open and closed sections, in the pattern of a complete structure [*binyan shalem*] just as a man has ligaments and joints in his hand and foot. And just as there are limbs upon which the soul is dependent and there are limbs upon which the soul is not dependent even though there is no gain or deficit to the health of the body, so there are sections and verses in the Torah that appear to one who does not know their explication as though they are worthy of being burnt, but the one who comprehends and knows their explanation sees that they are the bodies of Torah [*gufei torah*],[408] and the one who leaves out one letter or a single point from them is like one who diminishes a whole body. . . . All the commandments are called "truth" [*emet*] . . . and even though there are light and difficult commandments, the commandments are the glory. . . . Therefore, no one knows the reward for the commandments for all the commandments have a purpose, but their purpose has no limit. Whoever is occupied with the commandments the fear of the commandment should be upon him as if he were crowned and encircled in its glory.[409]

The ecstatic-theurgic nature of the commandments proffered by the Geronese disciples of Isaac the Blind is affirmed as well, albeit in a somewhat varied language, by Naḥmanides, who concluded that "a man is vanity and air, and he is nothing at all . . . for his eyes, his head, and all his limbs are nothing, but the commandments are his body, his limbs, and his soul."[410] In a manner consonant with Ezra and Azriel, Naḥmanides identifies the commandments as the tissue of the body as well as the fiber of the soul. Implicit in this comment is the mystical conception of Torah as body and the further identification of the latter with the sefirotic configuration of the divine in whose image the human body below, that is, the idealized body of the circumcised male Jew, is patterned. To mention one source here in support of this contention, Naḥmanides offers the following esoteric explanation of the injunction for the priests to wash their hands and feet before entering the Tent of Meeting (Exod. 30:19):

> By way of truth [al derekh ha-emet] this is on account of the fact that the top and bottom of man are the hands and feet, for the hands are higher than the rest of the body when one lifts them up and the feet are below, and they are in the form of man an allusion to the ten *sefirot* so that the entire body will be between them, as it says in *Sefer Yeṣirah*, "he decreed with him a covenant between the ten fingers of his hands and between the ten fingers of his feet, in the covenant of the tongue and the covenant of the foreskin."[411] Therefore, the servants of the supernal one were commanded to wash the hands and feet, and the washing is for the sake of holiness.[412]

Fulfillment of the commandments facilitates the transformation of the carnal body into the textual body of Torah, a state of psychosomatic equilibrium wherein the body becomes the perfect vehicle to execute the will of the soul and the soul becomes the perfect guide in directing the will of the body. The soul thus mirrors the embodiment of God's glory in Torah by donning the name that is envisioned in the form of an anthropos. As the incorporeal assumes the bodily contours of the scriptural text, the body of one who observes the commandments is transformed into a ritualized body composed of the very same letters.

Consider the following remark of Ezra on the expression *enhagkha*, "I would lead you" (Song 8:2): "The soul does not show its actions except through the body and the body has no action except through the soul, and thus the holy One, blessed be he, shows his wonders and signs by means of his attributes."[413] The word *enhagkha* is from the root *nhg*, "to lead" or "to guide," and one of its nominal conjugations is *hanhagah*, a technical term in medieval Hebrew for divine governance. Ezra's point, then, is that the mystery of providence entails the incorporeal God manifesting itself in the attributes in the same manner that the soul acts by means of the body. Insofar as the attributes are expressive of the divine name, and the name is the mystical essence of Torah, it follows that adhering to the commands affords one the opportunity to be incorporated into the "divine edifice," the "holy and pure body."

In a similar fashion, albeit in a different terminological register, Naḥmanides proffers an attenuated ascetic understanding of ritual, interpreting the overall rationale for the commandments as a harnessing of the body in the service of sacred matters. Accordingly, the priestly ideal of holiness (*qedushshah*) is understood by Naḥmanides as advocating a form of piety that exceeds the strict demands of law, an asceticism (*perishut*) that impels one to separate from hedonistic gratification even in areas permitted by halakhah.[414] The highest spiritual achievement, however, is for man to cleave in thought to God uninterruptedly and to love him constantly, so that even the most routine somatic act becomes an opportunity for worship.[415] In one passage, Naḥmanides makes it quite clear that in his opinion the pietistic ideal entails spiritualization rather than abrogation of the body:

> Those who are occupied with the commandments out of love according to the law and as it is appropriate together with matters of this world . . . will merit a good life in this world in accordance with the custom of the world and the life of the world-to-come where their recompense will be complete. Those who leave aside all matters of this world and do not pay attention to it as if they were not corporeal beings [ba'alei guf], and all their thoughts and intentions are toward their Creator alone, as in the case of Elijah, by the cleaving of their souls to the glorious name, they live forever in their bodies and in their souls, as it appears in Scripture in the case of Elijah and according to what is known of it from the kabbalah, and as it is in legends [midrashim] about Enoch and those belonging to the world-to-come who will rise in the time of the resurrection. Therefore scriptural verses say regarding the reward for the commandments "in order that your days will be lengthened" (Exod. 20:12), "in order that you may live" (Deut. 16:20), "in order that you may lengthen the days" (Deut. 22:7), for the language comprises all the types of life as is appropriate for each one.[416]

For those whose minds are completely focused on God—in technical terms, those who cleave to the glorious name (shem ha-nikhbad), which, for Naḥmanides, refers to Shekhinah, the object of conjunction[417]—it is as if they were incorporeal, without the impediment of the physical body, but in fact their reward is immortality of body and soul. Though not stated explicitly, the body that lives forever is not the natural body subject to generation and corruption, but the angelic body.

Support for this interpretation may be gathered from another passage in which Naḥmanides attempts to explain the aggadic tradition that Jacob did not die. According to Naḥmanides, the intent of the rabbinic claim is not to deny the demise of Jacob's physical body but to emphasize that consequent to that demise his soul, like the souls of all the righteous, was garbed in a "second garment" (levushat ha-sheni), that is, the ethereal body, by which he was bound to the "bundle of life," an eschatological expression (based on 1 Sam. 25:29) that signifies in this context the conjunction of the soul with and incorporation into the body of Shekhinah.[418] It is noteworthy that Menaḥem Recanati, an Italian exegete active in the early fourteenth century and influenced greatly by Spanish kabbalah, associates this second garment with the older eschatological motif of the "rabbinic garment" (ḥaluqa de-rabbanan), the garment/body donned by the soul and woven from one's deeds.[419] Naḥmanides does not make this association explicitly, but I think there is cogency in Recanati's suggestion.

I would infer, therefore, that the second garment does indeed refer to the *corpus astrale* the soul receives after being stripped of its fleshly encasement. Rendered kabbalistically, we can say the material of this body is the Hebrew letters, as the body is the garment woven from one's good deeds, and the substance of the latter derives from the words of the divine commands, words inscripted in the textual body of Torah, which, in the formulation of Naḥmanides himself, is composed entirely of the names of God.

In the primordial Torah, letters are not broken into discrete words and sentences, for the letters are the constituent elements—the particles—of the divine names. The Torah given to Moses had two aspects, the written text, which corresponds to the "way of our reading" (*derekh qeri'atenu*), which is also described as the "division according to the ritualistic reading" (*derekh ḥilluq qeri'at ha-miṣwah*), and the oral text, which is not a reference to the standard rabbinic Oral Torah but an occult reading by "way of the names" (*derekh ha-shemot*). There are two originary ways of reading Scripture—the term for the later is *miqra* from the root *qr'*, "to call out," "to invoke," "to read," whence the word *qeri'ah*, "recitation"—the mystical way of *shemot* transmitted orally and the ritual way of *torah* and *miṣwah* inscripted in written form; the textual ground of both is the primordial Torah, which as Naḥmanides describes, citing an ancient tradition (*qabbalah*), was written in black fire on white fire.[420]

Moreover, as I surmised in a study published in 1990, the theme of the second garment should be considered in conjunction with the "garment" (*malbush*) mentioned by Naḥmanides in his explanation of the epiphany of the divine glory to Abraham in the form of three men/angels (Gen. 18:1ff.). For Naḥmanides, expanding upon an earlier midrashic interpretation, the shift in identity of these characters from "men" to "angels" is to be explained as the mystery of the garbing of angels as men, the secret of the incarnation of the glory, which is seen exclusively by the "eyes of the flesh of the pure souls" (*einei basar be-zakkei ha-nefashot*), that is, a corporeal seeing that is possible for those who have achieved a state of spiritual perfection predicated on renunciation of physical pleasure and sensual gratification.[421] By linking the two exegetical excurses, we can posit that for Naḥmanides, pious individuals have the capacity to experience what the soul of the righteous experiences when returning to Paradise after the death of the physical body, being attired in the more refined body. Commenting on the biblical injunction "and cleave to him" (Deut. 11:22), Naḥmanides affirms precisely such a possibility when he writes concerning the individuals whose love for God is so continual that they are conjoined to him even when involved in worldly affairs:

> It is possible for people of this level that their souls even in their lives are bound to the bundle of life, for they are themselves an abode [*ma'on*] for *Shekhinah* . . . their thoughts and actions are constantly with God. Thus Joshua warned them that even now in the land when the wondrous acts will withdraw from them, their thoughts should constantly cleave to the awesome and glorious name and their intention should not depart from God.[422]

In a passage in *Sha'ar ha-Gemul*, the section in *Torat ha-Adam* that deals at length with the subject of reward and punishment, Naḥmanides describes the world-to-come (*olam ha-ba*) as a state of being consequent to the resurrection of the dead (*teḥiyyat ha-metim*) wherein the deceased rise in body and soul (*anshei ha-teḥiyyah be-guf u-ve-nefesh*), rather than (as Maimonides argued) as a world of disembodied souls (*olam ha-neshamot*).[423] As to the nature of the body and soul in this state, Naḥmanides offers the following account:

> The existence of the soul [*qiyyum ha-nefesh*] in its unification with the supernal knowledge [*da'at elyon*] is like the existence of the angels [*qiyyum ha-mal'akhim*], and the elevation of the soul over the body nullifies the corporeal faculties [*koḥot ha-gufiyyot*] . . . to the point that the body exists as the existence of the soul without eating or drinking . . . there is in this form deep secrets [*sodot amuqqim*] . . . for the existence of the body [*qiyyum ha-guf*] will be like the existence of the soul [*qiyyum ha-nefesh*], and the existence of the soul will be united with the supernal knowledge.[424]

The eschatological body will be like the original embodiment of Adam who, prior to the sin, was created to be immortal. The cleaving to the supernal knowledge, moreover, is depicted as an augmented luminosity of the face and as being garbed in the Holy Spirit, characteristics that are adduced from several biblical and rabbinic figures. We may conclude, therefore, that for Naḥmanides, the secret entails a somatic transformation that is in inverse relation to the mystery of incarnation, the glory assuming tangible shape when it appears in the world.

A striking example of the incarnational drift in the religious philosophy of Naḥmanides is found in his explanation of the manna consumed by the Israelites in their sojourn in the desert. Nahmanides deduces the "great matter" (*inyan gadol*) of the manna from a talmudic debate concerning the verse "Each man ate bread of the mighty," *leḥem abirim akhal ish* (Ps. 78:25): According to Aqiva, *leḥem abirim* refers symbolically to the "bread that the ministering angels eat," whereas Ishmael maintains that angels do not eat and hence the verse must be interpreted literally as a reference to the "bread that is absorbed by the 248 limbs."[425] Naḥmanides writes:

> This matter of which R. Aqiva spoke is that the existence of the ministering angels is through the splendor of the presence [*ziw ha-shekhinah*] . . . and the manna is from the by-product of the supernal light that is materialized through the will of the Creator, may he be blessed [*ha-man hu mi-toledot ha-or ha-elyon she-nitgashshem be-raṣon bor'o yitbarakh*], and thus those who ate the manna and the ministering angels were sustained from one thing.[426]

Even though the ministering angels and the Israelites who ate the manna are both nourished by the "supernal light" of *Shekhinah*, the last of the sefirotic gradations, there is a
critical difference between the two groups: The former derived their sustenance directly
and the latter indirectly through an emanation of the light that assumes material form in
compliance with the divine will. R. Ishmael, by contrast, as interpreted by Naḥmanides,
emphasizes that the "bread of the mighty" cannot refer to manna eaten by angels, since
they are sustained by the splendor itself and thus have no need for the lustrous substance
that emanates therefrom. Without denying the biblical contention that the manna was
physically consumed, Naḥmanides imparts spiritual significance to the eating by understanding it as an act that occasions (concretely and not figuratively) the unitive experience
of the soul and the light that streams from *Shekhinah*.

Naḥmanides utilizes this contemplative ideal to explain the tradition that the Israelites were able to educe different tastes in the manna in accord with their desires, for "the
soul by means of its thought is conjoined to the supernal beings." Partaking of the manna
is a foretaste of the eschatological reward awaiting the righteous in the world-to-come,
being conjoined to *Shekhinah*. Thus Naḥmanides interprets the dictum attributed to Rav
that in the world-to-come there is no eating or drinking but only the righteous sitting
with their crowns on their heads, sustained by the splendor of the presence,[427] in the following way:

> Those who belong to the world-to-come will be sustained in their pleasure by the
> splendor of the presence through their cleaving to the crown that is on their heads
> [*be-hidavqam bo ba-aṭarah she-be-ro'sham*], and the crown [*aṭarah*] is the attribute
> that is called in this way as the verse says "In that day, the Lord of Hosts shall become
> a crown of beauty" (Isa. 28:5), and it is said concerning her "wearing the crown that
> his mother gave him" (Song 3:11).[428]

The eschatological image of the righteous wearing the crown is rendered symbolically as
conjunction with *Shekhinah*, the attribute that is designated *aṭarah* or *aṭeret ṣevi*, an idea
well attested in other kabbalists from this period and beyond, as I have discussed in a
number of my previous publications.[429] What is crucial to emphasize here is that for Naḥmanides, this image bespeaks a more reified form of bodily nourishment, being sustained
by the splendor of the presence.

The spiritual spectrum, as it were, with eating manna on one end and cleaving
directly to *Shekhinah* on the other, is reiterated by Naḥmanides in *Sha'ar ha-Gemul*. It is
worth considering this reiteration, as the formulation is slightly different and affords the
reader another vantage point. In the relevant passage, Naḥmanides begins by noting that
with respect to the "pure of soul" (*zakkei ha-nefesh*), the same technical term he used in
his remark concerning the ones worthy of seeing the garment, the incarnation of the glory

in the anthropomorphic form of an angel, their "corporeal existence" (*qiyyum gufam*) is through "subtle things" (*devarim daqqim*), and the purest of them from things most subtle (*daqqim min ha-daqqim*). To illustrate the point, Naḥmanides mentions that the Israelites who ate the manna

> were sustained by the manna absorbed in their limbs, for it is from the by-product of the supernal light that is materialized through the will of the Creator, blessed be he, and they were nourished from it in the desert from the time that their souls were elevated by what they apprehended of the miracles at the sea . . . but the soul of Moses, who was more elevated and unified than them in the knowledge of his Creator, had no need for this matter because his body was materialized and sustained through the splendor of the presence [*ziw ha-shekhinah*] and the supernal comprehension [*hassagah elyonah*].[430]

The manna, which is the by-product of the supernal light that materializes, is a higher and more sublime substance than the coarse food that nourishes the mortal body of tissues and blood; but the supernal light, the splendor of the presence, is even more subtle than the manna. Moses, in contrast to the Israelites who devoured the manna, was sustained by the splendor itself and hence had no need for an alternative manner of provision, an idea that Naḥmanides expounds on the basis of earlier rabbinic sources.[431] What is worthy of emphasis is the statement that the body of Moses was "materialized and sustained" through this splendor, a state, according to the opinion of R. Ishmael, characteristic of the angels. It is apposite to conclude, therefore, that the supreme body that Moses inhabited is the angelic body, the body that is constituted by the divine radiance.

On this basis we can draw the following parallel between language and body in the religious philosophy of Naḥmanides and the other Catalonian kabbalists previously discussed: Just as the way beyond language is through language, so the way beyond body is through body. This holds a key to understanding the role of asceticism in the formation of the mystical pietism affirmed by kabbalists of the period: Separation from sensual matters is not seen as a way to obliterate the body—commitment to rabbinic ritual precluded such an unmitigated renunciation of the natural world—but as a means for the metamorphosis of the mortal body into an angelic body, a body whose limbs are constituted by the letters of the name, the anthropomorphic configuration of Torah. Adorned in the apparel of this body, the soul is conjoined to the divine name.

Flesh Made Word / Specular Iconization of the Body as Text

While it was surely the opinion of kabbalists that the ideas I have mentioned were part of the ancient esoteric lore of Judaism, and indeed there is textual verification that at least in some measure their ideas were expansions of older doctrines, one cannot help but note the resemblance between the pertinent kabbalistic symbolism and several dogmas shared ubiquitously by orthodox Christians in the twelfth and thirteen centuries, a point not lost to some of the rabbinic figures (for example, Meir ben Simeon of Narbonne) who openly attacked kabbalists for espousing heretical views and promulgating blasphemous practices.[432] Specifically I have in mind the kabbalistic teaching regarding the incarnation of the name in the body of Torah, which implies as its corollary the materialization of Torah in the body of the name, and the even more striking affinity between the embodiment of the splendor of *Shekhinah* in tangible form and the consequent transformation of the corporeal body into a glorified body (*corpus glorificationis*) by partaking of that light, on the one hand, and representations of the divine flesh as the consecrated host in the medieval Christian imagination and the sacramental transubstantiation of the body into spirit, on the other.[433]

To be sure, the philosophical issue underlying these mythic formulations can be framed in metaphysical terms that would not necessarily be limited to a Christian context. That is to say, thinkers in different religious settings laboring under the impact of Neoplatonic theories of emanation, which, for all the diversity and complexity, uniformly posit a continuous chain of being, had to deal not only with the challenge of how the One becomes many, but also with how sensible substance arises from the intelligible, the corporeal from the incorporeal.[434] I would surely assent to this caution, but I am not persuaded of the wisdom of separating the Christological and Neoplatonic channels of influence in this matter. It is not even necessary to limit the former to textual sources, as there were other forms of communication, including especially the visual medium, that would have readily conveyed the symbolic power of the image of Christ's body in the formation of Christian piety.[435]

Notwithstanding the legitimacy of this rather obvious though regrettably neglected avenue to explain the transmission of Christian creed to masters of Jewish esoteric lore in European cities and towns, I would contend that the issue need not be restricted to historical influence, whether through text or image. Far more important is the logical inevitability that speculation of this sort will invariably yield a mythopoeic representation of the literal body, that is, the body that literally is literal, the body that is letter, an analogical literalism that accounts for the phenomenological resemblance between kabbalah and Christianity, a resemblance exploited—but not concocted—by Christian kabbalists in the Renaissance.

Assuredly, one must be on guard against making definitive claims regarding the origin of kabbalistic motifs, given the sophisticated exegetical prowess of kabbalists and the intricate ways they develop secret traditions either hinted at in older texts or transmitted orally, a belief in the antiquity of their traditions and practices that is persistently affirmed by practitioners of the occult wisdom; nevertheless, it behooves one to note the obvious affinity of the mythic understanding of Torah as the name and the related motif of shedding the somatic body and donning the luminous body, sometimes portrayed as being crowned by light, with Christological beliefs.[436] As I have already noted, there is no escaping the incarnational implications of the esoteric identification of Torah and the name, since the latter is the divine essence, a point made explicitly in several zoharic passages and confirmed by other kabbalists contemporary with the literary production of the *Zohar*, for instance, Joseph Gikatilla, Menaḥem Recanati, Joseph of Hamadan, and the anonymous authors respectively of *Sefer ha-Yiḥud* and *Sefer ha-Temunah*.[437] Thus in one zoharic passage we read, "It has been taught that the holy One, blessed be he, is called Torah."[438] In a second passage, the matter is laid out in more detail based on the symbolic correspondence between the ten commandments revealed at Sinai, which contain the whole Torah, and the ten divine utterances, the emanations comprised within the Tetragrammaton:[439]

> The Torah is the name of the holy One, blessed be he. Just as the name of the holy One, blessed be he, is inscribed in ten utterances, so Torah is inscribed in ten utterances; these ten utterances are the name of the holy One, blessed be he, and the Torah is entirely one name, verily the holy name of the holy One, blessed be he. . . . The one who is meritorious with respect to Torah is meritorious with respect to the holy name. R. Jose said that he is indeed meritorious with respect to the holy One, blessed be he, because he and his name are one.[440]

The Castilian kabbalists whose views are preserved in the zoharic homilies make even more explicit the assumption of their predecessors. The equation of Torah and the name implies that God is embodied in Torah, and consequently, engagement in study and fulfilling the commandments serve as the means by which one is conjoined to the divine. In the words of the *Zohar*: "He who is occupied with Torah it is as if he were occupied with the holy One, blessed be he, for Torah is entirely the name of the holy One, blessed be he."[441] But how can we speak of God being embodied in the text? Can light that is without limit be contained in letters that are limited by the shape of their very orthography? The mystery that is basic to zoharic kabbalah (though by no means unique to its fraternity) is that God is absent from the text in which God is present, since for God to be present in the text, God must be absent.

In spite of—or perhaps precisely on account of—the proximity of the gnosis promulgated by kabbalists and Christian faith, the incarnational thrust of the identification of Torah as the name and the name as divine body, especially as expressed in zoharic literature, has to be understood as a subtle polemical ploy vis-à-vis the Christological myth of the incarnation of the Word. A poignant illustration of the point may be adduced in the following passage extracted from the *Zohar* in the opening homily on the verse "On the eighth day Moses called to Aaron, his sons, and the elders of Israel" (Lev. 9:1).

The homily begins by extolling the fortune of Israel for having received Torah, which is described as the "joy of the holy One, blessed be he," the object of his bemusement (*sha'ashu'a*, a term derived from Prov. 8:30),[442] the place wherein he strolls, *aṭyyaluta*, apparently a zoharic coinage derived from the Hebrew *leṭayyel* ("to stroll"), a widespread euphemism in kabbalistic texts, attested already in *Sefer ha-Bahir*, for sexual intercourse,[443] the foot symbolizing the male (or, more precisely, the phallic) potency and the ground the female.[444] The older aggadic theme is embellished with the esoteric truism that the Torah is entirely the one holy name of God. The discussion circles around to the point that an explanation (attributed to R. Ḥiyya) is offered for why the first letter of Torah is *beit*, the second letter of the alphabet, a query that appears in classical rabbinic literature:[445] This letter signifies the dual Torah, oral and written, a doctrine that is also used in this context to explain the plural in "Let us make Adam in our image," that is, Adam was created by means of the Written and Oral Torah, reflected in the mentioning of image and likeness in tandem with his creation, the former correlated with the masculine and the latter with the feminine. According to R. Isaac, the orthographic structure of *beit* as the letter that is opened on one side and closed on three sides[446] is interpreted as a sign that Torah receives those who seek to be conjoined to her but she is closed from the other side in relation to those who close their eyes and turn away from her. It is at this point in the homily that the passage critical to my analysis appears:

> R. Judah said: *Beit* has two sides[447] and one that connects them. What do they come to teach? One for heaven, one for earth, and the holy One, blessed be he, connects and receives them. R. Eleazar said: These are the three holy, supernal lights bound as one, and they are the totality of Torah, and they open an opening to everything. They open an opening to faith and they are the abode of everything. Thus they are called *beit,* for they make up the dwelling [*beita*]. And thus the beginning of Torah is *beit,* for it is the Torah, the remedy for the world. Therefore, whoever is occupied with Torah it is as if he were occupied with the holy name . . . for Torah is entirely the one supernal holy name. And since it is the holy name, it begins with *beit*, for it is the totality of the holy name in three knots of faith. Come and see: all those occupied with Torah are conjoined to the holy One, blessed be he, and they are crowned in the crowns of Torah, and they are beloved above and below.[448]

The kabbalistic identification of Torah and the name is joined to an orthographic teaching regarding why the Torah begins with *beit*. According to the opinion attributed to R. Judah, *beit* refers to heaven, earth, and the divine being that unites the two.

I am not inclined to interpret this opinion theosophically; it seems rather that it is meant to be understood at face value: The three lines that make up the letter symbolize the heavenly and earthly realms and the divine being who unites them.[449] The theosophic explication is offered in the name of R. Eleazar. The three lines of *beit* refer to three holy, supernal lights that are bound as one, and they are the totality of Torah (*kelala de-oraita*). Insofar as the three potencies are the opening for faith, which may here denote the lower seven emanations, they are characterized as the abode (*beita*) of all that exists, and hence they are the three lines that make up *beit*, the letter that is the "totality of the holy name in three knots of faith" (*kelala di-shema qaddisha bi-telat qishrei meheimanuta*). All of Torah is the name and thus its first letter must encompass the totality of the name; the three lines—the orthographic form of the letter—are knots of faith.

I would conjecture that the three knots of faith—faith is the fourth side, the opening created by three closed sides—may be decoded as the three letters contained in the Tetragrammaton, YHW, a name that is depicted pictorially by *beit*.[450] At the beginning is the second letter that is first; the letter made of three lines, which are three knots of faith, YHW.[451] Alternatively, the knots of faith may allude symbolically to *Ḥokhmah*, *Binah*, and *Tif'eret*, three configurations of the divine that are imaginally depicted in some zoharic passages as father, mother, son and are correlated respectively with YHW; the last letter of the name, the fourth party of the quaternity, the daughter, *Malkhut* or *Shekhinah*, is represented by the second *he*, the letter that has already appeared, a duplicate of the second, the element of faith, empty vessel, capacity to receive.

The beginning of Torah, therefore, is the letter that marks the mystery of the threefold unity, the totality of the name, the secret abode of faith. The Christological resonance in the zoharic locution *telat qishrei meheimanuta* has been noted.[452] Reinforcing this orientation, I would add that the author of the homily has combined the motif of Torah as the incarnation of the divine name and the trinitarian symbol of the three knots of faith. In this matter, as with regard to a number of crucial themes, the kabbalists whose ideas and interpretations are preserved in zoharic literature reflect a complex relationship to Christianity, which was viewed as the major competitor in the arena of salvation history, the perennial struggle between synagogue and church, Jacob and Esau, Israel/Adam and Gentile/Edom, not in binary opposition, but rather as attraction through repulsion, repulsion by attraction, a gesture that encompasses both at once, differently similar in virtue of being similarly different.

On the one hand, the kabbalists adopted a harsh stance and portrayed Christianity as the earthly instantiation of the demonic potency, Satan or Samael, long conceived to be the archon of Edom, progenitor of idolatry, *avodah zarah*, worship that leads one astray, the other that seduces the Jew (men seem to be especially vulnerable) both in the form of spiritual enticement (particularly in the guise of magic) and sexual temptation.[453] On the other hand, the very same kabbalists were duly impressed with and intrigued by aspects of this faith, including trinitarian and incarnational symbols, as well as Marian devotional imagery, and attempted to appropriate them as the authentic esoteric tradition,[454] perhaps even modeling the fraternity of Simeon ben Yoḥai and his comrades on the pattern of Jesus and his disciples.[455] In my judgment, the kabbalists hidden behind the personae of the zoharic fraternity sought to divest Christological symbols of their Catholic garb and redress them as the mystical truths of Judaism. The zoharic understanding of text as body, which provides the mechanism by which the body is understood as text, is a stunning illustration of this strategy.

I shall conclude with the citation and analysis of one final zoharic text that demonstrates the subtle and complex relationship between kabbalistic and Christological symbolism:

> "As for the tabernacle, make it of ten strips of cloth" (Exod. 26:1). Here is the mystery of unity, for the arrayment of the tabernacle was from several gradations, as it is written with respect to it, "and the tabernacle was one" (Exod., 26:6). This is to illustrate that all the parts of the body are all the mystery of one body. In a man, there are several upper and lower parts, the ones interior and the others revealed on the outside, and all of them are called one body, and the man is called one composition. So here, all the parts of the tabernacle are in the pattern of what is above and when all of them are joined as one, then it is written "and the tabernacle was one." The commandments of Torah are all parts and limbs in the mystery above, and when all of them are joined together, then all of them add up to one mystery. The mystery of the tabernacle, which consists of the parts and limbs, all compute to the mystery of Adam in the manner of the commandments of Torah, for the commandments of Torah are all of them the mystery of Adam, male and female. When they are joined together, they are one mystery of Adam.[456]

In this homily, the images of the tabernacle, the human body, the androgynous Adam, and the Torah are linked together like pearls in a necklace of symbolic equivalencies. The thread that ties the images together is the linguistic conception of embodiment, that is, what the four entities share in common is the assumption that they are constructed from letters of the Hebrew alphabet. In older rabbinic sources, one can find the notion that the tabernacle (*miqdash*), the earthly residence of the divine glory, the microcosm of the universe, was built by means of the letters.[457] What the zoharic author adds is the depiction of the tabernacle in the shape of an anthropos. To grasp the hermeneutical move, we must bear in mind that in the above passage the tabernacle symbolically stands for the totality of the divine pleroma, a secret alluded to in the hyperliteral rendering of the verse that dictates the making of the tabernacle from ten strips of cloth, which correspond to the ten emanations from *Keter* to *Malkhut*. The mystery of the tabernacle's construction, therefore, imparts the wisdom that the multiplicity of divine powers cohere in a unified whole, that is, God's unity may be represented schismatically as a composite of discrete elements the infinity of which denies the possibility of fixed enumeration.

The organic unity of the tabernacle is illustrated further by comparing it to the human body. The anthropomorphic representation is illumined by a similar characterization of

Torah, for the commandments are the limbs of the body of Torah, which is envisioned as the mystery of the androgynous Adam, the positive commandments engendered as masculine and the negative commandments as feminine. The conjunction of the two facilitates the constitution of the mystery of the divine anthropos, which is depicted both as the textualization of the tabernacle and the materialization of Torah—parallel processes in the hidden disclosure of the divine name. The secret of poetic incarnation imparted by masters of Jewish esoteric lore, beholding the luminous flesh from the word, may be seen as a countermyth to the image of the word/light made flesh in the Johannine prologue, a mythologoumenon that played an inestimable role in fashioning the hermeneutical aesthetic of medieval Christendom.

This is not to deny that in the history of Christian devotion the incarnational theme did express itself in terms of textual embodiment.[458] My point is, however, that the mythologic basis for this form of embodiment in Christianity is always the incarnation of the Word in the person of Jesus, whether this is understood veridically or docetically. As a consequence, medieval Christian piety was informed by the exegetical supposition that incarnation of the word in the flesh had the effect of removing the veil of the letter as expounded by Jews, who resolutely refused to accept the spiritual interpretation that the Christological understanding demanded; the literal meaning, intricately bound to the carnal law, thus killed the spirit by obstructing the true knowledge of the Last Things.[459] By contrast, in the kabbalistic wisdom that concretized in the course of the twelfth, thirteenth, and fourteenth centuries, incarnation of the flesh in the word preserved the letter of the veil, as the only credible means to apprehend the inner meaning of the law was thought to be through its outer covering, to behold mysteries of Torah from underneath the garment, to see the image of the imageless embodied iconically in the text that is the textual embodiment of the name.

PART II

Religious Vocabularies

CHAPTER 6

Semantic Differences, or "Judaism"/"Christianity"

Daniel Boyarin

For Chana

> The role of the intellectual is not to tell others what they have to do. By
> what right would he do so? . . . The work of an intellectual is not to shape
> others' political will; it is, through the analysis that he carries out in his
> field, to question over and over again what is postulated as self-evident, to
> disturb people's mental habits, the way they do and think things, to dissi-
> pate what is familiar and accepted, to reexamine rules and institutions and
> on the basis of this re-problematization (in which he carries out his specific
> task as an intellectual) to participate in the formation of a political will (in
> which he has his role as citizen to play).
>
> —Michel Foucault, *Politics, Philosophy, Culture:*
> *Interviews and Other Writings, 1977–1984*

A recent writer in a popular context was surely representing what is
postulated as self-evident—people's mental habits, the way they do and
think things—when he wrote the following sentence: "Christianity's
parent religion, Judaism, is actively hostile to celibacy, one of monasticism's chief institutions."[1] This is precisely the sort of self-evidence that
my work as an intellectual sets out to question, disturb, and dissipate.
Judaism, I will argue (and so do many other scholars today), is not
the parent religion to Christianity; indeed, in some respects the opposite may be as true. Nor can we speak of a religion, Judaism, at all in the
sense of a bounded institution existing before the Christian era (and
even fairly deep into that era), of which it could be said that it was hostile
to any one thing. The issue of celibacy actually provides an instructive
example. Various groups that we can only call Jewish were very friendly

indeed to celibacy in the period just before and at the time of the emergence of Christianity,[2] and *Rabbinic* Jewish hostility to celibacy is almost surely a product of the Christian era (and arguably a response to Christianity).

An increasing number of cutting-edge scholars are referring to the "fourth century as the first century of Judaism and Christianity."[3] If we are not to speak of Judaism as the parent of Christianity, how, then, shall we speak of the emergence of two religions, Judaism and Christianity, as two religions, as we know them in our modern world? The first major theoretical assumption I adopt is that, as postcolonial theorist David Chidester has put it, "Religions have been reopened as invented traditions or as imagined communities." No less than with the study of the idea of the "nation," the idea of the "religion"—as in the Jewish religion, the Christian religion—the question can be asked: Where and when did this idea emerge? Moreover, as Chidester points out as well, "rather than bounded cultural systems, religions are intrareligious and interreligious networks of cultural relations."[4] It is on the borders, at the contact zones, that we find "religions" being produced (rather like the production of continents at the borders between tectonic plates). As Homi Bhabha has written, "It is the 'inter'—the cutting edge of translation and negotiation, the *in-between* space—that carries the burden of the meaning of culture."[5] Studying such borders should be a productive way of thinking about the construction of "religions" and thus, in this case, of Judaism and Christianity.

This is an inquiry into how language produces social "facts" and how social facts produce language. It is about how "Christianity" and "Judaism," as the names for a difference that we call "religions," came into being. I am attempting a sort of social history of ideas as material facts.[6] One of the outstanding theoretical issues with which I struggle is the question of language as social practice.[7] The problem is to find a theoretical model for understanding the situation in which Judaism and Christianity are existent realities but not defined or clearly distinguished ones—that is, a situation of hybridity.

At the beginning of the Christian era, people in the Mediterranean area seem most often to have named themselves in ethnic terms and not as adherents of what we would call a religion. The name "*Ioudaios*" by and large meant "Judean," as did its Hebrew cognate," '*iri*.[8] There was no *Ioudaismos* as the name of the Jewish religion before there was *Christianismos*. Although the term "*Ioudaismos*" existed before the Christian era, it meant something other than what we call "Judaism." In its earliest use, in 2 Maccabees 2:22 of the second century B.C.,[9] the term "*Ioudaismos*" is contrasted with "*Hellenismos*": the ways of the Judeans (or of the Jewish state) as opposed to the ways of the foreigners.[10] According to this text, there are those who "vie with one another in fighting manfully for *Ioudaismos*" (2 Macc. 2:21). This means fighting not for the defense of the faith but, as the text puts it, to preserve "the temple, the city, and the laws."

That *Ioudaismos* here is not the name of a "religion" can be argued philologically with a certain degree of plausibility (if not ineluctably). In the same work, at 4:13, "*Hellenismos*" means, according to Jonathan Goldstein, "the aping of Greek manners." In the Greek of the time, "*Medismos*" meant aping of Persian manners and with it "Greek collaboration with the Persian enemy." In the ostracisms of Athens in the early decades of the fifth century B.C., "*Medismos*" indicated disloyalty to the city.[11] "*Hellenismos*" in the Maccabees text (4:13) occupies the semantic role of *Medismos* in those Athenian anathemas. It indicates disloyalty to the city, together with its temple and its laws, as well as the miming of Greek ways. The opposite of *Medismos* in Greek usage was, seemingly, "*Hellenismos*," meaning remaining loyal to the Greek cause and the Greek ways.[12] It follows, therefore, if Goldstein is correct, that "*Ioudaismos*" (2 Macc. 8:1) in the Jewish text, which occupies the semantic position of *Hellenismos* in the Greek texts, means what *Hellenismos* means in those: remaining loyal to the ways of the Judeans and the political cause of Jerusalem.[13] It is not a name, then, for what we would identify as "Judaism," the Jewish religion. Indeed, we habitually differentiate between "Judaism" and "Jewishness" to mark something like this distinction. That very distinction that we make between Judaism and Jewishness could only appear after, in the words of historian Seth Schwartz, the "emergence of religion as a discrete category of human experience."

Although conversion to "Jewishness" was already a possibility, this move constituted a sort of naturalization into the Jewish people more than it did a conversion in the later, religious sense. "Conversion" in the first century still seems semantically and socially more like becoming an Athenian or a Roman citizen than it was like becoming a Christian.[14]

When Paul was writing, "Greek" and "Jew" were as incompatible as identities for a single person at a single moment as "male" and "female" or "slave" and "free" (Gal. 3:28).[15] Similarly, in the somewhat later *Acts of Pilate,* Pilate asks the Jewish leaders, "What are proselytes?" to which the answer comes, "They were born children of Greeks, and now have become Jews."[16] The semiotic opposition is still Greek/Jew. On the other hand, "Christian" and "Jew" were compatible identities in Paul's formulation, as well as for centuries thereafter. Most, if not all, Christians of the first, second, and perhaps even third centuries considered themselves and were considered by others to be Jews. "Jew," accordingly, is a member of the paradigm that includes "Greek," while "Christian" identifies another semantic field—perhaps one that included such entities as "Pharisee," "Sadducee," and "Essene." Becoming a Jew was like becoming a Spartan or an Athenian (not in the full political sense of these latter, as there was no formal civic identity of "Jew").[17] "Jew" was clearly an ethnic identity, even if a mutable one. Of course, entry into the community carried with it the requirement that one behave according to the mores of one's new community. It nevertheless remained a matter of essentially ethnic or national identification and identity formation.

I have been arguing that "*Ioudaismos*" could not have meant Judaism, the religion, in the period before and just after the advent of Christianity, by observing the sets of semantic oppositions (or lexical paradigms) within which the term then functioned. Signifiers, as we have known since Saussure, only function differentially—that is, by virtue of their difference from other signifiers—within a signifying system such as a language. Consequently, a "term" in a signifying system exists only when there are others that it is not. This is not a psychological point about identity (e.g., Freud's "narcissism of minor differences") but a theoretical claim that by now is both unexceptional and unexceptionable. However, its implications for the history of religions have not been taken seriously. Insofar as the semiotic system did not include other "religions" to which Jews might adhere, there could be no name that means the "proper" Jewish religion. The oppositional term to the various religions of the Ancient Near East with which the Israelites were in contact has to have been "the Israelite cult," in the broadest sense of "cult/ure," not because of substantive difference between this and the religion that we call Judaism (although there is, of course, such and much), but because this was what it was: the cult, in all of its various forms and subvarieties, of the ethnic group called Israel, and not a "religion." The other terms within the paradigm to which this signifier belongs are "the cult/ure of Assyria," "the cult/ure of Egypt," "the cult/ure of Canaan," and ultimately "the cult/ure of Greece" as well. As the terms of this paradigm suggest, the set of oppositions that it comprised was peoples and their lands and the practices and beliefs associated with them, not religions and *their* beliefs, practices, and so forth.[18] Although in all of these formations (and in Israelite and early Ioudaistic cult/ure as well), elements of what we call religion were prominent (that's the point of the virgule in the middle of the word), "religion" was not a dominant and independent variable, "a discrete category of human experience"—to use Schwartz's formulation—disembeddable from the culture as a whole.

It is, therefore, meaningless semiotically as well as historically to claim that Judaism existed before there was another term in the semiotic system, the names of religions, for it to be *not* that, and there is no point in even attempting to define a pre-Christian "Judaism" or Judaisms.[19] In other words, *Ioudaismos* in the sense of "Judaism" could only appear after *Christianismos* had appeared. *Christianismos* too, as the name for a religion, can only appear in opposition to *Ioudaismos* as the name for another religion, and that, as we shall see, has had important material consequences. A strong analogy to this point is that heterosexuality and homosexuality could only have come into the world together, and together as elements in a new paradigm called "sexualities." Similarly, I claim, *Judaism* and *Christianity* as the names of religions could only come into the world together as elements in the paradigm "religions."

It should be emphasized that *Ioudaismos,* even before it became a "religion," nevertheless constituted a cultural complex that had important religious elements. The argument, then, is that, following the epistemic shift for which I am arguing, *Ioudaismos* was transformed into a religion containing important national, ethnic, and cultural elements.

The coming of Christianity, it would seem, made the difference. The most dramatic innovation that Christianity introduced into the world was the making of a new kind of identity, "religion." It would follow from this that it was this invention, moreover, that produced the Jewish religion as well. Accepting the positions of such scholars as Wilfred Cantwell Smith and, more recently, Talal Asad,[20] that our modern concept of religion is a historical product of Christianity, I will suggest a revision to this thesis, proposing that this historical production does not belong to the eighteenth century but was in process from nearly the beginnings of certain parts of the Jesus movement and largely complete—whatever that might mean, precisely—by the beginning of the fifth century. Late antique historian Seth Schwartz has strikingly phrased this point by referring to "Christianization, and what is in social-historical terms its sibling, the emergence of religion as a discrete category of human experience—religion's disembedding."[21] What Schwartz is claiming and what my work here will support is that the production of Christianity, and thus the production of Judaism as a religion in this sense, is itself the invention of religion as such a discrete category. The production of such a category does not imply that many elements of what would form religions did not exist before this time but rather that the particular aggregation of verbal and other practices that would now be named as constituting a religion only came into being as a discrete category as Christianization.[22] Tracing a similar trajectory lexically, Maurice Sachot has argued that the term *religio*, in the sense in which we use it, is entirely the product of Christianity.[23] Schwartz has written that the disembedding of religion that constitutes the very invention of religion "had a direct impact on the Jewish culture of Late Antiquity because the Jewish communities *appropriated* much from the Christian society around them."[24]

In other words, when Christianity separated religious belief and practice from *Romanitas*, cult from culture, Judaism as a religion came into the world as well. The Rabbis articulated their own sense of identity and definition in part through "appropriation," not of course at this period owing to any power or dominance that "Christianity"—even if it made sense to claim the existence of such an entity—possessed, but owing to the compelling force of the question of identity asked by at least some early Christians. The partial (not parodic, but partial and in some sense strategic) "appropriation" referred to by Schwartz is not, then, on the interpretation to be offered here, a mimesis of or the product of the influence of Christianity on Judaism. It should be read, I will argue, as a kind of mimicry (in the technical postcolonial sense) and thus as an act of resistance in the sense articulated by Bhabha:

> Resistance is not necessarily an oppositional act of political intention, nor is it the simple negation or exclusion of the "content" of another culture, as a difference once perceived. It is the effect of an ambivalence produced within the rules of recognition of dominating discourses as they articulate the signs of cultural difference and reimplicate them within the deferential relations of colonial power—hierarchy, normalization, marginalization and so forth.[25]

Schwartz has given us, too, a further and more fine-grained statement of his notion of "appropriation":

> We should not be debating whether some pre-existing Jewish polity declined or prospered, or think only about relatively superficial cultural borrowing conducted by two well-defined groups. In my view, we should be looking for *systemic change:* the Jewish culture which emerged in Late Antiquity was radically distinctive, and distinctively late antique—a product of the same political, social and economic forces which produced the no less distinctive Christian culture of Late Antiquity.[26]

Schwartz, appropriately for the purposes of his book, does not further specify those forces but does set a major agenda for my own work. By entirely reenvisioning the problematic of the "parting of the ways,"[27] thinking it as a much later and very different process from that which is usually portrayed, we find the formations of Judaism and Christianity ineluctably bound up in the question of Christianization, Peter Brown's "great society going over a watershed," the "systemic change" to which Schwartz refers. If Christianity becomes, then, the symbolic religious marker of the place of the universal, transcendent, and translocal in the making of imperial power, then Judaism becomes the placeholder of the other of that universal: the particular, the ethnic, the local.[28] One of the important constructive hypotheses of my work is that *both* orthodox Christianity and "orthodox" Rabbinic Judaism, or perhaps better put, the system of orthodoxies that comprised both the church and the Rabbinic formation, was an element in the aspect of the history of Roman imperial power that was concerned with the discourse of religion, the aspect of the history that is conventionally denominated as Christianization.

Thinking Hybridity in Language

In my 1999 book *Dying for God*, I suggest that we might think of Christianity and Judaism in the second and third centuries as points on a continuum from the Marcionites, who followed the second-century Marcion in believing that the Hebrew Bible had been written by an inferior God and had no standing for Christians, and who completely denied the "Jewishness" of Christianity, on one end, to many Jews on the other end for whom Jesus meant nothing. In the middle, however, there were many gradations that provided social and cultural progression across this spectrum. In other words, to use a linguistic metaphor, I proffered a wave-theory account of Christian-Jewish history, in which innovations disseminate and interact like waves caused by stones thrown in a pond, an account in which convergence was as possible as divergence, as opposed to the traditional *Stammbaum* or family tree model, within which virtually only divergence was possible—after 70 A.D. in some versions, or after 135 A.D. in others. I argue the case via a close analysis of Christian and Jewish texts about martyrdom produced in the second, third, and fourth centuries and propose that the best way to account for many features of these texts is the assumption of shared cultural, religious innovations flowing in both directions, providing social contiguity and contact and even cultural continuity between the two religious groups in formation.[29] To put the same point in terms drawn from postcolonial studies, we must imagine, I think, a "contact zone," a space of "transculturation," where, as Mary Louise Pratt defines it, "disparate cultures meet, clash, grapple with each other, often in highly asymmetrical relations of domination and subordination."[30] The advantage of the wave-theory model for my purposes here is that it does not presuppose an originary separateness of the two cultures in question, which the colonial description tends to.[31]

The religious dialect map is a hybridized one, and the point is that the hybridity extends even to those religious groups that would consider themselves "purely" Jewish or "purely" Christian in their self-understanding. This shift in model is significant, not only for purely scholarly reasons, by which I mean that it provides a better, "truer" description of "facts," but also because it represents a shift in fundamental understandings of human difference and its meanings. Writing in an analogous context, Robert Young has said, "We may note here the insistently genetic emphasis on the metaphor of 'families' of languages, and the oft-charted language 'trees' which were to determine the whole basis of phylogenetic racial theories of conquest, absorption and decline—designed to deny the more obvious possibilities of mixture, fusion and creolization."[32] It is, then, no minor matter to revise our basic metaphors for understanding how "religions"—Christianity, Judaism, and Paganism—came into being.[33]

The wave-theory analogy can be productively extended in ways that I hope will clarify my approach to modeling the hybridity of the late ancient religious world and narrating the history of the emergence of Judaism and Christianity in late antiquity. Jonathan M. Hall has undertaken a critical rethinking of the use of ancient genealogical texts for the reconstruction of archaic Greek history.[34] Among the other issues and methods that Hall has employed in his investigation are linguistic ones, in particular *Stammbaum* versus wave theory. Traditional historiography of Greek ethnicity has assumed that the various Greek groups, as well as their dialects (Ionian, Dorian, and so forth) derived from a once unified proto-Greek. Assuming this original unity and subsequent divergence has enabled historians to construct narratives of tribal migrations and invasions in the prearchaic period. Hall mounts a critique of this methodology. Hall's argument, however, could have been enhanced by a sharper articulation of wave theory itself. Clarifying the difference between his and my understanding may prove an effective way for me to propose a first rough draft of the theory that I am developing in my work. Hall believes that wave theory, just as much as *Stammbaum* theory, presupposes primal linguistic (cultural) uniformity and merely explains the differences between dialects as owing to diffusion of innovations over various parts of the language area.[35] However, it is the virtue of wave theory, as usually understood by historical linguists, that it does *not* presuppose a unified proto-language at any point in time and imagines dialects in contiguous geographical areas becoming more like each other than previously, not less, and thus producing dialect groups. Wave theory is thus more akin to the situation that Hall himself imagines as the historical origin of groupings such as Dorian in archaic Greece, where once unrelated groups became more like each other, linguistically and otherwise, and agglomerated into the "ethnic" groups known from the archaic period.

This is a model to which I appeal as well. I am not claiming an undifferentiated "Judaism" that formed itself into Judaism and Christianity through the "borrowing" of various religious traits but rather an assortment of religious "dialects" throughout the Jewish world that gradually developed structure as clusters through diffusion and were eventually organized as "languages" (religions) through processes very much analogous to those by which national languages, such as French and Italian, were also formed. In other words, I am not denying that in the second, third, and fourth centuries there were religious groups that were more Christian than others (I shall immediately below be talking about what this comparative might mean), or that there were groups that were not Christian at all, but rather that the various Christian groups formed a dialect cluster within the overall assortment of dialects that constituted Judaism (or perhaps, better, Judaeo-Christianity) at the time.

Hall himself argues that "the clustering of dialects within dialect groups is 'a scholars' heuristic fiction.'" The linguist William Labov has also written, "But in regard to geographical dialects, it has long been argued that such gradient models are characteristic of the diffusion of linguistic features across a territory and the challenge has been to establish that boundaries between dialects are anything but arbitrary." However, Labov goes on to state, "Nevertheless, even in dialect geography, most investigators agree that properties do bundle, and that it is possible to show boundaries of varying degrees of clarity even when all variable features are superimposed upon a single map."[36] In other words, one can model a situation in which there will be persons or groups who will clearly be "Christian" or "non-Christian Jewish," that is, who will form definable clusters of religious features, while the boundaries between the two categories will remain undefinable. The eventual triumph (or even partial triumph) of orthodoxies in defining a separate identity for the two "religions" is much like the formation of national languages. Remarking that many dialects of Italian are more understandable by French speakers than by other Italians, and citing other similar phenomena, Hall writes:

What allows for this at first sight surprising phenomenon is the fact that a "national language" is seldom a higher order linguistic category which embraces and subsumes its constituent dialects. It is, rather, an invention which rarely precedes the nineteenth century and which owes its existence to reasons "that are as much political, geographical, historical, sociological and cultural as linguistic." From a linguistic point of view, there is little or no difference between a standardised national language and a dialect in terms of their hierarchical ranking within the historical structure of a language.[37]

Adding only the proviso, following Labov, that dialects do group eventually into dialect clusters, analogous to Judaism and Christianity in formation, I would suggest, once more, that this provides a powerful analogy for thinking about the history of these nascent "religions." Not via a separation, a "parting of the ways," but via choices made by different groups of different specific indicia of identity[38] and the diffusion and clustering of such indicia (such as, eventually, noncompliance with the law—hardly an essential "Christian" trait) were groups gradually congealing into Christianity and Judaism,[39] but it was only with the mobilizations of temporal power (via both ideological and repressive state apparatuses) in the fourth century that the process can be said to have formed "religions."[40] One might say that Judaism and Christianity were invented in order to explain the fact that there were Jews and Christians.

In suggesting that Judaism and Christianity were not separate entities until very late in late antiquity, I am, accordingly, not claiming that it is impossible to discern separate social groups that are in an important sense Christian / not-Jewish or Jewish / not-Christian from fairly early on (by which I mean the mid-second century). In order to make the opposite claim, even if I believed it, I would have to do a very different kind of historical research from what I am doing here. Indeed, although I do not know quite how one would show this, such "separatist" groups may have been statistically dominant much earlier than the fifth century. Thus I cannot answer empirical questions such as: How much were Christian and other Jewish congregations mixed at any given time or place? Or, what was the social status of Jewish-Christian groups; were they accepted as Jews, as Christians (by whom?), or neither at any given time?

Instead, the question that I pose is a theoretical one, or at least an interpretative one: Even if we grant the statistical dominance (and perhaps a certain power dominance, although, once more, I don't know how we would show or know this) of the separatists, in terms of the semantics of the cultural language, the discourse of the time, are there sets of features that absolutely define who is a Jew and who is a Christian such that the two categories will not seriously overlap, irrespective of the numbers of members of the blurring sets? I think not. The perspective adopted here is not unlike that of Mary Beard, John A. North, and S. R. F. Price, who write:

> Our last section in this chapter does investigate the degrees of religious continuity in these cults traceable across the Roman world. By and large, however, in discussing the religions of the empire we have tried to avoid thinking in terms of uniformity, or in terms of a central core "orthodox" tradition with its peripheral "variants"; we have preferred to think rather in terms of different religions as clusters of ideas, people and

rituals, sharing some common identity across time and place, but at the same time inevitably invested with different meanings in their different contexts.[41]

Another body of theory may help us make progress in understanding a situation in which there are recognizably separate entities within a given field but no way to articulate the borders between them. Mobilizing some recent thought in semantics might help us in thinking about this issue. These theories begin with Wittgenstein's notion of family resemblance in the formation of semantic fields.[42] In Chana Kronfeld's succinct formulation, "Members of one family share a variety of similar features: eyes, gait, hair color, temperament. But—and this is the crucial point—there need be no one set of features shared by all family members."[43] There is, perhaps, one feature that constitutes all as members of the Judaeo-Christian semantic family: appeal to the Hebrew Scriptures as revelation. In all other respects, the category of Jews/Christians constitutes a family in which any one subgroup might share features with any other (on *either* side of that supposed divide) but not all features with any, and there is no one set of features that uniquely determines a Christian group (except, of course, for some appeal to Jesus, which is simply an analytic statement and therefore tautologous) over and against a non-Christian Jewish group.

Kronfeld's work has been devoted to an entirely different classificatory problem—namely, the description of "modernism" as a literary movement—but it is relevant for my inquiry in that it has to do with groups of people and their practices and the ways that they and others (including "scholars") array people and practices into named categories (as opposed, for example, to the ways that people [including scholars/scientists] categorize plants, animals, or colors).[44] The problems and solutions that she has envisioned will, therefore, be useful for me. Kronfeld writes:

> Despite the overwhelming evidence that modernism defies reduction to simple common denominators, one study after another, after asserting the complexity and heterogeneity of the various manifestations of modernism, proceeds to attempt the impossibly positivist task of providing a definition of modernism; and this usually means, explicitly or tacitly, an attempt at what logicians call an intensional definition—namely, a list of necessary and sufficient conditions for all modernist trends. . . . While it would be nice for a theory of modernism to have the explanatory power that an intensional definition can facilitate (by showing clearly what makes all the branches of modernism part of one distinctive movement or trend), such an approach would force us to restrict severely the extension of what we could term modernist. Many important works, authors, and even entire groups that identified themselves as modernist and that are commonly perceived to be subsumed under this admittedly tattered and oversized umbrella would have to be kept out. There simply is no set of distinctive features that can apply to all the subgroupings of modernism (from futur-

ism to surrealism) and separate them from all nonmodernist groupings (classicism, baroque, romanticism, and so forth).[45]

The problem with Judaism/Christianity is somewhat different, but analogous enough for this statement of the issue to be useful for me. While, as I have said, there is one (analytic) feature that could be said to be common to all groups that we might want to call (anachronistically) "Christian," namely, some form of discipleship to Jesus, this feature hardly captures enough richness and depth to produce an interesting category, for in so many other vitally important ways, groups that follow Jesus and groups that ignore him are similar to each other. Or, put another way, groups that ignore (or reject) Jesus may have some highly salient other religious features (for instance, logos theology) that bind them to Jesus groups and disconnect them from other non–Jesus Jews, or some Jesus Jews may have aspects to their religious lives (to wit, following Pharisaic *halakha*) that draws them closer to some non–Jesus Jews than to other Jesus people.[46] Moreover, some Jesus groups might relate to Jesus in ways phenomenologically more similar to the ways that other Jewish groups relate to other prophets, leaders, or Messiahs than to the ways that other Jesus groups are relating to Jesus, and the reverse: Some non–Jesus Jews might very well have had in their religious lives elements similar to the belief in an incarnated or present mediator from God.[47] The model of family resemblance that Kronfeld develops for talking about modernism seems, therefore, apt for talking about Judaeo-Christianity as well: Judaeo-Christianity "can remain one clear category even though no two subtrends within it may share the same features."[48]

There is, however, another issue for my project that can be illuminated via Kronfeld's version of semantic categorization, because there is another problem that I face here. I am not only trying to describe a category called "Judaeo-Christianity" (I would prefer just to call it Judaism), but also to account for a division within this category that will ultimately produce a binary opposition between categories, namely, between Christianity and Judaism. The part of the theory that seems relevant for this works with what is called the "prototype theory of categorization."[49] The "prototype, in the technical sense developed by Rosen and others, is a member of the category (for example, birds) which is considered a 'best example' of that category (sparrow, swallow, or robin, but not turkey, penguin, or chicken)."[50]

Prototype semantics makes, moreover, distinctions between categories, however like family resemblances, that have clear boundaries and categories that don't. Some things may be prototypical birds, and indeed different birds can be more or less central to the category—this is called the "centrality gradience"—but in the end a given object is either a bird or it isn't. The category "bird" is not, seemingly, one with "extendable boundaries," like the categories "number" or "game." Thus, George Lakoff has written with respect to Eleanor Rosch's work:

For example, take her results showing prototype effects within the category bird. Her experimental rankings shows that subjects view robins and sparrows as the best examples of birds, with owls and eagles lower down in the rankings and ostriches, emus, and penguins among the worst examples. In the early to mid 1970s . . . such empirical goodness-of-example ratings were commonly taken as constituting a claim to the effect that membership in the category bird is graded and that owls and penguins are less members of the bird category than robins. . . . It later became clear that that was a mistaken interpretation of the data. Rosch's ratings . . . are consistent with the interpretation that the category bird has strict boundaries and that robins, owls, and penguins are all 100 percent members of that category. However, that category must have additional internal structure of some sort that produces these goodness-of-example ratings.[51]

Similarly, there may be "best examples" (prototypes) of "Jew" and "Christian" already in the second or third century with, however, an internal structure to the category that will allow other than best examples to be members of the group as well.[52] This is the semantic analogue of Labov's point about dialect grouping in language geography: Are there or are there not "objective" criteria with which such distinctions can be made? This is particularly relevant, I think, when there are different political actors in antiquity and in the present as well (both in "scholarship" and outside of it) attempting to make such determinations. "Best example" is itself a context-bound, historically shifting, and therefore political category.[53] In a situation such as the one under investigation, moreover, it can be (and is) a contested one. Another way of putting this is to say that I am inquiring whether an emu would have a different sense of what the best example of a bird is than a robin would, and, moreover, do robins get to judge what a bird is?

There is, moreover, a further wrinkle. Another kind of category has "unclear boundaries," and then, in addition to a centrality gradience, there is a "membership gradience" as well. *Judaism* and *Christianity,* I want to claim, are categories more like *red* and *tall* than like *bird* (or perhaps a fuzzy category of categories somewhere on the boundaries between categories like "bird" and categories like "tall"): "It seems to me that modernism [Judaism/Christianity] presents so many difficulties for the literary theorist [historian of religions] partly because in its different constructions it involves both centrality and membership gradience."[54] As Lakoff has argued, "Prototype effects are superficial. They may result from many factors. In the case of a graded category like *tall man*, which is fuzzy and does not have rigid boundaries, prototype effects may result from degree of category membership, while in the case of *bird*, which does have rigid boundaries, the prototype effects must result from some other aspect of internal category structure."[55] Lakoff does not emphasize (at least at that juncture) that there is another consequence of this difference between types of categories. One cannot be both a *bird* and a *fish*, but one can be both a *tall* man and a *short* man. Moreover, I suspect that this latter form of category is typically the case for the human construction of categories of the human and that much human violence is generated simply by resisting the fuzziness of our own categories of sociocultural division. Just as certain entities can be more or less tall or red, I wish to suggest they can be more or less Christian (or Jewish) as well. And just as certain entities can be tall and short given different perspectives, so too can certain people or groups be Christian or Jewish from different perspectives, or both.[56] Indeed, the determination itself will be a matter of contention. Jerome's very important notice that the sect of the Nazarenes are to be found "in all of the synagogues of the East among the Jews" and that they consider themselves both Christians and Jews but are really "neither Christians nor Jews" is emblematic of this point.[57]

Let us imagine that "Jew" and "Christian" are both categories with gradations of membership. Moreover, while both have "central" members (which can be different at different times and even at the same time for different groups), there will be a semantic (and in this case, therefore, social)[58] chain that connects the most central and salient members to others: "Another case is where I call *B* by the same name as *A*, because it resembles *A*, *C* by the same name because it resembles *B*, *D* . . . and so on. But ultimately A and say D do not resemble each other in any recognizable sense at all. This is a very common case: and the dangers are obvious when we search for something 'identical' in all of them!"[59]

The net result will be that there might indeed be people who are prototypes of *Jew* but also *Christian* (say, a Pharisee who observes all of the Pharisaic laws and rules but believes that Jesus is the Messiah) and, moreover, that the "best example" of *Jew* and *Christian* would almost definitely be both a politically charged and a diachronically varying category. Further, while there would be *Jews* who would not recognize certain other Jews as such, there might be ones whom they would recognize as Jews who would recognize in turn those others as Jews, setting up the possibility of chained communion or communication. An example of this phenomenon (from the other "side") would be Justin, who recognizes as Christians precisely those Jewish Christians to whom Jerome, much later of course, would deny the name *Christian*, even though Jerome would have certainly recognized Justin as Christian. Those so-called Jewish Christians surely thought of themselves as both Jews and Christians, and some non-Christian Jews may very well have recognized them as Jews as well.

Therefore, with respect to religious history we must add yet another factor, which may be less relevant to a literary movement like modernism (although probably equally salient for something like "Marxism"), to wit, the activities of writers/speakers who wish to transform the fuzzy category into one with absolutely clear borders and the family resemblance into a checklist of features that will determine an intensional definition for who is in and who is out of the group as it defines itself and, therefore, its others.[60] Returning to the wave-theory metaphor, these are the legislators who wish, as well, to determine and enforce clear boundaries between languages, to decide what is orthodox French and what is orthodox Italian. These are the writers whom we now know of as heresiologists. The discursive practice known as heresiology was crucial in the formation of Judaism and Christianity as religions, for all that it appeared in very different textual guise in each of these cultures.[61]

CHAPTER 7

The Name *God* in Blanchot

Jean-Luc Nancy

This title is neither a provocation nor a cover for an insidious kidnapping attempt. It is not a question of trying to smuggle Blanchot over to the side of the new *political correctness* (and thus indecency) that takes the form of a "return to religion," as unsound and insipid as are all "returns."

It is merely a question of this. Blanchot's thought is demanding, vigilant, uneasy, and alert enough not to have thought itself obliged to adhere to the atheistic *correctness* or requisite expression of antireligious feeling that was *de rigueur* in his day. Not that his thought was in any way caught up in a countervailing declaration of faith—it is true that Blanchot affirms a form of atheism, but he does so only to dismiss atheists and theists alike.

That takes place in a major text in *The Infinite Conversation*, "Atheism and Writing: Humanism and the Cry," in which atheism is associated with writing.[1] I shall return to this point, without, however, quoting or analyzing this text, no more than I will any other. In the context of and space allotted for this essay, no analysis can be carried out. I will limit myself to allusions to a few Blanchotian topoi in order to suggest a direction for subsequent work.

To reject in the same gesture both atheism and theism means to consider first and foremost the point that the atheism of the West (or the double atheism of monotheism: the one it causes and the one it secretly bears within itself) has thus far never pitted against or set in the place of God anything other than a different figure, instance, or idea of the supreme punctuation of a sense: an end, a good, a parousia—that is, an accomplished presence, especially that of man. It is for that very reason that what is at stake in the association of atheism with writing—a provisional one, preliminary to the joint deposition of the claims of theism and atheism—is the displacement of atheism in the direction of an absenting of sense, of which, it is true, so far no notable atheistic figure has been capable (unless it may be in the figure, so close to Blanchot, of the *atheology* of Bataille—of which I will say no more here).

The "absent sense," that expression Blanchot sometimes risks, does not designate a sense whose essence or truth is to be found in its absence. That would be transformed ipso facto into a modality of presence no less substantial than the presence most assured, most *being*. But an "absent sense" makes sense in and by its very absenting, in such a way that, in sum, it never stops not "making sense." Thus it is that "writing" designates for Blanchot—as well as in the community of thinking that connects him with Bataille and Adorno, Barthes and Derrida—the movement of exposure to the flight of sense that withdraws signification from "sense" in order to give it the very sense of that flight—an *élan*, an opening, an indefatigable exposure that consequently does not even "flee," that flees flight as well as presence—neither nihilism nor the idolatry of a signified and/or a signifier. This is what is at stake in an "atheism" that owes it to itself to deny itself the position of the negation it proffers and the assurance of every sort of presence that could substitute for that of God—that is, the presence of the signifier of absolute signification or signifiability.

Now it so happens that Blanchot's text is devoid of any interest in religion (beyond the fact that a Christian—a specifically Catholic—culture shows through here and there in a remarkable way, which will have to be examined elsewhere), yet the name *God* is not simply absent from it. Precisely, one might affirm that it occupies, within the text, the very particular place of a name that flees and yet returns, finding itself alternately (not very frequently, but often enough to be noticeable) firmly distanced, then evoked in its very distance as the site or as the index of a form of intrigue of the absenting of sense.

(Again, although it is totally out of the question to go into the texts here, I simply suggest a rapid rereading of *Thomas the Obscure* [first and second versions], *The Infinite Conversation*, and *The Writing of Disaster* or *The Last to Speak*,[2] to verify at least from a formal point of view the presence of the word *God*—even if at times only latently—and the manifestly diverse, complex, or even enigmatic modalities of its role or tenor.)

If the name *God* comes in the place of an absenting of sense, or in the line of flight, so to speak, and in the perspective at once infinite and without depth of field of that same line of flight, that is primarily because this name does not involve an existence but precisely the nomination (and this is neither designation nor signification) of that absenting. There is, then, in this respect, no "question of God" that is to be asked as the ritualistic question of the existence or nonexistence of a supreme being. Such a question cancels itself out automatically (as we have known since Kant, and in fact from much earlier), since a supreme being would have to be indebted for its being or for being altogether to some authority or some power (terms obviously very inappropriate) impossible to classify within the order of beings.

This is why the most precious gift of philosophy is, for Blanchot, not even in the operation of the negation of the existence of God, but in a simple shrinking away, a dissipation of that existence. Thought does not think unless it is from this point of departure.

Blanchot, therefore, neither asks nor authorizes any "question of God," but he additionally posits and says that that question "*is not to be asked.*" This means that it is not a question—that it does not correspond to the schema of the demand for the assignment of a place within being ("What is . . . ?" or "Is there . . . ?"). God is not within the jurisdiction of a question. That does not mean that he falls within an affirmation that would answer the question in advance. Nor does he fall within a negation. It is not that there is or is not a God. It is, quite differently, that there is the name *God*, or rather that the name *God* is spoken. This name corresponds to a *statement* of the question, whether it is a question of the being (the "What?"), of the origin (the "Through what?"), or of sense (the "For what?"). If all questions intend a "what," a something, the name *God* corresponds to the order, the register, or the modality of what is not, or has not, any thing.

Moreover, this name sometimes appears in Blanchot alongside words such as *being* (as taken from Heidegger), or *neutral*. For them as well, the question is not to be asked, for it is already deposited within them. But they are words (concepts), whereas *God* is a name (without concept). The name *God* must, then, represent something other than a concept here; more precisely, it must bear and bring to a head a trait common to names as such: to be at the extremity and the extenuation of sense.

The same may be said, no doubt, of this name and of the name *Thomas*, who might be called the eponymous hero of Blanchot's writing. In the story titled *Thomas the Obscure*, a narration in the course of which God appears and intervenes on several occasions, the name *Thomas* is sometimes referred to as "the word *Thomas.*" The word *thauma*, in Greek, means "marvel, prodigy, miracle." As a concept, "Thomas" presents the miracle or mystery of the name qua name.

The name *God* is said by Blanchot, on occasion, to be "too imposing." That qualification, mixed with fear or reverence, is open to two interpretations. Either this name is too imposing because it claims to impose, and impose itself, as the keystone of an entire system of sense, or else it is majestic and awesome to the degree that it reveals the nonsignification of names. In the second case, this name names a sovereign power of the name that beckons—which is very different from signifying—toward that absenting of sense such that no absence can come to supply a supposedly lost or rejected presence. "God," then, would name neither the God subject to sense nor the negation of this in favor of another subject of sense or non-sense. *God* would be the name of that which—or of he or she who—in the name escapes nomination to the degree that nomination can always border on sense. In this hypothesis, this name would de-name names in general, while persisting in naming—that is, in *calling*. That which is called, and that toward which it is called, are in no regard of another order than what Blanchot designates, on occasion, "the emptiness of the sky." But the appeal to and in this emptiness inserts in this name a sort of ultimate punctuation—though without a *last word* . . . to the abandonment *of* sense that also forms the truth of an abandonment *to* sense insofar as the latter exceeds itself. The name *God* would indicate or proffer that call.

To the coupling of atheism with writing Blanchot adds, in the same text and under the same title, the association of humanism and the cry. The humanism of the cry would be a humanism that abandons all idolatry of man and all anthropo-theology. If it is not exactly in the register of writing, it is not in that of discourse, either—but it cries out. Precisely, it "cries out in the desert," Blanchot writes. It is no accident that he takes up a watchword phrase of biblical prophecy. The prophet is the one who speaks for God and of God, who announces to others the call of and recall to God. There is no motif here of any return to religion, but rather an attempt to extract for himself, out of the monotheistic heritage, its essential and essentially nonreligious trait—the trait of an atheism or of what one might call an *absentheism*, beyond all positing of an object of belief or disbelief. Almost in spite of himself, and as if at the extreme limit of his text, Blanchot did not yield on the name *God*—on the unacceptable name *God*—because he knew that it was still necessary to name the call unnamable, the interminable call to in-nomination.

Translated by Michael B. Smith.

CHAPTER 8

Humanism's Cry

On Infinity in Religion and Absence in Atheism—
A Conversation with Blanchot and Nancy

Laurens ten Kate

Religion as Bond? A Fragment in Blanchot

In 1980, in *The Writing of the Disaster*, Maurice Blanchot formulates a question concerning the word that haunts the pages of this volume on words: the word *religion*. "Haunting" is indeed an appropriate expression here, for Blanchot confronts religion—its concept, its definition—with what seems to be its opposite. Religion binds people, constituting their individual identity and collective unity; religion underlies,[1] supports and "builds" our "I" and our "we," contingent and finite as they are, in the direction of a tradition in which people recognize themselves, distinguishing them and ultimately closing them off from other traditions. Religion feeds the mechanism of the "bond," thereby making our lives livable: livable, because more or less self-evident and "natural"— the religious bond keeps our symbolic spheres and cages closed,[2] even in a time of globalization. The "secular" worldviews of modernity, like humanism, are religion's twin in this respect. Similar bonding mechanisms, aimed at building a distinctive tradition of one's own, apply to nonreligious religions. The appeal to the Enlightenment and its achievements, for instance, and the necessity of universal moral principles founded on the equally universal force of human reason often serve to bind "us" as against others who do not belong to this tradition.

However, in his own unique way, writing in fragments and posing uncertain questions, Blanchot challenges us to rethink religion, to go beyond this concept,[3] simply because religion as bond is becoming hopelessly inadequate in the face of the complex and turbulent inter- and cross-cultural movements that characterize our contemporary globalized existence. This concept of religion, with the experiences and desires belonging to it, is becoming an illusionary force, albeit still an appealing and strong one. The cages are being opened, and we would be well advised to relate to this opening.

So, Blanchot asks, what about the opposite? What about the non-bond? Is nonbinding really the opposite of religion as a binding force? Blanchot hints at a different definition of religion by suggestively wondering if the non-bond would automatically be nonreligious. His wondering involves critical doubt, too, almost silently. For even if one accepts that religion is a phenomenon that binds people, there may be something strange about this bond. Maybe religion is a bond only in the sense that it opens this bond to its dissolution, to the non-bond. Pursuing his ongoing, endless conversation with Levinas on what religion could possibly be, Blanchot starts from religion's etymology, that of the Latin *religare* ("connecting, binding"), inviting us to move beyond this concept and to address an unstable—that is, endless—possibility hidden in this definition of religion as a binding force. Blanchot suggests a disclosure of the definition of the bonding tradition by opening religion toward the infinity of a relation that is never at rest: Blanchot suggests that we understand the bond and the non-bond as a reciprocal dynamic, the one always presupposing, always haunting the other.

If, as Levinas affirms, religion is etymologically that which binds, that which holds together, then what of the non-bond, which escapes the synchrony of holding together, yet does so without breaking all relations or without ceasing, in this break or in this absence of relation, to open yet another relation? Must one be nonreligious for that to come about?[4]

Blanchot's suggestion that religion be opened up toward its own specific infinity affects humanism and its claim to being nonreligious. To question the bond of religion is immediately to question atheism. We will examine this double questioning shortly by reading a complex but programmatic text by Blanchot on the relation between religion and atheism. Let me summarize what is at stake in this examination by offering my own preliminary statement: a thesis that will have to be tested.

Insofar as modern humanism aims to be an atheism, defined as a polemical "no" to religion, it suppresses its complexity and complicity with religion. This implies that modern humanism can never claim to be atheistic. It will have to think and experience itself in connection with the history of religion and religions. There is no universal and neutral humanism rising above the particularities and turbulence of religion.

Religion, Relation, and Infinity

Blanchot asks for an understanding of religion beyond the bond, questioning the etymological reduction to *religare*. But this beyond is not a beyond. Blanchot argues that religion could be the stage for a restless relation between bond and non-bond. In religion, the non-bond—the implosion of tradition and the identities, relations, synchrony, and unity it produces—presents itself as an interruption, a break in religion's binding force, but this does not entail the destruction of all relationality. On the contrary, it opens up a new relation, and this relation has but one adjective, one name: infinite. It is both an infinite relation and a relation to infinity; attribute and address go together. Infinity is not some higher, divine realm here; in fact, it "is" nothing. It "happens" continuously as a destabilizing force between bond and non-bond, between settled traditions and hybrid figurations, between belonging and wandering exposure.

This also implies that the infinite and the finite coincide in religion. They no longer fulfill the same role in the metaphysical configurations of our "axial" history, as Karl Jaspers once named it.[5] They no longer form an opposition: Instead, infinity enters the finite; the finite opens the infinite. In the fragments of *The Writing of the Disaster* preceding and following his formulation of the question of religion, it becomes clear that the suggestion of a new concept—probably beyond any stable conception—of religion is connected to a new relation with the other (i.e., the other of identity, of the bond, of tradition: of that by which the self is distinguished and then immunized from the other). Let us assume, for he never describes it explicitly, that Blanchot is staging an experimental definition of religion in these passages. "Beyond the bond" would then not mean simply leaving any bond behind. Rather, religion would be the stage for a continuous oscillation *between* bond and non-bond, performed in millions of different rituals, practices, meditations, narratives, doctrines, images, art, music. Religion would be the *praxis* in which "a finite I . . . necessarily comes to recognize, in the other, its responsibility for the infinite."[6]

In this context, the other refers neither to some distant realm of alterity nor to the other person. The other happens within the self, as the disjoining of the self: the self opening itself to the other side of itself that consists in its nonnaturalness, its nonbelonging to itself. This predicament the finite "I" finds itself in (it can only be "I," but "I" already means I am another, I am never "presence-to-self," as Jacques Derrida would say)[7] is described a few fragments earlier by Blanchot, as if he were slowly building his argument in the form of a series of steps—hints—toward the central passage on religion's bond and non-bond: "In a sense, the 'I' cannot be lost, since it does not belong to itself. It only is, therefore, as not its own, and therefore always already lost."[8]

Is the infinite this gap in the I, this impossibility to be, to say "I" that, paradoxically, seems to be the only way in which the I is? And is religion indeed the stage where the "responsibility for the infinite," as Blanchot calls it, is performed by this I? Yes, but only by an I that recognizes its own other, and in this other the infinite relation that the I *is*. In consequence, the finite (the I, the bond the I needs to constitute itself) becomes entangled with the infinite (the other, the non-bond that every bond presupposes). Blanchot repeats the same complicated thought by inverting it in the next fragment, the last one before he comes to speak of religion. Here, he uses the word *limited* for finite: for the finite I limits itself by means of bonds it can identify with. The bond is always a limitation, a limit with regard to the other. Nevertheless, this I, *being* this limit, appears to defy it at the same time, being infinite: "It is only inasmuch I am infinite that I am limited."[9]

Then, directly after the key question on religion ("Must one be nonreligious for that?") a final, rather mysterious question: "Infinite-limited, is it you?"[10] Who is addressed here? Who is this "you"? Is it the I that has so far been located between infinity and finitude, as their relation? Is it the other, the other in the I? Or is it another name, another figure, another "you" who is invoked?

Religion and Atheism

What are the implications of these fragments surrounding Blanchot's remarkable questions about the nature of religion and unbinding: "Must one be nonreligious for that?" This question is almost a provocation, first of all against religion: One has to be atheist to understand the complexities of religion. Those who do not belong to the bond know more about its interconnectedness with the non-bond. Maybe they even know better how to appreciate, how to believe in such a new religion. Yet Blanchot almost seems to claim that this atheism does not leave religion behind but offers a new perspective on it. Is classic atheism still tenable in this ambiguous relation to religion? Or do we have to formulate a new form of atheism, analogous to our quest for a new concept of religion?

Putting pressure on the opposition between atheism and religion had been part of Blanchot's program since the 1940s.[11] The most extensive critical study of this opposition takes place in a chapter of *The Infinite Conversation* entitled "Atheism and Writing, Humanism and the Cry."[12] In "The Name *God* in Blanchot," Jean-Luc Nancy mentions this crucial text, confirming that it "dismisses atheists and theists alike."[13] As we will see, both Nancy and Blanchot offer ways into the classic understanding of both religion and humanism by sharing the experimental and often tentative project of a redefinition of religion and atheism in the twentieth and twenty-first centuries. Nancy's own project of a deconstruction of monotheism and of Christianity in particular is in many ways a continuation of the intuitive research Blanchot had initiated in the 1960s.

Nancy modestly refrains from analyzing Blanchot's "Atheism and Writing" and "limits himself to allusions to a few Blanchotian topoi in order to suggest a direction for subsequent work." Still, he has already made an important decision: To problematize the atheism-religion opposition is to engage in a new discussion of the "name" of "God." In a brief coda I will address that discussion.

But before I take up the challenge of analyzing "Atheism and Writing," let me articulate how, influenced by Blanchot, Nancy opens up the difficult issue of the entanglement of finitude and infinity, making it to one of the central themes in his entire work.

The "Human": "Nothing Other Than Infinity"

Man is a finite being. Human life is finite; one has to die. Human words and acts are finite, because they always reach a moment in which they meet their end and are no longer valid. In a straightforward sense, "finite" means never acquiring absolute status, never being able to "loose oneself" (Latin: *ab-solvere*) from the ends (Latin: *finis*, "end, or goal, aim")[14] and limits set to human existence. Both Blanchot and Nancy affirm this basic statement.

But having said this, what of the opposite of finite life, what of infinity? Is it the absolute, endless, unlimited life of the gods, of God, or of any higher power (Emperor, *Führer*, magnate)? No, Nancy tells us time and again, from his earlier readings of Kant and Bataille to his book *A Finite Thinking* and on to his later works on the "deconstruction of monotheism."[15] Staying close to Blanchot's reflections, he emphasizes that infinity is not a realm that stands opposed to the finite, and, in consequence, that one should avoid confining finite life in some dualistic structure. In order to support this argument, Nancy proposes a distinction between two concepts of the finite: *finité* and *finitude*,[16] provisionally translatable as "finiteness" and "finitude." This distinction is expressed clearly in the brief afterword Nancy wrote for a book by Martin Crowley.[17]

> Thinking finitude is not the same as thinking finiteness. . . . Finiteness is the order of the finite as being limited and as lacking infinity—the classic concept of the "finite." Finitude . . . indicates nothing else than the "finite" in the sense that it reaches, in its end [*dans sa fin*], the infinite. Here, the end does not become the marking of an essential incompleteness, but on the contrary the index of this: that (no completeness whatsoever being possible, and beyond any totality that could be achieved) the finite exposes the infinity that it actually *is*.[18]

Remarkably, Nancy thinks finitude as no more than an "index," a finger pointing at the impossibility of itself. It is in this "pointing at" its own limits that finitude shows its infinity. The impossibility of achieving its "end" *is* the *End-lichkeit* (to use Heidegger's term), the finitude that is brought into play here. It is the impossibility of a *finition* (lit.: "ending," the very act of bringing something to an end), Nancy writes, that is, of a final limitation or closure as produced by the bond we analyzed above: the bond as the essence of religion contested by Blanchot. It is, in other words, the impossibility of *finition* as identity, essence, or fixed tradition: in sum, the impossibility of the bond, of the *religare* of religion, in all its different forms and expressions. To take the argument one step further, it is the impossibility of the "classic concept" (as Nancy calls it above) of infinity as opposed to finiteness, where the infinite envelops, transcends, and supersedes the finite in view of compensating for its incompleteness.

Finitude is like a stamp on finite being, the stamp of the impossibility of attributing to this being something like an "essence" and thus also a "sense" or a "goal" [*fin*]. Finite being is that being to which one cannot give its ending [*finition*]. Because of the impossibility of any completeness (solution, achievement, satisfaction), it opens us to the infinite.[19]

We may then conclude that, according to Nancy, the impossibility of the "old" infinity opens the possibility of a "new" conceptualization of infinity.[20] This new infinity is nothing in itself: It is a relation with what *in* this ongoing "ending" (a life coming to an end in death; an act, word, or phrase that loses its meaning and hence is forgotten, replaced by other gestures and statements; the I who, despite all its self-identifications, remains a mystery to itself; a group or community that, despite its self-determination, fails to reach unity) just cannot come to an "end."

The consequences for finite being, for man, for the "human," are clear. The sense of a human, of *l'homme*, no longer resides in himself, in his "true self" as his "true humanity," binding his being together toward the fulfillment of completeness (in this respect, even humanism is a form of religion, that is, of a bonding practice).[21] The meaning of being human lies precisely in being infinitely in trouble with these bonding foundations. Why? Because these foundations, although they are an inextricable part of human existence—an existential "need," so to speak—do not found anything. They are *fonds-sans-fond*, a key concept in the philosophy of difference, from Heidegger's thinking of the *Ungrund* to Derrida. This being without a founding sense is articulated well by Martin Crowley in his formulation of *l'homme sans* (man without . . .): The *sens* is in the *sans*. Nancy adds in his afterword to Crowley's book, "'*L'homme sans*' . . . opens the question—gaping—of what 'human' could be. Doubtlessly, human can be nothing else than the infinite."[22]

The result of all this is that finitude and infinitude have become complementary concepts, which can only be grasped together, one out of the other. In the end both concepts tend to become synonymous, as if they formed a tautology. This is also true for another pair of concepts that plays a vital role in Blanchot's and Nancy's thought: that of presence and absence. Much of Blanchot's and Nancy's philosophical adventure is dedicated to the chances and possibilities offered by these tautologies. Needless to say, this type of tautology has little to do with static equality; it concerns a dynamic relation breaking out of an oppositional structure.

And what about God, what about religion?

Infinity and Religion

In principle, Nancy's conceptualization of infinity pertains to all themes discussed in his work: to the community, democracy, and the political in general; to sense, world, and globalization; to thought and reason itself. In all these fields of research, Nancy focuses on "opening up" his subject matter to a "remainder" it cannot control: to its "other." In this way he radically and consistently tries to expose an infinite or limitless moment or dimension within his topic. Nancy's treatment of reason, especially in its Kantian form, is one of the prime examples of this approach. According to Nancy, rationality can never be self-sufficient and self-closing, as if it were a "natural" foundation for human life, needing no further questioning. "It is, however, a question of opening . . . reason to the limitlessness that constitutes its truth," Nancy states at the very beginning of *Dis-Enclosure*,[23] strongly criticizing scientific humanism, neo-positivism, and political rationalism. Reason does not find truths in itself, but only by entering into a relation with unreason, by going outside itself and addressing the "remainder" that does not fit its strategies, methods, and discourse.

It is striking that Nancy often places the analysis of this "infinitizing" movement in the context of a discussion of religion. The quotation above, for example, is directed against Kant's project of rethinking religion "within the limits of reason alone." Although Nancy repeatedly explains that he does not intend to "revive" religion, to "save" it,[24] or to renew or even improve its definition, it is a religion, Christianity (so he claims), that "designates nothing other, essentially (that is to say simply, *infinitely* simply: through an inaccessible simplicity), than the demand to open in this world an alterity or an unconditional alienation."[25] Alterity and alienation are the features of the infinite relation analyzed above. Blanchot and Nancy are looking for the complex tautology of finitude and infinity, and in a way they strive to rethink it, if not to "revive" it, then certainly to bring it to life in an unexpected way. In doing so, they claim to shed new light on "religion," "faith," the "divine," and "God"—not on what these would "be," but on what these words, concepts, names could mean. But the reverse is true as well. It is religion that may well shed new light on the infinite relation:

> Christianity assumes, in the most radical and explicit fashion, what is at stake in the *alogon* [lit.: what is outside the *logos*, outside reason] . . . the "other world" or the "other kingdom" never was a second world, or even a world-behind-the-worlds, but the other of the world (*of every world: of all consistency tied up in beings and in communication*), the other than any world. Christianity can be summed up, as Nietzsche, for one, knew well, in the precept of living in this world as outside of it—in the sense that this "outside" is not, [or] not an entity. It does not exist, but it (or again, since it) defines and mobilizes ex-istence: the opening of the world to inaccessible alterity (and consequently a paradoxical access to it).[26]

In a note to these passages Nancy explains that the movement of this infinite opening, which is almost passionately present in his writings, has "the form of the active infinite," borrowing that expression from Derrida. Here we see that infinity is also approached by Nancy as the presence of absence ("nothing"): a thought that is central to Blanchot's work, as well: "the active infinite: thus, the act, the actual and active presence of the *nothing* qua thing (*res*) of the opening itself. Here and now, death, the truth, birth, the world, the thing, and the outside."[27]

Infinity and God

Finally, in "The Name *God* in Blanchot," Nancy shows how the movement of the infinite applies to humans ("human can be nothing else than the infinite"), as well as to God. To be more precise, the name *God* stands opposed to God as an "existence" in a realm detached from, but ruling over, the realm of humans (as it stands opposed to the infinite as binding completion, fulfillment, absoluteness). It is presented as the "actual infinite" presenting absence as presence and vice versa. Wondering why the name *God* is not at all absent from the language of an atheist thinker like Blanchot, Nancy states, "If the name *God* comes in the place of an absenting of sense, or in the line of flight, so to speak, and in the perspective at once infinite and without depth of field of that same line of flight, that is primarily because this name does not involve an existence but precisely the nomination . . . of that absenting."[28]

God is a line of flight, an infinite movement, but this movement does not aim to reach some "content." It is "without depth," a "simple" and concrete relation to what escapes me, every day, every hour: the other, my other, my "remainder." This infinite cannot be proven or appropriated (it doesn't need existence or reality). It can only be "nominated" (i.e., "named") and (here Nancy again uses a Christian concept) addressed in "adoration," the title of the second volume of his project of the deconstruction of Christianity.[29] In adoration, literally the act of "speaking to God" (Latin: *orare* plus *ad*), the addressant of adoration, the human, and the addressee, immediately revert to absence. No longer is either subject present to itself, simply part of a relation in which the event of the address takes over from both addressing and addressed subjects. "Man feels himself to be annihilated by the feeling of adoration: It reduces him to nothing."[30] But similarly, God as addressee of the adoration is a "presence" who is nothing in itself: His "presence gives or presents itself when it is 'addressed.'"[31] This God is only, is *named* only, in the relation. In the relation to finitude lies his infinity.

So we arrive at a rather surprising turning point in Nancy's account of the non-oppositional, "actual" relations that are the driving force behind his thought: finitude-infinity, presence-absence. At first, it was the human described as "infinite"; now it is God who merits the same description. In a way, this is consistent with Nancy's theorem: Both finite beings and the infinite God should be approached from the perspective of their mutual infinity—their *relation*. Outside of this relation (of address, of adoration, of *kenosis* and incarnation, to stick with the Christian discourse), they are nothing.

We started our analysis of infinity with Blanchot's critical comment on the *religare* as the accepted meaning of religion (which can also be found in Levinas): the bond. But what of the non-bond? We have seen how the confrontation with the non-bond introduces us to a new type of relation between finitude and infinity, in which reciprocal address (man to God, God to man) is more important than a logic of identification by "binding." Address, which Nancy conceives as adoration, is an "alienation," not an identification. This seems to be a critical stance toward *religare*, religion as a binding practice. However, the Latin etymologic root of religion has been debated since Antiquity, and different readings of the etymological roots of the word *religion* contradict the tracing of religion to *religare*, usually determined as a Christian invention.[32] They propose a different etymological meaning, one that has everything to do with address: *relegere*. This word is not completely devoid of a "binding" connotation, since it indicates "bringing together in order to return and begin again," as Derrida summarizes it.[33] But what is begun here is not the forming of a bond—between people, between God and man, as the realm of obligation—but the renewal of a relation by choosing new rituals, new formulas, and so on. *Relegere* is always an address to the divine power, bearing an element of creativity in it—hence the noun *religio*, which gradually will receive the meaning of "scrupulous attention, respect, patience, modesty."[34] Couldn't Blanchot's critical questions regarding *religare* and Nancy's articulation of religion as address be seen as unconscious rephrasings of *relegere*?

Infinite Religion, Infinite Humanism: Back to Blanchot

We have seen that Nancy presents both "God" and the "human" as names for the infinite. It may therefore be worthwhile to shift our discussion of religion to what is often considered to be its opposite: humanism. Can we treat humanism, however multiple its historical and contemporary forms and expressions, along the same theoretical lines: as a "worldview" oscillating between bond and non-bond, installing through this oscillation a rapport with infinity? And if so, what of a particularly modern feature of humanism: its antireligious attitude, its atheism?

Let us take a closer look at Blanchot's "Atheism and Writing, Humanism and the Cry," which also serves as the starting point for Nancy's brief explorations in "The Name God in Blanchot." Within the confines of this essay, it is impossible to do justice to the whole of Blanchot's text; I will concentrate on its first, programmatic sections, then conclude with the very last.

The Future of a Humanism without Future

Blanchot concludes the short introduction to "Atheism and Writing, Humanism and the Cry" with these surprised questions:

Why this sensitivity of a paranoiac character which . . . immediately leads some particular individual to feel he is being targeted, provoked, assailed, and wounded each
time it is a question of "man?" The end of humanism? As though ever since Feuerbach, who gave it its most energetic form, humanism had not been constantly knocked
about and rejected by all important research. Why then this uneasiness, this indig-
nant rumor?[35]

The essay that follows is a philosophical and historical study of what humanism *is*, in its
connection with modern history, and of what it *might be* in an unrevealed future. In its
final sentences, Blanchot again surprises his readers by announcing that the future of
humanism lies in the deferral of any thought of a future. Waiting for this future is "the
wait without hope that breaks up in the 'humanist' cry."[36]

Why does Blanchot not see humanism as a more or less well-defined tradition (one
worldview among others): a means of identification with a clear definition of man, a
moral ideal and a social movement? Why should it be determined only on the basis of
self-criticism and the criticism of others ("all important research"), that is, on the basis
of its "end"?

Why should humanism be no more than a "cry"?

When "Atheism and Writing" was first published, in 1967, as an article in *La Nouvelle
Revue Française*,[37] the Western world was full of hopes for the future. Expectations of a
better world were everywhere, and the pathos of emancipation of those advocating a new
humanism was rapidly conquering the scene of public debate. Blanchot's article formed a
critical interruption in and deconstructive analysis of this debate: What, he asks the
reader, do we say when we say "humanism," when we worry about its presumed "end" or
rejoice in its "future"? And what do we do when we speak about "man," about "humanity"? When did we start to speak about "man" and to study him? Blanchot poses the last
question in dialogue with a book that was then brand-new and causing quite a stir: Michel
Foucault's *The Order of Things*, in which the author claims that "man" is a very recent
invention, introduced by the emerging human sciences at the start of the nineteenth century. In "Atheism and Writing," Blanchot discusses Foucault's book at length, and he
largely follows Foucault's provocative thesis: Modern humanism is a sign of late modern
times, and when times change, modern humanism will disappear.

But Blanchot's avalanche of questions has not yet finished. Even if we assume that
humanism *is* something and take this something seriously, is humanism identical with
the humanism Foucault problematizes? And is it identical with atheism? Does it lead to a
farewell to religion and theology? Does its future lie there?[38]

One of the uncertainties of postwar humanism consists in its troubled relation to
another time of change and anticipation of the future whose violence and terror were still
fresh in memory: those of the Third Reich. Particularly in his later works, Blanchot consistently connects any belief in a new world to the horror of a few decades earlier. In this

sense he always remained close to the views of his friend Georges Bataille, who had died in 1962. Bataille tried to examine the excessive and explosive violence of the twentieth century from a position of critical complicity, thus creating an impossible role for himself within a culture that believed passionately in man, in reason—in a better future.

A key question begins to emerge from the dialogue between Blanchot and Nancy on religion that I proposed in the opening sections of this essay. We started with Blanchot's question "What of the non-bond?" with which he appears to challenge both religious and humanist traditions, a question that Nancy takes up. The result of this dialogue was a new theorem of the twin concepts of finitude and infinity, followed by theorems of self and other. These theorems were applied to the "names" "God" and "man." But what of man? What if man's infinity—the infinite relation he is as a finite being—implies that his presence is always at the same time an absence? What is a human being as a being who plays out his existence between presence and absence? A being who lives his own absence? What sort of humanism could feed on this paradox?

Blanchot Reading Hegel

The analysis of absence that commences in section 3 of "Atheism and Writing" and remains central in most of its following ten sections is prefigured by a reading of Hegel in section 2. Again, the finitude of man—conceptualized as a "place" for (the relation with) infinity—is at stake here: the finitude of a finite being who, qua finite, is always "vanishing," as the title of section 2 reads.

For Hegel, seen through Blanchot's eyes, the death of God is neither a historical *factum* inherent in the process of secularization nor the logical by-product of the emergence of modern man. The death of God belongs intrinsically to God and his sovereignty—to his divinity as being free of the limits, needs, obligations, and pleasures of the human world. Only God can prove and realize the meaning of his sovereignty even in dying, and by this he gives death its radiant glory. Only God has an active "right to death";[39] humans only undergo death. There is something in God that dies permanently, but this something is all he is: He is dying, and as such he lives. This limit between finitude (dying) and infinity (life, but life that means dying time and again, which is to say, infinite finitude) can be inhabited only by God. The narrative of Christ's death and the symbolism of the cross that Christianity has adopted are intriguing examples of this double dimension that only God can embody: in this case, the limit between divinity and humanity, the limit of incarnation.

Only God has the right to death. At least, that was the situation until the medieval world gradually fell apart. After the modern rupture with the Middle Ages, "now it falls to man to die."[40] Modern man claims the right to death, and from that moment sovereignty is nothing anymore, as Bataille repeatedly states. As soon as man no longer places the meaning of and power over finitude in a figure who is infinite (God and his representatives on earth: the clerical hierarchy, linked up with the nobility and with the monarch), he turns finitude into a daily project, a mundane event. Blanchot cites Bataille: "The sovereign is no longer a king: he is hidden in our great cities, he surrounds himself with silence."[41]

But what does this project of modern man look like? It is the act of *negation*, Hegel says, an act that can be seen as a secular transformation of Christian self-negation and ascetic life. The everyday labor of negation means that man claims the capacity to step outside himself and the world he lives in—a self and a world that are no longer given to us by God. In consequence, self, world, and God have lost their self-evident status of serving as a foundation. On the contrary, the self and the world change into empty, bottomless spaces, to be explored and ultimately appropriated by man. Man claims ownership over himself and the world, but in order to do so, he must negate, must lose himself. He must leave himself if he wants to acquire sovereignty. This is precisely what the prostitute Edwarda, the protagonist of Bataille's short story "Madame Edwarda" and the "sovereign" referred to in the quotation above, performs. Striving for sovereignty, desiring infinity—that is, longing for the limit between finitude and infinity that once belonged to God—Edwarda risks herself and her client (the "I" in the story) in an excessive ramble through the streets of Paris, defying the protecting walls of the brothel to "hide silently in the great city." The prostitute, the extreme outsider, is presented as the prototype of modern man, of the modern God. The knowledge and power modern man achieves in this way are, in the end, just as finite and unstable as what he wishes to subject: that is, himself, man, the world. When man steps out of man in order to gain control of himself as a strange auto-object, his sovereignty becomes fundamentally broken, becomes nothing. Humanity enters the night like Edwarda—the night that, in the end, humanity *is*.

Man negates himself and dies in the project wherein he readdresses himself and the world as *question*—as objects to be questioned and then grasped as knowledge. In the third section of "Atheism and Writing" Blanchot connects this Hegelian account of modern existence as a new, postmedieval, dialectical form of negation to Foucault's innovative analyses of the rise of the human sciences: In these new sciences man is questioned, researched, objectified, and hence irretrievably lost like the silent, excessive sovereign Bataille invokes. The "originality of the human sciences," Blanchot writes in conclusion to the third section, lies in the fact that in these sciences "man seeks himself as *absent*."[42] Needless to say, these sciences are much more than academic disciplines establishing themselves in a certain period: They are, for Foucault and Blanchot, a crucial sign of the time. They enact our predicament, performing who we are, as moderns.

This man negates himself, but, as dying, as *negator sui et mundi perennis*, he lives. Modern humanism, in which man seeks himself as sovereign power—that is, as a vanishing object—is in this sense the ideological parallel of Hegel's philosophical system:

Humanism can be seen as a dialectical process, which means that, although it is a "doctrine" of negation (antithesis), as such it entails a "higher" meaning of human existence (synthesis). Bataille and Blanchot, along with an important part of "poststructuralist" philosophy, refuse this "higher" meaning that would fulfill the dialectic movement, maintaining that the dynamics of negation (antithesis as the pivotal "event" in the dialectical scheme) abandons man to a never-ending play between finitude and infinity (to objectify oneself as finite entity only to subjectify oneself as infinite, sublated [*aufgehoben*] entity). Because the play is never-ending, it renders man radically unstable: He can never simply be present to himself, to others, and in the world. He is nothing but a question to himself, a question about the self: Who am I?[43]

From a Humanism without Man to an Atheism with God

Blanchot inverts the idea that man is absent in humanism: For him, God is present in atheism. He unfolds this inversion in the essay's first section, where he claims that humanism is a "theological myth," thereby dismissing humanism's atheism just as he dismisses theism.

"Theological" here does not refer to an academic discipline but to the modern tendency (1) to postulate a divine essence of man, world, and history as transcending the sense of human existence and (2) to conceal, even blur this postulation. The theological structure of humanism consists in the fact that its accounts of man and humanity as achievements of modern secularization are still impregnated with what humanism has inherited in its own unique way: the religious traditions of "axial history" and their quest for a radically sovereign, absolute God, who, as such, as radical outside, has to live and die *in* the world—inside. Thus, in a way, humanism suppresses its axial roots.[44]

Blanchot does not deny that the secularization with which humanism identifies has taken place and is still taking place. However, he thinks the "secular condition," the "immanent frame," as Charles Taylor has recently investigated it,[45] in unconventional terms: the terminology of a paradoxical appropriation of death and of absence. The prime activity of secular humanity is *absenting* itself. Modern man becomes a question for and to himself, as we have seen; he appropriates death and refuses the divine world that was the owner of death. In doing so, he finds himself suspended in open air and must give a new, human meaning to sovereignty. To accomplish this, he will have to renounce his "egoism" and abandon himself to his absence: "God disappeared or disappearing, it is as a finite and earthly being, but also as a being that has a relation to the absolute (having the power to found, and to found oneself, to create and to create oneself) that we direct ourselves to the self that is already there but simply separated from ourselves by egoism."[46]

Here Blanchot paraphrases Feuerbach, with whom he is in dialogue in this section. The dynamics of negation is a continuation of religion by different means, because in this modern dynamics man creates a new relation to the absolute. He becomes a new God who can sovereignly distance himself from the world and from himself, who can negate both world and self and who, in consequence, "dies" eternally. But in this perpetual death he founds both the world and himself and builds them up again. He founds and builds on nothing, so that the foundations he lays and the buildings he makes become infinitely unstable. They become the non-bond within the bond.

Man's absence to the world and himself (his presence being one of dying) is, according to Blanchot, the modern successor to the transcendent absence represented by premodern divine sovereignty. For it was precisely through their absence that the gods of the axial religions—in their strange mix of being an abstract principle (the Good, Light, the Force, etc.) and a personal figure (the Savior, the Comforter, the Partner)—could be creators, bearers, and ultimately redeemers of the world. This ambitious task fell onto man's shoulders as soon as he had negated the fictitious "subject of Christian predicates," God. He finally could "reconcile" himself with his "truth" and "construct the world: compensation for the long while man lived in working for the other world."[47]

But can modern man exist perpetually suspended in open air, to give new meaning to sovereignty? Can this secular sovereignty in the end escape its loss, absence, and death to achieve true human control of the world? Or, on the contrary, is it precisely the being without end of this sovereignty, the infinity of its finitude (loss, death, absence), that marks its "newness"? It seems we must confront Edwarda's night with the light of Western phenomenology, from Plato's ideal truth to Husserl's origin of truth. Blanchot carries out this confrontation in section 4, entitled, "Always Light, Meaning": "Phenomenology . . . accomplishes the singular destiny of all Western thought, by whose account it is in terms of light that being, knowledge (gaze or intuition), and the logos must be considered."[48] The deconstruction of humanism undertaken by Blanchot—through readings of Feuerbach and Hegel, both radical representatives of a secular philosophy, interpreted against the grain and against themselves—keeps open as long as possible these questions about the possibilities of modern man and the confrontation between night and light ensuing from them. Ultimately, man, who became sovereign by killing his predecessor (God), enters the space of nothingness, as Bataille has explored it. But it is *through* his endless ambitions, through the blinding light surrounding him, that he opens himself to the night.

Man loses himself in his revenge on God; in this loss he is a continuation of the ambivalences of our religious legacy, of our "axiality." Blanchot rephrases Feuerbach to clarify this: "Be he God's rival, his replacement, or his heir, creator of himself or in the process of becoming toward the point omega, man is but the pseudonym of a God who dies in order to be reborn in his creature."[49] This is the theological myth humanism bears in itself: "Humanism is a theological myth. Hence its attraction and usefulness . . . , but also its weighty simplicity."[50]

A New Atheism?

My conclusion can be straightforward. The outcome of our analyses has been to make even more radical the initial statement that modern humanism can never claim to be atheistic: Insofar as humanism aims to be an atheism, a polemical "no" to religion, it is a failure. Every atheism needs a god, because the modern dynamic of negation presupposes that God remains present "as sign and as future each time the same categories that have served in thinking the divine logos, be they profaned, are turned over to the understanding of man at the same time as they are entrusted to history."[51] Atheism needs a god, above all when that god is man—this is the old message of Christianity. God remains present because he is absent—and because, in the Christian tradition, he has always been absent.

Although this conclusion appears to be relatively straightforward, unmasking atheism as a form of religion that inherits key elements of Christianity is too easy for Blanchot, however. In the fifth section his argumentation takes a new path by raising the question "How is atheism possible?" If atheism is not a simple antireligious worldview, what, then, could it mean? Can humanism fuel itself with a different atheism? Blanchot does not offer a clear-cut answer to this question, but the direction he takes is to affirm the problem. If humanism simply "cries out" the problem of atheism, it may arrive at a new, modern atheism. But how does Blanchot hint at new possibilities for atheism? What is this cry?

The axial religions—those that emerge during the historical phase of a farewell to the gods and to the world as "given" by these gods—introduce transcendence as a sphere of absolute alterity with regard to this world. That not only leads to many varieties of metaphysical dualism, it also implies that these axial religions somehow "present" this absent God *in* the world. In this complex sense, the death of God was already "active" in these new religious configurations. We may add to Jaspers's conceptualization of the axial condition that dominated the Greek, Roman, Jewish, Persian, Indian, and Chinese cultures in transformation during the first millennium B.C., that in the West this condition prepares the ground for Christianity, Islam, and modernity. Axial religion bears atheism in its heart.

Christianity has gone as far as possible in this invention of a God who dies as a human on the cross. This implies that modern humanism can never claim atheism for itself. It will have to think and experience itself in connection with the axial religions. It will have to affirm itself as a problem, for it has to linger in the space between religion and atheism, where both meet only to be "dismissed" as separate, well-defined worldviews, to cite Nancy once again.[52] His "deconstruction" of monotheism and of Christianity in particular can be considered a thorough and multifaceted continuation of Blanchot's earlier critical reflections.[53] It is a deconstruction of this mutual dismissal and an exploration of the in-between space in which the dismissal takes place. Exploring this space may give us a sharper idea of what modernity is and what modernity's humanism may be.[54]

Blanchot describes this in-between space as follows: "Seeking the true atheists among the believers (always necessarily idolatrous) and the true believers among those who are radically atheists, we will, perhaps, exchanging the one for the other, happily come to lose the two figures they perpetuate."[55] A "true atheism" can evolve on the condition that one avoids any *is* statement, any ontic identification. Only on the condition that atheism accepts its double bind, its "two figures," can it hope to lose these figures and redefine itself. The affirmation of its failure is the only opening toward the possibility of an atheism to come.

Atheism is neither the "historical event" of an epoch liberating itself from theism nor the personal choice of a secular worldview to which one would adhere.[56] Atheism is faith in the "I" and must start from that affirmation: "I can very well tell myself, and believe with a strong conviction in so doing, that every form of affirmation in which the name or the idea of God would arise is foreign to me; yet 'I' am never atheist. The ego, in its autonomy, secures or constitutes itself by way of the unmitigated theological project. The self as a center who says 'I am' says its relation to an 'I am' of height who always is."[57]

The atheism to come, which "always eludes us,"[58] is thus never something I do or am. This atheism stalks us as an uneasy yet tempting experience of absence: the absence of God, the absence of man. But who can speak absence, give it a sense, signify it? Absence can only be cried out. Humanism is a cry.

Absence and Actuality

Why cannot we speak absence? Because absence is not simply nothingness as opposed to being. It is in its own peculiar way present, as an event, a gesture, a contamination, a stalking force—that is, as an *act*. In Blanchot's and even more in Nancy's writings, this act is often named by verbalizing the word *absence*: absenting, to absent. As a verb, *absence* "is," "is done," "happens"; here we encounter the conceptual parallel to the "actual infinite" analyzed above. Like the infinite *in* finitude, absence must be thought *in* presence. The same double structure can be applied to the other couples of words that dominate Blanchot's writings: light and night, day and the obscure. But we cannot speak this double structure: We cannot bring language to the point where it can express *is* and *is not* at the same time. The *in* of the actual (infinite *in* finitude, absence *in* presence) is too difficult for human language.

The Infinite Conversation can be read as one long investigation into this actuality of absence, intertwined as it is with presence. Where presence is understood and postulated outside this entanglement—a key strategy of Western philosophy and science according to Blanchot—it must be countered, "refused," as the fourth chapter of its first part indicates in its title: "The Great Refusal." The unique being of absence is itself like a space in-between, thought—again, parallel to the account of the infinite—as a *relation*. This is formulated most explicitly in the seventh chapter of that part, "The Relation of the Third Kind (Man Without Horizon)," where Blanchot designates this relation "neutral" (*neutre*). Absence is not one pole of an oppositional scheme but the tension between the poles, which cannot be reduced to either of them. (The Latin *neutrum* derives from *ne-uter*: "neither of two.")

Man is absent in the neutral relation. However, though absent he nonetheless *is* and *acts*. What examples does Blanchot give of this strange form of acting? Throughout his work he presents writing as the central practice of "absenting." Writing is much more than a capacity or a profession. It is also more than literature, although Blanchot equals writing and literature in his earlier work. In Blanchot, writing (*écriture*) develops into a philosophical assignment. It indicates as well as *performs*, *en-acts* a reservation, a "remainder" with regard to a culture based on the oppositional thinking that privileges presence. In "Atheism and Writing," too, Blanchot introduces writing as a space where atheism might encounter new possibilities. In "The Name *God* in Blanchot," Nancy addresses this "coupling of atheism with writing" in a more detailed manner: "What is at stake in the association of atheism with writing . . . is the displacement of atheism in the direction of an absenting of sense, of which, it is true, so far no notable atheistic figure has been capable (unless it may be in the figure, so close to Blanchot, of the *atheology* of Bataille)."[59]

A full treatment of the theme of writing in Blanchot lies beyond the scope of this essay. Let me conclude with a brief coda on the other act of absenting that touches on writing: the cry.

Coda: The Cry of Humanism—On Words and Names

One could say Blanchot seeks a particular language: Let's call it the language of absenting. At the end of "Atheism and Writing," he refers to such a language in words like *murmur* and *crying*: "the cry—that is to say, the murmur; cry of need or of protest, cry without words and without silence, an ignoble cry—or, if need be, the written cry, graffiti on the walls."[60]

The "name" God that Nancy traces in Blanchot, as well as the "name" man, we may conclude, are first of all names that are cried out. Because they are cried out ("Man!" "O God!"), they "abandon all idolatry," whether theist or atheist.[61] They open an empty place in language, which is occupied time and again by man, only to be left behind by him in the next moment. What remains of humanism is the infinite repetition of finite claims, identifications, meanings, senses, hints: claims as to who we are and what our history, our world, consists of. This repetition (which is never a succession, a sequence of the same, but creates difference) was analyzed meticulously by Gilles Deleuze the year before Blanchot's book came out, in his key work *Difference and Repetition*.[62] Repetition is the concrete form in which the relation we have been studying, that of infinity and finitude, of absence and presence, appears in human existence—every minute, every day. Repetition is nothing other than a restaging of the lack of foundation. For Blanchot, humanism *is* this lack, and it is precisely this lack that opens its possibilities, that gives it the possibility for a new beginning. But already this sounds far too certain, too hopeful: Blanchot sticks with questions: "But how is the 'repetition' that opens this very possibility [of transcendence] itself possible? . . . how does rebeginning—the non-origin of all that begins—found a beginning? Would it not first of all ruin it?"[63]

If Blanchot is right, humanism has to reformulate its view of "man." Being infinitely finite, having to repeat and differ from his "self," caught up in the rhythm of negation, man dances round the empty place he himself is, in a strange act of redoubling. In this "play of the world," as Blanchot describes it, quoting Nietzsche, man is without himself.[64] This is a rejection of "human reality determinable as such, and capable of becoming the object of a global scientific knowledge," Blanchot states, in line with Foucault's criticism.[65] In writing, in the cry, the empty place "man" is occupied by the words *man, human, humanity*: words that do not primarily refer to some content and value but that are literally carvings, groovings, scratches (Latin: *scri-bere, scriptum*; Greek: *graphē, gramma*), like "graffiti on the walls." Man is traced back to a notch in stone.

The neutral, the neutrality of writing and crying, is by no means a realm of indifference and relativism. The cry of humanism sprouts from what Blanchot, at the beginning of *The Infinite Conversation*, calls "a terrible responsibility." The absenting cry is engagement, resistance, even "ethos," but at the same time it entails danger and violence. He who invokes a limit where presence and absence touch enters a marginal space of "the greatest violence, for it transgresses the law, every law, and also its own."[66]

In the end, the cry inscribes the inhuman into the human—but not as two opposites that have to be reconciled. The inhuman cry hides in waiting: waiting for humanity. The Renaissance humanists, much less devoted to an atheist program, knew this well before the term *humanism* was invented: Man is a task, a task for himself: man is a being striving for true humanity. Blanchot will, as we have seen, make only one little addition: The truth of that humanity may well lie in the striving itself—in the waiting. In the cry:

> A humanism of what kind? Neither a philosophy nor an anthropology: for to tell nobly of the human in man, to think the humanity in man, is quickly to arrive at an untenable discourse and (how deny this?) more repugnant than all the nihilist vulgarities. What, then, is this "humanism?" How can it be defined so as not to engage it in the logos of a definition? Through what will most distance it from language: the cry.[67]

CHAPTER 9

Intuition, Interpellation, Insight

Elements of a Theory of Conversion

Nils F. Schott

This essay aims to provide a theoretical articulation of conversion. Conversion, on this reading, opens up new ways of understanding that respond to crises in our relation to ourselves, to others, and to the world. I argue that conversion is best conceived of as an experience of the radically new and that it is best understood if we approach it through the words used to describe this experience in conversion narratives.

I will proceed in three steps. First, I will delineate the concept *conversion* from related concepts with which it is often conflated. Taking a cue from the writings of, in particular, Paul of Tarsus, the sociologist Bernd Ulmer, and the philosophers Jean-Louis Chrétien and Jean-Luc Marion,[1] I suggest a narrow definition of conversion as the response to a call, as the singular event that allows the questions that arise in personal crises to be answered. I will then introduce two key notions I borrow from philosophy. As it is centrally concerned with a profound transformation of the self, the response can be articulated in analogy to Henri Bergson's notion of *intuition*; as it is concerned with establishing ties to others and the world, the call can be articulated in analogy to Louis Althusser's notion of *interpellation*. Finally, a discussion of conversion narratives illustrates this essay's overall claim, which is much indebted to Hent de Vries's work on the instant.[2] Conversion is an event that, like Bergson's intuition, is reducible neither to antecedents nor to consequences; conversion, like Althusser's interpellation, is experienced as an intervention from the outside; conversion, unlike Althusser's interpellation, provides a new *insight*; conversion, finally, calls for a *profound* transformation, which takes the form of a new orientation of our actions.

The possible meanings of the word *conversion* taken in a wide sense are numerous, and I do not pretend to exhaust them here. They range from "a turn toward a new goal" to "a total change," an entire process of transformation that is only complete once it is and remains manifest in thought and action, theory and practice.[3] In the first sense, conversion concerns only a particular object or objective. In the second, it concerns a complete transformation of all aspects of life. In this widest sense, conversion comes to an end only when the situation from which it emerged no longer exists and the goal toward which one oriented oneself is achieved. Conversion, however, centrally concerns subjects (including collective subjects such as a people, a nation, a race, or a class) that seek to orient themselves in an ever-changing world. Under these conditions, any transformation must either remain incomplete (changing conditions preclude the completion of a transformation by the means employed so far) or continually transform itself and thereby not come to an end, either. Conversion in the wide sense becomes synonymous with transformation.

Such a conception of conversion as transformation according to a new orientation, however, enlarges the concept to a worrisome degree—worrisome because it becomes difficult to distinguish conversion from other (trans-) formations of the self, for example in the ever-growing literature on *metanoia*.[4] And while conversion as transformation describes very well processes such as, on the individual level, the adoption of a new religion or, on the collective level, the unfolding of a revolution, it can contribute little to an understanding of the reasons for these transformations. It sheds no light on what questions the way we have lived our lives (and leads us radically to change it); it has even less to say about the way this intervention is experienced. Most theories based on definitions of conversion in the wide sense conflate or, as the case may be, confuse conversion in the narrow sense with its manifestations, effects, or consequences.

By contrast, a narrow conception of conversion as the experience of an intervention of something new seeks to delineate conversion from what conversion creates (a new knowledge about and action in the world, say). According to Augustine, "It is hidden from us when it is that one whom we now see present in the body does really come in spirit."[5] Conversion, in other words, is indiscernible. Even if it has already taken place, it remains indiscernible unless it manifests itself—and in this addition of a relation to the world, conversion becomes subject to criteria of discernment and knowledge that do not quite fit. It is possible, after all, to fake a conversion or to delude oneself as much as others about having turned one's life around. Yet conversion cannot be forced or controlled; it cannot even be foreseen.

That conversion is experienced as an intervention from the outside does not necessarily mean that it does in fact come from outside ourselves; it comes from outside our expectations and habitual experience. It opens up a new perspective and thereby refigures our *entire* lives: *From* this perspective, we reorganize every aspect of our lives. Put more acutely, this reorganization has to be undertaken, or else that perspective closes down again and the conversion, so to speak, never takes place. All conversions in the narrow sense are so complete that although nothing "really" changes, nothing will ever be the same. Conversion, as it were, brings it all together and gives new meaning to everything. Yet this also means that we cannot go on as before. The intervention of conversion calls for an intervention in the world. The call heard in the conversion experience calls for a response on our part.

Here Henri Bergson's notion of intuition can furnish additional elements of a description.[6] Intuition occupies an intermediary position between the inner life of the self (or subject) and the external world. Contrary to tradition, Bergson holds that intuition is not an overcoming of the intellect but both its impetus and most valuable supplement. The traditional appeal to intuition implies an appeal to *eternal* truths that serve to solve problems—but they only appear to do so: What can resolve *every* problem alike ends up solving *no* problem in particular. Rather than fleeing ever further from the fullness of inner life to an ill-understood empty eternity, Bergson suggests an alternative approach. To understand ourselves and our place in the world, we cannot take the world (with all its limitations) as a template. We must begin with ourselves and seize our own uninterrupted temporality; that which captures this life within us is what Bergson calls intuition.[7] Marking a turn to our inner selves, intuition consists in "the direct vision of spirit [*l'esprit*] by the spirit." This is not, however, a solipsistic retreat that indulges in some sort of beatific vision. Intuition propels us forward and into the world. Our life in the world is predicated on intuition because intuition opens up the possibility of a shared, and therefore social, space. On the one hand, it is an "intuition of ourselves"; on the other, it also establishes a relation to the world outside of the self, for "the material universe partakes of [*relève de*] intuition in all the real change and movement it contains." Intuition mediates between the two realms of the inner self and the material world and thus opens up an entirely new perspective on the world. Intuition begins with movement; it is thus able to grasp changing realities as such and to recognize in the unchanging, the eternal, the immobile an abstraction we operate on the mobility of the real. The real, in this sense, is the "spiritual," as Bergson calls it; it is "spirit, duration, pure change," "an uninterrupted continuity of unforeseeable newness." Intuition, in short, reveals the new. From the perspective opened up by intuition, reality is creation. To capture a changing reality, however, is not simply to apply general principles to a set of cases; it is hard work, which is why "Intuition is arduous and will not endure."[8] In that intuition captures duration, but does not endure itself; it reveals itself to be an activity of the mind that stands at the threshold to action. Just as the inner life it captures is to be expressed in action, intuition needs to be translated into words. In that it is arduous; however, intuition marks a resistance to a straightforward, linear expression in concepts. The arduousness of intuition explains why, like Socrates's famous *daimon*,[9] it is, above all, interdictive, telling us what is wrong, but not what is right. Expression must necessarily work with what Bergson calls "symbols," that is, with concepts. No matter how basic and simple they are, however, they can never fully convey the simplicity of the original intuition: We must keep translating, always anew, the fullness of inner life captured in the intuition.[10]

The practical imperative to view everything from the perspective of an originary intuition, *sub specie durationis*,[11] can also be found in conversion narratives and in converts' attempts to reorganize their lives *sub specie conversionis*, as it were. For Bergson, intuition captures the fullness of inner life, duration, which imparts the creative *élan* of "unforeseeable newness" to life in the world. Precarious and transitory, intuition opens a view on the "otherwise inaccessible" depths of our selves.[12] This experience is arduous because it is new and because it can be neither repeated nor ignored. An impulse that creates the future, it demands to be given form, yet the simple transitoriness of intuition makes it impossible to recapture intuition as intuition. We are left with nothing but an "image" to translate the insight that the systems we had lived by cannot be adequate. With only this image to guide us, the task is to create our own concepts out of the impossibility of the concepts of others. The task of the convert is to build up a new life out of the impossibility of the old life. This is the incisive change demanded by conversion, and the problems that come with this reorientation in the world are well described in Bergson's vocabulary of intuition, for the attempt to return to the source of the *élan* that informs life is complicated by two characteristics intuition shares with conversion: Both come from an outside beyond our control, and both are transitory and refuse to be permanently captured. Both Bergson's thinking of duration and space and the divine origin of the call in conversion narratives caution us against making any strong assertions about conversion's "place of origin." The claim that conversion comes from an "outside" is not to assign it a particular locale. "Outside" here means "external to our expectations, outside our habitual experience, non-locatable and therefore unforeseeable" and can therefore serve to designate the "inside" of the "depths" Bergson speaks of, which are forgotten in the world of action (the "outside world" in the usual acceptation). The designation "outside" also captures the loss of control experienced in the intervention. Finally, it captures the liminal nature of both intuition and conversion: They are on a threshold and, importantly, remain on a threshold. At the limits of experience, they are as if taken out of time and as if taken out of language as well. For all its mysterious origin and transitory nature, however, the intervention is no less incisive or important: It articulates a clear demand and becomes as if audible in conversion's call to turn one's life around.

To gain a better understanding of this intervention, let us now turn to Louis Althusser and his notion of interpellation. Althusser's engagement with the Christian tradition in a discussion of the process by which individuals come to an understanding of their subjectivity—an understanding at stake in every conversion—renders his 1969 essay "Ideology and State Apparatuses" particularly germane.[13]

The terminology employed by Althusser in the opening of the essay—he speaks of a "flash" that provided a momentary glimpse of something we now have to "bring into appearance"—indicates an affinity with our discussion so far, as does the theme of the reproduction of the conditions of production, the question *How do we go on living as subjects?*[14] Althusser's answer is that capitalism, like all other systems, survives thanks to ideology, that is, by endowing individuals with a conception of themselves and of their place in the world.

Thus ideology provides individuals with a conceptual apparatus (*dispositif*) to elaborate or simply accept as valid a representation of their beliefs in the (reductive) form of ideas such as "God, or Duty, or Justice, etc."; these ideas, steeped in ideology and thus both productive and normative, determine individuals' consciousnesses even to the extent of prescribing particular behaviors. If I believe in God, for example, it naturally follows that I go to church, kneel down, and so on. A belief's theoretical reduction in ideas and its practical application in certain rituals is a function of a community. Such a community is constituted by "all those who live within an ideological representation of ideology," in other words, it is constituted by *subjects*.[15]

But if, as Althusser argues, "You and I are *always already* subjects,"[16] how can we gain the necessary distance to come to an understanding of how ideology works, of how we become subjects? Always already subjects, we cannot simply step "outside" to tell the story of the subject. To speak about ideology is to speak from within ideology. What we need in order to capture the relation between subject and ideology such that we produce knowledge about it is *a different kind of narrative* that can balance the ideologically recognizable concrete and the scientifically thinkable abstract. Althusser's text changes notably as a result. Althusser begins with a "formula," a general statement, namely, that "all ideology interpellates concrete individuals as concrete subjects through the functioning of the category of the subject." He follows this up with an explanation of the implications of the formula; note how he accompanies this new step with commentary, as if he were narrating a scene on the street: "We are thus suggesting that ideology 'acts' or 'functions' in such a way that it 'recruits' subjects from among individuals (it recruits them all) or 'transforms' individuals into subjects (it transforms them all) by means of this very precise operation I'm calling *interpellation*, which we may represent on the model of the most trivial everyday interpellation by the police (or otherwise): 'Hey, you there!'"[17] Althusser suggests that ideology works by recruiting or transforming individuals into subjects by means of an operation he calls interpellation, which can be represented as it is in the next line: "Hey, you there!" He takes his procedure even further. Not only does he call out and enact the interpellation; he acknowledges that this scene takes place on a stage. At first, he plays on this double meaning of *scène*, but then he calls himself out on what he is doing: He acknowledges explicitly that he is putting on a piece of theoretical theater, which he then proceeds to analyze. Let's watch:

> If we suppose that the imagined theoretical scene takes place in the street, the interpellated individual turns around. By means of this simple physical conversion of 180 degrees, he becomes a *subject*. Why? Because he has recognized that the interpellation was "indeed" addressed to him, that "it was *indeed he* who was interpellated" (and not another). . . . For the convenience and clarity of the exposition of our little

theoretical theater, we have naturally had to represent it in the form of a sequence, with a before and an after, thus in the form of temporal succession. Individuals take a walk. Somewhere (generally behind their back) the call "Hey, you there!" rings out. An individual . . . turns around, believing-suspecting-knowing that it's about him, therefore recognizing that "it's indeed he" at whom the interpellation is aimed. But in reality, these things happen without any succession. The existence of ideology and the interpellation of individuals as subjects is one and the same thing.[18]

We see the individual become subject in a simple turning around, a "physical conversion." That is all, and Althusser's slow-motion recreation can add only little detail. How can this work? This question, Althusser seems to suggest, can arise only because we have imposed an artificial narrative on interpellation. True, interpellation triggers the *acknowledgment* of being a subject; in that sense there is diachronic succession. However, to understand why there is this acknowledgment, we must come to terms with the synchronicity of interpellation of individuals as subjects and the existence of ideology. To do so, we must appeal to the nonsuccessive, the nondiachronic. If Althusser's earlier reflection that ideology is "eternal" (insofar as it is *always* present) holds,[19] then ideology always already *has* interpellated individuals as subjects. That is why the theoretical theater was just that: an artificial narrative positing a succession that simply does not apply. If anything, the subject precedes the individual, who, in the series of rituals that begin with birth, is charged with becoming who or what he/she/it always already is within a horizon of (always already ideological) expectations: a boy or a girl, say, or a doctor, a lawyer, the next owner of the family business.[20] In "Christian religious ideology," there is a formula to express the subject's relation to these expectations: *Amen (Ainsi soit-il)*.[21]

Amen or *Let it be thus* is a plea that the perspective opened up by the ideological intervention (conversion) be kept open, for life will never have the same meaning outside of it. *Amen* therefore is not just "so be it" but also "it must be so": In order for subjects to remain the subjects they are, they pray that "it may be thus" and therefore pray that it may not be otherwise.

In the intervention that Althusser describes as interpellation, there is a fundamental identity of call and response, of the question of the subject's identity and its answer. His articulation of the eternity, the omnipresence of ideology allows us to specify the idea that the call comes from no particular place. It comes from everywhere and from nowhere in particular. Omnipresence also allows us to articulate the temporal nonlocatability of the call. The intervention cannot be foreseen, and it can be described, if at all, only retrospectively and with great difficulty. The convert finds her "true"—in any case, a new—identity to be revealed in conversion, and her narrative of the transformative conversion tries to make sense of the identity it confers, of the answer conversion provides. The conferral—the recognition or acknowledgment—of an identity is at stake in *every* interpellation. Every interpellation puts our identity in question, and each answer determines both our identity and our experience of interpellation each time anew. In most cases, interpellation withdraws and we are left with the self-evidence of who we are. In the case of conversion, however, the answer diverges from how we were previously defined and defined ourselves. A gap has opened up between expectation and answer: "I'm not who I thought I was." The disruption of our self-understanding has opened up a question. The interpellation of conversion is experienced as providing the resolution of a crisis and is therefore remembered.

Althusser's theoretical theater narrates what remains concentrated in the act of interpellation. This act, which constitutes a subject, is too small (it is imperceptible) and too large (in its implications) to be captured meaningfully by the individual in whose life it intervenes. The description of the "physical conversion" of responding to the call from no-where (and no-when) captures what happens in an "image," as Bergson would have it. Yet this image needs to be translated, and it must be repeated for us to remain within its perspective in each new adaptation, be it social, liturgical, or textual.

All this holds true for conversion, too. It is in practices that conversion—which has created a new self—is kept alive. In other words, the intervention of conversion questions everything and destabilizes everything, but it also provides answers. Since we need to go on and need to know how to do so, we need to translate the answers into the knowledge—about God, about ourselves, and about the world—necessary to make it in this world.

With Bergson and Althusser, we can go even further. It is not some obscure human need to narrate that prompts us to give an account of the intervention that led us to change the way we lived our lives; the intervention itself calls for being narrated and manifested in practice. Conversion narratives as accounts of interpellative interventions serve a purpose beyond mere communication. They articulate interpellation as the basis for a new life. Their challenge thus lies in establishing a new continuity that takes account of an event that seems as if taken out of time and space.[22] The "image" and "threshold" Bergson speaks of are themselves useful images. The image is a shadow of the originary intuition, and the threshold, like the place of conversion, is a limit that our words cannot quite describe. Both make possible a new continuity, provided we understand that they express the need for a different kind of continuity. To preserve the *élan* of intuition, to remain the subject constituted in interpellation, is not to establish a linear continuity with the past but to keep open a perspective, to maintain a relation to the threshold we have crossed. The task is to articulate the transitory for its very eternity, to translate it into words that are neither transitory nor eternal. The habits, rituals, and routines of daily life in all its facets are translations that establish a new continuity with the foundation of our actions, translations that allow us to return to or reiterate the fundamental experience of conversion.

Conversion is an experience of the fullness of inner life; it gives meaning to our individual existence. Conversion is experienced neither as an empty eternity nor as a transitory present. Rather, it is both a singular and a universal experience. It is singular because it resembles no other previous or subsequent experience; it is universal because from its perspective, the meaning of everything changes. Conversion, then, marks an absolute break. There is no going back to a *status quo ante*. The intervention of conversion is irreversible because it opens up a new perspective that so thoroughly alters our experience of the world that nothing will ever be the same for us. But at the same time, because it is so complete and because in opening up a new perspective it also withdraws (it is absolute and not to be recaptured as such), nothing "really" changes. The experience of the intervention as radical transformation—so radical that everything and therefore nothing changes at all—leaves us wondering, first, What happened? and, second, *What am I supposed to do now?* Conversion lifts us up, as it were, and gives us a new vantage point, but that also means that we are dropped back into the world of finitude, of material necessities and of contingencies. The reconfiguration of the way we view ourselves and the world thus calls for a reorganization of our individual and communal lives that establishes a continuity between the conversion experience and the lives we lead afterward.[23]

Narratives about conversion are an integral part of this reorganization. They are attempts at making sense of the (new) world and our place in it. The conversion narrative, in other words, fashions a new identity and presents a new image of the self, a shadow cast by the transformative experience that crosses the threshold into the world and connects the identifying intervention with particular actions.

Althusser's narrative challenge, as it were, is that in working through the memory of conversion, in the attempt to endow the answer revealed in conversion with the words it does not yet have, the memory of conversion becomes indistinguishable from its articulation. The identification of the individual as subject identifies recognition with what is to be recognized, identification with identity, the response with the call, the narrative with what it narrates. The elaboration of a new image of the self that can mediate between the recognition of identity and the demands of life in the world thus *constitutes* this new identity. The conversion narrative, which links conversion, self, and the world, is the vehicle of this elaboration.

An extensive discussion of such narratives would establish how the permanent translation of the intervention into everyday life is predicated on an account of life before the conversion, how the conversion experience is articulated as a resolution to a biographical crisis, how conversion narratives seek to keep open the perspective broached by this decisive intervention, how, in short, these narratives supplant conversion. Here, I will give only a schematic description that relies on two premises. First, by analogy to the expression of the fullness of inner life captured in intuition, there is a need to give voice to the call and to the experience of being called to live up to this conversion's call for a complete transformation of our lives. Second, by analogy to the production of subjectivity in interpellation, conversion cannot be narrated in any of the conventional ways significant events are narrated because it is more than significant—it is what gives meaning to all other events. The instantaneous intervention that radically questions the life we have lived in the past and what life we will live in the future, in other words, needs to be related to a before and after; it needs to be brought into time.[24]

Augustine's narration of his conversion and its preparation in the eighth book of the *Confessions* offers an example. His conversion is a long time coming. He knows of it before he experiences it. There is no surprise; or rather, the surprise is of an unusual kind: His will be an experience so radical that nothing changes, and yet nothing, even the past, will ever be the same. Augustine's biography in the first seven books of the *Confessions* up until his conversion in the year 386 places his life strictly within the perspective that conversion opens up. Only from this perspective can the events be recalled in the form of a confession, only with the understanding gained in the conversion experience can Augustine come to know trespasses, indulgences, and false conversions for what they are. Book 8, which narrates the events immediately leading up to the conversion in the garden, opens accordingly with an exposition of what we may call the difference between knowledge and insight. Having studied Scripture and accepted the theoretical tenets of Christianity, Augustine is convinced that he has all the requisite knowledge to become a Christian. Nonetheless, the resolve to take that road, whose constrictions annoy him, is still not there. The obstacle he finds himself confronted with is his continuing enslavement to desire. This attachment leaves him at a loss for insight, an understanding that alone makes action possible, and this luck plunges him into an agony of contrition and indecision.[25]

In the interweaving of several conversion stories with an account of his own uncertainties and continuing deferment of a resolution, Augustine prepares the description of the resolution of his spiritual crisis in the famous conversion by a voice—by the words *tolle, lege*—in the garden.

> Suddenly I heard a voice from a house nearby—perhaps a voice of some boy or girl, I do not know—singing over and over again, "Pick it up and read, pick it up and read." My expression immediately altered and I began to think hard whether children ordinarily repeated a ditty like this in any sort of game, but I could not recall ever having heard it anywhere else. I stemmed the flood of tears and rose to my feet, believing that this could be nothing other than a divine command to open the Book and read the first passage I chanced upon; for I had heard the story of how Antony had been instructed by a gospel text.[26]

Completely caught up in an inner struggle and yet oriented toward God, Augustine's crisis clears the way for the sudden intervention of an unidentified—and unidentifiable—voice that calls from outside habitual experience. The voice's words have never been heard before, and they "immediately" change Augustine's expression, marking a change toward an attitude that is open to what I have called "something new," an idea that can be clarified thanks to the example of Augustine. The voice is the intervention of something never experienced before, a divine command that reveals itself to Augustine as such. This is the interpellation that constitutes Augustine's conversion: The call from nowhere—from now-here and from an eternal omnipresent God—constitutes a new self, one that hears the call and is able to act on it. Everything falls into place; all precedents reveal themselves to be such. Augustine now understands what previously he only knew. The interpolation of another interpellation—Anthony's—is the precedent that determines Augustine's interpretation of his experience. What previously he only knew, he now understands: "*because* I had heard of Anthony"—but this precedent is only a necessary, not a sufficient, condition of his new insight.

The conversion narratives we find in the *Confessions* can be supplemented by a wealth of other documented conversions.[27] I mentioned at the beginning of this chapter how the very concept of conversion challenges different disciplines in different ways. The examination of conversion narratives, which provide the evidence for most theorizations, offers a perspective that lets us understand different theories of conversion as part of the same spectrum. To name but one example, for the sociologist Bernd Ulmer conversion narratives address a "communicative problem" whose solution in the conversion narrative takes the form of a "temporal and thematic tripartition" into preconversion biography, the "conversion event proper," and postconversion life. More importantly, the narrative shifts between an "external everyday reality" of pre- and postconversion biography and the "internal world of the convert." The function of the narrative is to manifest the conversion experience in external reality in terms of precedent crises and antecedent practices and thus to authenticate individual conversions and to legitimize converts' status as members of a community. To this end, conversion narratives include a series of "indicators" (especially emotional unsettlement) and a "rational interpretation" of events that posits a "sequence of decisions" and a "new biographical account of time."[28]

In the example of Augustine's conversion, these two elements can be described as destabilization and deferral; both are characteristic of Augustine's crisis. Crisis here is to be understood in the double sense of, literally, a divorce or separation—that is to say, as a decision—and in the sense of a situation that calls for such a resolution. In the latter sense, it is a period of opening, of indecision, of unsettledness, of flux that corresponds to the indeterminacy of the inner world as Ulmer describes it and as we know it from Bergson.[29] It is a situation in which questions remain unanswered. It is the turning point, the time of interpellation as the revelation of a particular calling that will or will not manifest itself. Yet this manifestation is problematic and only partially captured by its identification as transformation. The problem of conversion's achievement sketched earlier—if conversion is to provide answers for individuals in an ever-changing world, it can by definition never be complete—is present in the very structure of the conversion narrative. As Augustine demonstrates, the resolution of the crisis is deferred. And even when the resolution comes, it consists in letting go, in divorcing oneself from prior attachments and accepting the limits of what can be known and done. This resolution is in effect a suspension of resolution. It is a suspension that we arrive at thanks to another critical endeavor, namely, the narration of the conversion experience.

From this loss of control in the crisis derives identity or, in Althusser's terms, the subject. What is at stake in the crisis-decision is a sense of who we are and what we are supposed to do. Interpellation provides this sense, and we can assent to it voluntarily because nothing else makes sense to us. The decision of conversion therefore imposes itself because it answers a lack, and it calls for a new relation to the world *within* the perspective it has opened up. The elaboration of this new relation appears in conversion narratives as a sequence of decisions that are incorporated into a new biographical account of time. This new calendar, as it were, determines the narrative both quantitatively and qualitatively, as to what is said and how it is said.[30] But it also gives shape to how we live our lives going forward.

For Ulmer, the convert's new way of telling time is a means of rationalizing—and therefore representing—an "unrepresentable religious process." By way of conclusion, I would like to reflect on this question to make the point, once again, that conversion is not to be conflated with its effects. I have discussed a number of explanations for why attempts to represent the intervention of conversion fail. Among them are the idea that interpellation comes from outside the habitual and the notion that the failure results from the difference in kind between spiritual experience and life in the world, between the inner vision of intuition and the external act of symbolic representation. With Bergson, I have also insisted, however, that it is imperative to give voice to this experience. Conversion narratives, then, give an account of the new relation to the world—a world that is always already in time—established after conversion. The tripartite structure discerned by Ulmer leads us directly to the question of time, for the definition of conversion by a biographical "before and after" is a temporal definition.[31]

Conversion can be defined temporally in terms of a break between past and present, an event or instant, as Hent de Vries has brilliantly discussed in specific reference to Augustine. In the conversion narrative, this break is determined retrospectively by the future it opens onto, by the perspective it opens up.[32] The future, insofar as it can be anticipated, is always determined by the present. In the conversion narrative, however, the future of conversion is (or is at least shaped by) the present of narration. The present of the narrative, therefore, is a past the narrative constructs from the position of the author's present insight. Before Augustine can write the *Confessions*, he has to understand what there is to confess; yet he can have this understanding only thanks to a conversion in the past that continues to manifest itself in the perspective it has opened on what came before. This retrospective work of endowing experiences with meaning is the central function of the conversion narrative.

As a break that allows a new view on the world we inhabit to emerge, conversion closely resembles Bergsonian intuition. Like intuition, conversion belongs to a different order that is not a simple linear continuation of what came before. That is also why it does not simply determine a future course (*futur*) but opens up a future (*avenir, Zukunft*). It is creative; it allows for a reconfiguration of our biography. In the example of Augustine, I articulated this foundational function negatively as a lack of resolution, a crisis; more neutrally, it can be called a suspension. The task of defining this suspension, however, faces an analytical obstacle. It subtracts from the conversion experience all elements that can be clearly assigned to a before and an after. In other words, it seeks to isolate the moment of conversion between an old life and a new but is left with a curious nonpresent, a no-time.[33] Analysis has abolished time.[34] Attempts to isolate the present from time face the same challenge as the attempt to isolate the "moment" of conversion, and they arrive at the same paradox. The analytical approach strips experience of its temporality, and in so doing, it figures the extraordinary nature of the conversion experience. In other words, in failing to articulate conversion in temporal terms, it brings its uncommon temporality to the fore: not yet / no longer.[35] Conversion—like the present—cannot be pinpointed. Its precise location, its very being, remains in abeyance.[36]

Conversion thus presents an opening in (or destabilization of) a temporal structure in which the past determines a future course. It allows what comes to us to arrive.[37] It is not, however, an openness to anything whatsoever; rather, it opens a perspective, a way of understanding. The suspension of conversion is therefore a suspension in relation to a temporal horizon. Conversion, in the examples most commonly discussed, opens us up to understanding ourselves in relation to two horizons, eternity and the second coming.[38] The second coming is an event yet to come and entirely beyond our control, even though all of our action is directed toward it. All that really matters, we realize, is put on hold, suspended until then. The horizon of eternity, unexpectedly, is much more immediate. Like the present, it cannot be located and is experienced as nontemporal. Juxtaposed to the past and the future, both the present and eternity are no time at all. The association of present and eternity by the convert, who experiences conversion as the intervention of the divine from an outside, from nowhere and from out of time, becomes an identification of the present with eternity in a conversion to "one's true self."[39]

Conversion thus preserves the openness of crisis, the intuitive vision or insight that otherwise "would not endure," at the price of its determination as the "new" that is given meaning in the conversion narrative. Conversion is lived as new in the way one's life comes together in a configuration that is oriented toward a different temporal horizon. It allows us to see things that we did not see before, although they were there all along. Because conversion opens up a new perspective on our lives, it is almost immediately determined from this perspective; it cannot remain "pure" (in Bergson's sense) because it calls for its own articulation. Conversion must be brought into time: It must be put into words, and it is thanks to these words that it gives new shape to our lives.

CHAPTER 10

Allowed and Forbidden Words

Canon and Censorship in *Grundbegriffe*, Critical Terms, and Encyclopedias: Confessions of a Person Involved

Christoph Auffarth

After an age of lexicons, we have entered an age of companions.

Lexicons, dictionaries, and encyclopedias arrange our *scientia,* our knowledge in alphabetical order, placing side by side, for example, *Abend-mahl* ("Eucharist") and *Aborigines.* "Oh, what a wonderful encounter," William Robertson Smith, nineteenth-century pioneer of religious studies and editor of the *Encyclopaedia Britannica,* would certainly have remarked, "the Christian *Abendmahl* equated with the Aboriginal ritual of killing and eating the totem." But these two successive entries are just coincidental. The reader must himself construct a systematic order by combining one item with another. Only then is the en-cyclo-pedia ful-filled, having achieved the full "circle" of learning. But who reads an encyclopedia, who reveals the inner systematic order of all those pieces? *Verweise* (cross-references), *Dachartikel* (umbrella lemmata)*,* and the like were invented as tools to detect the systematic order and the place of bits and pieces in the whole structure.

A beginner, however, will find the guiding thread of Ariadne in introductions—*intro ducere,* "guiding to the inner [secrets]." Or in a companion, a comrade at my side (literally: one who eats the same bread [Latin, *panis*] as I do), a *Vade mecum*: "Come with me! I will show you, in the jungle of titles, works, and papers, a viable way to a clear-cut solution to your question!" A systematic approach is required.

Now, at a moment when we are leaving the land of the linguistic turn, I would like to venture a retrospective look at what has been accomplished in such work, why this approach via words was chosen, what has been achieved, and why this cannot be the solution for many aspects of the issues.

211

Object Language, Emic Designations, and Metalanguage

Levels of Object Language and Scientific Language

In order to find a way from *di-lemmata* (incertitude; in Greek, "double-entry") to one *lemma* (in Greek, "entry"), the task scholars set themselves was to define terms as unequivocally distinct from one another. The goal in doing so was to achieve a clear and unambiguous tool that would have the same meaning in every vernacular, a scientific language different from the colloquial, which does not speak concisely about "things." But this is just one specific problem in the field of the linguistic turn. For the linguistic turn in the context of linguistic theories see Table 1.[1]

Language "then and there"	Modern Western academic language
Object language: historical language, the language of a specific culture (*Historische Objektsprache, Eigensprache*)	Contemporary scientific language, metalanguage (*Metasprache, heutige Wissenschaftssprache*)
-emic[a]	-etic
single word	—
Metaphor and parable	term
guiding words (*Leitbegriffe*)	fundamental terms (*Grundbegriffe*)
Contexts of the individual text	Diachronic (historical) changes in meaning, history of critical terms (*Begriffsgeschichte*)
Intertextuality	*Begriffsgeschichte*
Discourse	Discourse
	Great narratives
Literary genre (*Formgeschichte*)	"History" as a form of literature[b]
Speech acts	Teaching/learning—in order to be reproduced
	Defining positions in discussion

[a]The term *-emic* was first applied in linguistics, when in 1954 K. L. Pike drew a distinction between "phonemic" and "phonetic." Later, ethnology developed a distinction between observations from the inside, that is, from those who live within a respective culture, and the observations of anthropologists, who perceive different things based on their experience of different cultures and their socialization; see Ernst Wilhelm Müller, "Die Verwendung der Begriffe emisch/etisch in der Ethnologie," in *Kultur, Gesellschaft und Ethnologie* (Hamburg: Lit, 2001), 53–68.

[b]The German title of Hayden White's *Tropics of Discourse: Essays in Cultural Criticism* (Baltimore: Johns Hopkins University Press, 1978) is *Auch Klio dichtet oder Die Fiktion des Faktischen: Studien zur Tropologie des historischen Diskurses* (Stuttgart: Klett-Cotta, 1986). Concerning the narrative and metaphorical language of the Annales School, which dismissed the great man as the actor of history and invented other actors like the sea instead, see Axel Rüth, "Metaphern in der Geschichte," in *Begriffe, Metaphern und Imaginationen in Philosophie und Wissenschaftsgeschichte*, ed. Lutz Danneberg, Carlos Spoerhase, and Dirk Werle (Wiesbaden: Harrassowitz, 2009), 125–43.

Terms are concepts that belong to a specific endeavor to encircle a topic as it is communicated in words viewed as conventions. But words have their own histories, which are linked to historical changes in society, at least in the scholarly community. Let us first review different approaches to correlating the language of the object of study and scholarly language.

The Hope of Creating a Precise Language and Family Likeness

In his search for a precise scientific language, Ludwig Wittgenstein went through two stages.[2] In *Tractatus logico-philosophicus* (published in 1921), he advocated the concept of an ideal language, which would be able to designate by each word one single, distinctive meaning; the relation between the denominator *signum* and the object *significatum* would thus be clear without any ambiguity. Moreover, unambiguous sentences could be generated without any trace of doubt concerning their meaning. In his *Taschennotizbuch*, written in 1937, he still formulates this goal: *"Die Sprache scheint . . . eine Art idealer Ordnung besitzen zu müssen. Eine ideal geregelte Grammatik. Und wir sind so geneigt z.B. von allen Regeln, der Gesamtheit der Regeln zu sprechen, die die Verwendung eines Wortes bestimmt, ohne zu fragen, wie diese Gesamtheit aussieht. . . . So fragen wir uns auch, was das* EIGENTLICHE *Wort* [the actual, really meant word], *der eigentliche Satz unserer Sprache sei, denn die geschriebenen + gedruckten Wörter + Sätze besitzen in ihrem Wesen nicht die Klarheit, die die sublime Sprache erfordert"* (*Taschennotizbuch*, 157a, S. 105–6).

By contrast, later in life Wittgenstein developed the concept of family likeness, which is nearly the polar opposite to his former project. Its basic assumptions are:

> Many terms of our language do not have firm borderlines. However, terms do not need firm borderlines in order to be understood. On the contrary, such a limitation of colloquial terms is not constructive. Terms of our language should not build firm borderlines.[3]

These considerations led Wittgenstein to formulate his theory of family likeness, which pointed out that words do not need sharp distinctions and that kinship is built not upon a connection between things but on words. Wittgenstein first introduced his new theory of language function tentatively in 1925, and he employed it on a general basis beginning in 1931. In *The Blue Book*, dictated in English during the academic year 1933–34, he used the term "family likeness." In lieu of an ideal language with one meaning for one word, he proposes to view language as a game (*Sprach-Spiel*) by analogy to playing chess: Words are used strategically, in tactical operations regarding answers, challenges, and counterstrategies. This image captures quite adequately the strategic borrowing and offering of terms in today's interdisciplinary stock exchange.

Fundamental Terms: The Call for the Revision of *Grundbegriffe*

We can observe a comparable shift in the understanding of the relationship between term and meaning in scholarly language in three major German works of reference, all completed after 1968, with its "youth revolt." The cultural upheaval of 1968 affected all of Europe; in Germany, its effects were colored by the fact that the generation that had experienced childhood during the thirties and forties now revolted against the generation of their parents, who still formed the elite in the postwar democracy, although they had gained their positions under fascist and other authoritarian governments. Although 1968 affected all of Europe, I will build my argument referring to the German academic community.

The *Historical Dictionary of Philosophy* (*Historisches Wörterbuch der Philosophie*), in thirteen volumes, planned by Joachim Ritter, was edited between 1971 and 2005 by Joachim Ritter, Karlfried Gründer, and Gottfried Gabriel. (The index appeared in 2007.) Already in the early 1960s, Ritter had intended to revise an older lexicon of philosophical terms in historical perspective.[4] As a young scholar, he had converted to National-Socialism from being a member of the Communist Party.[5] He maintained that defining terms and their changing meanings would save the inner coherence of the philosophy of science from an impending hostile takeover by the '68 revolutionaries, who called for a radical revision of science and scholarship. By defending the scientific approach, he minimized the enormous break caused by the construction of a so-called "German" philosophy during the Nazi period, evaluating this process of the thirties as a historical development not unlike many other changes.

Such a radical revision of critical terms had, however, already taken place when the Nazi movement had taken over the universities. At the congress of the German historians (*Historikertag*) in 1937 at Erfurt, the Austrian historian Otto Brunner formulated as the task of the new "political" historians a revision of fundamental terms (*die Revision der Grundbegriffe*).[6] His authority was the *Kronjurist* ("king's counsel") of the Nazi regime, Carl Schmitt. Brunner's book *Land and Lordship* (1939, 3rd ed. 1943) was reprinted "without changes" (*unverändert*) after the war and translated into English in 1992.[7] Although Schmitt asserted that he merely used the (emic) language of his sources and the historical terminology, his book was a call to arms both in society and in academia. Brunner asserted that war is a case of emergency (*Ernstfall*) for which everyone must be prepared.[8] He thereby issued a challenge to liberal teachers in that his aim in revising critical terms was to declare war on liberalism. To provide an example, Brunner claimed that what had been called "constitutional history" (*Verfassungsgeschichte*) among liberal historians of medieval history should be labeled "national history" (*Volksgeschichte*). In the editions after 1945, he changed this term to "structural history" (*Strukturgeschichte*).[9] Brunner tried to set his readers and pupils on the wrong track by claiming that he used only the language of his sources. As Otto Gerhard Oexle observes,[10] the common endeavor of Brunner and his hero Carl Schmitt proclaimed the offensive against the liberal research program because they themselves had been targeted by Karl Mannheim.[11] He rightly observes that their program of revising fundamental terms (*Revision der Grundbegriffe*) did not subject their own new terms and thus their own position in their turn to the never-ending project of historicizing.

Brunner, together with Werner Conze and Reinhart Koselleck, launched and edited the second great endeavor, the *Historical Fundamental Terms: A Historical Lexicon of Sociopolitical Language in Germany* (*Geschichtliche Grundbegriffe: Historisches Lexikon zur politisch-sozialen Sprache in Deutschland*), which appeared in Stuttgart in eight volumes between 1972 and 1997. But Brunner did little for the *Grundbegriffe* other than lend his name as editor. The decisive actors were Conze and Koselleck. Conze thought that during the revolutions of the *Sattelzeit* of 1750 to 1850 (a word Koselleck coined for an era during which terminology changed due to a new interest in public discussion), change in linguistic terms prepared the way for a political change in society at the time of the revolutions. The Enlightenment destroyed traditional modes of thinking in Old Europe and thereby paved the way for political upheaval.[12] Conze saw this as a threshold, not a borderline.[13] Koselleck, who was about a decade younger and who had also been heavily influenced by Carl Schmitt,[14] went even further: He constructed the *Begriffsgeschichte der Sattelzeit* as the real historical development of the time. Therefore, the objection of historicism is in his case justified.

The third great undertaking, the *Handbook of Fundamental Terms in Religious Studies* (*Handbuch religionswissenschaftlicher Grundbegriffe* [HrwG]), was edited by Hubert Cancik, Burkhard Gladigow, and in the beginning by Matthias Laubscher, though his role later passed to Karl-Heinz Kohl. It appeared in Stuttgart in five volumes between 1988 and 2001. Cancik and Gladigow were trained in *Altertumswissenschaften* (classics); Laubscher and Kohl in social anthropology. Later I will also speak about the *Encyclopedia of Religion*,[15] although it is predominantly an encyclopedia (*Reallexikon*), not a terminological lexicon. The same is true for the *Metzler Lexikon Religion*,[16] The Metzler Lexikon has been edited for the English-speaking world by Kocku von Stuckrad as *The Brill Dictionary of Religion* (2006). The *Wörterbuch der Religionen* is intended to combine the results of the HrwG with the Eigensprache of the specific culture and was edited by Christoph Auffarth, Hans Kippenberg, and Axel Michaels (Stuttgart, 2006).

A paradigm shift in the academic discipline *Religionswissenschaft* ("history of religions, academic study of religion") can be traced across the five volumes of this lexicon. It mirrors the paradigm shift of the history of religion, which dismissed the assumption that religion is a phenomenon sui generis (as in the phenomenology of religion, *Religionsphänomenologie*), about which one cannot speak unless inspired by personal religious experience. By drawing on the vocabularies of the *Kulturwissenschaften* ("humanities"), such as social anthropology, psychology, sociology, medicine, literary criticism, philology, and history, the encyclopedia sought to build up the terms of a scientific metalanguage while avoiding any object language. This is why there is no entry "priest" but rather "religious functionaries," no entry "fundamentalism" but rather "rigorous religion," no entry "afterlife," but "postmortal existence." And—most surprising—no entry "religion."

The editors argue that the term *religion* is part of Roman and Christian discourses and therefore must be regarded as a term on the object level of language, which cannot be valid as a term of the academic metalanguage. Jonathan Z. Smith's argument in *Critical Terms for Religious Study* sounds quite similar; his famous saying reads, "There is no data for 'religion.'"[17]

Is There Something Different about Religion?

The Dissolution of the Term Religion

The discussion about the definition of religion demonstrates that (1) the modern singular term *religion* should not be mistaken for the Roman notion of *religio* and (2) the term is specific to Western discourse. The linguistic notion of a word cannot be defined by its etymological derivation. Across history, the meaning of a word changes radically. In the age of Enlightenment, the meaning of *religion* paid tribute to a concept of the one universal religion that should unite mankind: natural religion. Religions in the plural were but forms of religion, though of poorer quality, or even obstacles in the quest for natural religion; this was said to be especially true of the positive religions that obscured the ideal religion by their dogmata.

Once the comparative study of religion developed, however, the "essential core" of religion faded away. Neither God or superhuman beings, offerings and prayers, nor miracles and healing could serve as an "essential" to enable a definition of religion that would not be contradicted by an example from a culture where this element is or was not present. The "Weltformel" for religion invented by Rudolf Otto in 1917 defined the neuter noun *das Heilige* not positively but by the effects men experienced when they encountered it: "The Sacred" could not be identified with a God, a person, or something that could be described in human terms. It could only be experienced as a *numinosum tremendum* and *numinosum fascinosum*. Such peak experiences might form 5 percent of all the elements that are conventionally called religion or religious. But even this negative theology did not satisfy, because only a nearly extinct species encountered such peak experiences: *homo religiosus*.

Another definition of religion that was proposed did not dwell on its constitutive essentials but on its cohesive social function. For the individual, religion can provide meaning where rational thinking fails: With its help, contingent processes such as accidents, suffering, or death can be filled with meaning. Religion then becomes the residue in a world in which humans can explain all but a few, though rather a significant few, experiences in life.

But what can be said to differentiate religion from other cultural phenomena? If one compares a religious service with a football game, many of the dimensions seem similar and comparable.[18] Does that imply the dissolution of religion in culture?[19]

Belief and Trust

In a paper dedicated to Jonathan Z. Smith on his sixty-fifth birthday, Catherine Bell hints at a lacuna in most encyclopedias of religion: belief.[20] In Mircea Eliade's concept, the universal Sacred is present, it can be observed, and, moreover, it reveals itself (*Hierophania*) whether or not people are open to perceiving it, revering it cultically, or believing in it.[21] Bell argues for significance of belief in the concept of religion in the English-speaking world, especially its absence in academic discourse. I want to add the following nuance: during the quarrels of confessionalization—not only in the sixteenth century but also vividly at the time of the institutionalization of *Religionswissenschaft* in England, Holland, and Germany—belief, Luther's *sola fide*, became a Protestant identity marker directed against the Catholic *ex opere operato*. The Protestant position can be summarized as asserting an individual religious life of the inner self in the form of belief, without any need of outward signs, actions, or rituals.

But when one observes and analyzes other religions, one finds no bridge to understanding through belief. Other religions' beliefs don't necessarily make sense to the monitoring scholar from a different culture and/or religion. The same is true for the scholar who does not believe in a religious "assurance of things hoped for, the conviction of things not seen."[22] The theologian is generally both, a scholar and a member of a religious community that shares and assures a faith.[23] The sociology of knowledge has provided a key to this compartmentalization of shared knowledge and values. Belief is more than knowledge, however. For the purpose of academic study, the distancing term *religiosity* was created: This refers to the often idiosyncratic belief and practice of individuals and should not be confused with real religion—as defined by theology. But religion must be envisaged the other way around: It has to be appropriated by individuals as their own; otherwise it would exist only in books and institutions. When I was working with Jutta Bernard and Hubert Mohr on *Metzler Lexikon Religion*, we planned (contrary to our teacher's decision in *HrwG*) to include an entry on *Glaube* ("belief, trust").[24] We could not come to an agreement, however, with the contributor who had promised to write it, and so finally I had to write this article myself. It appears in the third volume under the entry "Religiosität/Glaube."[25] Much of what I deal with in this essay is also visible and present here and now. Material religion is an indispensable part of religion, presenting and representing both collective and individual belief, as well as being also evidence of things hoped for and things unseen.

Future/Zukunft/L'avenir: An Example of Terminological Change in the Dynamic of Historical Development

The term *future* has been used in the programmatic title of the research project of which this volume is a part: The Future of the Religious Past. The English term *future* is not as resonant as its German equivalent, *Zukunft*, which can provide an excellent example of a fundamental change in terminology—specifically, the change that has been taken to be an indicator of religious change in what Koselleck termed the *Sattelzeit*, that is, the era around 1800.

But this change is true not only for the political sphere on which the lexicon "Geschichtliche Grundbegriffe" concentrates, but also for the change of religious terms and the concept of religion in the era of Enlightenment and in the era of "classical" modernity often called the era of secularization.[26] Except for the term "secularization," religious terms are not treated in the GGB as autonomous lemmata; a religious meaning or connotation is noted in some instances. One of Koselleck's students, Lucian Hölscher, is working on a lexicon that will investigate the change of religious terms in transition to modernity.[27]

The German term *Zukunft* bears two meanings.[28] In my Groningen dissertation on medieval eschatology I came to a similar conclusion as Lucian Hölscher by investigating the changes in its religious meanings. Until around 1800, in a usage that can be found up to the middle of the nineteenth century, *Zukunft* meant "he/that, who/which is about to come to us" (*wer oder was auf uns zukommt*), in Latin, *adventus*. The term conveys a convention about the future of our world: the end of times, the end of history in the Last Judgment, the Second Coming of Christ announced in the prophecy of the Apocalypse. It describes the final drama. The last act has already been revealed, step by step; the only remaining question is: When will this happen? The same meaning can be discerned in the religious meaning of the French word *l'avenir–adventus*.

Around 1800, the term *Zukunft* gained a new meaning: It was no longer conceived as the Second Coming of Christ but came to denote an open concept of the future, in Latin, *futurum*, "whatever will be." This opening of the future by means of an evolving script reflects the optimism of Enlightenment: The future will lead into the promised land of freedom. The eschatology of modernity is a promise. Parallel to *Zukunft*, one can show the same evolution in the term *crisis*, which changes its meaning from "the Last Judgment" to "an impending threat of the end of the world."[29]

At first, the term *Zukunft* may seem to be a secular word designating what will happen in the time to come, but on a second glance one detects an eschatological meaning that promises liberation and self-determination, a better world to come.

It is tempting to multiply examples of how changes in the meanings of specific terms reflect the dynamics of religious change. The notion of *Niedergang*, "decline," rather than *Fortschritt*, "progress," can offer a promising thread in narrating the history of religion.[30] In terms of religious history, this decline is employed to create a master narrative of a religion being doomed to extinction, a narrative that employs the word *secularization*. The utopia of origin sets the standards from which history declines, unless a reformation or awakening occurs. *Religion der Zukunft* was a counterconcept to that of the downfall of

Christian religion.[31] In religion, the master narrative usually tells of decline and fall, of survival,[32] very seldom of rise or even of achievement and progress.[33]

The master narrative of the decline and fall of religion was turned upside down by Enlightenment concepts of change toward the better, the new: progress. We have seen how change in the notion of *Zukunft* reflects this; it can also be seen across the nineteenth century in the terms for progress (*Fortschritt*)[34] or the evolution from primitive to modern.

The history of religions resolved the ambiguity of fall and progress by adopting new terms to designate the superiority of European or Western ideas. The missionary enterprise was assigned the task of converting the rest of the world to a Commonwealth of the Christian religion. But beginning with the 1893 World Parliament of Religions in Chicago, gradually the deeper insight arose that there is no single goal for everybody and every culture, but rather that religious cultures represent an especially strong source of diversity within the converging structures of globalization. This can be seen in terms that capture civilization in plural situations, not just inevitable clash or desirable peace, but also neighborliness: how groups living in the same region find a way of cohabitation.

Religion in Context: Syncretism and Globalization

The History of religions implies the history of every single religion, beginning with its founder and first and ideal revelation, and then building up to a decline and fall, emically called secularization. Each religion must be viewed separately. The Sacred may well be the ultimate common religious experience, but religion in the singular is the arena of different actors who struggle in the same field over the definitional power of religion, over who should be allowed to use its label and privileges—actors competing to attract the same people. These people are not only agents who define themselves as religious communities, but also other parties, such as theater and movie directors, sports fans, humanists, atheists, or bankers and brokers. We can see this in terms that reveal how "religion" functions as a common field with its rivalries and competition.

World Religion

The idea that there is only one world religion was conceived by the nineteenth-century Dutch scholar and historian of religion Petrus Cornelis Tiele in an entry in the *Encyclopaedia Britannica*. Out of a catalogue of religions that transcend the sphere of family and kinship (i.e., natural bonds), as well as the artificial bonds of city and nation, he claimed that only three aspire to worldwide dissemination: Buddhism, Islam, and Christianity. Both Hinduism and Judaism, he asserted, remained on the level of national religions. He reckoned that only Christianity would ultimately prevail as the true world religion.[35] In particular, he claimed:

> to distinguish the three religions which have found their way to different races and peoples and all of which profess the intention to conquer the world, from such communities as are generally limited to a single race or nation, and where they have extended farther, have done so only in the train of, and in connection with, a superior civilization. Strictly speaking, there can be no more than one universal or world religion, and when one of the existing religions is so potentially, it has not yet reached its goal. This is a matter of belief which lies beyond the limits of scientific classification. . . . Modern history of religions is chiefly the history of Buddhism, Christianity and Islam, and of their wrestling with the ancient faiths and primitive modes of worship, which slowly fade away before their encroachments, and which, where they still survived in some parts of the world and do not reform themselves after the model of the superior religion, draw nearer and nearer to extinction.[36]

Yet the so-called World Parliament of Religions turned out not to be the beginning of a convergence toward the single best world religion. Instead, it cemented the divergence of cultures: Not one out of three, but five or six world religions were acknowledged. Swami Vivekananda, the pupil of Rama Krishna, constructed a neo-Hinduism along the lines of modern spiritual and Christian principles, but—emically and etically—it remained a Hindu religion nonetheless.[37]

Syncretism

Drawing on Hegel's notion of *Aufhebung*, "sublation," in which, in a harmonious progress, something is abolished or annihilated, yet its best parts preserved in a higher synthesis, Adolf von Harnack gave the term *syncretism* a new and positive meaning by claiming that ancient Christianity was a syncretistic religion. He argued that it had destroyed—in the interest of progress—pagan and especially mystery cults while integrating their best elements.[38] He thereby redefined a term that had been considered an insult among theologians.[39] The ancient term, used by Plutarch, describes how the Cretans never united except to fight an enemy. Once they had won, they immediately disbanded again. During the Age of Reformation, the term acquired such negative connotations that it was equal to a veto: Lutherans and Calvinists refused to dismiss their differences in order to fight together against their common enemy, the Catholics.

Harnack could use the word *syncretism* positively because he added to the Hegelian heritage a further notion from his contemporary discourse about the forces of life, that of race and social Darwinism. While Harnack held that ancient Christianity assimilated the best of the pagan cults and dismissed their degenerate and dead elements, he believed that its decisive living force was the resurrected and living Christ. This theological credo stood for a historical explanation against Nietzsche's assertions that "God is dead" and "history/ historicism suffocates the forces of life." In Harnack's view, history provides the evidence: Christianity survived as an ancient religion because, on the one hand, it was syncretistic and, on the other, it comprises the force of life in the person of the resurrected Christ, who would lead his followers to eternal life.[40]

Globalization

The term *syncretism* is still en vogue as a means to explain historical changes in a global world. However, conceptions that viewed cultural systems as closed and essentially stable entities were challenged from the perspective of globalization. This led to a fresh look at the encounter of East and West in the Hellenistic empires and in Late Antiquity. Given the reality of cultural intermingling, one must analyze the elements of cultures rather than treat them as closed systems. One should not exaggerate this interchange, however, as did Peter Burke in his speech to the Einstein Forum on "cultural exchange" when he compared negotiating cultural goods to bargaining for porcelain, incense, or Coca-Cola.[41] Globalization is a process of convergence and becoming uniform, on the one hand, and of fragmentation and relocalization, on the other. The encounter with other traditions and contexts requires strategies for coping, a need that increases as the dynamics of interference intensify. As in other areas, such as food, clothing, music, and sports, religion is not immune to these dynamics, and each case yields a different result. Within religions, one party may try to build a fortress to shut out open exchange, while other parties open up religion as a "third space" that can provide a common field for negotiation of things and ideas that belong to both meeting cultures, but are neither external to one nor indigenous to the other. This field can be a relatively free space for experimentation, leading to something new that could change both cultures and form a new stage. By contrast, the biological metaphor of "hybridity" is used to tar such a space with the negative assessment attached to the infertile and decadent.

There is no Archimedean point for an objective view on cultures and religions. The first and fundamental operation must therefore be to distinguish between object language and metalanguage. Yet metalanguage is also incapable of producing terms that have precisely the same meaning for every researcher in every part of the world—or even for me and my French colleagues. Descriptive terms are more useful as *hermeneutical* tools for comparison than normative terms.

Terms have their own history, and most of those that have been used to analyze religion are derived from a Western perspective. It is better not to deny or conceal that restriction of perspective, and any attempt to rectify it by seeking a new term in a metalanguage merely results in yet another coinage from within a Western perspective. The crucial point is to reflect on and reveal the restrictions of one's own perspective by fostering an awareness of its historical context and contingency. In drawing comparisons, one must incorporate one's own standpoint, and therefore perspective, so that it too can be compared in both space (with other cultures) and time (with other epochs and generations).

Cogito (ut homo masculinus, evangelicus, Bremensis, . . .), ergo sunt facta simul et ficta: The awareness of this context enables my discussion partner or my reader to grasp more easily my restrictions and understand why I have formulated the problem of religious language in this particular way. One cannot aim at objectivity, but it is possible to foster discussion in an ongoing process, in which each side exposes its point of view to discussion as openly as possible.

Academic study is not a narrowing down to truth via objectivity. It consists of a series of problems that are raised differently by each generation and are subject to change in the course of history. It is *Problemgeschichte*, as Otto Gerhard Oexle puts it. In an attempt to join this ongoing process, in this essay I have attempted to understand myself and my standpoint better by seeking a distanced and comparative view of some of the terms I use: my conclusions, my words.

PART III

Transmitting and Translating the Implicit

CHAPTER 11

God Lisped

Divine Accommodation and Cracks in Calvin's Scriptural Voice

Ernst van den Hemel

It is in Scripture that all foundations for theological reflection are offered: One can know God only by Jesus Christ, who himself can be found only through the Scriptures.

—François Wendel, *Calvin*

For who even of slight intelligence does not understand that, as nurses commonly do with infants, God is wont in a measure to "lisp" in speaking to us? Thus such forms of speaking do not so much express clearly what God is like as accommodate the knowledge of him to our slight capacity. To do this he must descend far beneath his loftiness.

—John Calvin, *Institutes of the Christian Religion*, 1.13.1

In the sixteenth century *sola scriptura*, the doctrine of justification through Scripture alone, was proclaimed by a variety of religious factions in Europe. Many reformers saw a return to the direct, literal meaning of Scripture as a vantage point from which to stage their attacks on Scholasticism. But far from being restricted to developing Protestant factions, the return to Scripture was a phenomenon as broad as the humanist developments that engulfed both Catholics, like Erasmus, and reformers, such as Calvin and Luther.

Exegetical methods became more sophisticated, and access to better sources and the education that would enable these sources to be translated and circulated opened up discussions about not merely the doctrinal meaning of Scripture but also its status in general. To put it in terms of the Eucharist: In an age when the word *is* in the words of institution ("this is my body") could generate doctrinal divisions and conflicts that divided Europe, return to the literal meaning of Scripture was a complicated and explosive affair for who was to decide what the literal interpretation amounted to? Thomas More's succinct summary of the problematics of the literal sense of Scripture: *"Et quis erit iudex, quodnam id verbum sit: Lutherus, an ecclesia catholica?"* *("and who will be the judge as to which is that word: Luther or the Catholic Church?").*[1]

The claim to base oneself on literal truth seems to be seductively simple, but when one considers what implications literal reading has for the status of interpretation, reading, and textuality, things become quite complicated rather quickly. James Simpson, in *Burning to Read*,[2] emphasizes that the rise of literal-mindedness meant predominantly a change in textuality, not a return to the literal sense:

> Single-minded concentration on the simplicity of the literal sense, then, produced a much less simple multiplication of texts. The single, self-sufficient literal sense gave way in the first place to an anterior text, painfully written onto the heart. . . . Thus the entire world became pregnant with signs and portents, traces in which God's inscrutable decision might be legible. . . . Evangelical insistence on the simplicity of the literal sense paradoxically produced fathomless, unnerving, and ubiquitous textual complexity. . . . The literalist can only appeal to the words on the page or written on the heart.[3]

A similar diagnosis has led Brian Cummings to state in his *The Literary Culture of the Reformation* that "the Reformation was as much about literary truth as it was about literal truth."[4] Instead of taking the return to Scripture at face value, authors like Simpson and Cummings invite us to question the effects literal-mindedness has on texts that proclaim the return to Scripture. As Simpson sketches it, the claim to base oneself on literal sense involved, paradoxically, a dilemma for the texts that professed it, for the literal sense aims to exclude interpretation, but at the same time, depends upon it. The literal sense has a certain tendency not to remain on the page. In the words of Brian Cummings:

> A literal interpretation, like any other, pays words back with words. Luther has promised the ultimate linguistic fiction of a language without fiction, of words which really do render things. In the process he has apparently destroyed all confidence in any language which appears to do less.[5]

Taking my cue from the recent insights offered by authors such as Cummings and Simpson, who have focused on England during the Reformation, I will ask John Calvin some of the same questions they have asked figures such as William Tyndale and Thomas More. More specifically I will zoom in on one of the most elusive concepts in John Calvin's *Institutes of Christian Religion* : the accommodated statement. For it is in the notion of "accommodation," that is, the way in which God stoops down to a lower level to communicate with humanity, that a sense of the complexity of the literal sense of Scripture in Calvin's work, and by extension, of early modern practices of interpretation in general, can be sketched.

Calvin's Scripture

Calvin, although he is known in some circles as an "iron" theologian, explicitly acknowledged the temporality of human interpretations of Scripture. All his emphasis on human fallibility notwithstanding, he refused to state that Scripture itself was time-bound. Scripture itself is perfect, but it is unable to correct human imperfection, because no truth can be deduced from Scripture that is as secure as Scripture itself.[6] The reader of Calvin's text is thus confronted with the "paradox" that Simpson identifies in the practice of reading literally: The literal truth of Scripture stands in stark contrast to the sinfulness of human nature. The peculiar conflation of descriptive uncertainty and literal infallibility that characterizes Calvin's approach to Scripture is discussed by Calvin when he presents the idea that in Scripture God stoops down to human level, "as nurses commonly do with infants, God is wont in a measure to 'lisp' in speaking to us."[7] This is perhaps the clearest exposition of the accommodated statement, *accommodatio*, to be found in Calvin's oeuvre. Yet despite this elusiveness, the accommodated statement is of central importance in evaluating Calvin's claims to scriptural validity.

As I will show, Calvin's use of the term "accommodation" differs from modern uses of the term, in which accommodation becomes part of a certain rationalization of religion, and it distances itself, partially though crucially, from earlier uses of the term, where accommodation was part of the interpretative process for uncovering the fourfold sense of Scripture. The analysis of Calvin's accommodation as a peculiar moment in between these two ages shows the idiosyncratic nature of his use of accommodation. For Calvin accommodation is not limited to passages in Scripture; it points, more generally, to the mode in which God relates to mankind. As I will show, it is precisely the pervasive presence of accommodation in Calvin's theology that has made it so difficult to pinpoint its workings and limits in Calvin's theology.

Calvin and Accommodation: Scholarly Problems

Only relatively recently has the notion of accommodation attracted attention in Calvin scholarship. The first in-depth analysis of the notion of accommodation in Calvin's theology probably appears in the introductory chapter to Edward Dowey's 1952 *The Knowledge of God in Calvin's Theology*. In this chapter, Dowey gives a clear definition of the process of accommodation in Calvin's work: "The term accommodation refers to the process by which God reduces or adjusts to human capacities what he wills to reveal of the infinite mysteries of his being, which by their very nature are beyond the powers of the mind of man to grasp."[8] In his exposition of the topic, Dowey interprets accommodation as inherently concerned with the knowledge of God. It is the process of accommodation that enables the unknowable God to be known. Furthermore, Dowey identified two forms in which accommodation features in Calvin's theology: as the process by which God limits himself in order to communicate aspects of himself in spite of human finitude (the "essential" limitations of human nature) and as accommodation to human sinfulness, in which the aspect of redemption is important (what Dowey calls "accidental" limitations).

A second perspective on Calvin's use of the term *accommodation* is presented in David Willis's essay "Rhetoric and Responsibility in Calvin's Theology." Willis emphasizes the rhetorical roots of the concept, tracing it to classical rhetoricians and Augustine. More importantly, according to Willis, the notion of accommodation predominantly functions as a persuasive and educational device. The accommodated statement pushes readers toward the "maturity God wills for them."[9] Willis explicitly traces the function of the accommodated statement to a God who "strategically adjusts his dealing with his people in order to inform, delight and move them," thereby placing the activity of God in a specific rhetoric mode.

This perspective is deepened by Louis Battles's 1977 article "God Was Accommodating Himself to Human Capacity." Battles links the use of the notion of accommodation both to the early church fathers and to classical rhetorical authors such as Cato and Cicero. More importantly, he does not confine accommodation to specific moments in Calvin's work but sees it in practically all aspects of Calvin's theology: not only in his dealings with Scripture but also in his accounts of creation, civil government, and the "accommodated act par excellence," the Incarnation. He thus sees accommodation as one of the defining features of Calvin's theology:

> In so espousing the divine rhetoric, Calvin was no innovator; before him went a cloud of patristic witnesses who, in response to the destructive critique of Scripture by pagan and heretic alike, had contended that God in revelation was adjusting the portrait of himself to the capacity of the human mind and heart. But, unlike an Origen, or an Augustine, or a John Chrysostom, or a Hilary of Poitiers, Calvin makes this principle a consistent basis for his handling not only of Scripture but of every avenue of relationship between God and man.[10]

In the period between Dowey's uncovering of the notion and Battles's acknowledgment of its importance, it had become clear that the notion of accommodation is quite hard to pin down. Is it merely a rhetorical strategy that Calvin employs to explain certain aspects of Scripture, or is it central to the way God interacts with humanity? Battles's statement that accommodation is characteristic of "every avenue of relationship between God and man" is a tell-tale sign that accommodation tends to spill over into broader topics. If accommodation is *the* way God interacts with mankind, interpreting what the accommodated statement means becomes problematic.

A third perspective emerged at the end of the twentieth century. David F. Wright's articles on Calvin and accommodation opened an attack on the connection between accommodation and rhetoric espoused by Battles and Willis. Other authors have similarly objected to folding Calvin into a rhetorical tradition. Jon Balserak, for instance, first in "The Accommodating Act Par Excellence? An Inquiry into the Incarnation and Calvin's Understanding of Accommodation" and then in *Divinity Compromised*, argues that to see the Incarnation as the pinnacle, the prime example of accommodation, is unjustly to fold Calvin's theology as a whole into the concept of rhetorical accommodation:

> The link between accommodation and rhetoric made by some scholars is one which seems to this author, at best, unproven and one which (as noted earlier) tends to insist on clarity and ease of definition which are defied by the data of Calvin's *corpus*. Echoing one of the criticisms made against this position by Wright, it may be pointed out that all three of the major proponents of it (Willis, Battles, and Millet) invariably narrow the idea of accommodation down to such a degree that it does not come close to resembling the broad and diverse concept which one finds in Calvin.[11]

Oddly enough, Balserak objects less to the broad scope given to the concept of accommodation than to the narrow definition given to the process of accommodation. Accommodation, according to Balserak, is such a pluriform phenomenon in Calvin's theology that subsuming it under rhetoric does it no justice. In his book, he painstakingly collects practically all citations in Calvin's oeuvre in which accommodation is mentioned and attempts to characterize them all, while devoting great attention to the individual occurrence and character of each citation. He concludes that the portrait in Calvin's work of an accommodating God is not a unified one:

> Calvin is not only inclined to leave loose ends (as stated earlier) but also to emphasize points in such a way that there is a resulting tension present in his theology. So then is this tension merely stylistic or rhetorical? This is one of the numerous questions that remain. But for now, having considered matters briefly, we will close this discussion with a summary—considering these disparate images of Calvin's accommodating God, we can say that (1) these images are probably not irreconcilable; (2) they are consistent with the general character of Calvin's theology; and (3) the tension present in them is often the product, not so much of the biblical text, but of his own mind and method.[12]

Balserak's problems with the emphasis on rhetorical structure in Calvin's theology is that it seems to presuppose a theological unity, both in the form of accommodation and in its role in Calvin's theology as a whole, that glosses over the differences among Calvin's varying portraits of the accommodating God, which have little in common. Yet by asserting that "[t]hese images are probably not irreconcilable,"[13] Balserak leaves the door open to a future assessment that would succeed in further defining the "general character"[14] of Calvin's theology. He concludes by offering vistas that so far have not been investigated, naming, for instance, the possible connection between Calvin's legal training and the role of accommodation in his theology or the influence of Calvin's contemporaries on his use of the term.[15] In what follows I would like to stress that the "tensions" and "disparate images" that Calvin's use of the concept of accommodation generates might be best approached not by seeing them as puzzles waiting to be solved by the scholar, but that the disparity of these images might be interesting symptoms of something in themselves, precisely because they resist a systematic, coherent overview. I will focus on where and why these tensions occur, in order to examine how they relate to a more general nature of Calvin's textuality. Therefore, I will not, in this essay, seek to establish the next step in a search for a unifying rhetorical principle in Calvin's theology, but rather will see what insights we can gain into the textual mechanisms of Calvin's *Institutes* precisely by focusing on the rough patches in his theology. But first we must take a closer look at the origins of the concept of accommodation, including its roots in rhetoric, its transformation by the church fathers and its use by Calvin's contemporaries. We will then be able better to distinguish where Calvin's own appropriation of the concept begins.

Rhetoric and Accommodation

Classical rhetoricians employed the notion of accommodation as one element in the scheme for preparing a good oration. The fivefold scheme of rhetoric—invention, disposition, elocution, pronunciation, and memory—offers steps on the way to delivering an oral discourse. Invention is the selection of the topics to be treated; disposition, their correct (good) arrangement; elocution, the choice of the voice most appropriate for the intended audience; pronunciation, the actual delivery of the speech; and memory, the imprinting of the whole in one's memory. In the work of Cicero, for instance, it becomes clear that the whole practice of rhetoric is in fact a form of accommodating that which one wants to say to the audience. In *De Oratore* Cicero states, "this oratory of ours must be adapted to the ears of the multitude, for charming or urging their minds to approve of proposals, which are weighed in no goldsmith's balance, but in what I may call common scales."[16] In selecting the topic, in the disposition of the arguments, in the selection of the right style, and in the gesticulation involved in delivering the speech, the orator must constantly keep circumstances in mind and accommodate the way in which the message is communicated accordingly.

The church fathers began early on to use this idea of accommodation to explain the nature of the language of Scripture. In book 6 of the *Confessions*, Augustine describes how the simple and crude style of Scripture formed a stumbling block on his way to conversion. Its style was too crude to please the mind of a learned man like himself. He preferred the smooth rhetoric of Cicero over the simple style of Scripture. Yet in book 12, speaking of Scripture, Augustine praises the "wonderful profundity of your eloquence." In the interim, he has opened the door of interpretation by realizing that by choosing such a crude and unpolished style, God is appealing to readers of many different natures:

> And it seemed to me all the more right that the authority of Scripture should be respected and accepted with the purest faith, because while all can read it with ease, it also has a deeper meaning in which its great secrets are locked away. Its plain language and simple style make it accessible to everyone, and yet it absorbs the attention of the learned men in the wide sweep of its net, and some pass safely through the narrow mesh and come to you. They are not many, but they would be fewer still if it were not that this book stands out alone [as] so high a peak of authority and yet draws so great a throng in the embrace of its holy humility.[17]

Scripture is seen here as a particularly well-crafted piece of rhetoric, which contains something for all members of the audience. This means that at times simple imagery is used to convey a complex meaning.

Good readers know to identify when in Scripture something is put forward in simple language for educational purposes. In clarification, Augustine offers his favorite example, time: How can Scripture speak of "in the beginning," given that God is eternal? It is because, human nature being fallen, "we can only speak of it as if it were first in order of time, although it is last in order of value."[18] Scripture thus speaks of eternity in the mode of human cognition. Even though its style is simple and crude, this is done because of the limited capacities of its readers:

> For my part I declare resolutely and with all my heart that if I were called upon to write a book which was to be vested with the highest authority, I should prefer to write in such a way that a reader could find re-echoed in my words whatever truths he was able to apprehend. I would rather write in this way than impose a single true meaning so explicitly that it would exclude all others, even though they contained no falsehood that could give me offence.[19]

In chapter 13, Augustine puts this insight to work in an interpretation of Genesis—specifically, in an analysis through the prism of the fourfold sense of Scripture. When discussing the multiplication of the creatures of the sea and the land, Augustine identifies literal, allegorical, tropological, and anagogical senses at work in the same passage, all contributing to a better though not exhaustive understanding of the text:

> I believe that by this blessing you granted us the faculty and the power both to give expression in many different ways to things which we understand in one way only and to understand many different ways what we find written obscurely in one way . . . consider the verse "In the Beginning God made heaven and earth." Scripture presents this truth to us in one way only, and there is only one way in which the words can be shaped by the tongue. But it may be understood in several different ways without falsification or error, because various interpretations, all of which are true in themselves, may be put upon it. The offspring of men increase and multiply in this way.[20]

In this way the fourfold sense of Scripture is a way of uncovering the secrets of Scripture that God, through adapting his word, communicates to us. By analogy to the relation between the Old and New Testaments, Augustine explains his method:

> It is not the Old Testament that is abolished in Christ but the concealing veil, so that it may be understood through Christ. That which without Christ is obscure and hidden is, as it were opened up [Paul] does not say: "The Law or the Old Testament is abolished." It is not the case, therefore, that by the grace of the Lord that which was covered has been abolished as useless: rather, the covering which concealed useful truth has been removed. This is what happens to those who earnestly and piously, not proudly and wickedly, seek the sense of the Scriptures. To them is carefully demonstrated the order of events, the reasons for deeds and words, and the agreement of the Old Testament with the New, so that not a single point remains where there is not complete harmony. The secret truths are conveyed in figures that are to [be] brought to light by interpretation.[21]

"Not a single point remains where there is not complete harmony": Augustine draws upon the idea that the Old Testament contains "secret truths" whose meaning was brought to light by the advent of Christ. Like the discovery that Augustine makes over the course of the *Confessions*, Scripture entails a simplicity that should be interpreted as being accommodated to human capacity. The discrepancies between the Old Testament and the New are in fact a perfect continuity if one is prepared to see, for instance, the Law given to the Jews as a temporally bound accommodation of God's truth to a human situation. The basis of this insight is the idea that God, through a merciful act of dispensation, has given signs for fallen mankind to decipher:

If we cleave to the eternal Creator we must necessarily be somehow effected by eternity. But because the soul, implicated in and overwhelmed by its sins, cannot by itself see and grasp this truth, if in human experience there were no intermediate stage whereby man might strive to rise above his earthly life and reach likeness to God, God in his ineffable mercy by a temporal dispensation [*temporali dispensatione*] has used the mutable creation, obedient however to his eternal laws, to remind the soul of its original and perfect nature, and so has come to the aid of individual men and indeed of the whole human race.[22]

The notion of a dispensation granted by God that speaks differently over time in order to better reach his audience is presented in the *Confessions* as the discovery that opened up the truth of Scripture:

I knew nothing of the true underlying justice which judges, not according to convention, but according to the truly equitable law of Almighty God. This is the law by which each age and place forms rules of conduct best suited to itself, although the law itself is always and everywhere the same and does not differ from place to place or from age to age. I did not see that by the sanction of this law Abraham and Isaac, Jacob, Moses, David, and the others whom God praised were just men, although they have been reckoned sinners by men who are not qualified to judge, for they try them by human standards and assess all the rights and wrongs of the human race by the measure of their own customs. Anyone who does this behaves like a man who knows nothing about armour and cannot tell which piece is meant for which part of the body, so that he tries to cover his head with a shin-piece and fix a helmet on his foot, and then complains because they will not fit; . . . The people of whom I am speaking have the same sort of grievance when they hear that things which good men could do without sin in days gone by are not permitted in ours, and that God gave them one commandment and has given us another. He has done this because the times have demanded it, although men were subject to the same justice in those days as we are in these.[23]

Without this realization the style of Scripture remains crude and simple, and the two Testaments remain irreconcilable. Augustine uses the notion of accommodation to explain the mysteries of Scripture, as well as to secure the unity of the Old and New Testaments. For him, the notion of accommodation opens up Scripture to analysis, so that—through an allegorical interpretation, for instance—the divine intention behind the accommodated statement can be approached.[24] Essential to his approach to Scripture is the idea that language can be both transient and sacred: "For material symbols are nothing else than visible speech, which, though sacred, is changeable and transitory."[25]

Starting with the early church fathers, there is a strong apologetical element in the use of accommodation. In *Contra Celsum*, an early example of Christian polemical writing, for instance, Origen defends himself against the attack that Christians believe literally in fables:

> If Celsus had read the Scriptures in an impartial spirit, he would not have said that our writings are incapable of admitting an allegorical meaning. For from the prophetic Scriptures, in which historical events are recorded (not from the historical), it is possible to be convinced that the historical portions also were written with an allegorical purpose, and were most skillfully adapted not only to the multitude of the simpler believers, but also to the few who are able or willing to investigate matters in an intelligent spirit.[26]

Here we see that the adaptation of Christian truth to the ears of an audience is an essential part of early Christian apologetics. It serves to link apparent logical incoherences to a variety of interpretations that are better suited to defend them. While "simpler" believers are accommodated, the learned reader can find plenty to investigate in the adapted statement. The divine orator has clothed his truth in words that fallen mankind can understand, but this accommodation does not mean that the accommodated statement is not true. If the learned scholar zooms in on a statement, he can discover "secrets" through the apparatus of allegorical interpretation. Thus accommodation enables a text to allow authority on multiple levels, so that the deeper one delves into the text the more of its secrets it yields. Furthermore, it serves the tactical purpose of smoothing over rough spots in Scripture. Origen uses the idea of accommodation to counter the argument that God's emotional oscillations in Scripture are incompatible with his majesty and eternity:

> But as, in what follows, Celsus, not understanding that the language of Scripture regarding God is adapted to an anthropopathic point of view, ridicules those passages which speak of words of anger addressed to the ungodly, and of threatenings directed against sinners, we have to say that, as we ourselves, when talking with very young children, do not aim at exerting our own power of eloquence, but, adapting ourselves to the weakness of our charge, both say and do those things which may appear to us useful for the correction and improvement of the children as children, so the word of God appears to have dealt with the history, making the capacity of the hearers, and the benefit which they were to receive, the standard of the appropriateness of its announcements (regarding Him). And, generally, with regard to such a style of speaking about God, we find in the book of Deuteronomy the following: "The Lord your God bore with your manners, as a man would bear with the manners of his son." It is, as it were, assuming the manners of a man in order to secure the advantage of men that the Scripture makes use of such expressions; for it would not have been

suitable to the condition of the multitude, that what God had to say to them should be spoken by Him in a manner more befitting the majesty of His own person. And yet he who is anxious to attain a true understanding of holy Scripture, will discover the spiritual truths which are spoken by it to those who are called "spiritual," by comparing the meaning of what is addressed to those of weaker mind with what is announced to such as are of acuter understanding, both meanings being frequently found in the same passage by him who is capable of comprehending it.[27]

Here again, in stating that the language is accommodated to human capacity, we see an emphasis on explaining potential paradoxes of Scripture by stating that the language was not spoken in "a manner befitting the majesty of His own person" but rather chosen for our benefit.

The church father who used the concept of accommodation most abundantly is Chrysostom.[28] In his *Discourse on Virginity*, Chrysostom uses such an argument to assert the unity of the Testaments by stating that the Israelites of the Old Testament were like children to whom God spoke in a childish tone:

Although the new commandments are superior to the old, the aim of the lawgiver is the same. What is it? To reduce the baseness of our soul and to lead it to perfect virtue. Therefore, if God had been anxious not to dictate obligations greater than the former ones but to leave things eternally the same and never to release men from that inferior state, he completely contradicted himself. If at the beginning, in fact, when the human race was more childlike, God had prescribed this regimented sort of life, we would never have accepted it with moderation but would have totally jeopardized our salvation through immoderation.[29]

In the Old Testament God spoke to the Israelites as if they were children. This explains the sacrifices and dietary laws of the Old Testament: "Dietary laws, the acceptance of some foods while rejecting others, were a Jewish weakness."[30] In this citation the accommodated statement functions not only as an apologetic mechanism. It also includes a pedagogical element: Through the accommodated statement, God urges man to be moderate, to accept the right meaning and comportment to be found in Scripture. Explaining Isaiah 6:1–2, where Isaiah sees a vision of God surrounded by angels who cover their faces with their wings, Chrysostom emphasizes that what seems to be a logical inconsistency is in fact a pedagogical accommodation:

Why tell me, do they stretch forth their wings and cover their faces? For what other reason than that they cannot endure the sparkling flashes nor the lightning which shines from the throne? Yet they did not see the pure light itself nor the pure essence itself. What they saw was a condescension [*sygkatábasis*] accommodated to their nature. What is this condescension? It is when God appears and makes himself known not as he is, but in the way one incapable of beholding him is able to look upon him. In this way God reveals himself proportionally to the weakness of those who behold him.[31]

Why would angels cover their faces, whereas Isaiah could clearly see God on his throne? The condescension of God toward man for mankind's benefit (*sygkatabasis*) is defined as "the way one incapable of beholding him is able to look upon him." Whereas for Origen the accommodated act signifies the unfolding on multiple levels of secret meanings of Scripture, for Chrysostom there is a deep connection between the notion of accommodation and the very work of salvation inherent in the Christian religion. For him, condescension makes it possible for mankind to look upon God so as to acquire knowledge of him. It thus becomes a cornerstone of theology in general, and it has been a major influential interpretative device ever since.

Since the early church fathers, the notion of accommodation functions both to open up Scripture to different layers of analysis and to give these different layers a distinctive pedagogical twist: God not only accommodates himself in order to express information about himself, he actively means for these accommodated statements to convey an ethical impulse to the reader, impelling him to adhere to the correct way of living. Accommodation functions, then, as an invitation to inquire ever deeper into the text.

Calvin's use of the accommodated statement is similar to earlier uses in many ways. These similarities are to be found predominantly on the rhetorical level. The similarities with Augustine, especially, are striking. The crude and simple style of Scripture was a stumbling block for the classically trained intellectual Augustine. Calvin started his career of letters as a lawyer who published a commentary on Seneca. In *Institutes*, 1.8.1, Calvin reiterates a problem that Augustine had wrestled with more than ten centuries before, describing the style of Scripture as characterized at times by a "simplicity, almost bordering on rudeness" that nonetheless "makes a deeper impression than the loftiest flights of oratory":

> Read Demosthenes or Cicero, read Plato, Aristotle, or any other of that class: you will, I admit, feel wonderfully allured, pleased, moved, enchanted; but turn from them to the reading of the sacred volume, and whether you will or not, it will so affect you, so pierce your heart, so work its way into your very marrow, that, in comparison of the impression so produced, that of orators and philosophers will almost disappear.[32]

This rudeness has nothing to do with a lack of eloquence: "The Holy Spirit was pleased to show that it was not from want of eloquence he in other instances used a rude and homely style."[33]

However, Calvin immediately adds that this adaptation to human crudeness has nothing to do with a fictive aspect of Scripture. And he does not take this crudeness, as did Augustine, as a point of departure for the discovery of hidden treasures. Calvin traces Scripture back to the covenant with Abraham and states that there is no text that surpasses Scripture in historical validity: "Now if Moses (who is so much earlier than all other writers) traces the tradition of his doctrine from so remote a period, it is obvious how far the Holy Scriptures must, in point of antiquity, surpass all other writers."[34] Furthermore, Calvin asserts that the miracles Moses relates should be taken literally and not figuratively: "Moses published all these things in the assembly of the people. How, then, could he possibly impose on the very eyewitnesses of what was done?"[35] We will see time and time again that Calvin considers the accommodated statement to be a device that is akin to rhetoric, but he refuses to use the accommodated statement as the beginning of a search for deeper meaning. In his commentaries, Calvin generally refuses fourfold interpretation, often in favor of a defense of literal interpretation.

Turrettini and Calvin on Accommodation

This preliminary sketch of the way in which Calvin relates to earlier uses of the term serves the purpose of outlining the specificities of Calvin's use of the term. Before we continue with zooming in on Calvin's use of the term, I want to sketch the way in which Calvin's usage differs from later uses of the term. Specifically, Calvin differs from those uses of accommodation that seek to combine the claims of Scripture with the advances of science.

Whereas in early times the notion of accommodation was predominantly geared toward either metaphorical or analogical interpretation of seemingly problematic parts of Scripture, in the wake of the Reformation it became aligned with reason in order to reconcile Scripture with the rise of scientific thought. Accommodation came to serve as a tool to square seemingly unscientific claims in the Bible with the progress of science. The work of Jean-Alphonse Turrettini, one of the theologians who is credited with moving the religious climate at Geneva toward the Enlightenment and away from orthodoxy, can provide an apt example.[36] Turrettini became professor of church history at the Genevan Academy in 1697, was promoted to rector in 1701, and concluded his career as professor of theology, a post that he accepted in 1705. He wrote in a time when the Cartesian standard was accepted as a way of thinking about the world, and he tried to square its demands of scientific rational clarity with Scripture through the concept of accommodation. Much like Calvin, Turrettini argued that the Old Testament authors did not reveal the nature of creation accurately because, if God had so chosen, the Hebrew people would not have been able to understand it.

In a similar vein, Calvin had accounted for the fact that Genesis identifies the moon as one of the two great lights that God created (Gen. 1:16):

Moses makes two great luminaries; but astronomers prove, by conclusive reasons, that the star of Saturn, which on account of its great distance, appears the least of all, is greater than the moon. Here lies the difference; Moses wrote in a popular style things which without instruction, all ordinary persons, endued with common sense, are able to understand. . . . Had he spoken of things generally unknown, the uneducated might have pleaded in excuse that such subjects were beyond their capacity. Lastly, since the Spirit of God here opens a common school for all, it is not surprising that he should chiefly choose those subjects which would be intelligible to all. If the astronomer inquires respecting the actual dimensions of the stars, he will find the moon to be less than Saturn; but this is something abstruse, for to the sight it appears differently. Moses, therefore, rather adapts his discourse to common usage.[37]

For Calvin as for Turrettini, the biblical reference to the moon's being one of the two lights that God created is part of an accommodated statement that is meant to communicate, at a time when certain knowledge was not yet available, the splendor of God. However, Calvin finds it important to stress that "Moses, accommodating himself to the rudeness of the common folk, mentions in the history of Creation no other works of God than those which show themselves to our own eyes."[38] It is important to note here that Calvin believed Moses knew very well what was really happening, though in order to be understood he chose to speak in the language of the times. So even though Moses did not accurately provide an explanation of what was going, as far as *perception* is concerned, Moses did not speak falsely: "Nor, in truth was he ignorant of the fact, that the moon had not sufficient brightness to enlighten the earth, unless it borrowed from the sun; but he deemed it enough to declare what we all may plainly perceive, that the moon is a dispenser of light to us."[39]

For Turrettini as well, the visions of creation offered in Genesis are part of an accommodation that God gave to an ignorant civilization. However, for Turrettini the notion of accommodation is instrumental in accomplishing his goal of justifying the Bible in an age of science. Where the Bible contradicts reason, the literal account should be given up in favor of a moralistic explanation. This enabled him to address the increasing claims at the end of the seventeenth century that the biblical account of creation runs counter to common sense. He was thus able to defend the spiritual value of religion without having to contradict scientific discoveries.[40] As Turrettini emphasizes when he discusses the Old Testament, we are now "blessed" with "more complete and solid principle of wisdom": "We know the cause and the mystery of the legal rites; we know that they were the rudiments of a puerile age; we know that they were shadows of good things to come, whose body is Christ, and we are blessed with more complete and solid principles of wisdom, with the wisdom of men, or of the perfect, which succeeded in the place of former rude dispensation."[41]

In short, in the age of Descartes, the underlying attitude toward the notion of accommodation changed inherently. From a form of explaining a mode of revelation explicitly geared toward confronting a reader with his own imperfections, the accommodated statement becomes a tool with which one can square Scripture with scientific knowledge, which is deemed superior and "more complete." Whereas Calvin used the notion of accommodation to reconcile seeming contradictions, Turrettini disqualifies biblical passages that create problems for science. He focuses, for instance, on passages that offer external indications of the truth of Scripture, but he relegates to the realm of the pedagogical passages where irrational or illogical information is offered. This obtains especially for the Old Testament and for Genesis. Statements that fly in the face of science should be read as accommodations urging the reader to live a virtuous life. To put it simply, rather than a specific textual challenge to think literal truth and descriptive roughness together, as in the work of Calvin, Turrettini transforms accommodation into a tool for disqualifying truth claims of Scripture in favor of a new form of metaphorical interpretation. Where for Calvin the accommodated statement brings human iniquity to light, for Turrettini it shows that inconsistencies in Scripture should not be taken at face value but seen as moralistic illustrations of a spiritual argument.

This implies a much greater faith in reason than Calvin could ever warrant. Whereas for Calvin accommodated statement undermines faith in reason, for Turrettini it is a challenge to establish a rational defense of religion against rational arguments. Turrettini predominantly focuses on offering proofs for the nonbeliever, whereas Calvin focuses on the movement the text inspires. While Turrettini's attitude leads to rationalist discussions about whether what is happening in Scripture is rationally admissible, for Calvin reason should, above all, undermine itself. Whereas Turrettini's attitude opens the way to discussions of the rational reality of God's role in nature and in science, for Calvin this was never in doubt or a matter for discussion: Reflection on nature and science functions as a theater for attesting to God's wisdom, whereas for Turrettini reason must vouch for the coherence of this theater. Whereas for Turrettini all readers, whether Calvinist, deist, or atheist, have equal access to the rational validity of Scripture, for Calvin the accommodated statement separates those who can understand from those who cannot. Rational explanation has little to do with this emotive access to the text. Thus Calvin is not modern, like Turrettini, but he does not belong to the earlier tradition either. Let us focus a little bit more closely on this use of accommodation, which characterizes Calvin as a writer standing on the fluid brink between two ages.

Scripture and Logical Inconsistencies

Calvin's theology cannot be easily summarized into a logically coherent worldview. Compared to the systematic commentaries of, for instance, Melanchthon, Calvin's exegetical work refrains from providing a running commentary, trying to stay as close to the text as possible without forcing the rhythm of Scripture into a dogmatic pattern that might smooth out the creases through an appeal to "human invention." As a result, theologians have unsuccessfully sought for a systematic principle behind Calvin's theology. As Wendel puts it:

> It would be better, we think, to confess that Calvin's is not a closed system elaborated around a central idea, but that it draws together, one after another, a whole series of Biblical ideas, some of which can only with difficulty be logically reconciled. As he developed them in turn, the author of the *Institutes* was doubtless striving to bring them into harmony by some sort of application of the formal method taught in the schools; that is, by expounding the opposed conceptions one after the other and showing that they are joined together in a higher principle. At other times the breach of logic, to which he himself takes good care to call attention to by an "as though," is passed off as merely apparent, as an effect of the contrast between the human and divine points of view. . . . What have been called the "paradoxes" of Calvin remain.[42]

Wendel draws out a number of these paradoxes: man's greatness and his misery, the value attached to earthly goods and contempt for them, the presence of Christ at the right hand of God as well as his presence in the sacrament. In Calvin's theology, fidelity to Scripture does not mean creating a logical system out of the logical paradoxes arising from Scripture: "One could even say that his fidelity is proved by the fact that he allowed them to remain."[43] Wendel furthermore draws attention to a remarkable aspect of Calvin's relation to Scripture: Calvin repeatedly calls attention to breaches of logic via an "as though." God speaks "as though" he lisped, as we have seen in the quote opening this chapter.

Calvin frequently points to apparent contradictions in the text without solving them, without folding them into a logically coherent, systematic theology. A typical example of this "as though" is the seemingly problematic change in God's behavior toward men:

> We therefore see that God is described to us in two ways [*dupliciter*], namely, in his word, and in his hidden counsel. With regard to his secret counsel, I have already said that God is always like himself and is not subject to any of our feelings. But with regard to the teaching of his word, which is accommodated to our capacities, God is now angry with us, and then, as though he were pacified, he offers pardon and is propitious to us. Such is the repentance of God.[44]

In order to reconcile the change in God's behavior from a state of satisfaction to a state of anger, Calvin reminds the reader that God is portrayed *as though* he changed his feelings, in order to bring about a change in us. Or, as Calvin describes it in the *Institutes* (note the use of "accommodation"):

Now the mode of accommodation is for him to represent himself to us not as he is in himself, but as he seems to us. Although he is beyond all disturbance of mind, yet he testifies that he is angry towards sinners. Therefore whenever we hear that God is angered, we ought not to imagine any emotion in him, but rather to consider that this expression has been taken from our own human experience.[45]

Calvin draws a distinction between God as he is (*quid sit Deus*) and how he is for us (*qualis sit Deus*), between God as he is in his Word and as he is in his "secret counsel." God *appears* wily insofar as he chooses to present himself in such a manner in Scripture, but this does not imply a wily God who *actually changes* his secret counsel. This distinction is reminiscent of the debate about whether the power of God is ordained or absolute. The absolute power of God, *potentia absoluta*, implies a God who is capable of changing his will as he pleases, whereas *potentia ordinata* refers to a God, who is forced by his nature to be constant. Both positions lead to speculation about God's nature, and they are aimed at reconciling, in a logically sound way, the problem of God's omnipotence with his activity in creation. Yet Calvin makes clear that his use of "as though" and of accommodated statement have little to do with making systematic claims about the nature of God: "As if Paul did not lay a curb on perverse curiosity when after speaking of the redemption obtained by Christ, he bids us 'avoid foolish questions' (Titus 3:9). To such insanity have some proceeded in their preposterous eagerness to seem acute, that they have made it a question whether the Son of God might not have assumed the nature of an ass."[46]

Calvin repeatedly refuses to refer to the distinction between *potentia ordinata* and *absoluta*. He regularly hints at the fact that God does not change and that his counsel is forever fixed at the beginning of time, yet refuses to speculate about what God could have done or whether God is forced to do what he does by the laws of logic or of noncontradiction. Time and again, Calvin refers the reader back to what is simply there, in order to remind him that Scripture is there not to promote speculation but to spur us to "reflect upon our own iniquity." What remains most important for Calvin is that God's behavior toward mankind is designed for our benefit. For Calvin, the remark that God speaks in the terminology of change and emotion does not invite systematic speculation about the nature of God, nor does it invite speculation of a systematic nature into what an accommodated statement really means. Rather, the accommodated statement, seen as a way to account for changes in God's behavior, should in no way be used for speculation about the hidden counsel of God.

Balserak, taking a stand in the discussion concerning whether Calvin was in fact part of the *potentia ordinata / potentia absoluta* debate, states that the distinction in Calvin's work is subsumed by accommodated statement. In a discussion of Calvin's interpretation of Genesis he writes:

Here, then, Calvin again describes God as one who had options at his disposal which he did not choose to bring into effect—he could have made the earth so that it possessed its own strength without requiring rain to replenish it; he could have caused the heavens to yield rain without it rising from the earth, and so forth. Here, interestingly, Calvin asserts an "operational" understanding of the *potentia absoluta*, noting that God could work outside of the normal means he ordained if he saw fit to do so. And here, Calvin again describes God as one who chose *de potentia ordinata* to accommodate in his establishing of these aspects of the created order. Hence accommodation and the ordained power of God are, again, linked in such a way that God's decision to ordain was, for him, a decision to accommodate.[47]

In some places, Calvin affirms that God can do anything he pleases, yet elsewhere he states that God is unchangeable and trustworthy. But, as Balserak and Wendel note, what underlies both is not logical coherence but an attempt to take Scripture at face value, while combining human language with divine truth. What Calvin emphasizes in accommodated statement is that it is spoken thus for the benefit of our lowly condition. At times Calvin refers to this language as "rough" or "crude" (*rutis*), or he describes God as taking on "a character not his own."[48] This, then, is the primal tension in accommodated statement for Calvin: In accommodated statement one is not to take the word at face value, yet it should not lead to vain speculation about the author's intentions, since the counsel of God remains hidden from the sinful reader. At the same time, all the figures of roughness notwithstanding, accommodated statement is nonetheless true:

> Such modes of expression are accommodated to our capacity, that we may the better understand how miserable and calamitous our condition is without Christ. For were it not said in clear terms, that Divine wrath, and vengeance, and eternal death, lay upon us, we should be less sensible of our wretchedness without the mercy of God, and less disposed to value the blessing of deliverance. . . . In short, since our mind cannot lay hold of life through the mercy of God with sufficient eagerness, or receive it with becoming gratitude, unless previously impressed with fear of the Divine anger, and dismayed at the thought of eternal death, we are so instructed by divine truth, as to perceive that without Christ God is in a manner hostile to us, and has his arm raised for our destruction. Thus taught, we look to Christ alone for divine favor and paternal love. Though this is said in accommodation to the weakness of our capacity, it is not said falsely.[49]

Or, as Paul Helm formulates it, "The language of the divine attributes is not nominal, but real; it gives us real knowledge of God, but it is folly to attempt to go behind or beyond these attributes to know God as he is in himself. For only God can know himself."[50] As we shall see, this stance goes beyond the call to see Scriptural language about God as meta-phorical. The accommodated statement unrolls itself as an instance of divine truth under the auspices of temporality, in order to move the believer toward right reflection. An emphasis on movement underlies Calvin's resistance to the interpretation of the accom-modated statement as allegorical, metaphorical, or metaphysical truth.

Calvin frequently walks a tightrope between literal faith in Scripture and an under-mining of faith in the human capacity truly to receive the secrets of Scripture. This deli-cate balance leads him at times to depart from logical coherence, and it engenders an attitude toward Scripture that pervades his whole work. The reader is not to deduce logical meaning or systematic reflection from these passages. Instead, he should focus on the emotive aspect: God spoke in that manner in order to bring about a change in us.

Calvin's approach to the literal truth of Scripture is therefore not merely a logical approach: The accommodated statement is a rhetorical device supposed to bring about reflection on our own iniquity. The correct reaction to this is not metaphorical explana-tion, nor is it an attempt to translate the accommodated statement into a statement that is not accommodated (what God really meant to say is . . .). The accommodated state-ment is said "in accommodation to the weakness of our capacity, [but] it is not said falsely." This refusal to step out of the mode of accommodation toward a more formal language that would explain what an accommodated statement "really means," is key to the interpretative mechanism that Calvin returns to time and time again. As Helm states:

> For Calvin neither the philosophers nor the theologians occupy a privileged position with regard to thought and language about God. God "lisps" or "accommodates" himself not only to children in the nursery, or to those who have no particular intel-lectual aptitude for metaphysical reflection. He speaks in this way to us all, conde-scending from his loftiness to make himself known to us in familiar terms."[51]

Perhaps no single theologian, Chrysostom excepted, has used the notion of accom-modation as extensively as Calvin. Calvin's dealings with Scripture tend to spill over into his theology and the textuality in which it is presented. The results of this for the *Institutes* as a text are potentially far-reaching. Calvin describes his work as "a summary [*summa*] of religion in all its parts, and digested in an order which will make it easy for any one, who rightly comprehends it, to ascertain both what he ought chiefly to look for in Scrip-ture, and also to what head he ought to refer whatever is contained in it."[52] Whereas tra-ditional interpretations are able to provide textual security and a description of what to look for in Scripture, as we have seen, the accommodated statement conceals its own meaning. If Helm is right, and theology does not occupy a privileged position with regard to thought and language about God, and if God speaks in accommodated statements to all of creation, humanity is indeed surrounded by the "fathomless unnerving and ubiquitous complexity" outlined by James Simpson.

∞

Before we continue, let us take a look at the various instances of Calvin's use of the notion of accommodation. In his study Dowey states that there are two types of accommodation at work in Calvin's thought: those that are structurally, ontologically necessary and the historical accommodation to human sinfulness. Balserak suggests refining the model by including four more categories: human beings as creatures (roughly the same as Dowey's accommodation generated toward the finiteness of human nature); human beings as sinners; accommodation specifically aimed at Israel as a primitive nation (a distinction derived from Willis); and a fourth: human beings specifically targeted as either wicked or godly. In what follows, I will illustrate these categories with examples from Calvin's *Institutes*.

Human sinfulness. This category is historical. It pertains to specific accommodations geared toward overcoming such emotional weaknesses as sluggishness, lethargy, fear, grief, doubt, willfulness, and hypocrisy. For instance, Calvin discusses the apparition of angels in Scripture and warns against the attribution of any agency to angelic messengers:

> This danger we will happily avoid, if we consider why it is that God, instead of acting directly without their agency, is wont to employ it in manifesting his power, providing for the safety of his people, and imparting the gifts of his beneficence. This he certainly does not from necessity, as if he were unable to dispense with them (. . .). Therefore, when he employs them, it is as a help to our weakness, that nothing may be wanted to elevate our hopes or strengthen our confidence. It ought indeed, to be sufficient for us that the Lord declares himself to be our protector. But when we see ourselves beset by so many perils, so many injuries, so many kinds of enemies, such is our frailty and effeminacy, that we might at times be filled with alarm, or driven to despair, did not the Lord proclaim his gracious presence by some means in accordance with out feeble capacities.[53]

The overarching element in this notion is the idea that humans are incidentally interpellated by God in order to bring about a specific event or change. It is used to describe, for instance, the changing behavior of God with relation to humans, whether they are Old Testament Israelites or New Testament apostles. The events and miracles of the Bible fall under this category, and it should be kept in mind that these events existed in time, and for that specific time's sake.

Human creatureliness. God transfers to himself what properly does not belong to him, for he does not delight himself after the manner of men when he takes vengeance on wickedness; but we know that God's judgment cannot be comprehended, unless he puts on the character of man, and in some manner transforms himself.[54]

Because of the inherent gap between man and God, the only knowledge of God that we can form is under the guise of divine accommodation to a human, creaturely form. This broad category of accommodation includes, according to Dowey, not only the act of creation itself, but also the incarnation and the sacraments as well as the whole of Scripture. This category of accommodation is focused predominantly on the whole aim of creation being the praising of God. Now Balserak suggests a criticism of Dowey's twofold distinction:

> The inclusion of knowledge in this group as well as in the first group bears witness to the difficulty inherent in any attempt to distinguish between different kinds of *captus*. It was this which moved us to criticize, albeit mildly, Professor Dowey for distinguishing in too tidy a manner between different expressions of human capacity.[55]

According to Balserak, the myriad of examples of accommodation in Calvin's work defy easy applications to a twofold framework because the categories are both geared toward knowledge. The two categories—God stooping in specific Scriptural passages because of our iniquity and God stooping in general because of our iniquity—are linked; what unifies all these forms of accommodation is the perceived effect they have on the human mind. The accommodated statement, whether it be creation in general, or instances of divine action, are both a "stooping," a "lisping" from the side of God, to move the human subject. Therefore, although there might be no unifying aspect to the accommodated statements, in the sense that a logical coherent factor might be hard to find, one can point to a certain circular aspect in the accommodated statement: The accommodation might not point to a logical point outside of Scripture, in the sense that it imposes a dogmatic structure on the text, but it aims to retain the educatory, pedagogic element of Scripture without interfering with it from a human perspective. Balserak points to the blatant fact that, seen in this light, accommodation extends, spreads out, from a historical event to the entire creation itself. Let us take a look at Calvin's commentary on Genesis 1:5:

> God himself took the space of six days, for the purpose of accommodating his works to the capacity of humankind. We slightly pass over the infinite glory of God, which shines forth here; from whence does this arise but from our excessive dullness in considering his greatness? In the meantime, the vanity of our minds carries us away elsewhere. For the correction of this, God applied the most suitable remedy when he distributed the creation of the world into successive portions, that he might fix our attention, and compel us, as if he laid his hand upon us, to pause and to reflect.[56]

In the *Institutes*, Calvin emphasizes this point even more clearly:

God himself has shown by the order of creation that he created all things for human-kind's sake. For it is not without significance that he divided the making of the universe into six days, even though it would have been no more difficult for him to have completed in one moment the whole work together in all its details than to arrive at its completion gradually by a procession of this sort.[57]

Not only does Calvin defend the literal meaning of the creation of the earth in six days. More importantly, Calvin also states that the whole of creation was explicitly created for the "benefit of mankind." Now Scripture, or better put, the spiritual movement that Scripture engenders in the reader, spills over into the natural world to such an extent that it is not reason that is the access to God's wisdom, but the marvel of his accommodating gesture that ordained the world to be.

Balserak underlines that this implies a break with the *potentia ordinata* and *potentia absoluta* distinction. He even claims that Calvin's notion of accommodation engulfs the distinction in one act of accommodation:

Grappling with the details of God's ordaining of the structures of creation and redemption, he often comments on or alludes to the distinction between the absolute and ordered power of God—normally along with a range of related ideas such as God's freedom, the contingent character of these orders, God's commitment to them, his use of means and the like—and links God's decision to ordain to his decision to accommodate.[58]

As a result, according to Balserak, Calvin does not discuss the difference between ordained and absolute power often. Indeed he refutes it as a "perverse ingenuity."[59] Instead, Calvin prefers to refer to the act of accommodation that underlies the created order. In the example of the span of six days in which God created the earth, Calvin states that God ordained the creation of the universe in six days "for humankind's sake," even though "it would have been no more difficult for him to have completed in one moment the whole work altogether." However, this realization should not lead to speculation on what God could or could not have done:

Let us rather conclude that God himself took the space of six days, for the purpose of accommodating his works to the capacity of men. We slightingly pass over the infinite glory of God, which here shines forth; whence arises this but from our excessive dulness in considering his greatness? In the meantime, the vanity of our minds carries us away elsewhere.[60]

What is important for Calvin is not the distinction of what God could or could not have done, but the accommodated nature of what he has done. Speculations that attempt to go beyond this realization, according to Calvin, lead us away from the glory of God.

Balserak asserts that "accommodation penetrates Calvin's theology to an indiscernible degree."[61] This idea has quite far-reaching consequences: for it is no longer possible to take one's distance vis-à-vis accommodation, either through reason or through metaphor or allegory. Instead, accommodation becomes indeed, as Dowey stated, a central question in Calvin's theology. If the whole of creation, including Scripture, can be seen as an accommodation geared toward engendering a movement in the human mind, a movement that, furthermore, cannot be explained by a metadiscourse, such as the *ordinata/absoluta* distinction, what is the vantage point from which anyone could realize this? What can Calvin's text expound, explain, or communicate, other than the limits of human understanding in comprehending God's accommodation? The accommodated statement thereby threatens to become auto-referential, turning back on itself, and closing off Scripture at its surface.

In Calvin's use of the notion of accommodation, apparently contradictory dimensions show themselves. First, Calvin does not use the term *accommodation* as a tool to facilitate interpretation. The accommodated statement lacks intellectual depth. It is geared toward retaining an *immanent* truth that is nonetheless expressed in temporal form. The challenge becomes not to uncover what the puzzle means but instead to marvel upon the wisdom and benevolence of God in stooping to our level and to use our foolish language in order to communicate something. Second, there is a certain undecidability in accommodation. It is not geared toward excusing logically unsound Scriptural citations from scientific validity, nor does it do the inverse, claiming the literal truth of Scripture in the face of empirical evidence indicating otherwise. The split between the realm of science and the realm of religion, as Turrettini helped to define it, does not exist for Calvin. Rather, there is a notion of truth in Calvin that lies in between these two dimensions. The notion of accommodation is not to be used to detract from the validity of the direct literal sense of Scripture, but it is not to be used to turn Scripture into a scientific handbook, either.

The notion of accommodation functions in Calvin as a demand placed on the reader to see in God's word both the presence of divine truth and the admonition that this truth is not to be taken at face value. In short, what Scripture really means is beyond our reach, and what it *should* mean for us is up for debate. This conclusion can be folded back into the claim that the *Institutes* themselves function as a guide, as a *summa* of what is needed to read Scripture. For a true effort to define the meaning and effect of Scripture, if seen through the prism of accommodation, lies not in defining a clear content of the text, but in realizing the temporality of meaning and understanding that notions such as eternity and truth are inherently connected to our own temporal limitations. Thus for Calvin the truth of the accommodated element lies on the surface, not hidden away like a puzzle waiting for a scholar to solve it. Christ's incarnation, Scripture, even creation, can all be seen as accommodated statements demanding that believers respond with the correct mix of self-reflexivity and veneration, without falling into the trap of believing that this mix can ever be brought to an end by a final interpretative act.

The text redirects the reader time and again to an indescribable experience of the text itself, and not to a hidden stable meaning within it. As a result, the roads "into" this text, the protocols for reading it in the right way and thus the possibility for a reader to draw comforting conclusions from it, become highly problematic. How is a reader to compare, describe, or conceptualize this experience? This analysis has its repercussions not just for scholarship about Calvinism. As the works by Simpson and Cummings also indicate, *sola scriptura* is often associated with dangerous, fundamentalist practices of reading. Calvin has been seen as someone whose fidelity to Scripture has led to an iron and, according to some, intolerant theology. At the other end of the spectrum, Calvin has been associated with the process of secularization in which religious truth-claims have slowly started to withdraw from the public domain. Calvin's emphasis on human iniquity is presented as an essential ingredient in the development of modernity. A close reading of Calvin's use of accommodation in combination with Simpson's and Cummings's emphasis on the textual implications of *sola scriptura*, shows that Calvin's theology was considerably more complex and ambivalent than is often acknowledged. This has its repercussions for the narratives about the development of religious-political authority in early modernity, and it can shed light on how fundamentalist agency as well as secularization can be ascribed to the same theological texts.

CHAPTER 12

Rethinking the Implicit

Fragments of the Project on Aggada and Halakhah in Walter Benjamin

Sergey Dolgopolski

The term *implicit* refers to a whole range of implied thoughts, senses, or meanings that stand in opposition to those that are explicated. In the nineteenth and twentieth centuries, the concept was appropriated by logicians. Retrieving the implicit from the realm of logic back into the realm of rhetoric shows that a complicated structure of movements, exercised by the mind and indeed by the whole person, interacting with a given expression, stands beyond what a logical notion of the implicit can describe.

The concept of the implicit has been used broadly for the investigation of the nature of *language* as an object of linguistic science, where the language is understood as an independent and self-regulating structure. (I use the word "structure" in order not to use "substance," because structural linguists could not agree to treat a *structure* as a kind of *substance* in a philosophical technical meaning of the term, yet "structure" shares with "substance" an important feature of self-sufficiency, if not immanency.)

The approach to *language* as a structure is characteristic of both formal-mathematical approaches and formal-literary ones. The implicit is treated there as being strictly and definitely explicable at any moment of discourse. Thus, in formal-mathematical approaches, the ideal language is an artificial one; the implicit is strictly determined according to the formal rules of deduction and, hence, can be explicated easily at every point.

Similarly, formal literary approaches deal with literature as with a language or *form*,[1] which is subjected either to modification by creating a new *literaturniy fact* ("fact of literature"), as in Tynjanov, or to critical analysis of its poetics, as in Bachtin. Once again, the language is treated here as a substance or sill structure, which is either modified or revised. (It is a kind of "alchemy" of language.) In this approach, the implicit does not have any independent theoretical value.

Both approaches refer to language as a given structure that includes implied meanings, indicating that the meanings can indeed be explicated in a theory of language or in the form of a dictionary. If we do not agree for a moment with understanding the language as either a substance or structure, we cannot continue to think of the implicit in terms of meaning that could be actually and explicitly determined for any particular unit of language. (By *unit* I mean an expression, an utterance, a sentence, an argument, or even a particular language.) In this situation the implicit becomes a complicated matter. The logical terms of implicit become insufficient for elaborating the complicated topology of being implicit. Therefore, a new theoretical strategy is required.

We seem to have good resources for such a strategy, including taking into account the very *facticity* of the implicit "as is"—that is, to give theoretical respect to the fact that the implicitness of an expression has been kept implicit and has not been stated explicitly. However, this solution is not an easy one. If accepted, we have to elaborate a theory of the influence of the very status (*topos* or *location*) of a sense in an expression on the sense itself. Walter Benjamin, Franz Brentano, and Franz Kafka seem to be thinkers of great resource for fulfilling this task.

Plan of This Essay

I will emphasize the new vision of the nature of the *implicit* that Brentano's critique of the grammatical model of *language* gives us. In parallel to Brentano, I will look upon Benjamin's epistemological project of retrieving language from the realm of linguistic communication to the entirely implicit realm of *ideas*, wherein the philosopher, using a literary and philosophical form of *tractate*, returns to the biblical Adam's primordial use of names for naming/calling things rather than for communication. We will see how Benjamin projects his epistemology onto a reading of Kafka's work. Also I will note the point at which Benjamin stops projecting himself onto Kafka. At the same time, aiming at a better understanding of Benjamin's project, I will try to isolate points where Kafka's texts, as compared to traditional ones, can resist Benjamin's reading.

Theoretical results of the project are (1) outlining a new concept of the implicit that emerges from the Brentano-Benjamin perspective and (2) questioning the relation of the implicit to traditional sources, treated in and out of Benjamin's and Bialik's terms of Aggada and Halakhah—that is, in his understanding, the "folklore narratives" and "legalistic discourses" as two separate parts of the Jewish tradition.

Criticizing the Linguistic, Understanding the Language

Franz Brentano demonstrates a weak point of the linguistic-grammatical (in other terms, substantialist) approach to language in his *Kategorienlehre* (translated as *The Theory of Categories*).[2] Brentano argues against the simplified distinction made by grammarians between the use of the verb *sein* ("to be") as a main verb and as an auxiliary verb. In his argument, Brentano enters an important distinction between the thought of *in oblique* ("indirectly") and *in recto* ("directly") that leads to an understanding that being implicit (in his terms *in obliquo*) does not equal being *existent* yet.[3]

Following his argument, we will see that the implicit must be strongly protected from being taken as *actually* and *evidently* existent in any plane of presence in an expression.

Here are the points of Brentano's argument that seem to be most important for our discussion. As Brentano pointed out, grammarians would say that in the statement "A is," A is stated to exist. However, according to Brentano, "we are dealing with a simple affirmation of A thought of in the temporal mode of the present."[4]

Brentano takes us immediately from a grammatical dimension of substantial *language* to a dimension of "being thought of" as it is introduced by the *utterance* "A is." This change is decisive. In many cases, where grammatical theory sees a kind of linguistic predication, Brentano discovers the expression for a kind of "thinking of." In his analysis of more complicated cases of predication, Brentano points out two already mentioned distinct modes of "being thought of": *in obliquo* vs. *in recto*.

What distinguishes a relative determination from an absolute determination? The answer is this: Whenever one thinks a relative determination in *recto*, then one also thinks of something in *obliquo* at the same time. Thus, one who thinks of a person seeing is also thinking in *obliquo* of something colored that is thus seen.[5]

Brentano continues by saying that a thing thought of *in obliquo* can be either existent or not. Its existence or nonexistence does not make a difference for the very thinking of it in *obliquo*.

Now we are ready for the next step. If the predications of grammarians in many cases turn out not to be predications but rather *expressions* for being thought of, then what conclusions can we derive about the very thoughts or "thinking of" expressed there? To answer, one should consider that Brentano's analysis is capable of dealing not only with the direct and indirect modes of thinking of a *thing* or an *object*, but also with states of the thought itself. The thought of an object *in obliquo* is the thought that *is* in *obliquo*. Therefore, one is not obliged to read Brentano in terms of a reified opposition between the thought and the thing.[6]

Thus, it seems to be accurate to use Brentano's distinction for the description of states of thoughts. It allows me to say that, in terms of Brentano's discourse, the implicit is a thought *in obliquo* or is included in a "relative determination." That means the implicit is given indirectly in a statement that only seems to be a predication, but instead turns out to be an affirmative expression of the state of "thought of."[7] Thus, the implicit is included in a *relative* determination of an expression rather than in an absolute determination of predication.

For the present discussion, it means that to think of a relative determination is not necessarily to assume its existence. Now, relative determination is the determination of thought itself, rather than of its object. The object of relative determination is only an external determinative for the very effect created by the indirect character of thought itself.

The most general conclusion to derive from the above exposition of Brentano's argument is that whenever we deal with expression (as opposed to statement or predication) we have some indirect thought included. It stays an indirect thought and remains irreducible to any explicit thoughts presented in the expression directly.

Brentano's discovery of the states of "thought of" that are irrelevant to either existence or nonexistence of either the objects described or subjects manifested in an expression reveals a new aspect of thinking implicitly. His theory helps to see an indirect thinking hovering over any expression, however explicit or "existent" the references and the subjects of that expression might be. That indirect thinking always accompanies direct and explicit thoughts in expression. Brentano thus helps see the irreducibility of indirect thinking or of thinking indirectly. Yet there is more to thinking in that oblique register.

A Way to Represent the Implicit

In Walter Benjamin's *Erkenntniss-Kritische Vorrede* [*Critical-Epistemological Introduction*] there is another very important aspect of nonreducibility of the implicit to any kind of existence. In this work Benjamin suggests treating *ideas* as both separate from all the "phenomena of our world" and from all the "concepts" of our theories that embrace the "phenomena." Because *ideas* stand beyond explicit concepts of theory, to represent *ideas* one needs some specific form. In Benjamin the form is that of a medieval *tractate*.[8] The form of tractate, re-elaborated and implemented by Benjamin for his purposes, allows him to deal with *ideas*, which are never expressed directly either in a concept or in a phenomenon.[9] The *form of tractate* follows the idea, organizing concepts and phenomena without unfolding it in a concept—that is, keeping it in the immediacy of the implicit. Benjamin's *Introduction* emphasized very strongly that the dimensions of the explicit and implicit are unconvertible and do not communicate with each other directly.

In his projective readings from Kafka, Benjamin further elaborates the point. In fact, Benjamin reads Kafka as a person, as a writer running from the *phenomena* (including given expressions, utterances, and so forth) toward their *idea*, making up new points in *concepts*, in "spurious predications,"[10] running to embrace the phenomena, which never, ever can be embraced finally.

Applying this notion to reading Kafka, Benjamin talks on Kafka in terms of *"failure"*:

> To do justice to the figure of Kafka in its purity and its peculiar beauty one must never lose sight of one thing: it is the purity and beauty of failure.... There is nothing more memorable than the fervor with which Kafka emphasized his failure.[11]

Benjamin's reformulation, given after the completion of his "Kafka" in a letter to Gershom Scholem (published as a fragment as "Some Reflections on Kafka"), seems to be related to Bialik's work "Aggada and Halakhah" in Scholem's translation.[12] In his text, Bialik explains the generalized modem usage of the terms *halakhah* and *aggada*:

> The words "Halakhah" and "Aggada" are Talmudic, and their meaning in their proper places is very strict. But in the aspect of their inner quality their meaning fits to be extended and generalized to the rest of all the different phenomena both of the pre-Talmudic and post-Talmudic preriods. Halakhah and Aggada are two specific forms, two variants of style, which complement one another in life and in literature. Every generation has its own Aggada, and every Aggada has its own Halakhah.

It does not mean either this or that Halakhah, nor does it mean this or that Aggada. We are dealing with the very principle of Halakhah, with Halakhah as an extreme generalization, as a specific and concrete form of real life, taking place not in the imagination, depending only on infirmity of mood and beautiful words, but rather of life with a body and with a beautiful image of the body. And Halakhah of such kind, I say, is nothing else but necessary continuation, a "logical completion" of Aggada. Great Aggada leads to Halakhah. The Aggada that has not his own Halakhah is a poor one. At the end such Aggada is canceled. It also cancels the force of its producers' acts. Here is an expression of the same motif in Bialik, now in application to modernity:

> Our days we got a generation of Aggada alone. Aggada in literature and Aggada in life. The whole world is no more than Aggada in Aggada; and there is no memory and no sign of Halakhah in any of its meanings![13]

In these passages one recognizes Benjamin's motif of failure from the letter to Scholem: Aggada fails without Halakhah, wisdom fails without truth. What are the roots of the modern failure marked in Bialik as "Aggada without Halakhah"? Benjamin's thinking about failure in Kafka might help. This is how Benjamin describes the roots of Kafka's "beautiful failure": They are in Kafka's (and, in part, Benjamin's own) relation to tradition. Benjamin says:

Kafka's work presents a sickness of tradition. Wisdom has sometimes been defined as the epic side of truth. Such a definition stamps wisdom as inherent in tradition, it is truth in its haggadic consistency. It is this consistency of truth that had been lost. Kafka was far from being the first to face this situation. Many had accommodated themselves to it, clinging to truth or whatever they happened to regard as truth and, with a more or less heavy heart, forgoing its transmissibility. Kafka's real genius was that he tried something entirely new: he sacrificed truth for the sake of clinging to its transmissibility, its haggadic element.[14]

If Benjamin's characteristic of Kafka as an inventor who "sacrificed truth" for the sake of its "transmissibility" is taken in the context of Benjamin's epistemological project of failure, that reveals yet another, no less important dimension of the notion of failure in Benjamin. The failure turns out to be a failure to go directly from a phenomenon to its idea. Even if such failure is characteristic for the whole range of people (which is also in accordance with Bialik), it was only Kafka, Benjamin argues, who lives in it, experiences it in detail, and therefore grasps it in its beauty. Kafka's work seems to serve as an esthetic or literary utopia for Benjamin's epistemological project of the *ideas*. On the way to them, one not only commits a failure, but also must live in the beauty of it.

In terms of Benjamin's epistemology, failure would mean that Kafka sacrificed his will to reach the truth (i.e., *ideas*) directly or in the explicit (that is, in concepts), and instead went for getting and transmitting the *ideas* indirectly, *in the implicit*, without violating their indirect character. Benjamin's Kafka thus finds himself, among many others, facing a choice of Aggada or Halakhah, wisdom of ideas or truth of concepts. Unlike many others, however, his solution was, instead of choosing, changing the conditions of choice. Kafka thus sacrificed *transmissible* truth (Benjamin's own concepts) for the sake of transmissible wisdom (Benjamin's *ideas* in the philosophical form of *tractate*). Thereby Kafka won a new status for wisdom: Transmissible but failing wisdom is the only realistic foundation for the nontransmissible truth in our world. That is how wisdom (that is, Kafka's and Bialik's Aggada or, in Benjamin's epistemological project, the form of *tractate*) becomes the foundation of law, instead of being a secondary appendix to it. Benjamin's law, which for him is another name for *ideas*, exceeds the conceptual dimension of our world, but functions in our world due to the forms of Aggada and Tractate.

As an indirect way of expression, Aggada becomes a fundamental representation of the law in our world; therefore Benjamin reestimates the very nature and character of its indirectness. In his "Some Reflections on Kafka," Benjamin presents this argument:

Kafka's writings are by their nature parables. But it is their misery and their beauty that they had to become more than parables. They do not modestly lie at the feet of the doctrine, as the Haggada lies at the feet of the Halakhah. Though apparently reduced to submission, they unexpectedly raise a mighty paw against it.[15]

254

Nearing a crucial point wherein Benjamin dismisses his own projection onto Kafka, his form of wisdom or Aggada as a representation of the truth diverges from Benjamin's form of tractate. Wisdom in its new, law-representing position no longer remains wisdom. Instead we have only "products of its decay": "This is why, in regard to Kafka, we can no longer speak of wisdom. Only the products of its decay remain."[16] For Benjamin, being very close to the philosophic tractate, the Aggada, still cannot organize any positive representation for the *ideas*. The notion of "products of decay" is the particular instance in which Benjamin's program of making the philosophic tractate becomes imperative if he wants to do what Kafka's strategy of failure cannot: to express the law in the world in a positive way—to go beyond the failure and to represent *ideas*, not only by failing to represent them, but also by making the failure into a form of representing the *ideas*—the form of tractate.

Of Tradition

With Benjamin's epistemology of *ideas* and Brentano's theory of indirect thinking of, let us examine how the topology works in Kafka's "haggadic" pieces. Let us also see how well that topology of making sense of *ideas* through failure to grasp them might work in reading some relevant pieces of Jewish tradition.

In Kafka's "On Parables," an anonymous voice states that the words of the wise are mere parables, incompatible with the senses of our everyday world. A parable bespeaks the inconceivable, which is beyond our world and cannot help us here; a narrator of the parable, the sage bespeaks the inconceivable by means of a parable because she does not have any direct knowledge of the unconceivable, either. By means of a parable the wise narrator just says that the unconceivable is unconceivable, *"und das haben wir gewusst"* ["but that we have already known"], Kafka notes bitterly. As I should highlight, for the sage-narrator of a parable, that initial awareness of inconceivability of the unconceivable seems to be absolutely independent of the sage's words. In contrast to that sage-narrator of the parable, Kafka understands that initial awareness—"but that we have already known"—to be the best possible result of the sage's action of telling the parable. What for the sage is failure, for Kafka is a productive act—that is, the sage's performance is a success precisely because it is a failure to conceive the unconceivable. Part of that effect consists in hiding its cause.

The success of a parable cannot be measured in terms of achieving a goal the narrator has posited for herself. Rather, it is based on the work of a device, which those involved in the work cannot control. Neither the sage nor Kafka can. By definition such a device is a machine to start and let go rather than a tool to hold and control in one's hand. In the words of the parable, "The first said: 'you have won.' The second said: 'But unfortunately only in parable.' The first said: 'No, in reality: in parable you have lost.'"[17] Victory in reality is loss in the parable. That is how the machine of learning from a failure works.[18] Can this machine produce more than despair? Kafka and Benjamin differ in the answer. For Kafka, in telling the story there is only a negative way of relating to the unconceivable through failing to conceive the unconceivable, which is the only real way to relate to it. For Benjamin both the failure and the victory are parts of one form, one machine, that of tractate, of which both "reality" and "parable"—that is, law and homily, Halakhah and Aggada—are intrinsically interconnected parts: Through failing in the latter one wins the reality for the former. From Benjamin's standpoint—that is, failing in parable or Aggada—leads to gaining the reality for what is addressed in the law or Halakhah, so that the two parts intrinsically belong to one form, that of a Talmudic tractate.

Is Aggada Tractate?

Jill Robbins pointed out the difference between Kafka and a homiletic Midrash Aggada.[19] As a genre, Midrash Aggada is a form of exegesis of biblical phrases and passages. The characters, including often nameless narrators, in Midrash Aggada initially present the audience with what seems to be an incoherence in divine utterances in the Bible. They consequently bring the audience to the point where it sees the ultimate coherence of the utterances as reconstructed and defended in the *midrash*. Jill Robbins's example of Midrash Aggada on Genesis 22 is a story known as "Binding of Isaac" in Jewish tradition or as "Sacrifice of Abraham" in Christian tradition. Abraham as a character of the story was the one to take, and in particular miss-take, the divine order "bring him [Isaak] to sacrifice" as "incoherent" with earlier promises G-d made to Abraham. That is, as Robbins has it, Abraham had a "mistake of hearing." On this reading, shocked as he was by the discrepancy between an earlier promise G-d gave about Isaak and the new order "to bring Isaac to sacrifice," Abraham did not pay attention to the ambiguity of "bringing to sacrifice." The divine utterance might have meant either "slaughter Isaac" or "bring him to the place of slaughtering," Jill Robbins highlights. Yet, as she argues following the Midrash, Abraham commits the "mistake of hearing" that is later corrected by the angel. The "mistake of hearing" is a detail Midrash Aggada adds to the story to restore the coherence between an earlier divine promise to give Abraham seed through Isaac and the new command, which strikes both the audience, and therefore Abraham, as "incoherent" with the earlier promise.

This mistake of hearing has however, an intrinsic temporal element, which the Midrash Aggada, on Robbins's reading, does not address, but Kafka does. For Kafka, as Robbins interprets him, in the beginning of the story Abraham "heard," or paid attention to, the first meaning only ("slaughter Isaac") while he understood the second meaning ("take him to the altar") only at the very end, standing as he did in front of the altar with his hand stretched. According to Jill Robbins, in analyzing the Midrash Aggada Kafka goes further than Midrash does. As she argues, the Midrash Aggada only reveals the "mistake of hearing" to restore the coherence of biblical text, while Kafka defends the fundamental and basic character of such a mistake. For Kafka, in Robbins's interpretation, Abraham could not have eliminated this mistake in the beginning of the story, even if, by the end, he realized it was a mistake. To make the story work, the character cannot eliminate the mistake, even if it became known to the character from the start. Neither can the audience decide whether it was just Abraham's mistake or the mistake was set up by the Holy-One-Blessed-be-He to "tempt" and to teach him. For Kafka the mistake is a necessary part of the story; even for the Midrash Aggada it is only a way to explain a seeming incoherence in the Bible.

For Robbins Kafka thus differs from this particular Midrash on Abraham.[20] He gives the mistake and miss-taking a much greater role than Robbins finds in the traditional Aggada. Nevertheless, as I would still stress, a mistake that cannot be eliminated by illumination is one of the features not only in Kafka, but also in Talmudic discussion. Recognition of the importance of making a mistake in studying the Torah finds an explicit expression in an Aggada about two Talmudic sages in which a winner in the argument consoles his losing friend (potentially relating to himself as well): "One can understand the words of the Torah only if one is mistaken by them." In the light of this rule of the mistake, Abraham's "mistake of hearing" turns to be a *grano salis* of "Binding of Isaac," in which case the mechanics of the story runs like this:

1. Abraham was promised that "in Isaac shell thy seed be called."
2. Abraham was tempted. He heard an utterance, which he could hear either as a command "to bring Isaac as a burnt offering" or as a command "to bring Isaac to a place of a burnt offering."
3. Even if Abraham understood the ambiguity of the command right away—that is, from the start—by the end of the story, by having his hand stretched, he intimated his own will (or his own understanding of the divine will) to sacrifice the son, which proved different from the "will" of the utterance, even on its weak reading of "bringing to altar." Of course, Abraham's will (choosing to sacrifice rather than bring to sacrifice) is still related to the utterance "bring your son to a burnt offering" as one possible interpretation, but his will does no longer depend on the will conveyed. This double bind—relation without dependence—substantiates the essential role that the "mistake of hearing" plays here. It is the machinery of miss-taking that reveals to Abraham the divine utterance beyond Abraham's hearing it. Because of this machine of miss-taking prolonged in time, the divine word is revealed to the audience of the Midrash Aggada in its isolation from Abraham's will to interpret and act on it. More closely, two meanings in one utterance create a necessity of choosing one of them at Abraham's own will. His will to interpret, along with the necessity of a miss-take in the interpretation, make for

the core moving force of the story, as the audience, but not Abraham, can clearly see. In action—that is, "in reality"—Abraham wins: He fulfills both meanings by approaching the altar and stopping there at the very last moment, and thereby shows the audience the true meaning of the divine. However, in his will—that is, in what guided the actions of Abraham as a character—he loses, no matter which way he wills to interpret the utterance at the start. If, in the beginning of the story, he interprets divine words as a command to approach the altar, then he is missing the other possibility of interpretation, and thus he is mistaken. If, again, in the beginning of the story, he interprets the utterance in a different way, as a command to slaughter, he again is mistaken, as becomes clear at the end. If, in yet another way, in the beginning of the story he understood fully the ambiguity of the utterance and interpreted it both ways, this also would mean a mistake, because, in the beginning, acting on double interpretation automatically means choosing the weakest one: dismissing the command of "slaughter Isaac" altogether—that is to say, in Kafka's perspective, time plays a crucial role, as it also does in the above Talmudic principle of mistaking in studying the words of Torah. In the beginning of the story Abraham cannot control the end of it. Any attempt to control the end would be and must be a mistake. To arrive at the end of the story, "in the story" Abraham must commit a mistake and must lose. This leads Abraham to winning his future "in reality."

There is yet another reading. It is closer to Benjamin than to Kafka. Yet as I suggest, it approximates the rabbinic tradition of Midrash Aggada no less than Kafka's view does, even if from a different angle. The reading has to do not only with the irreversible, even if back-traceable, work of a time-machine, in which miss-taking must occur to make the story going. As it will immediately become clear, that reading also has to do with what Benjamin would have called the timeless ideas approached in that story. Abraham, in one option, was right away in the beginning capable of seeing the two possible interpretations of the divine utterance ("bring to altar" and "sacrifice"). However, a new understanding that the divine utterance stands beyond and above any graspable interpretation comes to Abraham and to the audience only after, and as a result of, the miss-take he commits. Otherwise the character of Abraham would read along the lines of Kierkegaard rather than Benjamin. For the latter, the divine utterance is an *idea*, which means it stands beyond any graspable sense, remaining as it does in the implicit. To borrow Brentano's terms, this utterance proves to be a relative determination rather than an absolute one. This means, as a parable, "Binding of Isaac" does not reveal what the divine idea behind the story actually is, nor does it claim either existence or nonexistence (or either knowledge or lack thereof) of the unthinkable. Rather and much more powerfully, it creates and induces in the reader the initial "thinking of" of the unthinkable approached by the story.[21]

The work of the machinery of miss-taking keeps the initial divine utterance in the implicit—that is, out of its initial interpretation ("sacrifice Isaac") that emerges in the beginning of the time-machine's cycle. Nor is the utterance fully explicated at the end of the cycle, when the story ends. All the end of the story does is reveal the implicit to be implicit. It is revealed, that is to say, to be an implicit place wherein Abraham's own will emerges, gets explicated, and grows.

In both Benjamin's and Kafka's perspectives, the case of Abraham turns out to be a symbolic birthplace for the rabbinic rhetoric of mistake as opposed to Kierkegaard's hermeneutics of interpretation in *Fear and Trembling*. Kierkegaard's technique of interpretation does not require miss-taking. Rather, Kierkegaard only recognizes that Abraham defies any interpretation of his actions and thoughts in terms of universal ethics, and is instead the "knight of faith." Kierkegaard does not see Abraham going through an experience of miss-taking or, for that matter, of the thought of any describable experience. Instead, Kierkegaard's method of interpretation concerns readers, not Abraham. Kierkegaard demands from the readers to understand the problem of unexplainably of Abraham's actions in terms of universal ethics, which in turn circumscribes him and readers to a hermeneutical circle. An emblem of that circle and a way to break it is Abraham as a "knight of faith," who exists—that is, finds his salvation from nonbeing—precisely because he escapes any universal understanding of his actions or motives. That hermeneutical circle of reading proves very different from the working cycle of the time-machine of miss-taking. The former circumscribes the reader of the story only, while the machinery of miss-taking describes the trajectory of the characters in the story as well.

In Kirkegaard's hermeneutics of interpretation, the implicit is directly explicable in an interpretation, at least in principle. This means this is not exactly implicit in Benjamin or Kafka's terms, but rather is only "implied." In Kafka, the implicit does not become any explicable "implied," because the time-machine of miss-taking guarantees keeping the implicit implicit as the only way in which one is to deal with it.

Failure Proves

Observably, Kafka's and Benjamin's manner of dealing with mistake and miss-taking pertains not only to reading a Biblical story, but also to some Talmudic passages. A rather general statement—that one cannot take the words of the Torah unless he will make a miss-take or fails in them, appears in the Babylonian Talmud not only as words one rabbi tells to another in the course of polemics. Rather, miss-taking plays a much more serious work, both as a heuristic device and as an instrument of proving. In what follows I address a case in Talmudic discussion in which the mechanics of miss-taking are shown in more detail. We can even find a Talmudic hero of miss-taking, ironical as that hero might prove to be, who, on different readings, either teaches or learns what the beauty and importance of failing and miss-taking are. His name is Raba Bar Rav Huna, and his story is narrated in a passage from the Talmudic tractate *Gittin* [*Divorce Writs*].[22] In it there appears a dictum:

No one can [properly] take the words of Torah, unless one miss-takes them.

וְיֵא סְדָא מוֹעַ לַע בְרֵיד תוֹרְ הַאֶלָּא סָ מָ כֶ הוֹ או נְכֶשׁ לַ הַבְו

Mis-taking is a condition of success in doing Torah! For Bialik this would be an Aggada appearing in the midst of Halakhah. However, does this Aggada lead to Halakhah, or does that Halakhah lead to that Aggada? I will read it closely in context and follow the story assuming that the text displays a coherent argument rather than an anthology of the three or four independent fragments loosely connected by association or by similarity in style, names, or characters. In reading, I will also presuppose that in the story there are no purely "ornamental" figures of speech.

It is important to begin with the broader context of a legal discussion pertaining to the story of Raba Bar Rav Huna. In terms of background, the story concerns a society in which there are not only free individuals, who therefore can marry and bear consequent financial responsibilities, but also there are slaves, who are not financially responsible and therefore cannot legally marry. Most importantly for the story, in such a society there can also be individuals who are half-slaves and half-free persons. Such a legal condition arises when a slave is owned by two owners, and one of them sets her part of the slave free. Noteworthy, in this society a free person may have, and be responsible for, more than one wife.

This creates a series of legal issues. What if a slave belonged to two masters, and then one granted him freedom? The slave becomes half-a-slave, half-a-free person; he then works one day for his master and another for himself, as it is said in the Mishnah, a third-century code of Jewish law. A much more difficult question is, can such a person marry? The Mishnah says he cannot marry a free woman, because he is partly a slave, nor can he marry a slave-woman, because free people do not marry slaves either, and he is partially free. To rectify this impasse, the Mishnah regulates that the court must obligate the remaining master to grant that person freedom.

Centuries and miles away from the point of Mishnah's composition, the nameless characters in the Talmud, interpretable as rabbis and students in Babylon, are challenged to reconfirm the recorded memory of the Mishnah. If the Mishnah is only available for them as recorded memory, is this record automatically accurate? Is there really no way for such a person to marry? Perhaps half-a-slave man could still marry a woman of a similar status—that is, a half-a-slave woman? The stakes of this question are very high, both locally and more generally. It is not only whether the remaining master really has to let the half-a-slave go, but also whether the recorded memory of the Mishnah is accurate and therefore authoritative.

As the Mishnah states, a slave-part of half-slave prevents him from marrying a free woman, and his free part prevents him from marrying a slave-woman. Their task is thus to test and dismiss the possibility of marriage between people who are half free. Following the tactics of failing proofs, these rabbis and students explore a possibility that Mishnah did not explicitly mention. What if half-a-slave man marries a half-a-slave woman? Perhaps this is legally possible, and the Mishnah on record misses that possibility? If so, the text of the Mishnah is not remembered right, is corrupt, and needs fixing. While the strategic goal of the rabbis is therefore to prove that such marriage would not be possible, tactically the characters in the Talmudic discussion begin by testing and dismissing possible legal grounds for such a marriage. Unlike other models of relationship between tactics and strategies, for them a tactical failure means strategic success.

In the sequence of arguments I will address for the purposes of this essay, the anonymous characters in the Talmud consistently follow the tactics of failing proofs and even, as one point in that sequence, make the elusive nature of failure a theme of a story they recall and reread anew.

Yet first, the anonymous rabbis and students begin the sequence of explorations in legality of marriage between half-free people by using more general rules of betrothal. Two such rules lead them to mutually exclusive suggestions about approving such a marriage or not. As a matter of one general rule, if a free man betroths a woman saying, "you are thereby betrothed to half of me," then legally the woman does become betrothed to him entirely. This, however, does not work for the half-slave, because the entirety of that free man was legally available to betroth her, yet half-a-slave was not, the rabbis confirm. That suggests to them that half-a-slave may not effectively betroth a half-free woman to his free half. Therefore a half-free man cannot marry a half-free woman. On the contrary, as a matter of another general rule, if a free man betroths only a half of a free woman by saying, "half of you is betrothed to me," that does not constitute legal betrothal, because he could have betrothed the whole of her, but did not. This, of course, does not apply to the half-slave woman, because he had no way to betroth more of her than he did. That suggests to them that half a slave may legally betroth "half of a woman." Therefore, a half-slave man can marry a half-slave woman, so he thus can and cannot marry a half-free woman.

Given these contrary suggestions, the rabbis go through a sequence of invariably failing attempts to prove that half-free people can marry. For that end they first explore and test a general rule from a more remote area of law. "If a bull killed the half-slave-half-freeman, the owner of that bull is to pay half the fine to the half-slave's owner and half the ransom to the descendants."[23] This rule is suggestive of half-a-slave having inheritors, so he must have been effectively married. However, after a very detailed consideration the rabbis do not accept the suggestion, arguing that an actual existence of, rather than a mere possibility to have, dependents cannot be inferred from the ruling, because, as confirmed by Rabba's more general pronouncement, "he might have to pay, but there still might be no to whom"; the owner of the bull might still be legally obligated to pay, even if there actually is nobody to whom he could pay. Rabba's more general formula allows them to rule out the rule as an indirect proof of such marriage. Rabba's is also a direct statement that betrothal of a half-free woman is not legally effective, which the rabbis timely recall in order to confirm the accuracy of their use of Rabba's formula in analysis by his direct statement coinciding with the outcome of that analysis.

With directly applicable rules of betrothing to half a man, or betrothing half a woman having led to an irresolvable contradiction (a half-slave man both can and cannot marry a half-slave woman), and with having dismissed an otherwise indirectly applicable proof of such marriage from damages payable to inheritors of half a slave, the rabbis in the story have already arrived at an impasse and have already failed one attempt to get out of it through approving marriage between half-free people. They have ended up so far with a statement of Rabba, as axiomatic as it sounded, that betrothing a half-free woman is not legally effective. The content of Rabba's statement serves well their strategic goal of defending the Mishnah; however, the axiomatic form of it does not. A sequence of proofs cannot end with an axiom. In order to reinforce Rabba's all too axiomatic statement on record, the sequence of failing proofs must continue. It does so with a story that not only provides a proof through failing another proof, but also makes failing proofs its more general topics.

Next in the sequence is a recalled—and for me here central—story of Rav Aba Bar Rav Huna and Rav Hisda. This is a story of miss-taking, failing, and self-refuting. As I will argue, in Bialik's terms, but perhaps unlike his thesis, the story functions as Aggada and Halakhah at the same time, not only one leading to the other, but one becoming inseparable from the other. This story represents a narrative about rabbinic authorities of the past in their attempts to fail each other. In the way the story is positioned, narrated, and explained in the Talmud, the story also represents a reading of it by the anonymous rabbis and students in the Babylonian academy. Because it not only performs a tactic of failing proofs, but also makes failing proof its theme, this story is an even stronger and the most interesting case of the rabbinic tactic of failing to prove the whole sequence. It goes as follows:

Raba Bar Rav Huna inferred (שרד): Just as "a [free] woman is not betrothed to one who betroths only a half of her," so also "half-a-slave-half-a-free-women who was betrothed is not [legally] betrothed."[24]

Rav Hisda objected to him: [Your analogy does not work!] What's in common [between the two]? There [in the antecedent] a free man would have been able to get the [free] woman in whole, but here [in the consequent] the female half-a-slave could not have been taken in whole at all!

Raba Bar Rav Huna held back [stopped his discourse], and put in front of him an *amora* [the reciter of post-Mishnaic legal materials] to recite as follows: The verse in *Isaiah*, "When a man shall take hold of his brother of the home of his father, saying, Thou [hast clothing, be thou our ruler, and *let* this ruin *be* under thy hand],"[25] suggests, "*let* this ruin *be* under thy hand" to mean no one can [properly] take the words of Torah unless one miss-takes them (וְהָב לְשִׁכָּן זֶּך מָא אָלָא הָרוּת יַרבַּד לַע דְמוּע סַדָא זְיָא), [therefore] even if it says "a [free] woman is not betrothed to one who betroths only a half of her," a-half-a-slave-half-a-free-woman who was betrothed still has a [legally valid] betrothal![26]

[The rabbis and students in the Rabbinic academy] comment on that as if in the name of Raba Bar Rav Huna and, in fact, even mimic the objection of Rav Hisda above]: What was the reason [for Raba Bar Rav Huna's final conclusion], they ask. There [in the antecedent] a free man was able to betroth the woman in whole, but here [in the consequent] a female half-a-slave cannot be taken in whole at all![27]

This exchange is a part of the tactic of "failing proves." As complex as this tactic already is, in this exchange the relationship between failure and success becomes even more complex, but also more clearly articulated.

Raba Bar Rav Huna suggests that just as a free person cannot effectively betroth only a half of a free woman to himself, so also half-a-slave cannot either. Rav Hisda breaks the analogy: The two cases are not comparable; in the former the man could have betrothed the whole of the free woman, but he did not; however, in the latter the man could not, he argued. This makes Raba bar Rav Huna's attempt to defend the Mishnah unsuccessful.

Bar Huna's response is ironic. Seemingly recognizing his failure as a scholar and his argument ruined by Rav Hisda's counterargument, he in fact reduces Rav Hisda's counterargument to absurdity by using it to prove exactly what nobody wants proven: Even if a free person cannot effectively betroth only half of a free woman to himself, still half-a-slave cannot, he ironically argues. The reason is that exactly because free man could but did not betroth the whole woman, while half-a-slave man could not have done that to half-a-slave woman at all, the betrothal of half-a-slave man to half-a-slave woman turns out valid! It means that in the story Bar Huna was the one who failed, but in reality the one who failed was his opponent.

And yet, even if in the story the question of who failed is playful, the role of failure is not; it helps to reconfirm what needs to be reconfirmed: The Mishnah was right—there is no way for half a slave to get married. What is more, the failure is indispensable on the way there. Without presenting as absurd what otherwise might have been a convincing argument—the betrothal of a half slave works precisely because it is different from betrothal of a fully free person—which does not. Failing the other is in reality disguised as failing oneself in the story and remains necessary for success both in the story and in reality. In the story the Mishnah gets defended against an allegation of error in its recording, and in reality the Mishnah authority is reaffirmed.

As already highlighted, in the story the failing proofs are not only accomplished, but their elusive nature playfully becomes the main theme. For the rabbis in the Talmud as readers, the story not only reconfirms that half-free people cannot marry, but also illustrates the heuristic role of failure, in particular of miss-taking, and of self-refuting in debates about the matters of Torah. What for Bialik is the element of Halakhah—legal discussion—and what for him is *Aggada*—storytelling—illuminate each other. What is more, in the eyes of rabbis as readers of that story, if Aggada and Halakhah were separated in it one from another, the story could not even work. For other readers, if Aggada and Halakhah are separated in it, the story may suggest that Raba Bar Rav Huna admitted his mistake and changed his opinion in favor of his opponent. To yet others it may suggest that Raba Bar Rav Huna proved Rav Huna to be self-refuting; he thus addressed the principle "miss-taking is a condition of success not to himself" but to his opponent, Rav Hisda. Yet for the anonymous rabbis and students as readers of this story in the Talmud, only the latter reading is possible, at least according to what they say explaining Raba Bar Rav Huna's argument in "what is the reason."

As rhetorical in their form as they are, the arguments made of failing proofs are naturally open to different readings, indeed to attempts either to prove that the proof was not failing or to fail it in a different way. Medieval Talmudic commentaries show us how that can be done, and early modern commentators even show us how studying the arguments of the failing proofs may also involve the need of a heuristic failure on the side of the student of the Talmud.[28] As a result, the text of the Talmud too becomes accessible only through failure and is thus comparable not only to what Benjamin called the form of tractate (accessing *ideas* by effectively failing to grasp them) but also to what Benjamin calls *ideas*. The Talmudic Tractate becomes accessible to its readers only through a series of carefully performed failures to read it.

In the story the readers see the ruins of argument created by miss-taking as well as the erection of new arguments on these ruins. The ruins created by miss-taking serve here as a basis for an either ironical or seriously taken conclusion, which also constantly threatens to be a miss-take. Miss-taking stands at the very core of this process of construction and constantly haunts its results. It cannot be eliminated from either the process or from its result.

How do both the constructive and always imminently destructive role of miss-taking in the Talmudic story compare to the agency of mistaking and failure in Benjamin's interpretation of Kafka? In the first approximation, the difference is that in the Talmudic story the uncertainty of miss-taking has a positive aspect: Either the initial conclusion of Raba Bar Rav Huna is reaffirmed, which means all his polemics with Rav Huna is only an irony, or alternatively miss-taking by both of them is a basis for a new conclusion. In either case, unlike the miss-taking of the ungraspable in Benjamin's Kafka, Talmudic miss-taking not only moves the discussion forward, but also constantly threatens its outcomes, making miss-taking perpetual. In such a comparison, what Benjamin would call the implicit *ideas* in the Talmud would never be approachable in any final or definitive way. If the

Talmud is a tractate, then it approaches no external *ideas*. Instead, as a form, it also functions as the *idea* that for the readers of the Talmud will always be imminently grasped, but never in any finalized way. That difference requires a much closer look. Hence the next question to ask is, what stands behind it?

Tractate and Aggada

Returning from Talmud to Benjamin, we now see a clearer difference between the Talmudic form of miss-taking and Benjamin's form of tractate as both divergent and convergent ways to approach ideas. As discussed, in Benjamin, due to the necessity of miss-taking, Kafka's Aggada fails, but *tractate* wins. Benjamin's project of tractate treats the machinery of mistake as a product of wisdom's decay, which is the decay of Aggada that occurs alongside dismissing the truth or Halakhah. However, if, unlike Benjamin and like the Talmud story, we take the very project of the machinery of miss-taking positively, we could contemplate the Talmud as a project wherein Halakhah and Aggada are not juxtaposed as they were in the whole project of Jewish modernism, including Benjamin's Kafka. In the Talmud, then, the machinery of mistake would no longer mean a "decay" of the Aggada, but rather would represent a normal device among other rhetorical devices, working in Talmudic ways of miss-taking, which also embraces the Talmudic texts as imminently its possible object. In terms of Benjamin's philosophy, the Talmud would then turn out to be a kind of tractate rather than a traditional source of irrationally separated Aggada and Halakhah. This is precisely the point at which Benjamin's retroactive and miss-recognized image of the Talmud reappears. For discerning that image a reconceived notion of the implicit becomes as absolutely crucial as decisive.

In Benjamin's perspective, the Talmudic story thus proves to be a prose-form that uses the time-machine of miss-taking to constantly keep itself in the implicit, both for the rabbis who read the story, being at the same time its part, inhabiting it, as it were from within, and for those readers who first come to read that story from the time after.

The Status of the Implicit

From failing in story yet winning in reality in Kafka, to making failure a way to win even in the story, now understood as a prose-form of medieval tractate, that is a failure in grasping ungraspable, which is a victory in showing that the ungraspable must remain implicit but still embraced in the literary form; to a specific form of failure, miss-taking through failing proofs in the Talmud, where the literary form is not only driven by failing but is itself in everlasting imminence of being miss-taken by its readers both by those accounted in the story and those who come to read it centuries later. This trajectory leads to analyzing Benjamin's projective reading of Kafka in more detail. It allows us to see a gap, a stoppage point, wherein Benjamin stops projecting. This is a point where Benjamin's ideal of a *tractate* no longer applies to Kafka's Aggada.

A difference in conceptualizations of the implicit draws a line between these two thinkers. Needless to say, in Benjamin's reading Kafka's Aggada is not technically equal to the implicit, unless the implicit stops being treated in terms of logic or in terms of grammar—that is, as an implicit content. In Benjamin's reading of Kafka, the implicit is taken as a form rather than as content. Even more specifically, here one speaks about the position in reading and writing rather than about the form of the product in either literature or poetry. Implicit here is the position (locus, topos) a reader or writer could not ever take unless she miss-takes it. The only one thing one can and should do, and at the same time cannot plan doing, is to miss-take that position.

A position that could be taken only by miss-taking it is essential in how Benjamin characterizes the entire work of Kafka. This strange position is indicated by Benjamin in reading the Potemkin story in the introductory part to his "Franz Kafka." On the tenth anniversary of Kafka's death, Benjamin calls the story "a herald racing two hundred years ahead of Kafka's work."[29]

According to Benjamin, Potemkin suffered from states of depression that recurred more or less regularly. At such times no one was allowed to go near him, and access to his room was strictly forbidden. This malady was never mentioned at court, and in particular it was known that any allusion to it incurred the disfavor of Empress Catherine. One of the chancellor's depressions lasted for an extraordinary length of time and brought about serious difficulties; in the offices documents piled up that required Potemkin's signature, and the Empress pressed for their completion. The high officials were at their wits' end. One day an unimportant little clerk named Shuvalkin happened to enter the anteroom of the chancellor's palace and found the councilors of state assembled here, moaning and groaning as usual. "What is the matter, Your Excellencies?" asked the obliging Shuvalkin. They explained things to him and regretted that they could not use his services. "If that's all it is," said Shuvalkin, "I beg you to let me have those papers." Having nothing to lose, the chancellors of state let themselves be persuaded to do so, and with the seal of documents under his arm, Shuvalkin set out, through galleries and corridors, for Potemkin's bedroom. Without stopping or bothering to knock, he turned the door-handle; the room was not locked. In semi-darkness, Potemkin was sitting on his bed in a threadbare nightshirt, biting his nails. Shuvalkin stepped up to the writing desk, dipped a pen in ink, and without saying a word pressed it into Potemkin's hand while putting one of the documents on his knees. Potemkin gave the intruder a vacant stare; then, as though in his sleep, he started to sign—first one paper, then a second, finally all of them. When the last signature had been affixed, Shuvalkin took the papers under his arm and left the room without further ado, just as he had entered it. Waving the papers triumphantly, he stepped into the anteroom. The counselors of state rushed toward him and tore the documents out of his hands. Breathlessly, they bent over them. No one spoke a word; the whole group seemed paralyzed. Again Shuvalkin came closer and solicitously asked why the gentlemen seemed so upset. At this point he noticed the signatures. One document after another was signed Shuvalkin . . . Shuvalkin . . . Shuvalkin.[30]

Shuvalkin, the hero of that story, is Kafka's K, according to Benjamin. The hero had to experience his miss-take in order to discover the implicit in the image of the inaccessible room of Potemkin. Despite Shuvalkin's intervention, the inaccessible room of the chancellor remains inaccessible, remains in its own locus or place of being implicit. Shuvalkin learns that the implicit cannot be explicated. Due to his miss-take of the situation, Shuvalkin discovered what he had done in reality.

Controlled by no intentions and thus by no subject, the effect of this machinery of mistake is similar to the effect of poetry for Benjamin. One cannot reduce that effect to the "ideal content" or to the "doctrine" communicated by a piece of poetry;[31] that is why Kafka's parables are not illustrations for a doctrine and why they are different from what Benjamin thinks a real parable is. Neither are they clarifications of "content," precisely because they are nothing else but machines of miss-taking. Similarly to poetry, Kafka's prose pieces are working in the manner in which the machinery of mistake works:

> [Kafka's prose pieces] have . . . a similar relationship to doctrine as the Aggada does to Halakhah. They are not parables, and yet they do not want to be taken at their face value; they lend themselves to quotation and can be told for purposes of clarification. But do we have the doctrine which Kafka's parables interpret and which K's postures and the gestures of his animals clarify? It does not exist; all we can say is that here and there we have an allusion to it.[32]

The point is that the doctrine beyond Kafka's prose pieces does not exist. However, as Brentano explains, the nonexistence of the implicit does not eliminate its importance and power in thought. Because of Brentano' s works we know that existence does not matter for the thinking of the implicit. That means that even if, and precisely because, the doctrine in Kafka's work does not exist, that doctrine still remains in the implicit and has its power. It is in order to give to this strange positioning of the implicit some traditional legitimization that Benjamin uses the generalized of similar of Bialik's concepts of Aggada and Halakhah, calling the inexplicable doctrine Halakhah and thereby suggesting, even if never explicitly, to call the whole of the Talmudic discourse Aggada.[33]

Both Benjamin and Brentano present projects of critiquing *language* as an object of linguistic science. Both of them take us into the field where one can speak in different ways of thinking about the implicit—"thinking of in *obliquo*" in Brentano, or as "revealed by miss-taking it" in Benjamin (or, by extension, as always imminent miss-taking in the Talmud). Their ways of rethinking the implicit are radically different from the way it was approached in the broad framework of the project of language. The project of language seems to be the intellectual milieu for the secularization of the tradition and for the radical separation of the truth from the wisdom reflected in Bialik's terms of the Aggada and Halakhah. Benjamin's and Brenatano's approaches open a theoretically valid alternative to the project of language. It opens an image of the tradition, standing beyond emergence of the project of language in an, as it were, secular field called "Kultur." Including the Talmudic tradition and its study in that secular field, controlled, as it is, by the global concepts of language and literature, explains the necessity that splits modern representation of the ancient prose-form of the Talmud in two: in Halakhah and Aggada, where, by the same necessity, one of these mutually opposing terms gets lost. Because of the crisis signaled by the unbridgeable split between Aggada and Halakhah, between prose and doctrine, between implicit and explication, in Benjamin, a utopian image of the Talmud is lurking. In this image, the split does not take place. The revised theoretical idea of implicit seems to be one of the adequate tools to grasp this image in theory.

CHAPTER 13

What Cannot Be Said

Apophasis and the Discourse of Love

Jean-Luc Marion

1

What we (wrongly, as we shall see) call "negative theology" inspires in us both fascination and unease. In it, we actually encounter a mode of language or even a language game that claims (perhaps deservedly) to express what cannot be experienced. It fascinates us first because it claims to express an event, or better an ineffable advent. But it also makes us uneasy with its assurance that the inexpressible can really be experienced according to the frequently attested paradox "What no eye has seen, nor ear heard, nor the human heart conceived" is, Paul announces, precisely "what God has prepared for those who love him."[1] In short, this language game occurs only in circumstances where "what had not been told them they shall see, and what they had not heard they shall contemplate" (Isa. 52:15). Hence it is something unseen, unheard of, ungraspable. To give an extreme but unavoidable example, at stake is the paradox of seeing in human flesh him "whom no one has ever seen" (John 1:18), for "no one shall see me and live" (Exod. 33:20).

The language game of what is called "negative theology" all too quickly claims not only to speak the unspeakable but to phenomenalize it, to experience what cannot be experienced and to express it inasmuch as it remains inexpressible. In philosophical terms, one can thus say (as did Descartes) that "in effect, the idea of the infinite, in order to be true, must in no way be comprehended, for incomprehensibility itself is contained in the formal reasoning of infinity [*idea enim infiniti, ut sit vera, nullo modo debet comprehendi, quoniam ipsa incomprehensibilitas in ratione formali infiniti continetur*]."[2] In more theological terms, one can say of God that "we thus call him . . . the inexpressible, the inconceivable, the invisible, and the incomprehensible, he who vanquishes the power of human language and surpasses the comprehension of human thought" (John Chrysostom).[3] Since the two conditions of this speech exercise are unambiguously extreme (to experience what cannot be experienced, to express the inexpressible) one can hardly avoid looking for an alternative when faced with such claims. On the one hand, one could simply challenge all "negative theology" as a language game that is both impractical (after all, one cannot experience what one cannot experience) and contradictory (one cannot, after all, express what one cannot express). In this case one chooses to respect the double prohibitions by Kant ("by means of principles to show the specific limits [of reason])"[4] and by Wittgenstein ("Whereof one cannot speak [*sprechen*], thereof one must be silent").[5] On the other hand, one could accept "negative theology" but restrict it to the domain in which it claims its validity, that of the purest and most extreme religious experience, the domain attributed to the "mystical." This acceptance would amount to a marginalization, since this domain remains inaccessible to most of us—certainly to most philosophers. Even if admitted in principle, "mystical theology" would thus remain an unfrequented territory, willingly abandoned by those who attempt to ignore it to those who are willing to lose themselves there, at the risk of irrationality. This refusal in principle is thus reiterated by a refusal in fact. Metaphysics has amply confirmed these two attitudes, as is proven indisputably by its modern history— which can be described as a rejection (indeed, a tenacious elimination from thought) of what cannot be comprehended as one of its objects.

Or rather, this situation has preceded us, for modernity itself has found its limits and is attempting to identify them. Thus the theme of "negative theology" has resurfaced in philosophy in recent years, at least in a vague manner. Among other indications, one can cite Heidegger, who was unable to avoid "comparing" the step back of the thought of presence toward that of giving (*Geben*) "with the method of negative theology."[6] Or Wittgenstein, who states, with a different accentuation, "There is the ineffable [*es gibt allerdings Unaussprechliches*]. It *shows itself*. It is the mystical."[7] It remains simpler, however, to rely on the most explicit testimony—Derrida's arguments (which, moreover, were elaborated in response to my own publications), for a new pertinence for "negative theology" in the forum of contemporary philosophy.[8] As we know, Derrida revived this theme in order to subject the apophatic moment of "negative theology" to deconstruction. He did so by establishing that it inverts itself and, in the end, achieves a second-order kataphasis so as to reestablish the metaphysical primacy of presence, a goal that was in fact never abandoned by theology. To say of God that he is and then that he is not in the long run would aim only at thinking of this nonbeing as the ultimate and finally unchanging figure of his being—a being beyond being, because, having undergone the ordeal of its negation, the being of God is thus able to prevail not only in transcendence but in presence over the being of all other beings: "Apophasis has always represented a kind of paradoxical hyperbole."[9] In this way the "metaphysics of presence" annexes "negative theology" without any other form of trial, reducing it to the ranks of a pure and simple auxiliary of metaphysics without too much circumspection. Hence deconstruction finally triumphs by getting rid of a possible rival that is all the more dangerous in having preceded it and having come from elsewhere. One can nonetheless show that this interpretation deals a double blow—and the more violence it exerts, the more fragile it becomes.

(a) First, it denies the patience and suffering of the apophatic negation, without taking into account the seriousness and the work of the theologians involved. One need only think of a very explicit remark made by John Scotus Eriugena on the irremediable nature of negation, which can be neither abolished nor mitigated by a final naming:

> For, when we declare "God is super essential," we imply nothing other than a negation of essence. Whoever declares "God is super essential" explicitly negates that God is essence. Consequently, although the negation is not found in the words themselves, its meaning does not escape the understanding of those who think about it seriously. In this way, in my opinion, I am constrained to admit that the divine names enumerated below, though at first they seem to imply no negation, belong more to the negative part of theology than to the positive part.[10]

In fact, the negation remains as radical and definitive for language as kenosis does for its referent.

(b) But in order to bring everything back to the "metaphysics of presence," this attempt to reduce apophasis to kataphasis must also cancel the third path, often called the path of eminence. How is one to understand, in effect, that everything is predicated of God while at the same time nothing is predicated of him—other than by recognizing that a third path surpasses the first two and only thus does away with the contradiction? Of course, it remains to be seen whether there is a language game that could dispense with affirmation and negation like this and thus dispense with truth and falsity. Would we still be dealing with a meaningful assertion and, more particularly, with a predication? Without a doubt; but as Aristotle foresaw, not all assertions refer to truth and falsity following the model of predication: "Prayer [is] certainly a discourse [λογος], but it is neither true nor false."[11]

Even before answering these questions, one can already point to evidence in this direction: First, the phrase "negative theology" does not describe the situation we are dealing with correctly, for the moment of negation (admittedly with variable positions) is inscribed within a triple determination that articulates discourse into (i) *via affirmativa*, (ii) *via negativa*, and, especially, (iii) *via eminentiae*, radically other and hyperbolic. It does not mirror the negation with another superior affirmation (whether disguised or admitted), but tears discourse away from predication altogether, and thus away from the alternative of truth or falsity. Two consequences follow. First, I will no longer say "negative theology," but rather, following the nomenclature of the Dionysian *corpus*, "mystical theology." And second, one will come to realize that "mystical theology" (when it claims to be following the third path) no longer has the ambition of making constative use of language; its ambition is, rather, to be freed from such use. But what type of language use can replace it? I have suggested that it involves moving from a constative (and predicative) use of language toward a strictly pragmatic usage.[12] This has yet to be proven. What follows is an attempt to do just that.

2

But, just as "negative theology" is finally not really negative, it is also possible that it cannot be confined to the theological—at least understood in the narrowest sense. Indeed, one must not exclude the possibility that the pragmatic system used by mystical theology extends to other states of affairs and to other utterances. Nor can one exclude that these other uses may allow us to establish with greater clarity the true function of the third path, which is neither affirmative nor negative. I will thus choose a privileged case of pragmatic language outside of theology, one that illustrates the third path indubitably. I propose considering the erotic event and its corresponding utterance: "I love you!" The question then becomes that of determining what it is one says when one says "I love you!" supposing that one says anything at all. Let me take a famous example from *The Charterhouse of Parma*, when Clélia meets up with Fabrice after years of separation: "'It's me,' a dear voice told him, 'I've come to tell you I love you, and to ask you whether you will obey me.'"[13] Are we dealing with a constative utterance here? Is Clélia really saying something? And is she saying something about something? And in this case, is it a predicate of herself or of Fabrice? I will attempt to respond to these complex questions by emphasizing successive difficulties.

One can first reduce her utterance to its central nucleus, "I love you," and ask what "I love you" says. If, first hypothesis, one reads the formula as it stands, it falls in the domain of pure private language: Neither Fabrice nor anyone else can understand what Clélia is saying. Of course, if I were to make an analogy with my personal experience, I could conjecture that she is describing her subjective attachment to the person of Fabrice. Yet one cannot exclude that she may be pretending or lying, either to Fabrice (to seduce him), to a possible witness (to embrace her standing), or even to herself (to love loving, without loving anyone in particular). In order to defend the constative character of Clélia's utterance, one can also reduce her sentence, "I've come to tell you that I love you" to a quasi-predicative proposition in the style "Someone exists—X, me, Clélia—such that she is in love with another—Y, you, Fabrice" (let me allow for the moment that the identification of X and Y with Clélia and Fabrice is not problematic). What signification does this utterance offer? One that is revealed by its method of verification. Here two possibilities open up.

(a) "I love you" could perhaps be verified by precise interactions between things and actors (to approach, to speak to, to watch, to take care of, to serve, etc.). Yet can one locate them, and then establish which and how many are sufficient to give a meaning to the predication "X is in love with Y"? Clélia undoubtedly invests herself—"It is I who have come to tell you," just as she has undoubtedly given sufficient proof of her devotion in the past, helping Fabrice in prison, helping him escape, thinking of him, etc. Yet one cannot say that "I love you!" exactly signifies "I helped you in prison, I helped you escape, I abandoned myself to you, I thought of you," etc. Not only because all of this is far from proving "I love you" (a lot is missing here), but also because one can oppose to these facts other, at least equivalent, facts: Clélia has in the meantime married someone else (Count Crescenzi), she has promised the Virgin never to see Fabrice in the light of day, she has avoided meeting him, etc. Thus, reduced to behaviors and states of affairs, the declaration "I love you!" remains ambiguous, precisely because it doesn't describe anything with precision.

(b) A second possibility remains: Since the reduction of "I love you" to a predicative proposition does not guarantee its verification, it remains possible to trust in Clélia's sincerity by considering that the meta-narrative "It is I who have come to tell you" guarantees what she says in the phrase "I love you." But how is one to recognize and prove this sincerity? All the facts and actions that one could inventory belong to the world. They cannot say anything, nor can they determine the validity of someone's sincerity, which in principle remains both out of this world and absolutely foreign to things. At its best, sincerity pertains to the private sphere and thus cannot be described or verified any more than lying can. One cannot even invoke private language in this situation, because the private sphere is precisely deprived of it. What is more, as soon as someone claims to speak and prove his or her sincerity by speaking utterances of the type "I am sincere," "you can trust me," experience has taught us that we should rather hear an indication of deceit, such that the utterance "I am lying" would suggest that I am in fact not lying. Thus Clélia is saying nothing about nothing to Fabrice when she says "I love you!"

Another interpretation is possible, however. Even if Clélia says nothing to Fabrice, she speaks to him as herself. "I love you" perhaps states nothing concerning any state of affairs and predicates nothing at all, but this utterance nonetheless speaks this nothing *to* someone, Fabrice, and it speaks it *on behalf of* someone else. Let me look once more at the example: "'It is I,' a dear voice told him, 'who have come to tell you that I love you, and to ask whether you will obey me.'" Especially if Stendhal is saying nothing about nothing, it is clear that he insists on the speaker and the person spoken to, to the point of saturation: first the speaker, for she says "it is I," "I have come to tell you," "I love you"; then the person spoken to, for he hears "tell *you*," "love *you*," "ask *you*." Clearly, predication and proposition fade away, leaving the naked intrigue of the two speakers, that is to say, the interlocutors, in the foreground. Could we not describe "I love you!" as a strict dialogue, without an object but perfectly intersubjective?

Several arguments compromise this position: (a) Understood in this way, Clélia's declaration to Fabrice is in effect reduced to a pure dialogue between "I" and "you," in other words, between two pronouns labeled personal and thus, properly speaking, both impersonal and improper. Not only could Clélia rightfully make the same declaration to someone other than Fabrice (and what proves that she has not done just that or that she will not do so?), but Fabrice could equally well receive it from someone else (why not from Sanséverina or from "little Annetta Marini," who faithfully listens to his sermons?). The roles could also be reversed. Yet, most importantly, anyone (not only Clélia and Fabrice) can take on these two roles, like characters in a play, or on the spontaneous stage of everyday life. In "I love you!" "I" and "you" remain empty terms, which essentially produce occasional expressions (occasionally significant) and nothing more.[14] Simple pronouns, they suffice neither to bind people, nor to attribute names, nor to create lovers out of them. Thus Clélia does not speak herself to Fabrice, for purely logical reasons. (b) What is more, if "I love you!" is not sufficient to establish a true signification or even the identity of the person one thus claims to love, that is not only because I can love anyone but especially because I can love someone who is not present or who remains anonymous. In fact, the more I sincerely love (or think I love, which amounts to the same for me), the less the identity of the presence of the loved one is required. I can love a woman or a man whom I know only superficially, or whom I do not know at all (based on his or her name or reputation), or even about whom I know nothing. I can love someone who is absent most of the time and who will probably always remain thus, and I can even love someone absent who has never yet been present, not even for a moment. I can love a woman whom I have lost or whom I have left. I can love someone dead out of loyalty and a child not yet born out of hope. Because I love, what I am in love with does not have to *be* at all, and can thus dispense altogether with maintaining the status of a being. Not only does this absence not stop us from loving and desiring, it reinforces this desire. For the loved one, the person to whom "I love you!" is spoken, it is no longer about being or not being, or about being or not being this or that, but only about the fact that one is loved. Thus (and this time for motives that are not only logical, but also erotic), what Clélia says to Fabrice does not designate Fabrice and is not even addressed to him. "I love you," then, neither produces a proposition with a reference (a signification), nor does it predicate a meaning, nor does it even mobilize identifiable interlocutors. It thus does not constitute a locutionary act.[15]

3

And yet, even if it is not a locutionary act, "I love you" remains a speech act. To see this, we can consider a second hypothesis: that "I love you!" constitutes an illocutionary act, in other words, a performative. By pronouncing "I love you!" the speaker does not in effect say anything (neither meaning nor reference), but accomplishes what he says, puts it into practice simply by saying it; the force of the utterance enforces what is said.[16] This hypothesis, one must admit, seems convincing. It would justify the fact that, strictly speaking, "I love you!" offers neither meaning nor reference, without, for all that, saying nothing, since in saying "I love you!" it is not a matter of communicating information or making a predica-tion but of loving in act and in force. So when I say "I love you!" to someone, or when I hear it spoken by someone else, an act is accomplished immediately: Whether my lover and I rejoice (as occurs with Clélia and Fabrice) or are worried (like Phaedra and Hippolytus in another context) is due to the fact that this love, simply because I declared it, becomes an effective and unquestionable fact, which modifies intersubjective reality and which one must, from now on, take into account. One can add to this: Because this illocutionary act is a performance, it intervenes in a precise time and place and thus attaches a precise and identifiable signification and precise, identifiable speakers to what hitherto remained an essentially occasional expression: Here and now, it is a question of Clélia accomplishing this speech act once and for all and definitively for the benefit of Fabrice and for no one else except her and him. In the same way, the "I don't know what inexplicable and fatal force" that seals the friendship between Michel de Montaigne and Étienne de la Boétie (as if according to a performative) identifies them absolutely and determines the reference to them: The famous but difficult utterance "because it was him; because it was me" thus eliminates at least the danger of an essentially occasional expression and ensures that we are dealing with them, in Bordeaux and in 1554, and no one else, nowhere else.[17]

However, the speech act "I love you!" cannot be analyzed as a performative or illocu-tionary type. Moreover, so far as I know, neither Austin nor Searle mentions it among the latter (in fact, they seem to ignore it entirely, no matter what heading one gives to it). To understand this impossibility, one need only address Austin's conditions for all illocu-tionary acts and measure whether or not "I love you!" satisfies the requirements under each heading.

(1) "There must exist a conventional procedure having a certain conventional effect, a procedure that includes the utterance of certain words by certain people in certain cir-cumstances." If by such a conventional procedure one is to understand a ceremony, whether public (marriage, contract, social pact, etc.) or private (engagement, marriage proposal), then "I love you" is not appropriate: I can say it or hear it in all circumstances, sometimes even in a semi-unconsciousness (pleasure, sleep, etc.), even almost in silence. (2) "What is more, the particular people and circumstances in a given case must be suit-able to invoke the particular procedure they would invoke." "I love you" satisfies this cri-terion so long as it implies two people capable of communicating and possessing at least a certain freedom of feeling. But it does not comply, inasmuch as it ignores all "particular procedures" and can be performed in all circumstances and in all language games. (3) "The procedure must be executed by all participants both correctly and" (4) "completely." But "I love you" can very well remain unilateral (this situation is all too common) and thus does not necessitate that "all" (the protagonists of the action) satisfy this require-ment: One is more than enough. As for the requirement of a "completely" executed "pro-cedure," it has no pertinence, not only because in this case no "procedure" is required but especially because a "complete" utterance either would change nothing, or by changing

something would weaken "I love you!" rather than reinforce it: To add to "I love you!" something like "a lot" or "very much" amounts to saying much less than simply "I love you!" and even insinuates that "I don't love you!"

Let me look at the two remaining conditions: First, (5) "when, as is often the case, the procedure is meant to be used by people having certain thoughts and feelings, or to trigger a certain behavior having consequences for any one of the participants, then a person who participates in this procedure and claims to have certain thoughts and feelings must in fact have them, and the participants must have the intention to behave accordingly; what is more" (6) "they must in the future so behave."[18] It is clear that "I love you" can satisfy these last two requirements even less than the preceding ones. First, as Stanley Cavell has judiciously remarked, I cannot say "I love you" unless motivated by passion, or at least from a passion.[19] Yet no one can verify this passion, not even (or rather especially not) the person who is supposed to benefit from it. Thus my "intention" remains utterly unverifiable. Here one finds the aporia of sincerity: It is a totally private mood, ineffable in everyday language. Thus to say "I love you" guarantees my sincerity no more than it presumes the acceptance (or refusal) of the other or, for that matter, his or her own sincerity. Following Cavell once more, one must next recognize that the freedom and fragility of "I love you" have no ambition to be of any value for anything other than "now," certainly not "in the future": How can I guarantee to someone that I love him or her, if I myself have no certitude? One could answer that I can very well promise to love someone in the future, in spite of the fickleness of my heart and my moods. Of course, but then one is dealing with a promise ("I promise to love you"), and thus with a completely different speech act from "I love you!" The promise is, in fact, the perfect illocutionary act, even the epitome of the performative, satisfying all the enumerated conditions, precisely those that "I love you!" does not satisfy (conventional procedure and effect, fixed circumstances, formal and complete fulfillment, guarantee of reciprocity and the future, etc.).[20] Thus, the promise differs essentially from "I love you!"; it can only be added on, and this supplement confirms that by saying "I love you!" I do not perform an illocutionary speech act.

4

Admittedly, then, "I love you" cannot be considered an illocutionary act, since it respects neither the conventions nor the conditions of such an act. However, the one who pronounces these words does indeed accomplish an act, even if it is not the act of actualizing what he or she says. One does not do what one says by saying it, but in saying it one nonetheless does do something. What can it be? By saying "I love you!" I do not thereby factually or actually love, but I nonetheless radically modify the intersubjective relation between me and my interlocutor; from now on nothing will be the same, for better or for worse. Wherein lies the difficulty, then? Perhaps in this: Whereas the illocutionary act effectively accomplishes what it says (to promise, condemn, curse, bless, etc.), the act that says "I love you!" accomplishes something other than what it says: for example, to be fond of someone without sincerely loving him or her, or to admit to holding someone in affection without hoping for the return of that affection, or else to satisfy a preliminary request or to gain a moral advantage by virtue of my sincerity, etc. When I pronounce "I love you!" I do not prove that I love (as with an illocutionary act), but I nonetheless always produce an effect on my interlocutor: returned love, saddened or fearful refusal, placing the other in a position of power over me, fear, gratitude, surprise, etc. The act therefore does not accomplish what it says, but it says what it says in order to have on the interlocutor an effect that is other than what it says—even if it is simply to draw his or her attention and to constitute the other as my interlocutor in an erotic dialogue.

Now this is exactly what is called a perlocutionary act, as defined by Austin: "an act that we instigate or accomplish by saying something: to convince, persuade, frighten, etc."[21] Searle usefully specifies: "If we consider the concept of the illocutionary act, we must also consider the consequences, the effects that such acts have on the actions, thoughts, or beliefs of the *listeners*, etc." That is, by saying something, we elicit a different effect: to persuade, convince, but also frighten, make aware of, lead to act in a certain way, etc.[22] Cavell gives us a perfect example: "the [perlocutionary] effect [brought about by Iago] of helping to drive someone [Othello] mad with jealousy."[23] When I say "I love you!" I try (and in fact always manage) not necessarily to perform the love that I speak but to move, to influence, and, at the very least, to summon my listener to consider my declaration. I declare my love as one declares war: It is not yet to engage in it, but already to oblige my adversary to mobilize him- or herself, and thus to determine him- or herself in relation to me. The declaration of Clélia, if we understand it as a perlocutionary act, must be reorganized: The sequence "to tell you that I love you" must be understood in terms of the sequence that precedes it—"I have come to"—because together they try to produce another effect than that of the declaration itself, an effect that Clélia renders perfectly explicit: "to ask you to obey me." By saying "I love you!" I do not love for all that, but I in effect ask the other to love me or at least to answer me sincerely. I thus accomplish neither a locutionary act nor an illocutionary act, but rather a perlocutionary act.[24]

In fact, other characteristics of this type of act fit what I do when I say "I love you!" (a) The perlocutionary act produces its effect by saying something, but this effect acts, beyond the *dictum*, on the other speaker or the speakers thus provoked; to be more precise, it "produces certain effects on the feelings, thoughts, and actions of the listeners, the speaker, or *other persons*; and it can be done with the goal, the intention or the will to produce them."[25] Instead of doing what I say, I say *in order to* do something to someone, in the same sense in which, in everyday French, as in English, "faire quelque chose à quelqu'un"—"to do something to someone"—means to provoke, to intrigue, to move, to overwhelm, and eventually to seduce someone. Instead of saying something about something, or bringing about what I say, it is rather, for me, about saying *to* someone, not necessarily what I say, since I mean for my listener to understand something *other* than what I say, but that I am here, that I am speaking to him or her, imposing my will or having his or her will imposed on me. Contrary to the illocutionary act, the perlocutionary does not involve itself so much with the utterance as with the person spoken to, and the speaker always takes the initiative: "The speaker is on his or her own to create the desired effect."[26] (b) Perlocutionary acts prove to be nonconventional, or at least "it is difficult to say where convention begins and ends."[27] We have seen that "I love you!" dispenses with almost all conventions proper to locutionary acts, in particular that of reciprocity. This does not signify the disappearance of such conventions in principle, but that in this case they belong neither exclusively nor primarily to logic or language theory, although they do come within the scope of such theory: They arise out of the space of dialogue itself and from the pragmatics that ensue. To sum up, if there must be conventions, they will first depend on the originary fact of the other. In this way, when I say "I love you!" what I say produces an effect that depends not so much on the obvious meaning of my utterance as on the identity, the situation, even the state of mind of my interlocutor. And I can predict this effect, because my interlocutor's moods follow from language conventions: For example, Don Giovanni plays better than Leporello, when it is a question of speaking to Elvira in particular and to women in general. (c) Indeed, in the perlocutionary act what essentially matters is not what I say (the intention and the meaning) but to whom I say it (others, an audience, or a specific someone); the listener is thus privileged over the speaker—hence the pedagogical rule of thumb that, to teach math to Pierre, one must know mathematics, and above all Pierre. The decisive factor, according to Cavell, consists in the fact that "in perlocutionary acts, the 'you' comes essentially into the picture,"[28] while in illocutionary acts, everything depends on my capacity, as the speaking "I," to perform what I say. And of course, with "I love you!" more than in any other act, what takes center stage is called "you," which constitutes the perlocutionary act par excellence. (d) One last point, decisive for my inquiry, must be addressed: Because one is dealing here not with what I utter but rather with the "responses" to it, hence the effects produced when "I have an effect" on my interlocutor, these effects (emotions, thoughts, reactions, etc.) taken in themselves "can be accomplished additionally or entirely by non-locutionary means." In short, there is nothing contradictory or unthinkable about a "non-verbal response."[29] Not only do perlocutionary acts accomplish intersubjective effects (which lie outside the particular utterance) and contradict what is said, but what is more, the responses arrived at in this way can be given in silence (outside of language). Who does not see that "I love you!" can, once its effect is produced, receive a response all the more satisfying in that it remains silent? It could even be that silence constitutes, if not the best response, at least always the first, and that, without this first silence, the following verbalization would not be convincing. Since all these characteristics are reunited in the utterance "I love you!" one can thus conclude that one is dealing with a performative of the perlocutionary type. And, granting it this status, I am justifying, against its omission by Austin and Searle, what Cavell specifically calls a "passionate utterance."[30]

5

It has now become possible to describe the perlocutionary act that I accomplish when I say "I love you!" or at least to trace a sketch. It is a matter of acting in which not only the fact *that* I speak is more important than *what* I say but in which the fact *that* it is spoken has an effect on *the person to whom* I said it. This characteristic, which goes beyond the field of language [*langue*] and its use [*langage*] to give preponderance to individual speech [*parole*], establishes a structure that is essentially pragmatic, and in this case dialogic. This act speaks inasmuch as it calls out. This call elicits a response and possibly a response to the response, without there necessarily being an end in sight. Thus erotic discourse unfolds according to a call, a response, and a counter-call that can be seen as following three paths.

Let me consider the first and affirmative path. How can I make an affirmation if I am, strictly speaking, not saying anything when I say "I love you!"? As we have seen, this proposition does not offer any reference that can be verified, either by myself (I promise nothing—it is not an illocutionary act) or by the person to whom I am speaking (I can lie, and even if I don't lie, he or she does not know the difference—it is not a locutionary act). It also does not offer a precise meaning (to love can mean to possess like an object, to desire, or, on the contrary, to want the best for and even to sacrifice oneself for someone).[31] Yet as a perlocutionary act, "I love you!" does affirm something: the effect that it produces as a speech act. But this effect is split. First, by affirming to someone that I love him, I choose him as my interlocutor; not only do I distinguish him from the crowd of others who remain anonymous or at least indifferent but, by placing him in a prominent singularity, I individualize him, name and compromise him along with myself, whether he wants this or not: I identify myself through him by identifying him with me. Then, in the dialogical space that has thus been opened, I impose upon my interlocutor a decision regarding whether or not he loves me in return. This decision comprises two questions: Does he accept that I love him, or does he refuse to accept it? but also, Does he love me in return, or does he hate me? Even a refusal to answer one or the other of these questions would be equivalent to a response (negative in this case). No affirmation can impose itself as powerfully as "I love you!" but, paradoxically, it imposes itself as a question whose contours are almost impossible to trace, as the most radical question that one can perhaps ever ask. Put otherwise, if my affirmation *that* I love him neither promises nor teaches him anything, it nonetheless forces him to answer a question, a question that is formulated from my point of view as "Does he love me?" while he hears it as "Do you love me?"

It follows that the initial affirmation "I love you!," as categorical and affirmative as it remains, ends up producing the effect of a "Do you love me?"—a question that leaves room for doubt, for choice, and for a possible refusal. Affirmation thus elicits negation in and of itself; kataphasis becomes apophasis.

One must thus examine the second and negative path. However, can one really consider the question "Do you love me?" to be an apophasis? This assimilation certainly seems paradoxical, but paradoxes are themselves imperative. Let me try to conceive this. To do so, one must remember that, in the case of a perlocutionary act, one does not consider *what* is said but the fact *that* it is said, the effect it has on the listener; but this effect belongs unambiguously to apophasis. By telling her "I love you!" I expect to hear (and to elicit) that she loves me, thus what I want to say is "Do you love me?" and I await confirmation. By this means I find myself in the exact same position as my listener, who, hearing my "I love you!" asks herself and me if I am telling the truth (in other words, if my thoughts concur and if my conduct will reflect what I think and say); she thus asks me as well, in words or in silence, "Do you love me?" Is it possible to give a categorical answer (affirmative or positive) to this double and yet unique "Do you love me"? If it is a question of deciding whether or not (referentially) I am sincere, or whether or not I understand (semantically) what "to love" means, neither she nor I know anything at the moment of the declaration—hence the apophasis. One might answer that what is at stake is not our sincerity but our concrete behavior and coherence: Each of us will learn more about the intention of the other over time, which means that if I ask "Do you love me?" at a particular moment t_1, I can hope to obtain the beginning of an answer at moment t_2 or t_3, etc. This, in its turn, implies that the answer to the question is reached, in the best of cases, only in the moment that follows after. Yet if precisely only the *following* moment can affirm something in response to what I asked only the moment *before*, the temporal gap between doubt and confirmation cannot be abolished and will extend from question to response, endlessly. Thus, even in the case of a happy confirmation, the temporal delay and lateness maintain a différance.

With all other questions about states of affairs or objects that are in principle characterized by a certain permanence, this différance does not seriously compromise the answer. But in the case of the erotic relation, where the fickleness of the heart holds sway even with no intention of lying (and this is precisely why I cannot stop asking "Do you love me?"), différance disqualifies the answer, even when it is positive. One need only think of the common experience of receiving a letter in which the sender reassures me, "I love you too!" This answer can never definitively get rid of my anxiety (I who just said "I love you!" and am waiting for a confirmation today), precisely because it was written and posted several days ago, and I know nothing of what the other was thinking during that time, such that today, now, at the exact moment when I read it, it is too late and still leaves me unsatisfied. "Do you love me?" thus remains decidedly apophatic. This is emphasized from the point of view of the speaking I, for whom doubt goes even further (and not, as one might too quickly assume, less far), for by saying "I love you!" I know that I provoke another question in return as the perlocutionary effect: "Do you love me?" And I also know that there is no way for me to respond to this question and that, on the contrary, I have every reason in the world not to know anything about it. Even if I am sincere in the moment, I know very little about my motivations (desire, the vanity of seduction, fear of solitude, moral altruism?) or about their future (for how long?), such that if I confirm, by answering, "Yes, I love you!" I know only one thing—that I am stepping out of bounds and that, at bottom, as far as the moment to come is concerned, I know nothing. The question "Do you love me?" thus effectively establishes an apophasis.

And yet, despite this apophasis, the erotic dialogue is no less persistent. How is this possible? By means of a third path, a hyperbolic redoubling, a sort of eminence. I can really only repeat "I love you!" precisely because the other repeats ceaselessly "Do you love me?"; and for her, it is the same. She and I, we repeat "I love you!" only because her first enunciation (kataphasis) could not avoid giving rise to the apophatic "Do you love me?" And this repetition is prolonged without foreseeable end, because the confirmation always arrives too late for the question. In the same way, we repeat "Do you love me?" although we know that we cannot obtain a definitive response and although we undergo an insurmountable apophasis on its account, because we do not want to renounce the declaration of love that we can never truly promise or act. It follows that the other and I repeat "I love you!" (over and over again) because it cannot be verified. We repeat "Do you love me?" because we do not want to resign ourselves to invalidating it. I keep saying and *repeating* "I love you!" precisely because, on the one hand, I cannot guarantee it, *and*, on the other hand, I cannot give up trying. Short of answering the question, "Do you love me?" I repeat the perlocutionary act that instigates it, "I love you!" It is a question neither of kataphasis nor of apophasis but rather of a temporalizing language strategy, a repetition that affirms nothing, negates nothing, but that keeps alive a dialogic situation.[32] What the present tense sees as impossible (an affirmation cancelled by a negation), and constative language as contradictory (a kataphasis that gives rise to an apophasis), repetition and the future it conquers makes possible, but in a pragmatic, more precisely perlocutionary, sense. I reach the other and the other reaches me because "I love you!" and "Do you love me?" continually provoke a (perlocutionary) effect in us, or to be more exact, incite each of us for and by the other. We tell each other nothing in a certain (constative) sense, yet by speaking this nothing, or rather, these nothings, we place ourselves (pragmatically) face to face, each receptive to the (perlocutionary) effect of the other, in the distance that both separates and unites us. Constative and predicative (locutionary) or even active (illocutionary) speech definitively gives way to a radical pragmatic (perlocutionary) use: neither speaking nor negating anything about anything, but acting on the other and allowing the other to act on me.

6

If we accept the conclusion toward which these analyses have been leading, a few remarks are in order. First, pragmatic usage (which elsewhere I have attributed to mystical theology in order to gain a better understanding of the third and last path) finds a lateral confirmation in the perlocutions of erotic discourse. In both cases there is a pragmatic use of language, in the form of three privileged perlocutions (and all of their variations, which could be itemized) "I love you!" and "Do you love me?" and their repetition, corresponding to kataphasis, apophasis, and hyperbole. In this sense, mystical theology would no longer constitute a marginal and insignificant exception in language theory but, on the contrary, would indicate a much more central and vast domain, where pragmatics, perlocutions, and what they render utterable unfold, among other things. It is no longer a question of a discourse about beings and objects, about the world and its states of affairs, but rather the speech shared by those who discourse about these things when they no longer discourse about them but speak to one another. The suspicion that modern philosophy has bred of the encounter with theology in general and mystical theology in particular differs little from its disinheritance of the question of love in all its forms. One could then interrogate the dimensions of this encounter between erotic discourse and mystical theology. Are we dealing with a formal similitude, limited to linguistics, or a deeper univocity? I cannot answer such a question in this context. I am already satisfied with having been able to ask it. Two comments, marking a convergence, can nonetheless be made.

First of all, the following: Just like mystical theology, erotic discourse mobilizes three types of names, to name the beloved in three different ways. (a) I love him and thus affirm him using all possible names, predicates, and metaphors in all registers of all possible languages. Consequently, I do not hesitate to attribute to him not only all appropriate names, but also and especially all inappropriate names, names taken from animals, even obscene or religious names, etc. But these excesses are not perhaps perverse at all, no matter how indecent, because they attempt, awkwardly to be sure but perfectly logically, to reach the very limits of the kataphasis that claims the saturated and exceptional phenomenon that is the other in its eroticized flesh. (b) Yet this uncommon phenomenon ends up exceeding all nomination. It thus becomes appropriate to name it precisely as having no name, as resisting all ownership, all character, and all determination. One then has recourse to minimalist designations, childish, animalistic, or silly names, to pure tautology, to deictics and possessive pronouns, or even onomatopoeias, etc.; offering no meaning, they say nothing and thus manifest a strict apophasis. (c) Yet if the flesh of the other remains definitively her own, and mine, my own, they nevertheless accomplish a single common and reciprocal erotics. In *jouissance*, we still speak to one another and, in a certain sense, still give each other names. But *jouissance* can only speak its own repetition, operating it without syntax and managing its temporality: It is a question of articulating together "I love you!" and at the same time "Do you love me?" using alternately "now" (kataphasis), "again" (apophasis), and "come" (eminence). And one could show without difficulty that at least here one is dealing with an analogy from the path of eminence, or more precisely, from the discourse of praise.

In this context (and this is the second comment) one can also question the episode near the end of the gospels in which Christ asks Peter three times, "Do you love me?" (John 21:15–17). In response to the first questioning, Peter answers, "Yes Lord, you know that I love you." Why does this categorical response not satisfy the initial question? First, because Christ already knows and has always known that Peter does not love him, or at least that at the decisive moment he did not love him as much as he had promised, betraying him (Mark 14:66–72) instead of risking his own death (Mark 14:30). Peter's kataphasis thus actually signifies an apophasis. He denied, in other words, "negated" (Mark 14:68, 69) Jesus's name and even "swore 'I don't know this man *you* are talking about'" (Mark 14:66). He refused even to say the man's name, so that he put the responsibility for uttering it on others. Thus when Christ repeats the question "a second time" (John 21:16), one can assume that Peter hears an allusion to this past lie, also spoken "a second time" (Mark 14:70). Thus he utters his love a second time, as if to compensate for his second denial: This latent confession thus accomplishes the apophasis. Speaking in this way, he either supposes that a locutionary act is expected of him (to inform Jesus of his love and to confirm this information), the stupidity of which is immediately apparent, since Christ knows everything, including this, or else he thinks that by repeating himself it will "sink in" and convince Jesus that today at least he truly loves him. Such an illocutionary act in fact performs nothing, and it is not enough to prove Peter's sincerity. Or else perhaps he finally understands what the third questioning asks of him: It is not about what Peter says about things (first questioning), nor is it about his behaving in all sincerity (second questioning), for Peter knows that Christ knows he knows ("Lord, You know everything, You know [thus also] that I love you" [John 21:17]), but rather it is about the perlocutionary effect that Christ expects to have on him: "Tend my sheep." Christ expects neither that Peter should admit not loving him nor that he pretend to love him, but that out of love of Jesus he loves the other believers, present and to come. These three stages within a single utterance follow the three paths of mystical theology and of erotic discourse. Is this so surprising, inasmuch as between God and humans everything remains ambiguous except, precisely, love? We repeatedly say, despite all the impossibilities that prohibit it, "The word that resounds even to the heavens, the word, the word of gods and men: 'I love you!'"[33]

Translated by Arianne Conty.

CHAPTER 14

Givenness and the Basic Problems of Phenomenology

Tarek R. Dika

Je dirais donc d'abord que la différence . . . n'est . . . ni un mot ni un concept.
—Jacques Derrida, La différance

For Kant, the content of revelation can only enter philosophy once it has been purified of any empirical, historical content that does not conform to the a priori requirements of human reason, whether theoretical or practical. In theoretical philosophy, God is the "transcendental ideal" (*prototypon transcendentale*) of reason, so called because, like an "idea" of reason, an ideal regulates the use of the understanding without being an object of possible experience, but is even "further removed from objective reality than the idea" because it is an "idea not merely *in concreto* but *in individuo*, i.e., as an individual thing." The ideal regulates the use of the understanding because it "contains," Kant says, "the entire storehouse of material from which all possible predicates of things can be taken." Because any given thing (any possible object of experience) has a certain number of predicates and, as such, excludes other predicates (e.g., if something is "square," it cannot also be "round"), reason, which always concerns itself with the unconditioned, generates the idea of a being that contains in itself all possible predicates and is, therefore, the "All of reality." Unlike the pure concepts of the understanding, this idea has no objective reality; it is an idea of reason *in individuo*, "hypostasized," as Kant says, into an individual being:

> Thus if the thoroughgoing determination in our reason is grounded on a transcendental substratum, which contains as it were the entire storehouse of material from which all possible predicates of things

can be taken, then this substratum is nothing other than the idea of an All of reality (*omnitudo realitatis*). All true negations are then nothing but limits (of this reality), which they could not be unless they were grounded in the unlimited (the All). . . . Hence the object of reason's ideal, which is to be found only in reason, is also called the original being (*ens originarium*); because it has nothing above itself it is also called the highest being (*ens summum*), and because everything else, as conditioned, stands under it, it is called the being of all beings (*ens entium*). Yet all of this does not signify the objective relation of an actual object to other things, but only that of an idea [of the All] to concepts [of things], and as to the existence of a being of such preeminent excellence it leaves us in complete ignorance.

Finally:

The concept of such a being is that of God thought of in a transcendental sense.[1]

In practical philosophy, God is a "postulate" of pure practical reason, as is the immortality of the human soul. The "highest good," "happiness proportioned to morality," is not possible without postulating God's existence; adherence to the moral law makes me worthy of happiness, but it does not establish a necessary connection between morality and happiness. But the "highest good" is an object of pure practical reason, and it is a rational duty to promote it. Promoting it, moreover, presupposes that it is possible, and if it is not possible without postulating God's existence, then God's existence must be postulated, and human reason is warranted in doing so.

Now, it was a duty for us to promote the highest good; hence there is in us not merely the warrant but also the necessity, as a need connected with duty, to presuppose the possibility of this highest good, which, since it is possible only under the condition of the existence of God, connects the presupposition of the existence of God inseparably with duty; that is, it is morally necessary to assume the existence of God.[2]

Here again, God's existence is not claimed to have objective reality, but is only postulated so that the requirements of pure practical reason may be satisfied. A few years later, in his preface to the second edition of *Religion within the Limits of Reason Alone*, Kant writes: "[R]evelation can certainly embrace the pure religion of reason, while, conversely, the second cannot include what is historical in the first." Shortly thereafter, he writes that a "pure rational system of religion" may "from the morally practical standpoint, be self–sufficient and adequate for genuine religion, which, indeed, [is] a rational concept a priori (remaining over after everything empirical has been taken away)."[3] Genuine religion is rational religion—that is, revelation, not as it presents itself (as it may, for example, in biblical theology), but insofar as it conforms to the antecedent requirements of theoretical and practical reason. Revelation enters the critical philosophy only insofar as it conforms to these a priori requirements, either as an ideal of reason in its theoretical employment or as a "postulate" of reason in its pure practical employment. This ensures the rationalization of its content, but only according to a highly determinate, transcendental concept of reason, which determines the limits within which it—revelation—can "appear."

Contemporary phenomenology contests this transcendental concept of reason. In particular, it contests the normative authority the a priori exercises over the given.[4] But this is not limited to a historical dispute about Kant (or even Husserl, for that matter); it needs to be understood in the context of a broader debate about the limits of "normativity" in general, defined here as a logic of prior requirements.[5] The phenomenological concept of reason does not determine the "limits" within which "the given," i.e., phenomena—including the phenomenon of revelation—may be said to appear according to antecedent norms of any kind, whether a priori or historical. Revelation, no more and no less than any other phenomenon, should not, from a phenomenological point of view, be constrained by the requirements of an a priori, transcendental concept of reason, nor yet by some historically conditioned figure of rationality. Not everything is given in accordance with an antecedent norm; phenomena can be given that do not conform to our requirements. Phenomenology respects, and seeks to develop the tools to describe, such phenomena.

Questions regarding the status of the concept of "givenness" (*Gegebenheit*) in phenomenology have decisively affected this debate,[6] which has largely focused on how this concept has been used in descriptions of the phenomena of revealed religion.[7] Jean-Luc Marion's descriptions of such phenomena employ a controversial concept: the "saturated phenomenon," a phenomenon that by definition cannot be determined by what he—referring, no doubt, to the transcendental tradition—calls the "finitude of the conditions of experience."[8] Marion distinguishes between "saturated phenomena" and "objects" (*Gegenstände*) because the former, unlike the latter, saturate the receptive faculty with a surplus of intuition and, in so doing, occasion a deferral of conceptual determination.[9] As such, they do not satisfy but rather contravene a basic requirement on being an "object."[10]

No doubt, concepts of "deferral" and "excess" have played decisive roles in the formation of twentieth- and twenty-first-century French philosophy since Emmanuel Lévinas, if not before, both within and beyond phenomenology.[11] Marion's phenomenology of givenness makes use of these concepts in order to articulate the phenomenality proper to saturated phenomena.[12] Generally speaking, the concept of deferral has functioned to render the authority of normative determinations chronically problematic in nearly every domain of philosophy. For Marion, this becomes possible in phenomenology by reversing the Kantian "Copernican" thesis that the conditions of experience and its objects be determined prior to their "being given." On the contrary, he asserts, phenomena must be described on the basis of their givenness *alone*. Again, this holds as much for the phenomena of revealed religion as it does for any other phenomenon. Either it holds for all phenomena, or it holds for none. (There is no "cherry picking" in phenomenology.) Revelation is given neither as an ideal of reason nor as a postulate of pure practical reason, both of which retain from the phenomenon only what the requirements of reason authorize. These requirements do not describe the phenomenon but rather limit, a priori, the scope within which it may rationally be said to appear. To describe the phenomenon of revelation in its pure givenness requires an *epoché*, a suspension of a priori requirements. Only then can it be described. Phenomena ought to determine the scope of reason, not the reverse. Phenomena whose possibility does not conform to our requirements should neither be excluded from the domain of rationality nor forced to conform to our requirements at the expense of their own phenomenality; rather, the domain of rationality must be expanded in order to "hospitably" make room for them. In this regard, Marion describes the phenomenology of givenness as a form of "radical empiricism."[13] Saturated phenomena enjoy a privileged place in the phenomenology of givenness precisely because they can be described only via the uniquely phenomenological concept of reason it deploys. Their saturated phenomenality, deferral of conceptual determination, and, therefore, irreducibility to norm, go hand in hand.

The ubiquity of the concept of deferral in contemporary French thought should not, however, give rise to the false impression that it has something like a univocal sense. On the contrary, its sense varies in accordance with the conceptual idiom in which it is articulated, and these idioms are the product of divergent philosophical concerns. Nowhere do these differences become clearer than in the work of Jacques Derrida and Jean-Luc Marion. Marion's debate with Derrida traverses nearly the entirety of his phenomenological oeuvre. *Reduction and Givenness* and *Being Given* both devote many pages to Derrida on fundamental issues such as the status of signification in Husserl's *Logical Investigations*, the possibility of a phenomenon of the "gift," and the relation between *différance* and the saturated phenomenon.[14] Furthermore, a debate between Marion and Derrida has been documented—one in which they explicitly disagree, among other things, over the meaning of deferral and saturation.[15]

Their disagreement concerning deferral hinges on the role, if any, played by intuition in occasioning the deferral of conceptual determination. Whereas the concept of the saturated phenomenon requires that a surplus of intuition ground the possibility of any such deferral, the deferral specific to *différance* has no such requirement.[16] What distinguishes the saturated phenomenon from the objects traditionally privileged by modern (especially transcendentally oriented) philosophy consists entirely in the excess of (usually, sensible) intuition it gives. For Derrida, however, conceptual deferral characterizes the very structure of concepts, a deferral intuition does not occasion but is determined by. Deferral does not arise as the result of an asymmetrical relation between given intuition and concept but rather determines the structure of both.

The dispute between Marion and Derrida over the "ground" of deferral indicates a deeper one. Not only has Marion explicitly distinguished his understanding of conceptual deferral from that of Derrida, he has sought to ground what Derrida calls *différance* on the concept of givenness.[17] These are bold claims. What motivates them needs to be understood. In my view, Marion has felt compelled to ground *différance* on givenness because, for Derrida, *différance* contests the primacy of givenness altogether. For Marion, givenness articulates the structure of the phenomenon as defined by Heidegger: "The expression '*phenomenon*' signifies *that which shows itself in itself*, the manifest."[18] "Givenness" expresses what it means for a phenomenon to be a phenomenon. Givenness in some mode or other is what every phenomenon accomplishes, and describing the phenomenon in its givenness is what the phenomenology of givenness—like all phenomenology—seeks to (must) do. For Derrida, however, there can be no phenomenology of the trace of *différance*. The trace "can never present itself [*se présenter*] . . . can never appear and manifest itself as such in its phenomenon."[19] In short, the trace does not give itself. Nevertheless, "*The trace is in fact the absolute origin of sense in general. Which amounts to saying once again that there is no absolute origin of sense in general. The trace is the différance* which opens appearance [*l'apparaitre*] and signification."[20] These claims are no less bold (and no less characteristic, let alone difficult) than Marion's. Whether they truly bear on the possibility of the phenomenology of givenness remains to be seen. I do not assume that they do but cite them here to indicate that the difference between Marion and Derrida resides in the general possibility of the phenomenology of givenness itself. In *Reduction and Givenness*, Marion makes claims about the primacy of givenness in signification and intuition very similar (if not identical, at least on the surface) to those made by Derrida for *différance* in the passage I have just quoted. The nongivenness of the trace, which "opens appearance and signification," contests the primacy of a givenness that claims to determine these two domains no less radically.[21] How, then, does Marion determine by givenness that which by definition cannot be given? In what follows, I schematically reconstitute some essential moments in the history of the phenomenological concept of givenness (§1) with an eye toward foregrounding the relation between the phenomenological method and the concept of givenness (§2). I then introduce the concept of the saturated phenomenon and describe the relation between concept(s) and intuition it deploys (§3) in order finally to raise a number of questions regarding the possibility of the phenomenology of givenness in relation to *différance* (§4).

Husserl and Heidegger on Givenness

For Husserl, givenness, defined as presence to consciousness, is the basic criterion of evidence in phenomenology. Phenomena are brought to evidence by means of two methodological procedures, the *epoché* and the phenomenological reduction, both of which bracket epistemologically questionable commitments regarding the existence of a physical and psychological reality to consciousness. Once these procedures have been carried out, only pure givenness remains, which includes not only the object of consciousness (the *noema* or "sense" of the object), but also the cognitive acts of which it is the object (the *noesis*), both of which are immanent to consciousness. These procedures furnish the sole *epistemologically secure* basis of phenomenological description. Under their auspices, the "world" is no longer the world of the "natural attitude," but a system of noetico–noematic correlations that together form the object of phenomenological description.

> Once the world in this full universality has been related to the subjectivity of consciousness, in whose living consciousness it makes its appearance precisely as "the" world in its varying sense, then its whole mode of being acquires a dimension of unintelligibility, or rather of questionableness. This "making an appearance [*Auftreten*]," this being-for-us of the world as only subjectively having come to acceptance and only subjectively brought and to be brought to well-grounded evident presentation, requires clarification. . . . For it is precisely as meant by us, and from nowhere else than in us, that it has gained and can gain its sense and validity.[22]

The world, which "makes its appearance" in my "living consciousness," "gains its sense and validity" from consciousness.[23] The modes in which an object can be given to consciousness depend on the mode of intentionality directed toward it. That there are different modes of intentionality—that the intentionality of "hoping for" something differs from that of "recollecting" the very same thing, or that the intentionality of perceptual judgment differs from that of axiological and aesthetic judgment, and that in each case the "whole intentional content" (the *noema*) becomes "peculiarly transformed to correspond to [the] mode"[24] of intentionality in question (the *noesis*)—this correlation between modes of intentionality and the modes of givenness of phenomena, which Husserl elsewhere calls the "correlational *a priori*,"[25] is the object of Husserlian phenomenology.

Husserl frequently defines the task of phenomenology in terms of an analysis of the various modes of givenness in which the intentional relation to the world can be had, and he consistently affirms the essential relation between phenomenology and the concept of givenness.[26] The "slogan" of phenomenology—"to the things themselves" (*zu den Sachen selbst*), coined by Husserl in *Logical Investigations* and adopted by every generation of phenomenologists since—identifies the *Sachen* of phenomenology with givenness.[27] The phenomenological method developed by Husserl in *Ideas* I foregrounds the primacy of the concept of givenness for phenomenology. In *Ideas* I, §24, Husserl famously states the "principle of principles" that givenness alone is a "source of right for knowledge."

> No theory we can conceive can mislead us in regard to the principle of all principles: that every originarily giving intuition [*originär gebende Anschauung*] is a source of right for knowledge [*eine Rechtsquelle der Erkenntnis*], that whatever presents itself in

"intuition" originarily (in its fleshly actuality, so to speak), is simply to be accepted as it gives itself out to be, though only within the limits in which it gives itself.[28]

The phenomenological *epoché* and the phenomenological reductions open up the domain of pure, indubitable givenness (and 'therewith' phenomenological evidence), the object domain of Husserlian phenomenology.[29] None of the methods of Husserlian phenomenology makes any sense without the concept of givenness, which they were designed to secure. The sense and significance of the phenomenological method depends entirely on its capacity to secure the domain of givenness. Without it, nothing could be described according to the phenomenological method. Without givenness, there can be no phenomenological description and consequently no phenomenology as such: "As far as self-givenness extends, so far extends our phenomenological sphere, the sphere of absolute clarity, of immanence in the genuine sense."[30]

As this brief sketch makes clear, Husserl determines the concept of givenness according to Cartesian epistemological requirements: namely, indubitability (certainty), clarity, distinctness, etc.[31] These requirements, which place Husserlian phenomenology squarely in the history of modern philosophy (defined as a philosophy of science) can be satisfied only by the *epoché* and the reduction. Epistemological requirement, phenomenological method, and givenness go hand in hand here. It is on this basis that Husserl draws some of his most basic—and most problematic—ontological distinctions such as the distinction between immanent and transcendent being. This distinction between the immanent being of consciousness and that of everything transcendent to consciousness is a basic ontological implication of Husserl's epistemological requirements. Its grounds are Cartesian in spirit, if not in letter. In his most sustained criticism of Husserl (in *History of the Concept of Time*), Heidegger takes issue with the propriety of Husserl's ontological distinctions. Heidegger's basic claim is that Husserl's distinctions are based on *non-ontological*, epistemological considerations, which are, for Heidegger, by definition improper when it comes to ontological reflection, which ought to be autonomous with respect to epistemology:

> Our question will be: Does this elaboration of the thematic field of phenomenology, the field of intentionality, raise the question of the *being of this region*, of the *being of consciousness*? What does *being* really mean here when it is said that the sphere of consciousness is a sphere and region of *absolute* being? What does *absolute being* mean here? What does being mean when we speak of the being of the transcendent world, of the reality of things? Is there somewhere in the dimension of this fundamental deliberation, in which the elaboration of the field of phenomenology is decided, in turn a clarification of the regard from which the separation of the two spheres of being is considered, namely, the *sense of being*, to which there is constant

reference? Does phenomenology anywhere really arrive at the methodological ground enabling us to raise this *question of the sense of being*, which must precede any phenomenological deliberation and is implicit in it?[32]

With an eye toward establishing the ontological impropriety of Husserl's distinctions, Heidegger distinguishes four senses of the being of consciousness as determined by Husserl: immanent being, two senses of absolute being, and pure being. He argues that the first characterizes, not the being of consciousness itself, but rather a relation between the phenomenological act of reflecting on a lived experience and the lived experience itself: "Immanence is not a determination of the entity in itself with regard to its being, but a relation of two entities within the region of lived experience or consciousness."[33] "Immanent being," therefore, determines not the being of consciousness but only a relation between two entities "in" consciousness ("immanence" is a location, a "where"). The being of consciousness itself remains undetermined here.

The second determination, "absolute being," signifies the character of the experience reflected upon. Lived experiences have an "absolute" character by virtue of the fact that their givenness does not depend upon (i.e., they do not appear relative to) anything transcendent to consciousness. "In contrast to the transcendent, lived experiences are there in an absolute sense. That is, they do not show themselves indirectly, symbolically, but are apprehended in themselves. They are called absolute because of this absolute givenness."[34] "Absolute being" signifies the mode in which the lived experience is given to the act of reflection. The act of reflection "has" this experience as something absolutely given, free from reference to anything transcendent. Whereas "immanence" locatively characterizes the relation between reflection and the object reflected upon, "absolute being" characterizes the way in which the latter gives itself in the former: "Now what is characterized is the specific mode of being an object by which an entity of the region of lived experience is an object for another such entity. Once again, the entity in itself does not become a theme. What does become thematic is the entity as it is a possible object of reflection."[35]

The third determination (the second sense of "absolute being") characterizes consciousness as something that can in principle exist independently of everything else: "It is evident *that the being of consciousness, . . . though it would indeed be inevitably modified by a nullifying of the world of things, would not be affected thereby in its own proper existence. . . . Immanent being is therefore without a doubt absolute in this sense, that in principle nulla 're' indiget ad existendum.*"[36] Later, Husserl clarifies that the independence of consciousness vis-à-vis all transcendence stems from the dependency of the latter on the former: "The whole *spatiotemporal world*, which includes human being and the human ego as subordinate single realities is, *according to its sense, a merely intentional being*, thus one that has the merely secondary sense of a being *for* consciousness. It is a being posited by consciousness."[37] This nonreciprocal dependency makes it so that consciousness constitutes, not the existence of the world, but the *sense* of its being. Husserl defines the absolute being of consciousness in terms of its function as a consciousness that constitutes objects and, because it does not depend on them for its function, in terms of its independent existence: "Absolute being accordingly means not being dependent upon another specifically in regard to constitution."[38] Does this "independence" sufficiently determine the meaning of the being of consciousness, or does it merely determine it in a purely negative manner, as in- or non-dependence? It apprises us, not of the being of consciousness, but rather of its absolute difference from everything transcendent to consciousness. The third determination merely assigns to consciousness the role of constitution and transcendental priority; Heidegger writes: "This third determination—absolute being— once again does not determine the entity itself in its being but rather sets the region of consciousness within the order of constitution and assigns to it in this order a formal role of being earlier than anything objective."[39]

Finally, the fourth determination, "pure being," characterizes the irreducibility of consciousness to its concrete individuation in individual, psychologically real subjects. Here, "pure" means "essential" as opposed to "existential." Not the existence of the intentional being, but rather the essence of intentionality considered in itself (the a priori laws of its noetico–noematic correlations), makes up the object of Husserlian phenomenology: "not the determination of the being of the entity which has the structure of intentionality, but the determination of the being of the structure itself as intrinsically detached."[40] This detachment results directly from the eidetic reduction, which protects against making judgments about objects (in this case, "consciousness," though in principle this holds true for any phenomenon) in the manner of the natural sciences.[41] For Husserl, phenomenology describes not facts but rather essences, the necessities immanent to the phenomena themselves, including consciousness.[42] For Heidegger, this requirement ensures that the being of the intentional being cannot in principle become a theme of phenomenological inquiry. The being that has this intentional structure must, for essential reasons, remain ontologically undetermined:

> At issue is not the particular individuation of a concrete intentional relation but the intentional structure as such, not the concretion of lived experiences but their essential structure, not the real being of lived experience but the ideal essential being of consciousness itself, the *a priori* of lived experiences in the sense of the generic universal which in each case defines a class of lived experience or its structural contexture. In other words, consciousness is called pure to the extent that every reality and realization in it is disregarded. This being is pure because it is defined as *ideal*, that is, *not real* being.[43]

Like Descartes, Husserl determines, not the *sum*, but rather the *cogito*, not the intentional *being*, but rather the *eidos* of intentionality alone.[44] For Heidegger, these distinctions are based not on reflection on the being of the intentional subject itself, but rather on the basis of the Cartesian requirements referred to above:

> Husserl's primary question is simply not concerned with the character of the being of consciousness. Rather, he is guided by the following concern: *How can consciousness become the possible object of an absolute science?* The primary concern which guides him is the *idea of absolute science.* This idea, that *consciousness is to be the region of an absolute science,* is not simply invented; it is the idea which has occupied modern philosophy ever since Descartes. The elaboration of pure consciousness as the thematic field of phenomenology *is not derived phenomenologically by going back to the matters themselves* but by going back to a traditional idea of philosophy. Thus none of the characters which emerge as determinations of the being of lived experiences is an original character.[45]

Whatever the status of Husserl's requirements and however one might determine their validity, they do not in themselves yield any insight into the being of the intentional being. Indeed, according to Heidegger, they cannot: The entire import of the phenomenological and eidetic reductions consists in the fact that they *exclude* all considerations of being—and, therefore, all ontology—so as to secure the domain of givenness in pure consciousness and focus exclusively on the *essence,* not the *existence,* of intentionality and its acts. Whether the being of the intentional subject can be determined by the epistemological requirements of a science of consciousness becomes an open question for Heidegger.

For Heidegger, the rule of epistemology in phenomenology has no basis *in* phenomenology. His criticism of Descartes in *Being and Time* §6 applies with equal legitimacy to Husserl: "With the '*cogito sum*' Descartes had claimed that he was putting philosophy on a new and firm footing. But what he left undetermined when he began in this 'radical' way, was the kind of being which belongs to the *res cogitans,* or—more precisely—the *meaning of the being of the 'sum.'*"[46] The significance of the *cogito sum* consists in the fact that its performance attests to the *existence* of the being that performs it: I think, I *am.* The attribute of "thought" refers back to (because it presupposes) the existence of the *ego.* Descartes' determination of the *ego* as a "thing" (*res*) distinguishes it from *res extensa* by subtracting everything that belongs to extension and determining it solely according to the attribute of "thought." Because, according to Descartes, a substance cannot be known independently of the principal attribute that determines it, the meaning of the being of the *ego* remains undetermined and doubly concealed: first behind its principle attribute, second by the category of "substance." Plus, for Descartes, nothing could be more self-evident than the meaning of "being."[47]

Although Husserl uses the phenomenological reduction to eliminate the reference to *res,* he nevertheless determines the ontological meaning of intentionality from a resolutely epistemological point of view. All four of Husserl's determinations stem from the epistemological dimension of his inquiry. For this reason, they are not original ontological determinations. From an ontological point of view, they have no basis whatever. Indeed, they do not (cannot) cross into the ontological dimension. By definition, the reductions exclude all ontological considerations. Heidegger writes:

> This conception of [eidetic] ideation as disregard of real individuation lives in the belief that the what of any entity is to be defined by disregarding its existence. But if there were an entity *whose what is precisely to be and nothing but to be*, then this ideative regard of such an entity would be the most fundamental of misunderstandings. It will become apparent that this misunderstanding is prevalent in phenomenology, and dominates it in turn because of the dominance of the tradition.[48]

The question regarding the sense(s) of being cannot be subjected to the epistemological requirements of transcendental phenomenology (of which the reductions are but the consequence) by virtue of the fact that all such requirements cannot have the question in view. If they determine the sense(s) of being, they determine it from the standpoint of consciousness (the ontological sense of which is itself determined by epistemological requirements). Posing the question regarding the sense(s) of being demands bracketing these requirements as requirements specific to a regional science of consciousness. Only then can a properly ontological inquiry begin.

For Heidegger, phenomenology cannot take pure consciousness as its basic starting point. As we have seen, the question regarding the sense(s) of being cannot in principle arise within the limits of transcendental phenomenology. With Heidegger's intervention, the question regarding the proper starting point of phenomenological inquiry once again becomes an open one. Given that the proper (hitherto neglected) question of phenomenology becomes the question regarding the sense(s) of being, this question must itself determine the starting point of phenomenology.

Marion on Reduction and Givenness in Husserl and Heidegger

Heidegger's definition of *Dasein* as the being who uniquely has an understanding of being, thus as the being in and for whom the question regarding the sense(s) of being can even arise, makes sense only in this context. For *Dasein* to so much as be able to pose the question regarding the sense(s) of being, however, being must first be *given*. In *Being and Time* §2 ("The Formal Structure of the Question of Being"), Heidegger writes, "Inquiry, as a kind of seeking, must be guided beforehand by what is sought. So the sense of being must already be available to us in some way." Does this prior (preontological) availability of the sense(s) of being amount to a prior givenness? Toward the end of his 1927 summer semester course at Marburg, Heidegger says:

> The essential feature in every science, philosophy included, is that it constitutes itself in the objectification of something already in some way unveiled, antecedently given. What is given can be a being that lies present before us, but it can also be being itself in the pre-ontological understanding of being. The way in which being is given is fundamentally different from the way beings are given, but both can certainly become objects. They can become objects, however, only if they are unveiled in some way *before* the objectification and *for* it.[49]

Here, Heidegger explicitly describes the prior availability of the sense(s) of being referred to in *Being and Time* §2 in terms of givenness. The significance of this givenness consists in the fact that without it the possibility of ontology as a science could not be secured. Being must be given for the question about its sense(s) to arise. It must be given to *Dasein* in the understanding of being that determines its existence. Significantly, Heidegger extends the scope of givenness beyond beings (entities) to being itself. Both being and beings are given according to givenness. Furthermore, the fact that both being and beings fall within the scope of givenness in no way prohibits us from distinguishing between them. On the contrary, it makes the distinction between them originally possible. Heidegger determines this difference as a difference between modes of givenness: "The way in which being is given is fundamentally different from the way beings are given." Givenness embraces both being and beings and makes the difference between them readable in terms of their respective modes of givenness. This difference in mode makes possible the articulation of ontological difference. No doubt, Heidegger does not (not yet) thematize this givenness in and for itself. Nevertheless, he affirms the priority of givenness *en passant*. Whatever the differences that separate them, both Husserl and Heidegger remain committed to the primacy of givenness, even if they never make givenness itself the primary theme of their respective researches. Indeed, this very negligence (if it is appropriate to speak of "negligence" at all here) could itself be read as the strongest index of the primacy of givenness, a primacy so radical as to seem too self-evident to require its own treatment. The criterion, introduced by Husserl in *Ideas* I, §24, remains that of givenness. The primacy of givenness, which undergirds the disagreement about the proper object and site of givenness, determines and controls the "dialectic" of phenomenology. Only on this basis does the shift from "consciousness" to "Being" make sense as a shift internal to the history of phenomenology itself.

Not until Jean-Luc Marion's reconstruction of this history do the primacy and implications of givenness in and for phenomenology become fully transparent, specifically in the relation between reduction and givenness. Let us recall that the entire import of the phenomenological method (the *epoché* and the reductions) consists in the givenness it alone secures. For Husserl, the method ensures the presence of a reduced phenomenon to a reduced consciousness. This determines his concept of evidence: The given phenomenon, methodologically cut off from all transcendence, appears within the limits of its proper givenness to consciousness, in which it can be described. Only thus does it satisfy the criteria for evidence. As we have seen, this concept of givenness remains controlled by the Cartesian concept of philosophy: The value of the givenness secured by the method consists in the epistemological status of the contents it yields. Givenness does not, therefore, extend beyond the domain prescribed for it by the requirements of the method. If the question regarding the sense(s) of being cannot be raised within the limits of transcendental phenomenology, it must clearly be raised beyond them. Does this, however, require abandoning the phenomenological reduction and therewith the phenomenological method? Not at all. On the contrary, it requires extending it even further, such that being itself, not consciousness, becomes its *terminus ad quem*:

> Apprehension of being, ontological investigation, always turns, at first and necessarily, to some being; but then, *in a precise way, it is led away* from that being *and led back to its being.* We call this basic component of phenomenological method—the leading back or re-duction of investigative vision from a naively apprehended being to being—*phenomenological reduction.* We are thus adopting a central term of Husserl's phenomenology in its literal wording though not in its substantive intent. *For Husserl*, phenomenological reduction, which he worked out for the first time expressly in *Ideas Toward a Pure Phenomenology and Phenomenological Philosophy* (1913), is the method of leading phenomenological vision from the natural attitude of the human being whose life is involved in the world of things and persons back to the transcendental life of consciousness and its noetic-noematic experiences, in which objects are constituted as correlates of consciousness. *For us* phenomenological reduction means leading phenomenological vision back from the apprehension of a being, whatever may be the character of that apprehension, to the understanding of the being of this being (projecting upon the way it is unconcealed).[50]

The phenomenological reduction, far from disappearing once the question regarding the sense(s) of being has been raised, ensures that all questioning about beings ultimately refers back to it. By projecting every being upon its being, it institutes the guiding regard, the final reference, of Heidegger's phenomenology. It methodically fixes the question regarding the sense(s) of being. Beyond the *epoché* and Husserl's phenomenological reductions, all of which have as their primary goal the suspension and exclusion of ontological questions,[51] the reduction to being refers beings, not to their reduced phenomenality in an equally reduced consciousness, but rather to their ground in being, of which we have a preontological understanding, and which must be given beforehand.

For Heidegger no less than Husserl, and despite the gulf that separates transcendental phenomenology from fundamental ontology, the relation between reduction and givenness remains constant.

For Marion, the ubiquity and constancy of this relation give rise to a series of questions regarding the proper "object" of phenomenology. If the primary aim of the reduction consists in securing givenness—whether that of the immanent acts that constitute the object of intentionality or being itself—remains phenomenologically anterior to what it gives. This anteriority, moreover, would seem to require that the reduction surpass both consciousness and being, that it not stop short of givenness itself, that it go to the end. Under such conditions, the *terminus ad quem* of the reduction would no longer be a givenness *of* (consciousness, being), but rather givenness as such, which, in its very anteriority to consciousness and being, gives both without being rendered possible by either: "Givenness thus goes farther than objectness and Being because it comes from farther away. Extreme figure of phenomenality, givenness precedes or overcomes all other specification of it."[52] The radicalization of the reduction would furnish the materials for a phenomenology of givenness, and givenness would no longer be the name for that by means of which the object of phenomenology comes into view (however distinctly, and at the expense of a givenness that both delivers and remains obscured behind it), but would rather become the object of phenomenology itself: "If givenness could let itself be covered over by instances which nevertheless remain by right subordinate to it, this no doubt must be attributed to the limits that restrain the corresponding reductions."[53] In *Reduction and Givenness*, Marion establishes that the identity of phenomenology consists less in the history of its substantive doctrines than in the irrevocable tie between reduction and givenness:

> Thus, givenness is deployed according to the direct measure of the reduction: the more the reduction is radicalized, the more givenness is deployed. Or rather, they progress in inverse proportion, for the reduction is radicalized in reducing (itself) to a point of reference that is all the more original and unconditioned insofar as it is more restricted, whereas the givenness that ensues is broadened to a field that is all the more vast insofar as it imposes fewer conditions. The more reduction reduces (itself), the more it extends givenness. The less the reduction brackets what is in question, the less givenness will be able to render it accessible. The preceding rule—"so much appearance, so much Being"—is therefore doubled by a more essential statement: so much reduction, so much givenness.[54]

Ultimately, the priority of givenness consists in the fact that it constitutes the outer limit of every possible reduction. Givenness consists, therefore, in its reduced unconditionality. Nothing conditions its possibility. In this sense, it names a strictly phenomenological figure of the absolute, opened up by the reduction, whose sole function consists in securing it and thereby making it available for description: "What phenomenologically validates a phenomenon as an absolutely given is therefore not its mere appearing but its reduced character: only the reduction grants access to absolute givenness, and it has no other goal but this."[55] "A phenomenon becomes absolutely given only to the degree that it has been reduced; but the reduction is in turn practiced only phenomenologically—namely, for the sake of giving, thus making the phenomenon appear absolutely."[56] "Husserl says as much literally: 'Absolute givenness is a last [term]—*absolute Gegebenheit ist ein Letztes.*'"[57] Givenness exhausts the power of the phenomenological reduction by being that beyond which it can go no further: "Once again, there is no givenness that does not pass through the filter of a reduction; there is no reduction that does not work toward a givenness."[58] If givenness becomes phenomenologically absolute, this can only be because it functions to relieve the reduction of any further domain into which it might extend its reach. Its limit character with respect to the phenomenological reduction determines its absoluteness: "The reduction reduces everything, except the given; conversely, what it cannot reduce it admits as given."[59] "The question of a radical phenomenological givenness can therefore be legitimately posed as that of a pure reduction."[60]

If the reduction can have nothing in view that does not admit of being given, does this indicate the priority of givenness or the point at which the reduction can go no further? In other words, does givenness appear to be absolutely unconditioned purely as a result of a requirement internal to the phenomenological reduction itself, a requirement that, in excluding from its field of vision everything that does not admit of givenness, ends up seeing only what it allows itself to see? The reduction, after all, has as its sole and proper task the reduction *to* givenness. Should one, then, be surprised that it terminates there where, by definition, it *must*, at the very destination it has always already determined itself to terminate in before it has even been carried out? In short, does the reduction establish or presuppose givenness? To respond to this question by invoking the unconditionality of givenness merely begs the question: This unconditionality has itself been determined in and by its relation *to* the reduction, the right of which to do so has been called into question.

I have been arguing that the reduction can have nothing other than givenness in view and that therefore it provides no answer to the question as to whether the givenness it secures can be called "unconditional." But can the givenness secured by the reduction be conditioned by something *not* given, when all nongivenness has already been excluded by the reduction? What would such a nongiven—one that would not yet be identifiable as or reducible to mere ontic transcendence—*be*? These questions can be boiled down to two: (1) whether all nongivenness *can* be reduced by the reduction and (2) whether nongivenness and transcendence are equivalent, convertible terms. For Marion, they are. For Derrida, they are not. That is the question.

Givenness, Signification, and Intuition in Marion and Derrida

In *Reduction and Givenness*, Marion's first foray into the phenomenology of givenness, he argued for a new interpretation of the meaning of Husserl's "breakthrough" into phenomenology in *Logical Investigations*, grounded in the concept of givenness. What constitutes the singularity of the early Husserlian breakthrough? The breakthrough has two dimensions. First is the broadening of intuition beyond its sensible delimitation to include what Husserl calls "categorial intuition." In *Logical Investigations* VI, §40, Husserl raises the following question: "*Are there parts and forms of perception corresponding to all parts and forms of meaning?*"[62] In the case of names (e.g., the city of "Cologne"), problems regarding the relation between the "proper meaning of the word 'Cologne'" and the city itself do not arise: "The straightforward percept [of the city] here renders the object apparent without the help of further, superordinate acts, the object *which* the meaning-intention means, and *just as* the latter means it. The meaning-intention therefore finds in the mere percept the act which fulfils it with complete adequacy."[62] Things become more difficult with what Husserl calls "structured, articulated expressions" (as opposed to "directly naming, unstructured expressions"), such as "The paper is white":

> [The] intention of the word "white" only partially coincides with the colour-aspect of the apparent object; a surplus of meaning remains over, a form which finds nothing in the appearance itself to confirm it. White paper is paper which *is* white. Is this form not also repeated, even if it remains hidden, in the case of the noun "paper"? Only the quality meanings contained in its "concept" terminate in perception. Here also the whole object is known as paper, and here also a supplementary form is known which includes being, though not as its sole form, in itself. The fulfillment effected by a straight precept obviously does not extent to such forms.[63]

The significance of this problem consists in the fact that it leads Husserl to identify modes of givenness and intuition whose origins (1) do not lie in sense perception and (2) cannot therefore be "fulfilled" or brought to evidence on the basis of sense perception. Forms like "is," which underlie all predicative, perceptual judgments, are categorially, not sensibly, given. Givenness and sensible intuition are not, therefore, identical. On the contrary, sensible intuition constitutes but a *mode* of givenness, a mode in which nonsensuous, categorial forms play a distinctive role.

Not only does the categorial form play a distinctive role in sensuous intuition; it can itself be intuited:

> But if the "categorial forms" of the expression, present together with its material aspects, have no terminus in perception, if by the latter we understand merely

sense-perception, then talk of expressing a percept must here rest on a different meaning: there must at least be an act which renders identical services to the categorial elements of meaning that merely sensuous perception renders to the material elements. . . . Plainly the connection between the wider and the narrower, the *supersensuous* (i.e., raised above sense, or categorial) and *sensuous concept of perception*, is no external or contingent matter, but one rooted in the whole business on hand. It falls within the great class of acts whose peculiarity it is that in them something appears as "actual," as "self-given."[64]

To the broadening of intuition corresponds a broadening of the field of objects that can be intuited by its means. Marion writes, "Here it is first necessary to bring up the fact that objectity [*Gegenständlichkeit*] is extended beyond real objectivity, in a manner parallel to the broadening of intuition beyond the sensible; and it is necessary to note above all that these two broadenings lead to the same—categorial—horizon."[65] Husserl clarifies the sense in which this is to be understood: "If we are asked what it means to say that categorically structured meanings find fulfillment, confirm themselves in perception, we can but reply: it means only that they relate to the object itself in its categorial structure."[66] The scope of intuition becomes so radically broadened that nothing can be said to be excluded from it; the discovery of the categorial form effects a broadening of intuition such that "nothing escapes its reconduction to the full light of presence; neither the sensuous, nor essence, nor the categorial form itself—*nothing will remain invisible from now on*, since a mode of intuition tracks and hunts down each of these objects as so many modes of presence."[67] For Marion, the first broadening establishes the "primacy of intuition as universal presentification."[68]

In addition, the first broadening serves to initiate a line of questioning that will occupy Heidegger's thought until the end. In his 1973 Zähringen Seminar, Heidegger explicitly makes the connection between *Logical Investigations* VI and his early reflections on the meaning of being. Marion's interpretation of this dimension of the Husserlian breakthrough corresponds to Heidegger's own:

> In order even to develop the question of the meaning of Being it was necessary that Being be *given*, so that one might question its meaning. Husserl's *tour de force* consisted precisely in this presencing of Being, phenomenally present in the category. By this *tour de force*, I finally had a ground: 'Being' is not a simple concept, a pure abstraction thanks to the work of deduction. The point that Husserl nevertheless did not pass is the following: having more or less obtained Being as *given*, he does not question any further.[69]

Husserl broadens intuition so radically that it seems as though nothing remains that cannot be brought to presence by means of intuition. For Husserl, however, not only does signification remain autonomous as regards all present intuition, it also exceeds intuition itself: The "*realm of signification is, however, much wider than that of intuition*, i.e., than the total realm of possible fulfillment."[70] Marion comments on this passage:

> Intuition here completes metaphysics by no longer tolerating any remainder—any fringe still available to mark the vastness of the realm of signification. To where would this realm extend itself if intuition already covers and discovers everything, including the categorial, in evidence alone? For, precisely, evidence could seem here to spring from *two* sources: intuition or signification—two sources that are autonomous to the point of competing for primacy.[71]

The second dimension of the Husserlian breakthrough pertains to the domain of signification. It establishes the "status of signification (*Bedeutung, meinen*), [as] valid without the confirmation of an intuition and therefore without the foundation of presencing."[72] Marion understands this interpretation of the breakthrough to have been elaborated by Derrida in *Speech and Phenomena*. For Derrida, this breakthrough consists in severing the tie that binds the philosophy of language to epistemology (and the concept of evidence in particular). In *Logical Investigations* I, Husserl clearly states that signification signifies entirely by itself, before and without a requirement for evident, intuitive fulfillment. The singularity of signification gets foregrounded by demonstrating that an intention need not receive intuitive fulfillment in order to signify something. As Derrida remarks, this absence of intuitive fulfillment "is not only *tolerated* by speech; [but] is *required* by the general structure of signification."[73]

Nevertheless, for Derrida, no sooner has this freedom from epistemological requirements been established than Husserl smuggles them in through the back door. Although signification can signify entirely by itself without intuitive fulfillment, this signification necessarily remains fundamentally empty and does not constitute "genuine" or "true" meaning, defined by Husserl as an intuitively fulfilled and therefore evident expression. Signification becomes stifled by the sort of intuitionism that endlessly conducts signification back toward the intuitive fulfillment and therefore intuitive presence. Despite the fact that Husserl frees signification from the requirement of present intuition, such that it can be said to signify entirely by itself, signification does not cease to be oriented by the *telos* of intuitive fulfillment and evidence: Only in evidence does signification fully realize its proper entelechy. That signification signifies entirely by itself, and that Husserl perfectly recognizes this, Derrida does not deny. On the contrary, Derrida focuses on the fact that Husserl recognizes this only to then reaffirm the rights of epistemology in a teleological mode.[74]

Marion responds by both criticizing and radicalizing the reading offered by Derrida. He charges that Derrida reads Husserl selectively and therefore fails to appreciate fully the breakthrough of *Logical Investigations*: Far from effacing the freedom of signification it announces, far from privileging the "*present* or *presence* of sense to a full and primordial intuition," *Logical Investigations* maintains the very freedom that Derrida claims it effaces.[75] Indeed Marion claims that *Logical Investigations* so radically dignifies the autonomy of signification as to authorize the claim that "even though pure of intuition, it attains 'the final authority in questions of knowledge: evidence.'"[76] Not only does signification not constitute an exception to presence, but it becomes a mode thereof. For Marion, the field of presence exceeds intuition in both its sensuous and categorial dimensions, embracing both intuition and signification. Marion thereby effects a broadening of the sense of presence by including signification in it as a mode of nonintuitive presencing.[77] Furthermore, signification not only does not constitute an exception, it confirms presence itself. Signification is defined as evidence and by presence, becoming reducible to the very "metaphysics of presence" to which Derrida claims it remains irreducible. Derrida does not take his reading of Husserl far enough: All of *Logical Investigations*, and not only the parts that privilege the role of present intuition, belongs to the "metaphysics of presence." For Marion, that signification also belongs to the field of presence requires our recognizing that "intuition, universal as it might be, does not constitute the ultimate name of presence."[78]

By broadening the sense of presence to include both intuition and signification, Marion inverts nearly every aspect of Derrida's reading. Locating a gap between presence and intuition, Marion can claim that signification becomes irreducible to intuition without thereby becoming irreducible to presence. Intuition and signification belong to givenness as modes: "The object, already 'given' in signification, is found 'given' anew by intuition, in 'the same mode' as the latter" because it was "in fact *already* [given] in the signification." Because a "broadened" or "deepened" presence of this sort (i.e., one that also embraces signification) may "not be defined exactly by the word 'presence,'"[79] givenness remains irreducible to the metaphysics of presence, defined by Derrida throughout *Speech and Phenomena* according to present intuition. The breakthrough of *Logical Investigations* does not, therefore, consist in the broadening of intuition or in the "freeing" of signification from intuition, but rather in the givenness to which both attest:

> The phenomenological breakthrough consists neither in the broadening of intuition, nor in the autonomy of signification, but solely in the unconditional primacy of the givenness of the phenomenon. Intuition and intention, as liberated as they may be, are so only through the givenness that they illustrate—or rather that never ceases to illuminate them—and of which they deliver only the modes—the "modes of givenness" of that which appears.[80]

To the problem regarding the relation between the two broadenings, Marion responds by referring the entirety of *Logical Investigations* to the anteriority of a givenness that governs or "gives" both signification and intuition: "More 'broadened' than intuition, more autonomous than signification."[81] Here, the two "domains" of phenomenology, the domains that exhaust the totality of its object—namely, signification and intuition—are said to be determined by the anteriority of a givenness without which neither could accomplish itself in presence: Signification without intuition ("empty" or "unfulfilled intention") gives the phenomenon intended in the mode of signification, and signification with intuition gives it "in person." Marion writes, "givenness very clearly marks its anteriority by defining each of the terms to be considered: the object, already 'given' in signification, is found 'given' anew by intuition, in 'the same mode' as the latter,"[82] and again, "Nothing precedes givenness, which is modulated in all the modes of the phenomenon, whatever they might be. More 'broadened' than intuition, more autonomous than signification, givenness gives the phenomenon through itself because it falls thoroughly to givenness to deal the thing in person."[83]

The unconditionality of givenness vis-à-vis both signification and intuition consists in the fact they themselves deploy it (and, in so doing, attest to it) without its being reducible to either. Marion reaffirms this unconditionality throughout *Being Given*, especially §5 and §§7–12. He does so both with respect to the predominant role it plays in Husserl's discourse and to its general irreducibility to anything that might condition its possibility from the outside. Insofar as *différance* remains irreducible to giveness, this sets Marion up for a confrontation with Derrida.

Saturation and Signification in *Being Given*

As we have seen, for Husserl, "*The realm of signification is . . . much wider* [sehr viel umfassender] *than that of intuition*."[84] Signification remains broader than *intuition* because no intuition fully satisfies or adequately fulfills the intentional aim that precedes it. In every case, the intentional aim can only be partially fulfilled by intuition (there are, to take a simple example, always sides of an object that are not intuitively present, but are nevertheless co–intended in present perception). Husserl constantly speaks of an ideal of adequation whereby the intention and its fulfillment would be perfectly equal to one another. This ideal, although normative, can never be achieved in fact. Intuition remains impoverished vis-à-vis the breadth of signification.[85] A reversal, in which intuition would be broader than signification—a "saturated phenomenon"—remains for Husserl unthinkable. For him, saturation amounts to nonsense: An object must have a sense that is determined in advance in signification and only confirmed in intuition. The possibility of meaning remains necessarily tied to the possibility of relating to and/or constituting an object in this way. Otherwise, it is not an object. This determines the sense of sense.[86] For Marion, the Husserlian determination of the relation between intuition and signification reflects an impoverishment of intuition, not its privilege: The possibilities of phenomenality are determined in advance according to intentionality and its possibilities, according to the standard of "our" limited powers of manifestation. "To the limited possibility of phenomenality" Marion opposes "a finally unconditionally possible phenomenality, whose scope would not be the result of the finitude of the conditions of experience": "To the phenomenon characterized most often by lack or poverty of intuition (a deception of the intentional aim), indeed, exceptionally, by the mere equality of intuition and intention, why wouldn't there correspond the possibility of a phenomenon where intuition would give *more, indeed immeasurably more,* than the intention would ever have aimed at or foreseen?"[87]

This "third possibility" can be characterized by an excess of intuition "and/or lack of signification."[88] To the differing degrees of givenness correspond different kinds of phenomena: poor, common, and saturated. Marion defines saturation in relation to both Kant and Husserl.[89] Generally speaking, the saturated phenomenon exceeds what intentionality can anticipate and therefore frustrates all efforts at object constitution.

For Marion, the importance of the saturated phenomenon is that it can be given as a perfectly legitimate phenomenon despite the fact that it disagrees with the conditions of experience:

> What would happen if a phenomenon did not "agree with" or "correspond to" the power of the knowing I? The likely Kantian response to this question is hardly in doubt: such a phenomenon quite simply would not appear; there would not be a phenomenon at all, but a confused perceptive aberration without object. . . . In fact, the situation is very different here. In saturation, the I undergoes the disagreement between an at least potential phenomenon and the subjective condition for its experience; and, as a result, it does not constitute an object. But this failure to objectify in no way implies that absolutely nothing happens here. To the contrary, intuitive saturation, precisely insofar as it renders it invisible, intolerable, and absolute (unconditioned), is imposed in the type of phenomenon that is exceptional by excess, not by defect. The saturated phenomenon refuses to let itself be regarded as an object because it appears with a multiple and indescribable excess that annuls all effort at constitution.[90]

Disagreement with the conditions of possible experience does not mean that nothing appears or that the saturated phenomenon is devoid of sense. It can be said to be "senseless" only on the basis of a philosophical decision whereby only intentional objects and their concepts are said to determine the essence of sense. Saturation is not to be understood as the "lack" or "other" of sense, but rather as a surplus of intuition over intention characterized not so much by its supposed senselessness as by the difficulty of ever rigorously determining its sense. For Marion, givenness can be said to condition the possibility of any constitution and to frustrate the very constitution it nevertheless conditions. Everything depends on the degree of givenness. This degree defines the relation of the given phenomenon to intentionality. Saturation occurs only at the most elevated degrees.

That something like a saturated phenomenon is so much as possible, Marion argues, means that the Kantian and Husserlian constraints no longer suffice as constraints on phenomenality: There are genuinely possible phenomena—saturated phenomena—that cannot be accounted for or described in terms of these constraints. This means that the transcendental conditions of possibility must be expanded; they must begin with and from the possibilities of givenness and its various degrees, not the formal conditions of possible experience, which only place limitations on these possibilities. The phenomenology of givenness reconfigures the relation between "possibility" and phenomenality such that the former is determined relative to givenness, not vice versa: "The condition of possibility does not consist in rendering the phenomenon possible by delimiting it *a priori* from the impossibilities, but in freeing possibility by destroying all prerequisite conditions for phenomenality."[91]

Saturation, Signification, and Deferral in Marion and Derrida

Throughout *Being Given*, Marion makes a number of remarks concerning the relation between the concept of givenness, the saturated phenomenon, and *différance*. In each case, he seeks to establish the priority of givenness and the general impossibility of a nongivenness that would either precede and condition givenness or constitute an exception to its "jurisdiction."[92] The reasons underlying his remarks are clear: For Derrida, *différance* both "precedes" and renders possible any and all givenness without itself being given.[93] As such, it constitutes an exception to the universal jurisdiction of givenness (and, therewith, phenomenology). This potentially gives rise to a serious challenge for Marion's phenomenology of givenness, for givenness would then become a function of a nongivenness that would both constitute its possibility and render its jurisdiction regional. For Marion, the fundamental issue remains one of determining the extent to which givenness can lay claim to *unconditionality*:[94]

> All meaning that is not validated by presence, or all meaning whose intuition—indeed whose concept—is endlessly deferred (différance), would remain in the field of givenness. Since, according to my fundamental thesis, givenness is not equivalent to intuition and does not necessarily require it, the fact that a phenomenon (or a statement) lacks intuition does not prevent it from still appearing as given, nor does it limit the scope of intuition. Deconstruction, which only considers sensible intuition

(for categorical intuition perhaps still resists it), does not broach givenness, which would secure for it any and all pertinence in phenomenology. Deconstruction therefore remains a mode of givenness—to be quite exact that of givenness deferred.[95]

What Derrida understands by the deferral of presence Marion understands as a deferral of givenness. Marion identifies this deferral of givenness as a distinct *mode* of givenness. On this understanding, *différance* appears to affect a phenomenon or statement only insofar as it has already been given, albeit in some nonintuitive mode. In other words, *différance* not does precede but rather *postdates* the givenness of the phenomenon. It does not affect the purity of its givenness, but rather the possibility of its intuition. *Différance* does not affect givenness as such, but rather presupposes and follows upon it.

In *Being Given* §28, Marion returns to *différance* once more, this time after having developed the phenomenology of givenness in considerable detail. Under the heading "To Differ/Defer [*Différer*]," Marion, in a few cryptic passages, attempts to determine the deferral of presence on the basis of givenness. These late passages presuppose everything that precedes them (the basic determinations of the given phenomenon in §§13–18, the description of the saturated phenomenon in §§19–24, and the description of *l'adonné* in §§25–27). Marion reconfirms and further extends the claims made in §5. Here, however, he explicitly cites the following passage from Derrida's "Différance": "*Differer* in this sense is to temporize, to take recourse, consciously or unconsciously, in the temporal and temporizing mediation of a detour that suspends the accomplishment or fulfillment of 'desire' or 'will.'"[96] After citing this passage, Marion raises the following question:

> As radical as it pretends to be and remains, this reconduction of difference to *différance* still suffers from a basic indeterminacy. That is, since here it is always a question of "difference as temporization-temporalization," how can we not ask if temporalization flows from temporization (time from différance, the "logical" position) or temporization from temporalization (différance from time, the "Husserlian" position)? Difference differs by its withdrawal (Heidegger), its lapse (Lévinas), or its delay (Derrida)—but do these come from temporality or should they be thought in and through themselves?[97]

What Marion refers to here as an "indeterminacy" he treats as a disjunction: Either temporization ("delay") follows from temporality (in which case temporality would precede temporization and render it possible) or temporality follows from temporization (in which case it would "determine temporality and the modes of temporalization.")[98] He does not propose any criteria on the basis of which to choose between these two disjuncts, nor does he justify the necessity of the disjunction itself. He does not do so, however, because he does not intend to choose between them: "It is not self-evident that the delay, which opens all difference, can and should be understood first temporally [*temporelle-ment*]—in other words, that the delay is equivalent to a pure and simple temporization."[99] The lack of self-evidence here pertains to the relation between the delay of *différance* and temporization. For Marion, unlike Derrida, the former may not be identical with the latter. As Marion understands it, the difference between the phenomenology of givenness and a thinking of *différance* hinges on the place accorded to time (or, more specifically, temporization) in relation to the possibility (or necessity) of deferral. For Marion, deferral stems, not from the delay of presence due to the temporization of temporality, but rather from the relation between the excess of givenness and *l'adonné*, specifically with respect to the limited, finite capacity of the latter to convert this excess into manifestation:

> The belatedness has nothing of a temporizing or temporalized delay; it stems from the gifted's strictly phenomenological conversion of what gives itself (the call) into what shows itself (the responsal). This conversion imposes a delay—a slowness, but a ripening slowness that puts the given on the path of showing itself by filtering through the prism of the gifted. The belatedness of what shows itself to what gives itself stems from the phenomenological work that the responsal exercises over the gifted. Only givenness, unfolded in all its instances, differs/defers.[100]

Here again, deferral follows upon givenness as a consequence and therefore presupposes it. Deferral emerges in the relation between a nonfinite, saturated givenness and a finite givee. This relation defines the paradigm of saturated phenomenality.[101] There where the intuition effected by a phenomenon exceeds the limited capacity of *l'adonné* to constitute it as an object falling under a determinate concept or sense (giving rise to an, in principle, interminable series of conceptual determinations), an event of "saturation" (and therefore deferral) has taken place. Time plays no role in making this deferral either possible or necessary—it is due, not to time, but to *intuition*. Saturated phenomena (or "paradoxes") are phenomena that present us with an intuitive excess: "The fundamental characteristic of the paradox lies in the fact that intuition sets forth a surplus that the concept cannot organize, therefore that the intention cannot foresee."[102] Although his interpretation of the Husserlian breakthrough in *Reduction and Givenness* §6 permits Marion to maintain that givenness exercises jurisdiction over the domain of both signification and intuition, and that, as he claims again in *Being Given* §5, givenness does not "necessarily require" intuition, this does not hold for the saturated phenomenon. The saturated phenomenon requires nothing if not a "multiple and indescribable excess" of "intuitive saturation" "that annuls all effort at constitution."[103]

In other words, signification alone cannot achieve the excess that intuition alone delivers. To acknowledge such a possibility would be tantamount to acknowledging the possibility of a "counter-intentionality" *of signification* owing nothing to the saturation of intuition, a possibility the phenomenology of givenness has resolutely denied due to the strict equivalence it maintains between intentionality and signification.[104] Thus, in sketching a "topics of the phenomenon," Marion distinguishes three types: poor, common-law, and saturated phenomena. These three types collectively exhaust the possible configurations of the relation between signification and intuition. Marion defines these types according to the "degree of givenness" given in each.[105] Poor phenomena are those "poor in intuition" that admit of a purely "formal intuition in mathematics or a categorial intuition in logic. . . . For this type of phenomenon, what shows itself in and from itself does not need much more than its concept alone."[106] Here, poor phenomena (the poorest there are) are those defined by pure significations permitting only a "formal" or "categorial" intuition. In other words, they are characterized by a "radical phenomenological deficit . . . since it [the poor phenomenon] conveys neither real nor individual intuition . . . in short, no accomplished phenomenality."[107] Such phenomena are barred from the possibility of saturation because of the absence of "real," "individual" intuition in them. As pure signification, they conform perfectly and foreseeably to the intention that aims at them. Common-law phenomena, by contrast, "should be defined by how much they vary in terms of givenness."[108] Here, adequation between intention and intuition remains possible in principle, but "most of the time . . . the intention, like its concept, remains partially unconfirmed by intuition, thus not perfectly given."[109] Common-law phenomena (e.g., "the objects of the physical and natural sciences" and "technological objects")[110] are defined by a de facto inadequate degree of intuitive givenness. Certain scientific laws, for example, can only be experimentally verified under ideal conditions, which, by definition, require "restricting the intuitive given to what confirms (or rather does not diminish) the concept": For example, "Galileo's law of falling bodies is experimentally verified only if one eliminates in thought the friction, the resistance of the milieu, the noninfinity of the space crossed, etc." Minimally given, common-law phenomena do not exceed the intentional frame that everywhere restricts them. In both cases (poor and common-law phenomena) the relation between signification and intuition remains one in which the former exercises its authority and "mastery" over the latter and, consequently, no deferral takes place.[111] This phenomenological topic requires or presupposes a strict equivalence between intentionality, signification, and conceptuality (terms Marion uses interchangeably) and refers the general possibility of deferral to the excess of intuition alone.

And yet it can be demonstrated that the deferral Marion reserves for the saturated phenomenon is not at all unique to it. Indeed, it can be demonstrated that, in the final instance, the very functioning of the domain of signification requires a certain deferral of its own, irreducible to (and therefore inexplicable in terms of) an excess of given intuition, exactly as Derrida claimed in his debate with Marion. Irreducible, not only to (1) intuition but also to (2) givenness as such, this deferral would be but the "effect" of that which cannot in principle be given as a phenomenon, either in signification or in intuition. *Différance*, according to Derrida, constitutes the possibility of signification without itself ever being given or giveable in signification: "The elements of signification function due not to the compact force of their nuclei but rather to the network of oppositions that distinguishes them, and then relates them to one another. . . . this principle of difference, as the condition for signification, affects the *totality* of the sign,"[112] and later, "What is written as *différance*, then, will be the playing movement that 'produces'—by means of something that is not simply an activity—these differences, these effects of difference."[113] *Différance* thus opens the scene wherein signs (and therefore signification) can be given to consciousness without itself being giveable in signification. This "differing" dimension of *différance* conditions the possibility of the givenness of signification as such. The differing of *différance* does not arise from, but rather conditions the possibility of, givenness itself here. The "deferring" dimension of *différance*—temporization— can be understood only on this basis. If, in language, "there are only differences" (phonetic and conceptual), that is, if every signifying element relates to another only by bearing within itself the trace of that other and others, a trace that affects the totality of the sign, then the deferral of presence takes place in signification itself. The system within which concepts "refer . . . to other concepts" in a play of reference without determinable end does not wait upon an excess that would affect it from the outside (from intuition), but rather functions according to a law internal to the domain of signification.

The line separating "signification" from "intuition" cannot be drawn in the way Marion *must* draw it for the concept of a saturated phenomenon to operate within the parameters of the essential distinctions of the phenomenology of givenness: If the deferral characteristic of the saturated phenomenon can with equal legitimacy be said to determine the domain of signification *as such*, then "signification" can no longer function as the name of a circumscribed or circumscribable territory against which to measure the intuitional excess of the saturated phenomenon. Any appeal to a saturated intuition of givenness as the ground of conceptual deferral already presupposes that deferral does not belong to the nature of the concept itself (or, better, that the nature of the concept does not belong to deferral, to *différance*), that this deferral does not constitute or institute the entire order of what we call conceptuality.

Indeed, for Derrida, the structure of deferral affects intuition no less than signification: The two must be understood together on the basis of the trace. For Derrida, the deferral of intuition does not arise as the *result* of an intuitive saturation. Deferral is not an effect of a certain degree of givenness, however elevated. On the contrary, the deferral of intuition takes place according to the trace of *différance*. The difference between Marion and Derrida could not be greater: Whereas Marion determines the possibility of time on the basis of given intuition in the *Urimpression* of givenness,[114] such that an excess of intuition effects deferral, Derrida determines intuition on the basis of the trace. For Derrida, deferral determines the temporalization of temporality, whether Husserlian or Heideggerean: The horizon of presence remains purely normative and teleological, an

Idea in the Kantian sense, as Husserl was fond of saying. Temporalization and temporization are ultimately identical. There is no question as to which gives rise to the other. Marion seeks to demonstrate that *différance* results from givenness. Can this be demonstrated? Does describing the deferral effected by the saturated phenomenon suffice to inscribe *différance* within the conceptual economy of givenness? Or does it merely describe *one* possibility of deferral (the only one possible under the conditions established by the phenomenological reduction), without establishing itself as the *sole* operator thereof? For Derrida, there is no such thing as "intuition" in the classical sense. "Intuition" is merely the name for presence deferred. Temporization determines intuition, not conversely. This, moreover, institutes the necessity for signs in self-relation. Let us recall that, according to Husserl, signs are dispensable within the reduced presence of consciousness. They are dispensable under a certain condition of time: self-presence. For Husserl, I do not need signs where the contents they signify are themselves present to my consciousness in the reduced ideality of presence achieved by the phenomenological reduction.[115] For Derrida, however, the deferral of self-presence and the necessity of signs go hand in hand.[116] Deferral determines the possibility of both intuition and signification. Thus, it cannot be said to arise on the basis of intuition. Nor, moreover, can it be said to require an excess of intuition.

Where does this leave us? We have only managed to raise a few questions. Either we determine intuition and signification on the basis of givenness (as Marion does in the first chapter of *Reduction and Givenness* and other texts), or we determine them on the basis of *différance* (as Derrida does in *Speech and Phenomena* and other texts). If the former, then the possibility of the phenomenology of givenness has in principle been secured. If the latter, this possibility, although secured, remains derivative. Between givenness and *différance*, however, there can be no common measure. What Marion has said of Heidegger no doubt could have been said of Derrida as well: "The question remains, today, to know if, in the final analysis, givenness might not arise from itself and from nothing else."[117]

PART IV

Situating Oneself via Language

CHAPTER 15

Prayer

Addressing the Name

Karmen MacKendrick

> Yet every sentence is not a proposition; only such are propositions as have
> in them either truth or falsity. Thus a prayer is a sentence, but is neither
> true nor false. Let us therefore dismiss all other types of sentence but the
> proposition, for this last concerns our present inquiry, whereas the inves-
> tigation of the others belongs rather to the study of rhetoric or of poetry.
>
> —Aristotle, *On Interpretation*, §4

Ethical speaking is a strange, intercut mode of address and listening. As
some of the peculiarities of the sign are made vivid in thinking of sacraments as divine signs, so too the strangeness of speaking is especially
evident when it calls upon an infinite addressee. In considering the
peculiarity of prayer as an address from finite to infinite, I have followed
Nancy, for whom "The singular address to a singular God—my god!—is
prayer in general."[1] The singular address links prayer to love, with an
echo of Augustine's "what then do I love when I love my God?"[2] But the
idea that this is "prayer in general" is not universally shared. Levinas,
notably, insists that true prayer is communal, because it opens and
shares, functions that he believes private prayer fails. Community is for
him necessary for an interrogative opening, and as such it is the only
proper place for this most open of addresses.[3] I would certainly join
Levinas in valuing opening and interrogation, but find my own thought
closer to Nancy's sense of the "self" as already made in being transited,
always opened or exposed to an outside. The particular opening that
community makes possible may turn out to be closer to the earlier considerations I have made of the fundamentally communal sacrament; the
point is not that one or the other opens more, but that they do so a little
bit differently. The distinctions are not as sharp as we might at first

think; the consideration of sacraments as formalized rituals in community also inflects the sense of the world as sacramental, with its ethical implications. And that sense in turn, with its emphasis on call and response and the resonant sounding of voices, becomes central to the consideration of prayer. Prayer is a curious interrogation, no matter who or how many may pray. Individuation is necessarily troubled in any relation, but the trouble is especially vivid in the call that would relate one to a singularly infinite divinity.

As Nancy realizes, the address or outcry "my God!"—characteristic of joy and devastation alike, of ecstasy and abandonment—is grammatically a little bit odd. We use the phrase, he says, "as we say 'my friend' or as we used to say 'my Lord.' . . . In each case, behind the apparent possessive there in fact lies what we ought to call an interpellative: You, here, now, are entering into a singular relationship with me."[4] In fact, "my God" (as Nancy fully recognizes) is still more puzzling than "my friend," despite the deep complexity of my relation to any other person. When I call my friend, I call by her individuating name; when I call "my God," as Nancy says, "I am entering into a singular relationship with the lack of a singular name."[5] The name of my friend calls in part because it also designates, though its call is not limited to its designating. How do we call a name without designation?

Nancy echoes Friedrich Hölderlin's argument that "holy names are lacking."[6] For Nancy, this has a profound impact on our ability to use such names, to call (on) *my God*. Divine names "no longer refer to gods," leaving us unable to use those names for the beings they once designated. "They are, as *divine* names (and not as the nomenclature of worship), strictly unpronounceable: they no longer call upon 'My God.'"[7] In this lack of names, says Nancy, prayer is suspended. We can celebrate the divine, but we cannot pray without names; at most, we cite those names and those prayers.[8]

I have argued here (not least under Nancy's influence) that holy names do lack a certain kind of referentiality. Prayer cannot provide a name as definite referent, but it can call upon and respond to the sign of infinite enticement. It can address, both as we always address, reaching toward without quite reaching, and as we address nothing else, reaching toward what is itself question. It is suspended in the sense of remaining always between, yet we do call upon the name in suspense, the name that is lacking designation but abundant in seductive evocations. There is a poetic quality to this kind of addressing. Blanchot quotes Kafka as answering the question "Do you mean that poetry tends toward religion?" with "I will not say that, but toward prayer, certainly."[9] More extensively, Celan writes of poetry, "A poem, being an instance of language, hence essentially dialogue, may be a letter in a bottle thrown out to sea with the—surely not always strong—hope that it may somehow wash up somewhere, perhaps on a shoreline of the heart. In this way, too, poems are *en route*: They are headed toward. Toward what? Toward something open, inhabitable, an approachable you, perhaps."[10] Poetic language is not an arrival but a reach, always approaching. So too is prayer. What the genres share is also what sets them aside from most prose—not just their frequent musicality and sensory beauty, but the very fact of address, evident in their frequent use of the second person.

This grammar of address is fundamental to prayer. Merold Westphal writes, "To address God as 'you' would seem to be a necessary condition for prayer. To present oneself as 'yours,' in which that you is *aufgehoben*, would seem to be the necessary and sufficient condition of prayer."[11] That "you" is the pronoun for a most elusive name. The prayer, as Celan says of the poem, "is lonely . . . . Its author stays with it. Does this very fact not place the poem already here, at its inception, in the encounter, *in the mystery of encounter*?"[12] The encounter with mystery, which is not quite grasp, not quite rest, is itself mysterious. It is not quite a meeting, with not quite a presence. The address to mystery must also render its language strange. "Each time Augustine addresses God," Pranger notes, ". . . he evokes the newly found source of his life. Yet, by nature of his timelessness, this same addressee of his prayers is also the black hole in his remembering mind, in his prayer, his thought and his narrative."[13] This beauty so old and so new is before what he can remember, later than his newest love.[14]

The one who reaches out, who calls, will be transited and complicated by the very question, the question proper to the caller (the *you* is *my* God, even as the *I* is *yours*), yet without the bounds by which propriety is set (*my God* is infinite, unbounded, always question and in question). Every question makes an opening and so is just a little bit improper. (So your mother might have told you, suggesting that you not be quite so inquisitive with strangers.) The most profound question, says Blanchot, "places us in relation with what evades every question and exceeds all power of questioning."[15] Prayer addresses itself to what not only exceeds it, but even evades it. No matter how manifest, Blanchot says, the profound question "still flees." Yet, he adds, "perhaps this flight brings us into relation with something essential."[16] Blanchot sees some measure of such evasive strangeness in all address. The other approaches indirectly by evasion and retreat—not out of a perverse hostility, but so that the separation or space necessary to speaking is maintained.[17] The distance in all speaking is "infinite" in a sort of Zeno's paradox fashion—it is uncrossable, uncloseable. This infinite distance imposes an impossible demand—the demand of response, that we "engage with speech."[18] The mere act of address carries its own demand; failing to meet it, as Barthes reminds us, we risk boring the addressee. He writes to the author of the boring text, "You address yourself to me so that I may read you, but I am nothing to you except this address . . . for you I am neither a body nor even an object . . . but merely a field, a vessel for expansion."[19] Instead, "the text you write must prove to me *that it desires me*."[20] Address is a desirous relation, or it is a failure. Prayer's address reaches beyond a single body or object, but it must address, still, must seek more or other than its own expansion.

Prayer brings us into relation with what exceeds both us and the language that is our means of relating; the nature of that relation—its modes of address, its implicit responsivity, its revelations, its embodiment—forms the questions for the rest of this chapter.

Calling the Name, Responding to the Impossible

> *You?* Can that be you?
> Imagine! And here, of all places!
>
> —David Markson, *Wittgenstein's Mistress*

In *Dis-Enclosure*, Nancy refines his sense of non-referentiality to declare that divine names have meaning *only* in calling: "'God!'" he writes, "only takes on 'sense' in calling, in being called, and even, if I may say so, in calling himself."[21] The call in its seductive reversibility (a reversibility that may even allow the name to call itself) is enfolded in the sense of the singular yet lacking name, a name lacking reference to a thing: We hear the call that we echo; the call that we hear echoes our own desire. The divine name is a name that calls and calls forth, even when it calls out to itself.

Attending to desire, the prayer doesn't only call, but necessarily listens, to the divine. In exploring Samuel's *here I am* (1 Sam. 3:4–10), Westphal points out that one prayerfully reveals oneself as an *answer* to a divine call, an answer that is in its turn an invocation. Samuel "is called, called forth, even called into being by a voice not his own,"[22] and he in response to the call presents himself "as a listener."[23] Augustine in the *Confessions* likewise (though more complicatedly) presents himself both as a listener eager, or maybe desperate, for the word, straining to catch God's meaning, and as a speaker who tells of himself, as he says, "for love of your love" (2.1). For both (and they are exemplars among many others), to speak *is* (once more) to listen—when Augustine prays, when Samuel answers, they strain to catch the traces of God's voice in their own.

In this grammatical interpellative, the act of prayer unsettles the very relation and distinction on which it seems to be founded: the self over here and finite, and God infinitely out there. Samuel's "here I am," says Westphal, is an entirely free statement; nonetheless, "He does not originate the conversation but is called."[24] The response to address "decenters" us. Samuel presents himself, reveals himself, but he is not alone in revelation. So too when Augustine confesses himself to God (and not so much to his readers, causing centuries of frustrated fascination): So that God might "come into" him, he reveals himself, too. It is to God Augustine wants most to reveal himself, God he wants to read him in the seductively graceful text. This desire displays the reversibility of seduction: Augustine hopes that God will read him in the beautiful text as he reads God in the beauty of scriptural text and created world. Failure to reveal himself to God has a curious effect, the reverse of what we might anticipate: "I would be hiding you from myself," he writes, "not myself from you" (10.2.2). Augustine reveals himself to seduce divine revelation, tells his story to call God toward him and to learn how to read sacred signs—how to hear God called out by the world. What he reads in the world calls out to the divine, which in turn calls Augustine into himself. As Pranger points out, "In a sense the first and third person are sublimated into the second, as in—confessional—prayer which is the ultimate literary rendering of the 'object' bestowing itself."[25] The address has a graceful gravitation.

The one who prays does not call and *then* find that God is revealed; rather, the revelation is in the calling, in the answer that is another call, which has a question built into it. "Surely when I call on him," Augustine writes, that is, when he uses the second person in relation to God, "I am calling on him to come into me" (1.1.1). This doubly reaching invocation is typical of prayer. The divine is the perfect *you*, *my God* the ultimate address. But address multiplies. "Do not be vain, my soul," writes Augustine; "Even you have to listen. The Word himself cries to you to return" (4.11.16). We too call upon ourselves, if only to remind ourselves to pay attention to the call.

Even a third party may be drawn in, as in the case of the Augustinian text, which seductively leads its readers into temptations, and not only those Augustine describes as his own: He entices us with his desire to praise (a desire, we come to realize, that he desires to share); he draws us with his desire to describe the infinite "object" of that praise; and he makes us want to join in, to enter into this relation.

All language is relational, belonging wholly neither to speaker nor to listener, but the language of prayer is unusually unlikely to speak from a clearly defined subject position. For Blanchot, Kevin Hart argues, "we might say that we do not experience God," with we the subjects knowing a divine object, "but rather encounter Him by way of an infinite relation."[26] We encounter in a proximity without meeting, without grasp. *"Nah ist/und schwer zu faßen der Gott,"* writes Hölderlin. The grammatical structure makes the English hard to render; Michael Hamburger wisely goes for a fairly literal translation: "Near is/and difficult to grasp, the God."[27] Prayer is reach and just possibly passing touch, but never grasping; nearness, but never colocation. Nancy links the very space that differentiates proximity from full contact with God—or what is left after God, after the death or loss of the solidity of the God who is some-thing: "The interval, the space between us—which makes 'us' possible—is all that remains when there is no more God. God filled the intervals; he was himself without interval."[28]

Nothing fills the intervals, but we cannot simply identify the divine with nothing (particularly not if we retain any trace of the Augustinian; for Augustine, nothingness is evil). There remains the interval itself, not a nothing between somethings but the space that makes us and speaking and communication in all of its imperfection, the sound interval of silence in which an infinite moving toward is signed, the space-interval moving between written words and between bodies; moreover, there is the interval as itself a trace, a space *left*, perhaps by a withdrawal itself seductive. Blanchot's approaching other is relevant here: "The other who draws near you does so, Blanchot says, by turning away, backing off out of your reach, out of your ken."[29] Backing off with, perhaps, a Nancyean "wink," the divinely enticing gesture that is what we have left in the lack of divinely referential names.[30]

Speaking is drawn by an other whose approach is not distinct from its withdrawal, across an infinite distance: Prayer then would be a conspicuously pure or intense speech, or a speaking with an exceptionally profound question. As we have seen with desire in other contexts here, the relation of this query and call to desire is complex; an infinite draw is enticing, but not altogether satisfying, certainly not satiating. It is perhaps more "the communication of a disappointment, of a nonpossibility, of a withdrawal of communication itself,"[31] as Nancy says that speaking is for both Bataille and Blanchot. The disappointment occurs because "no subject of the utterance comes in touch with another subject."[32] So if communication means completely crossing the abyssal interval between subjects, full comprehension, then every communicant is disappointed. All the more so anyone who prays, especially if that praying is trying to reach and to grasp the divine. If it is not just disappointment, prayer must seek something other than comprehension and conclusion.

Prayer addresses itself to a mystery, to an unknowable that is not just incidentally unknown, to a distance that is proximate too, to the impossible fullness of possibility—to the element within speaking that gives to all of it a trace of prayer, here without illusions of finality. Prayer, says James Mensch, makes the space in which the sacred can appear.[33] Or, we might also say, can speak. Making that space and enticing across it are paradoxically coincident. Speaking of Blanchot, Ann Smock remarks in a conversation with Nancy that our obligation of response to the other is "answering the demand, which his nearness is, that you should hear him—hear him and thus let him speak; make it so he can; let him come up close and be there, speaking."[34] The space opened by hearing also entices speaking nearer; the space opened by speaking (and prayer, like the question, speaks to open, not to speak over or foreclose) also entices the listener.

The tradition of such paradoxical, apophatic address turns out to be a long one. Oliver Davies notes that even one of the most stubbornly elusive Christian thinkers, Meister Eckhart, "cannot be seen to be operating with apophatic reference to the exclusion of address. . . . The individual is . . . in the most profound sense addressed by God through the *gotesgeburt* or birth of the Word in the ground of the soul. Christian apophatic language is not pure reference therefore, but rather reference which has been transformed by divine revelation as address."[35] Virginia Burrus writes that, for a still earlier figure, the fourth-century Evagrius Ponticus, "the Trinitarian naming—the matter of divine address—involves a relation, rather than a metaphoric, linguistic practice."[36] It is not only the referential element here that is deliberately apophatic, but the address itself, and the relation to which it calls: The call does not end, does not arrive, but it does draw toward, into a space in which we may speak, and be heard, and encounter the mystery of the voice.

That notion of non-arrival, or arrival infinitely deferred, belongs most famously to Blanchot and, in intellectual conversation with him, to Derrida. Davies notes of the latter:

Derrida points out too that negative theology is a mode of address, an encomium or hymn, which bears the distinctive trace of the other to whom it is uttered. It is preceded by a prayer. . . . This prayer Derrida describes as a living conversation, and he speaks of it in most un-Derridean terms as language that can never be written: "Does one have the right to think that, as pure address, on the edge of silence, alien to every code and to every rite, hence to every repetition, prayer should never be turned away from its present by annotation or by the movement of an apostrophe, by a multiplication of addresses?"[37]

Like Nancy, Derrida emphasizes the singularity of the addressee, even where that addressee is a *theos* whose logic is negative. Yet Derrida too acknowledges the echoes of Augustinian confession in prayer, and that echo problematizes the notion of the unwritten. Augustine's confession is a prayer recorded in writing not as some sort of definitive result, but as if (we must always be wary of underestimating Augustine as a polished rhetorician) caught up in the midst of its outpouring, a writing intriguingly close to speech, or a writing deliberately evocative of speaking. If prayer can be written, then it must be read; if in its reading it is to function as prayer and not simply as an account of prayer, then it must be read in an unusual kind of recreative performance, in which the reader takes on the voice and the curious decentered positioning of the one who prays.[38] Like the sacrament, it opens and unsettles even when it seems to be spoken as rite or by rote.

Conversion

> You spin me right round, baby
> Right round
>
> —Dead or Alive, "You Spin Me Round (Like a Record)"

Every address turns itself toward. This is as true carnally as in any ostensibly disembodied sense; calling out to somebody, to another body, I turn toward if I can—at least calling over my shoulder, if not in fact shifting my torso. When we speak without such a shift, it is often because we are angry, or resistant and resentful of the need to address the other at all. Prayer is conspicuous in its embodiment, though complex in its direction. Every call, and every response, is a small conversion. Derrida suggests that the Augustinian sort of confessional prayer "is a matter of a singular movement of the soul or, if you prefer, of a conversion of existence that accords itself to, in order to reveal in its very night, the most secret secret."[39] The revelation of a secret, though, is not its unsecreting, but the revelation that there are secrets, that there is mystery; the Augustinian conversion is vivid, yet the God to whom it directs its passion is no precisely defined or located thing. Chrétien calls prayer "a speech that . . . turns towards God,"[40] and Blanchot, still meditating upon the incompletion of speaking, notes that to turn and to find may be closer than we think: "To find is to turn, to take a turn about, to go around. . . . No idea here of a goal, still less of a stopping. To find is almost exactly the same word as 'to seek,' which means 'to take a turn around.'"[41] We turn about the unfindable, around the center that is everywhere.[42] When Augustine asks, "Where then did I find you in order to learn of you?" he finds the answer in memory, but he remains puzzled. "You were not already in my memory before I learnt of you," he declares, deciding that it is God's exceeding of place that answers, still mysteriously, the peculiar question of "where."[43]

In studying Augustine's *Confessions*, Pranger links conversion to the performance of a promise, which, like a seduction, must be sustained[44]—and which, like a secret, cannot be kept, or at cannot at any rate be kept by Augustine, who is constantly having to turn himself around again.[45] We keep promises by remaking them; we keep them as we keep making them.[46] Not definition but possibility, the promising, opens in prayer—not least the very possibility of turn and return, the possibility that "To be converted is something that is always ahead of us as well as behind us."[47]

Conversion, then, is not once and for all, but is a matter of re-turn. Prayer does not describe conversion, but enacts it. Thus, as I shall note again just below, it is not especially surprising to find that it so often takes up, and makes up, the language of scriptures. Augustine's act of reading scripture "itself turns into conversion,"[48] says Pranger, a conversion in which multiple voices sound at once—in which Augustine voices Paul's text, after hearing the voice of a child who seems to speak for a God.[49] Prayer's duality of revelation is also a duality or even a multiplicity of voice; one reveals oneself as a listener by speaking, and one may even speak in the voice of the addressee, or of other listeners who have sought the divine in address. This too is part of the search to know: to speak as a listener to multiple voices. Hart, in a scriptural citation, echoes our sense of the mutuality of revelation, here in the mutuality of speaking: "In the words of Isaiah, 'before they call, I will answer; and while they are yet speaking, I will hear' (Isa. 66:24)."[50] As Pranger has eloquently argued, in prayer or prayerlike speech the speaker takes on other language and voices—especially, as in his analysis of Augustine, the language of scripture—as the speaker's own.[51] The times of prayerful speaking and hearing are not linear and distinct.

Speaking Through

What matter who's speaking, someone said what matter who's speaking.
—Samuel Beckett, *Stories and Texts for Nothing*

To say that there is a connection between knowing and speaking is hardly unusual—we ask in order to know, we say what we know, we even learn what we know (and what we want to ask) by working it out in the saying. The nature of that connection is somewhat strange in prayer, where we do not simply speak what we know, nor simply learn by extracting information from what is spoken. We cannot altogether distinguish who is speaking here, who knows and who is learning, any more than, say, Augustine is able to distinguish the source of the childish voice that has urged him to "take and read" the transformative text from Paul. As Pranger points out, "the two aspects of turning inward on the one hand and the sheer exteriority of language on the other have to be taken together and analysed as one corpus presented to us in the shape of uninterrupted prayer."[52] This blending and slipping among voices, the appropriation of the scriptural voice that is itself in some way said to have God speaking through it, is not some confusion or mistake on Augustine's part, but a remarkable and graceful performance of the inwardness of desire in the outwardness of words. That is, it is a performance of prayer, and it shows us something of prayer more generally. Desire draws forth speaking; words, in turn, draw desire. Prayer, however brief, is taken up in, to steal Blanchot's lovely phrase, an infinite conversation. "Such, then, would be my task," he writes, "to respond to this speech that surpasses my hearing, to respond to it without having really understood it, and to respond to it in repeating it, in making it speak."[53] *In repeating it*, we make it speak: The prayerful appropriation of ritual words and scriptural phrases is something more than rote.

Prayer is mutually implicated with the divinity of its address, and as some measure of that implication, it repeats responsively; it arrogates other voices that are also addressing, and reading themselves as addressed by, divinity. In its reach across an infinite distance, "Prayer reflects exactly this process—or rather this ever repeated moment of arrogating voice," writes Pranger. He notes that, in Augustine's prayer, "It is language (seemingly) external to himself which is proven to have been carrying and creating his self all along: before you were born I have chosen you."[54] Even those divine names, lacking or exuberantly overly plentiful, may thus be reperformed. Westphal notes, for instance, that Pseudo-Dionysius's divine names "are those given to us in Scripture. The very call to which we may respond 'Here I am' . . . typically comes through the words of Scripture, directly or indirectly. . . . Before prayer is a . . . speech act on our part, it is listening to the word of God as found in Scripture."[55] Prayer is at once both our listening and our speaking, but the very nature of the speaking makes it something other than simply our own.

As thus multiple, prayer can no more be attributed to the divine than to the one who prays. (The number should begin to sound suspicious as our opening distinction begins to blur: Those multiple voices suggest something communal in the most solitary prayer; the singular address to a singular name nonetheless begins to sound polyphonically.) As Mark Cauchi points out, "The prayer, like the question, cannot simply come *from* the other."[56] If it did, my speaking would serve no point. We are not simply returning some possession in our words; even if I return to you your words, they must be changed by the resonance of my voice and the direction of my address. Prayer is not parroting, not quoting, but performing and sometimes, rather sacramentally, reperforming. And no repetition, we know by now, is ever exactly the same.

The address of prayer is thus complicated not only by the duality of its revelation, but also by the words it takes up and revoices as its own. It is complicated by its search for a language in which to address and to say an infinite that stubbornly exceeds and evades words. We might reasonably wonder if it doesn't make more sense, if we are trying to hear divine voices, just to shut up. Augustine himself sometimes warns of praying that talks too much and listens too little: "Lord, why should I so much as pray at all? You would not that I should use long prayers, yea rather Thou dost even bid me to use near none at all."[57] Moreover, if we share any of the Augustinian worries about the ease with which language misleads us, silence would seem to be the safer option.

If we want to make sense of prayer, then, we must seek a language that not only speaks in many voices (some of them the scriptural voices ostensibly of its own addressee), but also carries its silences in it, one that serves to listen even as it speaks. It is not only speaking that enters us, but silence, too. Chrétien writes, "Far from enclosing ourselves, in some dark crypt, [silence] is that which opens us, in the only way that anything can be opened: irreparably. Nor is it, even in the highest of its possibilities, a purely spiritual silence. Only what has a body can throw itself bodily into the fray. All attention takes place body and soul."[58] Both calling out and drawing breath pull the infinite in; both speaking forth and listening to the meaning are acts of gathering.

Prayer becomes the overflow of divine voices in our speaking; it requires its silences, its intervals, even more dramatically than does other speech. (It is becoming clear that much of what I have said of prayer is true of all speaking, especially of attentive speaking, just as much of what I said of sacraments is true of all signs. In both cases, the introduction of an explicit infinite intensifies the ordinary into something strange.) Prayer is desire welling up in the world of words. As I've suggested, the mutuality of revelation is already seductive and, indeed, I would further suggest, erotic; the gaze of eros, unlike that of scientific inquiry or even aesthetic judgment, is unusual, perhaps unique, in the urgency with which it seeks to be seen as well, to draw and not merely to be drawn by desire. But the better metaphors here may not be visual; prayer is an aural medium, meant to be heard even when we read it in print. The one who prays asks to be heard rather than seen, and asks the divine not to show its shape but to speak in turn, to offer answers that open the questioning further—answers, like beauty, that are vocation and provocation, that call us and recall us, always into question.

That to which we listen, says Nancy, is "first of all presence in the sense of a *present* that is not a being (at least not in the intransitive, stable, consistent sense of the word), but rather a *coming* and a *passing*, an *extending* and a *penetrating*."[59] When we are called and when we call (especially when we in our finitude call on the infinite to "come into me"), we complicate ourselves and are complicated, with a vulnerability that echoes the ethics of an openness onto the world.

We are transited, as Nancy says, or wounded, as Chrétien has it—in fact, he calls prayer "a wounded word." Chrétien's sense of prayer reminds us of the vulnerability of speaking and listening—of the important element of prayer that is lament, and not just joy, and of the entanglements of the two. Prayer "is the very event of a wound by which our existence is altered and opened, and becomes itself the site of the manifestation of what it responds to . . . the wound can bless and . . . benediction can wound."[60] Intriguingly, Jabès uses the same terminology to describe the project he shares with Celan, with whom he says that he is joined "by everything, . . . but in particular by 'one and the same interrogation and one and the same wounded word.'"[61] Prayer reaches toward what eludes saying, such that a word becomes only "the trace that it leaves;"[62] crossed through by the question and the silence that enters its words. Our speaking is traced through by silence, our silence by those sounds whose meanings it gathers.

Words and silences are traced through each other, and so too are those whose words and silences they are, those who are as unsettled in their possession of words as in their positions as subjects. Nancy writes that when we listen for sense, we are also attentive—attuned, even—to resonance ("in resonance, there is source and its reception"). Like the divine, such a sense withdraws even as it barely touches: "Sense . . . reaches me only by leaving in the same movement. Or there is only a 'subject' (which always means, 'subject of a sense') that resounds, responding to a momentum, a summons, a convocation of sense."[63] This sense of *resonance*, shared sound, shared sense, is the sense in which we communicate the ungraspable: "The incommunicable is nothing other, in a perfectly logical way, than communication itself, that thing by which a subject makes an echo—of self, of the other, it's all one—it's all one in the plural. Communication is not transmission, but a sharing that becomes subject: sharing as subject of all 'subjects.' An unfolding, a dance, a resonance."[64] Resonance keeps speaking from being speaking over, drowning out. Ann Smock summarizes Blanchot: "The other who approaches speaks and asks you to make it so that he can speak. Blanchot says you hear him asking you to find the words with which he'll make you hear him."[65] Making space for the sacred, for sound, for the other, comes in the strange listening character of invocation, the silence of speaking traced throughout prayer.

Prayerful Genres

Many have tried, but in vain, with joy to express the most joyful
Here at last, in grave sadness, wholly I find it expressed.
—Friedrich Hölderlin, "Sophocles," Epigrams from 1799

I have spoken primarily of the prayer of praise or adoration, a prayer that may describe, but does not inform (at least, its purpose is not to impart information about what it finds admirable). Rather, it invokes and reveals, though, to follow Nancy's distinction, it does not manifest; its praise resonates.[66] Praise is interestingly entangled with confession; listening to the praises we make in prayer, we perceive the praiseworthiness of their subject; telling the truths of ourselves, we perceive our entanglements with the *you* to whom we tell them. We continue to seek in the delight of finding, to desire even more of what we desire, and so to ask and to praise find their way into the same prayer, the same invocation. We can only hear prayerfully by listening to what resonates in what we say.

In this section, I argue that in fact this strange intersectionality applies beyond praise, that it is true too of prayers of both petition and lamentation. All three forms are movements of desire, and as that desire they are mutually revelatory movements of address, conversionary and subject-transiting.

All these forms of prayer are driven by desire, and it is through desire that they make their revelations. Praise is the most obvious instance. As I have suggested, it may well describe, but there is no presumption that it offers that description as new knowledge to the one it praises or to an uninformed audience; primarily, it expresses desirous, astonished delight. In the prayer of praise, meaning and language are themselves full of desire, reaching toward an impossible completion—in which all speaking would already have ceased, becoming pure resonance, words echoing the joyful, delightful character of that which they praise, of the one they address. The language of prayer, of praise and desire in excess of denotation,[67] is for Augustine (and not only for him) nonetheless the very deepest and most important meaning of language—as close, perhaps, as fallen speech can get to the mythically unfallen word, the least distorted echo of the word of God. Language will never grasp divinity, but it can still praise.

In fact, for Augustine, praise is primary in the glorified and redeemed speech of resurrected bodies. Prayer, as we see both in the attentive response to worldly beauties (in the *Confessions*) and in the eternal commentary of the resurrected on the beauty of risen bodies (in *The City of God*), *is* the joy of speaking, and of writing; it is the joyful call in response to the call of joy; it is mutual revelation. The beauty of glorified bodies causes those who live as those bodies to call out praise to the creator. Praise says of the world that it is good—a goodness caught up with vulnerability, not least with that in us that we cannot protect from beauty. The imperative to speak is not an imperative to report, or even to impart information. It is wholly unspecific as to what is or may be spoken; it may indeed speak about as well as to, or it may, better still, speak about to. Praise, most conspicuously of all speech, is drawn out of us, imparts no information. It may express astonishment, but it does not say that it is astonished (not, at any rate, as its primary point). Thus it is an expression, rather than an informational discussion, of desire. Augustine is again paradigmatic, declaring, "For he who desires, even if his tongue is silent, sings from his heart; and he who has no desire, whatever the cry with which he strikes men's ears, is mute for God."[68]

One might wonder whether prayer as praise is purely ornamental. Ornament, I hope I have indicated, is not without importance. But it is important to remind ourselves that praise serves a revelatory function as well, by calling upon an infinite name, and what it reveals, dually, are caller and respondent—in their mutual implication, which is no small measure of the content of the revelation. Delight is caught up in desire, the Augustinian essence of prayer. "If you would pray without ceasing," he writes, "do not cease too long. Your ceaseless longing is your ceaseless voice. You will be silent, if you stop loving."[69] Praise is speech seduced by delight in the desire of delight's returning.

Petitionary prayer too speaks desire, desire too intense for a simple, informational "I want X" statement to suffice. A petition at once exemplary and a little unusual is taken up in Derrida's "Sauf le nom," as Derrida considers Angelus Silesius's lines "Giebstu mir dich nicht selbst / so hastu nichts gegeben" ["If you don't give yourself to me, then you have given nothing"].[70] Derrida points out that "this particular prayer asks nothing, all the while asking more than everything. It asks God to give himself rather than gifts. . . . Which interprets again the divinity of God as gift or desire of giving. And prayer is this interpretation, the very body of this interpretation."[71]

This is stranger even than it seems; Angelus asks the gift for its giving, and the asking is a giving, too, a giving over of self in the very demand—because for Angelus, as for Eckhart, one does not receive God and retain separation.[72] That is, this petition, and any petition that interprets the divine as gift, also troubles the petitioner's subjectivity, because if she is given that gift, she is no longer simply the self that requested it but, in some strange measure, is crossed through and remade by the very gift requested.

Praise reveals to us the problems of trying to retain that separation, but also of the impossibility of overcoming it—it reveals the reach of desire. As Denys Turner argues in his discussion of Augustinian prayer, prayerful petition is also the discovery, if we pay attention, of the call of the desires that are deepest in us: In this sense too, it gives us ourselves. Noting that we have come to use "will" rather badly, as if it were opposed to desire, Turner insists that prayer is an act of will in an older and richer sense:

> For the great spiritual writers of classical and premodern times meant by "will" something more like our deepest desires. . . . And many of those desires lie very deep within us indeed, so that we do not know them, they do not fall within our experience. . . . Prayer is the process of discovering in ourselves that with which we can truly love God: that is our will, that is where our hearts are. . . . [For Augustine and Thomas] prayer is a kind of revelation to us of what our wills truly are, it is a kind of hermeneutic of the opaque text of desire.[73]

The petition, if it is not made glibly, tells us what we want, shows us to ourselves.

Petition is a special case in that it is so easily misconceived, in a manner not alto-gether unlike the misconception of faith as ill-grounded belief. Both errors oversimplify and demystify. As Nancy writes, "Prayer does not ask in order that its request be granted, nor does it produce that result. To have one's prayers answered—that is the expectation, as self-interested as it is illusory, of religion, which consequently is doomed to content itself with imaginary satisfactions."[74] He insists that prayer is essentially adoration, "not primarily a request made in order to receive a response, retribution, or reparation."[75] If petitionary prayer were simply a matter of presenting a request for fulfillment, it would scarcely be discursively unusual; we make requests of one another all the time. Indeed, it is generally more effective to call upon my spouse, for instance, to help me find my keys than upon St. Anthony of Padua, for all the latter's patronage of those who seek lost things. For that matter, we may even make requests of inanimate objects, as when we urge our cars to start on nasty cold days. What characterizes a petition as prayerful is also what characterizes the prayerfulness of praise: its revelatory character and its curious subject position. Like praise, the petition that arises out of meditation upon the depths of desire is a revelation of the praying self even as it addresses that self's outside; desire is itself drawn out in its expression in address, revealed in its saying. The prayer of petition, then, is caught up with the prayer of praise precisely by the commonality of desire. It too func-tions as a revelation, a revelation of will and desire to the speaker through the act of address, through address to what draws desire infinitely.

There remains an important third category: the prayer of lamentation. Desire prays, says Augustine, but so too does sorrow: "For, as soon as we feel sadness, we already pray."[76] At first lamentation evokes anything but revelation; as Michael Purcell notes, it is "associ-ated with the scriptural notion of a God who has hidden his face . . . and will not respond."[77] Purcell links this hidden God to the demands of the Law, the keeping of which is the way both to love and to experience the hidden God—an ethical way that does not keep us from experiencing the terror of absence.[78] Purcell argues that suffering, expressed in the lament, can be redeemed from meaninglessness only when it works toward justice, when suffering is for the sake of others.[79] Yet the same emptiness that creates the lament's sorrow and longing is, he says, the condition of hope, which ends if it is fulfilled in specificity.[80] Lament reaches back to memory, forward to the hope for justice. Purcell argues that it is solitary, occurring in the absence of interlocutors. I would suggest that, in the very speci-ficity of lament's address, we hear that its solitude is not the simple condition of being alone, but rather the more complex one of experiencing and addressing a particular with-drawn or hidden other: an absent interlocutor, to be sure, yet one who is importantly different from the absence of address at all.

Responding to Purcell, Kevin Hughes argues that lament is the first and paradig-matic Christian prayer, noting Christ's reiteration of the Twenty-second Psalm—"My God, my God, why have you forsaken me?"—just prior to his death in two of the gospel accounts.[81] Hughes wonders if the Lurianic sense of divine withdrawal or contraction fundamental to Purcell's understanding of the absent and hidden God is in fact useful to Christianity.[82] He argues instead that

> what we see on the Cross is precisely the Lament, and the Lament without answer. But, precisely as such, the Cross points to a God who is found in the Lament, and thus is no stranger to those who lament in turn. The paradox of the cross is that the one who laments and is not answered is himself the revelation of God, the coincidence of full humanity and full divinity in suffering is the coincidence of lament and God's presence.[83]

The "scandal" is not, he argues, the withdrawal of God, but the revelation of divine weakness, God's taking up in the incarnation of everything human, even the nonheroic, unimpressive aspect of mortality.[84] The divine embrace of this suffering and so of those who suffer "anticipates the end of suffering," he adds.[85]

Both accounts begin with lament, but diverge from it in an effort to make it meaningful, thus redeeming it by anticipating, hoping for, its end. Divine vulnerability appears differently in the two accounts—as a shattering in need of regathering, as the capacity to suffer—but it is important that it does appear. But both cases also look to some redemptive move, and for both, to redeem lamentation requires stepping outside of the lament. Lamentation in its own time of unbearable, inescapable attention does not anticipate suffering's end or wholeness reassembled; it may well ask "how long?" of its abandonment, but this is a sense of the hollow stretch of time, not of a measured discipline of endurance. It cries out. Both Purcell and Hughes, very reasonably, seek a way out of the sense of meaningless suffering that lamentation expresses; I am more engaged, here, in the moment of the lament itself, which like praise and petition is a revelation: of vulnerability shared, of the passionate desire for what is profoundly missing—a reminder that a name, a trace, a sign is not a full-fledged presence.

Here I recur to poetry as prayer's sister speech, to look at Rilke's poem "The Olive Garden." The poem retells the story of Christ's night in the garden at Gethsemane:

> . . . and why is it Your will that I must say
> You are, when I myself no longer find you.
>
> I find you no longer. Not in me.
> Not in the others. Not in this stone.
> I find you no longer. I am alone.
>
> I am alone with all of human grief,
> Which through You I undertook to lighten,
> You who are not. O ineffable shame . . .[86]

The theory of lamentation at work here seems closer to Purcell's; certainly it emphasizes solitude, though not its mending by justice. It calls to a *you*, but precisely in that addressee's absence, or withdrawal. Its grief is all the stronger in the absence of the one who was to lighten all grieving. The address could not be more direct, and if *my God* defines prayer, this is praying at its clearest. It is almost petition, but not quite: It is petition within abandon, petition that not only does not expect satisfaction, but that arises in the destitution of desire. And it is as destitution that it too is revelation. This is not suffering that hearkens toward its own end:

> For angels don't come to the prayers of such men,
> And nights don't grow large around them.
> The self-losing are let go by everything,
>
> And they are abandoned by their fathers
> And locked out of their mothers' wombs.[87]

The loss here is complete; the sense that resounds in the speaking and the reading and the hearing is the sense of forsakenness. To lose *my God* is to lose myself too.

Praise reminds us of the trace of the divine in all that is, the delight of reading it, the memory invoked by every sign in a mutual revelation of "within" and "outside." Petition reveals to us in the outpouring of words our own inmost desires and perhaps the entanglement of those desires with the no-less-desirous divine. And lamentation reveals to us the double, and sometimes devastating, vulnerability, at the extreme of loss, of human and divine. Just as there is some sense of praise, Nancy's "adoration," in all prayer, so too is there a touch of lamentation: Lamentation also shows to us the paradox of signification, because the sign is not what it signifies, whatever its mood or its mode. If we *read* divinity in ourselves, in others, in the stones, we do not *find* it there. The sign is not the thing: We are not God, say the beauties of the world to Augustine, and finally, even the query "Where then did I find you?" has as its only answer a memory without an origin. The lament, to be sure, cries out when the trace cannot be read, but it also reminds us that we are *never* wholly fulfilled, never lastingly in a presence, even when we read most clearly and take pleasure most fully. Seduction is often delight, but it is never satiation, and that must mean that it is sometimes sorrow. As we are ethically impelled, by our very vulnerability to beauty, also to be open to destitution and loss, so too we find expressed in prayer a sorrow that is not simply hurried toward its absence nor set as a prelude to praise. We do not have everything.

It is too easy for us—certainly for me, I find, writing—to focus optimistically. The open space of the possible, as Purcell points out, is the only space of hope, and that space of the possible is the space of seductive enticement. But true possibility opens onto darkness, too, and the dark nights of the soul are not just trials endured for the prizes that come after. Lament calls upon the retreating, withdrawn divine when the trace is too faint to read. It may well call bitterly—*you*, who are not, not even to be read anywhere, and yet retain this address, this remnant of a name by which *you* are called. It remains prayer because it calls, and infinitely. It calls despairingly, but not in the despair of not calling at all; it retains vulnerability and indeed woundedness. Here, too, the sacred speaks.

Here, too, if we pay attention. In his famous "Meridian" speech, Celan writes of the sites he has sought in his poetry:

> None of these places can be found. They do not exist. But I know where they ought to exist, especially now, and . . . I find something else.
>
> Ladies and gentlemen, I find something which consoles me a bit for having walked this impossible road in your presence, this road of the impossible.
>
> I find the connective which, like the poem, leads to encounters.
>
> I find something as immaterial as language, yet earthly, terrestrial, in the shape of a circle which, via both poles, rejoins itself and on the way serenely crosses even the tropics.[88]

The connective, immaterial as the breath of the word and earthly as the stretch of the desiring body, reaches out and crosses around. It addresses, it attends, and it prays. It speaks because it is paying attention, "the natural prayer of the soul."[89] It attends to fullness and to absence, too; we are connected not just to what is, but to passing and to passion.

Body

> And henceforth movement, touch, vision, applying themselves to the other and to themselves, return toward their source and, in the patient and silent labor of desire, begin the paradox of expression.
> —Maurice Merleau-Ponty, *The Visible and the Invisible*

The connective, again, is not wholly immaterial. Prayer is a strongly physical language; written on the page, it comes to life only when vocalized; breathed into voice, it is often accompanied by postures (spontaneous or prescribed) or gestures, movements, and repetitions.[90] It demands attention to its sounds and not only its sense. Or rather, "here there are two senses," as Nancy writes, "and listening aims at—or is aroused by—the one where sound and sense mix together and resonate in each other, or again through each other. (Which signifies that . . . if, on the one hand, sense is sought in sound, on the other hand, sound, resonance, is also looked for in sense.)"[91] Sense in sound: We neither desire nor find sense without embodiment. "Each time," says Nancy, "it can only be a matter of a close combination of analysis and touch, each one sharpening or strengthening the other."[92] The body that listens, like the body that prays (itself, we see by now, a form of listening speaking), is resonant, mutual in its speech and revelation: "Timbre can be represented as the resonance of a stretched skin . . . , and as the expansion of this resonance in the hollowed column of a drum. Isn't the space of the listening body, in turn, just such a hollow column over which a skin is stretched, but also from which the opening of a mouth can resume and revive resonance?"[93]

Chrétien notes of this mutual, resounding revelation: "If [prayer] corresponds to a theophany, it is first of all an anthropophany. . . . This act of presence puts man thoroughly at stake. . . . It exposes him in every sense of the word *expose* and with nothing held back. It concerns our body, our bearing, our posture, our gestures." That the addressee of prayer is not a material entity, or any entity in any conventional understanding, does not alter the corporeality of prayer: "Even he who turns toward the incorporeal does so corporeally, with all his body."[94] Prayer is no disembodied speech, even if it is silent, even if it forgoes traditional postures and gestures. Drawing us into the world with all of our senses, the divine name we call out resounds at once beyond the time of speaking and in the depths of our hearing. "The *body* [is] unique bearer of speech, . . . the very site of any response to the appeal," Chrétien declares. "This is what founds the central character of *voice, breath* [*soufflé*], and *nudity*: this will not be the speech of angels!"[95] We praise and desire and mourn this world, reaching into it for what transits it, for what it cannot hold.

When prayer is put into words, it is attentive to sound, to the music and the poetry of language, to its flesh. This is important not only because it reminds us to praise what our senses give us and to give sensory beauty to praise, to desire with all of ourselves, to allow the bodily vulnerability and physical ache of mourning—but because it reminds us to link prayer to the body, to the dual capability and vulnerability of the flesh. Prayer, says Chrétien, is "wounded by this hearing and this call that have always already preceded it, and that unveil it to itself, in a truth always in suffering."[96] The speech that is prayer is ordeal throughout, he argues, always called and always struggling toward an impossible perfection in which God speaks to God in an embodied human voice.[97]

Prayer gives to the divine to listen, as music gives itself to us, and prayer speaks and listens to music and not only to meaning. "Perhaps," as Nancy suggests, "it is necessary that sense not be content to make sense . . . , but that it want also to resound."[98] *Resonance* emphasizes the sensuality as well as the mutuality of sound. Nancy writes:

> It returns to itself, it reminds itself of itself, and it feels itself as resonance itself: a relationship to self deprived, stripped of all egoism and all ipseity. Not "itself," or the other, or identity, or difference, but alteration and variation, the modulation of the present that changes it in expectation of its own eternity, always imminent and always deferred, since it is not in any time. . . . In resonance the inexhaustible return of eternity is played—and listened to.[99]

Chrétien argues for a resonance of the will as well: "My obedience in this case could hardly be mute: To respect beauty is not to regard it silently but to sing it. This obedience, however, does not relate us to the will as such. . . . Here, too, obedience resonates in the sound of our own voice, through prayer, but also through the words that we exchange, since this is how the voice of the Word reaches us."[100]

Language resonates, and so does desire. In prayer there is no object presented to a subject, but the reach of the voice in address. To listen, Nancy argues, is to strain toward a meaning not immediately accessible[101]—to be seduced, I would suggest, by sound and meaning both, not stopping with either—coming and passing rather than finding and halting. It is not simply coincidental that Augustine searches in poetry and hymns for the ways in which language, distended across time, is nonetheless collected in meaning; some measure of the meaning even of words is, like the answer to his attention, in beauty. And for him as for us here the sense of the divine is *always* seductive, even into sorrow, always drawing us on, always a coming and a passing. We do not simply dwell in some "standing now," but neither are we simply distended over time; eternity too comes to us and passes as we live temporally.

Seduction in language, as language's poetic element—that is, as what evokes and speaks in sounds and spaces—does not, and cannot, confer meaning in the narrow sense. It is precisely what in language eludes discourse and representation, even narration and description.[102] Lacking the completion of meaning, the one who calls out in prayer has the seduction of faith, a lived experience of the infinitely incompletable, the eternal coming and passing—joyful, hopeful, and sorrowful, too. Prayer is, we might say, the resonance of the divine trace in the human voice.

In the in-finition of the call,[103] we are reminded of the impossibility of fully *knowing* the name we call out. The completion of what "infinite perfection" could possibly mean is as impossible as the saying of it; thus to say *is* all the knowing and showing we have, and we can never say enough. In language as it seeks understanding, divine enticement is dual, showing again the reversibility characteristic of all seductions. God draws Augustine's language, leading him to declare that "I tell my story for love of your love" (2.1.1), but Augustine's language is likewise a seduction, to God and to reader both. "Here I am," says Samuel, drawing God's attention to his attentive response, in response to God's searching attention. Give me what you will, says Angelus, but what I will is you (that very desire is my gift to you). Desire desires address, desires to direct itself. *My God* is that which pulls on desire to the extent of address—as the beauty read in the trace and mourned in its absence, called by the dispossessive name: *my God, you.*

A name that confronts us again with the depth of its strangeness. "This is an outcome we will once again be tempted to find disappointing if, at the moment when the sacred present declares itself for us in its now, we have with it no relation other than that of desire and are still only able to reach, in the very name by which we establish it, our fervent wish to name it. "Desire is very little," says Blanchot, ". . . but perhaps it is much more."[104] We will be disappointed if we think we might grasp, or even if we desire to end our desiring. The open name calls out desire, question, a revelation of a relation rather than of a presence. Or, as Nancy has it, a being-unto: "*Here*—on a face, but equally, perhaps, in a name—the divinity lets itself be seen, manifestly invisible and invisibly manifest. God reveals himself—and God is always a stranger in all manifestation and all revelation. Revelation—if such a thing must be conceived of—is not a presentation, or a representation: It must be the evidence of a possibility (never a necessity) of a *being-unto-god*."[105] It is a revelation of mystery.

To Call by Name

Father,
Great is our need and we beg,
. . . .
That your name be not
Darkened within us.
Tell us your name again
lest we forget.

—Hildegard of Bingen, "Antiphon for God the Father"

Name-calling too is reversible. In the scriptural example Westphal explores, Samuel is called by name, and in that call is made (a listener) and makes himself, presents himself, as he is made. To call and be called by name is itself a revelation. Prayer calls the divine not into being, but into coming, into proximity. Since Hegel, or at least since Kojève lectured on Hegel in the 1930s, those who take seriously the entanglements of subjectivity and human interrelation have reasonably assumed that being a subject is tied to the use of the subjective pronoun, the use of the "I." Kojève writes, "Man becomes conscious of himself at the moment when—for the 'first' time—he says 'I.' To understand man by understanding his 'origin' is, therefore, to understand the origin of the I revealed by speech."[106] But perhaps we come to another kind of consciousness, a more complex selfhood, when for the first time, rather than designating ourselves in the first person pronoun, we are called by name. The novelist Muriel Barbery gives us a vivid instance of such a possibility in *The Elegance of the Hedgehog*. Remembering a revelatory moment of her childhood, the character Renée Michel thinks:

We are mistaken to believe that our consciousness is awakened at the moment of our first birth—perhaps because we do not know how to imagine any other living state. . . . The fact that for five years a little girl called Renée, a perfectly operational machine of perception blessed with sight, hearing, smell, taste and touch, could have lived in a

332

state of utter unawareness both of herself and of the universe, is proof if any were needed that such a hasty theory is wrong. For in order for consciousness to be aroused, it must have a name.

However, a combination of unfortunate circumstances would seem to confirm that no one had ever thought of giving me my name.[107]

When Renée is finally called by name, at the age of five, the result is extraordinary. Not only does she come to consciousness, she is also given the world, "brought . . . into the world"; "I looked around me and saw a world that was suddenly filled with colors."[108] Though she has been designated, probably at birth, by her name, she has never been *given* it, as if it were a gift. She has never been *called* by it—and so never brought into the world that calls out beauty. Names are words we are given, not words given about us. As given language, they call us into the world as given, as something worth enjoying, and not just using up. As the dual call of names, finite to infinite, prayer gives the world as divinely significant.

But it does not, not even as a revelation, give us a full divine *presence*. As Elliot Wolfson points out, "In traditional kabbalistic lore, the mystery of prayer involves the invocation of the name that cannot be invoked, but such an invocation is based ultimately on the paradox of an absence that is present in its absence."[109] In the sense of prayer as I have tried to develop it here, too, the invocation of the name is an incompleteable call, a call into mystery. As mystery, this "necessitates an authentic lack, an absence that cannot be represented even as absence."[110] It is thus that the mystery and query avoid degenerating into the ontotheology of which Derrida suspects even apophasis. The seductive mystery draws language to what "in" language nonetheless exceeds it, at once *before* as if at an origin, *after* as if at a telos, yet *within* as if eternally. It does not posit an ontology, but neither is it certain that it calls only to other signs; in this, it remains mystery, otherwise than being or than words. The language of prayer functions rather like that of the Valentinian *Tripartite Tractate* in Patricia Cox Miller's description: "The accent here is on the search, for to speak is to search, and that is how the ineffable 'origin' can be conceived. What language as search yields, however, is neither the presence nor the absence of the unfathomable one, but rather 'traces' of him. All words are traces which mark out the paths of the search."[111] Without invoking the particularly Valentinian cosmology implied, we can nonetheless echo the sense of speech as search, a search provoked by traces and leaving further traces of its own.

Without the designation of a being, the name that calls mysteriously is not a representative sign. It is not a common or a normal noun. Burrus notes, "The name of God uttered in prayer is . . . a 'proper' name. And, as Nancy points out, a proper name is not 'part of language . . . in the way a common noun is.'"[112] A proper name calls even when it cannot call properly. But it cuts in, it transits, as well, as Barbery shows us: "Renée. That meant me. For the first time, someone was talking to me, saying my name . . . here was a woman with clear eyes and a smiling mouth standing before me, and she was finding her way to my heart, saying my name, entering with me into a closeness I had not previously known existed."[113] In calling out the name that traces through the world, the language of prayer echoes the world's elusive speaking, calling out (to) the trace, the interpellative name, of the God who is nonetheless not a presence.

Nancy reminds us of one last peculiarity of the divine trace. For Augustine, as Nancy puts it, the created world is a "world traced, simultaneously imprinted and transversed by a vestige . . . , that is to say, traced by that which remains withdrawn and by the withdrawal of an origin."[114] And so we are returned by the sign—the name traced and the name called out—to the impossibility of an ultimate return that would finalize the process of conversion and give us completely back to ourselves. We are returned to the elusion of the origin, not knowing where to start to speak. We answer with a call, and what is revealed to us in answer is a calling, a sensuous and full-bodied desire out of our own deepest will. We begin again.

"It is with prayer that the redemption of humanity and language must begin," writes Mackey. "But prayer itself is a problem. . . . The *Confessiones* begins . . . with the impossibility of beginning."[115] So too do less extended prayers. The impossible origin, the beginning that is never in the first place, calls out from within an infinite cycle of call and response and response again, calls to the *you*—to a singular and yet infinite name.

CHAPTER 16

A Quarrel with God

Cavell on Wittgenstein and Hegel

Asja Szafraniec

I'm sick of love, but I'm in the thick of it.
This kind of love I'm so sick of it.

—Bob Dylan

The aim of this essay is to work out a thought underlying two important motifs in the work of Stanley Cavell: his belief that the human individual keeps defining itself in terms of its relation to what he calls an "outsider" as the protector of its integrity (the outside is the traditional locus of God)[1] and his conviction that this relation is defined in terms of the possibility of dissent, including the possibility of severing the relation itself. The latter conviction is expressed in Cavell's critical observation, at the beginning of *The Claim of Reason*: "Some people are not even able to start a quarrel with God."[2] This remark, barely two sentences into *The Claim of Reason*, names one of the chief preoccupations of the whole book, paralleling Cavell's preoccupation with what he calls his lifelong "quarrel with philosophy."[3] In his commentary on the opening paragraphs of *The Claim of Reason*, Stephen Mulhall claims that Cavell tries to avoid a quarrel with God in the pages that follow,[4] but it seems to me, on the contrary, that *The Claim of Reason* records precisely Cavell's private "quarrel with God." The quarrel has its philosophical antecedent in the Hegelian struggle for recognition, and I will show how Cavell, by no means inattentive to this Hegelian motif, brings it in contact with a thinking that might be considered completely alien to it, that of Wittgenstein. I am interested in how Cavell channels the struggle for recognition into the environment of language: of our everyday use of words and our everyday quarrels about the meanings of those words (quarrels

335

aiming to persuade others to recognize as generally valid the meaning we attach to some of our words, quarrels in which we try to persuade others about the validity of a particular description of a given event). Disagreements about the meanings of words may seem of little importance—but then why is the landscape of political debate in so many countries often dominated by seemingly irresolvable arguments about the validity of projections of meaning from one context to another? Think, for example, of the debates about the validity of transferring the notion of "killing" from "killing humans" to "killing embryos" (in abortion or in an IVF procedure).

This attempt to channel the notion of struggle for recognition into the environment of language opens up the possibility of seeing the struggle for recognition, including the phase in which it is waged against the absolute, in terms of Wittgenstein's reflection on seeing aspects, most famously his discussion of the rabbit-duck drawing. Here I will focus on the part of this reflection that is concerned with seeing aspects of the meaning of what is said: Wittgenstein himself insists on the connection between "seeing an aspect" and "experiencing the meaning of a word."[5] Beyond his discussion regarding the instability of our everyday definitions, which influences our sense of the good (traditionally understood as what God expects of us), there is a more general way in which the discussion of "seeing aspects" influences our discourse on God. If it is true, as Wittgenstein shows, that there is no "absolute aspect" (i.e., an aspect that would include and account for all possible aspects), this means that one aspect must always overshadow another. Then we must ask what consequences that would have for our vision of the absolute or for our reformulation of that vision.

The idea of having a quarrel with God may seem counterintuitive: The name *God* is often thought to contain its sense analytically: Just as bachelors are per definition unmarried, if anything is God, you cannot have a quarrel with it. But that would be not only to ignore that the Old Testament does record quarrels with God, including both the complete book of Job and, perhaps more pertinently, Jacob's nightly struggle with the "stranger" (to obtain his blessing) but also to fail to realize that what we take our words to mean analytically may turn out to be disputable (does marriage analytically involve individuals of opposite sex?). For Cavell, the Christian idea of God descending to earth and becoming man is evocative of just such a possibility of having a quarrel with God, even of God's authorizing us to have a quarrel with him. That is what, according to Cavell, was "unacceptable" in "Christ's message": God's renunciation of final authority, his ceding this authority (and the responsibility for it) to humans. ("Christ was killed by us because his message was unendurable."[6]) From then on, the human relation to God has been progressively absorbed in expressions of our private life, in particular within the family (parents and children, a couple in marriage). Cavell calls this a "descent, or ascent, of the problem of the other."[7] But if this is so (and taking into account the fact that the idea of the human depends on the successfulness of this absorption of the powers of transcendence into the everyday), the status of our private lives and their relations to the public dimension deserve closer examination.

Cavell's ambiguous praise of a quarrel with God does not entail simply dismissing God or rejecting religious categories. On Cavell's account, the medium of our dispute with God is our everyday language, and in particular, the role our everyday exchanges and disagreements in this language plays in training us in moral judgment. This everyday language is the proper habitat of "the Outsider" in us—without ceasing to be at the same time the locus of dissent. It is in this sense that Cavell uses Matthew 12:37 as a motto for his discussion of morality: "For by thy words thou shalt be justified, and by thy words thou shalt be condemned."[8] The major source of dissent is in the way we must use our language to shape our sense of the good: for example, the moral significance of a particular way of describing a given action and the always-present possibility of contesting this description. As Cavell puts it, "Actions, unlike envelopes and goldfinches, do not come named for assessment, nor, like apples, ripe for grading."[9]

The Blindness of God and the Opacity of Spirit—Cavell and Hegel

Both Cavell's conception of Christianity as one of the central elements in the history of skepticism and his sense of the need for a quarrel with God are forms of an engagement with another philosophy essentially related to Christianity, that of Hegel. To say this is to go against the grain of the usual contextualization of Cavell's work—besides Austin and Wittgenstein, he is usually viewed in relation to Nietzsche, Emerson, and Thoreau. But if we fail to venture into this unexplored territory, we would not only be ignoring some of Cavell's well-hidden references to Hegel (e.g., his statements about the human "right to be satisfied"), but we might miss an intriguing connection between major motifs in the work of Wittgenstein and Hegel—those I have briefly indicated above.

Let me begin, then, with the claim that Cavell's position regarding Christianity stems from drawing the full consequences of two of the major tenets of the *Phenomenology of Spirit*: on the one hand, that it claims to tell "the soul's story as part of God's";[10] on the other hand, that the mechanism allowing this story to unfold is the struggle for recognition. What are those consequences? If history is not conceived as coming to a halt at a certain point, and if the soul is not fully identical with God, the fight for recognition must also take place on the level of the relation between soul and God. We witness this struggle in contemporary debates about religion (or in debates in which one of the sides is motivated by religious points of view).

Two objections can be made to this claim, one secular and one Christian. A secular person might want to say that the struggle already has taken place and that the soul emerged from it victorious. But the point of the struggle for recognition in Hegel is that it is never won or lost once and for all (if it were, human freedom would end, since this freedom exists only to the extent it is enacted in struggle). To think that it can be so resolved is to misunderstand the necessity of continuous renegotiation between the soul and the absolute, which is the most tragic way of losing the struggle. A religious person, by contrast, might object to Hegel's conceiving of God as equivalent to some aspect of shared human-mindedness and to accepting a certain attitude to this mindedness as an authentic relation to God. The spirit as it appears in Hegel would be too immanent, too secular, to still be called "religious"—to call it that merely means translating some religious values and ideas, considered extinct, into humanist values. To this one would have to reply that, if one draws the full consequences of the idea of God as descending to earth (in what Cavell calls "the ascent or descent of the problem of the other"), one must also accept the fact of the human other "becoming Christ for one another."[11] This means that the idea of the "ascent or descent of the problem of the other" is Christian precisely to the extent to which it takes on a secular appearance. I am not insisting that God should be seen as identical with some projected, shared human-mindedness (that would be to engage in a scholastic exercise), only making a grammatical point that religion, whatever it is, and even in its most private forms, can only be lived, given form, in and through this shared human-mindedness.

I am pointing out the motif of the struggle for recognition in Cavell's thought about religion (and skepticism) not in order to argue that Cavell is a Hegelian, but because I think that the part of the Hegelian myth it brings to the fore, and the way it is related to the problem of freedom and to the phenomenon of Christianity, helps us to understand why for Cavell the "quarrel with God" is, in view of the full consequences of his descending to earth, the only possible authentic way of relating to God.[12] If Christianity is to be the highest expression of subjective freedom (as Hegel thought) then the human subject must have its say in relation to God or, as Cavell might put it, the subject's expressions must count in the struggle for recognition.[13] A textual reason for bringing Hegel in at this point is that Cavell does address the complex of issues forming the background of skepticism—in particular, the issues addressed by Wittgenstein under the topic of "seeing aspects"[14]—against the background of shared human mindedness, or spirit. Consider, for example, the passage in the fourth part of *The Claim of Reason* where Cavell says that our skeptical attitude to another (to his pain or even to his being human at all) is rooted in our failure to see aspects (aspect blindness). He also indicates there that the ability or failure to see an aspect is a function of our participation in spirit. What prevents our seeing aspects, what "separates us, comes between us, . . . *can only be a particular aspect . . . of the mind* [spirit?] *itself.*" Then he adds, "*Call this our history. It is our present.*"[15]

To say that what separates us can only be our history, or an aspect of spirit, is to say that spirit, understood as the degree of our critical absorption in and of the human form of life (or "mindedness") must itself be understood as having aspects—hence to say that spirit is no more unifying than it is divisive. If spirit has aspects, then it can fail to see some of its own aspects (e.g., it may fail to see that to be human is to have a soul; it may also fail to see that there cannot be spirit without the expression of individual souls) and be blinded by others. It can end up, for example, believing that public expression—what is said in public—has a stronger, more measurable impact on the formation of our form of life and thus can take over private life without violating it. It can end up believing itself identical with public expression. Spirit can thus be blind to itself (to its real nature). But to say this is to say that we, as individuals who are responsible for spirit, responsible for responding to it, fail to see some of its aspects—that we are the ones responsible for its opacity. The odyssey of the spirit depicted by Hegel describes, then, not only an increase in human self-understanding but also an exactly proportional increase in the possibility that one aspect of self-understanding will fail to dawn (in Wittgenstein's sense)—will remain hidden by another. And every failure of self-knowledge is a limitation of the visibility of a given field of self-expression, hence a limitation of freedom—you cannot be free regarding aspects of yourself you are not aware of. (In this sense, the struggle for recognition that counters this limitation is nothing other than the cultivation of the transparency of spirit.)

But if every step toward self-understanding brings with it the risk of occluding some other aspect of this very self-understanding, then what the soul experiences as its emancipation, that is, its discovering itself to be one with spirit, may turn out to be in fact an alienation of freedom. Sometimes Christianity is seen in this way as a religion of obedience. Cavell emphatically rejects Christianity when so understood—this is part of his "quarrel with God." Here again, Cavell's concern is not to point out some flaw in the *Phenomenology of Spirit* (where the soul discovers itself to be one with the absolute), but rather to use the "grammar" of the *Phenomenology* to point out a possible flaw in construing our relation to God as a peaceful (re)establishing of a harmonious coexistence (the myth of Eden), which, for Cavell as for Kierkegaard, rests on a "comic presupposition."[16] Nothing sensible can be said about coexistence with God, only about its grammatical preconditions, and if the grammatical medium of this coexistence is spirit, we must remember that in spirit no harmony is possible without a struggle.

If we keep aligning, as the traditional interpretation of Hegel wants us to, spirit and God (Cavell's thought is closer to the idea that our relation to God is one of the aspects of spirit), then we will also have to grant that God may sometimes, including at crucial times, be blind in his demands on us. But since any conception we can have of God and any revelation, if we are to remain free, must in some way be a function of our human ways of relating to the world and to each other (otherwise we might as well be automata), then it is in fact our own blindness that we are projecting onto God or spirit. The blindness of God, like that of Shakespeare's Lear, is a metaphor for the opacity of spirit. This seems to be the sense of Cavell's reading of *King Lear*. Cavell suggests there that Lear's demand (in the opening scene of the tragedy) that the intimate bonds of love be translated into something public and objective is an expression of an abdication of the spirit (or of that part of the spirit that enacts itself in human privacy).[17] He thus reads the opening scene of the tragedy as a phenomenological meditation avant la lettre, with a twist: In this opening scene, the spirit as Lear, blinded (though not yet physically), violates the soul

(Cordelia). The source of the tragedy is Lear's demand that the private bond with his daughters be spelled out in a public idiom, in a political context, on the presupposition that the public currency can be substituted for private ties. Not only does the genuine part of his bond to Cordelia then become no longer viable, but this blindness to the private realm opens the way to political violence.

I am aware that bringing up Cavell's defense of privacy in the context of debates about the place of religion might be taken as trying to revive the idea that religion is an exclusively private experience. This is not my intention, because the possibilities for reading *Lear* as allegory stop here. In reality, the destruction of the private by the public and a consequent blindness do not have to be the state of things between spirit and the soul: "Those chains," Cavell says (the chains with which the spirit oppresses the soul), "we have created ourselves"; they are a function of our own doings. The spirit is not a blinded father to whose violence we are subjected. We are surrounded by a milieu in which we cultivate spirit in all its aspects: the everyday. Cavell is just as wary of emphasizing privacy as the source of our religious life as he is of emphasizing the public. He is, for example, wary of conceiving the source of moral values exclusively in terms of some kind of private spiritual source of moral intuitions, one incomprehensible to others. Our moral intuitions are nothing if not a sedimentation, always belated, of the continuous process of perfecting moral judgment—compared by Cavell to the necessity of continuous practice in playing an instrument. The "moral faculty" resides neither in the player alone nor in the instrument alone but in the practice of playing: It begins with an ability to describe our world and our actions in it, together with awareness of the exposure of those descriptions to the contesting judgment of others. Again, the proper habitat of "the Outsider" is the language we share as a condition for our ideas of perfection, ideas that only through this shared language can fulfill their intrinsic requirement of constant further determination. But without individual players this habitat would die.

But what does it mean to cultivate the spirit in the everyday? We have already said that we cultivate it by counteracting its opacity. In the opening pages of the fourth part of *The Claim of Reason*, Cavell provides an example of such opacity, together with its sources, throwing light on the ways in which it can be counteracted. He begins by asking about the causes of our need to "wedge" something between the other and his expression.[18] Why does it appear necessary to us to penetrate the other's body to see his hidden intentions—or to establish the truth of his suffering? The implied answer is that the reason for this attitude is the opacity of spirit that we ourselves project. Cavell explains that we project this opacity precisely by insisting on what might appear to us to lift it: on independent, "objective" verification. We desire this form of verification because it occurs independently of our agreements (of my individual, private agreement). But those agreements (or our explicitly withholding them) are essential for the cultivation of our shared human mindedness. As a result, the milieu that should allow us to "see" becomes opaque because of our failure to cultivate it. And we cultivate it, precisely, in contesting each other's points of view on issues regarding which an "objective" verification is neither available nor called for.

Another consequence of Cavell's aligning our history with our present ("call it our history. It is our present.") is the question of the continuity of Christianity as the form of life in which human subjective freedom expresses itself. If the only time in which spirit can be cultivated is the present, then it is not enough for the form of life in which our subjective freedom expresses itself (as Hegel defined Christianity) to *have existed*: It—or the part or aspect of it that makes it the unique milieu for our subjective freedom—must be kept alive. In the fourth part of *The Claim of Reason*, Cavell, again with Hegel, uses "Christianity" as the name for the condition of the "objectification of subjectivity,"[19] that is, for the form of life that makes possible the taking up of my individual expressions into the objective spirit. He continues:

> Then I might put the question "Is there such a thing as soul-blindness?" in the following way: Is this new form of civilization [i.e., Christianity as giving expression to the right of subjective freedom, the right of the subject's particularity, or the right to be satisfied] being replaced by another? In particular, is it being replaced by one in which nothing that happens any longer strikes us as the objectification of subjectivity . . . as the expression and satisfaction of human freedom, of human intention and desire? . . . If this future . . . were effected its members would not be dissatisfied. They would have lost the concept of satisfaction.[20]

Compare Hegel's following sentences on the religious commitment from the *Introduction to the Philosophy of History*:

> There is that in individuals which is not to be made subordinate but something intrinsically eternal and divine. This is morality, ethics, religious commitment. Already when we spoke of the role of individuals in the actualization of the rational goal, we touched upon the subjective aspect, the interests of the individuals, their needs and drives, their views and insights—and although we said that this was the formal aspect in them, *it has an infinite right to be satisfied*.[21]

Only when my individual expressions can be made to count, given significance as leading to the objectification of my subjectivity, that is, to being recognized as the expression—and the satisfaction—of my intention and desire can I recognize the words of our shared language as my own, as words that can be meant by me (or can I recognize another's pain as the same as my own). Again, much is said about the publicness of religious expression today, so as to counteract what is considered to have been a previously exaggerated notion of the role of privacy in religious experience. After all, so many recent public acts of violence have been religiously motivated. But it is perhaps precisely when privacy is perceived as irrelevant noise in the overwhelmingly public conception of our world that individuals withdraw their consent to and their investment in what is public, falling back into incomprehensibility and perhaps violence. (Needless to say, this perception of privacy as irrelevant noise is not something that is reserved for the secular part of our public world; it appears equally well in fundamentalist versions.) "If nothing strikes us any longer as the objectification of subjectivity," the "inner and outer worlds become totally disconnected, and man's life all public, among strangers, seen only from outside."[22]

Or, according to the scenario drawn in *The Claim of Reason*, subjective freedom will end and, in view of the speculative identity posited by Hegel of the subjective and objective freedom, human freedom will end altogether. Cavell projects visions of the subjugation of the human by science and of the moral by the tyranny of Hegelian *Sittlichkeit*, in which the latter becomes "perfectly tyrannical, a soul-destroying attempt to mortify the criminal into bringing peace to those who destroy him."[23] In both cases the condition that accounts for this is the opacity of spirit. Christianity properly understood—Christianity that could be acceptable to Cavell (and Nietzsche) is a force that counteracts it. The continuity of Christianity expresses for Cavell the continuity of individual conversation (of privacy) with the norms of our shared human-mindedness, each one feeding into another.

We often tend to think of Wittgenstein in terms of the "private language argument" particularly construed: There cannot be a private language because all our expressions are mediated by our being in the world with others. But this is for Cavell too extreme a way of putting things. It makes it seem as if the rules of our everyday language determined everything completely, making individual expression impossible, while, on the contrary, the latter is necessary to keep the concepts of our language alive. In other words, Cavell does not dispute the necessity of the mediation of the subjective by the objective or of the private by the public. But he protests against giving priority to this mediation, hence against viewing our language and our freedom as exhaustively determined from the outside (whether by the realm of the public or by God), and thus, as he puts it, "without my intervention, apart from my agreements."[24] (Cavell uses "agreements" in plural to indicate their radically finite nature: We cannot consent once and for all.) The other side of this mediation is the individual subject's expression, to which Christianity has opened the way. It is characteristic of Christianity that it allows subjective freedom to express itself in the realm of the ordinary, in our everyday ways of relating to one another.

Quarreling about Grammar—Cavell and Wittgenstein

The important distinction between Hegel's theses on the place of religion in the development of human spirit and Cavell's thinking about Christianity is that while Hegel's story of the relation between the soul and God is a picture of the world (or, in other words, a myth),[25] Cavell, like Wittgenstein, is interested not in the content of such a picture but rather in what we can learn by studying its *form* of representation (grammar, or *Weltanschauung*). The distinction between the grammar of our world and its picture is one between understanding, on the one hand, what is given to us in the guise of the sense of appropriateness in our engagements with the ordinary reservoir of language (what do we say when, what we then must imply, etc.—an always-individual appeal to shared norms) and, on the other hand, the inevitable temptation to turn the fragments of sense yielded to us by our language into fixed architectonic elements of our world, instruments we can control at will: for example, by distilling them into definitions that can be reapplied over and over again by anyone anywhere, without having to answer to this everyday sense of appropriateness of context. This is the distinction between what Cavell calls presentness (a spiritual exercise in appropriate response consisting in an unceasing attention to the life we live) and what he calls living a myth.

Then the question becomes "can religion be expressed in a non-mythological fashion?" If this is what Cavell could be taken to address, it is different from the fideism attributed to Wittgenstein that Hans-Johann Glock called "a religion for atheists." What Cavell offers cannot properly be defined as religion or nonreligion because it would then deteriorate into a mythology. It is for this reason that Cavell says, "the ordinary is the esoteric."[26] This means that if there are aspects of religious thought in Cavell's discourse, they must be subjected to a necessary indirectness, one that Cavell had in mind when he wrote about Kierkegaard's necessary indirectness.[27] The religious mode of speech is not saying anything in particular but "meaning everything you say in a certain way." This is not to say that it is speaking allegorically. It would be crude, for example, to take what Cavell says about marriage in a fixed way as an allegory for our relation to God or for political relations of power. He never pretends to talk about marriage in this sense, but always speaks about a unique couple with its particular set of problems, so that analogies pertain only to a certain point. Cavell's commitment to the ordinary reflects his struggle with the domain of myth: The ordinary is that which is lived, as marriages are lived and as the relations between parents and children are lived, and as for some people faith is lived: Each is in the first place a unique, exemplary configuration driven by the involvement of all concerned individuals—rather than a ready-made reservoir of sense.

All will depend then, for Cavell, on the question of whether the grammar of mourning ("our relation to God is that of parties to a testament—or refusers of it")[28] or the grammar of marriage can be projected onto the form we have given our relation to God and in what way. To say something about God directly, for example by making explicit "what the metaphor is the metaphor for" is to speak mythologically. But how else can we speak about the relation to God in Cavell? We can, perhaps, do so by putting in play our knowledge of the grammar of language, in particular language's "possibilities of projection." This is how Cavell refers to the slippage of sense from one context to another. Take, in Cavell's own example, what happens to the verb "*feed*" as it moves from "feeding the monkey" to "feeding the money into the meter."[29] Our language is "tolerant in that it allows projections, but it is also intolerant in that the projections are deeply controlled."[30] The verb cannot be projected into just any context: "An object or activity must invite or allow this projection."[31] And some projections are natural, while others, even though tolerated by our language, are not. But then the naturalness and even the very possibility of a projection must always remain open to question. If they were not, if our language were fully regulated, not allowing any doubts about the validity of a projection, it would be no different from myth or from a machine. Thus it is always possible to say that the comedy of remarriage can be projected onto the relation of the soul to God, but it is also possible to dispute it—debating the validity and naturalness of such projection is a matter of seeking community. And projecting means that something will be alike, but not everything (just as feeding money into the meter is in some ways similar, in other ways dissimilar to feeding a monkey). Another projection discussed—and rejected—by Cavell, one more appropriate to the question of his dismissing religion as seeking transcendence in favor of an esoteric immanence, is the slippage of the sense of the word "*to enter*" from "entering a place" to "entering another's mind" to "entering into marriage." "I do not enter another's mind the way I enter a place. This is so far not much help; it does not distinguish either from entering, say, into marriage."[32] Who decides whether a projection is legitimate? Again, the necessity of individual acceptance distinguishes proficiency in myth from proficiency in a form of representation. This distinction holds also when the form of representation in question involves an imaginary object, which is to say that for Cavell religion, too, can be lived grammatically rather than mythologically. It is in this that it differs from the "fideism" Glock attributes to Wittgenstein.

It is in order to call upon the individual reader's agreement in projection (without prejudging it), his exercise of his own subjective freedom, that Cavell prefers to say about Felicie in Eric Rohmer's film *A Tale of Winter* that she chooses a way of life that is not incompatible with Charles's return, rather than to say plainly "contemporary Christianity can be defined as practicing a way of life which is not incompatible with Christ's return."[33] The first sentence draws on the resources of an ordinary life. The question of whether it allows or invites a projection is suspended; it demands my seeing or failing to see certain aspects that present themselves—it requires my participation in its meaning. So it presents itself in the condition of conversation of individual souls with the spirit. The second sentence is "a fixation." One can be aspect-blind and still imagine one understands it—or, as Cavell puts it, drawing again on the resources of Wittgenstein's discussion of seeing aspects, "nothing in me needs to dawn."[34] Cavell's concern with the esoteric is precisely this: What makes the ordinary esoteric is not this or that particular dawning of sense but the event of dawning. When it fails to happen, "in terms of the myth of reading the physiognomy, this would be thought of as a kind of illiteracy; a lack of education."[35] Cavell's writing is all directed at countering this illiteracy by training individual ability and responsibility to project or refuse to—and give reasons for this refusal.

It might be objected that a projection might lead to establishing or solidifying a myth. Drawing analogies from the context of killing humans to killing embryos is, for example, a potent means in homiletics of the Catholic Church, solidifying a dogma. But again, for Cavell as for Wittgenstein, projections, just like seeing aspects, require individual agreement. It is precisely when addressing mythology (to counter its working on himself) that Wittgenstein says, "I should have said: *This is how it strikes me.*"[36] Individual expression and mythology oppose one another.

Sometimes myth and actuality can "live happily together"—when they are not in competition, or when myth has been given the last word. But "when you keep wondering too much, say, about where rules come from, then you have stopped living the myth." Again, the question "where the rules come from" can have a mythological answer (from God or from the social contract) or a grammatical answer: Even though they exercise control, they demand my agreement. The first often seems to have more explanatory power, but accepting it as an answer has consequences for our freedom. "To say 'All the steps are really already taken'" is to say that "the conclusion reached by a rule is always *forgone*. If you still ask 'What is foregone?' it may help to reply, 'Freedom. At each step the rule will dictate.'" For Cavell, every case in which the rule dictates at each step is a case of a "little mythology."[37]

I have established by now that the historical form of Christianity does play a role in Cavell's thought of the skepticism about other minds, and not merely as something in the past. In Cavell's account, the hypothetical impartial observer in the Cartesian meditations is not only the protector of the integrity of individual existence, but also the constitutive part of the idea of human nature.[38] Thus modernity's acceptance of the disappearance of God logically draws in its wake an acceptance of the disappearance of human nature. We might find this unproblematic and agree that this is what happened. But for Cavell dispensing with the idea of human nature has consequences that have not been sufficiently understood. This is why the myth of the opposition of nature and culture—and its variant, the opposition between childhood and adulthood—is so present in his work. The opposition between God and the human is one of the many cases of the "polarity of the human spirit"—its tendency to perceive itself in terms of opposed substances or alternating stages of history, with the accompanying danger that when one of them disappears, the other loses the content on which it thrives. If human nature disappears, so does human culture. If the inner is forced to abdicate, so does the outer. This is the essence of Cavell's reading of Shakespeare's *King Lear* as a play in which "the inner and the outer have become totally disconnected."[39] The remedy envisaged by Cavell lies in preserving communication between opposites, rather than either their conflation (where one must be expressed by means of the other) or their separation (so that the world is perceived either only from the outside, as in Machiavelli, or only from the inside, as in Luther).[40]

I have accordingly established that it is possible to discern in Cavell's work a certain accompanying reflection on the fate of contemporary Christianity, hence also on its fate in the condition of philosophy (when an aspect attributed to Christianity expresses itself in philosophy, in particular, in problems of skepticism). I have also established that what Cavell finds acceptable in Christianity, if it is not thought in the condition of a myth, must be a question of the meanings of our ordinary words—of our accepting or rejecting projections like those between reentering a room and reentering into marriage—or entering into another contract, that of mourning: "Our relation to God is that of parties to a testament (or refusers of it); and Luther's logical point is that you do not accept a promise by knowing something about a promisor."[41] The "quarrel with God" expresses itself in those disagreements. It is a matter of finding out what our words have absorbed of Christianity (and to what extent we accept this Christian absorption), hence a matter of mourning. It is, hence, in our agreements and disagreements about the meaning of ordinary words (about the way *we* mean them) that conversation takes place between the individual human soul and the spirit, and this conversation is not always harmonious.[42] The dissent between the soul and spirit may take the extreme form in which the soul insists on becoming the measure of spirit (as in Thoreau, whose words become a measure of reality, a "realometer"[43]), but it can also take the opposite form, in which it fails to recognize itself in spirit, separates itself, and falls into madness and isolation.

This dissent between the soul and spirit names a problem that is now more pertinent then ever: A somewhat similar stand valorizing dissent in the human relation to God makes a short and far from conclusive appearance in Charles Taylor's *A Secular Age*: "We might even be tempted to say that modern unbelief is providential, but that might be too provocative way of putting it."[44] Modern unbelief is providential in the sense that a possibility of dissent is a mark of every real conversation (as opposed to subjection to myth). It may be too provocative a way of saying it because dissent always carries with it the possibility of madness and isolation.

Is this still Christianity? Cavell himself acknowledges that it seems to be deprived of all its satisfactions, even those of negative theology and mystical contemplation: "Its hope is no longer in Heaven." But it does permit a quarrel with God and does permit it to take the shape of the struggle for recognition. It is in this sense not unlike the plots Cavell discusses under the common denominator of the comedies of remarriage. Cavell's essays on this topic pay a lot of attention to the evolution of roles in marriage, to the man and woman's constantly renewed struggle for recognition. We are dealing with a situation in which the myth of marriage as a straightforward institution is undermined; the distribution of power and positions has changed. In human marriage, this has to do with a change in the configuration of forces Cavell calls the creation of the woman; in the religious context, it concerns another such change, the man's having seen God naked (hence as human) and having thus understood the fact of the "descent" of the problem of the other. In both cases, everything must be renegotiated anew. In Cavell's "The Same and Different: *The Awful Truth*," the female character Lucy chases the totemic black cat out of her bed, to which Cavell responds, "no more symbols of marriage, the real thing is about to take over."[45] The myth of marriage is lost, the division of power has changed (the creation of the woman), and everything must be renegotiated anew: Without signs and totems, "real life begins." So what is it that allows the old marriage to show itself as viable in this film? Cavell mentions their rereading of an old love letter (it does not give the couple the laugh they thought it might), the rethinking of their common story of "festive existence," and finally, the woman's bold initiative, from her new, emancipated position, to give a new and unorthodox direction to their relation that redefines their mutual positions in the relation and the relation itself. As a result, the male character, Jerry, "must come to stand to himself in the relation that remarriage stands to marriage, succeeding himself."[46] This succession makes remarriage always at the same time a mourning.

This is, again, not to say that *The Awful Truth* should be read as an allegory. That is precisely what Cavell wants to avoid. Our language itself has a tendency to lure us into allegories, into mythical projections; the task of ordinary language philosophy is to expose them by constantly reminding us that those projections require our consent. This consent—or lack of it—is more important than the content of the projections themselves. Ordinary language philosophy, unlike Hegel's philosophy, cannot tell a story of how it envisages a human relation to God, though it can quarrel with the verdicts we accept as his (by quarreling about the description of acts that undergo these verdicts). At most, it can give us some grammatical remarks, on the basis of which such a "new dawn" can be brought to expression, or not.

CHAPTER 17

Thinking about the Secular Body, Pain, and Liberal Politics

Talal Asad

When we hear someone speak of a religious body, we tend to think of it as the body of a believer, of someone living a religious life. Can we also speak of a secular body? If so, what might that mean? And how is "the secular body," whatever it may be, related to liberalism and democracy—that is, to the political demands of our modern life? Is secularism inevitably hostile to pain and distress? Is Christianity, with its sacred narrative of suffering, the immanent frame of modern secularity? In what follows I speculate about the "secular body" as the site of sensibilities, attitudes, and convictions and the ways in which it may or may not be distinguishable from the "religious body." I do so by paying special attention to pain because it helps us to deepen our understanding of the secular. I consider in particular the relevance of pain for what it can make the sufferer say and do about her suffering.

Let me begin, then, with the painful body.

Consider this: I wake up one morning in deep pain; anxiety, wild speculation, and fear follow. The pain pushes me / my body into a particular *interpretive language*, an interpretation that is at the same time a translation. It leads me to the conviction that I am ill. In the absence of "real" evidence, conviction that the pain is more than itself—a *clue* to some hidden meaning—is usually called "hypochondria." I refer to hypochondria not to suggest that we sometimes misinterpret perceived objects in the external world, including bodily sensations, or that we sometimes imagine something exists when it really doesn't. I take "hypochondria" as alerting us to the fact that relations between the self and the objective world—or between the "mental" and the "physical"— are often accidental, post hoc, recursive, and *always practical*. It is one way of problematizing the standard distinctions between the spiritual and the material, belief and action, reason and unreason.

Charles Taylor, a leading authority on Hegel, has proposed that the "buffered self" is a precondition of modern secularity, a self that has learned to *interpret* the world objectively because it has separated itself from the world while remaining in a dialectical relationship with it.[1] This reference to disjunction is important but not quite adequate, because what matters is not simply "disconnection" of the body/self from the world, but the layered ways in which body and world have come to be severed and yoked together. The hypochondriac's encounter with his own feelings is real enough, but medical experts (and skeptical friends) tell him they are not real. The category of "hypochondria" as an illness is, in an obvious sense, modern *and* secular—by which I mean simply that it is a product of biomedicine, of an institutionalized practical knowledge that presents itself as rational and progressive, and sometimes as an epistemological model that can be opposed to theological definitions and explanations of experience.

The hypochondriac belongs to a modern, ruptured world; yet an individual's deep entanglement with the sensations of her own body (an object in the world) is not easily described as "buffered." Sometimes the hypochondriac's body may be called "religious," but this is not because he cannot distinguish the truth of his own body from forces external to him, and so should be called "superstitious/enchanted." It is identified as "religious" (or "secular") for other, more complicated reasons. What might these be? Rather than analyzing the institutional conditions in which the "religious" or "secular" body is disciplined, one might turn directly to the body's expression of pain for an answer. Pain is a function of the living body, and since the body's life is finite so too is its ability to feel pain. Thinking about pain as an unsolicited—and unwelcome—state of the body as *a living* body may allow one to conclude that it is not pain as such that is secular or religious but the way it is lived by the subject. Pain is especially interesting because of its ambiguous position not only between "body" and "mind," but also between "the secular" and "the religious."

"Hypochondria" (like "hysteria") tests the limits of sympathy for another's suffering. Although pain, anxiety, and fear are genuinely experienced by someone labeled a hypochondriac, in ordinary life these feelings tend to be dismissed as "imaginary" and *therefore* as not worthy of being taken seriously. It is the fact that he *believes* he is ill when he is not that makes him, for some, a figure of fun. Whatever evidence one brings forward, one cannot persuade the hypochondriac that he is not really ill; there is clearly something awry in his mind as well as his body. In its irrationality hypochondria resembles the secularist (Freudian) view of ritual.

But is "hypochondria" a *real* disease or just an *imagined* one? Modern medicine has now decided that it is itself a disease, one of several identifiable "anxiety disorders" (anorexia, claustrophobia, etc.) and that although there may be physical disorders that indirectly create the experience of pain, the disease known as hypochondria can be successfully treated—or more precisely, *because* it is the object of investigation and therapy, hypochondria is a (psychological) disease.[2] What was once thought to be an instance of mere illusion is now regarded as in an important sense *real*. The authoritative medical view (which today even "religious" people accept) is that the pain and fear experienced by the hypochondriac are not "healthy": There is no place in a healthy body for pain and fear that isn't based on "something real." The hypochondriac may *feel* pain, but in taking that pain to be a sign of hidden illness he reveals himself to be unwell. His painful feelings are not disputed; only his obsession with and his interpretation of them are. So here is a familiar perspective on pain: Pain as such is "real," capable of being cured or alleviated, and as a signifier of something "unreal" it should be disabused. But there is also another perspective on pain that doesn't involve the real/unreal opposition, to which I now turn.

Many religious and nonreligious persons have used their hypochondria to secure spaces for *living* in a particular, productive way. For them pain is not merely a sign of unwellness (something to be explained and treated) but a means of resolving problems they encounter. The hypochondriac is not simply an abstract subject; he has a particular body with a unique history. It is not merely that his alarmist reasoning may be mistaken, or that the effect of his beliefs on his visceral register is often not taken into account in explanations of behavior. In that *particular* body illness and pain might also be a claim to much-desired privacy, a distancing from the world and its unwelcome demands—in short, it may be *a distinctive way of living and working through suffering*. The hypochondriac in a sense *embraces* pain rather than rejecting it and seeing it entirely in a negative light. My central question is not the truth or untruth of the hypochondriac's relation to the world, not his lack of satisfaction with his life, not even the ethical status of his pain ("pain can sometimes be ethically valuable / pain is essentially and always evil"). It is what the grammar of statements about his pain are, what they show about his relationship to himself and to others in his life.

So—what might "the secular body" be? I want to draw attention here to something other than the business of explaining or justifying or abhorring pain, something that is evident in the public life of the body (*shown* by it and not *explained*, as Wittgenstein would say), something that doesn't constitute a consolation but a living-out, far-reaching or temporary, of life itself—and expresses that life in language.

In his history of nineteenth-century British secularism, Edward Royle has shown that this movement was initially linked strongly to *both* political and epistemological reform. Rationalistic (i.e., "antireligious") *explanations* of seemingly extraordinary experience, political demands for inclusion, and endorsements of an ideal universal morality (one that was "truly democratic") were *all* at the center of what one of its leaders, George Jacob Holyoake, named "secularism."[3] The general usage of the term *secularism* today is explicitly political rather than epistemological, perhaps because it is assumed that the battle for truth has been won but the battle for tolerance has not. Regardless of whether one "believes" in secularism or not, however, its commonly accepted grammar can be explored with the aim of tracing the *range of possible modes of living it articulates*, without making judgments about its truth or ethical value.[4] Thus Winnifred Sullivan has argued that the legal discourse of a secular state operates in ways that are contrary to the general sense of "secularism" as a political doctrine: The principles of complete separation from and strict neutrality toward all "religions" are not to be judged good or bad but declared *impossible*.[5] So how does the grammar of "the secular" work for the individual body that suffers pain? What role does pain have in the psychic structure of the political body? Pain is often deliberately inflicted, but more significantly, the deliberate character of inflicted pain takes many forms.

In Western societies, justifications of the desire to punish the body—to make it suffer pain—lie partly in Christian theology, especially in the theology of atonement. What kind of Christian and post-Christian body is being defined and regulated when punishment is shifted entirely to *this* world? Timothy Gorringe, in his history of the significance of the crucifixion for secular theories of punishment, describes how "the death of Christ dominated the 'structures of affect' of Europe for five hundred years, and in so doing they pumped retributivism into the legal bloodstream."[6] The legal bloodstream sustains the life of the liberal political body. So the gradual "humanization" of theological doctrines on punishment in the late nineteenth and twentieth centuries that Gorringe charts—and especially the increasingly permissive attitude toward the pleasures of sex that liberal Christianity took—alerts us to how one might think not only about "the secular body" but also about aspects of the secular state. Punishing the captive body is still regarded as necessary even if it isn't justified in theological terms. The secular justifications of legal confinement (prevention and suppression of crime, reaffirmation of social and political solidarity, locking up dangerous individuals, rehabilitation of criminals) cover up a strong desire to witness the "proper" infliction of suffering.

There is clearly more to the "secular body" than disbelief in supernatural beings (a self that is buffered) and the demand that causal explanations of pain be properly verified and that it be humanely administered. There is more than the desire that citizens should live tolerantly with the followers of other beliefs. What might this "more" be?

Consider this: In modern, liberal society Christians and non-Christians, believers and nonbelievers, live more or less the same kind of life in modern capitalist society and in that sense can be said to have similar bodies. What does this say about "the secular body"? One answer may be that religious belief, where it exists among *liberal* moderns, is so deeply repressed that it has at best a very tenuous connection with public—especially political—behavior. Consequently, the connection can be easily denied altogether, as in this statement of the chief minister of Ontario quoted in a local newspaper: "'As premier, I have made decisions that defy the beliefs of my own religion,' Mr. McGuinty said, citing his support for same-sex marriage and abortion. 'My Catholicism, my private faith, does not determine my position.'"[7] Inhabiting the body of the church is quite different from inhabiting the body of the state; even if religious belief can be publicly acknowledged it must not be politically imposed. According to the classic secularist argument, religion depends on unquestioned authority and liberal democratic politics on rational principles. However, the familiar opposition between "persuasion" and "imposition" is less secure than often supposed. "Reasoned discourse" covers a range of persuasive and dissuasive moves that aim at changing behavior: threats, promises, hidden appeals, and indirect influences. Persuasive discourses can be deceptive as well as rational at one and the same time—as anyone who has reflected on intimate relationships and political programs knows. Persuasion can be a mode of conquest as well as helping someone reach truthful conclusions.

According to secularists like Sam Harris, the matter is simple: "Belief is a lever that, once pulled, moves almost everything else in a person's life. Are you a scientist? A liberal? A racist? These are merely species of belief in action. Your beliefs define your vision of the world; they dictate your behavior; they determine your emotional responses to other human beings."[8] Thus religious beliefs, being preeminently irrational and emotional, are a notorious source of violent intolerance. McGuinty, by contrast, is able and willing to separate off his own Catholic beliefs from his political decisions—just as he expects non-Catholic fellow citizens in a secular state to cordon off their beliefs. But beliefs and decisions are embedded in language. Therefore, all citizens in a plural society must be prepared to translate their different religious or nonreligious beliefs into secular reasons so that they can subscribe equally to the state's core political ideals. So both Harris and McGuinty are defending a secular state—one by aggressively confronting religious belief as the source of intolerance, the other by elevating the principles of (1) separation between religion and politics and (2) state neutrality toward all religious and nonreligious group-ings in a plural society. According to Harris, the freedom of expression of all individual citizens—especially nonbelievers—must be protected by the state because it is a sacred political right. Because in his view the beliefs of religious believers lead them to try to restrict that freedom (usually violently), they must be repressed. For McGuinty the ideal society is one that doesn't allow the possible social implications of religious beliefs and sentiments to intervene in civil and political life. (However, it is evident that the formal separation of religious doctrines and sentiments from political activity cannot ensure that they won't carry over from the private to the public sphere.)

McGuinty's state is not, however, neutrally positioned toward religious and nonreli-gious *languages*; the demand that the former be accommodated to the latter, in which the main political ideals are articulated, gives secularist citizens an advantage over citizens who are religious (the political body's secular language is not required to be translated into the individual's religious language). For Harris there is no question of translating religious language into secular argument because that would simply mean unleashing religious persecution. Harris takes up a hostile attitude toward religion, McGuinty an attitude that seeks to neutralize religious beliefs in the sphere of state politics. The fear of *illegitimate* violence—especially violence produced by "religious passions"—lies at the heart of the modern state, and it is evoked again and again by modern liberal states in moments of crisis, although now that fear serves to consolidate dominant state power and expresses a paranoid preoccupation with the elusive bodies of enemies. So my question is not which of the two better defends the rights of the secular citizen body, but what distribution of pain follows from particular political decisions in particular societies.

But the relations connecting belief, pain, and worldliness to one another are more complex.

For epistemological secularists, the living human ends with death. The end is final, and there is nothing else. Pain accompanies the dying body. Left to itself, the body after death putrefies and eventually disintegrates into its chemical components. And yet the law has long recognized that a person's *will* extends beyond death, disposing of his or her properties in prearranged ways. The body may be cremated, but the personality of the deceased lives on in palpable ways; indeed, some aspects of that personality (its intentions regarding property) can be put into effect only after death. Henry Maine recounts how this legal fiction, indispensable to the continuity of what we now call secular liberal society, was genealogically traceable to ancient beliefs about life after death.[9] So, too, the law's requirement that cadavers be treated with respect: The dead body may not feel pain, but it appears nevertheless to retain *the right to dignity* that she possessed in life. The fact that the personality to which the cadaver once belonged continues legally after death indicates that the *living organism* may not always be essential to human personality. Yet this continuity of personality bestows on the cadaver something it otherwise does not possess, which is why even secularists are shocked at seeing images of dead bodies thrown carelessly in a heap. (The law finds it easier to protect the dignity of a dead body than a living one, because in death all cadavers are evidently equal.) Should one say that, because it feels no pain and entertains no illusions and has no fears, the human cadaver is the ultimate expression of the secular body? If so, would this mean that what defines its secularity is not a particular kind of discipline or belief but an absent capacity? And couldn't one also say that the dignity it possesses in the eyes of the living, and the reverence with which the cadaver is to be treated, bestow on it a measure of sanctity—and therefore a quasi-"religious" status?

There is a more recent problematization of the secular body as one that rejects certain illusions (principally, that there is life after death) and that clings to life in this world precisely because of its finitude. The anthropologist Abou Farmaian has recently produced a rich account of the U.S.-based groups that have developed the ideology he calls "immortalism." Immortalists seek an indefinite extension of human life by their faith in scientific progress—specifically, cryonics, biogerontology, and artificial intelligence. Paradoxically, immortalism is so committed to the world that it aims to overturn a basic principle of secular life as understood hitherto: that there is no life after death. Immortalists, Farmaian argues, believe that, given the development of scientific knowledge, human beings *can* enjoy life after death, and it is precisely their attachment to life *in this world* that leads them to their secular faith in the truth of this proposition.[10]

Let me return to pain and unwellness as expressed in what Henry Maine calls "corporation aggregate" (the collective body) and "corporation sole" (the individual body). Whether the body is metaphorical or "real," whether it is the object of state regulation or the subject of uncontrollable desires, corporation aggregate and corporation sole partly mirror and partly conflict with each other, invoking various accounts of pain.

In one of his meditations, John Donne reflects on faith and the body through the image of microcosmos. The individual body mirrors the city, the city mirrors the earth, and the earth mirrors the heavens, all in concentric fashion, and their common (worldly) center is disease and decay—a secret rebellion against *order*:

> God knew many heavy sins of the people, in the wildernes and after, but still he charges them with that one, with *Murmuring, murmuring* in their *hearts*, secret disobediences, secret repugnances against his declar'd wil; and these are the most deadly, the most pernicious. And it is so too, with the *diseases* of the *body*; and that is my case. The *pulse*, the *urine*, the *sweat*, all have sworn to say nothing, to give no *Indication*, of any dangerous *sicknesse*. My forces are not enfeebled, I find no decay in my strength; my provisions are not cut off, I find no abhorring in mine appetite; my counsels are not corrupted or infatuated, I find no false apprehensions, to work upon mine understanding; and yet they see, that invisibly, and I feele, that insensibly the *disease* prevailes. The *disease* hath established a *Kingdome*, an *Empire* in mee, and will have certaine *Arcana Imperii, secrets of State*, by which it will proceed, and not be bound to declare them.[11]

Implied in this text is an affinity, *within* the illness modern medicine now calls hypochondria, between "religious"—specifically Christian—and "secular" elements, between the refusal of the body's fluids (blood, urine, sweat) to disclose anything of its hidden disorder, on the one hand, and secret disobedience to God, on the other, between corruption within earthly bodies and disease itself as a political form. Yet Donne's account of his corporeal condition is not simply a medical category mistakenly expressed in theological guise. It assumes a particular mode of life and a polity in which *some* norms of health (social, theological, corporeal) are to be promoted and others discouraged, in which the illness, decay, and death of the state echo the disease, disintegration, and death of the individuals who make it up. It is not merely the body but the living (ensouled) body that is invoked. In seventeenth-century political theory, this affinity was expressed in the metaphysical view that the individual in a state of nature possesses the same inalienable right to defend himself from the threat of death as the sovereign (state) does.[12]

"Donne," notes Ramie Targoff, "was haunted throughout his life by feelings of the awkward dissociation between his body and soul: the tensions that arose between their respective needs; their irreconcilable states of health or illness; the occasional discrepancies between their objects of desire."[13] Donne's theological uncertainties led him to agonize over the possibility that the rupture between body and soul at death might not be healed at resurrection, to wonder anxiously whether, in being given a new sinless body at resurrection, his soul might not be reunited with his *own* familiar body. But his faith gave him the confidence that he, John Donne, would be present—*his* body and soul as one—beside Christ in heaven as he had promised his believers. Donne's theological anxieties and preoccupations entered into and shaped his poetry, his prose, and his life, making his very act of writing into what Targoff memorably calls an instance of "the word made flesh." We might (counter-intuitively) call Donne's body "secular"—not because he was emotionally attached to it but because its *earthly* experience was indispensable to him as a Christian preacher, poet, and lover, essential to his *worldly hope* in the resurrection of the body *after it has perished*. But what would be gained by calling it secular—other than the suggestion that it is merely worldly experience that explains Donne's hope and anguish, despite the fact that the latter were soaked in theological language?

During his tormented life, Ludwig Wittgenstein was convinced that his anguish—frequently expressed in bouts of wanting to commit suicide—was due to his own "baseness and rottenness." Modern medical science would certainly not categorize that state as one of "wellness." And yet for Wittgenstein his ailment was positive, because in trying to rectify the "unworthiness" he glimpsed in himself, he was in effect living religiously.[14] On occasion he was convinced that he was "physically" ill because of abdominal pains and high temperature (which then turned out to have been normal).[15] His biographer, Ray Monk, comments on the controversy over Wittgenstein's homosexuality: "Wittgenstein was uneasy, not about homosexuality, but about sexuality itself. Love, whether of a man or a woman was something he treasured. He regarded it as a gift, almost as a divine gift. But . . . he sharply differentiated love from sex. Sexual arousal, both homo- and heterosexual, troubled him enormously. He seemed to regard it as incompatible with the sort of person he wanted to be."[16] It was this deep internal conflict, and the signs by which it was to be recognized ("sensibility" is too weak a word here) that made Wittgenstein obsessed with the need for "confession," for being "ruthlessly honest" with himself and his bodily desires. As in depth psychology (he was familiar with Freud's writings, although not uncritical of them), corporeal signs were indicators of something hidden and therefore in need of interpretation.

Rightly or wrongly, his suffering and his continual attempts to interpret and understand himself were central to the way he lived, the way he interacted with others, and the way he thought as a philosopher. He was deeply absorbed by the signs of unwellness in his own body and by his repeated—and repeatedly failed—efforts to overcome it by his "religious task." Wittgenstein spoke of "the soul" not as *a part* of the human being (as Donne did) but as something best *represented* by the living body ("The human body is the best picture of the soul").[17] Should we call his a "religious body," even though as an adult he never practiced Catholic rites or presented himself as a "believer"? At the very least one must conclude that if we are to call him "secular" this is not because of his disciplined sensibilities—and certainly not because of his explicit denial of "supernatural" beliefs. He might be called "secular" (but why not for the same reason "religious"?) because he tried to live his painful body integrally, without invoking the duality of flesh and spirit (body and mind).

If "hypochondria" is a particular reading of the body in pain, how does it compare with other readings of pain that have emerged or disappeared in history—like "hysteria," say? What can hysteria tell us about "the secular body"?

Early modern medical treatises sometimes spoke of "hysteria" as the female version of "hypochondria," as a perversion of the virtue of "sensibility." By the beginning of the nineteenth century, "hypochondria" was applicable to women as well as men and considered a kind of heightened sensibility. In her study of the eighteenth-century concepts and practices of privacy, Patricia Meyer Spacks makes an illuminating comparison between what was understood by sensibility and later, in nineteenth-century medical thought, by hysteria—that is, between sympathy offered and sympathy denied, between private and public reaction to pain.[18] Spacks's comparison makes it clear that sensibility (an admired ability to respond generously to another's suffering) is the inverse of hysteria (an embarrassing expression of pain demanding but not deserving sympathy). Sensibility and hysteria are both said to be uncontrolled responses in the subject's encounter with pain; each articulates the relationship of the individual person with worldly power. Because hysteria is seen as transgressive, as an expression of indiscipline, it is taken as a sign of the subject's need for cure; the appropriate response of the observer is not compassion with the hysteric's anguish but distance from it. Whereas sensibility was an approved expression of the tactful feelings of the private self, the *publicity* of hysteria, the inarticulate passion it displayed, was a sign of a troubled interiority that therefore indicated something hidden. Yet the performance of sensibility also encouraged concealment by invoking *privacy*; unlike hysteria, sensibility discouraged the public display of emotions.

Thus the sympathy cultivated and offered (sensibility) and the sympathy desired and denied (hysteria) that made up emotional aspects of the emerging modern subject discussed by Spacks together reflect in miniature a political contradiction in modern liberal society. On the one hand, there are private spaces of "freedom" (including the subjective right to express criticism) that secular power should not invade; on the other hand, there are the secret spaces of "sickness"—potential irruptions of illegitimate disorder—that the state must penetrate if it is to defend the equal freedom of each body. The border between the private and the public is not as clear-cut as the law has it. The mind-body's sympathies and antipathies, fears and desires, and the reasonings and drives that attach to them, cannot be neatly boxed and shed as it moves from political space to civil to private and back.

The relation between the sick body and authority that can interpret signs of ailment *correctly* and respond to them in an appropriate manner is at once political, civic, and personal. The secular story goes that in premodern times the hysteric could not be scientifically treated because she was believed to be possessed by divine or demonic forces. Her irrational individual disorder—like the irrational collective violence of religious believers—could be treated properly only once secular knowledge and political practice had triumphed in human society. And as secularists overseeing a more humane world, we now require religious discourse (language) to remain in its assigned space and not encroach on either science or politics, so that unnecessary suffering can be avoided. But that story isn't quite adequate to the reality the hysteric now lives because there are different *structures of pain* that manifest themselves in our world.

Take sadism: Like the hypochondriac (though in his own special way), the sadist is obsessed with pain and lives in a disjunctive world. This disjunction, however, does not distinguish types of belief (religious and secular, as Harris does) or the sanctity of the private from the profaneness of the political (as McGuinty does). It links the sadist's unsatisfied desire, on the one hand, to his possession of the victim's body, on the other. Sadism is a late-eighteenth-century arrival, articulating the sovereignty of human reason and individual desire. It is repeated and repeatedly condemned in the centuries that follow, and attempts are made to box it in as a self-contained horror—but without success, for sadistic desire has a strong tendency to enter the motives and feelings of those considered "normal" and to seek from there its own readings of the truth.

In his history of madness, Michel Foucault writes that "sadism" was not simply the name given in the eighteenth century to a practice that had always existed but a striking cultural fact that appeared at that moment—what he called the mark of a great transformation of the Western imagination.[19] (It appears at the same time as those great classical texts of reason and humanity, the American Declaration of Independence and the French Declaration of the Rights of Man and Citizen.) Later, in *The Order of Things*, Foucault relates sadism to the complex rise of the life sciences in the late eighteenth century (exemplified by Cuvier's *Lessons of Comparative Anatomy*), when the human emerges as animal.[20] Sade was an individual, but sadism for Foucault is a collective phenomenon that marks an appetite without limit—a force that becomes a source of human singularity, of human monstrosity, that is at once implicit in yet goes beyond man's animal nature. If human reason explodes divine law by subordinating itself to *life functions*, then for Sade murder—"killing for life"—is a part of nature, not of law. The secular state's willingness to kill at home and abroad while subscribing to the sanctity of human life is an expression of that nature.

In an interesting commentary on Sade, Georges Bataille notes that, when the torturer inflicts punishment on his victim, he normally uses the language of an established authority; his violence is thereby given an impersonal, *silent* character; he speaks, that is, not in his own name but in the name of authority. In Sade's novels, however, those who inflict pain *do* speak for themselves, claiming that in enacting their cruelty they are truly following Nature. This claim, it might be said, renders their bodies "secular." However, there is more to the sadist's obsession with pain than the invocation of Nature in justifying it. Regardless of whether it is treated as a sickness or as a moral fault, the sadist's enjoyment of another's pain has a strong erotic dimension. And overcoming it (usually after the fact) involves the subject's forcible constraint.

Consider these facts: According to the U.S. Bureau of Justice Statistics on Homicide, of all children under age five murdered from 1979 to 2005 in that country, 60 percent were killed by a parent; the statistics on violence by spouses and lovers are also very high.[21] In Europe the violence sustained by women from their husbands or lovers is no less impressive. "That is what happens in Europe," writes Ignacio Ramonet:

> The violence perpetrated against women by a male partner has reached extraordinary dimensions there. For Europeans from the age of 16 to 44, brutality within the family has become the primary cause of death and disability—above even road accidents and cancer. Depending on the country, between a quarter and a half of all women are victims of abuse. . . . In all fifteen states of the European Union (i.e., before its expansion to twenty-five) more than 600 women die each year—almost two a day—from sexist violence within the family circle.[22]

As a human predisposition in liberal society, this is thought-provoking. The combined desires of loving, hurting, and killing to which these figures point make the options of liberal political reform, personal therapy, and correctional confinement seem inadequate. One might see them as being expressions of the fact that in modern secular society individual desire is a high value for every body. But something more complicated than *choosing* pleasure in inflicting pain and death (an abomination) is at work here. Sadistic acts and their *compulsive* repetition are more than simply the work of a few psychopaths.

Cultural historians have described how the idea of sympathy, first propounded by enlightened moral philosophers, gave rise to a distinctive genre of literature and art. "If pornography," one of them writes, "is best defined as the representation of sexual behavior *with a deliberate violation of moral and social taboos*, then the growing violence of pornography in the late eighteenth and nineteenth centuries is attributable to the new shock value of pain within a culture redefining it as forbidden and therefore obscene."[23] Thus pictorial depictions of sexual flagellation, virtually unknown before the eighteenth century, become common in the nineteenth and twentieth centuries and point, like so much else, to the pleasure taken in exhibitions of pain, precisely when it was forbidden or frowned upon.[24]

The question is not simply how widespread "sadism" has been since the late eighteenth century. It is whether the significance of "sadism" lies only in what we are conventionally asked to attend to—the reprehensible motives of a psychopath and the secular treatments that society provides for his sickness (medication and/or physical constraint). The interesting question is this: What precisely does the *cruelty* of sadism consist in? Is sadism simply a medical abnormality? Or does it tell us something about the body, privacy, and the liberal state?

Here is one interesting answer: Although it has become common since the nineteenth century to refer to "sadomasochism" as the name of a single pathology, Gilles Deleuze insists that sadism and masochism are two quite different conditions that should not be confused.[25] In the work of Masoch, he points out:

> We are no longer in the presence of a torturer seizing upon a victim and enjoying her all the more because she is unconsenting and unpersuaded. We are dealing instead with a victim in search of a torturer and who needs to educate, persuade and conclude an alliance with the torturer in order to realize the strangest of schemes. . . . The sadist is in need of institutions, the masochist of contractual relations. The Middle Ages distinguished with considerable insight between two types of commerce with the devil: the first resulted from possession, the second from a pact of alliance. The sadist thinks in terms of institutionalized possession, the masochist in terms of contractual alliance. Possession is the sadist's particular form of madness just as the pact is the masochist's.[26]

The masochist is an educator who fashions the dominatrix, dressing her and telling her what hurtful words she must utter and what physical pain she must subject him to. Thus, unlike the cruelty of the sadist, here "It is the victim who speaks through the mouth of his torturer, without sparing himself."[27] What Deleuze does not say is that the hypochondriac's symptoms and the masochist's schemes (so different in other respects) have a similar psychic structure of self-imposed suffering that *may* be capable sometimes of opening up creative talents—by shutting out the world, by obsessive attentiveness, and even by the continuous desire and repeated failure to control oneself.

At any rate, these two kinds of cruelty, the one emerging apparently from persuasion (masochism) and the other from coercion (sadism), are thus not the same. Both exchange (contract) and possession (property) are of course found in all historical societies, but they are together uniquely constitutive of liberal democratic states (based, as we are often told, on the idea of a founding social contract and the defense of property) and modern empires (driven as they are by the appropriation of land, raw material, and labor as property).[28] One might venture that, as channels for cruelty, contract and property are together in large part how bodies are distinctively connected to and disconnected from one another in modern societies. Might it be said that for this reason all bodies that *flourish* in the cruelties of capitalist society and modern empire are "secular"? Would it be too rash to say that—recalling the cadaver—the secular body is one that can thrive or decay only materially?

Authorized possibilities of emotional expression of pain depend not only on whether they are evoked by depictions or realities but also on how the pain expressed is *recognized*. Pain, and compassion for pain, can fit into different stories. Christ's suffering and death on the cross is essential to the redemption of mankind, and regardless of whether it is interpreted as divine satisfaction for human sins or as the divinely created paradigm of human injustice, the cruelty of the crucifixion *cannot* be expunged from the Christian story. In a secular key, Pamela's suffering, in Samuel Richardson's eighteenth-century novel by that name, allows the redemption of Mr. B., her persecuting employer. Both cases of suffering are directed at evoking the virtue of compassion, but Pamela's pain is felt to be gratuitous; Christ's is not. Indeed, Henry Fielding's parody *Shamela* suggests that there is something about the rhetorical structure of redemption stories such as *Pamela* that allows them to be satirized in a secularizing world. For secularists, publicly exhibited suffering endured for the sake of another individual or collectivity ("a sacrifice") may be suspected of having an ulterior motive—and this justifies discounting its claim to sympathy.

When pleasure is taken in and through another person's painful experience by integrating it into one's desire, it is no longer quite gratuitous. If the sentimental readers of *Pamela* tried to embrace her miseries as their own, how should we understand their instrumental use of that emotion? Entering into Christ's passion—the emotion invested in his tortured body—was an important part of religious devotion in the later Middle Ages, and again in the eighteenth-century religious revival.[29] Compassion is not unique to modern Western societies, of course—nor is cruelty. What seems to be original and what links bodies to one another in different modalities is the fusion of compassion and cruelty into what the eighteenth century sometimes named "delight." This theme has a long history, but the Scottish moralists addressed it in a revealing way. Thus David Fordyce wrote in 1754 of the man of sensibility, the benevolent man: "It is true, his friendly *Sympathy* with others subjects him to some Pains . . . yet to give a loose to it is a kind of agreeable Discharge. It is such a Sorrow as he loves to indulge; a sort of pleasing Anguish, that sweetly melts the Mind."[30] Can this be seen as articulating another aspect of the secular body?

The pleasure obtained from actively subjecting the other to pain is not, of course, the same as feeling oneself into another's suffering—even if that too can be experienced, in Fordyce's orgasmic metaphor, as "a sort of pleasing Anguish, that sweetly melts the Mind." The point I want to stress is that empathy is not a simple emotion, or one that is necessarily benign in secular, liberal culture. It is consistent with the satisfaction felt at observing the "justified punishment" of a monstrous criminal, the normal cinema audience's enjoyment of torture and death finally inflicted on the villain. How are we to understand this well-known desire to see certain kinds of individual treated cruelly, to find satisfaction (pleasure) in that spectacle? How are we to explain the enormous popularity of violent movies that realistically depict human agony, dismemberment, and death?[31] Of course, representations of cruelty on the screen belong to the imaginary world of cinema and should not be taken as clear evidence of incitement to cruelty, as many who denounce it often do. But it is still a *human* world—whose experience can be named and is meant to be enjoyed *aesthetically* precisely because it appears as an imaginary representation, presented in a particular time and place, but in itself as "real" as anything else, as the hypochondriac's sickness. They are occasions for enjoying passions among normal persons that neither polite society nor fastidious persons find worthy of respect—except in the guise of art. Could one say that this pornography of pain—drawing at once on the *legal prohibition* of cruelty and on its *secret enjoyment*—is an option typically available to the modern secular body? Of course, spectacles of cruelty are at least as old as the gladiatorial games in ancient Rome, but my question has to do with the attitudes to pain when it is located in structures that combine the forbidding of cruelty and the pleasure its display affords.

I have tried in this essay to think about the "secular body" by directing attention to disjunctions, parallels, permeations, and recursivities that seem to give some sense to the notion—but also to undermine it. I have suggested that, in convoluted ways, cruelty is deeply rooted in our modern liberal society—irrespective of the formal aim of the secular state and democratic politics of suppressing intolerance and abolishing pain.

This brings me finally to an old question, one that hasn't, in my view, been satisfactorily answered: To what extent does democracy presuppose secular bodies? But there is a prior question about "democracy" itself. People sometimes talk about democracy as an ethos, sometimes as a form of government. Are these always compatible? Although this question can't be answered briefly, here are a few points for consideration. When we speak of the former, we often think of the desire for mutual care and respect, the concern to understand the other—to listen and not merely to tell, and to suffer if need be for the sake of another. There is no a priori demand that the other translate herself into a language I can readily understand; on the contrary, to express a democratic ethos I must be ready to transform myself, and my language, in encountering the other. In the democratic ethos the individual is imbued with a sense of his finitude, of vulnerability and decay,[32] and the spectacle of pain and disintegration in the bodies and minds of others evokes compassion. But the individual takes his or her own pain not simply as a sign (something to be interpreted) of being unwell but as a way of living positively. By contrast, when reference is made to representative government, people normally think of the democratic state as the guardian of subjective rights and the focus of collective identity. They take sovereignty to be the absolute power of/over a unified body, the power to protect the freedom and equality of all citizens, and they are aware of the state's paramount concern with law and security. They know that national elections collect individual bodies within a sum of countable units, and that the representative state is a body with a transcendent will; this gives it the right to punish violators of national order and to wage war in defense of national interests.[33] In a representative democracy the individual is the object of state protection from the violence of others, and the monopoly of state violence is a means to that end. Pain in a liberal state is regarded as an unqualified evil to be used only to deal with a greater evil (the work of external and internal enemies).

The liberal state recognizes the citizen's right to dissent. It is, however, only in a law state and not in a society imbued with a democratic ethos that a sharp distinction is made between conscientious objection (protected as a right of the individual) and civil disobedience (regarded as a politically motivated violation of legal order). A democratic ethos predisposes one to civil disobedience, which often draws on religious sources. In a liberal democracy citizens are constitutionally represented by political parties, but *who* the parties actually represent, and *why*, is structurally ambiguous—largely because of the freedom afforded by money in a capitalist society. A democratic ethos, by contrast, works not through representation but directly through solidarity and confrontation. The two understandings of democracy presuppose different kinds of body, living in different ways. Or perhaps better: They can be seen as aspects of a single body pulled in opposing directions, at once "political" and "religious," a tension within the democratic state that can never be finally resolved because each depends for its difference on the other.

Although secularists lay claim to both senses of democracy, they often assert that democracy as a comprehensive concept can be traced to a particular religion, Christianity—thus supplying secularity with religious roots. However, a democratic ethos is not specifically Christian; it is found also in Judaism, Islam, Buddhism, and other traditions and in the languages those traditions use. And although Christianity is part of the history of the modern state, that doesn't prove the Christian origin of the "secular." It is one thing to seek essential origins, quite another to identify elements of a tradition that have been retrieved, reorganized, and put to modern use in contemporary formations. One of those elements, as Gil Anidjar has shown us,[34] is the obsession with blood in European history; another is the mutual constitution of love and cruelty. Such recursivities make political theology a justification for today's imperial wars, but from that it doesn't follow that Christianity is the fundamental frame for understanding our present "secular" world. The modern culture of commodity consumption, the new techniques of political-economic control and discipline on national and global levels, the degradation of the natural environment (making the planet an increasingly hostile place for human habitation) are not the products of a specifically Christian history. The accumulation of knowledge and power on which so much contemporary practice depends is generated by a complex institutional landscape with long-term consequences that are only partly foreseen. In fact, particular histories in different localities have shaped different norms of the healthy body, different experiences of unacceptable pain, and stories of when a just distribution of suffering depends on the "separation of religion and state." If I am skeptical of the claim made for secularism's essential roots in Christianity, this is not because I think that its real historical roots lie elsewhere, that secularism has no connection whatever with Christianity, but because I don't think we are entirely clear about what we are seeking to explain with such confidence—or for that matter, why the explanation in terms of Christianity has become so urgent.

So, instead of trying to determine the essential meaning of "the secular"—including "the secular body"—I conclude by proposing a more modest endeavor: an inquiry into what is involved when "the secular" is invoked—who tries to define it, in what context, and with what political consequences. How do lawyers, politicians, public intellectuals, social scientists, philosophers, and ordinary citizens *use* these terms, what do they *do* with them? To what narratives do these words—and their cognates—belong? I think it is more useful to inquire into how a historically shifting grammar identifies and regulates "the healthy body" and "the sick body" in political as well as personal life. Grammar tells us that there is no definitive answer to questions like, What is "a secular body"? What is "secularism"? There are particular usages of the terms that make sense in particular forms of life and that may be contested as and when aspects of that life are contested.

CHAPTER 18

The Rise of Literal-Mindedness

Peter Burke

This essay is a small part of a more ambitious investigation of a gradual shift in Western European attitudes, modes of thought, or mentalities from the late Middle Ages to the eighteenth century.[1] This shift might be described as the development of a propensity to reject or at any rate to devalue symbolism, whether in the interpretation of texts, rituals, other human behavior, or the natural world. (A description rather than a precise definition is offered here because the attitudes in question are neither clear nor distinct.) Literal-mindedness in this sense was an important element in the rise of what many historians call *modernity*.[2] It will be convenient to coin the term *symbol-mindedness* to refer to the opposite, declining mode of thought.

Historians and critics have long been aware of aspects of this shift. Max Weber discussed it in terms of the "disenchantment of the world" (*Die Entzauberung der Welt*). Johan Huizinga wrote in some detail about what he called the decline of a "symbolic mode of thought" in the late Middle Ages, contrasting it with the "causal" mode.[3] Looking at the culture of eighteenth-century Russia, Jurij Lotman has described what he calls the "desemioticization of life."[4] Scholars as diverse as Ernst Kantorowicz, Marjorie Nicolson, Michel Foucault, and Hans Blumenberg have interested themselves in the consequences of the decline of what they variously call the "moralized universe," "the prose of the world," or "the readability of the world"—in other words, a system of correspondences (microcosm and macrocosm, human body and body politic, and so on) that were supposed to be inscribed *in rebus* by the finger of God.[5] In a famous study of royal rituals, Clifford Geertz attacked what he calls "the notion . . . that symbolic opposes to real as fanciful to sober, figurative to literal, obscure to plain, aesthetic to practical, mystical to mundane, and decorative to substantial." He dated this notion to the nineteenth century. That this notion goes back much further is the principal argument of this essay.[6]

When, where, and why did literal-mindedness replace symbol-mindedness, among whom, and with what consequences? Was it possible for the two modes of thought to coexist? If so, can we speak of a shift in the relation between them, with literal meanings rising in the hierarchy and symbolic meanings declining? Would it be more useful to think of the two modes of thought as alternative strategies of interpretation? To what extent did the distinction between literal and symbolic emerge, or at any rate become sharper, more explicit, and more conscious at some moment (perhaps the sixteenth century)?

To answer all these questions is a little too much for a single chapter. Therefore, all I shall attempt to do here is offer a sketch of a possible "master narrative" of these developments before turning to a case study of the Catholic and Protestant Reformations and offering a closer analysis of a single, somewhat neglected episode within that story.

A grand narrative of this kind would of course be impossible to write without an analysis of the symbol-mindedness of Plato and the Platonists, the fathers of the church, and the masters of Kabbalah. This account would obviously have much to say about the fourfold interpretation of Scripture and its relation to the exegesis of secular texts, from the *Odyssey* to the *Divine Comedy*.[7] A history of Western literal-mindedness would need to include a chapter or chapters on the Middle Ages, drawing on Huizinga's famous book but examining earlier centuries, discussing the relation of literal-mindedness to the rise of literacy and print and placing more emphasis than Huizinga did on challenges to symbol-mindedness on the part of philosophers such as Jean Buridan and William of Ockham.[8] This hypothetical study would also include a chapter on the humanists of the Renaissance, in particular the philologists like Lorenzo Valla and Angelo Poliziano, who attempted to recover the "original" meaning of classical and Christian texts. The Netherlands humanist Christophe de Longueil, or Longolius, would have his place there as an extreme of the literal-minded interpretation of the injunction to imitate Cicero mocked by Erasmus in his *Ciceronianus.* The relations between literal-mindedness and the notion of a fixed text, encouraged by the development of textual criticism and the spread of printed matter, would also need discussion. The chapters on the Reformation—Catholic as well as Protestant—would be absolutely central to this enterprise. So would those on the scientific revolution and the Enlightenment, dealing especially with the "mechanization of the world picture," the concern for objectivity, and the attack on "superstition."

The story might well be continued into the nineteenth and twentieth centuries. It might treat, for example, Bentham's attacks on "fictitious entities" such as the crown, the church, and the law.[9] It might examine fundamentalist interpretations of Scripture in the Jewish, Christian, and Muslim worlds.[10] It should not omit investigating the practice of positivist historians, who have often read literary texts, such as dialogues and satires, as if they were objective descriptions or dismissed as "trivial" conflicts over "merely" symbolic matters, like the number of fingers used in the gesture of blessing, in the case of the Russian Schism.[11]

These examples suggest that literal-mindedness be defined, at least in its nineteenth- and twentieth-century manifestations, as "a sophisticated (or trained) incapacity to understand symbolism." The term "sophisticated" is required in order to distinguish the kind of literal-mindedness that changes over time from another, more naïve kind, which is always with us. Blindness or deafness to irony is a recurrent disorder of which the reactions to Defoe's *Shortest Way* and Swift's *Modest Proposal* furnish vivid but far from isolated examples.[12] It is said that when *Utopia* was published, a priest wrote to More asking him to find him a benefice in that country. In singular fashion, the BBC claim to have received letters from listeners who want to buy a house in Ambridge, the fictional village in which the long-running radio pastoral *The Archers* is located. (I am not vouching for the claim that such letters were written, or that they were intended seriously.) Again, a recurrent anecdote in histories of the theater is of individuals who mistake plays for reality and intervene to prevent the villain performing his role.[13]

❧

Summarized in this simple form, the master narrative is obviously vulnerable to criticisms—three in particular. In the first place, it lacks a social dimension. "Who, for example, was symbol-minded in the late Middle Ages? Everyone, or only the educated minorities of poets, mystics, and chroniclers on whom Huizinga drew overwhelmingly for his evidence? It is unlikely that historians will ever be able to give a full answer to this question, but it is worth pointing out that late medieval heresy trials reveal the existence—especially where the Eucharist is concerned—of what A. G. Dickens calls "popular materialist scepticism," a phrase that would seem to bear translation into "literal-mindedness." A wafer is a wafer is a wafer.[14]

In the second place, the story told so far is implausibly unilinear, implying that people have been becoming more and more literal-minded over the centuries. Yet there have been many reactions against the trend, including, for example, the rehabilitation of myth, the revival of correspondences, and the definition of "man" as a "symbol-using animal." Such reactions are already visible in Vico, but they are especially common in the nineteenth and twentieth centuries, from Goethe and Coleridge, through Baudelaire and other "symbolists," to Ernst Cassirer, Kenneth Burke, and beyond. Indeed, the pejorative term *literal-minded* would hardly have come into existence—in the mid-nineteenth century—had it not been for a reaction of this kind.[15] Even if the stream of time has been flowing steadily in one direction, rather than twisting and turning, the cross-currents of what might be called "reactive symbol-mindedness" deserve further investigation.

In the third place, it is not sufficient to discover who was literal-minded; it is equally important to ask "about what?" As will be seen, it has often been possible to be literal-minded in one domain and symbol-minded in another. More generally, it might be argued that the account offered so far lacks context. Half a century ago, in the age of Cassirer and Friedrich Meinecke, it would have been obvious how to go about telling the story of literal-mindedness on the grand scale, examining the "mountain peaks" of intellectual history, the great thoughts of great men. It would be otiose to do more than invoke the names of John Pocock and Quentin Skinner in the context of *context*. And the challenge of microhistory and history from below is difficult to ignore—even if microhistorians tend to prefer social to intellectual history—while Cassirer has been justly criticized for his neglect of *la petite histoire*.[16] It is therefore time (in this hypothetical study) to examine the mentality of literal-mindedness in relation to the religious debates of the early modern period; and time (in the historical profession) to examine *mentalités* in tandem with the vocabularies of intellectual history.

The central thesis I will argue is that the symbol-minded mentality was undermined by the Reformation. In making this provocatively simple statement, I do not mean to imply that events by themselves broke the traditional mental structures—if the structures had not already been dissolving, Luther's revolution could not have been as successful as it was. In any case, there were important continuities between the leading ideas of the reformers (including their view of symbols) and the ideas of certain late medieval thinkers—those mentioned above. (Luther's relation to Gabriel Biel and Biel's to Ockham are especially relevant here.) All the same, the great religious debates in Western Christendom that we call the Reformation were profoundly concerned with symbols. They both expressed and encouraged significant changes in what some philosophers would call the "logical status" of symbols, so that it may be worth looking again at these familiar controversies from this (historiographically) eccentric point of view.

Bearing in mind Lefort's criticism of Cassirer's *grande histoire*, let us see whether we can locate literal-mindedness in its context(s) by distinguishing three disputes, three regions, and three moments within the larger debate: first, a controversy over the interpretation of texts, with its center of gravity in northern Europe in the early sixteenth century; second, a controversy over the interpretation of images, with its center in Italy in the later sixteenth century; and third, a controversy over the interpretation of rituals, with its center in France at the end of the seventeenth century.

The history of the interpretation of the Bible is a thorny subject for lay historians to tackle. The field is vast and full of mines that explode in the face of the unwary. However, it lies directly on the route of our hypothetical study: Reformation controversies about the exegesis of the text and its application to everyday life cannot be evaded.

A simple contrast between medieval theologians interpreting Scripture in allegorical fashion and Renaissance or Reformation theologians offering literal interpretations cannot be sustained with plausibility. On one side, scholars have noted increasing interest in literal meaning on the part of medieval interpreters from Thomas Aquinas to Nicholas of Lyra.[17] On the other, they have emphasized the continuing concern with nonliteral meanings on the part of Erasmus, Luther, and others.[18] All the same, a gradual shift of emphasis over the long term can be detected. In the course of the sixteenth century, the Bible was increasingly treated as a historical document, whose meaning could be understood only by asking who was speaking to whom and by studying the history and geography of the milieus in which it was produced.[19] Indeed, the Bible was increasingly viewed not as a single text but a collection of texts, "having had each some several occasions and particular purpose which caused them to be written."[20]

It was precisely in this context that the idea of context (a term frequently used by St. Augustine) was revived: a metaphor from weaving that in this period referred to "the agreeing of the matter going before, with that which followeth," primarily in the Bible but sometimes in other authoritative texts such as Aristotle's or the code of civil law. The term gradually widened its meaning in the nineteenth and twentieth centuries, when terms like *moral context*, *contextual*, and *contextualize* came into use.[21]

Increasing concern with the literal meaning of the Bible was common to Catholics and Protestants, as the fate of the ideas of Copernicus showed. The Lutheran Osiander and the Catholic Bellarmine agreed that the heliocentric hypothesis of Copernicus could not be true because it contradicted the literal interpretation of passages from Scripture. In other ways, however, Catholics and Protestants diverged. In an obvious sense of the term, it was the Protestants who were literal-minded. They privileged the literal meaning of Scripture over the allegorical meanings, when they did not reject the latter altogether. The concern with context—and the use of the term *context*, or *circumstances*, or *scope*—becomes increasingly manifest in seventeenth-century discussions of biblical interpretation, notably those of Milton and Locke, who argued that the Bible is generally "to be understood in the plain direct meaning of the words and phrases."[22] John Toland dismissed the allegorical interpretation of Scripture by Christians as "a ridiculous imitation of the Jews."[23] It is also interesting to note the coinage of new terms such as *literalism*, *literalist*, *literality*, and *literalness* (all between 1630 and 1650, according to the *Oxford English Dictionary*), words that suggest increasing self-consciousness about the problem of interpretation.

However, there is another sense or, better, there were other occasions on which it was the Catholics who appeared to be literal-minded while the Protestants clung to symbolism. In the case of the text "This is my body," it was of course the Catholics who believed that it referred to the physical transformation of the bread and wine, while Protestants denied that. As early as 1524, Cornelisz Hoen was arguing that in the phrase "*Hoc est corpus meum*," "*est*" means no more than "*significat*."[24] In the age of Henry VIII, ordinary Protestants explained that "the body of God" was not present in the sacrament on the altar "but was a representation and signification of the thing": It was "only a figure of sacrament"; "The bread doth signify his body."[25]

Hell is another locus of Catholic literal-mindedness that contrasted with the symbol-mindedness of many Protestants, for "everlasting fire" is mentioned in the Bible. Some sixteenth-century Catholics discussed its precise location and measurements in considerable detail, while some Protestants suggested that the souls of the wicked perish with their bodies, or even that hell is not a place but rather a state of mind.[26] Catholic writers of the sixteenth and seventeenth centuries also described paradise as a real place with a physical location.[27]

A particularly striking example of ecclesiastical literal-mindedness emerged during the Galileo affair. Galileo, who might be described as a literal-minded interpreter of the Book of Nature, found himself in trouble for advocating an allegorical interpretation of passages of Scripture that he considered had been "accommodated" to the understanding of the common people. The church, represented in this case by Bellarmine, preferred the opposite solution to the problem of reconciling world and book, interpreting the Bible literally but Copernicus allegorically. Bellarmine claimed that Copernicus was not describing the true workings of the cosmos but offering the simplest hypothesis to explain appearances.[28]

There remains the problem of the relation between Scripture and everyday life. It seems useful to use the term *literal-minded* broadly enough to include the attitude, common among early modern Protestants, of following practices described in the Bible and condemning those that were absent from it, as if the context of these biblical descriptions were of no importance. This attitude underlay criticism of the Church of England by the so-called Puritans, who believed, as their opponent Hooker put it, "that the Scripture hath set down a complete form of church polity" and who failed to realize that human laws "may be varied by times, places, persons and other like circumstances."[29] In similar fashion, iconoclasm—not only by Protestants against Catholics, but by missionaries in the New World (and elsewhere)—was justified by a literal reading of God's prohibition of "graven images," interpreted to mean "idols," in other words, as objects "idolaters" were said to worship instead of worshipping the gods these objects symbolized ("The heathen in his blindness / Bows down to wood and stone," and all that).[30] Among the Christians who defended images, more and less literal-minded interpretations may be distinguished, as it is time now to demonstrate.

The discussion of the Reformation and the Bible outlined above, even in fleshed-out form, might be criticized by contextualists for its generality, dealing as it does with the whole of Europe over a hundred years or so. Let us see if a second, more concrete example would satisfy them.

For our second moment and domain of literal-mindedness, let us turn to reactions to religious art in Italy in the second half of the sixteenth century—a more concrete example, and one all the more important for the general argument, because in this case even Catholics appear to have become more concerned with literal meaning at the expense of the symbolic.

In Gilio da Fabriano's dialogue on the errors of painters (1564), three speakers illustrate the attitudes with which we are concerned. Troilo Mattioli criticizes representations of the crucified thieves in which ropes replace nails. Ruggiero Corradini introduces the problem of the distances between the three crosses, while Francesco Santi notes that St. John the Evangelist was thirty-one years old at the time of the Passion, so that it is absurd for painters to show him as a "beardless boy." Finally, Mattioli criticizes representations of St. Jerome with a red hat, pointing out that this element in a cardinal's equipment did not exist in Jerome's day.[31] The last example is particularly interesting because it links literal-mindedness to the increasing awareness of anachronism among Renaissance humanists (and some artists) and because it assumes that St. Jerome should be painted exactly as he would have appeared—thus failing or refusing to consider the point that the hat and the lion were the signs by which viewers could recognize a painting of a saint in the desert as Jerome. A painting of the Nativity is criticized for representing two apostles and a bishop at the birth of Christ, "because there were no apostles or bishops at the time that the saviour of the world was born"—an apt instance of what I meant earlier by a "sophisticated inability to understand symbolism."

Philip II's reaction, in 1586, to Federico Zuccaro's *Adoration of the Shepherds*, which included a shepherd offering a basket of eggs to the Virgin Mary, illustrates another form of literal-mindedness. The king complained that "it seemed improper that a shepherd, who had come running in the middle of the night from tending his herd, could have so many eggs, especially if he did not keep chickens."[32] Philip was concerned with plausibility or verisimilitude (a subject of considerable interest to literary critics at the time). But religious paintings were also criticized for lack of fidelity to the literal meaning of Scripture. The famous encounter between Veronese and the Venetian Inquisition in 1573—in which the painter, skillfully playing the role of a simpleton, appealed to a craft tradition of artistic license that he compared to that of "poets and jesters"—looks very much like part of a trend, as if the inquisitors were familiar with the work of Gilio and Borghini. At any rate, their question "Who do you really believe was present at that Supper?" suggests the similarity of their assumptions.[33] These assumptions might be described as the artistic consequence of Catholic biblicism, a movement that, whether spontaneously or in reaction to the Protestants, was then gaining ground in the church.[34]

Implied in these attacks on the "errors of painters" was the need for historical research on the manners and customs of the region and period represented. It was not sufficient for painters to consult theologians. What was needed was a knowledge of the "antiquities," or as we might say, the material culture of the time of Christ. How, for example, did the apostles sit, or recline, at the Last Supper? How was crucifixion carried out? In the case of Hooker versus the Puritans, as in that of Erasmus versus Longolius, the sense of anachronism is associated with the critics of literal-mindedness. In the case of Italy in the Counter-Reformation, by contrast, it is the literal-minded who seem to have the most acute sense of the past.

⁂

The examples discussed in the last section of this hypothetical study, though more precise and concrete than those in the previous one, might themselves be criticized for being too general and for paying insufficient attention to particular circumstances. Anyone who practices the contextual approach to intellectual history runs the risk of being criticized by a colleague who claims to be even more contextual by examining smaller episodes in even more circumstantial detail. In recognition of the value of this kind of criticism, it might be useful to offer a micro-study of the debate over ritual in late-seventeenth-century France, returning later to the limitations of what might be called "contextual reductionism."

At the time of Louis XIV's revocation of the Edict of Nantes in 1685, church and state together mounted a campaign for the conversion of the two million French Calvinists, while the pastors, many of them in exile in the United Provinces and elsewhere, did their best to resist it. On one side, Bossuet, bishop of Meaux, published his *Variations* to show that Protestantism was condemned to fragment until it withered away. On the other, Jurieu described Catholicism in general and the Mass in particular as corrupt and idolatrous practices that would soon be swept away on the arrival of the millennium.[35] In order to refute these arguments, Bossuet turned to Claude de Vert, a Benedictine scholar in the tradition of Jean Mabillon. De Vert published an open *Letter to M. Jurieu*, suggesting that the Mass was not as "unreasonable" a ceremony as Jurieu thought but that, on the contrary, it was compatible with "common sense" and the practice of the early church.[36] This kind of explanation was apparently received with enthusiasm by the "New Catholics" (in other words, the newly converted Calvinists), while de Vert's clerical colleagues (notably Bishop Feydeau of Amiens) asked him to develop his ideas, a task to which he devoted the rest of his life. The results were published starting in 1706 in a study entitled *Explication des Cérémonies*.

What did de Vert mean by this phrase? He glossed it as the search for "meanings" (*sens*) or "reasons" (*raisons*) that were at once "simple," "natural," and "literal" or "historical," as opposed to meanings that were "symbolic," "allegorical," or "mystical." This privileging of the literal or practical was what he called his "system," or "the economy of the *Mass*."[37] Why, for example, are candles lit on the altar during Mass in broad daylight? The answer offered by Durandus in the thirteenth century, and generally followed thereafter, was that the candles show that Christ is the light of the world. De Vert, by contrast, pointed out that the early Christians said Mass at night or in the catacombs during the age of persecution, so that candles were a practical necessity. Since the church "does not like to change," what had once been a necessity was retained as "simple custom," or

371

"pure ceremony."[38] In this ecclesiastical context, de Vert had given a clear formulation of what sociologists in the 1920s were to call "cultural lag." Similarly, de Vert explained the "original and primitive" use of incense in church as "fumigation," necessary in the catacombs or even in the early churches "because of the bad smell inseparable from the great multitude of people assembled there."[39]

De Vert claimed that his project was "neither new nor eccentric" and that it rested on an ecclesiastical tradition. Although he rejected what he called the "bizarre" opinions of medieval writers, he claimed to be criticizing misinterpretations of Durand rather than Durand himself. De Vert did not reject allegory altogether. However, he did argue that "the primary meaning, the simple, proper, natural, and necessary meaning" (*le premier sens, le sens simple, propre, naturel et nécessaire*) is "the base and the foundation of all metaphor and allegory" and that "generally speaking a ceremony has only a literal meaning."[40] For a seventeenth-century Catholic, de Vert was very near the far end of the spectrum of attitudes running from symbol-mindedness to literal-mindedness. Although it is technically anachronistic to call de Vert a "functionalist," his concern with *commodité* has much in common with later functionalism (and if a history of this approach were to be written, beginning perhaps with Aristotle and Galen, de Vert would have his place in the tradition). From another point of view (examining lateral connections rather than genealogies), his work is a monument of what might be called "Catholic rationalism," Cartesian in its clarity and in its concern with system.

That de Vert had some sympathizers in the church is apparent from the formal approbations of his treatise by the censors in 1706, which were printed immediately before the preface. Dr. Bigres commented that "in our time it is astonishing how far our ceremonies have been disfigured by the ideas which some mystics have believed themselves able to attach to them." Dr. Briilon, more cautious, criticized two extreme views, "allowing only mystical explanations" and "rejecting mystical explanations" altogether. Other theologians, however, were much more critical of de Vert's critique. Some accused him of following the Protestants, notably the great (if today neglected) scholar Jean Daillé.[41] The most elaborate, sustained, and effective critique of de Vert was that of Pierre Lebrun.

Pierre Lebrun was an Oratorian priest, a colleague of Nicolas Malebranche and Richard Simon. Lebrun is probably best known for his *Histoire critique des pratiques superstitieuses* (1702), which pays homage to Simon but is in fact closer to Malebranche in its concern with the question of whether apparently supernatural phenomena, such as ordeals, are capable of naturalistic explanation. Lebrun was also a gifted historian, as is shown by his contribution to the contemporary debate over the morality of the theater. In 1694 the Theatine priest Thomas Caffaro published a letter in defense of plays that provoked Bossuet, among others, to reply.[42] Caffaro's defense, like that of the abbé d'Aubignac, involved an argument about historical context. Caffaro claimed that the condemnation of the theater by the fathers of the church was no longer valid because plays were no longer impious or idolatrous. Lebrun was asked to reply and did so in an anonymous *Discours sur la comédie* (1694) that included, in order to refute Caffaro more effectively, a history of the theater and of attitudes to the theater from the early church onward that is notable for its attention to philological detail: "In order to understand his reply, it is necessary to point out that by *histriones* St. Thomas means...."[43]

From these secular rituals, Lebrun turned to the history of the Mass. His refutation of de Vert, the *Explication littérale, historique et dogmatique des prières et des cérémonies de la Messe*, was published in 1726. It is a key text, not only in the history of literal-mindedness, but also in that of hermeneutics, which has tended to overemphasize the importance of German Protestant contributions (those of Luther, Flacius, Chladenius, Wolf, Schleiermacher, and Dilthey) at the expense of those made in other parts of Europe. As one begins to read Lebrun's preface, one has the impression that de Vert has found an ally. "As soon as I applied myself seriously to their study, I realized that one would not understand the precise and true meaning (*on n'entroit point exactement dans le vrai sens*) of the words of the Mass without explaining them all word by word." An explanation of "actions" and "ceremonies" is equally necessary. Lebrun criticizes Durand and others who have offered what he calls "supposed mystical explanations" (*de prétendues raisons mystiques*) and notes the importance of "returning to the origins" of "the" customs of the church" (*remonter aux origines des usages de l'Eglise*).[44] We are back in the tradition of philology, or more exactly, that of late-seventeenth-century sacred philology, as exemplified by Simon.[45]

Then Lebrun turns to the late "M. de Vert" and blasts him with criticism—two criticisms in particular. In the first place, de Vert's concern with "system" got him off to a "bad start," because "everyone who begins with a system looks and sees virtually nothing but what supports it." He was more speculative than scholarly and offered too many "conjectures," whether his own or those of other modern writers.[46] Lebrun's second major charge against de Vert is that of reductionism, since ceremonies "cannot ... be reduced to a single cause" (*ne peuvent ... être réduites à une même cause*), that of an original necessity or practical convenience. Lebrun wrote of *des origines physiques de commodité ou necessité*, the word "physical" suggesting that he was reacting against de Vert's application to culture of a mechanical model derived from physics.[47] How, then, did Lebrun explain the rituals of the Mass? For him the "causes" include not only necessity and convenience, which he did not wish to deny, but also what he called *raisons mystérieuses*. What he meant by this formulation, itself somewhat mysterious, transpires when he returns to one of de Vert's favorite examples and reanalyzes it. Why are candles lit and placed on the altar? Not only to give light but as a sign of rejoicing (*pour marquer la joie*) on feast days, and to honor the relics of the saints. Likewise, the candles lit at baptism "are a symbol which shows the newly baptized that through baptism they have just passed from darkness to light."[48]

This may sound like a return to Durand, but it is not. The contrast with Durand, and also with de Vert, becomes most apparent when Lebrun summarizes his approach to interpretation in the form of a paradox. "The true literal and historical sense of a text or a ritual is the one which the author or founder had in mind" (*Le vrai sens littéral et historique d'un écrit ou d'une cérémonie est celui que l'Auteur ou l'Instituteur a eu en vue*)—even if this meaning is a symbolic one. One might say that he read ritual as Simon (and of course Spinoza) had read the Bible, with an eye on the "figures" or metaphors.

Lebrun's paradox authorizes us to translate his phrase *raisons mystérieuses* as "symbolic reasons." The contrast between de Vert's explanations in terms of system and Lebrun's explanations in terms of intentions is reminiscent in some ways of the famous debate between Lévi-Strauss and Ricoeur a generation ago.[49] Like other kinds of history, the history of ideas sometimes repeats itself—with variations. In any case, Lebrun's paradoxical resolution of the conflict between functional and mystical explanations should earn him a place in a future history of hermeneutics. Here his role has been to illustrate a reaction against literal-mindedness that accepted part of the critique of symbol-mindedness. In the context of current debates in intellectual history, he may be taken as a symbol of possible reconciliation between an approach focusing on vocabularies and one emphasizing mentalities.

Even this last account of a controversy between contemporaries—just two contemporaries—might be criticized as insufficiently contextual. My discomfort with what I called "contextual reductionism" (but do not identify with the work of any individual scholar) is precisely the fact that any account of past meanings, even the account of the writing of a single text, is vulnerable to criticism on these grounds, since each chapter, paragraph, sentence, and so on was written in a slightly different context. Like the Protestant appeal to individual judgment, the appeal to context would seem to lead to intellectual fragmentation, to intellectual microhistories that become smaller and smaller until they disappear altogether. What is to be done? We cannot return to the Grand Narrative of Cassirer's time; the criticisms of the contextualists have been effective and binding. But do we have to accept fragmentation? Can the conflict be resolved between *grande histoire* and *petite histoire*, between the long term and the short term, between the commitment to "get it right" and the belief that there are no right answers?

"Resolution" is a rather grand term. It might be more useful as well as more modest to speak of possible "links" between the two kinds of history. Paradoxically enough, a way to avoid fragmentation is to recognize the multiplicity of contexts, in other words of the possibility that a text (image, ritual) may have (or rather, be given) a meaning outside its original context, as histories of "reception" show. The controversy between de Vert and Lebrun, for example, needs to be placed in the context of intellectual debates within the French church at the end of the seventeenth century, even, perhaps, at a microlevel that the writer is not competent to explore, in the context of conflicts between or within the

Benedictine and Oratorian communities. However, these are not its only contexts. A wider context is that of historical studies of the liturgy in the seventeenth century. A still broader context is the more general debate between Catholic and Protestant scholars of that time, itself unintelligible outside the context of the Reformation, in which the appeal of both parties to tradition makes the fathers of the church, for instance, contextually relevant.

One might analyze this process of appropriation and adaptation (like the Renaissance appropriation and adaptation of classical antiquity) in terms of "decontextualization" and "recontextualization," or, in the language of the time, "accommodation." Adding intellectual microhistories to one another will not produce a satisfactory macrohistory, but *looking* for connections might well allow us to do so.

CHAPTER 19

From *Star Wars* to Jediism

The Emergence of Fiction-based Religion

Markus Altena Davidsen

May the Force Be with You

When Luke Skywalker takes off in his space fighter to attack the Death Star, the seemingly unconquerable imperial space station, Princess Leia wishes him good luck with the words "May the Force be with you." The heroes in *Star Wars* believe that the Force will aid those who combat evil. Those who fight on the side of the Force can overcome even a vastly superior foe—and of course the mission succeeds. In the crucial moment Luke turns off his ship's targeting computer, lets the Force direct his actions, and manages to strike the Death Star at its only weak point. The Force is with him and secures him the victory.

Many *Star Wars* fans playfully greet each other with the phrase "May the Force be with you" and sign their posts on online discussion forums with the abbreviation "MTFBWY." Nevertheless, these fans attribute the Force existence only within the fictional *Star Wars* universe. They do not anticipate that the Force could actually intervene in their own world, the empirical world. By contrast, there is a movement based on *Star Wars* that explicitly distances itself from the mainstream fan culture and in fact does postulate the existence of the Force in the empirical world. The members of Jediism, as this movement is called, not only believe in the Force but also ritually interact with it, mostly through meditation.

The present essay has three aims: (1) to present an overview of the core elements (Force teachings, ritual practices, and legitimization strategies) of Jediism;[1] (2) to compare Jediism with *Star Wars* fan culture and argue that Jediism must be classified as a religion, whereas fan culture must not, because Jediism substitutes ritual and belief for the play and fascination of fan culture; and (3) to introduce the category "fiction-based religion" and establish Jediism as a member of this subcategory of religion.

Jediism as Religion

Inspired by Steve Bruce, I consider religion to constitute any activity (i.e., cognition, communication, or action) that assumes the existence of transempirical realities (e.g., other worlds, Heaven), supernatural entities with power of action (e.g., gods, spirits), and/or impersonal processes or principles possessed of moral purpose (e.g., karma, *ma'at*).[2] According to this definition, Jediism must be categorized as a religion because its ideas and concerns are formulated with reference to a supernatural power (the Force) and the core of Jediist practice is ritual interaction with the Force (through meditation and, in some cases, prayer and various rites of transition). Jediism is not formally organized into a churchlike institution but is developed, maintained, and transmitted by a network of individuals and groups. Members mostly use the Internet as their medium of communication, but some also meet face to face. They have no physical places of worship, but some Jediists express a wish to build temples in the future.

Fiction-based Religions

Jediism is a new religion. The world premiere of the first *Star Wars* film in 1977 can be taken as its absolute beginning, but not until the rise of mass access to the Internet in the mid-1990s did it develop into a visible, organized, and extensive movement. Jediism is, however, interesting for the study of religion not only because it is a new religion but also because it represents a new form of religion, which I suggest calling "fiction-based religion."[3] In my understanding, a fiction-based religion is a religion that uses fictional texts as its main authoritative, religious texts. That a text is authoritative for a religion means that its members use terminology, beliefs, practices, roles, and/or social organization derived from the authoritative text as a model for their own real-world religion. The term *fiction* refers to a narrative that an author presents without any aspiration to refer to events that have taken place in the real world prior to their enshrinement in a text.[4] In some cases fiction-based religions are grounded in what we can call "fictional religions," that is, religions within fictional narratives, invented by the author and practiced by fictional characters. The Force religion of the Jedi Knights in *Star Wars* is an example of a fictional religion. Jediism, the fiction-based real-world religion, is modeled on the fictional Force religion. Even though the members of Jediism, the Jediists, see *Star Wars* in general as fiction, they consider the theology and practice of the Force religion to be valid in the empirical world.

There are many other examples of (partly) fiction-based religions that all use fictional narratives (science fiction, fantasy, horror) as authoritative texts. One well-known science fiction example is the neo-pagan movement the Church of All Worlds, which is modeled on the organization of the same name in Robert Heinlein's novel *Stranger in a Strange Land*, from 1961. From the fictional religion in Heinlein's novel, the Church of All Worlds has taken over the water-sharing ritual, polyamory, and the recognition of the divine within all human beings, which they express with the greeting "Thou art God/dess."[5] H. P. Lovecraft's horror story "The Call of Cthulhu," from 1928, and other short stories from his "Cthulhu Mythos" have inspired both Anton Szandor LaVey's Church of Satan and groups of chaos magicians. LaVey explains in *The Satanic Rituals* how one can call upon Cthulhu, Nyarlathotep, and other of Lovecraft's monster gods, and chaos magicians claim to be possessed by these gods, though they still stress their fictionality.[6] A spiritual milieu exists based on J. R. R. Tolkien's fantasy works. Its members believe that Middle-earth is a real place, being either a prehistory to our world or existing on another plane, and communicate ritually with the Valar, the Powers or "gods" of Tolkien's narrative world.[7] Some also believe themselves to be Elves, and in the 1990s the Internet-based Otherkin movement developed out of the Tolkien-inspired Elven community. The Otherkin believe themselves to be nonhumans, such as werewolves, dragons, or angels.[8] Jediism is thus not the only example of a fiction-based religion, but it is probably the largest of its kind and therefore suitable as a case through which to examine more closely this new type of religion.

Star Wars

The Star Wars Narrative

The opening roll-up of all six *Star Wars* movies begins with the same formulaic phrase:[9] "A long time ago in a galaxy far, far away. . . ." This is obviously a transformation of the traditional fairy-tale introduction "Once upon a time in a land far, far away," and *Star Wars* certainly shares a number of traits with fairy tales. The main character and hero, Luke Skywalker, has been raised by foster parents on a desolate farm in the Outer Rim of the galaxy and does not know the truth about his special ancestry and extraordinary powers. The story is full of princesses, noble warriors (Jedi Knights), evil villains, and all kinds of fantastic creatures. When George Lucas, script writer and producer of *Star Wars*, was interviewed around the time of the release of the first movie in 1977, he therefore never referred to his movie as "science fiction" (understood as dystopian anticipation of the future) but always as a "space opera" or "space fantasy." In these terms, *Star Wars* should resemble *Flash Gordon*, not *2001: A Space Odyssey*.

Star Wars is about the battle between good and evil. The peaceful Galactic Republic has become a tyrannical empire, ruled over by a Sith Lord, a kind of evil wizard who can manipulate the Force. A small band of rebels fights for the freedom of the galaxy. Among them is Luke Skywalker, who in the course of the film is initiated into the order of the Jedi Knights, warrior monks inspired by samurai warriors, Franciscans, and Arthurian knights. The Jedi Knights also use the Force, but only in the service of good. The Force gives the Jedi telepathic and telekinetic abilities and stimulates their perception, cognition, and skill, especially when they use their intuition and let themselves be guided by the Force.

In *A New Hope*, the old Jedi Knight Obi-Wan Kenobi introduces the Force to young Luke Skywalker with the following words: "The Force is what gives a Jedi his power. It's an energy field created by all living things. It surrounds us and penetrates us. It binds the galaxy together."[10] Put briefly, the Force is a nonpersonified divine energy. It takes special training to be able to sense the Force itself, but its effects (levitation, lightning bolts shot from one's fingertips, etc.) are visible to everybody, leaving the reality of the Force unquestionable within the *Star Wars* universe. The existence of the Force is a matter of fact, but its deeper nature remains a mystery into which one can gain (partial) insight only through meditation.

Star Wars *Fandom*

For most fans, *Star Wars* is first and foremost a fairy tale, and fans see the *Star Wars* universe as a fascinating world in which one can playfully immerse oneself. A twenty-year-old woman with the user name Dust from the Danish *Star Wars* fan club skywalker.dk expresses it like this:

> The Jedi, the Force, and the light-sabre battles are probably the things that captivate me the most about the *Star Wars* universe. I have always loved fantasy and love to immerse myself in other worlds or to dream that this boring, commonplace world will turn out to contain something more magical and exciting. I find the idea of a universal Force that binds us all together and gives us supernatural powers deeply fascinating.[11]

Entering the colorful and detailed universe of *Star Wars* is an important aspect of being a fan. Not only do fans like to discuss movies and books, to watch them again and again, and to collect heaps of merchandise and an encyclopedic knowledge of the fictional universe, they also play role-playing games within the *Star Wars* universe, dress up and fight with light sabres, compose their own fan fiction, draw and paint fan art, and so on. They enter the universe, explore it, and expand it.[12]

For many *Star Wars* fans, however, being a fan is not only about entering the fictional world from the empirical world, but also about how elements from the fictional world can enter the empirical world. It is the values of the *Star Wars* narrative, in particular, that are transferred from fictional space to everyday life. These values include an ideal of personal growth, a religious involvement, and a social ethic. The social ethic is emphasized by many fans, who either claim to have changed their ethical views after watching *Star Wars* or report seeing their own values confirmed in the choices and actions of the *Star Wars* heroes. Will Brooker cites several fans who talk about the ethical impact of *Star Wars* on their lives. One fan formulates it as follows:

> Yoda's theme song calms me from a day and gives me strength to continue helping others in a warm and caring way. He, Obi-Wan, Qui-Gon and Luke are such respectable figures that some of us can't help but aspire to be like them. Sure, we may not be able to lift droids, rocks or X-Wings, but we could "Use the Force" in other ways such as helping, loving, caring and supporting, and be our own personal Jedi.[13]

The four characters named here, Master Yoda, Obi-Wan Kenobi, Qui-Gon Jinn, and Luke Skywalker, are all Jedi Knights. This fan denies that the Force and the supernatural powers of the Jedi have a counterpart in the real world, but he perceives the social ethic of the Jedi ("helping, loving, caring and supporting") as equally valid and important in the real world and in the world of fiction.

Jediism takes its point of departure from the fascination with the Force and the identification with the Jedi Knights as role models that are common in fan culture, although there are, of course, many *Star Wars* fans who are not at all interested in Jedi ethics and Force theology.

"Jedi" as Religious Self-identification

Surprisingly many people are prepared to identify themselves as "Jedi" in a religious context. In the summer of 2009, the *Washington Post* reported that "Jedi" was the tenth most common religious self-identification globally on Facebook.[14] Better known, however, is the "Jedi Census Phenomenon," which has its own entry on Wikipedia. Before the 2001 census in Great Britain, Canada, New Zealand, and Australia, an e-mail circulated urging people to report their religious affiliation as "Jedi." The e-mail was probably a combination of practical joke, a test of the power of e-mail as medium, and political protest against the religious affiliation tick box (even though reporting one's religion was not mandatory). The result was that more than 500,000 people in the four countries reported themselves to be "Jedi." With more than 390,000 self-identified adherents, Jediism emerged as the fourth-largest religion in Great Britain. The largest concentration of Jedi proved, however, to be in New Zealand, where they made up 1.3 percent of the total population.[15] There was no e-mail campaign prior to the following census in 2006, and the number of Jedi dropped dramatically. In New Zealand, for instance, it dropped from 53,715 to 20,262.[16] More remarkable than the fall-off, however, is the fact that so many people continued to state their religious affiliation as "Jedi."

No researcher has attempted to establish how many of the self-identified Jedi Knights on Facebook and in the census really practice a Force-directed spirituality. The president of the Australian Star Wars Appreciation Society estimated in a newspaper interview in

2002, just after the publication of the census results, that of the 70,000 Australian Jedi, 50,000 had identified themselves as Jedi just for fun; 15,000 aimed to "give the government a bit of curry"; and 5,000 "would be hard-core people that would believe the Jedi religion," though for the most part probably only "at a metaphorical level."[17] If we generalize to all countries that participated in the census his approximation that between 5 and 10 percent of self-identified "Jedi" are serious Jediists, we get an estimated 30,000 Jediists in Great Britain, Canada, Australia, and New Zealand combined. To this figure should be added an even greater number in the United States, but so far such figures are pure speculations.

The Mythologization of Star Wars

Star Wars has not achieved its status as myth and cult solely because of its content and its fans. It has also benefited from a process of mythologization orchestrated by film critics, journalists, and George Lucas himself.[18] Though Lucas does not consider himself a Jediist, he has explicitly stated that *Star Wars* can legitimately be viewed as a spiritual resource.

The mythologization process began with the reviews of the second *Star Wars* film, *The Empire Strikes Back*, in 1980. Steven Hart describes the new rhetoric as follows:

> Associate editor [of *Time* magazine] Gerald Clarke, who had praised the original flick for its light-hearted refusal to offer anything like a serious message, now finds "a moral dimension that touches us much more deeply than one-dimensional action adventures can." A sidebar, ponderously headlined "In the Footsteps of Ulysses," cites everything from "The Odyssey" to "Pilgrim's Progress" before concluding that the "*Star Wars*" films "draw from the same deep wells of mythology, the unconscious themes that have always dominated history on the planet."[19]

Since then, Lucas has himself actively participated in the construction of *Star Wars* as a myth. In a famous interview with the journalist Bill Moyers, Lucas explains at length his view of the mythical and religious elements in *Star Wars* and formulates the following programmatic statement:

> I put the Force into the movie in order to awaken a certain kind of spirituality in young people—more a belief in God than a belief in any particular religious system. I wanted to make it so that young people would begin to ask questions about the mystery. . . . I didn't want to invent a religion. I wanted to try to explain in a different way the religions that have already existed. I wanted to express it all. . . . I'm telling an old myth in a new way.[20]

During the interview, Lucas makes three points. First, he considers *Star Wars* to be a "myth" because the narrative carries certain basic values. Second, he asserts that he has let religion and faith play a central role in *Star Wars* because he deems the authentic human life to be a religious life and because he takes the existence of a divine power for granted: "I think there is a God, no question."[21] Third, he makes clear that even though *Star Wars* is inspired by "real" religions, the movies are fundamentally human-made entertainment and not the result of divine revelation. Therefore, they are unsuitable as the foundation of a religion. When confronted with the fact that young people today draw inspiration for how to live their lives from films, including *Star Wars*, rather than from organized religions, he therefore answers, "Well, I hope that doesn't end up being the course this whole thing takes, because I think there's definitely a place for organized religion. I would hate to find ourselves in a completely secular world where entertainment was passing for some kind of religious experience."[22] According to Lucas, it is desirable for entertainment, including *Star Wars*, to awaken a religious interest, but he sees this interest as no substitute for organized religion.

The Force Religion of the Jedi Knights: The Fictional Religion in Star Wars

Mythic narratives play almost no role in the "Force religion," by which I mean the system of theological teachings, ritual practices, and ethical rules of the Jedi Knights in the *Star Wars* universe.[23] Instead, it focuses on theology, social ethics, and spiritual practice. The sources of this fictional religion are the canonical films and their "extended universe," which comprises official comics, computer games, and more than two hundred novels. The central metaphysical power in the Force religion is, obviously, the Force. In the extended universe, it becomes clear that many different schools have fought over how to understand its true nature. Here I shall briefly touch on just two themes in these theological or, more precisely, dynamological debates. One central theme is the question whether the Force is monistic or dualistic in nature. The Force is usually represented as dualistic, with both a light side (Ashla) and a dark side (Bogan). This dualism is always moral insofar as the light side is good whereas the dark side is evil. The real question concerns the ontological status of the dualism. It is generally agreed that one can either follow the light side and do good or let oneself be seduced by the dark side and work evil. Jedi Masters debate whether a turn to the dark side should be understood as the corruption in an individual of an essentially monistic and good Force, or whether the dark side has its own extra-psychic, cosmological existence. The dominant theology is an intra-psychic dualism (the individual is free to choose between good and evil) encapsulated in a cosmological monism (the Force itself is essentially good). The other important theme is the question of whether the Force is an independent agent. One position views the Force as a passive, dynamistic energy that can be manipulated, whereas according to another viewpoint the Force is a semi-personal, active, and animistic will power with a project of salvation. The second view is implicitly expressed in the common farewell greeting "May the Force be with you."

As a member of the Jedi Order, a Jedi Knight is obliged to live by the Jedi Code. One of the novels summarizes the code in this way:

Jedi are the guardians of peace in the galaxy.
Jedi use their powers to defend and to protect.
Jedi respect all life, in any form.
Jedi serve others rather than ruling over them, for the good of the galaxy.
Jedi seek to improve themselves through knowledge and training.[24]

Here an ideal of physical and spiritual self-development is combined with a social commitment to serve, protect, and help others. The last line of the code deserves comment. Jedi Knights are required to acquire knowledge and to train. They have to practice fighting and investigative skills, for the Jedi Order forms a kind of intelligence agency in the Galactic Republic. But through study, meditative contemplation, and guidance by a master, they are also required to gain insight in the Force and learn to interact with it ritually. In doing so they become capable of being guided by the Force and of using it to perform seemingly supernatural acts like clairvoyance, levitation, and the influencing of weaker minds, the so-called "Jedi mind trick."

Jediism: The Fiction-based Religion

Outside the *Star Wars* universe, the fictional Force religion serves as the basis for a loosely organized religious movement that is made up of several small, independent, but networked groups. Although throughout this essay I have used "Jediism" to designate the entire movement and "Jediists" to refer to all its members, several different terms are in use. Some members prefer to name their religion "Jedi Realism" or "Jedi Philosophy" and to self-identify as "True Jedi," "Real Jedi," or "Jedi Realists" (to emphasis the difference between the fictional Jedi and themselves) or simply as "Jedi" (to emphasize their likeness to the fictional Jedi). Jediists use the different terms in order to position themselves in relation to each other, but the particle *Jedi* is used in them all. The ideas and practices of Jediism stem primarily from *Star Wars*, but are also inspired by other religious traditions, such as Christianity and Westernized Buddhism and Taoism.

In April and May 2008 and February 2010, I visited the homepages and discussion forums of seven Jediist groups: the Temple of the Jedi Order, the Jedi Foundation, the Jedi Church, the Jediism Way, the Jedi Sanctuary, the Force Academy, and the Ashla Knights. The Jedi Church is based in New Zealand, the Force Academy in Great Britain, and the rest in the United States. All use the English language, but participants in the online discussions can in principle live anywhere in the world. In my analysis of the homepages, I aimed to answer the following four questions: (1) How does the group categorize itself?

(2) How does the group view the Force? (3) How does the group legitimate the fact that its religion is based on a fictional text? and (4) What are the practices of the group? Based on this source material, I can sketch what a collection of elite Jediists (homepage owners and active online discussants) understand to be the most important Jediist ideas and practices and how they position themselves in relation to fans and more conventional religions. The data collected do not allow me to say anything conclusive about whether common group members (let alone solitary Jediists) share these points of view or anything about their social backgrounds. Since I used only online sources, my knowledge of offline practices was limited. With these reservations in mind, let me present a sketch of Jediism as a religion in the empirical world.[25]

Dissociation from Fandom and Self-identification as "Religion" or "Spirituality"

Jediists describe the *Star Wars* films as "wonderful,"[26] and they display an extensive knowledge of the *Star Wars* universe in their discussions—traits that normally characterize fans. Nevertheless, they find it imperative to distance themselves from general *Star Wars* fandom and to emphasize their own seriousness and sincerity in opposition to the playful and ironic fans. Accordingly, interested visitors on the Jedi Sanctuary site are addressed as follows: "Some of you might think that the Jedi Sanctuary is like a SW fan club, or just a joke. It's not. It's a real path that we follow, and we take it seriously. When we say, 'May the Force be with you,' we believe it and mean it."[27]

In opposition to the category "fan club," three of the seven groups I have analyzed define Jediism as a "religion" (or "church"). The Jedi Church does not speak of Jediism, but simply of "the Jedi religion,"[28] and the Temple of the Jedi Order considers Jediism "a real living, breathing religion."[29] Both groups are legally authorized to perform marriages, and since December 14, 2005, the Temple of the Jedi Order has been recognized as a non-profit religious and educational corporation under Texas law, granting members the right to deduct contributions from their tax bill.[30] The Temple of the Jedi Order clearly considers a high degree of institutionalization and official recognition as a prerequisite for counting as a real religion. The Jedi Church and the Jediism Way, by contrast, see no problem in combining self-description as religion/church with dissociation from the dogmatic and collective aspects of institutionalized religion. The former stresses that the "Jedi church has no official doctrine or scripture,"[31] and the Jediism Way explains that it is a religion because of its members' shared belief in the Force despite the absence of collective rituals.[32]

In the other four groups, Jediism is more often referred to as a "spirituality," "philosophy," "path," or "way," and these terms are all used in opposition to "religion" understood as a collective and institutionalized (and therefore inhibited and alienated) engagement with the divine. As one Jediist formulates it in a post on the Jedi Sanctuary's forum, Jediism is a spirituality and not a religion because Jediism is not "the unthinking following of dogma."[33] Later in the same thread, one of the leaders of the group adds, "I don't consider the Jedi Path a religion, as far as traditional religions are viewed. When I think of religion, I think of an organized set of rituals, public worship conducted according to certain rules, incense burning, religious symbols, group prayers, etc. . . . I think Jedi believe in a more intimate connection to the Force than what organized religion offers."[34] These groups understand Jediism as an essentially individualistic, free, authentic, and mystical spirituality.

Teachings about the Force

Whether Jediist groups define Jediism as religion or spirituality, they do so with reference to their belief in the Force—even though different groups understand the Force differently. These dynamological differences stem partly from the fact that the individual groups typically stress one of the two Force conceptions in *Star Wars*, the dynamistic or the animistic, and partly from their inspiration from other religions.

The four self-identified "spiritual" groups, the Ashla Knights, the Force Academy, the Jedi Sanctuary, and the Jedi Foundation, are inspired by Eastern religions and holistic spirituality ("New Age") in addition to *Star Wars*. These groups all tend to view the Force in dynamistic terms. For them the Force is thus a vitalistic power or life energy. The Force Academy, the Ashla Knights, and the Jedi Sanctuary compare the Force to Eastern concepts like *qi* and *prana* and observe similarities between their own practice and taiji, aikido, and zen.[35] The Jedi Foundation believes the Force to be "essentially a 'by-product' of life—a side effect, if you will, yet symbiotic,"[36] and considers "the study of science and other beliefs and practices on energy" as different paths to knowledge of the Force.[37]

The three self-identified "religious" groups view the Force in *animistic* terms as an independent agent, sometimes interpreting the Force through a more or less Christian lens as a kind of Holy Spirit. The Jediism Way declares, "We believe the guidance of the Force will bring us to a course of right action," but still stresses that the Force is no person.[38] The Temple of the Jedi Order has a similar vision and refers to the Force as an active "living Force."[39] The Jedi Church is open to both dynamistic and animistic understandings of the Force.[40]

The Relation to Star Wars

As we have seen, the groups' self-identification as religion or spirituality corresponds with their conception of the Force as either a semi-personified agent or an impersonal energy. Along another axis, the seven Jediists groups can be divided into two groups depending on whether they seek to explicitly affirm that their spirituality is based on *Star Wars* or whether they dissociate themselves from *Star Wars* as a means of legitimation.

Three groups—the Jedi Sanctuary, the Jediism Way, and the Jedi Foundation—all stress that their ideas and practices come from *Star Wars*. The Jediism Way simply understands "the community of Jediism" as "those who connected with the stories in Star Wars, share the belief in an open concept of divine power known as 'the Force' . . . [and aspire to live their] lives similarly to that which they connected with in these tales."[41] The Jedi Foundation joins in with the following statement:

> Jedi [Jediists] strive to emulate those [Jedi Knights] seen in the movies, but we are aware of the differences from fiction to reality. This site takes a lot of [its] views from three main sources, *The Star Wars Power of the Jedi Sourcebook* [a source book for the *Star Wars* role-playing game], The *Jedi Apprentice* series [three novels that tell of Luke Skywalker's reinstigation of the Jedi Order after the movie storyline], and the Movies. We use these as guides, to explore, learn from and more importantly expand from. As *Star Wars* Jedi are what inspired us, it is what we chose to look towards.[42]

The members of the Jediism Way and the Jedi Foundation feel no need to legitimate and defend the fact that Jediism is based on the fictional *Star Wars* movies, but the Jedi Sanctuary refers to Joseph Campbell, who has supposedly said, "I've heard youngsters use some of George Lucas's terms—'The Force' and 'The dark side.' So it must be hitting somewhere. It's a good sound teaching, I would say."[43] The quote is regarded as Campbell's acknowledgment of *Star Wars*' status as a myth and thus by implication as his recognition of Jediism as a religion/spirituality.

In all seven groups, but strongest in the Temple of the Jedi Order, the Jedi Church, the Ashla Knights, and the Force Academy, one encounters a contrasting strategy, namely, disassociation from *Star Wars* and the claim that the *real* source of inspiration for Jediism is not *Star Wars* itself but the religions that inspired George Lucas to make it. The Ashla Knights and the Force Academy claim to build on "real world philosophies and influences" or "life force philosophies,"[44] namely, different forms of Eastern philosophy, religion, and martial arts. The Jedi Church and the Temple of the Jedi Order claim to base themselves not only on Eastern religion but on universal truths shared by all religions:

> The Jedi Church makes no denial that its name and terminology originate from a fictitious past, but the concepts and ideals that are identified by Jedi followers are known for their innate truth. . . . The Jedi religion . . . existed before a popular movie gave it a name, and now that it has a name, people all over the world can share their experiences of the Jedi religion, here in the Jedi Church.[45]

> Jediism is a syncretistic religion—a faith involving elements from two or more religions including Taoism, Shintoism, Buddhism, Christianity, Mysticism, and many other Religions' universal truths and a combination of martial arts and the Code of

Chivalry. These philosophies [the different religions] are the heart of Jediism; not the wonderful Star Wars movies themselves except to serve as parables.[46]

Because the Temple of the Jedi Order equates Jediism with the true essence of all religion as such, Jediism can be seen as ancient, and the line of "Masters of Jediism" can count "Buddha, Jesus, LaoTsu, St. Francis of Assisi, Gandhi, Martin Luther King, and so many others."[47]

In Table 1, I have plotted the seven groups into a matrix with self-identification/ dynamology on one axis and the place of *Star Wars* in their legitimation strategy on the other. Groups that are no longer active in September 2012 are marked by italics. It would seem that the combination of dissociation from *Star Wars* and "religious" Jediism makes for the "fittest" form of Jediism, or at least for the most stable Jediist communities.

	"Spiritual"/dynamistic	*"Religious"/animist*
affirmative toward *Star Wars*	Jedi Foundation *Jedi Sanctuary*	Jediism Way
dissociative from *Star Wars*	Ashla Knights *Force Academy*	Jedi Church Temple of the Jedi Order

Practice and Ethics

All Jediist groups emphasize physical and spiritual self-development, but this aspect is particularly dominant in the Jediism Way, the Jedi Sanctuary, the Jedi Foundation, and the Ashla Knights. As the leader of the Jediism Way formulates it, "I don't pray to the Force or worship it every day in the traditional sense, but I meditate and do other things [to] strengthen my connection to it every day!!"[48] Similarly, the Jedi Sanctuary emphasizes that the group does not have rituals, but instead aims to "discuss all aspects of being a Jedi, fitness, meditation, conflict resolution, negotiation, staying positive, making good decisions, having healthy relationships, trusting in the Force, and personal growth."[49]

The Ashla Knights has a comparable vision,[50] and the Jedi Foundation focuses on:

Physical Well-Being (diet, exercise, and practical self-defense), Mental Well-Being (stress-relief, conflict resolution, and learning new subjects such as different philosophies that exist), and Spiritual Well-Being (meditation, self-awareness and self-honesty, learning about the Force). The Jedi work towards self-betterment.[51]

The homepage for the Jedi Church gives no information about the practice of the group, and in the Force Academy the practice depends on which "path" the member belongs to—whether he or she is a "Light Jedi," "Dark Jedi," or "Shadow Jedi."

While some groups deny that social ethics founded on the idea of charity should have anything to do with Jediism (e.g., the Jedi Foundation),[52] others see no contradiction between the ideals of self-development and charity (e.g., the Jedi Sanctuary).[53] In the Temple of the Jedi Order, which downplays the self-development aspect, it is emphasized that "love and compassion are central to our lives. We must love each other as we love ourselves."[54]

A social ethics formulated in terms of charity is not the only loan from Christianity in the Temple of the Jedi Order. We are also told that Jediists "believe in the eternal life,"[55] and the homepage contains a modified version of one of Francis of Assisi's prayers under the title "Jedi Creed."[56] One of the functions of the forum is that members can present personal problems and ask other members to pray for them. Such calls for intercessory prayer get answers like "I will keep you in my thoughts and meditations."[57] The group also has a clergy and a "Clergy Ceremonies and Rituals Committee" that is responsible for the development of "the Temple of the Jedi Order Clergy Handbook," with rituals for "baptisms, naming, weddings, and funerals."[58] The Temple of the Jedi Order is thus clearly the Jediist group that to the largest extent models itself on a conventional religion (denominational Christianity), which entails institutionalization, public recognition, and the development of collective rituals.

We have seen that *Star Wars* includes a fictional religion, the Force religion of the Jedi Knights, and that both *Star Wars* fans and Jediists are interested in the dynamology, practice, and ethics of this fictional religion and see parallels between the *Star Wars* universe and the empirical world. On these grounds, and using a broad, functionalistic definition of religion, John Lyden has argued that both *Star Wars* itself (as a film conveying values) and *Star Wars* fandom (as a community sharing a "canonical" myth) constitute religious phenomena.[59] Such a conclusion is confusing and misleading, however, for it obscures real differences between *Star Wars* fandom and Jediism, differences that justify labeling the latter, but not the former, as religion according to a substantive definition.

For fans the *Star Wars* universe is first and foremost a fascinating place that one can playfully enter and leave again. Many fans see such visits to the *Star Wars* universe as inspiring and edifying because *Star Wars* confirms basic values in their own world. Jediists differ from mainstream fans by claiming that not only the ethics of the Jedi Knights, but also their dynamology and religious practice, are valid models for real world religious activity. Despite disagreements over self-identification, dynamology, and legitimization strategies, Jediists agree on two things: first, that a divine power guarantees the order of existence and that this power is the Force; and second, that being a Jediist is defined by belief in and ritual interaction with this Force through meditation and sometimes additional ritual techniques. The fictional religion of the Jedi Knights, which is merely an object for play within fan culture, is here transformed into a real religion, Jediism. Despite the facts that some groups distance themselves from *Star Wars* in an attempt to legitimate Jediism as a "real" religion and that all Jediist groups to a smaller or larger extent integrate ideas and practices from other religions, the Force religion from *Star Wars* remains the main source of inspiration and terminology for Jediism. Because its main authoritative text is a fictional narrative, Jediism can therefore be categorized as a fiction-based religion.

Jediism and other fiction-based religions constitute the institutionalized tip of a much larger iceberg of religious ideas and practices created and maintained by popular culture.[60] Popular cultural narratives with religious themes or embedded fictional religions—narratives such as *Star Wars*, *The Lord of the Rings*, *Battlestar Galactica*, *Buffy the Vampire Slayer*, *The X-Files*, and *Discworld*—are today very important sources of religious knowledge and edification for many (especially young) people. Just as *Star Wars* mixes material from the religious past—from Christianity and Eastern religions—other popular cultural narratives recombine and revitalize elements from both organized religion and folk belief. By influencing the religious beliefs and practices of their readers and viewers, these narratives contribute to the transmission and transformation of the religious past into a fiction-mediated religious future.

CHAPTER 20

The Words of the Martyr

Media, Martyrdom, and the Construction of a Community

Pieter Nanninga

On Tuesday July 8, 2008, jihadist Internet forums were abuzz. On some of the websites, a banner had announced the release of a new video called *Jihad wa-Istishhad* (*Jihad and Martyrdom*). A prominent golden logo on the purple banner indicated that the video was produced by al-Sahab ("The Clouds"), a media production house associated with al-Qaeda. The websites further provided hundreds of hyperlinks to online storage sites, where visitors could download the release in different formats, varying from DVD to mobile phone. They could then watch the forty-five-minute documentary-like video, which focused on one of al-Qaeda's recent "martyrs": an Egyptian commander named Abu al-Hasan who had carried out a "martyrdom operation" against a NATO convoy in Afghanistan. In a lengthy interview, the commander discussed his jihadi career and explained his motivations for the attack he was hoping to perform. In the sophisticated editing of the video, this interview was spliced together with statements by high-ranking al-Qaeda members and extensive accounts by an off-screen narrator and supplemented with Qur'an recitations, computer simulations, text banners, and various other sorts of footage. The result immediately won high admiration from its viewers. In comments posted on the forums soon after the video's release, they praised God, asked him to reward this martyr, and celebrated the video as "one of the most beautiful releases of al-Sahab yet."[1]

With such martyrdom videos, jihadist organizations have moved far away from the traditional farewell videos of suicide bombers in the eighties and nineties. In those decades, Lebanese and Palestinian organizations started to distribute brief videos of their martyrs, who read their last wills in front of the camera, surrounded by weapons and flags.

Pioneered by al-Qaeda and the newly established al-Sahab, this genre was taken to another level at the beginning of the twenty-first century in polished, hour-long videos such as *Jihad and Martyrdom*. Within a matter of years, several jihadist organizations had followed al-Sahab's example, and by now dozens of extensive martyrdom videos from Afghanistan, Iraq, Pakistan, Saudi Arabia, Somalia, and elsewhere circulate in the virtual world of anonymous webmasters and faceless surfers—a world that seems fascinated by the last words of the martyr.

Why have Islamist and jihadist organizations put so much effort into publishing these words since the rise of suicide attacks in the early eighties? Some scholars have argued that the recording of farewell videos was an important means of increasing the psychological pressure on future bombers, ensuring that they would actually carry out their mission.[2] Others have argued that the distribution of these videos was part of a strategy to foster a "culture of martyrdom," which would facilitate the recruitment of new bombers.[3] Although these explanations have some appeal, they hardly elucidate scenes like those in the summer of 2008, when people from all over the world celebrated the release of a new martyrdom video that had taken a team of producers weeks to script, record, and edit. In this essay, I will argue that the importance of martyrs in jihadist media must be understood in relation to the role of martyrdom and violence within the jihadist community. Together, the violence and the videos not only powerfully express contemporary jihadism but also shape the jihadist community and provide it with a sense of empowerment. A close reading of one video, *Jihad and Martyrdom*, will allow us to explore the symbolic violence of suicide attacks and to gain insight into the crucial role of martyrdom in contemporary jihadism.

Meanings of Martyrdom

Abu al-Hasan rammed his bomb truck into a NATO convoy somewhere in southeastern Afghanistan in the summer of 2007.[4] With his action, he followed in the footsteps of hundreds of men and women who, in the twenty-five years before his death, had blown themselves up in the midst of their enemies. In the early eighties, Lebanese organizations pioneered the method in their fight against foreign troops during the Lebanese civil war. Due to their success, Tamils, Palestinians, and Kurds successively copied the practice, after which it spread around the world in the wake of September 11, 2001, and the al-Aqsa intifada. Up to the present, suicide attacks have caused the deaths of at least twenty thousand people.

The political scientists and terrorism scholars who have dominated the study of suicide attacks have emphasized the role of the organizations behind the violence. They consider the employment of suicide attacks to be, in Martha Crenshaw's terms, a "strategic choice."[5] It is a rationally chosen means that, as her colleague Ami Pedahzur writes, "is a product of an organization's political strategy after it has defined its goals, clarified the options it has in order to realize these goals and checked the price label attached to each operational method."[6] So rather than the result of irrational behavior, suicide attacks are a deliberate and effective instrument used by organizations as a means toward certain ends. Although this functionalist approach has thus far characterized the research on suicide attacks, scholars' opinions about the goals and effects of this form of violence diverge significantly. In his groundbreaking study *Dying to Win*, the political scientist Robert A. Pape argues that all kinds of organizations have used suicide attacks throughout history in order to compel stronger, usually democratic enemies to withdraw their military forces from territory that these organizations consider their homeland.[7] Mia M. Bloom, however, has nuanced Pape's thesis by arguing that suicide attacks not only are used against an enemy but fulfill certain functions within the perpetrator's own community. They may enhance the prestige of an organization and can therefore be used to compete with other groups for support within the community, as was the case, for instance, with Hamas vis-à-vis the Palestinian Authority.[8] Leading terrorism expert Bruce Hoffman points to still another function of suicide attacks by describing them as a strategic "signaling game" in which organizations communicate their character and goals to a particular set of audiences. As a specific means of communication, the attacks can thus be considered an "instrumental tactic" serving the organizations' political interests.[9]

In recent years, some scholars have pointed out the limitations of these theories. Assaf Moghadam, for example, has argued that such explanations are based mainly upon the national struggles of the Lebanese, Tamils, Palestinians, and Kurds, whereas a new, globalized pattern of suicide attacks has emerged. This new pattern was instigated by al-Qaeda's attacks, he suggests, and is characterized by the Salafi jihad rather than by political motivations. Therefore, their value is symbolic, in addition to the strategic benefits that had been emphasized in earlier publications.[10] Mohammed M. Hafez has further developed this argument in an extensive analysis of suicide attacks in Iraq, which, according to him, are part of such a globalized pattern. He shows how, in addition to their tactical advantages, suicide attacks are an effective means of strategic communication, valuable because of their psychological impact. For these reasons suicide attacks have become a useful weapon for jihadists in Iraq, less to coerce foreign powers to abandon their territory than to spark sectarian violence and work toward the collapse the emerging democratic order.[11]

Whereas these scholars emphasize different goals and effects of suicide attacks, they all approach violence as an instrument directed toward certain ends. Beyond its instrumental aspects, however, violence always has expressive aspects.[12] As a form of social action, violence by definition expresses a relationship with others. But it also entails background ideas about, for instance, legitimacy and cultural values, and it presupposes certain images of the perpetrator's own community as well as the enemy. For that reason, every act of violence has something "to say" and communicates ideas to the audience that directly or indirectly witnesses it. In other words, violent acts can also be viewed as "performances," or "social processes by which actors, individually or in concert, display for others the meaning of their social situation."[13] They offer the audience insights into central themes of the perpetrator's culture and community. Like Clifford Geertz's Balinese cockfights, they can be approached as a "story they tell themselves about themselves"—a story, however, that not only passively reflects its surrounding culture, but also actively changes things.[14]

Religiously motivated violence, in particular, has an expressive or symbolic character.[15] Instead of waging a worldly battle, violent religious movements often envision themselves as engaged in a cosmic war. They are fighting on God's side, while the enemy is demonized and experienced as threatening the community of the faithful. The perceived marginalization and humiliation of this community can, in particular circumstances, be expressed by violent means. The goal of this violence is therefore not to transform society but rather to give vent to these experiences of frustration, rage, or abandonment. The violence itself can be experienced as liberating and may give religious communities a sense of empowerment.[16]

Seen in this light, jihadist suicide attacks are an exceptionally expressive form of violence. This results from the character of "martyrdom operations" themselves. As "witnesses"—the literal meaning of both the Greek *martys* as well as the Arabic *shahid*—martyrs communicate their total commitment to a cause by publicly demonstrating their preparedness to suffer or even die for it. With their acts, they draw attention to their belief system and show that it is worth dying for. This "communicative force" of martyrdom, as David Cook calls it, makes martyrs a powerful advertisement for contemporary jihadism.[17] Every suicide attack highlights the jihadists' belief system and forces upon those directly or indirectly witnessing the violence their alternative view of the world as a world at war.[18] This expressive nature is further increased by the heavily contested nature of suicide attacks. By employing such extreme means, jihadists distinguish themselves from what are, in their view, the unconcerned Muslim masses, which often condemn the use of suicide attacks. The jihadists thus portray themselves as the vanguard of the *umma*, as the faithful few who defend the Muslim community that is humiliated in Afghanistan, Iraq, Palestine, Saudi Arabia, and elsewhere. The extreme nature of the means underlines the gravity of the situation.

Furthermore, the form of the violence provides it with symbolic meanings. Like other forms of expressive violence, such as bullfights, public executions, and dueling, suicide attacks usually have a ritualized character. They are accompanied by several ritual or ritual-like practices, such as reciting passages from the Qur'an, ritual cleansing, the writing and sometimes recording of a last will, and (if possible) a funeral in bloodstained clothes. These practices have been selected from various sources and traditions and subsequently reordered and reinterpreted in order to form the "script" for the performance of a suicide attack. Some practices, such as the reciting of specific passages from the Qur'an, the shouting of *Allahu akbar* or the *shahada* (the Islamic creed) at the moment of the

attack, and several funeral customs are based upon traditional Islamic battle and martyrdom traditions. Others, however, are derived from recent Shiite martyrdom practices,
traditional cultural customs, or modern popular culture. Taken together, these "tools"
enable jihadists to shape present-day suicide attacks in a way that fits their particular
situation. By being related to classical practices and roles, suicide attacks are presented
as traditional, while they are perfectly adapted to the modern world. In this manner, the
form of the violence provides it with meanings for the actors as well as the audience. It
empowers the jihadist movement and gives its audience insight into some of the central
themes of their community by referring to martyrdom and jihad, faith and commitment, the nature of the enemy and its deeds, the state of the umma and its humiliation,
and so on.

In short, suicide attacks are more than an instrumental, effective means in a conflict
situation. To a lesser degree than the suicide attacks in the eighties and early nineties,
jihadist violence is aimed at clear strategic objectives. Even aside from the diversity of
contemporary jihadism and the dynamic and fragmented character of its leadership and
organizations, jihadists are often not pursuing the straightforward goals for which suicide
attacks are employed. While groups like al-Qaeda may occasionally refer to the reestablishment of the Islamic caliphate, they do not have a concrete program or strategy for
establishing such a state.[19] Yet even without such tangible functions, suicide attacks are
meaningful actions. The martyrs express the perceived humiliation of Muslims all over
the world and provide the Muslim community and its jihadist vanguard with renewed
respect and self-worth by dying for it. However, the attacks acquire these meanings only
by being witnessed, and here we encounter the crucial role of the media.

The Media Battle

In the summer of 2005, one of al-Qaeda's most prominent leaders, the Egyptian Dr.
Ayman al-Zawahiri, wrote a letter to the Jordanian leader of al-Qaeda in Iraq, Abu Musab
al-Zarqawi, after the latter had shocked the world by releasing videotapes that showed the
beheading of hostages. Zawahiri resisted the release of such videos, stating, "I say to you
that we are in a battle, and that more than half of this battle is taking place in the battlefield of the media. And that we are in a media battle in a race for the hearts and minds of
our Umma."[20] His comment demonstrates that jihadist leaders are well aware of the indispensable value of media in present-day conflicts. For that reason, their organizations have
developed numerous media-related activities, especially in the last decade. Movements
such as Ansar al-Sunna, the Islamic State of Iraq, al-Qaeda, al-Qaeda in the Arabian
Peninsula, and al-Shabab have issued hundreds of written statements, published numerous books and magazines, and established extensive, multilingual websites. Moreover,
hundreds of videos have been released, containing statements, operational footage, train-

ing instructions, and, probably the most sophisticated and professionalized of all, martyrdom videos.

Al-Qaeda's al-Sahab Establishment for Media Productions was the first "media production company" set up to exploit these media possibilities. Apart from its videos, very little is known about it.[21] Al-Sahab released its first video in 2001; it dealt with the suicide attack on the American naval destroyer *USS Cole* in the port of Aden in October of the previous year. After this release, hundreds of others followed with increasing speed. Although most of the videos comprise short statements and operational clips, al-Sahab has also produced dozens of extensive martyrdom videos, featuring suicide bombers from various regions, working for different organizations. They include six of the September 11 hijackers and two of the London bombers, but also several men who had carried out attacks in Afghanistan, Pakistan, and Saudi Arabia. Moreover, some videos focus on several "martyrs," such as the series *Winds of Paradise*—probably al-Sahab's most celebrated productions.

Jihad and Martyrdom is one of al-Sahab's most professional videos so far. Its structure is to a large extent representative of the genre, although the martyr's farewell message that constitutes its body consists of a lengthy interview instead of the more traditional reading of a written text. As usual, the video starts with a Qur'an recitation, after which an off-screen narrator explains the necessity of "martyrdom operations" in the contemporary situation. Then the main part of the video follows, in which Abu al-Hasan tells his life story. The sympathetic-looking commander is recorded in front of a rock wall, with a Kalashnikov beside him. He speaks freely into the camera, frequently smiling and showing his excitement about the operation he is about to perform. In addition to his story as told by himself, the narrator and three of Abu al-Hasan's colleagues—Shaykh Mustafa Abu al-Yazid and the commanders Khalid al-Habib and Abu Khalil al-Madani—offer comments on his life. They also describe the culmination of the commander's career: his suicide attack on a NATO convoy. At the end of the video, this attack is shown by means of a computer simulation depicting the bomb truck crashing into four Humvees guarding a truck. "Nothing remained of them," Abu Khalil commented, "nothing was left of any of them."

Jihad and Martyrdom

In the introduction to *Jihad and Martyrdom*, both the narrator and Shaykh Mustafa Abu al-Yazid set the stage for the last words of the martyr. In about two and a half minutes, the former draws a picture of a world at war. A confrontation is going on, he states, between the "umma and its mujahid vanguard," on the one hand, and the "Zionist-crusader forces" and the "treacherous rulers" of the Arab world, on the other. Because of the discrepancy in strength between the two sites, this war seems almost useless, according to the narrator—a statement that is underlined with footage of American war planes and soldiers, as well as destroyed buildings, heavy bombardment, and wounded people. Yet there is a solution to this unbalance, the narrator indicates: "martyrdom operations." While impressive images of the planes crashing into the World Trade Center are shown, he explains that actions like these restore balance to the conflict. Only by paying the price of "the noblest and dearest blood," he concludes, can the umma be victorious. Then, after Abu al-Hasan is introduced and shown reciting a verse from the Qur'an, Yazid takes over, saying that striving for martyrdom can bring victory to the umma. "It is the way to remove the weakness and humiliation the umma is currently experiencing," he states, while the opposite, "love of this life and an aversion for death," counts as weakness and will lead to humiliation and disgrace.

This narrative articulates what in the foregoing I have described as the symbolic meanings of jihadist suicide attacks. First, the video portrays a conflict that is described in religious terms. Christians and Jews, aided by deviants from within their own communities, are attacking and humiliating Muslims and their jihadist vanguard. Then martyrdom is presented as the way to restore the umma's dignity. While the narrator also briefly refers to the establishment of an Islamic state, the main point these two men make is that martyrdom empowers the umma and the jihadist movement.

Besides explaining the significance of suicide attacks, the introduction to *Jihad and Martyrdom* emphasizes Abu al-Hasan's status as a martyr. Martyrdom is not a status automatically gained by dying in a fight, but a social construct and therefore part of negotiations between different parties. Since suicide attacks are also a disputed means in the Muslim world, it is not very remarkable that the video takes part in these negotiations by relating this "martyr" and his "martyrdom operation" to several classical martyrdom traditions: For example, the opening of the video and Abu al-Hasan's first words consist of classical jihad and martyrdom verses from the Qur'an: sura 9:20 and 9:111.[22] Moreover, during his first physical appearance, the body of the Egyptian is surrounded by a green aura, in accordance with traditional Islamic martyrdom iconography. Further on in the video, to provide a final example, Abu al-Hasan explains that his longing for a martyrdom operation was not motivated by a desire to escape from this life, thus resisting the often-heard objection against suicide, which is strictly forbidden in Islam. Rather, he was driven by his desire to be in God's presence, he says, repeating Moses's words of sura 20:84: "And I have hastened to you my Lord, that you might be pleased." By referring to such authoritative symbols of martyrdom, the video stresses the special status of the commander.

Once suicide attacks are embedded in the narrative of a global religious war and the crucial role of martyrs in it has been explained, the video narrows its scope to focus on the life story of the commander and the movement of which he was part. In a long account, lasting about half an hour, Abu al-Hasan's life as a mujahid is portrayed by constantly switching between the narrator, the commander himself, and the three al-Qaeda leaders who had known him personally. In concert, they describe how Abu al-Hasan had moved from Egypt to Iraq, where he became impressed by cassette recordings of the legendary

Palestinian mujahid Abdullah Azzam and the stories he heard about the sufferings of the Palestinian people. These were his main reasons for joining the jihad, he states. From this moment on, Abu al-Hasan's life story runs remarkably parallel to the history of al-Qaeda. As a born-again Muslim, he went to Afghanistan in the late eighties, at the time al-Qaeda was established there. He thereupon joined Bin Laden and took part in the jihad against the Russians. In the early nineties, the video tells, Abu al-Hasan moved with al-Qaeda leadership to Sudan, whence he played a role in battles against the Americans in Somalia in 1993, as well as in the bombings of the American embassies in Nairobi and Dar es-Salaam in 1998. After that, he moved with Bin Laden to Afghanistan again, where he set up the al-Faruq training camp—the place where some of the September 11 hijackers were trained. Finally, after the American invasion of Afghanistan, he took part in the struggle against the coalition forces, first on the battlefield and thereafter in guerilla warfare in the mountains. In short, according to the video, Abu al-Hasan played a leading role in al-Qaeda's major fights and attacks.

On the one hand, this narrative could be considered a means of enhancing the status of the Egyptian commander. He has dedicated his entire life to the good cause and has become a prominent leader in the umma's vanguard. On the other hand, it could also be argued that the story of this man grants authority and credibility to the self-representation of al-Qaeda in the video. Because of the parallels between his life and the history of al-Qaeda, the narration of his life course provides plenty of opportunities to dwell on the movement and its activities, motivations and ideologies. Indeed, the editors of the video have fully grasped these opportunities. The description of al-Hasan's stay in Sudan, for example, is used to expand on the expulsion of the Americans from Somalia and the embassy attacks in Kenya and Tanzania, while the account of his second stay in Afghanistan is used to portray Bin Laden's activities here. This pattern is constantly repeated throughout the middle part of the video, to such an extent that more than half of it deals with the general history of the mujahidun and al-Qaeda instead of with Abu al-Hasan. Even more interesting is the division between the voices presenting this part. A content analysis shows that Abu al-Hasan is the main speaker here: He tells 34 percent of the story.[23] Surprisingly, however, he speaks for more than 62 percent of that time about the general history of the jihad and al-Qaeda, whereas his own biography takes up only 38 percent. By contrast, his three colleagues speak primarily about Abu al-Hasan and his biography and only incidentally about the jihad in general (79 versus 21 percent of the time, respectively). Thus the producers of the video have chosen to present al-Qaeda's history mainly through the words of the martyr. After his special status has been underlined in the first part of the video, his words are given the central place in the second part, providing extra authority to al-Qaeda's self-representation.

After this long account and the computer simulation of Abu al-Hasan's suicide attack, the "martyr" appears for one last time, issuing his final request in the last minute of the video. Here, he presents himself as a humble man or, in his own words, as an "errant son of Adam." He asks everyone who has any grievance against him to forgive him and finally prays to God to accept him as a martyr. This last minute powerfully rounds off the narrative, which had started with the global conflict between the umma and its enemies, then narrowed the subject to al-Qaeda and its commander, and now concludes with a personal word from the modestly smiling Egyptian. It shows the viewers that, after all, it is a story about an ordinary Muslim, like themselves. This man also saw images of and heard stories about the humiliation of his fellow believers in other parts of the world—images and stories like the ones shown in this video. Yet this man did not stay in front of his screen but actively joined the jihad. This ordinary Muslim became a prominent mujahid and finally a martyr. He was praised by his superiors for his key role in the global conflict, and he even gained the opportunity to represent the cause he was willing to die for in a professional martyrdom video, which would spread around the world within a few hours.

The Construction of a Community

Abu al-Hasan's martyrdom video makes clear that films like these express the symbolic meanings of the violence more explicitly than do suicide attacks themselves. In the videos, the attacks are embedded in an all-embracing narrative that amplifies the meanings of the violence. Yet, although the videos closely follow the symbolic meanings of the attacks, the framing of the violence within this narrative also provides it with new meanings. The original context, motivations, and effects are reconstructed by embedding the attacks in a new, global landscape. In the video *Jihad and Martyrdom*, for instance, Abu al-Hasan's suicide attack in a remote Afghan province is raised to a global level by incorporating it into the narrative of a worldwide conflict between the Zionist-crusader forces and the umma and its jihadist vanguard. In this manner, personal, local, and regional events are adapted to the globalized world of the jihadist community. When thus recontextualized, these events become relevant in every situation and for every person who is attracted to these narratives. This process enables the construction of a global community based upon these shared experiences, events, and ideas.

The role of the videos in the construction of a jihadist community can be illustrated by looking at the recurring theme of humiliation. "Martyrs" express the humiliating situation of the Muslim community by dying for it. In the videos, this deplorable condition is demonstrated more explicitly: in words and especially images. The videos acquire an emotional charge through footage of old women being beaten by Israeli soldiers, crying children in Iraqi hospitals, and corpses lying on the side of an Afghan road. Moreover, such footage connects all these different conflicts and situations and merges them into a single grand narrative about the Muslim community. In consequence, Muslims in other parts of the world are able to identify with this community and to feel for themselves the humiliation of their fellow believers. This "humiliation by proxy," as it has been labeled by Farhad

Khosrokhavar, is also visible in the story of Abu al-Hasan, who, while living in Iraq, was upset by the suffering of the Palestinians and then decided to go to Afghanistan.[24]

The case of Abu al-Hasan also shows that this "deterritorialization" is not limited to perceived humiliation but also affects the jihad itself.[25] Due to the rise of new media in recent decades, such as the audio cassettes of Azzam to which Abu al-Hasan refers or the satellite stations that enabled him to view images from Palestine, differences between local, national, and regional conflicts vanish. Contemporary jihadism is clearly a product of this development. Like Abu-al-Hasan, many jihadists have left their birthplaces, severed ties with their families, and traveled to other places to join the jihad. The places to which they have gone are not especially relevant in themselves, but seem interchangeable as places where the jihad can be practiced. In videos such as *Jihad and Martyrdom*, the differences between Afghanistan, Iraq, Palestine, Somalia, and Washington disappear: They are nothing more than accidental sites where the jihad comes to the surface. The place where Abu al-Hasan carried out his attack is insignificant for the story of the video, as well as for its viewers. In other words, while every suicide attack has specific meanings in its particular context, the martyrdom videos of al-Sahab and others recontextualize the attacks, thereby adapting them to a globalized world. Both the preceding humiliation and the sense of empowerment resulting from an attack can now be experienced thousands of miles away by people who feel part of the same community. Therefore, the violence and its representation in the videos should not be regarded only as expressions of the jihadist community only; they also actively shape it.

This community, created by acts of violence and the witnessing thereof in the media, is an abstract community. Most members do not know one another. Moreover, they have no shared socioeconomic, national, or even religious background. Usually their beliefs are not inherited or transmitted by traditional social or religious authorities, such as parents, clergy, or teachers. Rather, they shape their own beliefs by drawing from widely available sources and by selecting those ideas and practices that fit their own experiences and feelings. Only then do they make a personal decision to join the jihad.

In this case, too, jihadism is shaped by its time—by developments such as the fragmentation of traditional authorities, the democratization of Islam, and an emphasis on personal experience, authenticity, and self-realization. Obviously, the jihadist message as expressed in al-Sahab's videos is also a product of such developments. Although jihadism is often described as the offspring of Middle-Eastern, Arab, and Sunni movements such as Salafism and Wahhabism, its genealogy is not as straightforward as it is often presented.[26] Similarly, the jihadist message is drawn from various sources and traditions, such as Shi'ism and Sufism, as well as modern Western movements and traditions.[27] Suicide attacks and farewell videos were developed by Shiite movements, for instance, and the green aura that surrounds Abu al-Hasan on his first appearance in *Jihad and Martyrdom* clearly reminds us of the iconography of imam Husayn, whose death at Karbala is remembered every year in the Shiite world. But elements from Sufism are also appropriated in the video: Before his attack, for example, the commander has dreams foretelling that he would soon become a martyr. Like the miracle stories that are also regularly narrated in martyrdom videos, throughout history dreams have been closely connected to mystical forms of Islam (which are, ironically, strongly condemned by jihadists).[28]

This amalgamated jihadist message is not enforced from above but is a product of the diversity of the jihadist community and the dynamic and nonhierarchical character of its leadership and organizations. One consequence of this composite character is that the message can attract viewers from various regions and different backgrounds, who can all find some aspect that appeals to them. This is exactly the point and explains the attractiveness of the jihadist message. Due to the diversity of its members, the jihadist movement must depend for its success on its ability to bind individuals with various backgrounds and convictions. The jihadist message centering on martyrdom is exceptionally suitable for this task. It offers young men such as Abu al-Hasan a message that is relevant in every situation and can attract them as they sit behind their computers. It answers their quest for self-realization and provides them with guidelines for shaping their own lives, answering a modern demand for which people must increasingly themselves be responsible. It recognizes their perceived humiliation and, moreover, it shows them a way out. It demonstrates that they can be part of a powerful community and gives them a sense of empowerment—a feeling that they together can handle this situation and will be victorious in the end, whether in this life or in the next.

"Our words remain dead, waxen dolls, void of life, frozen, until we die in their cause, then they become alive and dwell amongst the living." This statement, first uttered by Sayyid Qutb and nowadays frequently returning in al-Sahab's martyrdom videos, powerfully illustrates the communicative force of martyrdom. Only after demonstrating your willingness to die for your words will they make an impact. And in these days, when streams of information from numerous media are struggling to find their way into people's minds, these words written in blood attract attention. "Who do we take seriously?" writes Don DeLillo in *Mao II*. "Only the lethal believer, the person who kills and dies for faith."[29]

Abu al-Hasan was one of the many "lethal believers" of the past decade, and the reception of his last words on the Internet in July 2008 showed that he indeed attracted attention. Approximately one year earlier, the Egyptian commander had died in a suicide attack. This attack in an Afghan province might conceivably have been part of al-Qaeda's strategy to advance toward the establishment of an Islamic caliphate. But certainly it was "words," too, saying something to the audience that, directly or indirectly, witnessed the attack. As an expressive practice, suicide attacks draw attention to the perpetrators' belief system and, because of their contested and ritualized character, provide the audience insights into central themes of their community. They express the perceived global war and the humiliating situation of the umma but also show the power of ordinary men to make a difference. In martyrdom videos, this violence is "reperformed" by means of footage, simultanions, or stories. Meanwhile, the martyr is embedded in the grand narrative about a global war and the decisive role of the mujahidun in it. In this manner, violence and the media reinforce each other: While the narratives amplify and reconstruct the meaning of the attacks, the violent actions actualize and dramatize these narratives and self-representations.

Suicide attacks and martyrdom videos are not only expressions of the jihadist community, they also play a role in its construction and reinforcement. The message of martyrdom is able to attract and unite individuals from all over the world and enable them to identify with one another. They can feel themselves to be members of this community that claims to follow in the footsteps of the Prophet and his companions, but in the meantime perfectly suits their globalized and individualized attitudes and beliefs. Like other contemporary religious movements, jihadism binds individuals with diverse backgrounds not with rigid dogmas, but by offering a coherent and comprehensible worldview that responds to people's search for spirituality and self-fulfillment, while leaving space for diversity. It does not provide clear-cut creeds to the young men behind their screens, but rather empowers them and therefore the jihadist community.

The ultimate medium for this message are men who have gone through this process themselves. It is martyrs like Abu al-Hasan who, identified with this community, personally experience its humiliation, initiate a search for liberation and truth, and finally find empowerment in the message of martyrdom, to such an extent that they are thrilled to express this message in both words and deeds.

PART V

Religious Language and Nationalism

CHAPTER 21

Militant Religiopolitical Rhetoric

How Abraham Kuyper Mobilized His Constituency

Arie L. Molendijk

Militant and deceitful political rhetoric, of course, is always with us. Demagogues use all possible means to obtain their goals. Propaganda presents the image of reality that serves the needs of the often authoritarian rulers. If our news is to be trusted, some 70 percent of the Russians presently believe that the United States started World War I. But democratic regimes may also construct their own reality. The most famous recent example is Sadam Hussein's alleged possession of weapons of mass destruction, which were the pretext the Bush government used to start the Iraq War. Perhaps the even more horrific fact is that the Bush administration felt perfectly justified in doing so. A senior adviser to Bush (probably Karl Rove) explains this imperial view as follows: "[Our critics live] in what we [in the White House] call the reality-based community, . . . those who believe that solutions emerge from your judicious study of discernible reality. That is not the way the world works anymore. We're an empire now, and when we act, we create our own reality. And while you are studying that reality—judiciously, as you will—we'll act again, creating other new realities, which you can study too, and that's how things will sort out. We're history's actors . . . and you, all of you, will be left to just study what we do."[1] The condescending arrogance of these words displays the contempt for what outsiders may see as "real"—a reality that in this view is only something to be manipulated by those in power.

In the modern history of the Netherlands the Christian politician Abraham Kuyper was one of the greatest orators. He used his extraordinary gifts not to start a war, but to mobilize his followers in a way that changed the Dutch political landscape dramatically. His rhetoric of militant antagonism was remarkably successful in a country that was and still is to a certain extent known for its conciliatory way of government and politics. To some readers it may come as a surprise that such fierce rhetoric and "shameless" (as some would say) exploitation of the sentiments of his constituency could be so effective.

Abraham Kuyper (1837–1920) was the first modern mass politician in Dutch history; his speeches captured large crowds. In the Netherlands his renown is comparable to that of William Gladstone in England. Kuyper is probably the most influential Dutch politician and theologian of the modern era. His strong engagement in church affairs led to a decisive break in Dutch Protestantism, which was healed only recently by the reunification of the churches that were split in the Doleantie of 1892. Kuyper founded his own newspaper, his own neo-Calvinist Free University in Amsterdam, and the first modern political party in the Netherlands. He was a long-time member of Parliament, and from 1901 until 1905 he was prime minister. The segmented social structures, based on differences in religion and worldview, that constituted "pillarized" Dutch society were to a large extent determined by Kuyper.[2] His polarizing way of acting was entirely new in Dutch politics and was an affront to the old elites, who still clung to the ideals of a consensual and homogeneous state and an inclusive Protestant people's church.[3]

Even when Kuyper's style and rhetoric are criticized, the fact that he was a great orator is never really called into question.[4] On the occasion of the twenty-fifth anniversary of the journal *De Standaard* (*The Measure*), which Kuyper founded in 1872, his colleague, the Reformed theologian Herman Bavinck stated: "And that man did not *write* to us on paper, he *spoke* to us and reached out through that word to our understanding and will, our heart and conscience, not satisfied until he knew what he had in us."[5] Although outsiders sometimes had difficulties in appreciating Kuyper's rhetoric, they were nevertheless impressed. Albert Venn Dicey, then Vinerian Professor of English Law at Oxford University, for instance, in a letter to his wife described the ceremony during which he and Kuyper received honorary degrees at Princeton University in 1898. Both were asked, he wrote, to say a few words.

> This led to the most remarkable speech I have heard for a long time. Kuyper spoke. He looked like a Dutchman of the seventeenth century. He spoke slowly and solemnly. His English was impressive, with here and there a Dutch idiom. He told us he was a Calvinist; that he had been persecuted by the anti-Calvinists—this itself sounded like the language of another age. All the good in America had its root in Calvinism, which was as much a legal and an ethical as a religious creed. The Continental States had sympathized with Spain. Not so the Dutch Calvinists. "We have not forgotten our contest with Spanish tyranny; we fought it for a hundred years. In six weeks you have given Spanish power its *coup de grace*, but neither England nor the U.S. would have been free but for Dutch heroism. Spain has in all countries and in all ages been a curse to the world. The just shall rejoice when he seeth the vengeance." This was the tone of the whole speech. There was not a word of flattery to America.

One felt as if the seventeenth century had visibly arisen upon us to give the last curse to Spain.[6]

Dicey's vivid sketch conveys not only a fine impression of Kuyper's performance but also a mixture of admiration and bewilderment concerning Kuyper's world of thought, in which the seventeenth-century Dutch resistance to the Spanish occupation and the way Dutch Calvinism had paved the way for the victory of freedom in the world were seen as realities that pertained immediately to the actual political situation at the end of the nineteenth century.

Kuyper did not hesitate to put forward strong, even outrageous (from the point of view of outsiders), claims and to use vivid and melodramatic images to enhance his case. A good example of this technique can be found in the Stone Lectures that he delivered at Princeton Theological Seminary in 1898. In the fourth lecture he explains how Calvinism had contributed to the rise of science, and he turns to one "glorious page" from its history to prove this fact:

The page from the history of Calvinism, or let us rather say of mankind, matchless in its beauty, to which I refer, is the siege of Leyden, more than three hundred years ago. This siege of Leyden was in fact a struggle between Alva and Prince William about the future course of the history of the world; and the result was that in the end Alva had to withdraw, and that William the Silent was enabled to unfurl the banner of liberty over Europe. Leyden, defended almost exclusively by its own citizens, fought against the best troops of what was looked upon at that time as the finest army in the world. Three months after the commencement of the siege, the supply of food became exhausted. A fearful famine began to rage. The apparently doomed citizens managed to live on dogs and rats. This black famine was soon followed by the black death or the plague, which carried off a third part of the inhabitants. . . . They patiently waited for the coming of the Prince of Orange, to raise the siege, . . . but . . . the prince had to wait for God. The dikes of the province of Holland had been cut through; the country surrounding Leyden was flooded; a fleet lay ready to hasten to Leyden's aid; but the wind drove the water back, preventing the fleet from passing the shallow pools. God tried his people sorely. At last, however, on the first of October, the wind turned towards the West, and, forcing the waters upward, enabled the fleet to reach the beleaguered city. Then the Spaniards fled in haste to escape the rising tide. On the 3rd of October the fleet entered the port of Leyden, and the siege being raised, Holland and Europe were saved. The population, all but starved to death, could scarcely drag themselves along, yet all to a man, limped as well as they could to the house of prayer. There all fell on their knees and gave thanks to God. But when they tried to utter their gratitude in psalms of praise, they were almost voiceless, for there was no strength left in them, and the tones of their song died away in grateful sobbing and weeping.[7]

This extensive quotation not only demonstrates the huge claims that were made by Kuyper ("the history of Calvinism, or let us rather say of mankind") but also shows the dramatic devices that he deployed to tell this tear-jerking history, which could have been taken from a child's adventure book. Although a strong story even for Kuyper, it illustrates his typical use of hyperbole, which he employed so often that one is sometimes tempted to think that his words are not meant as hyperbole at all. The story also shows the intimate connection that existed for Kuyper between Dutch military, political, and religious history, with Calvinism being the backbone of Dutch resistance against the Catholic Spanish oppressor. Identities are mostly defined by Kuyper in opposition to outsiders who threaten "us."

I will look at Kuyper's rhetoric not only in terms of the formal devices, such as hyperbole, that he employs to highlight his points, but I will also focus on the images, metaphors, and stories that he uses—in sum, on his "mythopoetics." This term is used by John Bolt, who analyzes Kuyper's public theology from a rhetorical and mythopoetic perspective, "turning attention away from seeing him *solely* through the more customary lens of philosophical and theological *ideas*."[8] Bolt claims that Kuyper "effectively captured the political *imagination* of the Dutch *Gereformeerde volk* with powerful rhetoric, well-chosen biblical images, and national mythology."[9] This seems to me to be a very fruitful approach. Another study that has been important for my own discussion is Jacobus van Weringh's very critical book on Kuyper's view of society.[10] To some degree it can be argued that he is too critical (he pictures Kuyper as a near-totalitarian dictator), but he rightly draws attention to the antagonistic way in which Kuyper cast his opponents, using military and pugilistic metaphors to show his followers that no compromise would be allowed and that a fierce battle had to be fought. The implications of this "style" should not be underestimated.

Kuyper and the Arts

To understand Kuyper's rhetoric, it is helpful first to have a glance at his view of art and the artist. From his early years on, art played a major role in his life. In one of his autobiographical texts—*Confidentially* (1873)—he described how he was moved by the English novel *The Heir of Redclyffe*, by Charlotte Yonge, which he had been given by his fiancée. The tale brings together "two diametrically opposed characters," the strong, haughty Philip de Morville and the sensitive, pious, and "rather unattractive" Guy. Slowly, their roles are reversed, "so that the once so extraordinary Philip is disclosed in all his vanity and inner emptiness while Guy excels in a true greatness and inner strength." First, Kuyper thought he felt a purely aesthetic sentiment, but then he realized that he was experiencing more than that. Kuyper remembers his overwhelming emotion when Philip repented and "fell to his knees before the poor Guy": "Oh, at that moment it seemed as if in the crushed Philip my own heart was devastated, as if each of his words of self-condemnation cut through my soul as a judgment on my own ambitions and character," and he envied "the fortunate repentant."[11] Reading *The Heir of Redclyffe* was the first stage in Kuyper's conversion history, as he tells it in *Confidentially*. Even if most scholars would not see self-critique, let alone self-condemnation, as a key element in Kuyper's life, he clearly had a capacity to be moved and transformed by such stories.

He must have read quite a lot of literature, since his speeches are full of quotes from Romantic poets. On one occasion he interprets—almost blasphemously, as he himself says—Torquato Tasso's love for Leonore von Este, the illustrious daughter of his king, as evoked by Goethe, as a longing for "a manifestation of his ideal in the flesh."[12] Art represents for Kuyper a sense of vividness and a longing for the real. In cold and irreligious times "the warmth of devotion to art has kept alive many higher aspirations of the soul."[13] Art sides with religion against intellectualism. One of Kuyper's main objections to theological modernism was that it is intellectual and out of touch with the piety of ordinary people. Intellectual art is no art, according to him, and he energetically claims that art is no "fringe that is attached to the garment, and no amusement that is added to life."[14] Art represents a sphere in its own right. In the Stone Lectures Kuyper discerns four spheres (the intellectual, ethical, religious, and aesthetic) and emphatically states, in a vitalist fashion: "Art . . . is no side-shoot on a principal branch, but an independent branch that grows from the trunk of our life itself, even though it is far more nearly allied to Religion than to our thinking or to our ethical being."[15]

It is evident that Kuyper inclined toward a Romantic view of art and the artist, valuing the spontaneity of artistic expression and stressing the role of genius. In his speech on "our instinctive life" he claims that all "genuine artistic expression arises spontaneously from the soul of the artist." Art schools and training may have their place, but they have at most a secondary importance: "Art can be ennobled by reflection, but art born of reflection is a monstrosity."[16] In this context Kuyper, interestingly, also presents his ideas of what a gifted orator whose power is rooted in the instinctive can achieve:

Simply compare the genuinely gifted public speaker with one who publicly reads what he has to say from a manuscript. The latter, after quiet reflection, has entrusted his thoughts to paper, line by line, and now communicates line upon line to the ears of his listeners, as if by telephone. But the really eloquent man, the born public speaker, takes up his position before the gathering, feels the contact between his spirit and that of his audience, and opens the tap. Almost automatically the words begin to flow, the thoughts leap out, the images frolic—psychological art in action. This is even more true of the *genius*. He does not plod and pick away at things; he does not split hairs or prime the pump, but senses within himself a fountain ready to flow. By spiritual X-ray vision he sees through doors and walls and virtually without effort grasps the pearl for which others grope in vain.[17]

A mechanical recitation is clearly not Kuyper's ideal of good rhetoric. The eloquent speaker is able to sense or intuit his audience and communicates directly with them, whereas the real genius seems to have almost magical qualities ("X-ray vision") and is able to come into contact with an inner source that starts to flow. Evidently, the rhetorical gift is presented here as purely intuitive, as being able to connect to the inner selves of the audience and thus succeed in moving them. Such gifts and talents are not equally distributed among people, and, in consequence, Kuyper did not shy away from elitism and the idea of strong leadership, a leader being to some extent an artist in his own right. In the next section we will have a closer look at one particular occasion that presents a powerful example of Kuyper's capacity for oratory.

Rhetorical Performance

On the evening of April 1, 1897, some five thousand men and women gathered in the Amsterdam Palace of Popular Industry to celebrate the twenty-fifth anniversary of Abraham Kuyper's editorship of the daily *De Standaard*. A commemorative volume documents the preparations, the history of the newspaper, the evening itself (including festive speeches by Herman Bavinck and Kuyper), and over two hundred pages, amounting to more than two-thirds of the book, that give "impressions" of the event from the Dutch press, photographs of Kuyper, and a final word of thanks by Kuyper as it was printed in the next-day edition of *De Standaard*.[18] After Bavinck's speech, the assembly sang a well-known hymn composed by Isaac da Costa, which expressed the feelings of the orator and the assembled guests rather well:

> They shall not get it,
> Our old Netherlands!
> Through all the trials [of the just]
> It remains our father's trust [*Gods en der Vadren pand*].

> They shall not get it,
> The gods of this age!
> God has not liberated it for us,
> To provide a legacy for *them*.[19]

The launching of the journal on April 1, 1872, again clearly linked Kuyper's neo-Calvinist movement to Dutch national history, as it was the three-hundredth anniversary of the Sea Beggars' capture of the port of Den Briel, another key event in the Dutch struggle against the Spaniards. And it is evident that according to Kuyper the Dutch are still struggling against the spirit of the times, against non-Calvinists who falsely claim God for their cause.

After the handing over of a gift and the singing of the first hymn of the national anthem, "Dr Kuyper" took the stand "amidst breathless silence" and addressed the crowd in the typical epithet "men, brethren" (*mannenbroeders*). He quoted Da Costa's verse to the effect that the sweet wine of adoration makes man drunk, saying that it takes a lot of self-restraint to remain sober when surrounded by so much loyalty and love. In a somewhat tongue-in-cheek way, he recalled the rumor of Kuyper idolatry, and, although he had not noticed this phenomenon "among you," he confessed that he had had some fears concerning this evening. As soon as he had seen the program, however, he was convinced that no key would be struck in honor of a human being, but that the whole event was to thank and honor God. Indeed, Calvinists are all instruments in the hand of God, and he thanked the men and women, the elderly and the youth, who supported this cause.

Newspapers are by no means an invention of evil, Kuyper claimed, but are instruments that fulfill at least two tasks. They provide the necessary information in a fast way, and—equally or even more important—they are a good instrument for bringing about unity, especially nowadays, as the spirit of individualism is growing stronger. *De Standaard* (like newspapers in general) has created what Kuyper preferred to call "the return to the standpoint of the ancient prophets."[20] Rephrasing things, suggesting in a somewhat esoteric way that "we Calvinists" have our own common bond, is one of Kuyper's many rhetorical devices. *De Standaard* provides guidance and creates a community of opinion. In Kuyper's view, however, this did not mean that he steers or manipulates readers. On the contrary, as was already suggested in the image of the orator who connects easily to the spirit of his listeners, the content of the newspaper is inspired by the people. Kuyper strongly rejected the claim that his readers are puppets on a string. To those who believe such fairy tales, he said: "Try it yourselves, to make puppets out of our Calvinists!" Whereupon, according to a report, there was "loud laughter."[21] Later in the speech Kuyper stated that if he was able to achieve something, it was because he was trying to voice the feelings and convictions of his audience, and he was able to succeed "because *your* life was *my* life and one breathing of the soul was common to us both."[22] This suggestion of an almost mystical unity between Kuyper and his followers, which downplayed his own role to the utter minimum, was followed by long applause.

This must have been the oratorical high point of the speech. Kuyper was very well aware of recent insights into the psychology of the masses (he refers to the work of Gustave le Bon),[23] and he must have known that to suggest that the crowd and he were one and that he only voiced their intimate feelings and thoughts could feed their sense of identification when applauding him as leader. The rhetorical logic erases the boundaries between speaker and audience and permits him—in the very sentence that followed this outburst of enthusiasm—to ask, "What did this newspaper mean for *me*?"[24] It turned out to be not more than a horse that he used to reach his goal. He wanted to make "my whole people and fatherland happy again" by "seducing" them back to the "ordinances of God."[25] Then he started to tell the story of his own life, which turned out to be the story of the rise of the Dutch neo-Calvinists. Making politics personal and using one's own biography politically is not an invention of the twentieth century.

It would be interesting to follow the track of his life story in this speech and to compare it with other of his autobiographical narratives, but here I will highlight only a few points. Basically, it is the story of a self-willed, perhaps somewhat lonely child (against the will of his father he read newspapers at the age of ten), who, after quite a few turns, matured to become the leader of the orthodox Protestants in the Netherlands. An approved way to obtain credibility is to establish lineage to respectable forebears, like the well-known conservative Christian poets Willem Bilderdijk and Isaac da Costa, and, above all, the politician and historian Guillaume Groen van Prinsterer, who is famous for his trenchant critique of the ideas of the French Revolution. This critique was a keystone of Kuyper's own worldview and a reason that his movement—including the political party he founded—was termed "antirevolutionary." Before moving to Utrecht in 1869, Kuyper claimed to have been enlightened by the simple, pious people of his first parish in Beesd. In Utrecht he hoped to defend the stronghold of the Dutch Jerusalem, supported by fellow orthodox companions. But he found only officers (professors and ministers) and soldiers who distrusted one another; there was a complete lack of unity. This was not an option for an army that saw itself as "the phalanx of the living God."[26] Kuyper tried to bring these men together on the basis of Holy Scripture, but—leaving aside a few exceptions—this was *impossible* (emphasized in the original).

This was a turning point in his life, after which, "perhaps a bit over-bold," he became a *franctireur* (literally, a "freeshooting" member of a militia) and waged the battle at his own risk. Kuyper changed tactics and was no longer on the defensive (no apologetics any longer), but decided to attack. He started throwing "hand-grenade after hand-grenade," first at modern theologians and then at modern life itself as it appears in liberalism and conservatism alike.[27] "Now I was at the point where Luther was when he exclaimed: 'Das Wort sie sollen lassen stehen [The Word it shall stand forever].'"[28] But something was lacking: From Germany the "termite of false philosophy" had crept across "our borders to undermine our theology." Even if the church had remained Christian, life itself had become dechristianized. But happily the spirit of Calvin was still alive in the Netherlands, and he taught that the ordinances of God concern not only religious life but human life as such. The military metaphors and the comparison with no lesser a figure than Luther made clear that the fight was by no means easy and that it would take someone of character and determination to achieve progress.

The comparison with key figures in the history of Dutch orthodox pietism (the so-called Réveil, which may be compared to the English Awakening and the American Great Awakenings), such as Bilderdijk, Da Costa, and Groen, makes two things clear: first, that

Kuyper could sow where these men had plowed, and second—even more important—that they had not succeeded in building a strong organization to establish their noble goals. Kuyper emphasized how difficult it had been for him: Many former companions were not there that evening (leaving it unclear whether they had died or "left" him), and he himself was inclined to be sympathetic toward other people. Therefore, it had been good to be surrounded by like-minded people, who helped steer the right course, for even the warmest sympathy is not enough to achieve lasting, stable cooperation if there is not enough adhesion to principles. If necessary, principles must prevail over friendship.[29] Referring to the absolute authority of God, Kuyper claimed that even the smallest deviation from the straight could be fatal. Those who have deviated are invited to assemble "under the one banner for the honor of God and the well-being of His people."[30]

At the end of his speech, Kuyper pondered the possibility of his own death (he was fifty-seven at the time) and gave the audience the double reassurance that his powers were not yet exhausted and that if he should die, the furrows were so deeply plowed and the seeds so good that God would not allow this work to be undone. The struggle may still be fierce, but it is important that (in my words) "we, the people," are united under one banner. Kuyper may have sung the praises of diversity and liberty on other occasions, but this does not mean that there could be various paths leading to the same goal. The implication is that the Anti-Revolutionary Party must stand united around their leader, whose authority is linked to that of God Almighty. Kuyper finished with a text of Da Costa, which he varied for his own purpose:

> My life is ruled by but one passion,
> One higher urge drives [my] will and soul.
> May breath fail me before I ever
> allow that sacred urge to fall.
> 'Tis to affirm God's holy statutes
> In church and state, in home and school,
> despite the world's strong remonstrations,
> to bless our people with His rule.
> 'Tis to engrave God's holy order
> heard in Creation and the Word,
> upon the nation's public conscience,
> till God is once again its Lord.[31]

Confronted with worldly resistance, the Dutch people must again bend their will to God and his ordinances. This is the powerful, unifying language of a leader who has no intention—at least not at the moment—to yield. Notwithstanding Kuyper's outspoken claim to give a voice to the people that resounds with them, the assembly could not miss the—somewhat more hidden—message that he is the man who will ultimately determine the future course. Indeed, this impressive speech shows Kuyper to be an eminently political man, whose main concern was to unite his party under the "ordinances" (another new word introduced by him) of the rulership of God that Kuyper was so eager to explain to his people.

Rhetorical Practice and Strategy

How did his contemporaries perceive and characterize Kuyper's rhetorical style? I will give two examples, both by men who were at least sympathetic to Kuyper. The first is Ph. J. Hoedemaker's review of Kuyper's attack on theological modernism. Hoedemaker wrote that Kuyper had brought out a whole armory of weapons to make his case and had cleared out the musty atmosphere of midcentury Dutch theology and let the cold, fresh morning air come in. Although Hoedemaker (a more irenic person than Kuyper, who would not follow him in his separatist inclinations) welcomed this, he also hoped that in the near future the cold would be somewhat tempered by the warmth of the rising sun.[32] An even more precise characterization is given by Herman Bavinck in his eulogy at the celebration of the twenty-fifth anniversary of De Standaard. Bavinck claimed that Kuyper had surpassed Bilderdijk, Da Costa, and Groen in "vividness of representation, richness of imaginary, in dramatic action, in the power to stir and carry along [the reader]." "[Kuyper's language] is built up of sentences that are lightly armed and approach the foe deftly and movingly, joyfully and courageously, with song and music, either to attack or defend, advancing or retreating, but always alert, preferring to be found in the heat of the battle." Bavinck's statement that Calvinists had a good fighting spirit was met with applause, and the metaphors of struggle and war are abundant in his speech. But in the same vein as Hoedemaker, he also said, "I do not want to deny that in the heat of battle the blows on occasion fell too sharply and that in the haze of gunpowder a clear distinction between friend and foe was not always made."[33] This remark was included in Bavinck's speech as merely counterpoint to stating how well Kuyper had struggled to defend the holy principles of Calvinism.

Kuyper made frequent use of military metaphors to energize his constituency. His is not the language of compromise and dialogue but of struggle and survival. Van Weringh has convincingly argued that Kuyper conceived of the Calvinist movement and its organizations as a hierarchically organized army.[34] The existence of an army makes sense only if there is an enemy who threatens "us."[35] Kuyper constructs the outside world (as we would say nowadays) as a "hostile other." Therefore, "we" must avoid contact with outsiders, *even if they are friends or relatives.*[36] Boundaries must be drawn, and it comes as no surprise that Kuyper wrote one of his fiercest attacks against the "blurring of boundaries."[37] In this speech against "pantheism" (a term that for him stands for all the evils of modern thought), Kuyper took a shortcut by saying that God created the boundaries. "He himself is the ultimate boundary for all his creation, and to erase boundaries is virtually the same as erasing the idea of God."[38] The enemy (the outside world) is seen as a "cancer" or a "poison" that threatens our organism. There is only one remedy, and that is to unite in holy comradeship, to have confidence in one's own cause and to be enthusiastic "for the colors of your own glorious flag which redoubles the strength of any army."[39]

Preparing his troops to attack, Kuyper admitted that the struggle would require "frightening sacrifices." To provide "a feel" of this really powerful rhetoric, let me give a quotation, which ends with one of Kuyper's most famous sayings:

> [This approach] forces you to break with much that is attractive. It frequently cuts off fascinating contact with some of the nobler pagans. You pay a heavy price for it. Much worse, if you are firm and act boldly, it will bring down on you all kinds of family grief and make it very hard to find a lifelong post for yourself and your children. But with Scriptures before me I say: This sacrifice *must* be made. "Whoever loves father or mother more than me is not worthy of me" [Matt. 10:37]. Christ did not come to bring peace in a pantheistic sense but to bring division, that is, *to draw a line that no one can expunge* between those who seize the hem of his garment and those who reject him.[40]

Although Kuyper rejected the idea that this should have anything to do with self-isolation, all the sacrifices that must be made in the spheres of relationships and work suggest the contrary. How could you be friendly with your archenemies?

Given the abounding dangers, "Radical determination must be insisted upon. Half-measures cannot guarantee the desired results."[41] Boundaries must be enforced. Therefore, we need *principles*. Kuyper saw world history as a struggle between worldviews, the main battle being at the moment that between modernism (pantheism) and Calvinism (the highest form of Christianity).[42] Ultimately, this is a struggle between principles, as these are the basis of unified worldviews (or systems of thought). Although Kuyper acknowledged a plurality of (opposing) worldviews, he did not like plurality within a particular worldview, and certainly not in his own party. Within an army this is not a good idea. According to Van Weringh, conflicts emerged as soon as the hierarchical structure of these Calvinist organizations was questioned. Diverging opinions were perceived as disobedience. Van Weringh gives strong examples, for instance, the "disobedience" of a clergyman who opposed what Kuyper had published on the Great War (condoning Germany's occupation of Belgium). Kuyper said this minister was an officer calling his men to denounce their general. In his view this was a breach in martial law, an "offense" (*delict*) that had to be investigated as soon as possible.[43]

Kuyper believed in strong organizations. He did not like pietism and Methodism, because of what he saw as subjectivistic, individualistic, and quietistic tendencies. For him, Scripture, dogma, confession, and principles mattered more than personal religious experience. The fact that organizations and institutions such as churches and political parties are considered to be based on voluntary participation does not necessarily imply that they are organized in a democratic way. In his one-sided but insightful book, Van Weringh sketches Kuyper as an antidemocrat, mainly because of his rejection of the principle of the sovereignty of the people.[44] Authority is ultimately based on God and has to be accepted. Kuyper even claimed that one human being has the right to dominate another one: "There is no equality of persons. There are weak, narrow-minded persons, with no broader expanse of wings than a common sparrow, but there are also broad, imposing characters, with the wingspan of the eagle. Among the last you will find a few of royal grandeur, and these rule in their own sphere, even if people draw back from them or thwart them, usually waxing all the stronger the more they are opposed."[45]

Kuyper's anti-egalitarianism, his conception of life as an organism, and his appreciative view of the struggle for life suggest that he was more or less a social Darwinist, a view of him held by Van Weringh. Indeed, it is clear that Kuyper saw himself as a leader who represents the head of the organism and sets out the course for his followers. Notwithstanding all this, Kuyper could be rather critical of such ideas:

> Since Bismarck introduced it into higher politics, the maxim of the right of the stronger has found almost universal acceptance. . . . And the end can only be that once more the sound principles of democracy will be banished, to make room this time not for a new aristrocracy of nobler birth and higher ideals, but for the coarse and overbearing *kratistocracy* of a brutal money-power. . . . And while Christ in divine compassion showed heart-winning sympathy with the weak, modern life in this respect also takes the opposite ground, that the weak must be supplanted by the strong.[46]

The question if and to what extent Kuyper's thinking can be described as social Darwinist is not easy to answer and would require a more extensive investigation than can be conducted in these pages. The answer will also depend on one's understanding of social Darwinism and the interpretation of seemingly conflicting texts. In his address on evolution, for instance, Kuyper opposed not only Darwin's idea of the origin of man but also the celebration of power as such. "Over against Nietzsche's Evolution-law that the stronger must tread upon the weaker we cling to the Christ of God who seeks the lost and has mercy on the weak."[47] Yet Kuyper was very conscious of the fact that unity was necessary to get power and to stay in power. He liked organic metaphors that showed this unity growing from life itself, and he also claimed that no rank or class should dominate the process. Yet a central committee has to provide leadership, and at crucial moments (such as campaigns) there must be agreement. Looking at Kuyper's political career, it is evident that he did not shy away from conflicts and tried to impose his will to a degree that was repugnant to many of his close collaborators.[48]

Nevertheless, Kuyper was the undisputed leader of the Dutch Calvinist movement and energized crowds with his stump speeches. On one occasion, he brilliantly described how unity was established by joint meetings and speeches:

For a party to be able to carry its platform forward energetically, it needs above all to be powerfully conscious of its unity. It must have the means—as *the psychology of the crowd* demands—to convert sober realism into enthusiasm, cool calculation into holy passion. That is the purpose served by our local meetings and especially our party convention. . . . Someone who joins the battle in an isolated village, with only a couple of sympathizers, easily feels weak, dejected, and abandoned. But bring the solitaries out of their hideouts and to a great gathering. Unite not just the fashionable and high class but representatives of all ranks, the notables along with the simple, the wise alongside the learned, the small and the great, and set them all aglow with the sense that they are *in fact* a mirror image of the whole country. Then faint-heartedness gives way to a sense of power. Good cheer, real animation, and high spirits arise. And if the circle swells (as among us) into a group of two thousand, their gathering amidst the tensions of an election will leave so fundamental and overwhelming an impression that the delegates return home not just encouraged but prepared to make any sacrifice, and exuding their enthusiasm to all who stayed at home.[49]

In sum, rhetoric was an integral part of the work of the mass politician Abraham Kuyper. By way of modern media such as stump speeches, brochures, and journals, he mobilized people and built a homogeneous group. He preferred energizing, military metaphors of struggle against mighty opponents, who were depicted in the bleakest way, and he liked to tell almost mythic stories—molded by a biblical imaginary—of Dutch history, showing how a small nation could resist a big empire, just as David had defeated Goliath. Kuyper's religiopolitical rhetoric was extremely succesful in mobilizing his constituency.

A Critical Appraisal

Kuyper understood the psychology of the masses (*Massenpsychologie*) and knew how to attune to the masses and manipulate them. The heritage of Le Bon's influential book is controversial, to say the least. It is claimed that not only Lenin, Mussolini, and Hitler but also Roosevelt, de Gaulle, and Herzl admired parts of it. The mechanisms of attunement that Kuyper describes may strike many of us—after the experiences of the twentieth century—as a bit scary. But that does not make them less real, of course. Kuyper had a keen sense of the instinctive and subconscious mechanisms that play an important part in modern politics, and he made use of these. There is, however, a danger in downplaying the rational aspect of politics and persuasion. If politics is primarily seen in terms of a life-and-death struggle, then one has to defy "the enemy," and compromise is undesirable. In my view it cannot be denied that Kuyper's rhetoric contained—to say the least—nasty elements of exclusion and of vilifying opponents. In practice (although this would require more investigation), Kuyper must often have been more conciliatory, in view of the political results he achieved: for instance, collaborating with the Dutch Catholic party. Yet the whole drift of his rhetoric is extremely militant, decrying "opponents" in the harshest terms. He constantly suggests that the enemy is everywhere and that "we" must be prepared for any sacrifice to defend our holiest principles.

The military metaphors are undergirded by religious language. To erase boundaries is to erase God, or, to give another famous example: "There is not a square inch in the whole domain of our human existence over which Christ, who is Sovereign over *all*, does not cry: 'Mine.'"[50] These huge claims led to an extremely antagonistic style. To his credit, one might say, Kuyper was very clear in this respect and consequently constructed the outside world as the "hostile other." Contact with outsiders must be avoided, even if they are friends or relatives.[51] Principles are more important than friendship. Kuyper's world of thought has a rather systemic character, in which persons seem to play a subordinate role in relation to the higher organization and its goals, which can only be reached by determination and sacrifice. By this dualistic rhetoric and by relating political goals to religious principles almost everything can be of decisive importance. As Kuyper said, even the smallest deviation from the straight can be fatal. Confronted with overwhelming dangers, we can only do one thing, and that is defend ourselves against those who threaten our life, by which is meant "those who disagree with our principles." (His opponents were not actually attacking and trying to kill Kuyper and his followers.) In a situation of war there is no room for difference of opinion: We must stand united around our leader.

Looking at recent Dutch history (e.g., the period of pillarization), we must discriminate clearly between militant speech and actual war. Kuyper, of course, used military imagery not to go to war but to mobilize his followers. This a key difference between a superpower like the United States and a small country like the Netherlands. Kuyper could use such fierce language, as there was no real threat that it would lead to an armed conflict. The militant rhetoric was primarily meant for internal use, whereas the emerging structures of pillarization could function only as long as the "leaders" of the various pillars were on speaking terms and their authority was accepted by their constituencies. Yet Kuyper steered his own course, fought again and again with people who once were his friends, and was not inclined to tolerate opposition.[52] His rhetoric was not only "rhetoric" but determined his politics to a great extent.[53] Kuyper's way of acting and speaking constituted a powerful blend of religiopolitical history, militant metaphors, autobiographical narrative, and determinative action. His rhetoric was a powerful instrument to shape his party and to energize his followers. The militant hyperbole made them feel important and contributed to the emancipation of ordinary people, who were convinced that their contribution really mattered. In this way the neo-Calvinist community and organizations (political party, newspapers, schools and university, unions, sporting clubs, and so on) could emerge.

CHAPTER 22

Thinking through Religious Nationalism

Roger Friedland and Kenneth B. Moss

Modernity has traditionally been understood as a phenomenon of disenchantment and secularization in which religion—absolute, metaphysical, irrational—was supposed to wane and to retreat into the heart of the believer, becoming a private matter, a discretionary source of ethics, a salve for existential anxieties, an answer to meaninglessness. Today we live in a world in which the divine is not only a resurgent source of individual identity and meaning but also a basis for making claims in the public sphere. And because our political world remains a world of nation-states, claims made in the name of the divine involve some sort of claim about the nation as a form of identity and the nation-state as the ground of bounded societies and sovereignties.

But what sort of claims about the nation-state does "religion" make? A number of voices in the public sphere easily pair "religion" and "nationalism" as compatible and mutually reinforcing passions. In recent years such pairing has focused on Islam, whether in Iran, Turkey, or Palestine, but similar claims were heard around the time of the Balkan wars and the Serbian and Croatian violence at the beginning of the 1990s and can also be heard applied to religio-political mobilizations by religious Jews in Israel or by Hindu nationalists in India.

Within academic circles the question is formulated with considerably less certainty and more care, but a growing number of scholars in diverse fields—in particular history, sociology, and political science—have become open to the idea that modernity may admit (and may long have admitted) a productive connection or intertwining of religion and nationalism. Consequently, there is a rapidly growing body of empirical work on particular intersections between religion and nationalism in one or another historical or contemporary locality.

However, in the realm of political and social theory, which has critically revisited both the categories of religion and the secular, there is very little basis for understanding these connections between religion and nationalism. Indeed, some of the most theoretically sophisticated work on religion and nationalism shares the conviction that nationalism is intrinsically secular or dependent on secularism. This conviction is in evidence in diverse places: in Talal Asad's rich genealogy of the secular as a cultural formation and secularism as a doctrine, in Benedict Anderson's resonant histories of nationalism as an imaginary, and in recent work on the definition of nationalism by one of the phenomenon's foremost sociologists and theorists, Rogers Brubaker.

To begin with Asad, there is no need to rehearse here the details of Asad's critical historicization of secular European modernity. Critiquing, but also taking seriously as an effective discourse, secularism's self-image as humanity's self-emancipation from myth, Asad excavates the secular as a specific system of beliefs and practices linked to historically specific assumptions—indeed, myths—about progress, knowledge, and the human capacity for self-determination. What is relevant here is that in the process Asad posits an essential relationship between secularism and nationalism: Nationalism, he argues, "with its vision of a universe of national societies, in which individual humans live their worldly existence, requires the concept of the secular to make sense."[1] Religion and nationalism, properly understood, he suggests, are incommensurable. Religious nationalism is therefore conceptually unthinkable, at least as regards religions of revealed law, and particularly Islam in its ostensible matings with nationalism. Asad dismisses the very notion of Islamist nationalism, insisting that Islamist views are by definition incompatible with nationalism because nationalism posits the individual and the community as the source of law and values, whereas genuinely religious people insist that individuals must orient themselves to "discover" divinely given commandments and "conform to them." On this view, religion is always and necessarily a challenge to "the deep structures of secularism, including the assumptions of nationalist discourse."[2] Such a theoretical project erects a high wall between religiosity and nationalism as praxis and discursive field—or what Asad calls a "grammar of concepts."

Asad's cautions accord with assumptions that have long dominated scholarship on nationalism. Certainly the understanding of nationalism has advanced over the last two decades: Scholars have gone from treating nationhood as the expression of a natural underlying collectivity to seeing it as a contingent identity formed through nationalism itself, from being a fact of social nature to an event, or even a diffused institutional form.[3]

But one assumption central to the scholarly study of nationalism has remained largely unchanged: Nationalism is a product of secularization and an ideology particularly suited to secular needs, secular modes of thought, and secular discontents. The older nationalism scholarship between the two world wars sometimes construed nationalism as a "secular religion"—that is, as a substitute for the ostensibly dead or dying meaning systems of religion, with its own rites, transcendences, and afterlives.[4] This essentially Durkheimian sensibility remains alive and well in some quarters.[5] The work of the 1970s and 1980s that refounded the study of nationalism was less concerned with religion; it took as its central problem nationalism's persistence as against the Marxist prediction of its demise.[6] But this work, too, took it for granted that to explain nationalism's continuing appeal one had to locate it in relation to a notional secular modern subject. This generation of historians of nationalism also assumed that nationalism was a secular form and that efforts to twin it with religion were either purely instrumental or at most an oddity, a side-show to the real story.[7]

In one of the most important of those historians' accounts, Benedict Anderson's *Imagined Communities*, Anderson argues that religion was a critical historical determinant of the emergence of the nation, but through its nonreligious consequences. European confessional struggle within Christianity was essential to the vernacularization of print literacy and the collapse of sacred universality, both of which contributed to the emerging imagination of national communities. Anderson would later argue that the spatial and temporal imaginations of religions and of nationalism are essentially different. In his essay "The Goodness of Nations," he posits that nationalists and the religious have non-congruent ideas of the afterlife and different logics of temporal moral obligation. Whereas nationalists emphasize their obligations to their community's unborn descendants, such a rhetoric makes little sense within the framework of the individually centered modes of salvation and redemption central to much theology and religious practice, especially but by no means exclusively Christian and Buddhist practice. Nationalism and salvation or redemptive religions hinge on irreconcilable conceptual orders, on different ends.[8]

Scholars of nationalism have not been blind to the role of religion, pointing to the ways in which religion per se has shaped the emergence of nationalisms through state-mediated confessionalization and the provision of tropes and templates of chosenness.[9] Yet they, too, tend to assert nationalism's essential secularity. Rogers Brubaker, who was critical in pointing to the nation as an achievement in political categorization, the result of a successful struggle over classification, an event rather than a natural social state, has recently reiterated the intrinsic secularity of nationalism. He writes, "There is no compelling reason to speak of 'nationalism' unless the imagined community of the nation is widely understood as a primary focus of value, source of legitimacy, object of loyalty, and basis of identity." Thus, Brubaker argues that most forms of political Islam are not nationalist in that their primary focus is God, not the nation. "Most Islamist movements, although they work through the state, are not oriented to the nation."[10]

Brubaker goes on to insist on a conceptual divide between nationalism and religion. He writes:

> Nationalist politics—based on claims made in the name of "the nation"—remain distinct from, even as they are intertwined with, forms of religious politics that seek to transform public life not in the name of the nation, but in the name of God. To be

sure . . . nationalism and religion are often deeply intertwined; political actors may make claims both in the name of the nation and in the name of God. . . . Yet intertwining is not identity: the very metaphor of intertwining implies a distinction between the intertwined strands. . . . Languages of religion and nation, like all forms of language, can be pervasively intertwined. But even when the languages are intertwined, the fundamental ontologies and structures of justification differ.[11]

This marginalization or segregation of religion in accounts of political Islam is quite common. Jürgen Habermas has argued that radical Islam is not really about religion at all. Rather, the politicization of Islam and its turn to violence are the result of the absence of democratic mechanisms by which the "life-world" can resist the "system-world" of an increasingly intrusive capitalism and state. Radical Islam emerges where the public sphere has been impoverished, internally by gross income inequality and an authoritarian state, externally as the result of the economic subordination and impoverishment imposed on the late-comer, geographically peripheral entrants in the world capitalist order. Political Islam, Habermas contends, is just "a new and subjectively more convincing language for old political orientations," namely, Arab nationalism.[12] The analytic move is to recognize the empirical appearance of politicized Islam operating through the medium of a nation-state that it seeks to govern, but to strip it of religious meaning.

In short, some of the most compelling scholarship on religion, secularity, and nationalism converges on the view that nationalism cannot and should not be aligned too closely with religion. Nationalism and nationhood, on this view, depend on secularity to function and are incommensurable with religion and religiosity properly understood. We should never conflate or fuse, they argue, the this-worldly secular nation and an other-worldly religious deity as conceptual orders, as ontologies, or as sources of identity and value. It follows that something like religious nationalism, while there may be isolated cases, is generally unthinkable—an illusion, a misnomer, indeed, even an analytic monster.

In this essay, we will call into question the incommensurability of nationalism and religion. There are many ways in which this claim of incommensurability might be subjected to critical scrutiny.[13] With all due attention to the dangers of imputing a relationship between nationalism and religion, we would argue there is just as much danger in not allowing for the possibility of such a relationship or in prematurely closing the book on how such relationships operate in the modern past and present and how they might operate in the future. At the most basic level, we take issue with claims about incommensurability because we find so much contemporary evidence of intersection between religion and nationalism on a global scale, across every major religious tradition, that it seems to us that any account of religion and religiosity in the contemporary world must find some way to ask how nationalism and religion can be substantially co-implicated projects that admit of mutual constitution and even fusion. But we also think it is necessary to reconceptualize these formations, so that we might understand the conditions of possibility of productive relations between religion and nationalism, up to and including phenomena that we believe can and should be conceived of as religious nationalisms.

The Institutional Logic of Nationalism

Nations do not exist on the ground; they must be constructed and maintained in the mind through categories of groupness and feelings of identification. The existence of nations depends on our thinking of them as if they were groups that are really real. Nations are ontologically subjective. Their reality inheres in a shared subjective understanding, indeed, a solidarity of feeling that a people with particular attributes—common residence, language, ethnicity, culture, religion, or history—constitute a collectivity, indeed a collective subject capable of action, in other words an imagined agent to which an identity and interests are ascribed, both by themselves, as well as by their allies, competitors, and enemies. That collective agency implies—whether actually or potentially—a polity as its visible locus and medium.

Nations are political achievements. A nation, as Anderson has famously remarked, is "an imagined political community," composed of people who will never know each other but "in the minds of each, lives the image of their communion."[14] Carl Schmitt likewise points to the political formation of a people. He located the political not in the laws of the state but in the sovereign decision on the enemy who is perceived to pose an existential threat to a "way of life." For Schmitt, it is the recognition of an enemy that is the "essence" of a people's "political existence," an enmity, however, preceded by a solidarity—the "intensity of human groupings, grounded in that "way of life."[15] The groupness of a nation, in the felicitous words of Rogers Brubaker, is an "event."[16]

Both the fact and the criteria of nationhood are stakes in "classification struggles."[17] These criteria vary so dramatically, Philip Gorski concludes, that "a substantive definition of nationalism must always fail." The historical record suggests that the political processes organized through or against the state in the name of nation creates the nation.[18] "Nationhood," writes Craig Calhoun, "cannot be defined objectively, prior to political processes, on either cultural or social structural grounds. This is so, crucially, because nations are in part made by nationalism."[19]

Nationalists seek to form nations as collective subjects through collective representation, through processes of political mobilization and ordination that aim at and work through or against sovereign states, either by struggling to take over an existent state or by establishing a new one. Nationalists may seek to nationalize an existent state, what Brubaker has termed, "nationalizing nationalism," in which claims are made in the "name of a 'core nation' or nationalism, . . . understood as the legitimate 'owner' of the state, which is conceived as the state of and for the core nation."[20] Or nationalisms may counter existing states, seeking some form of recognition within the state or to break away from the state and form their own. A nation is always a potentially sovereign subject. Sovereignty is immanent in nationhood; nations without sovereignty are states-in-waiting, even if that wait may be forever, as the Armenians, Palestinians, Kurds, Tibetans, and Quebeçois can all attest.

Nationalism is the collective movement that forms, and is in turn formed by, the making or remaking of the nation-state.[21] It is a program for the co-constitution of the state and the territorially bounded population in whose name it speaks, fashioning a collective subject as it seeks to create or sustain a nation-state. Unlike empires and other premodern states, nation-states imply a collective agency, a people whose identification with that collectivity, as opposed to the sovereign, is an essential attribute of it. As the history of authoritarian nationalisms attest, the collective agent may be invoked, orchestrated into existence, and spoken for. But the inner logic of nationalism and the collective body it seeks to form imply a tendency toward persuasive participation and popular sovereignty, both of which in turn imply identification of its members with each other. As Charles Taylor writes:

> In the good old days of the Austro-Hungarian Empire, the Polish peasant in Galicia could be altogether oblivious of the Hungarian country squire, the bourgeois of Prague, or the Viennese worker, without this in the slightest threatening the stability of the state. On the contrary, this condition of things only becomes untenable when ideas about popular government start to circulate. This is the moment when subgroups that will not, or cannot, be bound together, start to demand their own states. This is the era of nationalism, of the break up of empires.[22]

The territory is both the nation's site and its collective representation, critical to the imagination of this collective subject as a bounded, singular, and integral body to which one belongs and of which one partakes.[23] The territory is the mirrored, unitary, bounded body of the collective subject.

Nationalism offers a form of representation—the joining of state, territory, and the culture of a population. It does not dictate the content of representation, the identity of the represented collective subject, or the sources of state law and legitimacy. Max Weber believed that nationalism involves a pathos, a rhetorical appeal to people's emotions, here a "pathetic pride in the power of one's own community."[24] While Weber understood that the prestige of state power and of cultural values fuse in the invocation, elicitation, and production of national group solidarity, he was acutely aware that the nation was "empirically . . . ambiguous" and that a "sociological typology would have to analyze all the individual kinds of sentiments of group membership and solidarity in their genetic conditions and in their consequences for the social action of the participants."[25] Weber did not develop such a sentimental typology. He did, however, enumerate four media by which that nationalist pathos might be accomplished: language, common custom, political memory, and religion.[26]

Religion offers more than a grounding for sentiments of solidarity; it provides an institutionally specific way to organize this modern form of collective representation—how a collectivity represents itself to itself, the symbols, signs, and practices through which it is and knows itself to be. Religion need not change the national form of collective representation, only its content, privileging a basis of identity and a criterion of judgment that cannot not be collectively chosen by the people or the state.

A proper account of nationalism as it has evolved over the past two hundred years or so appreciates that it is—or has become—an institutional form, a discursive code sited in and enacted through the state, indeed through a field of states, that draws its organizing power and legitimacy from the recognition of that form by others.[27] The content of this form—for Weber, the criterion of solidarity and identity—cannot be specified in advance. As regards religion, then, there is no reason to assume a priori that this content cannot consist of divine writ as interpreted by those who claim religious authority in any given society.

That Max Weber anticipated this insight probably has something to do with the way in which his sociological thought about religion was attuned to the tension between typological specification and empirical mutability, and indeed that typological oppositions may contain consonances that make for unstable boundaries. Thus, although Weber asserted a typological incompatibility between the nation-state and religions of salvation as value spheres, his account also uncovers inner phenomenological commonalities between them that give us reason to expect fluid and productive relations between them.

Weber writes, for example, of the opposition between what he discerned as the hidden brutality of modern erotics versus the ascetic orientation to a loving God. Yet he also argues:

> The highest eroticism stands psychologically and physiologically in a mutually substitutive relation with certain sublimated forms of heroic piety. In opposition to the rational, active asceticism which rejects the sexual as irrational, and which is felt by eroticism to be a powerfully and deadly enemy, this substitutive relationship is oriented especially to the mystic's union with God. From this relation there follows the constant threat of a deadly sophisticated revenge of animality, or of an unmediated slipping from the mystic realms of God into the realm of the All-Too-Human.[28]

If Weber espied the possibility of slippage between eroticism and heroic piety, the warrant for not only slippage but rapprochement and even fusion between religion and nationalism is even more compelling in the Weberian account of religion and nationalism. Weber located the wellsprings of religion in the solidarity of the sib, of the neighbor, in the practical love of those to whom one belongs, one of the original understandings of the term *love*.[29] Religions of salvation are based on a loving creator God.

Weber espied a conflict between the nation-state and salvation religions that was born as much of their institutional commonalities as it was from their substantive conflict. It is those commonalities—in their love and their violence—that make religious nationalism a sociologically probable form. On the one hand, the "brotherly ethic" of universal salvation religions with their "God of 'love'" conflicts with the violence of the state.[30] Yet it is love, by and of the political leader, Weber argues, that is the source of his charisma, his extraordinary capacity to lead.[31] Moreover it is the impersonal brotherly love of the national community that is an essential ground of that leadership. Weber understood that salvation religions and the modern nation-state both draw on an original logic of kinship, extending and ultimately universalizing the solidarity and sentiment of the sib on the one side, and on particularistic "notions of common descent and of an essential, though frequently indefinite, homogeneity," on the other.[32]

Weber also underlines the unique capacity of the nation-state through violent conflict to create a "pathos and a sentiment of community" comparable to that of religion:[33]

> War thereby makes for an unconditionally devoted and sacrificial community among the combatants and releases an active mass compassion and love for those who are in need. And, as a mass phemonenon, these feelings break down all the naturally given barriers of association. In general, religions can show comparable achievements only in heroic communities professing an ethic of brotherliness.[34]

War provides death with a "consecrated meaning" through this "community unto death."[35] Love—of the cause, of the leader, of one's community and combatants—makes death meaningful. Religious nationalism can thus be read as a kind of "Puritan" solution to the "competition between the brotherliness of religion and of the warrior community."[36] Religious nationalisms capture not only the almost impersonal brotherliness of Calvinist love, but also the particularized grace of the nation, which has a chosen role to play in the working out of salvation, here identified with an objective, cosmic historical trajectory.[37] The love of the nation and the love of God are thereby fused and made objective.

Religions and Nationalism: Christian, Islamic, and Jewish Nationalisms

In seeking to explain the occurrence of religious nationalism, a number of scholars look to the attributes of the religion, either doctrinally or historically. At a doctrinal level, scholars point to Weber's critical dimension of "inner-worldly" and "other-worldly" religions, inner-worldly religions being more likely to engage in political projects, to sacralize the state.[38] The way in which that inner-worldly orientation is delimited is also critical, particularly as to whether there is a religious warrant for identifying the locus of sacred life in this world as a distinct community of descent or territory rather than a universal, ethnically and territorially unbounded community. Here one would expect Judaism or the Sikh religion to be most prone to nationalism, whereas a universalist Buddhism, Christianity, and Islam would be least prone.

Others point not to doctrine but to historical tradition, noting the differences in the ways in which different religions have been differentially tied to territorial states, including national ones. Christianity is more prone to generating religious nationalism than Islam, it is argued, because of the ways in which Christianity fragmented into different churches whose formation and institutionalization were tied to distinct states, many of the Protestant cases being themselves nation-states.[39] Indeed, in Europe comparative historians have pointed out that distance from the universal Church in Rome—with its Latin-based rite and its control over marriage and education—linked to the earlier and more stable formation of national states that could more easily establish legitimate authority.[40] Although there have certainly been state-dependent religious differentiations in Islam—the emergence of Shi'ism, for example—Islam has a more recent history of transnational order based on the Ottoman Empire, a transnational order of Meccan-based pilgrimage and a transnational tradition of jurisprudence.

The question of what dimensions of religious doctrine, organization, and practice are associated with politicization, and specifically nationalist politicization, requires a comparative approach both between religions and between forms of state. An adequate approach should be able to compare the ways in which religion and nationalism conflict, coincide, conjoin, concatenate, and even fuse across a variety of contemporary and historical cases. Three cases studies—one each from Christianity, Islam, and Judaism—point to the ways in which nationalism and religion can be mutually constitutive and not merely coexistent. Rogers Brubaker has recently warned that "languages of religion and nation, like all forms of language, can be pervasively intertwined. But even when the languages are intertwined, the fundamental ontologies and structures of justification differ."[41] We agree that the mere invocation of nationalist and religious languages at the same time by the same actors does not, in itself, constitute a co-implication of religion and nationalism. But we think that these cases suggest several ways in which the "fundamental ontologies" of nationalism and religion can and indeed do interpenetrate to such a degree as to be mutually reconstitutive.

Robert E. Alvis has written a detailed historical study of the local intersections between religion and nationalism in the first half of the nineteenth century in what is now the Polish city of Poznan (German: Posen).[42] Alvis traces the process whereby competing Polish and German nationalisms took shape in Poznan/Posen between the French Revolution and Europe's 1848 revolutions. Today monolithically Polish and Catholic, Poznan/Posen was once a religiously and ethnolinguistically diverse city. In 1793, its population was 60 percent Catholic, 24 percent Jewish, and about 15 percent Lutheran; by 1846, the percentage of Lutherans had risen to 30 percent. This Lutheran population was ethnolinguistically German, while the vast majority of the Catholic population was ethnolinguistically Polish.

Initially, the Jewish population was also ethnolinguistically diverse, speaking Yiddish and wearing distinct attire, but it underwent rapid Germanization in the course of the period under study.

The city's ethnic, linguistic, and religious distinctions took on political meaning during Prussian rule starting in 1793, when the Prussian state implemented policies deemed advantageous to German-speaking people or disadvantageous to Catholics or Polish-speaking people (who were, by and large, the same), which inaugurated the regional emergence of Polish nationalist and German nationalist discourses about politics and culture.

This general picture is familiar to anyone who has studied Eastern Europe, and Alvis's book is only one of many that study the emergence of conflicting nationalisms in one or another of the Eastern or East Central European cities. But Alvis, a religious historian by training, goes beyond the obvious fact that religious identification could also be used as a marker of ethnonational identification to offer concrete reconstructions of the ways in which "religion and nationalism could peacefully coexist and fruitfully interact with one another on a number of levels."[43] His work is especially interesting because it focuses on the interaction between Catholicism and nationalism, something that contrasts with assumptions about Catholicism's innate antinational tendencies. The first striking feature of local Catholicism is the way in which this "religious affiliation . . . instilled within [its followers] a particular sense of their geopolitical circumstances," tied to a sacred history specific to Poland. Catholic prelates "regularly struck upon the theme that Poland was a Catholic country" that had defeated pagan Mongols, Muslim Turks, and Protestant Swedes and now stood to be subjected to Orthodox Russia and Protestant Prussia.[44] The interweaving of this-worldly geopolitical danger and religious calling was not confined to preaching but was also manifest in the popular Poland-wide cult of the Black Madonna of Częstochowa, crowned the "Queen of Poland" and seen as a protector of Poland conditional on its inhabitants' Catholic piety.[45]

This narrative and popular intertwining of geopolitical fate and religious calling was, of course, not a guarantee of fusion between religion and nationalism. But it was a transcript available to believing Catholics who also found themselves compelled by the claims of an evolving Polish political nationalism fairly secular in its origins. From the 1820s through the 1840s, perceived Prussian attacks on the primacy of Catholicism locally and regionally generated a politicized Catholicism—a "lay Catholic alienation from the Prussian state."[46] The expressions of this alienation were not necessarily nationalist in the sense that the rhetorics of resistance to church closures or transfers of Catholic premises to Protestants to meet the needs of the growing German-Lutheran population (and to encourage its growth) did not necessarily invoke Polishness rather than Catholicism. But Alvis charts a number of distinct ways in which politicized Catholic and Polish-nationalist visions did indeed fuse.

First, local elites, including Catholic prelates, articulated a narrative connection between right faith and national territorial-ethnic difference at the level of divine providence. Both in their intellectual production and in concrete acts, such as the creation of Poznan's famed Golden Chapel, they construed the historical-territorial achievements of Polish kings and their temporal power as part of a divine plan in which Poles had a special collective calling to spread "true religious teachings." Alvis's analysis of the narrative and figural logic of the paintings and statues in the Golden Chapel also suggests that, however much we might imagine an incommensurability between conceptions of individual salvation in an otherworldly heaven and nationalism's this-worldly concern for the fate and behavior of one's descendants, in practice the two are often co-present for the believer. Standing between God at the apex of the chapel's dome and "human petitioner" below is a ring of "twenty saints associated with Polish history, individuals who excelled spiritually while on earth and who now serve as heavenly envoys for the petitions of subsequent generations."[47]

Second, Alvis pinpoints the way in which Polish nationalism and Catholic belief could intersect powerfully for nonelites as well—in this case, for illiterate Polish Catholic peasants—through the active interlacing of sacred/liturgical and worldly time. This is evident in how peasants in the Poznan region reacted to the 1831 Polish nationalist uprising on the other side of what was then the Russian-Prussian border. Working with Prussian police archives, Alvis notes the spread of a rumor among the peasants that the uprising would spread to Poznan on Good Friday of that year and the concomitant proliferation of miracles reported that specifically combined religious signs and nationalist symbols:

> In the small town of Jarocin, not far from Poznan, religious fervor swelled with the news that a devotional painting of the Virgin Mary in a private room of a young woman had shed tears of blood. The county councillor [*Landrat*] quickly dismissed the phenomenon, claiming the woman had unknowingly splashed the painting with water which, as it rolled down the dusty surface, turned brown. His explanation did not prevent a flood of pilgrims to the image or the popular conclusion that Mary was shedding tears over the fate of Poland. A similar sensation washed over Poznan when it was reported that one of the crosses atop the Parish Church was seen to have turned toward Warsaw [the cultural and political capital of Poland]. Other reports soon followed, and the consensus emerged among less sophisticated residents that the struggle for Polish independence would be successful.[48]

Alvis's analysis confounds any simplistic opposition between the phenomenology of liturgical time's cyclicality and the linearity of empty secular historical time. It suggests, contrary to Anderson's positing of an incommensurability between national and religious temporality, that conceptions of individual salvation in an otherworldly heaven and nationalism's this-worldly concern for the fate and behavior of one's descendants can be co-present for believers. And, most significantly, it points to the ways in which the contingent historical configurations of competing geopolitical units ruling religiously distinct populations who are drawn to different nationalist projects can mobilize and narrate their historical struggle as sacred histories in a way that allows for the sedimentation of nationalist ideologies with genuinely religious convictions about chosenness, sacred collective and intergenerationally transmitted calling. That this occurs within the ambit of Catholicism is particularly striking because of its transnational organization, its universalist theology of salvation, and the absence of doctrinal purchase for territorial or population-specific limitation. Alvis's work suggests how difficult it is to make a clean separation between religion and nationalism in history, whether nationalism is religionized or religion nationalized.

It is not so different in the second, Islamic example. Edward Aspinall's *Islam and the Nation: Separatist Rebellion in Aceh, Indonesia* traces separatist Acehnese nationalism in Indonesia over several decades up to the present.[49] His analysis points to the changing relations between Islam and nationalism, to the dangers of reifying a religious tradition, in this case Islam, as having an essential incommensurability with nationalism. Aspinall shows that Islamism was an important part of Acehnese nationalism during the anticolonial/anti-Dutch moment of the mid-twentieth century. Acehnese nationalist leaders were Islamists who tended to correlate the greatness of the Acehnese people with their especially strong commitment to Islam. In contrast, contemporary Acehnese nationalism is much more compatible with the doubts of Asad or Brubaker concerning the compatibility of Islamism and nationalism. By the 1990s, Acehnese nationalists were vocally distancing themselves from Islamism, most fundamentally because Islamism was more theologically and politically compatible with an antiseparatist statist claim than with demands for national separation from an Islamic state.[50]

The antinational, statist sensibilities available in Islam were easily subordinated to a fusion of Islam and nationalism in a context where Muslims were fighting a Christian colonial regime. When nationalists faced an Islamic sovereign, by contrast, juridical restraints within Islam to political resistance contributed to a secularization of nationalist discourse and identity. This points to the importance of analyzing the ways in which religious traditions variously construct legitimate sovereignty. But, as Aspinall shows, there is no secular necessity in nationalist resistance to Islamic states. In the 1970s and 1980s, the long middle period of Acehnese nationalism, the emergent anti-Indonesian separatist Acehnese nationalism involved a complex mixture of Islamism and nationalism. During this period nationalist leadership still construed Acehnese identity in terms of the depth of one's Islamic commitment. Moreover, this nationalism was still linked to religious specialists, albeit recruited from a different stratum: vernacular Muslim clerical intelligentsia located in the countryside. They were increasingly distant from the urban religious leadership, who either cleaved to an Indonesian statist nationalism or remained politically obedient on grounds of religious quietism.[51]

The relation between Islam and Aceh nationalism depends on where one cuts into its historical trajectory. Aspinall agrees with the point made by Asad and others that different religious traditions have different "specific gravities" as regards the ease with which religious identity, piety, and practice can be identified with nationalist modes of political imagination and practice, Islam being on the more resistant side of that spectrum. But, unlike Asad, he studies a particular setting in which conditions were such that a large group of actors overcame the "specific gravity" of Islamic antinationalism to forge an initially robust Muslim nationalism that later declined.

There are striking parallels between the Catholic case elaborated by Alvis and the Acehnese Muslim case elaborated by Aspinall. One parallel is the instability and temporary character of the religion-nationalism fusion in both cases. This is explicit in Aspinall's account. Alvis's account, however, stops around 1848, when the synthesis between Polish nationalism and Polish Catholicism in Poznan was still strong. Certainly there is historical warrant to argue that, were we to trace the history of Catholicism and nationalism in Central Europe further into the 1870s, we would find that the "specific gravity" of a religiously moral Catholic universalism reasserted itself in Germany in response to the Prussian repression of Catholic orders, the Jesuits in particular, who were at the center of a Catholic revival that occurred in the wake of what was perceived as the moral degeneration associated with the populist and democratic movements that had launched the revolutions of 1848.[52] Bismarck's *Kulturkampf* involved efforts by the newly unified German state to institute a common, statist German nationalism against both local and transnational commitments. In this context, where the church came under state control and its clergy were stripped of their rights to control even the education of its priests and were denied political speech, Catholicism again operated as a supranational and substantially antinational commonality between southern German Catholics and the Polish Catholics of the Posen region.

What the cases analyzed by Alvis and Aspinall show is a time-specific, unstable interlacing of nationalism and religion. These analyses are studies in the half-life of an unstable fusion of discursive and value orders that were indeed in tension. Here, to think about temporality and temporariness is to acknowledge the limits of our claims relative to scholars such as Asad, Anderson, and Brubaker, who suggest that nationalism and religion are basically incommensurable. There are good reasons to claim that one or another religious tradition—Islam, for instance—sustains ontological claims that are in tension with nationalism, as both Asad and Brubaker have argued. We do not disagree that this tension exists, but we have found that, in history, it is not absolute and that the extent to which it is operative in political practice varies not only between religions, but across historical conditions that remain to be specified.

At the same time, Alvis and Aspinall also bespeak the reality, power, and ongoing possibility of religion-nationalism fusions, however temporary these may be. Whatever intrinsic tension there may be between nationalism and religion operates at the level of code—it is a cultural *potentiality*. The distinctness of the codes must be promoted, practiced, and defended by interested agents. The extent of, the conditions under, and the consequences with which nationalist and religious discourses and practices actually interpenetrate is a historical question, not something to be decided by fiat or textual interpretation. It is a question of history and sociology, not heremeneutics, to be pursued at the level of individuals, groups, and states.

Beyond this methodological point, the very temporariness of these two cases also underscores the importance of including the dimensions of temporality, speed, and timing in any account of how nationalism and religion might relate. Our theoretical accounts cannot assume that the intrinsic tensions between nationalism and religion(s) as value spheres or as grammars will manifest themselves immediately and completely, but must also elaborate ways to think about the durative and contested process by which these tensions will lead to the actual breakdown (or *felt* incommensurability) of religious and nationalist commitments. Accounts of nationalism and religion must be attentive to the open-ended family of phenomena that come into existence and affect the world *in the meantime, after* another iteration of the "impossible" fusion has been made and *before* the tensions build to the point where the breakdown actually happens.

A third case, drawn from the relationship between Judaism and Zionism in the twentieth century, again shows that the tension between religion and nationalism is contingent, offering a multiplicity of stances that can change over time. As a religion grounded in the divine formation of a territorial nation, Judaism would seem ready-made for fusion with nationalism. And indeed, when Jewish nationalism emerged in the late nineteenth century out of the cross-currents of East and Central European nationalism, Jewish cultural modernization, and an increasingly vulnerable Jewish political position, this potential was in some respects realized. It is no accident that the earliest and most popular form of Jewish nationalism was Zionism, which linked Jewish "national revival" to Jewish territorialization and perhaps sovereignty in Palestine. In so doing, and by contrast with other versions of Jewish nationalism (some diasporic-autonomist, some territorialist but not Palestinist), Zionism could draw on the singularly powerful mythic structure at the heart of Judaism that sees a return to what Jews have called the Land of Israel as a restoration toward which a divinely determined Jewish history must lead.[53]

Yet if this apparent fusion of modern nationalism and a deeply rooted, constantly renewed people- and territory-specific religious myth may be doctrinally warranted, actual historical developments proved far more complicated. In fact, the response of religiously orthodox Jews to Zionism was decidedly mixed. Zionism attracted many observant rank-and-file Jews in the Jewish demographic centers of the Russian and Habsburg empires. But few religious leaders greeted Zionism favorably, and only a handful saw in

Zionism, however secular it seemed, the fulfillment of divinely promised redemption. Much of the region's variegated Jewish religious leadership rejected it outright or, more commonly, came to reject it by the turn into the twentieth century. After two decades of neutrality or guarded interest, it became increasingly clear that many of Zionism's most committed adherents in Europe and in Palestine were unwilling to abide by stringent religious law, unwilling to recognize the authority of traditional religious leaders, and bent on carrying out a full-fledged cultural and moral revolution in Jewish life that would replace divine revelation with a Jewish version of *Kultur,* the valorization of study and sacred service with an idealization of manual labor, obedience to religious authority with humanist ideals of individualism, and an incommensurable religious chosenness with a secular and frankly imitative concept of nationhood.[54] While a few traditionalist leaders who rejected Zionism did so on theological grounds in the first instance—identifying Zionism as an especially dangerous manifestation of cosmic evil in the context of a baroque mystical historiosophy of Jewish exile and redemption[55]—most of the traditionalists who came to oppose the movement did so not on "onto-theological" grounds but, as Gideon Shimoni puts it, because of "the perceived secularizing influence of Jewish nationalism and its undermining of traditionalist norms and rabbinical authority."[56]

In turn, a slightly expanded historical perspective renders this traditionalist rejection of Zionism still less surprising. This rejection was largely an extension of a more general and increasingly categorical antimodernist traditionalist posture, already in place by the mid-nineteenth century, before Zionism emerged. The nineteenth century saw the development of several distinct but increasingly interpenetrated forms of traditionalist Judaism that converged in the view that modernity as a normative project threatened to destroy Judaism and that a stringently traditionalist and fideistic "saving remnant" had to separate itself spiritually and socio-culturally from modernity's seductions.[57] By the time Zionism emerged as a distinct discourse and movement in the 1880s, these forms of traditionalist Judaism—often referred to en bloc as "haredi Judaism"[58]—were already well on their way to a categorical rejection of modern ideologies as such in the face of accelerating acculturation and normative assimilation among growing swaths of European Jewry.[59]

But does this mean that a categorical rejection of nationalism was, and is, intrinsic to traditionalist Judaism? While no one can gainsay the powerful predispositions within this Judaism to reject a modern concept like nationalism root and branch, recent fine-grained historical research suggests that the range of potential Jewish-traditionalist postures toward this ostensibly intrinsically antireligious ideology was initially wider than the above story suggests. The maverick Hungarian traditionalist ideologue Akiva Yosef Schlesinger (1837–1922) offers a striking example. Schlesinger has long been claimed as a forerunner by Zionist publicists due to his precocious 1873 call for the creation of a Jewish society in Palestine characterized by linguistic Hebraization, military preparedness, economic productivization, and a transformation of gender relations—and claimed with equal conviction by the most vociferous anti-Zionist elements within Israel's haredi community in light of his unyielding and theologically creative opposition to any reform in Jewish religion, to which he also annexed such seeming externalities as distinctive Jewish garb, language, and names. But recent work by historian Michael Silber that looks back to Schlesinger's earlier writings in the 1860s and places them in their immediate Austro-Hungarian context presents a different history: Silber demonstrates that the young Schlesinger was inclined to see his ultra-Orthodox opposition to any change in Jewish religious and cultural life as compatible with other "Herderian" cultural nationalisms in contemporary Europe like that of the "Magyars" (Hungarian nationalists) or "Englishmen." Schlesinger "brought explicitly nationalist declarations" in texts directed at an Orthodox public. Thus, defending his view that Austro-Hungarian Jews should not be forced to abandon Yiddish for German in the name of Enlightenment, Schlesinger noted in 1866 that no one would accuse an Englishman of lack of culture for not speaking German ("He is a man of culture in his own English fashion") and defended Jewish rights to preserve language and custom via a direct parallel: "This is what we Jews claim and demand. Even though it is true that we are dispersed among many peoples in the world, we too are a nation despite everything [*Ein Uma sein mir doch*]. When all is said and done, there exists a land that bears our name and we still await each day our righteous Redeemer."[60]

As Silber demonstrates, this was neither an occasional nor a mono-dimensional invocation of nationalist concepts. When Schlesinger transposed his own writings from Hebrew into Judeo-German (German in Hebrew characters, again intended for a traditional Jewish audience), he translated classical Hebrew terms that could be construed nationalistically or not (like *umah*) into unmistakably nationalist concepts: *Nation, Nationalsprache, Nationalrecht, Nationalität,* and so forth.[61]

Even more striking is how Schlesinger tied these nationalist construals of the Orthodox Jewish situation to a mystically inflected religious narrative drawn from a minor but legitimate strand of traditional Jewish thought. Schlesinger invoked a Rabbinic narrative tradition dating from some time before the tenth century that posited that, during their exile in Egypt, the Children of Israel had made a conscious choice to maintain their separate Jewish language, names, and dress and in so doing had merited in God's eyes redemption and granting of the Torah, the divine revelation. Rejecting the idea that Jewish peoplehood was purely a product of that religious revelation ("It is a commonplace to say that the Torah preceded [Jewish peoplehood]. . . . I say Israel preceded"), Schlesinger instead argued that it was "due to these things [distinctive language, clothing, and names] that we became a people." Finally, he insisted that these "merely" ethnic distinctions had not lost one iota of importance: "should these be taken, God forbid," stringent Jewish observance would also collapse, as garments would collapse without a body to support them. As Silber points out, Schlesinger here makes the double move of drawing a distinction between religious and "ethnonational" elements of Judaism and according essential significance to the latter not less than the former precisely in the name of religion: Jews as an ethnonational group were the "body" that wore the garments of Torah, and only Jews who maintained that ethnonational difference—whom he called "Hebrews"—would maintain the religion. Hence the creative defense of ethnonational difference—including innovative forms of settlement in Palestine—was a permanently essential aspect of orthodox religiosity.[62]

Schlesinger was, of course, only one thinker—and an admittedly peculiar one to boot. But he was not marginal: Silber offers evidence to show that the book in which he first articulated such ideas quickly became very popular among traditionally educated readers in Eastern Europe. Silber also notes that Schlesinger's ideas were foreshadowed by similar if inchoate arguments among his close compatriots. Thus, against Central European rabbis who wished to preserve orthodoxy but proclaim Jewish belonging to the German or Hungarian nation, several of Schlesinger's contemporaries ruled that Jews were forbidden to claim a different nationality and that, if forced to embrace a nationality in legal-discursive terms, they were obliged to choose "Jewish."[63] This stance, which we might call "anti-anti-Jewish-nationalist," further suggests how, under certain historical conditions—in a face of a particular kind of historical challenge and set of options—nationalism suddenly offered itself as at the very least a useful discourse, and maybe even a welcome one, to religious people.

Of course, the case of Schlesinger, writing in the 1860s, does not demonstrate anything other than the fact that traditionalist Judaism—like Catholicism and Islam as historicized by Alvis and Aspinall—was not permanently and essentially "immunized" against nationalism. And to our historicist doubts about the givenness of a tension between ostensibly secular nationalism and religion 'properly understood, one might here counterpose the equally historicist point that even if nineteenth-century Judaism had been open to nationalist concepts at some early stage, it might nonetheless be the case that the subsequent history of zero-sum secularist-traditionalist confrontation has rendered any such rapprochement unreproducible. Schlesinger could flirt with a nationalism in a simultaneously sociologically canny and mystically minded fashion circa 1868, but a subsequent century-plus of confrontation between an increasingly self-conscious haredi Jewry and a Zionism that proved itself the most successful and hence threatening form of Jewish modernism means that as such there can be no second coming of such Schlesingerian fusions.

But there is yet another way in which history as it has actually unfolded may in fact be undermining this sedimented opposition between Jewish traditionalist religiosity and nationalism. As a number of analysts have been arguing since the 1990s, the creation of the State of Israel as a Jewish nation-state, once imagined by both sides as the ultimate victory of Jewish secular nationalism and an interminable "exile at home" for haredi Jews, may in fact have paved the way for new and unforeseen formations of traditionalist Judaism that are quite "at home" in the ethnic and territorial logic of nationalism in its most extreme forms. In light of the picture sketched above, we would expect that the actual *achievement* of Zionism's efforts at reterritorialization and nation-state building should

435

have generated a radical bifurcation within the religiously Orthodox part of the Jewish population, between religious Zionists, on one hand, and the substantially larger camp of traditionalist non- and anti-Zionists on the other. This has indeed been the case, for a century now. In some realms of Orthodox Jewish thought and praxis, this bifurcation seems both complete and rigid, for instance, in the realm of Jewish religious law. How have Jewish religious legal figures, operating on their own understanding with divinely granted and exclusive authority to interpret the legal demands on Jews of an unfolding and inexhaustible revelation, understood the implications of renewed Jewish sovereignty in the Land of Israel for their legal practice? On the one hand, when Israel was established in 1948, for the then-small group of religiously Orthodox Zionists, who stood uncomfortably at the margins of both the secular Zionist establishment and the largely anti-Zionist traditionalist world, the attainment of secular Jewish sovereignty in the form of the State of Israel was a moment of radical fulfillment. For these actors, committed simultaneously to a Jewish nationalist project and to the principle of an all-embracing divinely revealed— if humanly interpreted—Jewish law, the achievement of Jewish sovereignty marked a moment of radical transition, at least in theory, whereby the law of the land must be the divinely revealed law, a religious nationalism par excellence. As Alexander Kaye puts it:

> This model was based on two fundamental assumptions. First, the norms of Jewish law, or *halakha,* which originate in the divine command, are a given. . . . Rather than the *halakha* developing to take into account new phenomena, new phenomena must all be interpreted and responded to according to the dictates of the *halakha.* . . . Second, the *halakha* as it stands can be directly applied to any situation. Unlike human beings who devised other systems of law, God was able to foresee any future situation and embedded the proper response to that situation in the closed system of the *halakha.* So although it may seem that the new state of Israel, for example, created new circumstances that the *halakha* does not address, this is an illusion. . . . This led to a widespread push in religious Zionist circles in the late 1940s and early 1950s to produce a comprehensive national legal code that was based exclusively on halakhic material.[64]

For religious Zionists, the achievement of Jewish nation-statehood meant that in principle there was no longer any barrier between Jewish sovereignty and the this-worldly institution of God's perfect law. All that remained was the practical task of hammering out the practical jurisprudence and capturing the state and the nation. There was no room morally and even ontologically for national law that was not Jewish religious law, *halakhah.*

While this stance might seem obvious for religious Jews, who are heirs to a tradition where divine law is specifically given to a specific people in a specific land, this position was anathema to most Jewish traditionalists. The overwhelming response of the haredi leadership to the creation of the State of Israel was one of theological "neutralization": a categorical rejection of the claim that the "Jewish state" was in any theological sense different from any other secular state, much less the fulfillment of a divine plan and the beginning of an ontologically new era. It therefore follows that the creation of the state and the nationalist principles its governments espouse ought not to have any bearing on the normative core of haredi religious practice and thought. As the pioneering scholar of this phenomenon, Aviezer Ravitsky, puts it, "the achievement of political independence in the Holy Land does not represent a transformation. It demands neither new categories of thought nor a specific halakhic [i.e., religious-legal] confrontation. Even more so has it nothing to do with messianic hopes."[65]

This has been the stance in principle, at least, for the broad middle of the haredi leadership. But there are signs that this posture of neutralization is not so easy to maintain in the face of the actual fact of Jewish mass resettlement, sovereignty, and ongoing society building in the Holy Land. Haredi Jewry's rejection of secular nationalism did not, of course, mean a rejection in any way of the traditional Jewish identification of the Jewish people with the Land of Israel, traditional precepts of chosenness and eschatologies of redemption, and a strong, if not exclusive, tendency within the tradition to see this redemption as involving a this-worldly restoration of the people to the Land and Jewish sovereignty over it. And this in turn opens the way for unexpected forms of rapprochement between antimodernist, antisecularist haredi Jews and that ostensible epitome of secular modernity, nationalism.

Thus whatever their stance on the theological legitimacy of the Israeli state, within Orthodox Israeli Jewry there is a general tendency to insist that the law that governs public life in Israel—in the holy Land—should be Jewish religious law as interpreted by the rabbis. As the Marakesh-born Israeli rabbi Avraham Haputah put it in 1965, "The religion and the Land are connected; religion and state cannot live together unless the regime is Torah-based as is proper to our land which is holier than all other lands."[66] A respected figure in the world of haredi Judaism, Haputah was certainly distant from Zionism as a movement and ideology. But we should also ask whether the effort to Judaize the law of a self-declared Jewish nation-state in the name of a God connected directly to land, law, people, and sovereignty does not constitute a decisive nationalization nevertheless—or at least open the path to such a nationalization.

Jewish religious law is not the only place—or even necessarily the most important— to look for rapprochement between antimodernist Orthodoxy and nationalism. Even leaving aside the ideological issues in question, there is also the structural restraint of a case-law tradition in which legal decisions must be legitimated in relation to classical texts and traditions of argument, with very little room for adducing extra-legal ideological factors. But if we look at other sites less bound by conservative norms, we find evidence of a much more fluid ideological situation. And significantly, this fluidity seems to relate above all to the difficulty for religious Jews of *not* reacting ideologically and affectively in some way to the *fact* of Jewish national sovereignty over the mythically and sacrally resonant Holy Land.

Writing in the 1990s, two knowledgeable observers of the Israeli Orthodox scene, Ravitsky and Lawrence Kaplan, pointed to two immediate factors making for this destabilization of haredi Judaism's theological neutralization of the Jewish nation-state's significance. Ravitsky noted the destabilizing impact of unforeseen political and social power on haredi society: In Israel's perennially divided society and parliamentary system, haredi parties backed by a growing haredi public began to manifest themselves as king-makers, spoilers, and essential junior partners. This new political power was matched by a growing social solidity and cultural power: A community that had always imagined itself as an embattled tiny minority was now a major part of Israeli society (estimates hover around some 10 percent and growing) and increasingly a tone-setter in an Israeli Jewish cultural sphere characterized by growing disillusionment with secularism, by moral searching, and by attraction to religious authority. What followed from this was a sea change in actual haredi relations with the worldly realities of the Jewish nation-state that could not but change haredi Judaism ideologically. These developments, he wrote,

> have suddenly provided Haredim with power and influence, both material and spiritual, to a degree far exceeding that required by, or appropriate to, a life based on a qualified acceptance of a strange and alien reality. These developments have increased their direct involvement in questions of society and economy, land settlement and foreign policy, and peace and war to a degree that is inconsistent with their intellectual and psychological inclinations. On the other hand, once power and responsibility have been conferred, they are not easily waived or abandoned.[67]

Writing at roughly the same time, Lawrence Kaplan noted a still more particular irritant in haredi thought: the question of what stance to take vis-à-vis the newly invigorated idea of trading the Israeli-occupied West Bank to the Palestinian national movement in exchange for peace. Kaplan suggested that here, for the first time, was an issue that did not admit of an obvious unified traditionalist position and hence opened the way for a destabilizing proliferation of clashing opinion within haredi thought: "For, pray tell, which is ... the less 'modern' and more 'frum' [religiously stringent] position on the question of the territories: the 'dovish' *Daas Torah*[68] viewpoint of Rav Shach and his followers or the 'hawkish' *Daas Torah* viewpoint expressed by various hasidic leaders? For, in truth, each side can and does—with some justification—claim that its position is the more 'traditional.'"[69] The unstated point underlying the tension here is that for a traditionalist Jew, the land occupied by Israel on the west bank of the Jordan is no less a holy part of the Jewish Holy Land (indeed, arguably more so) than that within Israel's borders, and that precisely insofar as that Jew rejects the legitimacy and raison d'état of the secular Jewish state, the fact of Jewish political possession of and settlement possibilities in that land demands a religious interpretation that may have profound worldly consequences.

Does all of this ideological complexity entail a renegotiation of the relationship between traditionalist Judaism and nationalism? To this larger—and, for Israel, fateful—question, we will try very modestly to sketch a response at the conclusion of this essay. For now, we close this section by noting that we might usefully ask the same question about any contemporary traditionalist population, such as the Islamists who may deride nationalism yet seek to Islamicize the nation-state. Whether or not nationalism can be linked to the formation of a nation-state that grounds its law and legitimacy in revealed law is a vexed issue not only among scholars but among the pious followers of those religious traditions as well.

The Unstable Secularity of American Nationalism

As befits Weber's explorations of the consonances between the nation-state and salvific religions, despite their otherwise contradictory values, the essential secularity of nationalism can be most unstable, even in the hands of those who have been most insistent in asserting it. Talal Asad has recently begun to unearth the deep religious grammar of Western liberal states as they conduct what some would call their imperial projects. But in the process, Asad continues to insist on the essentially nonreligious quality of violent resistance by Muslim fighters who struggle against that nation and what they see as its allies and agents because of the way he casts the incommensurability of nationalism and Islam. As a result, there is a fundamental asymmetry: America's military violence has a religious meaning, while that of those Muslims who struggle against it does not. It thereby becomes impossible to specify the religious quality of Muslims who fight to expel occupation forces from nation-states.

In Talal Asad's book *On Suicide Bombing,* Weber's contention that the legitimacy of the state hinges on the meaning of death finds an analytic executor.[70] Asad argues that the discursive and practical deployment of a "war" on Islamic terrorism, with its domestic abrogation of civil rights and exemption from the conventions of war abroad, must be understood through the particular meaning that the liberal state accords death. Asad argues that the legitimacy of Western liberal state violence hinges not on mere death-dealing to protect a generic way of life, but on a self-attribution of motive, namely a belief that human life is sacred and that one kills regretfully, whereas terrorists kill civilians intentionally.

The liberal state, Asad argues, is able to hold together the contradiction between "reverence for human life and its legitimate destruction" for a religious reason.[71] Reworking Carl Schmitt's dictum that Western models of sovereignty are secularized forms of Christianity, but relocating the political theology in the nature of the human rather than the sovereign, Asad argues that this duality is built on a secularized Christian culture wherein a sacrificial "indirect" suicide—that of Jesus—is understood to have redemptive significance, voluntary exposure to individual death affording collective immortality, the gift of human life achieved through sacrificial, suicidal death:[72]

> I want to suggest that the cult of sacrifice, blood, and death that secular liberals find so repellent in pre-liberal Christianity is a part of the genealogy of modern liberalism itself, in that violence and tenderness go together. . . . Today, this contradiction is a part of a modern liberalism that has inherited and rephrased some of its basic values from medieval Christian tradition: on the one hand, there is the imperative to use any means necessary (including homicide and suicide) to defend the nation-state that constitutes one's worldly identity and defends one's health and security and, on the other, the obligation to revere all human life, to offer life in place of death to universal humanity; the first presupposes a capacity for ruthlessness, the second for kindness. The contradiction itself constitutes a particular kind of human subject whose functioning depends on the fact that the contradiction has to be continually worked through without ever being resolved.[73]

"The violence at the heart of liberal political doctrine," Asad argues, links the right to self-defense to a "project of universal redemption."[74] There is an expansionary, secularized Christian suicidal violence at the core of the liberal state. Western liberal humanism is a secularized Passion play, evolving out of our ability to identify with Christ's suffering. Christ is our Man.

Asad, who has insisted on the secularity of the nation, here lays out the religiosity of the liberal state. But it is not so easy to cleave the one from the other. Liberalism, of course, is associated with civic nationalism, in which the nation is composed of the members of a collectivity who have together—often violently—chosen those freedoms in history. The sacred human is realized through a national state. But it is even more difficult to make the divide in the American case, a nation fashioned through Christian revival, which long understood itself as a Christian polity, a nation many of whose leaders have understood and continue to understand themselves as having a divinely given redemptive mission to bring liberty to the world. The liberal American project might be seen as an imperial project, but it is also a nationalist project. If liberalism operates according to a deep Christian code, so do a number of Western nation-states through which the liberal project is enacted.

States are made, Asad argues, by making particular forms of subjects. Our subjectivity is bound up with the meaning of death in the war making of our state. The state's war making must be understood not only as geopolitics, but as political psychology, that is, as a political subjectification. The military interventions of the Western liberal state "aim" not at the protection of life, but at the creation of "specific kinds of human subjects."[75] We kill the way we do—indiscriminately and at a distance—in part because we value human life so much, ours, of course, above all. Western war functions to create our version of the human, and the "war on terrorism," including its use of torture, likewise operates to perform the unhumanness of "their" form of violence, in part by instituting a new "epistemic object"—terrorism, which is marked by their torturability.[76] Torture is not a response to terror; it is the practice of its categorical performance: Terrorists are torturable outside the law. We are guilty when we kill; they are not. We are Christian soldiers; they are Islamic barbarians. We kill because we have to; they kill because they want to.

Islamist suicide tactics then operate effectively by damaging not our geopolitical security, but our collective subjectivity. Suicidal operations by Islamists work, Asad argues, through "horror," as potentially mortal cultural wounds, not as strategic threats as much as threats to our sense of what it means to be human. Our kind of human is bound up with the way death is configured in our war making. The nature and legitimacy of individual and collective state subjects are co-implicated.

But what about their violence? Is it aimed at our culture, the particular state of our humanness? In Asad's analysis, we cannot know, because Asad excoriates efforts to discern religious "motives" for the practices of Islamic suicide warriors, given that they are unknowable and tend to recapitulate the civilized-barbarian duality that the discourse of terrorism produces: "The motives of suicide bombers in particular are inevitably fictions that justify our responses but that we cannot verify."[77] Such accounts, he says, "tell us more about liberal assumptions of religious subjectivities and political violence than they do about what is ostensibly being explained."[78]

For Asad, not only is attribution of motive linked to individual culpability, and hence likely to be freighted with Western legal, religious, and psychological vocabularies of motive,[79] but the drive to discern motives typically is occasioned by a situation where we cannot understand the action, where it appears "bizarre."[80] But this is exactly the logic of the analytic operation in which Asad is engaging: Asad attributes motives for America's war on terrorism even though it's difficult to understand the disgorging of treasure and blood that is both wildly disproportionate to the military threat and counterproductive. The "war" on terror is for us as much a symptomatic working out of who we think we are as it is an instrumental tactic deployed against "them." In arguing this, Asad relies on what we say to defend the civilians killed in this war as we execute it, on what we don't say (namely, the dimly perceived religious sources of our own counterwar), and on our "horror" as a "state of being" in response to a violence that we cannot objectify. For this last imputation he provides no evidence other than a long footnote enumerating Western books on Islamist violence that he takes to be an indicator that we in fact inhabit this horrified state of being in the aftermath of these suicide attacks. Although he dissociates "horror" from the category of motive, horror is an emotional response to the experience of an attack on our humanness, to a violence out of place.[81] Indeed, that horror has a Christian constitution because violence repudiates our logic of redemption, there being no restorative death, no possible punishment. And "horror"—which Asad claims has no discursive component—is then a motive for the way we respond to such violence. In other words, Asad uses precisely the West's legal, religious, and psychological armature to understand why we respond in the way that we do.

He helps us understand what their violence means to us, but not what their violence means to them. Asad has provided what he has called a "grammar of concepts"—the way in which concepts and practices are conjoined and co-implicated—for the violence of the hegemonic liberal state, but he seems here to have refused it to the violent Islamist citizens of subordinate states, whose practices he strips down to desperate resistance.[82] Asad's analytic asymmetry is unnerving. He mimes the liberal ideologue or military commander who does not take the motives of the terrorist into account in categorizing his violence.[83]

The reason Asad excludes motive on the side of the Muslim fighters is clear: Motives here involve attributions of a reason derived from the religious discourse accompanying the act. Not only is he contemptuous of those who assume that the "highly ritualized proclamation" that "typically uses a religious vocabulary" corresponds to "real motives" of suicide bombers, he sees such attributions as implicit or explicit judgments, coterminous with the very "war" on terror that seeks to reproduce our particular form of subjectivity.[84] Reacting to historian of religions Ivan Strenski's interpretation of suicide bombing as a sacrificial act, a religious choosing of death, a kind of sacralizing gift to the nation, Asad argues this is a "forensic reading of motive":

> Its explanatory concern . . . is with identifying culpability that can be established through the reconstruction of a particular kind of motive. . . . The suicide bombers are fully responsible—answerable—for their acts because they *choose* to justify their violence in terms of a discursive religious tradition, in which they choose to offer individual lives (their own and the lives of others) in exchange for a transcendental value. It is the free intention of the perpetrator that leads to the criminal act and not (as is often alleged) brutal subjection to Israeli occupation.[85]

Such an interpretive move, Asad declares, makes the suicide bomber "morally underdeveloped—and therefore premodern." Likewise May Jayyusi's argument—playing with Agamben's sacral state order—that Palestinian suicide bombers can be sacrificed, but not killed, Asad argues, makes their actions into a "perverse form of national politics."[86]

Western theorists like Strenski, Asad argues, Christianize their Islamic objects of explanation through their academic categories. Thus Asad delineates the divergent conceptual grammars of Christianity and Islam, showing that the Christian sacrificial logic does not transpose to Islam, that sacrifice in Islam does not make holy, that Muslim martyrs are not understood in sacrificial terms. Asad's point is that we are not the same, that Muslims do not have the Christian sacrificial discourse of "partial death, absolution and rebirth" to draw on.[87]

But what is the internal order of their violent grammar? We don't know because Asad assiduously avoids citing any words uttered or penned by Islamists who engage in, organize, or explain the violence of the jihadis who kill themselves while killing others. Asad does explain that the Palestinians Muslims who die in conflict are *shuhada*, triumphant witnesses, not sacrifices, whose mode of death is understood to grant them immortality. But such witnesses don't have to kill themselves intentionally to become so.[88] The *shahid* exceeds the intent of the witness, the violence of the act, let alone the suicidal nature of that violent act; it describes an encounter, not a motivation. Not only do we not have any sense from Asad of how that religious understanding might shape the way Muslims war inside or outside the law or, when violence is conjoined with this understanding, what difference such an understanding makes to the order of that violence, but we are also not provided any understanding of how suicide bombing, in particular, as a practice might draw significance from this understanding. The category of *shahid*, after all, does not even require motivated agency. There is, Asad notes in passing, a struggle over whether suicide bombing can be accounted as an act of witness.[89] That interpretive conflict and the way it inflects the course of Islamic death-dealing deserves our attention as part of the account of suicide bombing. If he were to pay attention to what Muslims say religiously about their violence, he would have to explore the explicitly sacrificial language that the jihadis use. Thus al-Qaeda leader Ayman al-Zawahiri spoke of Muslim martyrs in the following manner: "Generation of mujahideen that has decided to sacrifice itself and its property in the cause of God. That is because the way of death and martyrdom is a weapon that tyrants and their helpers, who worship their salaries instead of God, do not have."[90]

Although al-Zawahiri did invoke Christian martyrdom, in this he is not different from early Muslims at the periphery of the Roman Empire who invoked Christian monks as models of the kinds of subjects they sought to be in the conduct of jihad.[91] One cannot purify Islam by pointing to the historic marginality of jihad or to the fact that the term holy is never applied to war in the classical texts.[92] One could say precisely the same about early Christianity before it was appropriated by the state. By that standard Protestantism, particularly fundamentalist Christianity, is not Christianity. It is the conjunction of category and practice, as Asad has taught us for a long time, that must be our level of observation and analysis.

Asad seeks to remain in the domain of causes rather than motives, by which he means to encompass both the legal analogue of "intention" to kill and the external structural reasons that lead a person to these acts. "I use 'intention' to refer to the causal structure of a social act and 'motive' to refer to the actor's reasons for acting in a particular way."[93] Asad's use here of "causal" transforms "he" into "me" in the sense that they have been "coerced," that "he has reached the limit; he has no other option left. . . . If he kills enough civilians (so he reasons), perhaps those who are politically responsible will respond in the desired way."[94] Suicidal violence, Asad argues, has no unique essence. Its uniqueness lies only in its "contingent circumstance."[95]

This asymmetry is methodologically indefensible in that—as Asad himself has shown us—meanings do afford motivations, discourses do subjectivize, and hence the subjectivity achieved through words and practices can be causal in the sense of sustaining or enabling the practice. One, of course, awaits a parallel analysis of the ways in which Islam is or is not implicated in the legitimacy of the state, the way in which Islam constructs death and how that has or has not shaped Islamic states or states that claim sovereignty over a majority Muslim population. Instead, Asad makes the Muslim suicide warrior into a quasi-liberal, rendering him like the liberal statesmen who claim the right to use nuclear weapons to defend an order founded on a generalized "individual natural right to violent self-defense" or as an act of an individual with "an uncoerced interiority."[96] The implication is that as foundational and defensive violence, the Islamic suicide is no different than the perpetrators of Dresden and Hiroshima.

That we have motives and they have causes is an act of symbolic violence, the kind of ontological assimilation by Western scholars Asad has consistently condemned in previous works. Ultimately we must be able to conjoin motives and causes in that this is a political ecology of truth games, a contest between alternative discursive grammars, between liberalism and political Islam, not to mention political Christianity within the United States. It is an analytically complex problem because—as Asad points out—they are interdependent, both historically and phenomenologically, because we must lay out not only their practical hermeneutic orders, as Asad has done, but also the conditions of their recruitment of individuals to the way they construct reality, as well as the conditions of their success in subjectifying in the way that Asad explains they are intended to do.[97]

Moreover, to argue that "the creation of terror and perpetuation of atrocities are aspects of militant action in the unequal world we inhabit," that Muslims who invoke religious language and rite as part of their violent practice respond to "brutal subjection," that they too feel they "have no choice" or are reacting to "injustice," in a "spontaneous action when legal political means are blocked," renders those Muslims the very apostates whom the jihadis contend they have a right to kill.[98] Not only is there the empirical problem for Asad's account that Salafi jihadi suicide bombers have in fact murdered many more civilian Muslims than soldiers and agents of the imperial liberal state.[99] But for Muslims, as for Christians of the liberal American state, attributions of motives are essential. To kill other Muslims, let alone themselves, for instrumental political purposes is for them religiously inadmissible. For the jihadi motive—or intention, *niyya*—is the essential criterion of legitimacy. It is the internal intention, one's belonging to God, not the external objective, the defeat of an enemy, that determines whether blowing oneself up is a cherished martyrdom or a condemned suicide. To blow oneself up to achieve union with God, "seeking the face of God," is the only intention that will stand.[100] Asad accuses Strenski of Christianizing Muslim martyrs. By refusing to take their motives seriously, Asad ends up criminalizing them by their own standards.

There must be ways to understand the meanings of death that ground sovereignty in a way that is not asymmetrical, that recognize the religious quality of religious political violence in a manner that does not render incommensurable the America hegemon and its Islamic enemies. It is a strange state of affairs when the violence of the avowedly secular hegemon is religiously nationalist, while that of its self-conscious Islamic opponents is analytically stripped of religious intent, not to mention motives.

Four Pillars of Religious Nationalism

So what is the nature of religious nationalism? Religious nationalism fuses two ontologies, two kinds of imagined agents, two logics of action—that of divinity and of the nation-state. Religious nationalism exists where the nation-state itself becomes invested with religious meaning. This can, but need not, involve four elements.

First, there is the religious identity of the nation, such that the nation-state as a collective subject is understood to represent the aggregation of its religious citizens, not only their religious identity but their religiously moral and legal concerns, as well as their metaphysical and ontological understandings.[101] At its most basic, religion constitutes the "we" of the nation-state. Both German Poles and the Aceh nationalists understood themselves in this way. The nation is a religious subject because its members are; the coherence of the collective subject is grounded in its common religiosity. In early modern Europe, trans-local, cross-class religious mobilization was critical to the formation of the nation.[102] Islamists likewise understand that the population of an Islamic nation-state is bound together not by participation in a national culture, but by common submission to *dīn*, to the way of life revealed and modeled by the Prophet. *Dīn* is not without political meaning.

Second, the nation itself can have religious meaning if its constitution, survival, and actions are understood to have redemptive or soteriological significance. The nation's historical trajectory is invested with cosmological significance. In this case, the nation is "chosen" or "elect," a critical element, for example, in Christian, Hindu, Shi'ite, and Jewish nationalisms.[103] The Polish nationalist case reviewed above exemplifies this as well. A particular nation-state is understood to serve a divine purpose. Asad has argued that the liberal Western nation-state builds on the Christian crucifixion narrative, enabling citizens of countries like the United States to understand themselves as a "progressive redemptive force, waging war in the ranks of Christ's army."[104] Given the Islamist hostility to the nation as a divisive source comparable to pre-Islamic tribalism, a Western-imposed impious medium for abrogating the unitary sovereignty of Allah and for secularizing the state by grounding it in human choice, this is the element typically missing from Sunni Islamist politics.[105] But it is not always missing from that politics or incompatible with it. Hamas, for example, casts its violent jihad against Zionism as a fulfillment of the Prophet's proclamation, according to *hadith*, about the advent of the Day of Judgment. According to Article 7: "The Islamic Resistance Movement aspires to the realisation of Allah's promise, no matter how long that should take. The Prophet,

Allah, bless him and grant him salvation, has said: The Day of Judgment will not come about until Moslems fight the Jews (killing the Jews), when the Jew will hide behind stones and trees. The stones and trees will say, 'O Moslems, O Abdulla, there is a Jew behind me, come and kill him.'"

Where Shi'ites traditionally endured—waiting for the return of Muhammad al-Mahdi, the twelfth imam and a descendant of Ali, who disappeared in 874, as the Messiah who will install a religious reign of justice—the Shi'ite revolutionaries in Iran developed an activist model by which a devout Muslim was to emulate the foundational Islamic martyrs, to struggle to the death, as Ali Shariati proclaimed, in "the name of God of the disinherited."[106] Khomeini's doctrine was that one was to actively emulate the model of Hussein in Karbalah, cut down by the Ummayads, to struggle against injustice and consciously to seek martyrdom. If the traditional Shi'ite posture was to accept nonreligious government until the coming of the Mahdi, Khomeini constructed the role of *Velayat-e Faqih*, a clerical guardian whose religious government would rule in the name of the Mahdi until his arrival. Over the years, an apocalyptic messianism has emerged in opposition to the traditional clergy and their rule, manifested in the posture of former Iranian President Ahmadinejad, who declared that he is in direct contact with the Hidden Imam and who understands the actions of the Iranian nation-state as "hastening the coming of Imam Mahdi," one of whose accomplishments will be the destruction of the State of Israel and the killing of Jews.[107] Popular among lower-level clerics and traditionalist milieus, this apocalypticism has strong support among Iran's Islamic Revolutionary Guard Corps and the Baiji militia.

Third, there is the explicit religious derivation of the nation-state's authority and laws from divine sources and revealed law. Here, the content of state law and the source of sovereignty are derived from divine sources, not from the historical decisions of a particular people. This can be written into law or into the organizational structure of the state such that religious authorities control law making, as in the Iranian theocracy. For religious nationalists, the religious criterion of judgment, like human rights, racial purity, or technical rationality, is beyond the reach of popular voice or compelling state interests. It cannot not be chosen.

Fourth, contemporary religious nationalisms hold to a specific and internally related understanding of the human and the nation-state. Through a double register of divine embodiment, they view the human body and the territorial state not just as parallel sacred entities but as divine creations, whose boundaries and life force must be both protected and assured.[108] The aspects of revealed law on which politicized religious movements that seek to rule the nation-state insist typically concern the making and taking of life, including sexuality, marriage, divorce, birth, death, burial, and inheritance. If one looks at both Christian and Islamic politics, whether in the United States, Iran, Egypt, or Turkey, one finds that these issues are central, whether the question involves gender, marriage, premarital and extramarital sexuality, homosexuality, modesty, or evolution. Religious nationalisms have a tendency to eroticize political authority, territorial and collective identity, and collective solidarity in a specific register, involving a particular ontology of life.

The Divine Body Politic

The fourth dimension of religious nationalism—its investiture of the human body and the territorial state as divine creations and the religious regulation of the nation's sexuality—requires further elaboration.

Religious nationalists seize on life's exception to the law, to what the Italian political philosopher Giorgio Agamben calls "bare life," which he identifies as the referent of sovereignty.[109] In the nation-state, Agamben has argued, bare life becomes the bearer of both human rights and national sovereignty.[110] The modern nation-state grounds sovereignty when it seizes hold of *zōe* in a culturally unmediated biological people—not the people of the polis—by joining the status of citizenship to the biological fact of birth, if not of race, as well as of bodily pleasure, the pursuit of happiness.

It is Agamben's bare life that politicized religious movements refuse, rejecting the modern state's foundation in biological life, the sufficiency of birth, the primacy of bodily existence, and the valorization of corporeal pleasure, utility, and biological need—precisely what Hannah Arendt disparaged as "the social"—as the basis of state authority and political action.[111] For the followers of politicized religion, neither the abstract individual nor the physiological person but human life understood as divine creation must be the ontological ground of political authority. Politicized religions contest the secular state's capacity to take life because, they insist, it is not grounded in the divine making of life. They, too, seize on life's exception to the law; but it is not the same exception, not the same life. Both their violence and their sex point to a different substance, an alternative basis of sovereignty.

Agamben identifies bare life as the state of nature, which Thomas Hobbes located both outside the sovereign order as its brutishly violent source and inside it in the sovereign's legally unmasterable, savage powers. But for religious nationalists, God's capacity to make life is part and parcel of his capacity to take it—a power excessive to the law, a fecundating power that is pervasive, for example, in Moses's relation to God, a relation that Hobbes used as his model for the sovereign and that was the template for numerous early modern European nationalisms.[112] The sovereign God in whom religious nationalists would ground state sovereignty is not only a law-giver who can deliver spectacular pains in its defense, but a figure who guarantees sometimes extraordinary birth, who rewards his followers with fertility, including collective birth, who not only takes but also makes life, and who loves his people fiercely and jealously.[113] Not just death but erotic love and the birth in which it issues provides an originary template for institution and for making place for the law and the collective subject that adopts it as its own. The politicized religious model of state sovereignty is also a model of human procreation. Law and life both derive from an exceptional divine source. God's violence is but one side of his boundless love, his possessive desires, and his exclusive demands.

The effort of religious nationalists to subordinate sexuality to divine law is part of their desire to derive sovereignty from divinity and their struggle to create a pious civil society as the ground for the national community over which the state claims sovereignty. Their sex, like their violence, partakes of, and must be ordered by, this divinity.

This stance toward divinity, sovereignty, and sexuality is found not only in many forms of religious nationalism, including Protestant, Hindu, Jewish, Shi'ite, and Sunni forms, but in central strands of antinational political Islam that seek to Islamicize existing nation-states. *Milestones*, the most influential text of Sayyid Qutb, whose political-theological thinking has inspired so many Islamists, links sovereignties without God to natural, materialist understandings of procreation, both of which reduce citizen men to their animal needs, precisely to what Agamben calls modernity's beast, the wolf-man.[114] The negation of the transcendent God and the consequent grounding of political order in nature have led, Qutb argues, to Communist ideologies in which "the basic needs of human beings are considered identical with those of animals, that is, food and drink, clothing, shelter, and sex" and to capitalist societies in which "physical desires" reign supreme.[115] Without God, citizens are animals. For Qutb, man is not only more than animal, he is more than man. Man's "creation," Qutb writes, "is the result of the Will of Allah rather than of his father and mother. The father and mother may come together; but they cannot transform a sperm into a human being."[116] Only by recognizing the divinity involved in conception, in birth, and in the making of life can a Muslim live a life worth living.

Religious nationalisms, including politicized religious movements that wish to transform the laws of nation-states to conform to their interpretation of revealed law, seize upon the proliferation of a secularized sexuality—one subjected to state regulation, commodified incitement, and cultural sacralization—and seek to reinscribe God in response to modernity's sexualization of social life, a sexualization derived from making sex into an object of government intervention, on the one hand, and elevating it into a substitute transcendence, on the other. Politicized religions emerge against a backdrop of market liberalization that feeds on the expansion of desire, floods the labor market with newly employed women, and undercuts the welfare functions of the state. In a newly commodified world, energized by an expansive sensual desire, in particular by woman's desired and desiring bodies, they seek to set their bodies apart, to construct a purity and a piety held in common in response to the increasingly unequal pleasures of a commodified world and to discipline the unnatural excesses of monetary and erotic exchange.[117] In a world that has transformed sex into pleasure and physical reproduction, they would recast it as divine creation. The secularity of the modern, unregulated market is to them an immodest world of selfish bodily pleasures.[118] For example, when Muslim Brotherhood member Sheikh Hazem Abu Ismail announced his intention, against the leadership, to run in Egypt's 2011 presidential elections, he declared, "We seek to apply Islamic law, but those who don't want it prefer cabarets, alcohol, dancers and prostitution, as the implementation of Islamic law will prohibit women to appear naked in movies and on beaches."[119]

Supporters of Islamism, the surveys show, want our democracy; however, they refuse our liberal, secular sex. Even Bin Laden's supporters do not see democracy as a Western imposition.[120] But they do refuse homosexuality, gender equality, divorce, and abortion. Ronald Inglehart and Pippa Norris, astute survey researchers, conclude, "These issues are part of a broader syndrome of tolerance, trust, political activism, and emphasis on individual autonomy that constitutes 'self expression values.' The extent to which a society emphasizes these self-expression values has a surprisingly strong bearing on the emergence and survival of democratic institutions."[121] It is not, we would argue, tolerance and trust, but the ontological construction of sexuality and an inability to cede sex to civil rights that are at issue.

Religious nationalism and political Islam have the organization of sexuality, indeed, of bodily desire, at their center. For Islamists, the propriety of one's sex, the ability to properly order it, is constitutive of one's relationship to God, of the strength and political coherence of the community, and of the kind of subject that predominates. For Qutb, for whom every external struggle is also an internal one in consciousness and community, the founding of relationships between men and women on the basis of "lust, passion and impulse" is a defining trait of a *jahili*—backward or ignorant—society.[122] Qutb reminds his followers that Allah will eventually reduce to "stubble" those societies whose members are unable to control their "unruly desires," who follow the counsel of those "given to excesses." In contrast, quoting Noah in the Qur'an (71:10–12), he asserts that those who ask God for forgiveness will be made "powerful through wealth and children."[123] This follows Islam's foundational narratives, in which the initial conquests, the *futuh*, were understood to be consequences of internal individual transformations that resulted from embracing the Prophet's message, encouraging a pious asceticism so that these men would be warriors by day and "monks by night."[124] "Every community has its monasticism," Mohammed reportedly told his companions, "and the monasticism of my community is jihad on the path of God."[125]

In Islamic thought, there is both an etymological and a causal link between *fitna*, identified as sedition or deviation, which divides the community in Islam's foundational civil wars, and sexual temptation.[126] *Fitna,* as trial or temptation, has its template, as in an Augustinian Christian reading, in man's inability to control his sexuality, to contain his sex inside of marital bonds, a template for lawlessness associated with sedition, wrong belief, and secession.[127] This is associated with the *hadith,* in which troops returning from battle were told by the Prophet, "You have come for the best, from the smaller jihad [*al-jihad al-asghar*] to the greater jihad [*al-jihad al-akbar*]." His followers did not understand, so Mohammed clarified that he was referring to "The servant's struggle against his lust" [*mujahadat al-'abdi hawah*].[128] For Islamists like Qutb, the struggle against erotic desire within prepares one for the struggle against the enemy without.[129] Islamic jurists link seduction to sedition.[130]

The centrality of sex is tied to that of the family, in which these movements seek to contain it. Religious nationalists give primacy to the family, not to democracy or the market, as the social space through which society should be conceived and composed. Familial discourse, with its particularistic and sexual logic of love and loyalty, is pervasive in religious nationalism. "The family," the Ayatollah Khomeini declared, "is the fundamental unit of society and the main center of growth and transcendence for humanity."[131] For Qutb, too, the family's production of moral beings "is the only measure by which true human progress can really be gauged."[132] In the United States, the unifying core of Protestant fundamentalism is likewise its defense of the heterosexual and male-dominated family. Pat Robertson, the founder of the Christian Broadcasting Network, writes, "The basic unit of social, local, national, and international organization in God's world order is the family."[133] In the political programs of Islamic movements, there is no consistent economic policy or form of government. The two pillars of contemporary Islamic politics involve a restrictive regulation of sexuality, eliminating it as a public presence and containing it within the family, and the promotion of a welfare state—or a religiously organized civil society—that enables families to survive physically and provides for those—orphans and widows, in particular, as enjoined by the Qur'an—who cannot rely on families for support.[134] Islamic politics is a politics of love.

This sort of politicized religion seeks to promote the materiality of the family—not only its sexual and gendered codes, but its capacity to cohere across time—against the logic of the capitalist market, which has commodified sexuality and transformed love into a consumption good, and against the state, which steadily intrudes upon its erotic life, extending the logic of rights and regulation into this intimate sphere. It is partly for this reason that so many women support these patriarchal movements, seeking to shore up the loyalty of their husbands and the value of their mothering. Against the gender-equalizing force of the market and the demos, they reassert a divinely ordered patriarchalism.[135] These movements—whether the evangelical Christians of America or Islamist movements in Egypt and Iran—do authorize female religious agency, including their moralization of men.[136] Nonetheless, the patriarchal family is for them a template for political order, the ground of a revitalized and moralized male agency.

Because the family is an order of creation, not merely an order of production or governance, religions all seek to stitch its transitions, its relations, into rites through which their transrational order is given concrete form. Religion situates the order of human creation within the cosmos, joining the life cycle to cosmogony, rites that point before life and after death. As Asad has shown us, institutional differentiation is an open game.[137] He asserted that our understanding of religion reflects the Western differentiation, in which religion came to be defined as the regulation of the ethical self, the interiority of the soul, and as marking the meaning of the life course, in which the rites of the life cycle—of birth, marriage, and death—are all that remain of the religious domain. This differentiation separates two spaces, the secular and the sacred. It is within the former that humans self-consciously make history and exact the truth of both nature and society, through the freedoms authorized by the nation-state.[138] Two temporalities, two times—that of collective history and individual biological life—are also differentiated. The political-religious imaginary rejoins the meaning of one's life to the origin and telos of a redemption set in historical time, to a history that points beyond both birth and death, joining a collective and an individual afterlife.

Qutb writes that, as a result of modernity, the "clouds that weigh over creation are thicker and denser than before." He also refuses modernity's progressive historical transcript, instead organizing time into successive periods of *jahilya*, or pre-Islamic and post-Enlightenment ignorance. Secular societies, he argues, have forgotten that their wealth, their children, and their political power are all "gifts of Allah." The "organic body" of Islamic society must therefore be "born" again from the Islamic movement, whose origins are "not the result of any human effort or thinking" but come from "the will of Allah": "This Divine element sows the seed of the Islamic movement in human hearts and simultaneously prepares them for action and practical life."[139] In contrast to modernist Egyptian nationalist history, which locates the wellsprings of history either in a national culture traceable back to pharaonic Egypt or in a nationalized—and largely spiritualized—Islam, Qutb underscores that true history is man's giving being to God's will.[140] God is, as Abraham said, "He who gives life and death" (Qur'an 2:258). For Qutb, nonmaterialist creation and the resacralization of history are linked.

There appears to us to be a common pattern in contemporary forms of politicized religion focused on sexuality, sovereignty, and the resacralization of political history, independently of whether or not the nation-states in that these politics are played out are invested with theological or particular redemptive significance. As the case of Qutb suggests, there is plenty of room for indifference to, suspicion toward, and even rejection of nationalism in such politics. But it is also compatible with an embrace of nationalist ideals, as the case of Hamas makes clear. One finds this linkage in Hamas, whose covenant declares its nationalism "part of the religious creed": "If other nationalist movements are connected with materialistic, human or regional causes, [the] nationalism of the Islamic Resistance Movement . . . is connected to the source of spirit and the granter of life, hoisting in the sky of the homeland the heavenly banner that joins earth and heaven with a strong bond."[141]

By the same token, Jerry Falwell, who led the Moral Majority, drew a straight line between the moral making of a divinely given life and the making of premillennial history. Falwell declared:

I believe as we trust in God and pray, as we Christians lead the battle to outlaw abortion, which is murder on demand, as we take our stand against pornography, against the drug traffic, as we take our stand against the breakdown of the traditional family in America, the promotion of homosexual marriages. . . . As we pray and preach and lead, Christian friends, I think there is hope that God may one more time bless America. . . . I believe that between now and the rapture of the Church, America can have a reprieve. God can bless the country and before the rapture, I believe we can stay a free nation.[142]

The preoccupation of politicized religions with sexuality and their violence point to an alternative temporality, a rejection of the regime of infinite progress, of methodical accumulation of uncertain knowledge, and of history that can be read off and in parallel with the predictability of nature. It is a modern rejection of our modernity, a modernity that itself derives, as Hans Blumenberg pointed out, from the playing out of the theological contradictions of Christianity, of progress not as a secularized, Christian salvation narrative but as a self-assertive outgrowth of late-medieval nominalism, in which the *potentia absoluta* of God, freedom from his ordained laws, ultimately stripped the world's order not only of a certain knowledge but also of its providential meaning, such that it fell to man to subject its unfinished materiality to ends he sets himself rather than those set by nature.[143] Hypothetical knowledge and the assertion of human purposes were historically connected. Modern man's self-assertion was a reaction, over the long durée, to the absoluteness of God's power that exculpated man. Against this backdrop, one can read politicized religion's preoccupation with sexuality as an effort to restore the link between human creation and human history, between individual and collective bodies—their sexuality being potentially part and parcel of the redemptive meaning of history issuing from their participation in God's will.

A religiously ordered sexuality is integral to reestablishing the divine telos of human history. It seeks to reground political foundation in creation, collective birth in human birth, and the making of a new collective body in the formation of individual bodies. To forge a nation, the state depends on an abstract space, upon physiological birth and the bland fact of residence—mere location—to build a universal citizen transcending other group loyalties. This anybody depends upon any place. Modern citizenship depends upon the empty space of the state. Religious nationalism fills that space—joining God to the territorial nation, fusing two collective representations, a couplet of spirit and matter, a male collective subject joined to a female territorial body.[144] "The nation," as Richard Koenigberg puts it, "is the fantasy of an omnipotent ego, projected into the world."[145]

Religious nationalism involves an outraged reaction to the effeminization of the collective public body as a result of the military, economic, and cultural penetration of its boundaries. Individual and collective bodily egos are religiously reformed in concert.[146]

One turns to God, the Superman, for the individual agency to protect, inform, and activate the nation's collective body and for the power to sacrifice, to engage in purifying violence, to perform masculinity, and to be—in the end—more than man, that is, to have more than human value and power. In this mating of two sacrificial orders, religious nationalism is a way to mark the land and defend or redefine a nation's boundaries. Religious nationalism's obsessive control of women's bodies is a parallel figuration, the policing of a bodily frontier. By clothing, controlling, and sequestering the female body—taking it out of the sites of collective representation—religious nationalists reassert the maleness of the public body and the femaleness of territory as a loved body that must be maintained inviolate, a perpetual possession.

A religious collective identity, a divine election of a nation, a divinely derived authority of the state, a religious regulation of the nation's sexuality: All four elements invoke God as "the cardinal point of reference."[147] All four invest the nation-state with religious significance. Within this logic, there is no necessary contradiction between nation-state and God.

The Logic of Nationalization: Religious Nationalism without Motive

Some have argued that religious nationalists are not nationalists at all because the nation is not, as Brubaker contends, "the cardinal point of reference and justification for their political program." "These programs," he says, "claim to reorganize public life not 'in the name of the nation' but in the name of God. They work *through* the state, but this does not make them nationalists; as Said Amir Arjomand observed, it makes them statists."[148] The primacy of God, it is argued, reduces the nation-state to an instrument and an arena, thereby rendering the nationalism of religious nationalists inert.

Using the nation-state to enforce religious law, Brubaker has argued, does not make a political movement or party nationalist.[149] Deciding "ultimate value" is a tricky business. Do we determine this by language use, in terms of what religious activists declare to be their ultimate value? Or do we examine their actual practices, the extent to which they invest resources and build the authority of a nation-state, to the exclusion of non-national or transnational projects? Just as the existence of religious language does not make nationalism religious, so the absence of nationalist language does not make a politicized religious movement non-nationalist. Nor, as the legal and policy discourse of Erdogan's AKP regime in Turkey makes clear, does the absence of religious language in the justification and framing of law make a nationalist political project by a religious party nonreligious. While the Islamist AK Party in Turkey has cast its legislative program and constitutional reforms in the secular terms of civil rights, these laws and programs are intended to intensify the religious identity of the nation, to expand publicly funded religious education, to assert religious control over public pedagogy, and to deprivatize Islam in Turkey. A secular state is being used to secure a religious civil society, in a religious nationalist project that operates through secular political idioms.[150]

Moreover, transnational religious projects, in themselves, do not diminish the religious quality of a nation-state's claim to authority. The Iranian regime is composed of Shi'ite nationalists who have promoted cross-national projects that not only seek to align non-Iranian Shi'ites with their regime but challenge Sunni states like Saudi Arabia. The Saudis base their claim to rule a particular nation-state both in a particular variant of Islam and in their claim to custodianship of a transnational pilgrimage center. Despite their global promotion of Wahhabism, they remain an Islamist nation-state.

When religious movements, parties, or regimes use the state as an instrument for the promotion of a particular religion or the enforcement of a religious law or practice, they must align their program with the nationalist code in order not only to mobilize popular support but to negotiate and build consensus with non-Islamists. The decision to reach for political power within the nation state generates tendencies toward a fusion of nationalism and religion on the level of practice, if not on the level of discourse. One can observe, for example, how the nationalist code has captured the transnational Muslim Brotherhood as they have sought to use various nation-states for their own purposes. The same thing has occurred with haredi political parties that theologically reject the Zionist state in Israel. Increasingly dependent on state funding to sustain their institutions and even to survive, radicalized by Palestinian violence and the value of defending Jewish life as opposed to Jewish land, they have moved into national electoral politics as defenders of Judaism within the nation-state, even voting for secular candidates like Netanyahu since the 1990s.[151]

Religious nationalism is an amalgam of religion, nation, and state. Brubaker and others argue that using the state to serve God as one's ultimate ground is to be statist, not nationalist. Even on its own terms, thinking through what it means to be a religious statist, as opposed to a religious nationalist, requires that we think of the state's role in the institution of religion itself. Capitalism offers a parallel case. Capitalists use the state to form and legalize capitalist property relations, indeed, to legally restrict the ability of the state to intervene in markets and production. Does that make them statists? By securing state authority for capitalism, they promote a capitalist state, in part because they use the state to secure the legitimacy of capitalism, to constitute what it is, and because they delimit capitalist domains of activity where the state cannot intrude. But reciprocally the authority of the state is tied to capitalism in that its viability depends on the capitalism whose institutional solidity it guarantees. By using the state to constitute and guarantee capitalism, capitalists construct a capitalist state.

Religion, too, is statist, in its formation, reproduction, and differentiation. Just as the creation of capitalism depended on the state, so, too, did the creation of the institution we know today as "religion." The Christianities of the West secured their institutional status through the exercise of—or the decision not to exercise—state power. Against the backdrop of Europe's early modern confessional struggles, Thomas Hobbes's state of nature was not a prepolitical, creaturely condition but a struggle over the political status of divergent forms of Christianity. The *Leviathan*'s sovereign decision on the enemy was a decision on divinity. The struggle over which God represented the absolute contributed to the absolutization of the sovereign state.[152] The formation of the sovereign Western state, with its monopoly on legitimate violence, was achieved by a compact—the 1648 Peace of Westphalia—that denied the right to violence to religious communities and the transnational church, arrogating the right to make war to sovereign states alone. The state's legitimate monopoly of violence was built on the enforced delegitimation of religious violence, not simply of the transnational church, but the right to go war to secure a faith at all. On the one hand, the violence of enemies was practically tied to sovereign states, not to religious communities. Only geopolitical enemies had a right to kill each other collectively. And on the other hand, religion became an interior faith, a spiritual domain, one of the first freedoms.

Religionists who seek state authority to bolster their religion to constitute and stabilize it as an institution have promoted a religious state, at least in the minimal sense that the state's authority is bound up with the definition of what constitutes a legitimate religion—not only which religion is legitimate, but whether religion is legitimate, and in what sense this domain of activity is outside the state's domain.[153] Even if the state is not itself religious, it remainders itself religiously. Moreover, as in capitalism, the state in part stakes its authority on the constitution, defense, and regulation of the religion that shapes the social world it must ordinate. Depending on the state, which in turn depends on it, religion contains an inherently political potential. Religious nationalists often seek to reverse the differentiation of nation-state and religion. But this can only be labeled statist from a differentiated condition; the charge is itself statist.

Modern religion is a political formation, shaped by the emergence of a "this-worldly" secular space, outside of and underneath the religious, upon which the nation-state and religion are now both assumed to rest.[154] But that space, which we today understand as secular, was religiously conditioned. It is not just that the Christianities of the West provided alternative models and media for disciplining the population and organizing the state apparatus, from bureaucratic form to military discipline and welfare.[155] The secular, democratic nation-state historically derives from a Protestant formation of the secular subject. It was the Protestants' abjection vis-à-vis their absolute God that made Protestantism such a great machine for democratic subjectification, for Protestants both made God's distribution of grace unknowable and thus beyond human reason and good works and yet made the individual's freedom into his most divine and religiously necessary attribute.

Just as late medieval nominalism provided the early modern model of the sovereign, it also provided the schematic ground for Protestantism and, through Protestantism, for the modern subject.[156] Unlike the orthodoxy of Thomas Aquinas, in which the universe is founded on God's reason, the nominalist universe is founded on God's unknowable productive will. In the place of God as Logos, knowledge of whom was the ultimate aim of every believer, nominalism sets up God as omnipotent free will, belief in whom must depend on faith beyond reason. Moreover, nominalism, as the name implies, suggests that universal essences or ideas—of which individuals are but instances—are, in fact, just names. Only individuals and their sense experiences have ontological status as the real.

Martin Luther would insist on God's free, unknowable, and unmanipulable bestowal of grace as the medium through which one's sins are forgiven, unmediated by any ecclesiastical structure. "Salvation," Mark C. Taylor writes, "is a function of the absolute will of God, which is grounded in nothing other than itself."[157] Protestantism created a new kind of religious subject, whose salvation is justified by his own faith, a faith indicated by his certainty.[158] Nominalism's free, omnipotent God established the theological and ontological ground for the correlatively free human subject, in a word, for what would become the secular subject.

It was the Protestant transcendent God's absolute, inscrutable power to elect that also helped make human election into a model of political organization. Luther proclaimed the priesthood of all believers, leveling access to God and stripping ecclesiastical authority of its sacrality. God no longer permeates the cosmos or the community of believers. Protestantism made religion into faith, choice, and a direct relationship between the individual and God. This transformed religion into fissiparous nodes of voluntary association. Indeed, the *anti-philosophes,* the Catholic opponents of the French Revolution, understood it as a Protestantism without God.[159]

The individual becomes a sacred person, whose ultimate truth is located in his subjectivity, both his faith and his senses. Modernity's sacralization of the common man—of which Durkheim makes so much—and the valorization of his choices derives, at least in part, from this religious understanding about his faith, his ability to choose God and to read the founding texts that he revealed. One approaches God through the revealed text, through the Word that all are required to read and interpret in the vernacular. This ground made constitutional democracy possible, a polity comprising and deriving its authority from the aggregation of monadic individual choices and individual readings of the text. With Protestantism, God became transcendent, unavailable in the natural world or in the organization of a delegated church but incarnate within the soul of the individual believer. There is a sense, then, in which the democratic nation-state is a secularized religious state.

Although Protestantism prepared the way for the reduction of all the Abrahamic, monotheistic religions to an interior, individual, other-worldly form of piety—to "relegate aqida," one's relationship to God, as Qutb, put it, "to the heart"—this interiorization also historically depended on the state's progressive shearing away of religion's world-making capacities by its enforced differentiation as "religion."[160] Religion was steadily reduced to a marker of collective identity or, more commonly, a private belief that barely rustled the waters of social exchange and was relegated to unobservable experiences of faith located in the chambers of one's heart. As the history of the Western nation-state makes clear, the contemporary religious reconstitution of the space of the social—not as a question of identity but as the nature of our subjectivity, the qualities of our sociality, and the attributes of the good—is a political act that can recast the ground and hence the nature of the nation-state. The extent and content of the religious regulation of social life always have political potential.

Piety can become political. There is a politics immanent in pietistic movements, not just in the sense that this kind of subject formation opens political possibilities in terms of organizational capacities, in defining religion and securing interpretive authority outside the scope of state regulation, but in its formation of subjects whose forms of life regulation may ultimately conflict with the state.[161] This is why Muslim states have increasingly sought to regulate the *dawa* movement in places like Egypt. Within Islamist movements, the inseparability of the two is manifest in Islamic discourse itself. Asad refers to the Islamic *umma* as a "theologically defined space enabling Muslims to practice the disciplines of *din* in the world."[162] But the *umma* is not just a theological or ethical space. Ibn Taymiyyah, a critical source for today's Islamists, writing in the late thirteenth and early fourteenth centuries, wrote that in a just community "exercise of a public office is one of the most important duties of religion [din]; we would add that public office is essential to the very existence of religion [din]."[163]

In the writings of Qutb, precisely this interdependence of inner belief and outer political enforcement of moral practice, between internal and external "tyranny," makes "all sin" political. "For Qutb," Andrew March argues, "it is almost always the corruption of the social, political world that causes humans to be overpowered by their capacity for vice."[164] This transom between personal piety and public politics points us to the ways in which Islamist tendencies like the Muslim Brotherhood—or Christian fundamentalism, for that matter—historically can and have moved into and out of the political sphere over time. Whether a religious movement is pietistic or political depends on where in time one slices into the historical record. Theorizing that movement suggests that we not engage in a priori purifications of religion, or even kinds of religion, as being nonpolitical.

When religious traditionalists, pietists, and/or fundamentalists who reject nationalism seek authority in the nation-state and in a nationally defined civil society, it can generate the sorts of politics and political culture that we identify with nationalism. We return to the *haredi* or non- and anti-Zionist Orthodox Jewish sector in Israel as one example. Much of this community remains hostile toward Zionism and to the secular-national institutions it created.[165] In some small parts of this community, this translates into an anti-Zionist politics characterized by a theological rejection of the heretical Zionist state so complete as to even generate identification with its avowed external enemies.[166] Yet much more substantial parts of this community now seem to be moving in the opposite direction.

First, a number of recent scholarly investigations have revealed desires for rapprochement with the Israeli state and with its ideals of national citizenship in certain parts of the haredi world, especially among those haredim of a Mizrahi background, meaning descendants of immigrants from the Arab world, and among haredi youth, including the yeshiva students who are its most respected bearers and symbols.[167] Thus, some analysts find change in haredi attitudes toward the army, which stands at the center of the dominant Israeli national narrative and its Zionist public culture. Among Israeli yeshiva students—young men studying classic Rabbinic texts in the setting of an intensive religious academy—the Israeli sociologist Nurit Stadler discovered a subculture of deep, even obsessive interest in the Israeli army and fantasies of joining it. Given the intense opprobrium that haredi spokesmen heap on the army as a social institution inimical to proper religiosity, the tenor of this military fantasy is striking. It includes an "idealization of soldier's masculinity," a reciprocal rendering of the students' own spiritual struggles in militaristic and soldiering terms, and, most importantly for us, investment in the national narrative and the narrative of the army's "purity of arms" and the rightness of its cause, which actually exceeds that of an increasingly critical secular Jewish public. Stadler quotes one yeshiva student who takes the final discursive step: "If we all joined the army, it would make it stronger, and the Jewish nation would have a better army."[168]

Now, there are good reasons to question the significance of these signs of rapprochement. As Yakir Englander notes, a broadening of the temporal lens might suggest the converse: that earlier forms of demonstrative haredi emotional and practical identification with the Israeli nation-state visible in the first decades of the Israel's existence—from the display of the Israeli flag on Independence Day at a major haredi institution of learning to higher levels of army service by Orthodox men—have in fact faded away.[169] On this argument, the structural integration of haredi Judaism into the mainstream of Israeli politics and society has led in fact to greater combativeness and less felt pressure to acknowledge the norms of the hated secular-national public culture. Moreover, as of the completion of this essay, a widening confrontation regarding the extension of mandatory army service to haredi men threatens any rapprochement that may have taken place between haredi and non-haredi Jews over national service and belonging.

But the question of haredi Jewish rapprochement (or not) with national institutions and ideals associated with secular Zionism is not the only question we might ask about religion and nationalism within traditionalist Jewry—especially at a moment when secular Zionist traditions seem to be suffering the same erosion in their ability to order social sensibilities as other secularisms. When we look at haredi Jewry from the broader perspective of political attitudes as such, we see signs that haredi society is moving toward an intensely chauvinist and territorial politics that one Israeli commentator defines as "more right-wing than the [secular Zionist and religious Zionist] right-wing."[170] Polling data reveal that a strong majority of Israeli haredi respondents are deeply opposed to any territorial compromise with the Palestinians—even though over the past few decades some of the greatest Rabbinic authorities in that community have given Jewish religious-legal sanction for territorial compromise on the grounds that the saving of life overrides the sanctity of the land. Moreover, a variety of recent studies suggest much higher levels of ethnic antipathy and distrust toward Arabs among haredi Jews than among their secular Zionist Jewish counterparts.[171]

Consider this statement: "The State of Israel belongs to the Jews and only the Jews have rights over it." Unsurprisingly, whereas 56 percent of respondents identified with the distinct religious Zionist sector agreed, only 28 percent of the secular respondents did so. But what is most striking was the stance of the anti-Zionist and nominally antinationalist haredim: Over three-quarters of the haredi respondents agreed.[172]

Certain grass-roots developments within and around haredi Jewry in Israel might be adduced here as well. First, recent years have seen some unexpected fusions of full-throated rightist Jewish nationalism and stringent religious traditionalism from groups who stand outside classical haredi Judaism but who aspire to join that camp religiously. Over the course of the past several decades, substantial numbers of Israeli Jews from a Middle Eastern or Mizrahi background have "returned" to an orthodoxy modeled on haredi traditionalism yet retained or even deepened an openness to Jewish/Israeli nationalist ideals. Where the mainstream of historical haredi Jewry still rejects any fusion of these ideals, this growing traditionalist bloc may be finding ways to embrace nationalism by desecularizing it. In the realm of liturgy, one of the most unacceptable Zionist innovations in the eyes of the haredi leadership was the insertion of prayers for the State of Israel and the safety of Israeli soldiers. Haredi prayer books generally have had no truck with such innovations. But a 1990s liturgy published by the son of Rabbi Ovadiah Yosef, the leading figure in the rapidly expanding subculture of haredi Judaism among Mizrahi Jews, included such a prayer in an edited form.[173] More directly, the political party and movement that reflects and channels this newly minted version of traditionalist Judaism, the Shas party, recently became the first haredi party to join the World Zionist Organization.

More recently, a second variety of "aspirationally haredi" Judaism has taken shape among young people raised in the religious Zionist camp (in Israel and in the Anglo-American world) who combine the messianic Zionism of that camp (centering on the view that Zionism and the maintenance of worldly Jewish sovereignty over the religiously defined Land of Israel are in fact bearers of divine providence and part of the eschatological process) with the stringent religiosity and antimodernism of haredi Judaism. Much remains to be investigated about the character, scope, sociological origins, and future ideological development of this relatively new phenomenon—generally referred to as "hardali" (an acronym of "haredi and national-religious")—but it seems to revolve around an assertive fusion of haredi antimodernism, messianic activism, and a fiercely right-wing ethnonationalism and integral territorial nationalism.

It is true that both of these phenomena are at best complicated iterations of our point, in that both represent not a transformation within haredi Jewry as a historically evolved community but rather syntheses by populations who have come to haredi Judaism relatively recently. So one could say that these represent not the triumph of nationalism in haredi ranks but a haredization of segments of Israel's nationalist political camp. Thus, concretely, the decision of Shas to join the World Zionist Organization might be said to reflect a "de-haredization" of the party rather than a nationalization of haredi Judaism: Observers note that this was in part an effort to pick up religiously Orthodox but non-haredi voters from the old Zionist-religious camp.[174]

There are now substantial groupings in Israeli society that are consciously seeking to achieve the very fusion that both haredi leaders and some analysts of religion and nationalism insist is impossible. A 2010 Shas party spokesman's defense of the party's decision demonstrates that will and asserts not its impossibility but its commonsensical, already-achieved character: "The party's ruling Council of Torah Sages 'concluded that there is no contradiction between our being ultra-Orthodox and our being Zionists and lovers of Zion,' [Knesset member Yaakov] Margi said, adding, . . . 'is there an ultra-Orthodox MK today who doesn't see the importance of Jerusalem, who doesn't see himself as part of Zion?'"[175]

A second and more extensively studied form of rapprochement cuts still more closely to the heart of the question. For decades, one important element within the classical haredi camp—the Chabad-Lubavitch Hasidic movement—has been moving toward an extreme position with regard to Israel's relations with the territories it occupies, with its neighbors, and with the Palestinians under its rule. Importantly, this extremism is framed and motivated in expressly theological terms.[176] Here too, it might be objected that this particular movement has always been a theological outlier within the haredi world; certainly, it can and has been argued that this movement has an altogether unique understanding of the relationship of the current era and its worldly Jewish realities, on the one hand, and the messianic advent expected by classical Judaism, on the other.[177] But once again, it is analytically self-defeating to ignore the possible implications of the fact that a substantial movement within haredi society has been transformed from one of the standard-bearers of haredi anti-Zionism into a movement that regularly aligns itself with the most ultranationalist positions in Israeli political life.

This last case raises another analytical question, however, that returns us to the starting point of this essay and to some of the powerful arguments against the view that nationalism and traditionalist religion can be substantially fused. For all of its effective ultranationalism, the Chabad-Lubavitch movement remains vociferously anti-Zionist in a formal ideological-theological sense. In his path-breaking analysis of this maverick movement, Ravitsky cites the pithy summary of one of its spokesmen that the movement combines "total opposition to Zionism and nationalism, coupled with a stringent prohibition against handing over a single inch of the territory that the Lord has granted us."[178]

Thus we are thrown back on the question of whether it makes sense to think about something like the Chabad-Lubavitch movement through the lens of nationalism if its spokesmen insist that they utterly oppose it as an idea. Again, we might counterpose to this declaration other evidence that suggests how a particular interpretation of classical

Jewish concepts of the very incomparability of Jewish peoplehood to that of other peoples and the uniqueness of Jewish fate among "the nations" nonetheless leads Chabad toward an especially uncompromising religious-nationalist politics of its own creation. Thus, agreeing that Chabad's "radically hawkish political stance . . . stemmed from different motivations, both halakhic and military, than that of messianic religious Zionists," Ravitsky argues further that "this political radicalism is directly connected with [the movement's] acute messianic consciousness," which posits that messianic redemption is imminent and that this demands that "Jews liberate themselves once and for all from the lowly stature traditionally characterizing the relationship of the Jew to other nations."[179]

What all these disparate phenomena within an expanding and dividing traditionalist Jewry in Israel have in common is a tendency to reject "nationalism" and sometimes "Zionism" as secular discourses while finding new space from within the Jewish tradition and its 'native' discourses for assertive and even eschatologically freighted ethnic and ethno-territorialist politics. Thus, we may not see any return to a guarded but open embrace of the discourse of nationalism as such in haredi Jewish circles à la Akiva Yosef Schlesinger circa 1868; certainly, we may expect haredi Jews committed to ideals of Jewish uniqueness and chosenness wholly to avoid Schlesinger's readiness to draw direct and positive analogies between Jewish self-determination and the self-determination of "other nations."[180]

But another aspect of Schlesinger's thought as reconstructed by Michael Silber was the connection he drew between the traditional sacralization of Jewish life in the Land of Israel and new concepts of this-worldly Jewish self-determination, itself recast in his ultra-Orthodox imagination as an essential bulwark of traditional Judaism in the face of modernity's secularizing and de-ethnicizing thrust. There are good reasons to question whether the fact of Jewish settlement and sovereignty in what is for religious Jews the Land of Israel can really be sequestered in the Jewish religious imagination as a nonevent. In 1939, when the British Mandate government in Palestine renounced its commitment to the creation of a Jewish national home in Palestine, the leader of the Modzhitser Hasidic group in Poland, Shaul Yedidiah Elazar, called on Jews to resist and thundered, "ultimately, no nation or language [*umah ve-lashon*] will be able to extend the hand of rule in our Land and foreigners will not come within our borders." Elazar wrote in the face of unprecedented anti-Semitism and an increasingly violent and total extrusion of Jews in Eastern and Central Europe. He and others in the haredi world were moving in the 1930s toward rapprochement with Zionism less because of theological factors than because of an increasingly clear-eyed appreciation that, as he put it two years later, "now we see the great and terrible woes of the people of Israel as a result of our lack of a land of our own; dispersed among the nations, everywhere a national minority. This situation awakens the wicked and piratical of the world to attack Jews, and indeed to use antisemitism as a means to conquer and enslave the world."[181] But we must also ask whether the theological sensibility of the first quote, even if it was activated by political powerlessness and state-lessness in a world of nation-states, might not also be awakened and nourished by the fact of political power and statehood in a sacred space—and if so, does this not open the way to a traditionalist Jewish hyper-ethnicist religious nationalism?

Perhaps we overstate the fluidity of what remains a highly conservative and wary intellectual culture. But there remains the evidence of growing ethnic intolerance and ethnopolitical militancy in a religious community "vitalized" by an overdetermined, powerful relationship to ideas of land, people, and sovereignty powerfully present in the tradition it claims to defend and in its everyday life. It is too early to know, but it does again suggest that we should be suspicious in this case too of a priori judgments of how nationalism and religion intersect. What seems clear in the Israeli haredi case is that the attitudes and sentiments of a good part of that population are "out ahead" of its leadership in terms of effectively ultranationalist tendencies and concomitant demands that the Jewish state enact these in the name of religious imperatives.[182] Of course, it may be that too much rapprochement with either the secular nation-state or the coinages of secular modernity will provoke haredi leaders to rein in their followers. But in the meantime—and every indication is that this is an ongoing "meantime"—we see a half-articulated but potent fusion of pietistic, antimodern religion and modern state-directed territorial eth-nicism that is a far cry from anything we could usefully call "antinationalism" or "nonna-tionalism." What may be taking shape is a hyper-nationalism with no roots in secular nationalism at all, a nationalism with no need of Zionism's complex mix of religious motifs and secular motives, because its adherents are *living* the reality of Jewish sover-eignty in the Jewish holy land, even if they continue to believe that it is an incomplete and flawed sovereignty prior to the coming of the messiah.

Brubaker writes, "The ultimate datum of nationalist politics—the ultimate point of reference and justification—is the claimed existence of a 'nation,' not the commandments of God. Does this not make nationalist politics fundamentally secular, or at least funda-mentally distinct from forms of religious politics that seek to transform public life not in the name of the nation, but in the name of God?"[183] This is an instance of secular nation-alist discourse, not an analytically viable distinction. It is the relation of God to nation-state that is at issue. God's proclaimed primacy does not negate the potentially religious nature of the nationalism. Nationalist politics cannot be religious only if there is a *neces-sary* contradiction between nation and God, or if we accept that making the state religious means rendering those means without religious meaning. Religion and nation-state can be co-implicated in a multiplicity of ways. Their manifest and hidden conjunctions and contradictions remain to be studied in careful comparative ways. At this juncture, purifi-cation protects our political imaginations; it does not promote our understanding of the world that has been shaking beneath our feet.

Notes

Introduction: Any More Deathless Questions?

Asja Szafraniec and Ernst van den Hemel

1. Daniel Dubuisson, *The Western Construction of Religion: Myths, Knowledge, and Ideology*, trans. William Sayers (Baltimore: Johns Hopkins University Press, 2003).

2. Hent de Vries, *Religion beyond a Concept* (New York: Fordham University Press, 2008), 11.

3. Webb Keane, "Religious Language," in *Materiality*, ed. Daniel Miller (Durham, N.C.: Duke University Press, 2005), 48. Kean is referring to Talal Asad's *Genealogies of Religion: Discipline and Reasons of Power in Christianity and Islam* (Baltimore: Johns Hopkins University Press, 1993).

4. Jan van Henten and Meerten B. ter Borg. eds., *Powers: Religion as a Social and Spiritual Force* (New York: Fordham University Press, 2010); Dick Houtman and Birgit Meyer "Introduction: Material Religion—How Things Matter," in *Things: Religion and the Question of Materiality*, ed. Dick Houtman and Birgit Meyer (New York: Fordham University Press, 2012).

5. See the volume introducing the series, de Vries, *Religion beyond a Concept*.

6. Webb Keane "Semiotics and the Social Analysis of Material Things," *Language and Communication* 23 (2003): 419.

7. Webb Keane *Christian Moderns: Freedom and Fetish in the Mission Encounter* (Berkeley: University of California Press, 2007), 21.

8. Ludwig Wittgenstein, *Philosophical Investigations: The English Text of the Third Edition*, trans. G. E. M. Anscombe (Nerw York: Macmillan, 1958), §432, 128.

9. Houtman and Meyer, "Introduction: Material Religion"; Keane, "Religious Language"; Manuel A. Vasquez, *More Than Belief: A Materialist Theory of Religion* (Oxford: Oxford University Press, 2011); Birgit Meyer, "Medium," in "Key Terms in Material Religion," ed. Birgit Meyer, David Morgan, Crispin Paine, and S. Brent Plate, special issue of *Material Religion* 7, no. 1 (2011): 58–67.

10. Houtman and Meyer, "Introduction: Material Religion," 5.

11. Birgit Meyer, "Mediation and Immediacy: Sensational Forms, Semiotic Ideologies, and the Question of the Medium," in "What Is a Medium?: Theologies, Technologies, and Aspirations," ed. Patrick Eisenlohr, special issue of *Social Anthropology* 19, no. 1 (2011): 28.

12. Houtman and Meyer, "Introduction: Material Religion," 10.

13. Maurice Merleau-Ponty, *Phenomenology of Perception*, 2nd ed., trans. Colin Smith (London: Routledge, 2002), 205.

14. John Locke, *Essay concerning Human Understanding,* ed. Peter H. Nidditch (Oxford: Oxford University Press, 1985), 614. While other ideas of Locke on the relation between words and ideas have become outdated, this one still stands. Words are not merely articulate sounds that return. Merleau-Ponty would probably restate Locke's argument in terms of an amnesiac patient—arguably, such a patient would be the best candidate for those religious rituals that purport to do away with meaning. One may also ask whether the context of those practices does not provide them with meaning, even if it is only implicit.

15. Jean-Luc Nancy, *Dis-Enclosure: The Deconstruction of Christianity*, trans. Bettina Bergo, Gabriel Malenfant, and Michael B. Smith (New York: Fordham University Press, 2008), 87.

16. Keane, "Semiotics and the Social Analysis of Material Things," 411.

17. "Scholars tended to overlook—or perhaps better, look *through*—religion's material forms." Houtman and Meyer, "Introduction: Material Religion," 11, emphasis in the original. See also Meyer, "Mediation and Immediacy."

18. Meyer, "Mediation and Immediacy," 26.

19. See Roy Rappaport, *Ritual and Religion in the Making of Humanity* (Cambridge: Cambridge University Press, 1999), 114–38; Keane, "Religious Language," 199; Houtman and Meyer, "Introduction: Material Religion," 11; Meyer, "Mediation and Immediacy," 28–29.

20. It also might seem that this approach offers a way to circumvent the traditional conundrums related to the philosophy of language—that it presents a solution to a set of discontents we might call "skeptical." It would seem to provide a pragmatic tool to cut short the endless detours of interpretation, the resulting indefinite suspension of judgment, the problem of the unfathomability of human sincerity, the inability to pinpoint meaning by capturing intention, and the resulting indetermination of every human act. See Roy Rappaport on rendering insincerity "publicly impotent": Rappaport, *Ritual and Religion in the Making of Humanity*, 122. Yet materialism thus understood might instead amplify skepticism, not rebut it. Austin's notion of performativity show how this could happen. The expression "My word is my bond" means that when I pronounce the phrase required by a given ritual at a right time and place, I am bound by it, regardless of my intentions or of how those are interpreted by others. Words here are objects designated to fit the predestined slots of the ritual. There is no place for inwardness, and hence no place for skepticism: all that counts is out there. But not only is this view branded as simplistic by Austin's student and follower Stanley Cavell (who points out that Austin seemingly forgets at this point the role he gives to excuses—my word is not always and shouldn't always be my bond), but the quite different approaches informed by phenomenology, neurology, and embodied cognition do not share this legalistic and ritualistic view, even though they are equally concerned with the concrete and the embodied. Instead, they point out that inwardness might be largely unconscious and preconceptual, that inwardness might be an inwardness of the body, rather than of the thinking subject. If we can venture an analogy between the way in which significance arises in a percept and the way we "perceive" what is said to us, to hear or read words is always to be put in movement by them, made resonant in a certain way, rather than to perceive their sense as something that is described and transmitted by them. This movement is always at first chaotic and inconclusive. As Francesco Varela explains, every impact of this kind (in which significance arises) is always "adjudicated in an extremely rapid, unconscious oscillation" in which the complex patterns of activity, displayed by the units that make up the (neural) network, compete with each other for possible outcomes. Francisco Varela et al., *The Embodied Mind: Cognitive Science and Human Experience* (Cambridge, Mass.: MIT Press, 1992), 99. For this "background of incoherent and chaotic activity in fast oscillations (that is, with periods of

about five to ten milliseconds) until the cortex settles into a global electrical pattern," see also Varela, *Ethical Know-How* (Stanford: Stanford University Press, 1999), 50, and "Reenchantment of the Concrete," in *Incorporations (Zone 6)*, ed. Jonathan Crary and Sanford Kwinter (New York: Zone Books, 1992), 333. For instance, what is it that decides how the overheard words *tolle lege* are to be taken? As a response to prayer —as a command or injunction—or simply as an irrelevant noise? It is unlikely that Augustine's reception of those words was a matter of a conscious choice— rather, some inward and obscure (to consciousness) process (an "unconscious oscillation") will have taken place. If this kind of rapid and unconscious oscillation indeed plays a role in our listening to words, conceiving their significance, and responding to them, it follows that the felicity of a given speech act must always inevitably be in question—on this latter account, it is open to a virtually infinite array of factors, which leaves space open for the possibility of performative failure.

21. Roy Rappaport grants that the human ability to lie, deceive, pretend and playact also has a role in religious ritual contexts, but defends his position by saying that while his approach "does not eliminate insincerity, it renders it publicly impotent." Rappaport, *Ritual and Religion in the Making of Humanity*, 122.

22. Merleau-Ponty, *Phenomenology of Perception*, 216. Merleau-Ponty speaks of the "linguistic gesture" and of "gestural sense." For example, "the spoken word is a gesture," which means that it is not "given to me as a thing" (214).

23. Jan Assmann, "Ancient Egypt and the Materiality of the Sign," in *Materialities of Communication (Writing Science)*, ed. Hans Ulrich Gumbrecht and Karl Ludwig Pfeiffer (Stanford: Stanford University Press, 1994), 26.

24. It has been argued by Rappaport that one of the merits of the ritualization of religious practices is the ability to counter, by repetition, precisely this skepticism regarding the obligation one incurs by engaging in the ritual. At the same time, every repetition has also something of an obsessive compulsion—Michael Lambek mentions an Islamitic ritual in which a phrase is being repeated some seventy thousand times, which may suggest that while serving to instill certitude in the faithful, it still stages what it is supposed to dissipate: a fundamental uncertainty.

25. Jan Assmann, "Inscriptional Violence and the Art of Cursing: A Study of Performative Writing," in the present volume.

26. Stanley Cavell, *Philosophy the Day after Tomorrow* (Cambridge, Mass.: Harvard University Press, 2006), 172.

27. Ibid., 176–67, 184.

28. Ibid. 185.

29. See also Asad's discussion of how the "sacred" and the "secular" depend on each other or on the movement in the conceptual ranges of "sacred" and "profane."

30. Keane, "Semiotics and the Social Analysis of Material Things," 419.

31. See "Deathless Questions," *The Immanent Frame: Secularism, Religion, and the Public Sphere*, http://blogs.ssrc.org/tif/deathless-questions.

1. Word as Act: Varieties of Semiotic Ideology in the Interpretation of Religion

Michael Lambek

1. This essay is a response to Jan Bremmer's kind invitation to speak at the conference "Words," the fourth themed conference in the NWO initiative "The Future of the Religious Past," held in Groningen from June 15 to June 16, 2009. I also acknowledge support from the Canada

Research Chairs program, the CFI, and the University of Toronto at Scarborough. A shorter version has been published as "Varieties of Semiotic Ideology in the Interpretation of Religion," in *A Companion to the Anthropology of Religion*, ed. Janice Boddy and Michael Lambek (Boston: Wiley-Blackwell, 2013), 137–53. Many thanks to the late Helen Tartar for her editorial support.

2. Webb Keane, *Christian Moderns: Freedom and Fetish in the Mission Encounter* (Berkeley: University of California Press, 2007), 16, summarizing Michael Silverstein, "Language Structure and Linguistic Ideology," in *The Elements: A Parasession on Linguistic Units and Levels*, ed. Paul Clyne et al. (Chicago: Chicago Linguistic Society, 1979), 193–247.

3. Webb Keane, "Semiotics and the Social Analysis of Material Things," *Language and Communication* 23, nos. 2–3 (2003): 419.

4. Stanley Cavell, *Must We Mean What We Say?* (Cambridge: Cambridge University Press, 1976).

5. Simon Blackburn, "You Are Not Helpful!" *London Review of Books*, January 29, 2009, 18.

6. Roy Rappaport, *Ritual and Religion in the Making of Humanity* (Cambridge: Cambridge University Press, 1999).

7. See Clifford Geertz, "Religion as a Cultural System," in *The Interpretation of Cultures* (New York: Basic Books, 1973), 87–125, for a notable attempt to develop a general formulation, and Talal Asad, "Anthropological Conceptions of Religion: Reflections on Geertz," *Man* 18 (1982): 237–59, for a stringent critique. See Clifford Geertz, "Shifting Aims, Moving Targets: On the Anthropology of Religion," *Journal of the Royal Anthropological Institute* 11, no. 1 (2005): 1–15, and Steven Caton, "What Is an 'Authorizing Discourse?'" in *Powers of the Secular Modern*, ed. David Scott and Charles Hirschkind (Stanford: Stanford University Press, 2006), 31–56, for responses to Asad.

8. Indeed, their respective semiotic ideologies are presumably more critical than whether the respective theorists adhere to a particular community of religious practice.

9. This does not imply that speakers agree on the meaning of any given utterance.

10. Geertz, "The Impact of the Concept of Culture on the Concept of Man," in *Interpretation of Cultures*, 33–54.

11. Mikhail Bakhtin, *The Dialogic Imagination*, ed. Michael Holquist, trans. Caryl Emerson and Michael Holquist (Austin: University of Texas Press, 1981).

12. Greg Urban, "The 'I' of Discourse," in *Semiotics, Self and Society*, ed. Benjamin Lee and Greg Urban (Berlin: Mouton de Gruyter, 1989), 27–52.

13. The linguistic exercises carry their own intentions and histories, of course.

14. J. L. Austin, *How to Do Things with Words* (1955; Oxford: Oxford University Press, 1965).

15. Claude Lévi-Strauss, *The Savage Mind* (Chicago: University of Chicago Press, 1966).

16. E. E. Evans-Pritchard, *Theories of Primitive Religion* (Oxford: Oxford University Press, 1965), and E. E. Evans-Pritchard, *Witchcraft, Oracles and Magic among the Azande* (Oxford: Oxford University Press, 1937).

17. E. E. Evans-Pritchard, *Nuer Religion* (Oxford: Oxford University Press, 1956).

18. Rodney Needham, *Belief, Language, and Experience* (Chicago: University of Chicago Press, 1972); Jean Pouillon, "Remarks on the Verb 'To Believe,'" in *Between Belief and Transgression*, ed. Michel Izard and Pierre Smith (Chicago: University of Chicago Press, 1982), 1–8; Malcolm Ruel, "Christians as Believers," in *Religious Organization and Religious Experience*, ed. John Davis (London: Academic Press, 1982), 9–32.

19. See Michael Lambek, "Anthropology and Religion," in *Oxford Handbook of Religion and Science*, ed. Philip Clayton (Oxford: Oxford University Press, 2006), 271–89.

20. Franz Steiner, *Taboo* (Harmondsworth: Penguin, 1956); Claude Lévi-Strauss, *Totemism* (Boston: Beacon, 1963).

21. See note 7 for the example of "religion."

22. Eva Keller, "Scriptural Study as Normal Science: Seventh-Day Adventist Practice on the East Coast of Madagascar," in *The Anthropology of Christianity*, ed. Fenella Cannell (Durham, N.C.: Duke University Press, 2006).

23. Geertz, "Religion as a Cultural System," 87–125.

24. Geertz, "Thick Description: Toward an Interpretive Theory of Culture," in *Interpretation of Cultures*, 1–30.

25. Respectively, Geertz, "Religion as a Cultural System," 87–125, and Geertz, "Deep Play: Notes on the Balinese Cockfight," in *Interpretation of Cultures*, 412–53.

26. Geertz, "The Cerebral Savage: On the Work of Claude Lévi-Strauss," in *Interpretation of Cultures*, 345–59.

27. Lévi-Strauss, *Savage Mind*.

28. Lévi-Strauss, *Mythologiques*, 4 vols. (Paris: Plon, 1964–71).

29. Blackburn, "You Are Not Helpful!" 18. The theme, metaphor, or allegory of music is key to Cavell, as well—and of course music has been central to religion itself—words put to music and chanted or sung rather than simply spoken, and sometimes no referential words at all. From the trance dance of the Bushmen to hymns of the Church of England, from Sufi odes to Bach cantatas, music plays a central role in religious performance. For some anthropological takes, see Maurice Bloch, "Symbols, Song, Dance and Features of Articulation: Is Religion an Extreme Form of Traditional Authority?" in *Ritual, History and Power: Selected Papers in Anthropology* (London: Athlone, 1989), and Wendy James, *The Ceremonial Animal: A New Portrait of Anthropology* (Oxford: Oxford University Press, 2004).

30. Eduardo Viveiros de Castro, "Cosmological Deixis and Amerindian Perspectivism," *Journal of the Royal Anthropological Institute* 4, no. 3 (1998): 469–88; Philippe Descola, *Par-delà nature et culture* (Paris: Gallimard, 2005).

31. Mark Nuttall, *Arctic Homeland: Kinship, Community and Development in Northwest Greenland* (Toronto: University of Toronto Press, 1992), 187; see also 69–70.

32. Godfrey Lienhardt, *Divinity and Experience: The Religion of the Dinka* (Oxford: Oxford University Press, 1961), 138, 139. Lienhardt shows that to speak of religion is to sift through words. There is no way to clarify with consistency Dinka notions of divinity and the relationships among the various manifestations (96): "As rain, or thunder and lightning, or a meteorite, which fall in one place, are not, and yet are, the same as those which fall elsewhere at some other time, so DENG is one and many" (162).

33. Austin, *How to Do Things with Words*.

34. Rappaport, *Ritual and Religion*.

35. Cavell, *Must We Mean What We Say?* and Cavell, *A Pitch of Philosophy* (Cambridge, Mass.: Harvard University Press, 1996).

36. It absolves some of the weight of individual choice. For a theorist like Maurice Bloch, ritual is a form of coercion, and hence the responsibility ultimately lies elsewhere.

37. Rappaport, *Ritual and Religion*; Lienhardt, *Divinity and Experience*, 251, 280.

38. Rappaport, *Ritual and Religion*, 296.

39. Lienhardt, *Divinity and Experience*, 139.

40. Rappaport, *Ritual and Religion*, 280–81, italics in original.

41. Ibid., 280.

42. Saba Mahmood, *Politics of Piety: The Islamic Revival and the Feminist Subject* (Princeton: Princeton University Press, 2004); Charles Hirschkind, *The Ethical Soundscape: Cassette Sermons and Islamic Counter-Publics* (New York: Columbia University Press, 2006).

43. Robert Pigott, religious affairs correspondent, "Atheists Call for "Debaptism," *BBC News*, http://news.bbc.co.uk/2/hi/uk_news/7941817.stm.

44. Stanley Tambiah, "Form and Meaning of Magical Acts," in *Culture, Thought and Social Action* (Cambridge, Mass.: Harvard University Press, 1985), 60–86.

45. Lambek, "Toward an Ethics of the Act," in *Ordinary Ethics: Anthropology, Language, and Action*, ed. Lambek (New York: Fordham University Press, 2010), 39–63.

46. Tambiah, "Form and Meaning of Magical Acts."

47. Informed by the religious milieu in which we are socialized as well as by prevailing stereotypes of non-Western and religious people, we have found it all too easy to ascribe excessive metaphysical weight to their key words and central concepts. Some of the best anthropologists, like Lienhardt and Michelle Rosaldo, are able to support Wittgenstein's antimetaphysical view, linking "religion" more with human creativity, ritual, myth, poetry, and ethical engagement than with explanation or the supernatural. Take also Ruel's work on sacrifice, or on what he specifies, with Austinian precision, as nonsacrificial ritual killing (Malcolm Ruel, "Non-Sacrificial Ritual Killing," *Man* 25 [1990]: 323–51), because, as he says, what is at issue is not the life *of* the animal, offered up to some deity, but the life *in* the animal, which is taken and redirected in a simultaneously natural and ethical flow of force or substance. In other words, "religion," for the East African Kuria, is a set of relatively formal acts that members of the community take to ensure collective and individual flourishing and well-being.

48. Alton Becker, *Beyond Translation: Essay Toward a Modern Philology* (Ann Arbor: University of Michigan Press, 1995).

49. "Dutch Leave Messages on God Phone," *BBC News*, March 7, 2009, http://news.bbc.co.uk/2/hi/europe/7929799.stm. It continues, "Although the hotline is officially launched on Saturday, the phone number has been active for the past week, with 1,000 messages left on the answerphone. But the messages are to remain confidential and will not form part of the art project. Van der Dong told Radio Netherlands: 'I'm not a pastor, I'm an artist and I won't listen to the messages. It's a secret between the Lord and the people who are calling.' Exhibition spokeswoman Susanna Groot said there was no intention to offend anyone. 'In earlier times you would go to a church to say a prayer and now [this is an] opportunity to just make a phone call and say your prayer in a modern way.' Instead, the aim is to provoke debate about the priorities of modern life. The phone line will remain open for the next six months."

2. Medieval Irish Spells: "Words of Power" as Performance

Jacqueline Borsje

1. This contribution is a revised version of "Miraculous Magic in Medieval Ireland: The *Epaid*, 'Spell, Charm,' Part 2," an invited paper presented at the Second Colloquium of *Societas Celto-Slavica* held at Moscow State University and the Institute for Linguistics of the Russian Academy of Sciences in Moscow on September 14 to 17, 2006. This contribution is part of my VIDI-research project "The Power of Words in Medieval Ireland," subsidized by the Netherlands Organisation for Scientific Research (NWO). The project consists of two subprojects: a study of the performers of verbal power conducted by Dr. J. K. Reid and my study of the words of power themselves. I would like to thank John Carey and Jennifer Reid for their comments on an earlier version of this paper.

2. I use the term *supernatural* as a neutral tool to describe the a-empirical dimension of life, which is the crucial part of religious belief systems. This term can be applied to notions found in any religion.

3. See Claire Fanger, "Things Done Wisely by a Wise Enchanter: Negotiating the Power of Words in the Thirteenth Century," *Esoterica* 1 (1999): 98.

4. For an example of a study of the power of words in a contemporary oral context, see, e.g., Suzanne Kuik, "The Magical Power of Words: About Children, Their Conflicts and Their Bodies," *Etnofoor* 12 (1999): 53–72. With thanks to Ambro Bakker, dean of Amsterdam, for sending me the details of his blessings (e-mail, April 4, 2012).

5. For successful use of research on modern ritual to explain ancient literature, see John Miles Foley, "Word-Power, Performance, and Tradition," *Journal of American Folklore* 105 (1992): 290–94; Richard P. Martin, "Keens from the Absent Chorus: Troy to Ulster," in *Lament: Studies in the Ancient Mediterranean and Beyond*, ed. A. Suter (Oxford: Oxford University Press, 2008), 118–38; Haralampos Passalis, "From the Power of Words to the Power of Rhetoric: Nonsense, Pseudo-Nonsense Words, and Artificially Constructed Compounds in Greek Oral Charms," *Incantatio: An International Journal on Charms, Charmers and Charming* 2 (2012): 7–22. My study of a medieval legal tradition concerning the evil eye benefited greatly from early modern and modern descriptions of the belief; see Jacqueline Borsje, *The Celtic Evil Eye and Related Mythological Motifs in Medieval Ireland* (Leuven: Peeters, 2012), 50–53.

6. Foley, "Word-Power," supplies a useful survey of relevant research.

7. J. L. Austin, *How to Do Things with Words* (Cambridge, Mass.: Harvard University Press, 1962); see also John R. Searle, "A Classification of Illocutionary Acts," *Language in Society* 5 (1976): 1–23.

8. See Wade T. Wheelock, "The Problem of Ritual Language: From Information to Situation," *Journal of the American Academy of Religion* 50 (1982): 49–71; Alderik H. Blom, "*Linguae Sacrae* in Ancient and Medieval Sources: An Anthropological Approach to Ritual Language," in *Multilingualism in the Greco-Roman Worlds*, ed. A. Mullen and P. J. James (Cambridge: Cambridge University Press, 2012), 124–40.

9. "Neutral" refers here to an unbiased, critical attitude toward religious phenomena, burdened as little as possible by existing controversies and ideological involvement and taking such phenomena as the subject of research without a priori judgments as to their legitimacy or validity from a moral point of view.

10. See also Jacqueline Borsje, "Druids, Deer and 'Words of Power': Coming to Terms with Evil in Medieval Ireland," in *Coping with Evil in Religion and Culture: Case Studies*, ed. N. van Doorn-Harder and L. Minnema (Amsterdam: Rodopi, 2008), 31–40.

11. E.g., Brill's *Religions in the Graeco-Roman World*; the Pennsylvania State University Press's *Magic in History*; Palgrave's *Historical Studies in Witchcraft and Magic* book series; the publications of the International Society for Folk Narrative Research Committee on Charms, Charmers and Charming; and the journal *Magic, Ritual, and Witchcraft*.

12. See, e.g., J. N. Bremmer, "The Birth of the Term 'Magic,'" in *The Metamorphosis of Magic from Late Antiquity to the Early Modern Period*, ed. J. N. Bremmer and J. R. Veenstra (Leuven: Peeters, 2002), 1–11; W. J. Hanegraaff, "Magic I: Introduction," and "Magic V: 18th–20th Centuries," in *Dictionary of Gnosis and Western Esotericism*, 2 vols., ed. W. J. Hanegraaff (Leiden: Brill, 2005), 716–19, 738–44; Bernd-Christian Otto, *Magie: Rezeptions- und diskursgeschichtliche Analysen* (Berlin: De Gruyter, 2011). *Emic* refers to the perspective of the believers. The perspective of scholars studying this belief is referred to as *etic*.

13. See, e.g., J. N. Bremmer, "Appendix: Magic *and* Religion," in Bremmer and Veenstra, *Metamorphosis of Magic*, 267–71.

14. See, e.g., Plutarch, *Symposiacs*, bk. 5, question 7; English translation available at http://ebooks.adelaide.edu.au/p/plutarch/symposiacs/chapter5.html#section52. The poisonous power of the eye is here attributed especially to the emotion of envy.

15. See David Frankfurter, "Narrating Power: The Theory and Practice of the Magical *Historiola* in Ritual Spells," in *Ancient Magic and Ritual Power*, ed. M. Meyer and P. Mirecki (Leiden: Brill, 1995), 457, on the perhaps fundamental principle of magical/ritual speech: "when one . . . utters a spell, the words uttered draw power into the world and towards (or against) an object in the world." See also the admonition in Wheelock, "Problem of Ritual Language," 66, to "avoid such fallacious perspectives as interpreting ritual discourse to be primarily a dialogue with supernatural beings, with its misleading use of an ordinary, conversational model of language use."

16. I borrow the terms *background name* and *subject name* from Tatyana Mikhailova, "On the Function of Name in Irish and Slavonic Written Incantation Tradition," in *Parallels between Celtic and Slavic: Proceedings of the First International Colloquium of* Societas Celto-Slavica, ed. S. Mac-Mathúna and M. Fomin (Coleraine: Stationery Office, 2006), 163–73.

17. This provisional survey of structural elements of verbal power is expanded on the basis of two other concrete examples (a spell and a prayer) in my forthcoming book, *Saints and Spells: Miraculous Magic in Medieval Ireland*. The aim of this exercise is to devise a list of structural elements as a tool that may help map this diverse material, which falls under the umbrella term "words of power." This investigation is intended to function as a dynamic study that takes into account contextual shifts and different readings/performances that may occur at various times and in various places.

18. Dublin, Royal Irish Academy, D.II.3 (1238); the text has been edited by G. F. Warner, *The Stowe Missal*, 2 vols. (London, 1906–15). See further Edward J. Gwynn, "The Stowe Missal," *Irish Church Quarterly* 9, no. 34 (1916): 119–33 (with thanks to Jürgen Uhlich for sending me this article); J. F. Kenney, *The Sources for the Early History of Ireland: Ecclesiastical; An Introduction and Guide* (New York: Columbia University Press, 1929; repr., Dublin: Four Courts Press, 1997), s.v.; and Sven Meeder, "The Early Irish Stowe Missal's Destination and Function," *Early Medieval Europe* 13 (2005): 179–94.

19. Kenney, *Sources*, 699; see also Meeder, "Stowe Missal's Destination."

20. It has been suggested that these texts were added in the eleventh century or later. This dating was done with diffidence on palaeographical grounds by Kenyon; see W. Stokes and J. Strachan, *Thesaurus Palaeohibernicus*, 2 vols. (Cambridge: Cambridge University Press, 1901–3; repr. Dublin: Dublin Institute for Advanced Studies, 1987), 2:xxviii. Edward Gwynn, however, argues that the texts are contemporary with the Irish tract on the Mass in the missal. If Gwynn's meticulous study is correct, the healing texts would date from the Old Irish period; Gwynn, "Stowe Missal," 130–33; see Warner, *Stowe Missal*, 2:xxxix ("my own impression of the whole MS. is that from first to last it contains nothing later than the ninth century"), and Kenney, *Sources*, 695; see also Stokes, "The Irish Passages in the Stowe Missal," *Zeitschrift für vergleichende Sprachforschung auf dem Gebiete der indogermanischen Sprachen* 26, n.s. 6 (1883): 498, who, despite the "Middle Irish corruptions," suggests that the scribe may have copied from an Old Irish codex.

21. Heinrich Zimmer, "Zum Stowe Missal," *Zeitschrift für vergleichende Sprachforschung auf dem Gebiete der indogermanischen Sprachen* 28, n.s. 8 (1887): 378, also reads *súil*, as against *súla*, in Stokes and Strachan, *Thesaurus*, 2:250.

22. Zimmer, "Zum Stowe Missal," 378, reads *admunmar*, "we invoke."

23. Stokes and Strachan, *Thesaurus*, 2:250, transcribe *sen dee et c.*

24. When editing medieval texts, modern scholars italicize those letters and words that are expansions of the abbreviations that medieval scribes wrote in the manuscripts. In this particular case, for instance, the word is formed in the manuscript by the letters "cr" with an abbreviation stroke above the "r"; modern editors expand this abbreviation into crist.

25. Warner transcribes conclerc, but see Gwynn, "Stowe Missal," 132, on the form of d in this manuscript. See also Gwynn's note h in Stokes and Strachan, Thesaurus, 2:250: an s or an i is written in superscript above the e, which has a dot underneath.

26. The acute accent above the a is not reproduced in Warner.

27. Warner, Stowe Missal, 2:39. I added an [s] twice (in expuit and puto).

28. I tentatively suggest reading arond as arind (preposition and article), "against the"; for a different view of arond, see Stokes and Strachan, Thesaurus, 2:250, n. a.

29. Reading ara rroícca, "in order that he/she/it may heal," and taking sén Dé, "the blessing of God," as the subject of this sentence. If we should read the following word as et (with Stokes and Strachan and with Zimmer), then this is combined with the c . . . gi of Christ.

30. My translation, with thanks to John Carey and Johan Corthals. Stokes and Strachan, Thesaurus, 2:250, translate: "For an . . . eye. I honour bishop Ibar who heals. . . . May the blessing of God and of Christ's . . . heal thine eye . . . whole of thine eye." They do not translate the Latin part.

31. According to Edina Bozóky, "Mythic Mediation in Healing Incantations," in Health, Disease and Healing in Medieval Culture, ed. S. Campbell, B. Hall, and D. Klausner (Basingstoke: Macmillan, 1992), 84, and Don Skemer, Binding Words: Textual Amulets in the Middle Ages (University Park: Pennsylvania State University Press, 2006), 105, the earliest medieval evidence of historiolae dates from the ninth or tenth century; our example, however, may stem from the eighth century.

32. These examples are to be found, respectively, in Stokes and Strachan, Thesaurus, 2:349, lines 4–5; Julius Pokorny, "Ein altirisches Gebet zu St. Columba," Zeitschrift für celtische Philologie 8 (1912): 285–88, 420: 286, §2, which reads literally, "I invoke a great prayer: the name of the son of Eithne" (i.e., Columcille's mother); John Carey, King of Mysteries: Early Irish Religious Writings (Dublin: Four Courts Press, 1998), 136; Carey, "Téacsanna draíochta in Éirinn sa mheánaois luath" [Magical Texts in Early Medieval Ireland], Breis faoinár nDúchas Spioradálta: Léachtaí Cholm Cille 30 (Maigh Nuad: An Sagart, 2000): 116; and Stokes and Strachan, Thesaurus, 2:249, line 8.

33. See also H. Ilomäki, "The Self of a Charm," in Charms and Charming in Europe, ed. J. Roper (Basingstoke: Palgrave Macmillan, 2004), 47–58.

34. For more on Saint Íbar ("yew-tree") and his purported prepatrician role in Ireland, see Kenney, Sources, 309–15; R. Sharpe, Medieval Irish Saints' Lives: An Introduction to Vitae Sanctorum Hiberniae (Oxford: Oxford University Press, 1991), 115–16; and A. MacShamráin, "Íbar," in Dictionary of Irish Biography, ed. J. McGuire and J. Quinn (Cambridge: Cambridge University Press, 2009), 4:892–93.

35. For examples, see Mikhailova, "On the Function of Name," 164–66.

36. See Foley, "Word-Power," 283–84.

37. For more on curses, see B. Mees, Celtic Curses (Woodbridge: Boydell Press, 2009).

38. Zimmer, "Zum Stowe Missal," 378.

39. Stokes and Strachan, Thesaurus, 2:250.

40. E-mail correspondence, September 6, 2010.

41. http://www.isos.dias.ie/.

42. See E. Knott, Togail Bruidne Da Derga (Dublin: Dublin Institute for Advanced Studies, 1936), 40, line 1351.

43. An example is *Fidula fadula fidaili bibili belabili . . . tilalup tilalup tilalup*, in the last text in Richard Best's collection; Best, "Some Irish Charms," *Ériu* 16 (1952): 32.

44. Kathleen Hughes, "Some Aspects of Irish Influence on Early English Private Prayer," *Studia Celtica* 5 (1970): 53; see also 57.

45. See, e.g., S. J. Tambiah, "The Magical Power of Words," *Man* 3 (1968): 175–208; John G. Gager, ed., *Curse Tablets and Binding Spells from the Ancient World* (Oxford: Oxford University Press, 1992), 5–12.

46. Cf. Hughes, "Some Aspects of Irish Influence," 49.

47. On *historiolae* as bridging the gap between pre-Christian and Christian in medieval Irish "words of power," see Phillip A. Bernhardt-House, "Magic and Narrative: Ulster Cycle Texts as *Historiolae*," in *Ulidia 3: Proceedings of the Third International Conference on the Ulster Cycle of Tales*, ed. G. Toner and S. MacMathúna (Berlin: Curach Bhán Publications, 2013), 213–20.

48. See also Jonathan Roper, "Typologising English Charms," in *Charms and Charming in Europe*, ed. J. Roper (Basingstoke: Palgrave Macmillan, 2004), 131–34. Roper (131) further distinguishes comparison and enumeration charms.

49. Ibid., 133.

50. Cf. also the idea of *Christus medicus*, "Christ the healer"; Hughes, "Some Aspects of Irish Influence," 53.

51. Cf. Frankfurter ("Narrating Power," 469–70) on ritualists entering the *historiola*, while narrating, by identifying themselves as a God. Frankfurter calls this "characteristically Egyptian."

52. For instance, the Evangelist Mark gives six Aramaic transliterations in his Greek gospel text: two healing formulas, two prayer formulas, the cry on the cross, and a place name. This usage may be connected with belief in the healing power of exotic words; R. E. Brown, *The Death of the Messiah: From Gethsemane to the Grave* (New York: Doubleday, 1993), 2:1062n.86.

53. The first reading was suggested by David Stifter in his paper "Towards an Understanding of the Early Irish Charms in the Stowe Missal (RIA MS 1238 [D ii 3])," presented at the symposium "Magical Moments in Maynooth," National University of Ireland, Maynooth, April 6, 2013; for the second reading, see Borsje, *Celtic Evil Eye*, 206.

54. See Borsje and F. Kelly, "'The Evil Eye' in Early Irish Literature and Law," *Celtica* 24 (2003): 2–4; for *drochrosc* and *in drochśúil* as expressions for the evil eye, see ibid., 30, 35–36.

55. Ibid., 32–33.

56. See Mikhailova, "On the Function of Name," 170–71.

57. The narrative is given in *Cormac's Glossary* §698; text in K. Meyer, "*Sanas Cormaic*: An Old Irish Glossary," *Anecdota from Irish Manuscripts* 4 (1912): 58–60, translation in P. Russell, "Poets, Power and Possessions in Medieval Ireland: Some Stories from *Sanas Cormaic*," in *Law, Literature and Society*, ed. J. F. Eska, *Celtic Studies Association of North America Yearbook* 7 (Dublin: Four Courts Press, 2008), 34–35.

58. For more on medieval Irish satire, see Roisin McLaughlin, *Early Irish Satire* (Dublin: Dublin Institute for Advanced Studies, 2008), and the literature cited there.

59. Neil McLeod, "Interpreting Early Irish Law: Status and Currency (Part 2)," *Zeitschrift für celtische Philologie* 42 (1995): 16.

60. Liam Breatnach, *Uraicecht na Ríar: The Poetic Grades in Early Irish Law* (Dublin: Dublin Institute for Advanced Studies, 1987), 114–15; for variant versions, see 137; see also McLaughlin, *Early Irish Satire*, 82–84, 140–41, §21.

61. Breatnach, *Uraicecht na Ríar*, 114–15.

62. See also Tomás Ó Cathasaigh, "Curse and Satire," *Éigse* 21 (1986): 10–15

63. See McLaughlin, *Early Irish Satire*, 14.

64. See E. A. Gray, *Cath Maige Tuired: The Second Battle of Mag Tuired* (Dublin: Irish Texts Society, 1982, repr. 1995), 46–51.

65. See McLaughlin, *Early Irish Satire*, 14, and Borsje, "Approaching Danger: *Togail Bruidne Da Derga* and the Motif of Being One-Eyed," in *Identifying the "Celtic,"* ed. J. F. Nagy, *Celtic Studies Association of North America Yearbook* 2 (Dublin: Four Courts Press, 2002), 89–96.

66. See various specimens in Gager, ed., *Curse Tablets and Binding Spells*; on the Church Fathers, see Riemer Roukema, "Early Christianity and Magic," *Annali di Storia dell'Esegesi* 24, no. 2 (2007): 374–77.

67. I am indebted to Jennifer Reid for the suggestion of this possibility. See further my forthcoming study *Saints and Spells: Miraculous Magic in Medieval Ireland*, for the later development of Caíar's satire into an impersonal, repeatable verbal weapon.

68. See also Mikhailova, "On the Function of Name," 171–72.

69. This healing text is extant in two manuscripts: Dublin, National Library of Ireland, MS. G 11, p. 394b, and Dublin, Royal Irish Academy, 24.B.3, 53, lines 35–36. An edition and translation has been published in James Carney and Maura Carney, "A Collection of Irish Charms," *Saga och Sed* (1960): 148–49. James Carney edited the texts from the manuscripts; Maura Carney translated them and added a commentary. James Carney edits the version from MS G 11 and gives the readings from 24 B 3 in the notes. I have checked and corrected the readings of some charms in this collection with Aoibheann Nic Dhonnchadha. I am grateful to Dr. Nic Dhonnchadha for going through these readings with me. I have also italicized those letters that were added by Carney himself without indicating that he is expanding the manuscript abbreviations.

70. James Carney omits this heading in "Collection of Irish Charms."

71. Carney and Carney, "Collection of Irish Charms," 148–49; my translation of the heading.

72. MS 24 B 3 reads, "Obaid ar galur sula A Coluim Cille a Padraig a muire a bri̅d a ri na ndula dinḡaib in galar dingglan fuil ar (leg. oc?) tindruid (leg. tindriud) mo shula. n. a cantain fo tri ₇ paidir roime ₇ na diaig."

73. The passage *frit suil. N. ar gac nduil bis* is lacking in Carney's edition.

74. Carney transcribes *rosg* and *amrosg* with *g*, but they are spelled with *c* in the manuscript.

75. Carney transcribes *go*.

76. Carney translates: "A charm for (a piece of) dirt on the eye."

77. Carney translates "sets" and offers "chants" as an alternative. For more on the translation "casts," see below.

78. Carney translates "creature," but in the light of the list that follows, "thing" seems more apt as a translation of *dúil*.

79. The first part of *ar rosc ar amrosc*, "against an eye / vision, against blindness / defective vision," seems problematic. The only way that *ar rosc* makes sense to me is if it is directed against an evil eye; Maura Carney, "A Collection of Irish Charms," 148, translates "against (an injury) with vision, without vision," and interprets this as "an eye injury that does not deprive the eye of sight and one that does." She furthermore refers to the expression *fuil ruisc fuil amruisc*, "a wound of eye, a wound of non-eye," in a law text. The glosses on this law text explain the former as a wound above the eye and the latter as a wound below the eye. Daniel Binchy suggests, however, wounds that are visible and invisible to the eye, respectively; Binchy, "Bretha Crólige," *Ériu* 12 (1938): 50–53, 76. If correct and applicable to our spell, this might also mean something visibly or invisibly harming the eye.

80. MS 24 B 3, p. 53, lines 32–35, from Carney and Carney, "Collection of Irish Charms," 148, trans. modified.

81. See also Ilomäki, "Self of a Charm."

82. For a more elaborate discussion of this text, see Borsje, "The Second Spell in the Stowe Missal," in *Lochlann: Festskrift til Jan Erik Rekdal på 60-årsdagen*, ed. C. Hambro and L. I. Widerøe (Oslo: Hermes, 2013), 12–26.

83. Dennis King (http://nimill.blogspot.com/2009/06/ortha-na-deilge.html) suggests that the manuscript reads *mo*, "my," here instead of *mc*. Because it is very difficult to see this on Irish Script on Screen, Aibheann Nic Dhonnchadha kindly studied the manuscript in the Royal Irish Academy and established the reading *mc*. David Stifter recently also consulted the manuscript and pleads for reading *mo*, his strongest argument being the absence of an abbreviation stroke over *mc*. My interpretation is based on the reading *mc*; the difficulty with reading *mo suele án*, "my splendid spittle," is practical: how would saliva help in squeezing out a thorn? One does not want the skin to be slippery when squeezing; it is afterward that the application of saliva is to be expected, as an anti-infectant and a ritual means of exorcising bad influence.

84. The second *t*, given in the edition of Stokes and Strachan, is not present in the manuscript.

85. Dennis King (http://nimill.blogspot.com/2009/06/ortha-na-deilge.html) rightly points out that the manuscript reads *mo* here (*nip* according to the editors). I have emended the transcription accordingly.

86. Stokes and Strachan, *Thesaurus*, 2:250.

87. My translation, based on ibid.

88. The interpretation of "son of spittle" as a salve appears to stem from Zimmer, "Zum Stowe Missal," 378. Stokes, "Irish Passages in the Stowe Missal," 518, previously read *ele án*, "a splendid salve."

89. Unless we should interpret the salve as being the "son" of the mixing of earth and saliva, as John Carey has suggested to me (e-mail correspondence, September 6, 2010). If this is the correct reading, the second and first spell in the Stowe Missal would be connected through the *historiola* from the Gospel of John with the "splendid son of spittle," taking its components from the earth and saliva mentioned there.

90. For this expression, stemming from Aramaic usage when "the speaker refers to himself as the *son of man* out of awe, reserve, or humility," see Geza Vermes, *Jesus the Jew: A Historian's Reading of the Gospels* (London: Collins/Fontana, 1973, repr. 1980), 186.

91. For a medieval example, see the first so-called St. Gall incantation, which employs the "holy words that Christ spoke from his cross" in order to remove a thorn "from me"; Stokes and Strachan, *Thesaurus*, 2:248. An example from recent times for extracting a thorn goes as follows: "The briar that spreads, the thorn that grows, the sharp spike that pierced the brow of Christ, give you power to draw this thorn from the flesh, or let it perish inside; in the name of the Trinity. Amen"; Lady Wilde, *Legends, Charms, and Superstitions of Ireland* (1887; London: Chatto and Windus, 1919; repr. Mineola: Dover, 2006), 190–91.

92. Matthew 27:29; Mark 15:17; John 19:2.

93. Matthew 26:67; Mark 10:34, 14:65, 15:19; Luke 18:32.

94. For binding formulas in legal texts, see Robin Chapman Stacey, *Dark Speech: The Performance of Law in Early Ireland* (Philadelphia: University of Pennsylvania Press, 2007), 122–23. This work brilliantly demonstrates how jurisdiction was performed in medieval Ireland through the utterance of (sometimes obscure) words in a ritual context. It also shows how legal texts sometimes can be identified as "words of power" and how they may overlap with other genres of verbal power. For more on the *lorica* genre, see Louis Gougaud, "Étude sur les *loricae* celtiques et sur les prières qui s'en rapprochent," *Bulletin d'ancienne littérature et d'archéologie chrétiennes* 1 (1911): 265–81; Gougaud, "Étude sur les *loricae* celtiques et sur les prières qui s'en rapprochent (Suite)," *Bulletin d'ancienne littérature et d'archéologie chrétiennes* 2 (1912): 33–41, 101–27.

95. M. Draak, *Betovering voor een etmaal* (Amsterdam: Meulenhoff, 1955), 9–12.

96. R. Best, "The St. Gall Incantation against Headache," *Ériu* 8 (1915): 100, edits this text from Dublin, Trinity College, H.3.17 (1336), fifteenth to sixteenth century. Two variant versions exist in eighth- or ninth-century manuscripts: the third of four "incantations" on a single leaf from an Irish manuscript preserved as Codex Sangallensis nr 1395 (Stokes and Strachan, *Thesaurus*, 2:xxvii, 248–49) and another in the *Book of Nunnaminster*, an eighth- or ninth-century prayer book from England (London, British Library, Harley 2965; Walter de Gray Birch, *An Ancient Manuscript of the Eighth or Ninth Century: Formerly Belonging to St. Mary's Abbey, or Nunnaminster, Winchester* [London: Simpkin and Marshall, 1889], 96). A third variant version was written in a blank space in London, British Library, Add. 30512, fol. 72, in the seventeenth century; R. Flower, *Catalogue of Irish Manuscripts in the British Library (formerly British Museum)* (London: British Museum, 1926; repr. Dublin: Dublin Institute for Advanced Studies, 1992), 2:471–72.

97. My translation.

98. Isaiah 6:3. The Vulgate text reads, "Sanctus sanctus sanctus Dominus (Deus) exercituum plena est omnis terra gloria eius"; Vetus Latina reads, "Sanctus sanctus sanctus Dominus Deus Sabaoth." Cf. the Stowe Missal: "Sanctus sanctus sanctus Dominus Deus Sabaóth pleni sunt caeli et universa terra gloria tua"; Warner, *Stowe Missal*, 2:10.

99. Apocalypse 4:8. The Vulgate reads, "sanctus sanctus sanctus Dominus Deus omnipotens qui erat et qui est et qui venturus est"; the reading "Dominus Deus Sabaoth" is present in Vetus Latina texts.

100. The variant versions (see above) give a different function and ritual context: the first prescribes the Latin part for head ailments; the second variant version of the Latin part follows a prayer against eye ailments; and the last appears in a vigil context.

101. Edition and translation by Carey, *King of Mysteries*, 130–35. The text is rather lengthy, which is why I summarize it here. For more on this text as a form of verbal power, see Borsje, "Druids, Deer and 'Words of Power,'" 31–40.

102. Carey, *King of Mysteries*, 130.

103. Such descriptions can be found in Ephesians 6:11–18 and 1 Thessalonians 5:8.

104. M. Herren, *The Hisperica Famina II: Related Poems* (Toronto: Pontifical Institute of Mediaeval Studies, 1987), 26, 31.

105. See Jacqueline Borsje, "Rules and Legislation on Love Charms in Early Medieval Ireland," *Peritia* 21 (2010): 172–90; Jacqueline Borsje, "Love Magic in Medieval Irish Penitentials, Law and Literature: A Dynamic Perspective," *Studia Neophilologica* 84, Supplement 1, Special Issue (2012): 6–23; and Jacqueline Borsje, "The Power of Words: Sacred and Forbidden Love Magic in Medieval Ireland," in *Everyday Life and the Sacred: Re/configuring Gender Studies in Religion*, ed. A. Berlis, A.-M. Korte, and K. Biezeveld (Leiden: Brill, forthcoming). On carrying protective prayers, see also Hughes, "Some Aspects of Irish Influence," 53n3.

106. See, e.g., R. Stübe, *Der Himmelsbrief: Ein Beitrag zur allgemeinen Religionsgeschichte* (Tübingen: Mohr, 1918), 1–4; Skemer, *Binding Words*, s.v. Sunday Epistle.

107. An edition and translation can be found in J. G. O'Keeffe, "Cáin Domnaig. I.—The Epistle concerning Sunday," *Ériu* 2 (1905): 189–214; see further Borsje, *From Chaos to Enemy: Encounters with Monsters in Early Irish Texts: An Investigation Related to the Process of Christianization and the Concept of Evil* (Turnhout: Brepols, 1996), 188.

108. The AGLA formula is a so-called *notarikon*, being originally a method of abbreviation by composing a word from the initial or final letters of several words, or to decompose one word into several. Powerful names were created in this way. AGLA, used by Jews and Christians, is most commonly explained as the abbreviation for the Hebrew "You are mighty forever, O Lord," stem-

ming from the second benediction in the well-known Jewish Amidah prayer; Joshua Trachtenberg, *Jewish Magic and Superstition: A Study in Folk Religion* (New York: Behrman's Jewish Book House, 1939), 261–62. The explanation for the formula as *Aieth* [*sic*] *gadol leolan* [*sic*] *Adonai*, "Thou art powerful and everlasting, Lord" (Best, "Some Irish Charms," 27, quoting P. Collin de Plancy, *Dictionnaire infernal* [Paris: 1825–26], 127*b*), literally "The Lord ??? great forever," is dubious because of the corrupt Hebrew. For this information, I thank my colleagues Peter Forshaw, Gemma Kwantes, and Irene Zwiep.

109. Best, "Some Irish Charms," 27–28; I have expanded and modified the translation.

110. Cf. Heinrich Zimmer, "Keltische Studien. 13. Ein altirischer Zauberspruch aus der Vikingerzeit," *Zeitschrift für vergleichende Sprachforschung* 33 (1895): 144–45.

111. "A love charm in salt" is used as an invective in a satire; McLaughlin, *Early Irish Satire*, 168–69, no. 82.

112. Stokes and Strachan, *Thesaurus*, 2:249. At least two people are involved in this healing: the singer of the *Caput Christi* text and the patient, who is addressed as "you" and who performs the rest of the ritual. For a different view, see Ilona Tuomi, "Parchment, Praxis and Performance of Charms in Early Medieval Ireland," *Incantatio: An International Journal on Charms, Charmers and Charming* 3 (2013): 60–85.

113. In the oldest version of the anecdote in the seventh-century *Life of Patrick* by Muirchú (L. Bieler, *The Patrician Texts in the Book of Armagh* [Dublin: Dublin Institute for Advanced Studies, 1979], 92–93, I.20), the saint merely blesses the drink. There are three variant versions that give the incantation discussed here: two later *Lives of Patrick* (Stokes, *The Tripartite Life of Patrick with Other Documents Relating to That Saint* [London: Eyre and Spottiswoode, 1887], 1:54–55, and K. Mulchrone, *Bethu Phátraic: The Tripartite Life of Patrick* [Dublin: Royal Irish Academy, 1939], 32–33; plus a fragmentary *Life*, Best, "Betha Pátraic," *Anecdota from Irish Manuscripts* 3 (1910): 35), and an etymological gloss in a legal context (W. Neilson Hancock et al., *Ancient Laws of Ireland: Senchus Mor: Introduction to Senchus Mor, and Athgabhail; or, Law of Distress, as contained in the Harleian Manuscripts* [Dublin: Her Majesty's Stationary Office, 1865], 1:2–3; Binchy, *Corpus Iuris Hibernici ad fidem codicum manuscriptorum* [Dublin: Dublin Institute for Advanced Studies, 1978], 2:339). This textual tradition is extensively discussed in my forthcoming study *Saints and Spells: Miraculous Magic in Medieval Ireland*.

114. Binchy, *Corpus Iuris Hibernici*, 2:339, lines 13–14.

115. I thank Folke Josephson for the suggestion that this may be an intensified form of *ibid*. The verb *fris-ibid* is not attested.

116. It is possible that the word *anfis* also alludes to "splendid knowledge," "the cup of knowledge," or even "death."

117. *Úatha*, "terrors," are supernatural entities that function as a test for members of the elite in medieval Irish texts; Borsje, *"Fled Bricrenn* and Tales of Terror," *Peritia* 19 (2005): 173–92. Here Saint Patrick is being tested as a holy man; for a similar conclusion, but based upon possible sources used by Muirchú, see Thomas O'Loughlin, "Muirchú's Poisoned Cup: A Note on Its Sources," *Ériu* 56 (2006): 157–62.

118. My translation; cf. Pokorny, "Ein altirischer Zauberspruch," *Zeitschrift für celtische Philologie* 20 (1936): 488.

119. Binchy, *Corpus Iuris Hibernici*, 2:339, lines 15–16.

120. My translation. Interestingly, this invocation—*in nomine Dei Patris*—is part of the exorcism formulas of salt and water and the baptismal rituals with salt and oil in the Stowe Missal (Warner, *Stowe Missal*, 2:25, 29, 31).

3. Inscriptional Violence and the Art of Cursing: A Study of Performative Writing

Jan Assmann

1. Deafness also occurs in the Kanais text of Seti I as an element of the actor-specification *(sh-hr)*. The Hittite treaty of Ramses II refers to "whoever will not observe these words."

2. See the specification "the eyes looking" (*jrtj hr dg3*) in late Egyptian texts like the *Amenophis Son of Hapu Decree* or the *Stèle d'Apanage* (see below).

3. For the concept of divine agency, see the important study by B. Albrektson, *History and the Gods: An Essay on the Idea of Historical Events as Divine Manifestations in the Ancient Near East and in Israel* (Lund, 1967).

4. This touches upon the problem of "magic"—i.e., the idea of an automatic link between cause and effect established by some ritual device, in our case by the pronunciation of a curse; see the literature quoted by W. Schottroff, *Der altisraelitische Fluch-spruch* (Neukirchen, 1969), 16n2. But this is not how inscriptional curses work. They require metaphysical agency and therefore do not suggest a distinction between magic and religion.

5. This, R. Wagner informs me, seems to be the case in ancient China, where cursing in these functions is virtually unknown.

6. A. Alt, "Zum Begriff des apodiktischen Rechts," in *Kleine Schriften* (Munich, 1953), 1:314.

7. The affinity of Deuteronomy to the form of a treaty and its many resemblances to political treaties of the ancient Near East have often been remarked; see esp. M. Weinfeld, *Deuteronomy and the Deuteronomic School* (Oxford, 1972), 116ff., and D. J. McCarthy, *Treaty and Covenant* (Rome, 1978); see also M. Weinfeld, "The Common Heritage of the Covenantal Traditions in the Ancient World," in *I trattati nel Mondo Antico: Forma, ideologia, junzione*, ed. L. Canfora, M. Liverani, and G. Zaccagnini (Rome, 1990), 175–91; for treaties in general, see this collection overall. The literal character of "treaty-curses" is also stressed by Assurbanipal in one of his historical inscriptions: The gods did bring "the complete number of curses which were laid down in writing in the record of the treaty over the illoyal Uaite' and the Arabs." A. E. Pritchard, ed., *Ancient Near Eastern Texts Relating to the Old Testament*, 3rd ed. (1955), 300a.

8. D. R. Hillers, *Treaty-Curses and the Old Testament Prophets* (Rome, 1964); H. C. Brichto, *The Problem of "Curse" in the Hebrew Bible* (Philadelphia, 1963). The most impressive example of an imprecative catalogue is to be found in the Vassal treaties of Asarhaddon; see Pritchard, ed., *Ancient Near Eastern Texts*, 534ff.; R. Borger, in *Texte aus der Umwelt des Alten Testaments*, ed. O. Kaiser, vol. 1, fasc. 2, *Staatssertrage* (Gütersloh, 1983), 160ff.; R. Frankena, "The Vassal-Treaties of Eaarhaddan and the Dating of Deuteronomy," *Old Testament Studies* 14 (1965): 122–54; S. Parpola and K. Watanabe, eds., *State Archives of Assyria*, vol. 2, *Neoassyrian Treaties and Loyalty Oaths* (Helsinki, 1988), 28ff.

9. M. Weinfeld, "The Loyalty Oath in the Ancient Near East," *Ugariische Forschungen* 8 (1976): 379–414; H. Tadmor, "Treaty and Oath in the Ancient Near East: An Historian's Approach," *Shnaton* 5–6 (1981–82): 165ff. (in Hebrew); see also J. Pedersen, *Der Eid bei den Semiten* (1914).

10. F. C. Fensham, "Malediction and Benediction in Ancient Near Eastern Vassal Treaties and the Old Testament," *Zeitschrift fur die Alttestamliche Wissenschaft* 74 (1962): 1–9.

11. Many examples can be found in Kaiser, ed., *Staatssertrage*. The Assyrian treaties, especially, provide an exact model for Deuteronomy; see Weinfeld, *Deuteronomy*.

12. This essay was originally delivered at the conference "Writing Ecriture Schrift," sponsored by the Department of Comparative Literature, Stanford University, February 27 to March 2, 1991.

13. The execution of this order is narrated in Joshua 8:30–35: "Then Joshua built an altar unto the LORD GOD of Israel in mount Ebal, as Moses the servant of the LORD commanded . . . and he wrote there upon the stones a copy of the law of Moses, which he wrote in the presence of the children of Israel. And all Israel . . . stood on this side the ark and on that side before the priests the Levites, which bare the ark of the covenant of the LORD, . . . half of them over against mount Gerizim, and half of them over against mount Ebal. . . . And afterward he read all the words of the law, the blessings and the cursings, according to all that is written in the book of the law."

14. The memory function of these stones is clearly stated in the biblical record: "When your children shall ask their fathers in time to come, saying, What mean these stones? Then ye shall let your children know, saying, Israel came over this Jordan on dry land" (Joshua 4:21–22).

15. The most important civil documents referring to boundaries are the Kudurru documents, which abound in curses; see L. W. King, *Babylonian Boundary-Stones and Memorial-Tablets in the British Museum* (London, 1912); F. X. Steinmetzer, *Die babylonischen Kudurru (Grenzsteine) als Urkundenform* (1922); M. Noth, *Gesammelte Studien zum Alten Testament*, 2nd ed. (Munich, 1960), 155–71.

16. B. Landsberger, "Das 'gute Wort,'" *Altorientalische Studien B. Meissner*, Mitteilungen der Altorientalischen Gesellschaft 4 (1928–29), 295–321; A. A. B. Mercer, "The Malediction in Cuneiform Inscriptions," *Journal of the Ancient Oriental Society* 34 (1915): 282–309; Watanabe, "Die literarische Überlieferung eines babylonisch-assyrischen Fluchthemas mit Anrufung des Mondgottes Sin," *Acta Sumerologica* 6 (1984): 99–119.

17. Kaiser, ed., *Texte aus der Umwelt des Alten Testaments*, vol. 1, fasc. 1, *Rechtsbücher* (Gütersloh, 1982), 30: "The day on which I erected justice in Sumer and Akkad, I verily erected this stela. May he be given a long life who does not commit bad actions against it, who does not destroy what I erected, who does not efface its inscription and write his own name upon it. May he lift his neck to heaven in Ekur and may the radiant front of Enlil from heaven return his look; but whoever commits bad actions against it, who destroys or stores away what I erected, who changes its place, effaces its inscription, writes his own name upon it or lets another do it, be he a king, or a priest . . . may he flee" (a series of curses follows).

18. Borger, in Kaiser, ed., *Rechtsbücher*, 39ff.

19. After A. Parrot, *Malediction et violation des tombes* (Paris, 1939), 17.

20. Parrot 151 (Syll. 3rd ed., 1240); *IG* XII.9:955 and 1170; L. Robert, "Malédictions funeraires grecques," *Comptes rendus de Académie des Inscriptions et Belles-Lettres* (1978): 241–89. The text continues (following Parrot): "Que ses biens soient anéanties, que la mer ne soit pas navigable, ni la terre franchissable et qu'il n'a pas de posterité, Que sa maison ne s'augmente pas, qu'il ne profite ni des fruits, ni des biens, ni de la lumière, ni de l'usage, ni de la possession. Quant à celui qui soignera, gardera et conservera (le tombeau) qu'il reçoive Ies meilleures choses, qu'il soil loué parmi tout le peuple, que sa maison abonde en enfants et qu'il jouisse des fruits": "Let his possessions be wiped out, let the sea not be navigable nor the land passable and let him have no offspring. Let his household not increase, let him profit neither from fruit, nor from goods, nor from the light, nor from use, nor from possessions. As for the one who will care for, protect and conserve (the grave), let him receive the best things, let him be praised among all the people, let his household abound in children and let him enjoy the fruits."

21. For Mesopotamia and the ancient Mediterranean, see Parrot.

22. Kurt Sethe, *Urkunden des ägyptischen Altertums*, vol. 1, *Urkunden des Alten Reichs*, 2nd ed. (Leipzig, 1933), 23.11–16. In a later inscription from the Middle Kingdom, crocodile and snake appear as avatars of the deceased himself: "I shall be against him as a crocodile in the water, as a snake on the earth, and as an enemy in the necropolis" (Heqaib Stela no. 9); H. Willems, "Crime,

Cult and Capital Punishment (Mo'alla Inscription 8)," *Journal of Egyptian Archaeology* 76 (1990): 34. The most comprehensive collection of ancient Egyptian "monument-curses" is H. Sottas, *La préservation de la propriété funéraire* (Paris, 1913).

23. From the inscription of Khentika, T. G. H. James, *The Mastaba of Khentika called Ikhekhi* (London, 1953), pl. 5.

24. Sethe, *Urkunden,* 1.256.

25. E. Edel, "Untersuchungen zur Phraseologie der ägyptischen Inschriften des Alten Reichs," *Mitteilungen des Deutschen Archäologisches Institut Abteilung Kairo* 13 (1944): 5–15; see also G. Fecht, *Der Vorwurf an Gott in den Mahnworten des Ipuwer* [*The Reproach to God in the Admonitions of Ipuwer*], Abhandlung der Heidelberger Akademie der Wissenschaften (diss., Heidelberg Academy for Sciences and Humanities, 1972), 136–37, who comments on the particular "Gewalttätigkeit" (violence) and "Selbstherrlichkeit" (hubris) of these formulas, which express an unmistakable "Unabhängigkeitsdrang" (urge to project independence [of judgment]) and "Unabhängigkeitsbewusstsein" (sense of independence [of judgment]).

26. Cairo CG 1651, Willems, "Crime, Cult and Capital Punishment," 35.

27. Heqaib Stela no. 9, Willems, "Crime, Cult and Capital Punishment," 34.

28. E. Edel, *Die Inschriften der Grabfronten der Siut-Gräber* (Opladen, 1984), fig. 5, pp. 25–37.

29. Ibid., fig. 7, pp. 37–66.

30. Siut IV, lines 79–80, Edel, *Inschriften,* 120–27.

31. Tomb of Hasaya, Edel, *Inschriften,* 190–91.

32. Louvre G 108; Pierret, Rec. d. inscr. II.1; Sottas 55f, G. Möller, *Das Dekret für Amenophis Sohn des Hapu*, Sitzungsberichte der Preussischen Akademie der Wissenschaften (1910), 932–48, appendix 4, p. 943.

33. The inscription of Ankhtifi of Mo'alla, which Willems, "Crime, Cult and Capital Punishment," takes as his starting point, might be a borderline case. In this inscription, he "who commits an evil act against this coffin, and against any part of this tomb, his arm will be cut off for Hemen at his procession from the district" (several other processions are then mentioned as occasions for the cutting off of the arm). Because the potential culprit is not threatened with total destruction but with a mutilation that seems to be an adequate penalty, Willems interprets this text (and after this model all the other texts) as decrees naming penalties laid down by law and not as curses evoking destruction by drawing on the imaginary. But the inscription of Ankhtifi goes on to say, "Hemen will not accept any of his meals; and his heir will not inherit from him," which looks more like imprecation.

But in later antiquity there are clear cases where an act of imprecation is combined with an act of legislation (perhaps out of mistrust in the efficiency of the metaphysical agents, which take care of curses, as compared to political institutions, which take care of penalties). This is especially common among the Nabataeans, e.g.: "que Dushara maudisse quiconque ... vendra ce tombeau ... ; et quiconque agira autrement que ce qui est dessus écrit, devra être imposé ... du prix total de mille drachmes" ("Let Dushara curse whoever ... will sell this grave ... ; and on whoever will act otherwise than as is written above will be imposed the total price of a thousand drachmes"). Parrot 80–81; many similar examples are on 78ff.

34. A. de Buck, *The Egyptian Coffin Texts*, 7 vols. (Chicago, 1935–61).

35. E. Hornung, *Altägyptische Höllenvorstellungen*, Abhandlungen der Sächsischen Akademie der Wissenschaften (1968).

36. After Wilson, in *ANET* (1955): 328 (h); see S. Schott, Kanais, *Der Tempel Sethos' I. im Wâdi Mia*, Nachrichten der Göttinger Akademie der Wissenschaften (1961), 158–59. Similar curses appear in Theban inscriptions belonging to expressions of popular religion; see A. I. Sadek, *Popular Religion in Egypt during the New Kingdom* (Hildesheim, 1987), 242–44.

37. G. Steindorff, *Aniba* (Gluckstadt, 1937), pl. 101.

38. C. Robichon and A. Varille, *Le temple du scribe royal Amenhotep fils de Hapou* (Cairo, 1936), 3–4; James Henry Breasted, *Ancient Records of Egypt* (Chicago, 1906–7), 2:925–26; G. Möller, *Dekret für Amenophis Sohn des Hapu, SPAW* (1910): 932–48.

39. That is, they will be raped by a donkey. See W. Spiegelberg, "Die Tefnakhthosstele des Museums von Athen," *Recueil des Travaux* 25 (1903): 190ff. Spiegelberg adduces more examples of this formula, which appears to be fairly common in dynasties 22 to 24. The earliest example, however, is a Ramesside graffito from Deir el Bahri; see Sadek, *Popular Religion*, 244. See also Sottas, *Préservation*, 149–50, 153, 165–68; A. H. Gardiner, "Adoption Extraordinary," *Journal of Egyptian Archaeology* 26 (1940): 23–29; J. G. Griffiths and A. A. Barb, "Seth or Anubis?" *Journal of the Warburg and Courtauld Institutes* 22 (1959): 367–71. A. Leahy has drawn my attention to the examples discussed by J. J. Janssen, "The Smaller Dâkhla Stela (Ashmolean Museum No. 1894. 107 b)," *Journal of Egyptian Archaeology* 54 (August 1968): 171–72, and K. A. Kitchen, "Two Donation Stelae in the Brooklyn Museum," *Journal of the American Research Center in Egypt* 8 (1969–70): 60–61.

40. Stela of Tefnakhte in Athens, in Spiegelberg, "Tefnakhthosstele," 190–91.

41. In late antiquity, imprecation formulas therefore degenerate into the abbreviation *tekna teknon,* children's children, *Kindeskinder.* The mere mention of "children's children" was deemed sufficient to evoke the whole spectrum of unrelenting persecution and destruction.

42. Plato, *Phaedrus,* trans. W. C. Helmbold and W. G. Rabinowitz (Indianapolis: Bobbs-Merrill, 1977), 69–70.

43. G. Offner, "A propos de la sauvegarde des tablettes en Assyro-Babylonie," *Revue d'Assyriologie et d'Archéologie* 44 (1950): 135–43. The famous formula warning the reader "neither to add nor to subtract" from the written version is found in the Erra epic; see M. Fishbane, "Varia Deuteronomica," *Zeitschrift für die Alttestamliche Wissenschaft* 84 (1985): 350–52.

44. Ptahhotep Dév. 49–50; M. Lichtheim, *Ancient Egyptian Literature* (Berkeley, 1973), 1:63. Similarly in *Amenemope*: "It profits to put them in your heart, but woe to him who neglects them!" *Amenemope* 3.11.12, in Lichtheim, *Ancient Egyptian Literature* (Berkeley, 1976), 2:149.

45. NHC 6.6.62.22–63.14; see G. Fowden, *The Egyptian Hermes: A Historical Approach to the Late Pagan Mind* (Cambridge, 1986), 97.

4. Words and Word-Bodies: Writing the Religious Body

Loriliai Biernacki

1. See especially Judith Butler, *Excitable Speech: A Politics of the Performative* (New York: Routledge, 1997), and Judith Butler, *Bodies That Matter* (New York: Routledge, 1993), 1–2, where she addresses the body as interpellated by language: "Could language injure us if we were not, in some sense, linguistic beings, beings who require language in order to be?" Also see Jacques Lacan, *Écrits: A Selection*, trans. Alan Sheridan (New York: W. W. Norton, 1977), revised version, trans. Bruce Fink (New York: W. W. Norton, 2002), and Jacques Derrida, *Of Grammatology*, trans. Gayatri Chakravorty Spivak (Baltimore: Johns Hopkins University Press, 1976). Lacan's infamous pronouncement that "woman does not exist" merely articulates, even if as provocation, an implicit assumption underlying our culture's pervasive equation of the feminine with body and especially with mute body by locating woman as outside of language, outside the symbolic; see also, e.g., Julia Kristeva, *Revolution in Poetic Language*, trans. Margaret Waller (New York: Columbia University Press, 1984); Luce Irigaray, *Speculum of the Other Woman*, trans. Gillian C. Gill (Ithaca, N.Y.: Cor-

nell University Press, 1985); and Luce Irigaray, *This Sex Which Is Not One*, trans. Catherine Porter (Ithaca, N.Y.: Cornell University Press, 1985), for a perspective that privileges further linkage of the body with women. Of course, writings on the Cartesian binary of spirit and matter as founded on speech are legion. One might suggest that it is *the* problem bequeathed by modernity, which thinkers in our postmodern context have been trying to reconcile. To document this explosion of conceptual critique of the Cartesian binary via language, however, is not the focus of this essay.

2. Apart from Judith Butler (*Bodies That Matter*, 30), Michel Foucault also proposes this understanding in *Discipline and Punish: The Birth of the Prison*, trans. Alan Sheridan (New York: Random House, 1979), and Michel Foucault, *A History of Sexuality*, vol. 1, *An Introduction*, trans. Robert Hurley (New York: Random House, 1990), 122–31.

3. Loriliai Biernacki, *Renowned Goddess of Desire: Women, Sex, and Speech in Tantra* (New York: Oxford University Press, 2007), 111–30.

4. *Bṛhannīla Tantra*, 7.103ff. The text discusses the practice of the sex rite; after the God Śiva in several lines protests he cannot reveal the practice, the Goddess sings a hymn of praise to him, which convinces him to change his mind (*Bṛhannīla Tantra*, ed. Madhusudhana Kaul [Delhi: Butala, 1984]). The quote is from *Bṛhannīla Tantra*, 7.86, "Ahaṁ deho maheśani dehī tvaṁ sarvarūpadṛk" "sarvarūpadṛk" as the appearance of all forms, may be a wrong reading for "sarvarūpadhṛk," "having all shapes and forms," a reading that does not substantially alter my interpretation.

5. *Bṛhannīla Tantra*, 6.114: "Śrī Bhairava uvāca / mantranyāsam samācarya ṛṣyādinyāsamācar et / ādau ca āsanaṁ dattvā pūjayet paradevatām."

6. *Brahmāṇḍapurāṇokta Śrī Lalitāsahasranāmastotram nāmāvali-triśatī-khadgamālā-sahitam[c fl]*, ed. Dattatreyānandanātha (Varanasi: Śrīvidyā Sādhana Pīṭha [Vikrama Saṁvat],1996), 126: "Mūlena ṣaḍaṅ gnyāsaḥ."

7. "Mahālakṣmyaṣṭaka Stotram" 4b: "*Mantra mūrte sadā devi Mahālakṣmi namostute*," in *Bṛhatstotraratnākara*, ed. Śivadatta Miśra Śāstrī (Varanasi: Jyotiṣa Prakāśana, 1997), 258.

8. The Sanskrit word *śabda* includes both a notion of word and an idea of sound. So a *śabda* constitutes both, and can be either a simple sound or a word. This notion is part of a cosmological conception of all sound as inherently aligned with being as meaningful. Thus a Saussurean notion of the arbitrariness of signs and what they signify is rejected in favor of a more magical understanding of all sound as meaning embodied in an auditory code.

9. *Īśvara Pratyabhijñā Vivṛti Vimarśinī*, 283: "Idantā eva hi śarīrabuddhiprāṇāditsu pradhānabhūtā. Na hi ete śabdanarūpavat saṁvedanagāminaḥ iti saṁvidam saṁkocayanto nibiḍatamam āvṛṇvate nanu. Evaṁ śabdanaśarīro mantrātmā hṛdayākāśe vimarśūpatayā viparivartamānaḥ, ata eva anāhataśabdavācyo nityodito mantraḥ"; Abhinavagupta, *Īśvara Pratyabhijñā Vivṛti Vimarśinī*, 3 vols., ed. Paṇḍit Madhusudan Kaul Shāstrī (Delhi: Akay Reprints, 1985). The unstruck sound refers to the *so'ham mantra*—which would be connected with *Sadāśiva*.

10. In this case, the *vācaka* stands as the sign and signifier in opposition to the object, the signified pointed to by words.

11. Abhinavagupta, *Īśvara Pratyabhijñā Vivṛti Vimarśinī*, 3:282.

12. See, e.g., ibid., 3:296, 3:301.

13. This is explicit in Abhinavagupta but also implicit in the structure of the ubiquitous basic cosmological template that classical Indian cosmology, Samkhya, proposes as well.

14. Abhinavagupta, *Īśvara Pratyabhijñā Vivṛti Vimarśinī*, 3:282: Sa ātmā aham bhāvabhājanam yesāṁ te tena śabdaśarīratvāt saṁkucitā vedyavargād anyonyaś ca, śabdasya ca atyantaṁ prakāśaṁ prati niviḍāvaraṇarūpatvābhāvāt na sarvajñāhāniḥ. Etac ca viśeṣagrahaṇena pramātrity ādi viśeṣaṇopādānena ca āsūtritam.

15. *Bṛhannīla Tantra*, 8.141–55.

16. *Bṛhannīla Tantra*, 8.146a: Mantrāṇāṁ mātṛkāyantrāduddhāro jananaṁ smṛtam."

17. *Bṛhannīla Tantra*, 8.147b–8.148a: "Mantravarṇān samālikhya tā *Bṛhannīla Tantra* ḍayec-candanāmbhasā/pratyekaṁ vāyubījena tāḍanaṁ nāma tat śṛṇu."

18. *Bṛhannīla Tantra*, 8.152: "Kuśodakena japtena pratyarṇaṁ prokṣayed manoḥ/tena mantreṇa vidhivadetadāpyāyanaṁ matam."

19. See Biernacki, *Renowned Goddess of Desire*, esp. chap. 4, "To Speak Like a Woman," 111–30.

20. *Bṛhannīla Tantra*, 6.39b: "Raktākhyacandanenaiva likhet bījam sureśvari," verses 6.35ff., give the specific seed letters for the various body parts.

21. *Bṛhannīla Tantra*, 6.37a: "Saṁlikhya vidhivadbhaktyā śirīṣavṛntakena vai."

22. *Bṛhannīla Tantra*, 6.35: "Stanadvandve ramābījaṁ hanudvaye bhagadvayam/kakṣādhaḥ parameśāni likhet gaṅgādharadvayam."

23. Elsewhere, in *Bṛhannīla Tantra*, 7.45–52, one writes the mantra on the tongue of a young boy, in order to invest him with the skills of a poet.

24. Lévi-Strauss, *Tristes Tropiques*, cited in Derrida, *Of Grammatology*, 127.

25. Ibid., 131ff. Even though Derrida, like Lévi-Strauss, associates violence with writing, he eyes with considerable suspicion a freedom from violence or hierarchy in societies purportedly without writing.

26. Abhinavagupta, *Īśvara Pratyabhijñā Vivṛti Vimarśinī*, 3:285: "Bhagavacchaktirūpā eva māyā."

27. Foucault, *History of Sexuality*, vol. 1, *Introduction*.

28. See, e.g., Ann Taves, "Religious Experience and the Divisible Self: William James (and Frederick Myers) as Theorist(s) of Religion," *Journal of the American Academy of Religion* 71, no. 2 (2003): 303–26.

29. See Biernacki, *Renowned Goddess of Desire*, and, in more detail, "The Absent Mother and Bodied Speech: Psychology and Gender in Late Medieval Tantra," in *Transformations and Transfer of Tantra in Asia and Beyond*, ed. Istvan Keul (Berlin: De Gruyter, 2011), 215–38.

30. "U.S. Views on God and Life Are Turning Hindu," *Newsweek*, August 14, 2009, updated March 13, 2010, http://www.newsweek.com/id/212155.

31. Samuel Huntington's argument for a clash in civilizations, in Huntington, "The Clash of Civilizations?" *Foreign Affairs* 72, no. 3 (1993): 22–49, is not the same as this argument, which represents understandings of religion as cosmologies instantiated in bodies—not as civilizations, but rather as habits of practice, in the sense that Butler suggests in *Bodies That Matter*.

32. I do not think that tatoos are an example of writing the body because they do not incorporate the element of language as performative, nor do they transform the body into a super-powerful body. I say this with the caveat that a notable exception occurs in Kafka's "In the Penal Colony."

5. Flesh Become Word: Textual Embodiment and Poetic Incarnation

Elliot R. Wolfson

This essay is reprinted (with some slight revisions)from Elliot R. Wolfson, *Language, Eros, Being: Kabbalistic Hermeneutics and Poetic Imagination* (New York: Fordham University Press, 2005), chap. 5.

1. Ulrike Wiethaus, Introduction to *Maps of Flesh and Light: The Religious Experience of Medieval Women Mystics,* ed. Ulrike Wiethaus (Syracuse, N.Y.: Syracuse University Press, 1993), 1;

Rosemary D. Hale, "'Taste and See, for God Is Sweet': Sensory Perception and Memory in Medieval Christian Mystical Experience," in *Vox Mystica: Essays on Medieval Mysticism in Honor of Professor Valerie M. Lagorio,* ed. Anne Clark Bartlett, with Thomas H. Bestul, Janet Goebel, and William F. Pollard (Cambridge: D. S. Brewer, 1995), 3–14. The polarizing of the carnal and spiritual had grave implications for the implementation of ecclesiastical discipline in the High Middle Ages. For discussion of this theme, see Edward Peters, "Destruction of the Flesh—Salvation of the Spirit: The Paradoxes of Torture in Medieval Christian Society," in *The Devil, Heresy, and Witchcraft in the Middle Ages: Essays in Honor of Jeffrey B. Russell,* ed. Alberto Ferreiro (Leiden: E. J. Brill, 1998), 131–48.

2. Françoise Jaouën and Benjamin Semple, "Editors' Preface: The Body into Text," *Yale French Studies* 86 (1994): 1–4. On the Eucharist, the glorified flesh of Christ, and the indwelling of the divine presence in the saintly body, see Henri de Lubac, *Corpus mysticum: L'eucharistie et l'église au moyen âge,* 2nd rev. ed. (Paris: Aubier, 1949); Ernst H. Kantorowicz, *The King's Two Bodies: A Study in Medieval Political Theology* (Princeton, N.J.: Princeton University Press, 1957), 193–272; Rowan Williams, "Troubled Breasts: The Holy Body in Hagiography," in *Portraits of Spiritual Authority: Religious Powers in Early Christianity, Byzantium, and the Christian Orient,* ed. Jan Willem Drijvers and John W. Watt (Leiden: Brill, 1999), 63–78, esp. 67–72. David N. Power, *The Eucharistic Mystery: Revitalizing the Tradition* (New York: Crossroad, 1995), 184–240, discusses Eucharistic devotion and representation of Christ's passion contemporary with the time and place of the early kabbalist fraternities in Europe. On the "swell of eucharistic devotion" in the later twelfth and thirteenth centuries, see Caroline Walker Bynum, *Jesus as Mother: Studies in the Spirituality of the High Middle Ages* (Berkeley: University of California Press, 1982), 192–93 and 256–57, and Miri Rubin, *Corpus Christi: The Eucharist in Late Medieval Culture* (Cambridge: Cambridge University Press, 1991).

3. Eric Jager, *The Book of the Heart* (Chicago: University of Chicago Press, 2000). For an illuminating study on the corporealization and fetishization of the book in a fourteenth-century Christian milieu, see Michael Camille, "The Book as Flesh and Fetish in Richard de Bury's *Philobiblon,*" in *The Book and the Body,* ed. Dolores Warwick Frese and Katherine O'Brien O'Keeffe (Notre Dame, Ind.: University of Notre Dame Press, 1997), 34–77.

4. I have discussed this notion in chapters 1 and 2 of *Language, Eros, Being: Kabbalistic Hermeneutics and Poetic Imagination* (New York: Fordham University Press, 2005).

5. This account is a philosophic synopsis of my exegetical presentation of the imaginal body of God in "Judaism and Incarnation: The Imaginal Body of God," in *Christianity in Jewish Terms,* ed. Tikva Frymer-Kensky et al. (Boulder, Colo.: Westview Press, 2000). For a similar account in a different cultural context, see John Lagerwey, "Écriture et corps divin en Chine," in *Corps de dieux,* ed. Charles Malamoud and Jean-Pierre Vernant (Paris: Éditions Gallimard, 1986), 383–98. It is of interest to note that the author begins his essay with an epigram from Jeremiah 7:23–24.

6. Renaud Barbaras, *Le tournant de l'expérience: Recherches sur la philophie de Merleau-Ponty* (Paris: Librairie Philosophique J. Vrin, 1998), 95–136.

7. On poetry as the embodiment of the mystery of incarnation, see Regina M. Schwartz, "From Ritual to Poetry: Herbert's Mystical Eucharist," in *Mystics: Presence and Aporia,* ed. Michael Kessler and Christian Sheppard (Chicago: University of Chicago Press, 2003), 138–60.

8. Maurice Merleau-Ponty, *The Visible and the Invisible,* ed. Claude Lefort, trans. Alphonso Lingis (Evanston, Ill.: Northwestern University Press, 1968), 193.

9. Ibid., 28. Sundar Sarukkai, "Inside/Outside: Merleau-Ponty/Yoga," *Philosophy East and West* 52 (2002): 459–78, thematizes the overcoming of the internal-external binary in Merleau-Ponty's thought in conversation with the yogic practice of attaining the inner body, which does not yield to or foster transcendent/immanent duality. The comparative analysis of Merleau-Ponty and Asian religions has been a fruitful area of scholarly inquiry.

10. On the nexus between perceptual faith and the invisible, see Françoise Dastur, *Chair et langage: Essais sur Merleau-Ponty* (La Versanne: Encre Maine, 2001), 111–26; see also Galen A. Johnson, "Desire and Invisibility in 'Eye and Mind': Some Remarks on Merleau-Ponty's Spirituality," in *Merleau-Ponty in Contemporary Perspectives*, ed. Patrick Burke and Jan van der Veken (Dordrecht: Kluwer, 1993), 85–96.

11. Merleau-Ponty, *Visible and Invisible*, 28.

12. Ibid., 226–27 (French ed., *Le visible et l'invisible* [Paris: Librairie Gallimard, 1964], 280).

13. Ibid., 252–53.

14. Ibid., 167.

15. Ibid., 37.

16. David M. Levin, *The Opening of Vision: Nihilism and the Postmodern Situation* (New York: Routledge, 1988), 331.

17 Merleau-Ponty, *Visible and Invisible*, 127–28.

18. Alphonso Lingis, "Intentionality and Corporeity," *Analecta Husserliana* 1 (1971): 75–90, esp. 83–87; Don Ihde, *Sense and Significance* (Pittsburgh: Duquesne University Press, 1973), 124–27.

19. Merleau-Ponty, *Visible and Invisible*, 147–48.

20. Ibid., 142.

21. Ibid., 148.

22. Ibid., 248–49.

23. Ibid., 118.

24. Ibid.

25. Ibid., 119. On the entwining of the visible and invisible, see Levin, *Opening of Vision*, 175, 211–323.

26. Merleau-Ponty, *Visible and Invisible*, 107 (emphasis in original). Various scholars have written about the nexus of body and language in Merleau-Ponty's thought. For a representative list, see Remigius C. Kwant, *The Phenomenological Philosophy of Merleau-Ponty* (Pittsburgh: Duquesne University Press, 1963), 46–62; Mary Rose Barral, *The Body in Interpersonal Relations: Merleau-Ponty* (Lanham, Md.: University Press of America, 1984), 171–212; Martin C. Dillon, *Merleau-Ponty's Ontology* (Bloomington: Indiana University Press, 1988), 130–50; and Stephen Priest, *Merleau-Ponty* (London: Routledge, 1998), 73–74, 166–78. On the isomorphic relation between language and world, see Remigius C. Kwant, *From Phenomenology to Metaphysics: An Inquiry into the Last Period of Merleau-Ponty's Philosophical Life* (Pittsburgh: Duquesne University Press, 1966), 54–61; Dillon, *Merleau-Ponty's Ontology*, 178–223, esp. 209–19; and Martin C. Dillon, "The Unconscious: Language and World," in *Merleau-Ponty in Contemporary Perspectives*, ed. Patrick Burke and Jan van der Veken (Dordrecht: Kluwer Academic, 1993), 67–83. On the inextricable link between language and silence, see Kwant, *From Phenomenology to Metaphysics*, 184–90. On language as gesture, see also the discussion in Jerry H. Gill, *Merleau-Ponty and Metaphor* (Atlantic Highlands, N.J.: Humanities Press, 1991), 82–104.

27. Merleau-Ponty, *Visible and Invisible*, 216–17.

28. Ibid., 139 (emphasis in original).

29. Ibid., 138.

30. Ibid., 249.

31. Ibid., 140 (emphasis in original).

32. Ibid., 147.

33. Ibid., 146.

34. Alain Cantillon, "Corpus Pascalis," *Yale French Studies* 86 (1994): 44–45.

35. Merleau-Ponty, *Visible and Invisible*, 271; see Alphonso Lingis, "The Sensitive Flesh," in *The Collegium Phaenomeologicum: The First Ten Years*, ed. John C. Sallis, Giuseppina Moneta, and Jacques Taminiaux (Dordrecht: Kluwer Academic, 1988), 225–40.

36. For discussion of the fuller context and implications of this theme in Merleau-Ponty's hermeneutical phenomenology, see Renaud Barbaras, "Le dédoublement de l'originaire," in *Notes de cours sur L'origine de la géométrie de Husserl suivi de recherches sur la phénoménologie de Merleau-Ponty*, ed. Renaud Barbaras (Paris: Presses de Universitaires de France, 1998), 289–303; and Barbaras, *Tournant de l'expérience*, 81–94.

37. My English renderings of *Urpräsentiert* and *Nichturpräsentierbar* are indebted to the suggestions made by Charlotte E. Fonrobert.

38. Merleau-Ponty, *Visible and Invisible*, 228; see Patrick Burke, "The Flesh as *Urpräsentierbarkeit* in the Interrogative: The Absence of a Question in Derrida," in *Écart and différance: Merleau-Ponty and Derrida on Seeing and Writing*, ed. Martin C. Dillon (Atlantic Highlands, N.J.: Humanities Press, 1997), 60–70.

39. Merleau-Ponty, *Visible and Invisible*, 251 (emphasis in original).

40. Ibid., 228 (emphasis in original).

41. It is important to recall here Merleau-Ponty's exploration of the metaphysical implications of human sexuality and the play of eroticism in the fifth chapter of *Phénoménologie de la perception*: "The importance we attach to the body and the contradictions of love are . . . related to a more general drama which arises from the metaphysical structure of my body, which is both an object for others and a subject for myself. The intensity of sexual pleasure would not be sufficient to explain the place occupied by sexuality in human life or, for example, the phenomenon of eroticism, if sexual experience were not, as it were, an opportunity, vouchsafed to all and always available, of acquainting oneself with the human lot in its most general aspects of autonomy and dependence. . . . Metaphysics—the coming to light of something beyond nature—is not localized at the level of knowledge: it begins with the opening out upon 'another,' and is to be found everywhere, and already, in the specific development of sexuality" (*Phenomenology of Perception* trans. Colin Smith [New York: Humanities Press, 1962], 167–68). For a constructive, feminist reading of Merleau-Ponty's notion of lived bodies and the phenomenon of the flesh, see Elizabeth Grosz, *Volatile Bodies: Toward a Corporeal Feminism* (Bloomington: Indiana University Press, 1994), 86–111; and the nuanced analysis of Sara Heinämaa, *Toward a Phenomenology of Sexual Difference: Husserl, Merleau-Ponty, Beauvoir* (Lanham, Md.: Rowman and Littlefield, 2003), 21–79. By contrast, a feminist critique of Merleau-Ponty's thinking about sexual difference is offered by Tina Chanter, "Wild Meaning: Luce Irigaray's Reading of Merleau-Ponty," in *Chiasms: Merleau-Ponty's Notion of Flesh*, ed. Fred Evans and Leonard Lawlor (Albany: State University of New York Press, 2000), 219–36.

42. Merleau-Ponty, *Visible and Invisible*, 132; see Jean-Marie Tréguier, *Corps selon la chair: Phénoménologie et ontologie chez Merleau-Ponty* (Paris: Éditions Kimé, 1996), 135–48.

43. Merleau-Ponty, *Visible and Invisible*, 263.

44. For an elaboration, see Elliot R. Wolfson, "Before Alef /Where Beginnings End," in *Beginning/Again: Towards a Hermeneutics of Jewish Texts*, ed. Aryeh Cohen and Shaul Magid (New York: Seven Bridges Press, 2002), 135–61.

45. Jacob Böhme, *The Aurora*, trans. John Sparrow (London: John M. Watkins, 1960), 8.123–26, 173.

46. Elliot R. Wolfson, "Anthropomorphic Imagery and Letter Symbolism in the Zohar" (Hebrew), *Jerusalem Studies in Jewish Thought* 8 (1989): 147–81; Elliot R. Wolfson, "Letter Symbolism and Merkavah Imagery in the Zohar," in *Alei Shefer: Studies in the Literature of Jewish Thought Presented to Rabbi Dr. Alexandre Safran*, ed. Moshe H. Ḥallamish (English section)

(Ramat Gan: Bar-Ilan Press, 1990), 195–236. The reader interested in gathering more information about the molecular biological image of the genome would do well to consult the wide-ranging study by Ram S. Verma, *The Genome* (New York: VCH Publishers, 1990).

47. *The Book Bahir: An Edition Based on the Earliest Manuscripts* (Hebrew), ed. Daniel Abrams with intro. by Moshe Idel (Los Angeles: Cherub Press, 1994), sec. 53, 149. Gershom Scholem duly noted that kabbalists draw no distinction between a thing and its proper name ("The Name of God and the Linguistic Theory of the Kabbala," *Diogenes* 79 [1972]: 77) and that the most proper of all names is YHWH, the "essential name" that is the "original source of all language" ("The Name of God and the Linguistic Theory of the Kabbala," *Diogenes* 80 [1972]: 194). It is of interest to note here that the number twenty-two was used to signify perfection in Christian devotional texts. This numerical symbolism was based both on the letters of the Hebrew alphabet and the Platonic tradition that twenty-two terms compose the double interval series related to the formation of the soul and the principle of order in the cosmos; see Kate Gartner Frost, *Holy Delight: Typology, Numerology, and Autobiography in Donne's Devotions upon Emergent Occasions* (Princeton, N.J.: Princeton University Press, 1990), 109–10.

48. The point was well understood by Shem Tov Ibn Shem Tov, *Sefer ha-Emunot* (Ferrara, 1556), 19b, who cites and briefly explicates the bahiric text.

49. Elias Lipiner, *Metaphysics of the Hebrew Alphabet* (Hebrew) (Jerusalem: Magnes Press, 1989), 124–40, presents a thorough summary of the linguistic theory in the second part of *Sefer Yeṣirah*; see also Moshe Idel, "Reification of Language in Jewish Mysticism," in *Mysticism and Language,* ed. Steven T. Katz (Oxford: Oxford University Press, 1992), 45–49; Moshe Idel, *Absorbing Perfections: Kabbalah and Interpretation,* foreword by Harold Bloom (New Haven, Conn.: Yale University Press, 2002), 34–37.

50. Scholem, "Name of God," 65–66. The ancient Israelite tradition about the power of the name crossed over into syncretistic Hellenistic magic; see John G. Gager, *Moses in Greco-Roman Paganism* (Nashville: Abingdon Press, 1972), 142–46. Another facet of the correlation of letters and limbs that I will not discuss in this chapter is the richly evocative traditions about the golem that have been cultivated and transmitted through the centuries. For analysis of this motif, see Gershom Scholem, *On the Kabbalah and Its Symbolism,* trans. Ralph Manheim (New York: Schocken Books, 1969), 158–204; Moshe Idel, *Golem: Jewish Magical and Mystical Traditions on the Artificial Anthropoid* (Albany: State University of New York Press, 1990); Yehuda Liebes, "*Golem* in Numerology Is Ḥokhmah" (Hebrew), *Qiryat Sefer* 63 (1991): 1305–22; and Yehuda Liebes, *Ars Poetica in Sefer Yetsira* (Hebrew) (Tel Aviv: Schocken, 2000), 63–71.

51. Jacob ben Sheshet, *Sefer Meshiv Devarim Nekhoḥim,* ed. Georges Vajda, intro. Georges Vajda and Efraim Gottlieb (Jerusalem: Israel Academy of Sciences and Humanities, 1968), 154; see Jacob ben Sheshet, *Sefer ha-Emunah we-ha-Biṭṭaḥon,* in *Kitvei Ramban,* ed. Ḥayyim D. Chavel (Jerusalem: Mosad ha-Rav Kook, 1964), 2:392–93: "There is no letter in the *alef-beit* that does not allude to the holy One, blessed be he."

52. Technically, the word "enstatic" is from the Greek *en-stasis*, "standing within," the etymological opposite of "ecstatic" from *ek-stasis*, "standing without." For a brief account of these terms, see Paul J. Griffiths, *On Being Mindless: Buddhist Meditation and the Mind-Body Problem* (La Salle, Ill.: Open Court, 1986), 149n27.

53. Maurice Merleau-Ponty, *Signs,* trans. and intro. Richard C. McCleary (Evanston, Ill.: Northwestern University Press, 1964), 89.

54. My language respectfully modifies the saying discussed by Roy W. Perrett, "Is Whatever Exists Knowable and Nameable?" *Philosophy East and West* 49 (1999): 401–14, being influenced in particular by Blanchot's notion of the limit-experience (see also Elliot R. Wolfson, *Language, Eros,*

Being: Kabbalistic Hermeneutics and Poetic Imagination.[New York: Fordham University Press, 2005], chap. 6).

55. Shem Tov ben Abraham Ibn Gaon, *Sefer Baddei ha-Aron u-Migdal Hananel*, a limited facsimile edition of Codex Paris Bibliothèque nationale no. 40, ed. D. S. Löwinger (Jerusalem: Makor, 1977), 14.

56. For a thorough treatment of this matter, and citation of other relevant scholarly analyses, see Moshe Idel, "Maimonides and Kabbalah," in *Studies in Maimonides,* ed. Isadore Twersky (Cambridge, Mass.: Harvard University Press, 1990), 31–81, and Elliot R. Wolfson, "Beneath the Wings of the Great Eagle: Maimonides and Thirteenth-Century Kabbalah, in *Moses Maimonides (1138-1204)—His Religious, Scientific, and Philosophical Wirkungsgeschichte in Different Cultural Contexts,* ed. Görge K. Hasselhoff and Otfried Fraisse (Würzburg: Ergon, 2004), 209–37, esp. 212–21. Scholars of medieval kabbalah and Jewish philosophy would benefit from the nuanced and sophisticated discussion on the interplay of the mystical and philosophical enunciated in the essay by Franz Rosenthal, "Ibn ʿArabī between 'Philosophy' and 'Mysticism,'" *Oriens* 31 (1988): 1–35.

57. *Lirmoz* literally means to hint, to allude, to represent symbolically. I have rendered it "to imagine," out of the conviction that in kabbalistic sources there is no disjuncture between the verbal and visual.

58. *Kitvei Ramban,* 2:454.

59. Gershom Scholem, *Origins of the Kabbalah*, ed. R. J. Zwi Werblowsky, trans. Allan Arkush (Princeton, N.J.: Princeton University Press, 1987), 452; Joel Goldberg, "Mystical Union, Individuality, and Individuation in Provençal and Catalonian Kabbalah" (PhD diss., New York University, 2001), 518n104, 520n109.

60. *Kitvei Ramban,* 2:453 (commentary on *Sefer Yeṣirah* 1:1).

61. *Kitvei Ramban,* 2:454; see also 455, where Azriel frames the ontological chain in terms of visionary ascent (in his commentary on *Sefer Yeṣirah* 1:6)—that is, the natural (*muṭba*) ascends in order to contemplate the sensible (*murgash*), and the sensible ascends to contemplate the intelligible (*muskʿal*), and the intelligible ascends to contemplate the hidden (*neʿlam*). According to Azriel, the word *ṣefiyyah* ("vision") denotes the effluence of the "potency that extends from above to below."

62. Scholem, *Origins*, 265, refers to Azriel's composition as a "Neoplatonic catechism."

63. See Elliot R. Wolfson, "Negative Theology and Positive Assertion in the Early Kabbalah," *Daʿat* (1994): xi.

64. Azriel of Gerona, *Perush Eser Sefirot*, in Meir Ibn Gabbai, *Derekh Emunah* (Berlin, 1850), 3a.

65. *Devarim*; this is one of the technical terms in the lexicon of Isaac the Blind and his disciples to refer to the *sefirot*; see Scholem, "Name of God," 166–67; Scholem, *Origins*, 265, 277–78.

66. *Sefer Yeṣirah*, 1:6.

67. Gershom Scholem, "A New Document for the History of the Beginning of Kabbalah" (Hebrew), in *Sefer Bialik* (Tel Aviv: Emunot, 1934), 143.

68. Ibid., 146; see also Scholem, *Origins*, 394–95.

69. Stephen Gersh, *Middle Platonism and Neoplatonism: The Latin Tradition*, 2 vols. (Notre Dame, Ind.: University of Notre Dame Press, 1986), 1:170–74.

70. James C. VanderKam, *The Book of Jubilees: A Critical Text*, 2 vols. (Leuven: Éditions Peeters, 1989), 73.

71. Many competent scholars have turned their attention to the evolution of the sapiential tradition in ancient Israelite religion and Second-Temple Judaism. For a useful survey and relevant bibliography, see John J. Collins, *Jewish Wisdom in the Hellenistic Age* (Edinburgh: T & T Clark, 1997).

72. It should come as no surprise that this matter has been the focus of many important studies. Here I mention but one study, Seth L. Sanders, "Writing, Ritual, and Apocalypse: Studies in the

Theme of Ascent to Heaven in Ancient Mesopotamia and Second Temple Judaism" (PhD diss., Johns Hopkins University, 1999). I am indebted to the author, who graciously sent me a copy of his informative and impressive work. Needless to say, one will find in Sanders a judicious engagement with other relevant scholarly accounts.

73. For discussion of the depiction of wisdom as the image of fullness, see Jan Liesen, *Full of Praise: An Exegetical Study of Sir 39, 12–35* (Leiden: E. J. Brill, 1999), 145–87.

74. Patrick W. Skehan, *The Wisdom of Ben Sira*, trans. Alexander A. DiLella (New York: Doubleday, 1987), 138. On the myth of the descent of the personified wisdom, see Randall A. Argall, *1 Enoch and Sirach: A Comparative Literary and Conceptual Analysis of the Themes of Revelation, Creation, and Judgment* (Atlanta: Scholars Press, 1995), 53–98.

75. Paul Davies, *About Time: Einstein's Unfinished Revolution* (New York: Simon and Schuster, 1995), 248.

76. I offer this remark as a rhetorical prod to stimulate thinking about kabbalah in a somewhat broader conceptual framework and not as a commitment to the belief that medieval kabbalists anticipated current developments in quantum physics, as is sometimes suggested by the overly zealous preachers of the gospel of New Age Jewish spirituality. For a helpful and measured account of the philosophical issues that emerge from the depictions of space and time in string theory, see Barry Dainton, *Time and Space* (Montreal: McGill-Queen's University Press, 2001), 320–34.

77. Gershom Scholem, *Explications and Implications: Writings on Jewish Heritage and Renaissance* (Hebrew), vol. 2, ed. Avraham Shapira (Tel Aviv: Am Oved, 1989), 38.

78. Kabbalistic lore preserves and intensifies the nexus between the chosenness of the Jewish people and the privileging of Hebrew as the ontological language. For a comprehensive and nuanced study of the development of this "metasemantic" notion of *leshon ha-qodesh*, see David H. Aaron, "Judaism's Holy Language," in *Approaches to Ancient Judaism*, ed. Jacob Neusner, new series, 16 (Atlanta: Scholars Press, 1999), 49–107, esp. 96–105, where the author discusses the mythological conception of Hebrew as a cosmogonic force in *Genesis Rabbah* and select mystical and magical texts. On the related but conceptually distinct topic of the holiness of the divine word, see Hannah K. Harrington, *Holiness: Rabbinic Judaism and the Graeco-Roman World* (London: Routledge, 2001), 130–60.

79. *Genesis Rabbah*, ed. Julius Theodor and Chanoch Albeck (Jerusalem: Wahrmann Book, 1965), 18:4, 164. For other sources, see Louis Ginzberg, *The Legends of the Jews*, 7 vols. (Philadelphia: Jewish Publication Society of America, 1968), 5:205n91.

80. On the theme of the heavenly tablets, see Shalom Paul, "Heavenly Tablets and the Book of Life," *Journal of the Ancient Near East Society of Columbia University* 5 (1973): 345–53; and other references cited in Elliot R. Wolfson, *Circle in the Square: Studies in the Use of Gender in Kabbalistic Symbolism* (Albany: State University of New York Press, 1995), 161n31. I note here two worthwhile discussions of this imaginal symbol in more recent studies: F. Garcia Martinez, "The Heavenly Tablets in the Book of Jubilees," in *Studies in the Book of Jubilees*, ed. Matthias Albni, Jörg Frey, and Armin Lange (Tübingen: Mohr Siebeck, 1997), 243–60, and Hindy Najman, "Interpretation as Primordial Writing: Jubilees and Its Authority-Conferring Strategies," *Journal for the Study of Judaism* 30 (1999): 379–410.

81. For a still-useful review of the image of the world as a book, see Gabriel Josipovici, *The World and the Book: A Study of Modern Fiction* (Stanford: Stanford University Press, 1971), 25–51. The augmented use of the metaphor of the book of nature has been traced to the renaissance of twelfth-century humanism; see Ernst Robert Curtius, *European Literature and the Latin Middle Ages*, trans. Willard R. Trask (Princeton, N.J.: Princeton University Press, 1990), 302–47; Ashlynn K. Pai, "Varying Degrees of Light: Bonaventure and the Medieval Book of Nature," in *The Book and*

the Magic of Reading in the Middle Ages, ed. Albrecht Classen (New York: Garland, 1998), 3–19. On the later reverberation of this motif as a key to understanding the respective convergence and divergence of science and theology, two fundamental fountainheads of knowledge, see Kenneth J. Howell, *God's Two Books: Copernican Cosmology and Biblical Interpretation in Early Modern Science* (Notre Dame, Ind.: University of Notre Dame Press, 2002),

82. On the textualization of God in kabbalistic symbolism, see Wolfson, *Circle in the Square*, 49–78; Wolfson, "From Sealed Book to Open Text: Time, Memory, and Narrativity in Kabbalistic Hermeneutics," in *Interpreting Judaism in a Postmodern Age*, ed. Steven Kepnes (New York: New York University Press, 1995), 145–78, and the recent remarks in Idel, *Absorbing Perfections*, 44, 116–24, 483–87. On the link between representation of nature as a text or book in medieval Christian sources, a belief that rests on the assumption that things in nature and words in Scripture are to be interpreted as metaphorical signs denoting God's existence, and on the doctrine of incarnation, see Jesse M. Gellrich, *The Idea of the Book in the Middle Ages: Language Theory, Mythology, and Fiction* (Ithaca, N.Y.: Cornell University Press, 1985), 29–50; Sabine Melchior-Bonnet, *The Mirror: A History*, trans. Katharine H. Jewett (New York: Routledge, 2001), 108–18; Barbara Newman, *God and Goddesses: Vision, Poetry, and Belief in the Middle Ages* (Philadelphia: University of Pennsylvania Press, 2003), 51–137. On the impact of this motif in occult philosophies that crystallized in the Renaissance and early modern periods, in part under the influence of kabbalah, see James J. Bono, *Word of God and the Languages of Man: Interpreting Nature in Early Modern Science and Medicine* (Madison: University of Wisconsin Press, 1995), 72–84, 123–66; Deborah E. Harkness, *John Dee's Conversations with Angels: Cabala, Alchemy, and the End of Nature* (Cambridge: Cambridge University Press, 1999), 64–97, 157–94.

83. Franz Rosenzweig, *The Star of Redemption*, trans. William W. Hallo (New York: Holt, Rinehart and Winston, 1970), 409.

84. For a comprehensive study of this influence, see Diana Lobel, *Between Mysticism and Philosophy: Sufi Language of Religious Experience in Judah ha-Levi's Kuzari* (Albany: State University of New York Press, 2000). The author provides a brief review of previous scholars who have discussed the influence of Islamic mysticism on Halevi (6–9). The theme of the sacrality of Arabic, the language of God's revelation transmitted to Muḥammad and preserved in the Qur'ān, in Sufism and its proximity to Halevi's view, not to mention Jewish mystical texts, is not discussed by Lobel. In spite of the justified emphasis placed on the auditory-verbal dimension of language attested to in the central role accorded recitation of the Qur'ān in Muslim ritual, one should not ignore the importance of the graphic-visual dimension; indeed, there is a subtle and dialectical relationship between the recited *qur'ān* and the written *kitāb*; see William A. Graham, *Beyond the Written Word: Oral Aspects of Scripture in the History of Religion* (Cambridge: Cambridge University Press, 1987), 81–115; Daniel A. Madigan, *Qur'ān's Self-Image: Writing and Authority in Islam's Scripture* (Princeton, N.J.: Princeton University Press, 2001). Furthermore, Muslim belief in the Qur'ān as the primal text, the heavenly "guarded tablet," *al-lawḥ al- maḥfūẓ* (Q 85:21–22), an archaic mythical notion (see above, n. 80), surely complicates the relation between the written and oral aspects of scriptural language even at the revelatory stage. It has even been suggested that the notion of the uncreated Qur'ān as the embodied word of God amounts to a doctrine of "illibration" that corresponds to the Christian concept of incarnation; see Harry A. Wolfson, *Philosophy of the Kalam* (Cambridge, Mass: Harvard University Press, 1976), 235–63; Stefan Wild, "'We Have Sent Down to Thee the Book with the Truth . . .': Spatial and Temporal Implications of the Qur'anic Concepts of Nuzūl, Tanzīl, and 'Inzāl," in *The Qur'an as Text*, ed. Stefan Wild (Leiden: E. J. Brill, 1996), 137–53. See the incisive and rich analysis of logo-centrism and the construction of religious truth in Islam offered by Mohammed Arkoun, *Unthought in Contemporary Islamic Thought* (London: Saqi Books,

2002), 170–203, esp. the discussion on writing, text, and reading, 171–78. The sacred nature of the written script is also attested in the central place accorded calligraphy in Islamic culture as well as in the sustained impact of magical talismans, which feature the sundry names of God written in Arabic; see Annemarie Schimmel, *Deciphering the Signs of God: A Phenomenological Approach to Islam* (Albany: State University of New York Press, 1994), 150–58; Annemarie Schimmel, *Mystical Dimensions of Islam* (Chapel Hill: University of North Carolina Press, 1975), 411–25. For a somewhat different perspective on the efficacy assigned to the isolated letters of the Qur'ān, see Louis Massignon, *Passion of al-Hallāj: Mystic and Martyr of Islam*, trans. Herbert Mason, 4 vols. (Princeton, N.J.: Princeton University Press, 1982), 3:98.

85. Judah Halevi, *Sefer ha-Kuzari*, trans. Yehudah Even Shmuel (Tel Aviv: Dvir, 1972), 4:25.

86. The influence of Halevi is conspicuous in *Zohar* 2:129b, where the "holy language" of the Jews is contrasted with the "foreign language" of the "other nations," i.e., the language of the other side, identified in the continuation of the passage as the "language of the Targum," i.e., Aramaic. The fact that most of the *Zohar* was composed in the language attributed to the demonic potency is a matter that demands analysis. For a related motif, attested in earlier sources, that may have influenced the formation of the zoharic topos, see below, n. 88. In *Zohar* 3:204a, the supremacy of the Jews vis-à-vis the idolatrous nations is emphasized by the claim that only the former possess the written and oral form of the language whence one can know the truth of reality. Part of the text is cited below, at n. 100.

87. Halevi, *Sefer ha-Kuzari*, 2:68. The resemblance, indeed underlying unity, of the three languages, Hebrew, Aramaic, and Arabic, is also noted in the writings of Halevi's contemporary, Abraham Ibn Ezra, but he is of the opinion that Aramaic is the "primordial language"; see discussion in Moshe Idel, "The Infant Experiment: The Search for the First Language," in *The Language of Adam: Die Sprache Adams,* ed. Allison P. Coudert (Wiesbaden: Harrassowitz, 1999), 59–61. On the contrast between the views of Halevi and Ibn Ezra on the nature of language, see Uriel Simon, *Four Approaches to the Book of Psalms: From Saadiah Gaon to Abraham Ibn Ezra*, trans. Lenn J. Schramm (Albany: State University of New York Press, 1991), 267n53. See below, n. 102.

88. Halevi follows a line of thinking in rabbinic literature according to which the language of the angels is Hebrew and not Aramaic; see Babylonian Talmud, Shabbat 12b, Sotah 33a; *Avot de-Rabbi Natan*, ed. Solomon Schechter (Vienna: Ch. D. Lippe, 1887), version A, chap. 37, 55a; Joseph Yahalom, "Angels Do Not Understand Aramaic: On the Literary Use of Jewish Palestinian Aramaic in Late Antiquity," *Journal of Jewish Studies* 47 (1996): 33–44. The motif is repeated on a number of occasions in zoharic literature; see, for example, *Zohar* 1:9b, 74b, 88b, 89a.

89. Halevi, *Sefer ha-Kuzari*, 1:53–56; Yochanan Silman, *Philosopher and Prophet: Judah Halevi, the Kuzari, and the Evolution of His Thought*, trans. Lenn J. Schramm (Albany: State University of New York Press,1995), 90n29, 292n7; Raphael Jospe, "The Superiority of Oral over Written Communication: Judah Ha-Levi's Kuzari and Modern Jewish Thought," in *From Ancient Israel to Modern Judaism Intellect in Quest of Understanding: Essays in Honor of Marvin Fox*, ed. Jacob Neusner, Ernest S. Frerichs, and Nahum M. Sarna, 4 vols. (Atlanta: Scholars Press, 1989), 3:127–29. Another twelfth-century author who demonstrates affinity with the mystical tradition on this account is the Yemenite Nathanel Ibn al-Fayyūmī. In his *Bustan al-'uqul* (Ibn alFayyūmī, *Bustan Al-Ukul*, ed. and trans. David Levine [New York: Columbia University Press, 1908], 3–4, English section; 2, Judeo-Arabic section), al-Fayyūmī relates the view in the name of "some of the learned" that the "characters of the alphabet [*ḥuruf al-otiyyot*] . . . were originated before the world of changeable things, inasmuch as every rational being needs them in discourse and in uttering the praise of God." In the continuation of this passage, al-Fayyūmī links this thought exegetically to the first verse in Genesis, "In the beginning God created the heavens and the earth" (*bere'shit bara elohim*

et ha-shamayim we-et ha-areṣ). It is possible that the exegetical point is related to the particle *et*, which consists of *alef* and *tau*, the first and last letters of the Hebrew alphabet. The technical term used by al-Fayyūmī reflects the Shiʿite notion of the "science of letters" (*ʿilm al-ḥuruf*), that is, the "magical and divinatory application of the numerical value of the alphabet" (Mohammad Ali Amir-Moezzi, *The Divine Guide in Early Shiʿism: The Sources of Esotericism in Islam*, trans. David Streight [Albany: State University of New York Press, 1994], 95). A possible source for al-Fayyūmī may have been Saadiah Gaon's commentary on *Sefer Yeṣirah*, especially the eighth of the nine positions he delineates in the introduction to this work, a position that he identifies as compatible with the one expressed in *Sefer Yeṣirah*, viz., that the first of all things created were the numbers and letters. For some representative studies of al-Fayyūmī, see Shlomo Pines, "Nathanael ben al-Fayyūmī et la théologie ismaëlienne," *Revue de l'histoire juive en Égypte* 1 (1947): 5–22; Ronald C. Kiener, "Jewish Ismaʿilism in Twelfth-Century Yemen: R. Nethanel al-Fayyumi," *Jewish Quarterly Review* 74 (1984): 249–66; and the comments by Moshe Idel, *Kabbalah: New Perspectives* (New Haven, Conn.: Yale University Press, 1988), 121, 334nn76–77.

90. In light of this long-standing belief attested in works of Jewish esotericism, it is of interest to consider the remark of Françoise Dastur, *Telling Time: Sketch of a Phenomenological Chronology*, trans. Edward Bullard (London: Athlone Press, 2000), 99n14, that the "inflection" of Semitic languages "concerns a root which—contrary to the Indo-European radical which is merely a product of analysis and becomes apparent only through etymological research—is part of the living linguistic consciousness of the speaker without, however, being embodied otherwise than in consonantal script."

91. Some relevant passages from Gikatilla on this point are cited by Moshe Idel, "Abulafia's Secrets of the Guide: A Linguistic Turn," in *Perspectives on Jewish Thought and Mysticism*, ed. Alfred L. Ivry, Elliot R. Wolfson, and Alan Arkush (Amsterdam: Harwood Academic, 1998), 298–99.

92. Halevi's influence is detectable in Joseph ben Shalom Ashkenazi, *A Kabbalistic Commentary of Rabbi Yoseph Ben Shalom Ashkenazi on Genesis Rabbah* (Hebrew), ed. Moshe Ḥallamish (Jerusalem: Magnes Press, 1984), 44: "On account of our sins we are mixed together with the nations and we have seen that their letters are only signs [*simanim*]. . . . The people of our nation made a great error and thought erroneously about God, his Torah, and the letters of Torah by saying they are only signs. God forbid that our holy Torah, that is, its letters, are signs fabricated in the hearts of men. How could the letters engraved by the finger of God be fabricated letters?"; compare 146. The former passage is cited by Lipiner, *Metaphysics of Hebrew*, 48–49; see also the commentary to *Sefer Yeṣirah* by the same kabbalist erroneously attributed to Abraham ben David in *Sefer Yeṣirah*, 31a: "Thus it should be clear to you that there are letters of spirit [*otiyyot shel ruaḥ*], and they are the letters of the Holy Spirit [*otiyyot shel ruaḥ ha-qodesh*]. Therefore [Hebrew] is called the holy language [*leshon ha-qodesh*], which is not the case with any other language of the seventy languages, because it comes forth and emanates from the source of holiness."

93. Scholem, "Name of God," 134–35; Moshe Idel, *Language, Torah, and Hermeneutics in Abraham Abulafia* (Albany: State University of New York Press, 1989), 12–14, 16–27; Idel, "Abulafia's Secrets," 300–4; Elliot R. Wolfson, *Abraham Abulafia—Kabbalist and Prophet: Hermeneutics, Theosophy, and Theurgy* (Los Angeles: Cherub Press, 2000), 58–65. On the possible impact the Maimonidean conception of language had in eliciting a response on the part of kabbalists, see Idel, *Absorbing Perfections*, 106.

94. For instance, consider Abulafia's depiction of prophecy in *Sitrei Torah* (MS Paris, Bibliothèque Nationale 774), fol. 155a (printed ed., Jerusalem 2001, 138): "The beginning of the truth of prophecy is the inner speech [*dibbur penimi*] created in the soul in the seventy languages by means of the twenty-two holy letters, and all of them are combined in the heart through the permutation

491

of letters." On the relation of the seventy languages to Hebrew in Abulafia's writings, see Wolfson, *Abraham Abulafia*, 62–64, and reference to studies of Scholem and Idel cited at 62n178.

95. Abraham Abulafia, *Imrei Shefer* (MS Munich, Bayerische Staatsbibliothek 40), fol. 238a (printed ed., Jerusalem 1999, 69–70; I have translated from the manuscript version). Compare Abulafia's comment in *Oṣar Eden Ganuz* (MS Oxford, Bodleian Library 1580), fol. 25a (printed ed., Jerusalem 2000, 51) on the statement in *Sefer Yeṣirah* that God created the soul of all that exists by means of the twenty-two Hebrew letters: "This is a great secret that God revealed to his prophets, and his prophets revealed it to his people Israel, and it is not known by any nation except this one." In the continuation of the passage, Abulafia refers to this "wondrous secret" as the "stake upon which everything is hung."

96. Idel, "Infant Experiment," 70.

97. Ibid., 71.

98. I am not engaging the third model, which Idel identifies as magic, since in my opinion the tripartite typological structure is a variation of the earlier twofold structure—that is, the magical is operative in either the theosophic or prophetic framework and one therefore does not gain much by according it an independent taxonomic status.

99. On occasion Abulafia limited somewhat the claim about the "natural" state of Hebrew by ascribing this quality only to the verbal dimension of the letters, as opposed to the written forms, which are considered to be conventional. The distinction is made, for instance, in Abulafia, *Oṣar Eden Ganuz*, fol. 62a (printed ed., 124): "I will speak now initially about the matter of the letters. That which is written in books are merely signs and that which is mentioned by mouth are also signs, but the difference between them is that the written letter *alef* is a conventional sign [*simman muskam*], and even if it is prophetic [*nevu'i*] it is conventional, However, the *alef* that is mentioned through pronunciation that comes forth from the throat is natural [*muṭba*] and not conventional."

100. *Zohar* 3:204a.

101. On the identification of word and will, see Halevi, *Sefer ha-Kuzari*, 2:6.

102. Halevi, *Sefer ha-Kuzari*, 1:101; 4:25. The insistence that the exclusive language of prophecy is Hebrew (see also 5:20) is a corollary of the claims that it is limited to the Jewish people and that it must occur within the boundaries of the land of Israel; see Silman, *Philosopher and Prophet*, 178–79. The distinctiveness of Halevi's approach and its similarity to Jewish mysticism are underscored when he is compared to other thinkers of his time. For a comparison of Halevi and Abraham Ibn Ezra, see the reference in n. 87 above to Simon, *Four Approaches*. In contrast to Halevi's classification of Hebrew as the divine language, Ibn Ezra views it as the "first language," created by Adam, though he maintains the unique sanctity of Hebrew as the "holy tongue" exemplified by the divine name; see Moshe Idel, "A la recherché de la langue originelle: Le témoignage du nourrisson," *Revue de l'Histoire des Religions* 214 (1996): 416–20. An even sharper contrast to Halevi is Maimonides, who incontrovertibly affirms that language is a matter of convention; no special status is accorded Hebrew; see Jospe, "Superiority of Oral," 128n2; Silman, *Philosopher and Prophet*, 90n29. For another example of a philosopher affirming the conventionalist view, see Aron Dotan, "Saadia Gaon on the Origins of Language" (Hebrew), *Tarbiz* 65 (1996): 237–49. The similarity of Halevi's identification of Hebrew as the divine language and the linguistic theory formulated by kabbalists, especially Isaac the Blind, is noted by Mark B. Sendor, "The Emergence of Provençal Kabbalah: Rabbi Isaac the Blind's *Commentary on Sefer Yeṣirah*," 2 vols. (PhD diss., Harvard University, 1994), 1:244–46.

103. Giovanni Manetti, *Theories of the Sign in Classical Antiquity,* trans. Christine Richardson (Bloomington: Indiana University Press, 1993), 166–67.

104. See Wolfson, *Language, Eros, Being,* chap. 1, n. 331.

105. Robert S. Corrington, *Ecstatic Naturalism: Signs of the World* (Bloomington: Indiana University Press, 1994), 67.

106. Schimmel, *Deciphering the Signs*, xii–xiii. On the nexus of body and writing in Islamic sources, see also Malek Chebel, *Corps en Islam* (Paris: Presses Universitaires de France, 1984), 175–90.

107. Schimmel, *Mystical Dimensions*, 411. For the introduction of gender and specifically the feminine character to depict the nature of the sign and the spirit, see Michael Sells, *Approaching the Qur'ān: The Early Revelations* (Ashland, Ore.: White Cloud Press, 1999), 201–4.

108. It is of interest to consider the following prophetic tradition on the special status accorded the Qur'ān in Merlin Swartz, ed., *Medieval Critique of Anthropomorphism: Ibn Al-Jawzī's Kitāb Akhbār as-Sifāt: A Critical Edition of the Arabic Text with Translation, Introduction, and Notes* (Leiden: Brill, 2002), sec. 170, p. 239: "In a tradition reported by 'Uthmān, the Prophet said: 'The superiority of the Quran to other forms of speech is comparable to God's superiority over His creatures, for the Quran proceeded from Him (*minhu kharaja*) and will return to Him.' The point of the saying is that the Quran has come (*waṣala*) to us from Him (*min 'indahu*) and will return to Him again; moreover, [the saying] is to be taken as resting on the authority of the Prophet." The qualitative difference between God and the Qur'ān must be upheld, even though the latter is to be accorded a special status, since it proceeded from and will return to God and thus it stands apart from the world of created things. The issue of the divinization of the qur'ānic text and the implied corporeality of God is underscored in sec. 237, p. 276: "As for the prophetic tradition: 'God's servants do not approach Him with anything like what proceeds from Him,' the expression 'what proceeds from Him' (*mā kharaja minhu*) should be construed to mean what becomes manifest through Him (*ẓahara 'anhu*). We are not to suppose that the expression implies one body coming out of another, for God is not a body (*jism*) and His word (*kalām*) is not a body (*jism*)." On the charge of heresy on the part of Muslims who refused to acknowledge the created nature of the Qur'ān, thereby affirming a view akin to the Christian depiction of Jesus as the uncreated Word of God, see the evidence adduced by G. R. Hawting, *The Idea of Idolatry and the Emergence of Islam: From Polemic to History* (Cambridge: Cambridge University Press, 1999), 80.

109. My analysis is indebted to the discussion of Augustine in Manetti, *Theories of the Sign*, where the author asserts that Augustine's semiology shows "a striking anticipation of some of the most recent semantic research tendencies (instructional model) in the contemporary world" (168).

110. Cited in William C. Chittick, *The Self-Disclosure of God: Principles of Ibn al-'Arabi's Cosmology* (Albany: State University of New York Press, 1998), 5.

111. Cited in Reynold A. Nicholson, *Studies in Islamic Mysticism* (Cambridge: Cambridge University Press, 1921), 140n1.

112. Gershom Scholem, *Major Trends in Jewish Mysticism* (New York: Schocken Books, 1954), 152–53. In that context, Scholem is describing the prophetic kabbalah of Abraham Abulafia, but his words could easily be applied to the theosophic kabbalah propounded, for instance, by Moses de León, Moses of Burgos, or Joseph Gikatilla, to mention just a few of the prominent figures active in the latter part of the thirteenth century. For an attempt to distinguish different views of language in theosophic and prophetic kabbalah while affirming the shared assumption regarding the ontologized or reified nature of language and the assumption that the Hebrew letters are the constitutive elements of creation, see Moshe Idel, "Reification of Language in Jewish Mysticism," in *Mysticism and Language*, ed. Steven T. Katz (Oxford: Oxford University Press, 1992), 42–79.

113. Babylonian Talmud, Menahot 29b. Regarding this text and other cognate rabbinic dicta, see Wolfson, *Circle in the Square*, 159n23.

114. Joseph Gikatilla, *Sefer ha-Niqqud* (Jerusalem: Yerid ha-Sefarim, 1994), 4.

115. See references cited in Wolfson, *Language, Eros, Being,* chap. 1, n. 251.

116. Ithamar Gruenwald, "A Preliminary Critical Edition of *Sefer Yezira,*" *Israel Oriental Studies* 1 (1971), sec. 19, p. 148. Scholem, "Name of God," 75, suggests three possible interpretations of this passage: the name refers to the Tetragrammaton; the reference is to the alphabet itself, which constitutes a mystical name; or the term *shem* does not denote a name in a precise sense but a method of the formation of words. I do not think the first two possibilities need be treated as distinct—that is, the mystical name can refer simultaneously to the divine name and to the letters of the Hebrew alphabet, for the latter are comprised within the former. Aryeh Kaplan, *Sefer Yetzirah: The Book of Creation in Theory and Practice* (York Beach, Maine: Weiser, 1990), 125, advances the interpretation of the "one name" as a reference to the Tetragrammaton. Although Kaplan is often anachronistic in his approach, it seems to me that in this particular instance he is not far off the mark. However, I do not agree with his assessment that this passage alludes to the process of combining the twenty-two letters with the letters of the Tetragrammaton, a technique we find in medieval prescriptions for creating the golem. This possibility is suggested as well by Idel, *Golem,* 11. In my estimation, the intent of the text in *Sefer Yeṣirah* is that the twenty-two letters themselves constitute the one divine name, which is the source of all that exists.

117. I am in agreement with Haviva Pedaya, "'Flaw' and 'Correction' in the Concept of the Godhead in the Teachings of Rabbi Isaac the Blind" (Hebrew), *Jerusalem Studies in Jewish Thought* 6, no. 3–4 (1987): 160n17, that the "one name" here refers to the Tetragrammaton, the root word of the metaphysical language, Hebrew, the divine source whence all being comes to be; see Haviva Pedaya, *Name and Sanctuary in the Teaching of R. Isaac the Blind: A Comparative Study in the Writings of the Earliest Kabbalist* (Hebrew) (Jerusalem: Magnes Press, 2001), 75. See also Seth L. Brody, "Human Hands Dwell in Heavenly Heights: Contemplative Ascent and Theurgic Power in Thirteenth-Century Kabbalah" (PhD diss., University of Pennsylvania, 1991), 431–32. In my judgment, this is the original meaning of the expression in *Sefer Yeṣirah.* For a different approach, see Scholem, "Name of God," 75; and Idel, *Golem,* 13.

118. Gershom Scholem, *The Kabbalah in Provence* (Hebrew), ed. Rivka Schatz (Jerusalem: Akkadamon, 1970), Appendix, 10.

119. See above, n. 65.

120. Azriel of Gerona. *Commentary on Talmudic Aggadoth* (Hebrew), ed. Isaiah Tishby (Jerusalem: Mekize Nirdamin, 1945), 99.

121. See Wolfson, *Language, Eros, Being,* chap. 2, n. 197.

122. Scholem, *Kabbalah in Provence,* Appendix, 13; Charles Mopsik, *Le grands textes de la Cabale: Le rites qui font Dieu* (Paris: Éditions Verdier, 1986), 74–75. For analysis of the emanationist doctrine articulated in this passage, see Sendor, "Emergence," 1:120–21.

123. Lipiner, *Metaphysics of Hebrew,* 100–103; Wolfson, "Anthropomorphic Imagery." In *Oṣar Eden Ganuz,* fol. 46a (printed ed. 94), Abulafia asserts that it is known to the "enlightened ones of our faith who receive from the truths" (*maskilei dateinu ha-mequbbalim min ha-amitiyyot*) that the "compositions of the body" (*harkavot ha-golem*) are identical to the "compositions of the letters" (*harkavot ha-otiyyot*).

124. *Kitvei Ramban,* 2:454. The linguistic conception of the human body is a principle affirmed by so-called theosophic and ecstatic kabbalists (see below, n. 338), and hence it may be considered an axiom of the esoteric tradition that cuts across the typological lines that have dominated contemporary scholarship.

125. See Wolfson, *Language, Eros, Being,* chap. 1, n. 345.

126. Some kabbalists have affirmed the view that the soul, and not the body, is the image of God, an approach well attested in philosophically inspired exegesis traceable as far back as Philo;

see Isaiah Tishby, *The Wisdom of the Zohar,* trans. David Goldstein (Oxford: Oxford University Press, 1989), 679–82.

127. Elliot R. Wolfson, "Ontology, Alterity, and Ethics in Kabbalistic Anthropology," *Exemplaria* 12 (2000): 129–55. It is regrettable that other scholars who have written on this subject have neglected to mention this critical point, thereby leaving the impression that the kabbalists have advocated a humanistic anthropology more equitable toward Jewish women and non-Jews. While this apologetic orientation is understandable and perhaps even desirable in certain homiletical circumstances, I find it to be a moral failing when scholars tender such a gross and blatant misrepresentation of kabbalistic tradition. An exception is the essay by Moshe Ḥallamish, "The Relation to the Nations of the World in the World of the Kabbalists" (Hebrew), *Jerusalem Studies in Jewish Thought* 14 (1998): 289–311. Working independently, we have reached similar conclusions, albeit expressed differently.

128. On the taxonomic centrality of knowledge of the name to understanding the phenomenological contours of kabbalah, see Moshe Idel, "Defining Kabbalah: The Kabbalah of the Divine Names," in *Mystics of the Book: Themes, Topics, and Typologies,* ed. Robert A. Herrera (New York: Peter Lang, 1993), 97–122.

129. Gershom Scholem, "The Concept of Kavvanah in the Early Kabbalah," in *Studies in Jewish Thought: An Anthology of German Jewish Scholarship,* ed. Alfred Jospe (Detroit: Wayne State University Press, 1981), 165–80; Scholem, *Origins,* 299–309, 414–30; Idel, *Kabbalah: New Perspectives,* 42–49, 51–55; Pedaya, *Name and Sanctuary,* 73–102; Haviva Pedaya, *Vision and Speech: Models of Revelatory Experience in Jewish Mysticism* (Hebrew) (Los Angeles: Cherub Press, 2002), 137–207; Brody, "Human Hands," 123–58; Mopsik, *Grands textes,* 88–95.

130. Idel, *Kabbalah: New Perspectives,* 41–42; see also the detailed study by Goldberg, "Mystical Union." A similar argument with regard to Sufism in relation to Arab-Islamic philosophy is made by Carl W. Ernst, "Mystical Language and the Teaching Context in the Early Lexicons of Sufism," in *Mysticism and Language,* ed. Steven T. Katz (Oxford: Oxford University Press, 1992), 192–94.

131. With respect to this dimension of the lived religious experience, Provençal and Spanish kabbalists were indebted to the ideal of contemplative worship cultivated by thinkers of a philosophical bent. A particularly interesting use of the account of intention in Maimonides is cited and explicated in a mystical vein in Asher ben David's *Sefer ha-Yiḥud;* see *R. Asher ben David: His Complete Works and Studies in His Kabbalistic Thought* (Hebrew), ed. Daniel Abrams (Los Angeles: Cherub Press, 1996), 80; and analysis in Wolfson, "Beneath the Wings," 222–23.

132. See below, n. 385.

133. Years ago I began to utilize the term "morphology" as a theoretical alternative to the typological approach championed by Scholem and Idel. For an elaboration of this terminological shift, see Goldberg, "Mystical Union," 32–54.

134. James H. Charlesworth, "The Portrayal of the Righteous as an Angel," in *Ideal Figures in Ancient Judaism,* ed. John J. Collins and George W. E. Nickelsburg (Missoula, Mont.: Scholars Press, 1980), 135–51; Willem F. Smelik, "On Mystical Transformation of the Righteous into Light in Judaism," *Journal for the Study of Judaism* 26 (1995): 122–44; Deborah Dimant, "Men as Angels: The Self-Image of the Qumran Community," in *Religion and Politics in the Ancient Near East,* ed. Adela Berlin (Bethesda: University Press of Maryland, 1996), 93–103; Crispin H. T. Fletcher-Louis, "4Q374: A Discourse on the Sinai Tradition: The Deification of Moses and Early Christology," *Dead Sea Discoveries* 3 (1996): 236–52; Crispin H. T. Fletcher-Louis, *Luke-Acts: Angels, Christology, and Soteriology* (Tübingen: Mohr Siebeck, 1997), 185–98; Crispin H. T. Fletcher-Louis, "Some Reflections on Angelomorphic Humanity Texts among the Dead Sea Scrolls," *Dead Sea Discoveries* 7 (2001): 292–312; and Crispin H. T. Fletcher-Louis, *All the Glory of Adam: Liturgical Anthropology in*

the Dead Sea Scrolls (Leiden: Brill, 2002). On angelomorphic Christology, see Margaret Barker, *The Great Angel: A Study of Israel's Second God* (London: SPCK, 1992); Richard N. Longenecker, *The Christology of Early Jewish Christianity* (London: SCM Press, 1970), 26–32; Fletcher-Louis, *Luke-Acts*; Darrell L. Bock, *Blasphemy and Exaltation in Judaism and the Final Examination of Jesus* (Tübingen: Mohr Siebeck, 1998), 113–83; Charles A. Gieschen, *Angelomorphic Christology: Antecedents and Early Evidence* (Leiden: E. J. Brill, 1998); Darrell D. Hannah, *Michael and Christ: Michael Traditions and Angel Christology in Early Christianity* (Tübingen: Mohr Siebeck, 1999) ; and Nicholas Constas, *Proclus of Constantinople and the Cult of the Virgin in Late Antiquity: Homilies 1–5, Texts and Translations* (Leiden: Brill, 2003), 300–307. On angelification as an ideal of mystical piety, see Christopher A. Morray-Jones, "Transformational Mysticism in the Apocalyptic-Merkabah Tradition," *Journal of Jewish Studies* 43 (1992): 1–31; and Elliot R. Wolfson, "*Yeridah la-Merkavah*: Typology of Ecstasy and Enthronement in Early Jewish Mysticism," in *Mystics of the Book: Themes, Topics, and Typologies*, ed. Robert A. Herrera (New York: Peter Lang, 1993), 23–26. As one might expect, in later rabbinic texts the angelic status is absorbed into their pietistic conception. Hence the one garbed in a fringed garment for the sake of prayer, study, or other ritual behavior is said to resemble the ministering angels of God; see *Pesiqta Rabbati*. ed. Meir Friedmann (Vienna: Josef Kaiser, 1880), 14, 61b–63a; Babylonian Talmud, Shabbat 25b; Nedarim 20b; Qiddushin 72b; and Nissan Rubin and Admiel Kosman, "The Clothing of the Primordial Adam as a Symbol of Apocalypic Time in the Midrashic Sources," *Harvard Theological Review* 90 (1997): 155–74, esp. 166–68.

135. In some rabbinic texts, inferential knowledge—"understanding one thing from another"—is accorded a privileged place in the epistemological hierarchy; see, for instance, Babylonian Talmud, Shabbat 31a: According to the dictum attributed to Rava, the last of five queries that every Jewish male will be asked at the moment of judgment is *hevanta davar mi-tokh davar* ("have you understood one thing from another?"). And compare Ḥagigah 14a, where the word *nevon* in Isaiah 3:3 is interpreted as *ha mevin davar mi-tokh davar* ("the one who understands one thing from another"), which is superceded only by "words of Torah that are transmitted silently" (*divrei torah she-nittenah be-laḥash*), a mode of learning encoded in the word *laḥash* from the aforementioned verse, which literally connotes enchanting. In his talmudic commentary, Solomon ben Isaac (Rashi) explains this as a reference to *sitrei torah*, the "mysteries of Torah," communicated clandestinely. According to the teaching attributed to R. Ami in Ḥagigah 13a, the expression *nevon laḥash* is listed as the last of five things (all derived from the same verse in Isaiah) that one must possess before one receives secrets of Torah. In the immediate context, no attempt is made to explain the idiom. On the use of *leḥishah* as a *terminus technicus* in the rabbinic lexicon to demarcate communication of esoteric lore "in a whisper," see Gershom Scholem, *Jewish Gnosticism, Merkabah Mysticism, and Talmudic Tradition* (New York: Jewish Theological Seminary of America, 1965), 58 (consider especially the comment of Hai Gaon cited in n. 10 *ad locum*); Alexander Altmann, *Studies in Religious Philosophy and Mysticism* (Ithaca, N.Y.: Cornell University Press, 1969), 129–30; Elliot R. Wolfson, "Beyond the Spoken Word: Oral Tradition and Written Transmission in Medieval Jewish Mysticism," in *Transmitting Jewish Traditions: Orality, Textuality, and Cultural Diffusion*, ed. Yaakov Ellman and Israel Gershoni (New Haven, Conn.: Yale University Press, 2000), 173–74.

136. Scholem, "Name of God," 71, 167–68. Sendor, "Emergence," 2:57n163, remarks that *ṣefiyyah* for Isaac the Blind "refers to the contemplation or inference of one thing from another, in this case, an object of inner hearing grasped through an object of inner sight." Basing himself on an explicit remark of Abulafia, Idel, "Reification of Language," 52–53, distinguishes the presumed two types of kabbalah, theosophic and ecstatic, on the grounds that the visual aspect of language is paramount for the former and the vocal aspect for the latter. Assuredly, there is cogency to this typological distinction, but the matter is more complex, inasmuch as both theosophic and ecstatic kabbalists

(to use the nomenclature for the sake of the argument) affirm the phenomenon of synesthesia, which is predicated on the mélange of the visual and auditory fields, ontically and experientially; see Elliot R. Wolfson, *Through a Speculum That Shines: Vision and Imagination in Medieval Jewish Mysticism* (Princeton, N.J.: Princeton University Press, 1994), 287–88. While it is true that some kabbalists emphasize the visual and others the auditory, or it may even be the case that the same kabbalist will at one point stress the former and at another point the latter, the texture of the experience should thwart any proposed dichotomization of the two epistemic modes along presumed typological lines. Even more vexing is the recent formulation in Idel, *Absorbing Perfections*, 76. Challenging my thesis regarding the centrality of the iconic dimension of Jewish mysticism, related specifically to contemplation of Torah as a technique for seeing God (some of my work is mentioned on 510n158, together with one of Idel's own studies), Idel writes that the visual "should be understood as a less influential tradition in the general economy of Jewish mystical literatures ... than the recurrent resort to the recitation of the Torah as another technique to induce a mystical experience." Apart from the dubious scholarly practice of making a general pronouncement with no textual backing, this claim rests on the false separation of the visual and auditory; I contend that in the mystical experience, seeing is hearing, and hearing, seeing. Another attempt, learned though it may be, based on an equally faulty dichotomy is found in Pedaya, *Vision and Speech*. The remark of Suhrawardī, cited in Schimmel, *Deciphering the Signs*, 156, encapsulates the collapse of the dichotomy precisely: "To listen to the Koran means to listen to God; hearing becomes seeing, seeing becomes hearing, knowing turns into action, action turns into knowing—that is the 'fine hearing.'" Though the conclusion of this statement would seem to privilege hearing, which indeed reflects the central role accorded the oral recitation of the Qur'ān in Muslim prayer ritual (see above, n. 84), the mystical wisdom imparted by Suhrawardī is that listening to the recital of the inscripted word of God is like listening to God, and in listening to God, hearing is seeing and seeing is hearing, just as knowing becomes acting and acting becomes knowing. This succinct formulation well captures what I have tried to articulate with respect to the phenomenology of vision and imagination in kabbalistic sources; see also William A. Graham, "Das Schriftprinzip in vergleichender Sicht," in *Gott ist schön und Er liebt die Schönheit: Festschrift für Annemarie Schimmel zum 7. April 1992*, ed. Alma Giese and J. Christoph Bürgel (Bern: Peter Lang, 1994), 209–26, esp. 220–21. For a well-informed discussion of a similar phenomenon in early Christianity, see David Chidester, *Word and Light: Seeing, Hearing, and Religious Discourse* (Urbana: University of Illinois Press, 1992). The tendency of kabbalists not to distinguish absolutely between writing and speech was duly noted by Scholem, "Name of God," 71, 67–168; Scholem, *Origins*, 277; David Biale, *Gershom Scholem: Kabbalah and Counter-History* (Cambridge, Mass.: Harvard University Press, 1979), 99–100. Scholem's view is repeated by Harold Bloom, *Kabbalah and Criticism* (New York: Seabury Press, 1975), 52. The ritual basis for the mystical wisdom can be sought in the fact that the word for Scripture, *miqra*, literally means "what is recited." Hence, just as in the case of the Qur'ān in Islam, so Torah in Judaism embodies the oral and written in an inseparable confluence.

137. These words are repeated verbatim in Ezra's commentary to Song 6:3, *Kitvei Ramban* 2:504.

138. That is, the composite and individual entities in the world of differentiation (*olam ha-perud*) which is beneath the world of unity (*olam ha-yiḥud*), the realm of *sefirot*, which are not ontically distinct from the infinite divine being. As Scholem observed ("Concept of Kavvanah," 35, 62–65), the expression *nifradim* to designate differentiated beings reflects an interesting misuse of a technical medieval philosophical Hebraism, *nifrad*, which denotes the incorporeal being; for instance, the nomenclature *sekhalim nifradim* refers to the immaterial intellects attached to each of the spheres. See also extended discussion in Sendor, "Emergence," 1:130–36.

139. Scholem, *Kabbalah in Provence*, Appendix, 5–6. For analysis of this passage, see Scholem, "Concept of Kavvanah," 165–66; Scholem, *Origins*, 300–301; Brody, "Human Hands," 429–30.

140. We can distinguish between writing and speaking, the former associated with a higher emanation than the latter and thus that can be thought of as preceding it. However, just as the emanative scheme can be imagined in a linear way, it also can be imagined cyclically, and when viewed through that prism, there is no lower or higher, before or after. To apply this to the particular example of language, every spoken utterance is an inscripted word and every inscripted word a spoken utterance, a critical dimension of the kabbalistic worldview duly noted by Scholem; see above, n. 136.

141. Scholem, *Origins*, 264–65.

142. Wolfson, *Through a Speculum*, 285n54.

143. Scholem, *Kabbalah in Provence*, Appendix, 1.

144. Ibid.; Scholem, *Origins*, 275. Elsewhere in the *Sefer Yeṣirah* commentary, the term *yeniqah* is used to depict the manner by which the lower entities draw the efflux from the sefirotic potencies; see Scholem, *Kabbalah in Provence*, Appendix, 9; Sendor, "Emergence," 1:122–23.

145. The distinction between *yediʿah* and *yeniqah* is not meant to convey anti-intellectualism, a mystical sensibility that is pitted against a speculative or philosophic orientation. On the contrary, the contrast between discursive and intuitive forms of apprehension is an integral part of the Platonic tradition, especially significant in Neoplatonism; see Sara Ahbel-Rappe, *Reading Neoplatonism: Non-discursive Thinking in the Texts of Plotinus, Proclus, and Damascius* (Cambridge: Cambridge University Press, 2000), 25–66. Consider also the pertinent discussion on the divergence of discursive philosophy (*al-baḥth*, literally, "investigation") and "divine philosophy" (*taʾalluh*, literally, "becoming God") in John Walbridge, *The Leaven of the Ancients: Suhrawardī and the Heritage of the Greeks* (Albany: State University of New York Press, 2000), 176. The intuitive philosopher attains a higher state than the discursive philosopher, but supreme perfection belongs to one who has mastered both. One can apply a similar model to the speculative kabbalah traced to Isaac the Blind.

146. To be more precise, for the most part Plotinus describes the One in apophatic terms as the "what" that is beyond being, thought, and language, but there are places where he describes the One in kataphatic terms (reminiscent of Aristotle's account of the first principle) as intelligible and as capable of thought. The inconsistency in Plotinus yielded two different approaches in Neoplatonic thought as it evolved in Islamic and then latter Jewish and Christian philosophy, one emphasizing the transcendence of the One (as in the Plotinian *Theology of Aristotle*) and the other identifying the One with the intellect and the ground of being (as in the Proclan *Liber de causis*); see Peterson, "Ḥamīd al-Dīn al-Kirmānī on Creation," in *Perspectives arabes et médiévales sur la tradition scientifique et philosophique grecque: Actes du colloque de la Société internationale d'histoire des sciences et de la philosophie arabes et islamiques, Paris, 31 mars–3 avril 1993*, ed. Ahmad Hasnawi, Abdelali Elamrani-Jamal, and Maroun Aouad, preface by Roshdi Rashed (Leuven: Peeters, 1997), 560–61. An extensive discussion of the One in Plotinian thought is provided by John Bussanich, "Plotinus's Metaphysics of the One," in *The Cambridge Companion to Plotinus*, ed. Lloyd P. Gerson (Cambridge: Cambridge University Press, 1996), 38–65.

147. Plato, *Republic* 509b 9–10. See also the characterization of the One as above being and description in Plato, *Parmenides* 142a 3.

148. For reference, see Wolfson, *Language, Eros, Being*, chap. 1, n. 307.

149. Aristotle, *De anima* 429a, 13–17. On the appropriation of the Aristotelian epistemology by Plotinus, see William Ralph Inge, *The Philosophy of Plotinus*, 3rd ed. (London: Longmans, Green, 1948), 1:137–38; Henry J. Blumenthal, "Plotinus' Adaptation of Aristotle's Psychology," in *The Significance of Neoplatonism*, ed. R. Baine Harris (Norfolk, Va.: Old Dominion University, 1976), 41–58.

150. Plotinus, *Enneads* I.6.8. The passage may be viewed as an interpretation of Plato's *Symposium* 218e–19a. In the context of discussing the distinction between the "semblance of beauty" and the "thing itself," Plato remarks that the "mind's eye begins to see clearly when the outer eyes grow dim."

151. For a detailed study of this theme in late antiquity, see Ioan P. Culianu, *Psychanodia I: A Survey of the Evidence concerning the Ascension of the Soul and Its Relevance* (Leiden: E. J. Brill, 1983).

152. William Blake, *The Complete Poetry and Prose of William Blake*, ed. David V. Erdman, commentary by Harold Bloom, rev. ed. (Berkeley: University of California Press, 1982), 225.

153. Plotinus, *Enneads* I.6.9. A similar sentiment is expressed in *Gospel of Philip* 61:21–25, in *Nag Hammadi Codex II, 2–7*, 1:163: In the pleroma, in contrast to this world, when one sees something, one becomes that which one sees even to the point of becoming the Father.

154. Plotinus, *Enneads* I.6.6.

155. For discussion of divine simplicity in Plotinus, see John P. Kenney, *Mystical Monotheism: A Study in Ancient Platonic Theology* (Hanover, N.H.: University Press of New England, 1991), 93–111.

156. Plotinus, *Enneads* V.5.6; see also V.3.14, V.4.1–2, VI.7.38.

157. Plotinus, *Enneads* V.5.6.

158. Frederic M. Schroeder, "The Vigil of the One and Plotinian Iconoclasm," in *Neoplatonism and Western Aesthetics*, ed. Aphrodite Alexandrakis and Nicholas J. Moutafakis (Albany: State University of New York Press, 2002), 61–74.

159. Wolfson, *Through a Speculum*, 270–72.

160. Richard T. Wallis, "ΝΟΥΣ as Experience," in *The Significance of Neoplatonism*, ed. R. Baine Harris (Norfolk, Va.: Old Dominion University, 1976), 121–53.

161. See Margaret Miles, *Plotinus on Body and Beauty: Society, Philosophy, and Religion in Third-Century Rome* (Oxford: Blackwell, 1999).

162. Peter Kingsley, *In the Dark Places of Wisdom* (Inverness, Calif.: Golden Sufi Center, 1999), 6. For parallel formulations of the mandate to experience death before one dies in Jewish and Islamic traditions, see Wolfson, *Language, Eros, Being*, chap. 8, n. 151. The theme is expressed as well in *Meister Eckhart: Sermons and Treatises*, trans. Maurice O'Connell Walshe, 3 vols. (Rockport, Mass.: Element Books, 1991), 1:140: "Our Lord ascended into heaven, beyond all light, beyond all understanding and all human ken. . . . Therefore a man must be slain and wholly dead, devoid of self and wholly without likeness, like to none, and then he is really God-like. For it is God's character, His nature, to be peerless and like no man." The theme is rendered in a poem either composed by Eckhart or by one of his disciples, cited at xxxi: "My soul within / come out, God in! / Sink all my aught / in God's own naught, / sink down in bottomless abyss. / Should I flee thee, / thou wilt come to me; / when self is done, / then Thou art won, / thou transcendental highest bliss!"

163. Pierre Hadot, *Plotinus, or The Simplicity of Vision* (Chicago: University of Chicago Press, 1993), 32. The passage upon which Hadot bases his comments is *Enneads* IV.4.2: "when one contemplates, especially when the contemplation is clear, one does not turn to oneself in the act of intelligence, but one possesses oneself; one's activity, however, is directed towards the object of contemplation, and one becomes this, offering himself to it as a kind of matter, being formed according to what one sees, and being oneself then only potentially." In *Enneads* VI.8.13, Plotinus expresses the same paradox in volitional terms. The desire of each being is to participate in the Good, but this must be both a freely willed act and reflective of a merging or synchronicity of wills that effaces the ontic independence of the individual will vis-à-vis the will of the Good whence all things emerge and to which they return: "Observe this also: every being in its desire for the Good wants to be that Good rather than what it is, and thinks that it is in the highest degree when it participates in the Good, and in such a state each being will choose for itself to be in so far as it has being from the Good; so the nature of the Good is obviously far more worthy of choice for himself,

if it is true that whatever share of the Good there may be in something else is most worthy of choice, and is its freely willed substance which comes to it in accordance with its will and is one and the same thing as its will and is established in existence through its will."

164. Dionysius the Areopagite, *The Divine Names and Mystical Theology*, trans. John D. Jones (Milwaukee, Wisc.: Marquette University Press, 1980), chap. 5, 825B, 171.

165. Ibid., chap. 7, 872A, 179. A similar negative dialectic is affirmed in John Scotus Eriugena, the ninth-century Neoplatonic thinker whose Latin translation of the *Corpus Dionysianum* had a decisive influence on medieval philosophy and theology. Eriugena's own *Periphyseon*, which betrays the Dionysian teaching, is presumed to have had a major impact on thinkers in the twelfth and thirteenth centuries, including kabbalists; See Dermot Moran, *The Philosophy of John Scottus Eriugena: A Study of Idealism in the Middle Ages* (Cambridge: Cambridge University Press, 1989), 186–87, 208.

166. From another perspective, contemplation on the part of the human mind can be seen as the mirror opposite of contemplation on the part of the One—that is, the former has the goal of purging the mind of multiplicity and restoring it to unity, whereas the latter is the process by which the unity becomes a multiplicity; see Plotinus, *Enneads* VI.2.6, where contemplation on the part of the One is described as being "the cause of its appearing many, that it may think: for if it appears as one, it did not think, but is that One." To be other than one, the other must not be part of the one, but if there is an other that is not part of the one, the one cannot be one. In the effort to explain the one and the many, one is forced logically to posit two aspects of the one, or two ones, as it were, if one adopts an emanationist scheme, such that the one both is and is not, it is one but it is not many, and yet the many could not be unless it were the one it cannot be. In great measure, the speculative trajectory of these matters springs from Plato's dialectical hypotheses about unity in his dialogue on Parmenides. For relevant texts and detailed analyses, see Plato, *Plato's Parmenides*, trans. Reginald R. Allen, rev. ed. (New Haven, Conn.: Yale University Press, 1997), 207–339; see also Plato and Parmenides, *Parmenides' Way of Truth and Plato's Parmenides*, trans. Francis MacDonald Comford (Indianapolis: Bobbs-Merrill, 1977), 109–15; Harold Tarrant, *Thrasyllan Platonism* (Ithaca, N.Y.: Cornell University Press, 1993), 150–61.

167. The influence of the Plotinian account was quite pronounced in Christian mysticism and occult philosophy. For instance, consider the depiction of the soul's immediate vision of God occasioned by the mental ascent that is consequent to leaving aside cultivation of the body in Marsilio Ficino, *Platonic Theology*, trans. Michael J. N. Allen with John Warden, Latin text ed. James Hankins with William Bowen (Cambridge, Mass.: Harvard University Press, 2003), 3:185: "Having returned thither, it sees God through what is now the very light of God like someone who uses the sun's ray to look at the sun itself and no longer at the colors of bodies."

168. Plotinus, *Enneads* V.8.11.

169 It lies beyond the scope of this chapter to engage the critical question of whether the mystical vision propounded by Plotinus should be viewed as "monistic" or "theistic." For representative studies, see Plato Mamo, "Is Plotinian Mysticism Monistic?" in *The Significance of Neoplatonism*, ed. R. Baine Harris (Norfolk, Va.: Old Dominion University, 1976), 199–215; John M. Rist, "Back to the Mysticism of Plotinus: Some More Specifics," *Journal of the History of Philosophy* 27 (1989): 183–97. See also Henri Oosthout, *Modes of Knowledge and the Trasncendental: An Introduction to Plotinus Ennead 5.3 [49]* (Amsterdam: B. R. Grüner, 1991), 75–164, and the discussion in Julia Kristeva, *Tales of Love*, trans. Leon S. Roudiez (New York: Columbia University Press, 1987). 119–21, on Plotinian ecstasy and the loss of self.

170. Plotinus, *Enneads* V.8.12; on intellect as an image of the first principle, see also V. 4. 2.

171. On the One as everything and nothing, see Bussanich, "Plotinus's Metaphysics," 57–61.

172. Plotinus, *Enneads* V.2.1.

173. Ibid., V.3.13.

174. Ibid., V.8.6; see Schroeder, "Plotinus and Language," in *The Cambridge Companion to Plotinus*, ed. Lloyd P. Gerson (Cambridge: Cambridge University Press, 1996), 336–55, esp. 350–51.

175. Plotinus, *Enneads* V.8.21.

176. Ibid., V.5.7. For a later influence of these Neoplatonic themes in the *Golshan-e Rāz* of the fourteenth-century Persian poet Mahmūd Shabestarī, explicated in the commentary of Shamsod-din Lāhījī, see Henry Corbin, *The Man of Light in Iranian Sufism*, trans. Nancy Pearson (New Lebanon: Omega Publications, 1994), 110–20, esp. 116: "The black light . . . is that which cannot itself be seen, because it is the cause of seeing; it cannot be object, since it is absolute Subject. It dazzles, as the light of *superconsciousness* dazzles. . . . Only a knowledge which is a theophanic experience can be knowledge of the divine Being. But in relation to the divine Ipseity, black light, excludes this correlation" (emphasis in original).

177. A learned treatment of the Western apophatic orientation is presented by Deirdre Cara-bine, *The Unknown God, Negative Theology in the Platonic Tradition: Plato to Eriugena* (Louvain: Peeters Press, 1995).

178. Plotinus, *Enneads* V.5.6; see VI.9.5.

179. Ibid., V.3.17. For discussion of the development of this theme, see Frederick E. Brenk, "Darkly beyond the Glass: Middle Platonism and the Vision of the Soul," in *Platonism in Late Antiquity*, ed. Stephen Gersh and Charles Kannengiesser (Notre Dame, Ind.: University of Notre Dame Press, 1992), 39–60.

180. Curtis L. Hancock, "Negative Theology in Gnosticism and Neoplatonism," in *Neopla-tonism and Gnosticism*, ed. Richard T. Wallis and Jay Bregman (Albany: State University of New York Press, 1992), 180. Hancock's study is important, for it provides a model to problema-tize the schematic polarization of the "two philosophical Hellenistic schools" (167), Neopla-tonism and Gnosticism, by demonstrating the affinity of the two with regard to the inability to converse or to speculate about the highest God. Hancock suggests, moreover, that respect for the "transcendent goal of moral life" entailed by the negative theology in both schools helps explain the influence of these two trends on medieval Christian apophasis. This approach could prove helpful in understanding the complex interweave of different threads that make up the intellectual cloth of medieval kabbalah in such a manner that one would avoid the radical split between Neoplatonic and Gnostic influences such as we occasionally find in Scholem, for instance, in *Origins*, 264. Also apposite is the opinion of Hans Jonas, *The Gnostic Religion: The Message of the Alien God and the Beginnings of Christianity* (Boston: Beacon Press, 1963), 91–92, that gnostic imagery has to be contextualized in the history of allegory in Greek philosophy, an exegetical strategy that facilitated the appropriation of concrete tales and figures of mythical lore as a symbolic mode to express abstract ideas. Jonas goes on to distinguish "gnostic allegory" from the more conventional type inasmuch as the former is often of a subversive nature and hence does not uphold the primary aim of integration and synthesis. I am not certain of the necessity to contrast subversive and conventional uses of allegory, but what is important for my purposes is the recognition on the part of Jonas that an intrinsic component of the gnostic imagination is the rendering of philosophical ideas in con-crete mythic symbols. In this regard, there is once again a striking correspondence between late-antique Gnosticism and medieval kabbalah. For a fuller discussion of Gnosticism and the "classical mind," see Jonas, *Gnostic Religion*, 239–89.

181. Bernard McGinn, *The Foundations of Mysticism: Origins to the Fifth Century* (Cambridge: Cambridge University Press, 2000), 118, 141.

182. Compare Gregory of Nyssa, *Commentary on the Song of Songs*, trans. Casimir McCambly (Brookline, Mass.: Hellenic College Press, 1987), I.331, 206: "Through baptism the bride has once and for all removed her sandals." On Gregory's interpretation of the blatantly erotic images of the Song as instruments by which carnal desire can be domesticated into the spiritual love of Christ, symbolized by the male lover, culminating in the discarding of images altogether as one enters the "apophatic space" of the Holy of Holies, which is identified as the Song, to encounter God in the luminal darkness of unknowing, see Graham Ward, "Allegoria: Reading as a Spiritual Exercise," *Modern Theology* 5 (1999): 286–87; R. Norris, "The Soul Takes Flight: Gregory of Nyssa and the Song of Songs," *Anglican Theological Review* 80 (1998): 526; Martin Laird, "Under Solomon's Tutelage: The Education of Desire in the *Homilies on the Song of Songs*," in *Rethinking Gregory of Nyssa*, ed. Sarah Coakley (Oxford: Blackwell, 2003), 81–88.

183. Gregory of Nyssa, *The Life of Moses*, trans. Abraham J. Malherbe and Everett Ferguson (New York: Paulist Press, 1978), 2.19, 59. I have availed myself of the Greek text printed together with the French translation in Gregory of Nyssa, *La vie de Moïse; ou Traité de la perfection en matière de vertu*, trans. Jean Daniélou, 3rd ed. (Paris: Éditions du Cerf, 1987). All references to Greek marked parenthetically are taken from and refer to the pagination of this edition. For a nuanced gender analysis of Gregory's account of the vision of Moses at the "virginal" thorny bush and his subsequent entry into the cloud of thick darkness, see Virginia Burrus, *"Begotten Not Made": Conceiving Manhood in Late Antiquity* (Stanford: Stanford University Press, 2000), 125–29.

184. Gregory of Nyssa, *Life of Moses*, 2.24, 60 (Greek text, 120).

185. Ibid., 2.25, 60 (Greek text, 120).

186. Ibid., 2.26, 60.

187. Ibid., 2.27, 61 (Greek text, 122).

188. Gregory of Nyssa, *Contra eunomium libri*, ed. Werner Jaeger (Leiden: E. J. Brill, 1960), I:11, 416A; and see discussion on the theme of the transposition of the image in Hans Urs von Balthasar, *Presence and Thought: An Essay on the Religious Philosophy of Gregory of Nyssa* (San Francisco: Ignatisu Press, 1995), 163–69; see also Bernard Pottier, *Dieu et le Christ sedon Grégoire de Nysee: Etude systématique du "Contre Eunome" avec traduction inédite des extraits d'Eunome,* preface by Mariette Canévet (Namur: Culture et Vérité, 1994), 233–43.

189. Gregory of Nyssa, *Life of Moses*, 2.162, 94–95.

190. Ibid., 2.162, 95 (Greek text, 210).

191. Ibid., 2.163, 95 (Greek text, 210). Gregory's exegesis of the entry of Moses into a cloud of darkness as symbolic of the soul's contemplation of the unseen and unattainable realm, the mystery in which God dwells, is repeated in his *Commentary on the Song of Songs*, J.181, 130, and J.322–23, 202. See also Gregory's explication of the sixth beatitude, "Blessed are the pure in heart, for they shall see God" (Matt. 5:6), printed in Gregory of Nyssa, *The Lord's Prayer, the Beatitudes,* trans. Hilda C. Graef (New York: Paulist Press, 1978), 143–53.

192. *De mutatione nominum*, 7–8; *De posteritate Caini*, 14; *De gigantibus*, 54; *De vita Mosis* I, 158; Harry A. Wolfson, *Philo: Foundations of Religious Philosophy in Judaism, Christianity, and Islam*, 2 vols. (Cambridge, Mass.: Harvard University Press, 1947), 2:155; Gregory of Nyssa, *Life of Moses*, 177n192.

193. David Bentley Hart, "The Mirror of the Infinite: Gregory of Nyssa on the *Vestigia Trinitatis,"* in *Rethinking Gregory of Nyssa*, ed. Sarah Coakley (Oxford: Blackwell, 2003), 111–31.

194. McGinn, *Foundations of Mysticism*, 157–82.

195. Dionysius the Areopagite, *Pseudo-Dionysius: The Complete Works*, trans. Colm Luibheid; foreword, notes, and translation collaboration by Paul Rorem; preface by René Roques; introduction by Jaroslav Pelikan, Jean Leclerq, and Karlfried Froehlich (New York: Paulist Press, 1987), 49–50.

196. Ibid., 53.

197. Ibid., 108–9. The Dionysian perspective is elaborated in less technical terms in the four-teenth-century anonymous English treatise *The Cloud of Unknowing*; see James Walsh, ed., *Cloud of Unknowing* (New York: Paulist Press, 1981), chap. 70, p. 256.

198. Dionysius the Areopagite, *Pseudo-Dionysius*, 54.

199. Ibid., 109.

200. Ibid., 137.

201. Ibid., 109.

202. Ibid., 263.

203. For a detailed study of this kabbalistic doctrine, see Moshe Idel, "The *Sefirot* above the *Sefirot*" (Hebrew), *Tarbiz* 51 (1982): 239–80.

204. Scholem, *Kabbalah in Provence*, Appendix, 3.

205. I borrow this richly ambiguous locution from Michael Sells, *Mystical Languages of Unsaying* (Chicago: University of Chicago Press, 1994).

206. On this important philosophical point, see Denys Turner, *The Darkness of God: Negativity in Christian Mysticism* (Cambridge: Cambridge University Press, 1995), 35; see also Steven T. Katz, "Mystical Speech and Mystical Meaning," in *Mysticism and Religious Traditions*, ed. Steven T. Katz (Oxford: Oxford University Press, 1984), 3–41; Steven T. Katz, "Utterance and Ineffability in Jewish Neoplatonism," in *Neoplatonism and Jewish Thought*, ed. Lenn E. Goodman (Albany: State University of New York Press, 1992), 279–98; Wolfson, "Negative Theology and Positive Assertion," v–xxii.

207. The meaning of the expression *remez ha-maḥashavah* is clarified by its use in the commentary on the *sefirot* by Azriel of Gerona, cited above at n. 64.

208. *Kitvei Ramban*, 2:409. For further explication of this passage, see Idel, "*Sefirot* above the *Sefirot*," 265–67; Idel, *Absorbing Perfections*, 119–20; Wolfson, "Beyond the Spoken Word," 199.

209. Maimonides, *Mishneh Torah* (New York: Schlusinger, 1947), Yesodei ha-Torah 2:10.

210. Maimonides, *The Guide of the Perplexed*, trans. Shlomo Pines, intro. Leo Strauss (Chicago: University of Chicago Press, 1963), II:6, 262–63.

211. Consider Scholem's sketch, *Origins*, 377: "With Jacob ben Shesheth, the kabbalists appear on the battlefield for the first time, undisguised. The enemy is unmistakable: the radical philo-sophic enlightenment of the adherents of Maimonides." In support of his characterization, Scholem cites one of Jacob's works, *Meshiv Devarim Nekhoḥim*, which is an explicit rebuttal of Samuel Ibn Tibbon's *Ma'amar Yeqqawu ha-Mayim*, a cosmology (*ma'aseh bere'shit*) based on Maimonidean thought. Scholem himself nuances his argument when he notes that the polemical thrust is directed more at Ibn Tibbon than Maimonides. The heretical views were introduced into the "system" of Maimonides, which in itself was "in Jacob's opinion very close to the true theology and therefore to the Kabbalah, as he frequently and triumphantly notes whenever he believes that he can demon-strate that his adversary misunderstood the views of Maimonides" (378); see 381, where Scholem notes that Jacob ben Sheshet sides with Maimonides with respect to the right of each interpreter to devise his own reasons for the commandments.

212. Scholem, *Kabbalah in Provence*, Appendix, 5.

213. My reflections here were inspired by the observations of Walter James Lowe, *Theology and Difference: The Wound of Reason* (Bloomington: Indiana University Press, 1993), 79–80. A similar affirmation of ostensible clashing views is found in the Sufi antinomy of *tanzīh* and *tashbīh*, the former declaring the incomparability of the one true entity (*wujūd*), the essence whose existence is necessary, vis-à-vis all other things, which are considered contingent, and the latter declaring the similarity between God and all things. See below, n. 280.

214. See Wolfson, *Language, Eros, Being,* chap. 1, n. 263.

215. *Zohar,* 3:152a.

216. Yehuda Liebes, *Studies in the Zohar Lexicon* (Hebrew) (Jerusalem: Akkadamon, 1976), 45–46. This is one of several attempts in zoharic literature to delineate four levels of meaning in Scripture. Whatever the historical or textual origins of this seminal idea, from the relevant kabbalistic sources it is evident that it was formulated as an elaboration of the principle of dual meaning, the internal and external, esoteric and exoteric; see Wilhelm Bacher, "L'exegese biblique dans le Zohar," *Revue des études juives* 22 (1891): 33–46, esp. 37–40; Wilhelm Bacher, "Das Merkwort PRDS in der Jüdischen Bibelexegese," *Zeitschrift für die alttestamentliche Wissenschaft* 13 (1893): 294–305; Scholem, *On the Kabbalah and Its Symbolism,* 50–65; Tishby, *Wisdom of the Zohar,* 1077–89; Albert van der Heide, "Pardes: Methodological Reflections on the Theory of the Four Senses," *Journal of Jewish Studies* 34 (1983): 147–59; Moshe Idel, "Pardes: Some Reflections on Kabbalistic Hermeneutics," in *Death, Ecstasy, and Other Worldly Journeys,* ed. John J. Collins and Michael Fishbane (Albany: State University of New York Press, 1995), 249–68; Moshe Idel, "The Zohar as Exegesis," in *Mysticism and Sacred Scripture,* ed. Steven T. Katz (Oxford: Oxford University Press, 2000), 89–91; Idel, *Absorbing Perfections,* 429–37; Boaz Huss, "NiSAN—The Wife of the Infinite: The Mystical Hermeneutics of Rabbi Isaac of Acre," *Kabbalah: Journal for the Study of Jewish Mystical Texts* 5 (2000): 155–81; Steven T. Katz, "Mysticism and the Interpretation of Sacred Scripture," in *Mysticism and Sacred Scripture,* ed. Steven T. Katz (Oxford: Oxford University Press, 2000), 21–32. Some scholars, including Bacher and Scholem, suggested the kabbalists derived the four levels of meaning from parallel Christian modes of interpretation. Regarding the fourfold sense of Scripture in Christian mysticism, see the lucid and relatively recent account in Ewert Cousins, "The Fourfold Sense of Scripture in Christian Mysticism," in *Mysticism and Sacred Scripture,* ed. Steven T. Katz (Oxford: Oxford University Press, 2000), 118–37.

217. *Zohar,* 1:20b; 2:75b–76a; Moses ben Shem Ṭov de León, "*Sefer ha-Mishkal:* Text and Study," ed. Jochanan H. A. Wijnhoven (PhD diss., Brandeis University, 1964), 44, 159.

218. For an insightful exposition of kabbalistic hermeneutics against a broader framework of religious culture in the Middle Ages, see Frank Talmage, "Apples of Gold: The Inner Meaning of Sacred Texts in Medieval Judaism," in *Jewish Spirituality from the Bible through the Middle Ages,* ed. Arthur Green (New York: Crossroad, 1986), 313–55.

219 A relevant passage appears in *Zohar,* 2:61b, where the following response is given to the hypothetical question of whether it is really the case that the members of the mystical fraternity engaged in Torah study are sustained by the spiritual food that angels eat, the "bread of the mighty," *leḥem abirim* (Ps. 78:25), the overflow of divine wisdom: "No, it is like that very food, for two are balanced on one" (*de-shaqil al ḥad terein*). The concluding phrase conveys the image of the scale upon which two independent things are weighed together and brought into balance. The food consumed by kabbalists is not exactly what is eaten by angels, but it is plausible to say that the former is in the likeness of the latter. For extended discussion of the motif of eating in zoharic kabbalah, see Joel Hecker, "Each Man Ate an Angel's Meal: Eating and Embodiment in the Zohar" (PhD diss., New York University, 1996); Joel Hecker, "Eating Gestures and the Ritualized Body in Medieval Jewish Mysticism," *History of Religions* 40 (2000): 125–52. The word *shaqil* in the sense of comparing one thing to another is used in other passages in zoharic literature; see *Zohar,* 1:153b, where the word is employed in the context of discussing the parallelism between the mundane and divine spheres, and especially *Zohar,* 3:64a, where the three books traditionally ascribed to Solomon—Song of Songs, Ecclesiastes, and Proverbs—are correlated respectively with Wisdom (*ḥokhmah*), Understanding (*tevunah*), and Knowledge (*da'at*). The description of the latter sheds light on the zoharic approach to parables: "Proverbs corresponds to Knowledge. How is this man-

ifest? All of the verses have two aspects [*terei gawwanei*], the beginning and end, two aspects that are disclosed [*ithazyyan*]. When one contemplates the verses, the [beginning] is contained in the [end], and the [end] is contained in the [beginning]. Thus it corresponds to Knowledge [*shaqil laqavleih de-da'at*]." Interestingly, the author of this passage follows the standard view regarding the twofold structure of the parable, as one finds, for instance, in the introduction to the *Guide of the Perplexed* by Maimonides, but there is a shift from the inner/outer orientation to the beginning/end distinction. The nature of parabolic truth illumines one in the wisdom that the one is contained in the other. Finally, it is worth mentioning the title of a treatise composed by Moses de León in 1290, *Sefer ha-Mishqal*, literally the "Book of Balance." The author gave the work another name, *Sefer Nefesh ha-Ḥokhmah*, which was used in the edition of the work published in Basel 1608. The latter title signals the main purpose of the book, which is to elucidate the kabbalistic mysteries pertaining to the nature of the Jewish soul. The former title, I surmise, relates to the enterprise of speaking about the divine emanations, which by necessity requires the symbolic correlation of disparate realities, the figural representation of the incorporeal God in anthropomorphic terms, an envisioning that makes possible the more specific discourse about the soul and its resemblance to the divine. It is possible that de León has this poetic process in mind when he uses the expression *mishqal ha-ḥokhmah*, the "balance of wisdom"; see Moses de León, *Sefer ha-Mishkal*, 34–35. It is of interest to recall as well that Moses de León begins *Sheqel ha-Qodesh*, 1–3, with a philosophical discussion (in the vein of Maimonides) on the incorporeality of God and the meaning of biblical anthropomorphism. Perhaps the meaning of the title is not "sacred coin" but "holy weight," the imaginal envisioning of God based on the inherently analogical nature of language. For a somewhat different explanation of the titles of Moses de León's works, see Wolfson, *Circle in the Square*, 182n128. In that context, I suggested that the words *mishqal* and *sheqel* denote the phallic potency, which is compared to the "tongue" that balances two sides of the scale.

220. *Zohar*, 2:98b. For fuller discussion of this passage, see Elliot R. Wolfson, "Beautiful Maiden without Eyes: *Peshaṭ* and *Sod* in Zoharic Hermeneutics," in *The Midrashic Imagination: Jewish Exegesis, Thought, and History*, ed. Michael Fishbane (Albany: State University of New York Press, 1995), 169–72. The more typical approach on the part of scholars has been to dichotomize the exoteric and esoteric layers of meaning; see, for instance, the discussion of *sod* as "coded meaning" in Betty Rojtman, *Black Fire on White Fire: An Essay on Jewish Hermeneutics, from Midrash to Kabbalah* (Berkeley: University of California Press, 1998), 68–98.

221. See Wolfson, *Language, Eros, Being*, chap. 1, n. 260.

222. My analysis finds support in Marion's discussion of the paradox of the face. See Jean-Luc Marion, *In Excess: Studies of Saturated Phenomena*, trans. Robyn Horner and Vincent Berraud (New York: Fordham University Press, 2002), 113–19, esp. 115–16.

223. Perhaps implicit in the symbol of the tongue when associated with *Shekhinah* is the kabbalistic understanding of Oral Torah. For an explicit correlation along these lines, see Joseph of Hamadan, "Joseph of Hamadan's *Sefer Tashak*: Critical Text Edition with Introduction," ed. Jeremy Zwelling (PhD diss., Brandeis University, 1975), 318.

224. My explication is supported by *Zohar*, 1:228a: "The holy spirit is called *zo't*, which is the mystery of the covenant [*raza di-verit*], the holy inscription [*reshima qaddisha*] that is found constantly with the person." The exact formulation recurs in *Zohar*, 2:236b. The gender transposition of *Shekhinah* is thus related to the fact that the word *zo't*, the feminine demonstrative pronoun, is identified as the covenantal sign affixed to the male organ. It is in this capacity that *Shekhinah* assumes the character of the holy spirit. Needless to say, the symbolism is older than the period of the zoharic fraternity; see, for instance, Azriel of Gerona, *Commentary on Talmudic Aggadoth*, 49.

225. *Zohar*, 3:60b–61a.

226. A number of scholars have analyzed this section of zoharic literature; see Michal Oron, "'Place Me as a Seal upon Your Heart': Reflections on the Poetics of the Author of the *Zohar* in the Section of *Sabba de-Mishpaṭim*," in *Massu'ot: Studies in Kabbalistic Literature and Jewish Philosophy in Memory of Prof. Ephraim Gottlieb*, ed. Michal Oron and Amos Goldreich (Jerusalem: Bialik Institute, 1994), 1–24; Pinchas Giller, *Reading the Zohar: The Sacred Text of Kabbalah* (Oxford: Oxford University Press, 2001), 35–68; Daniel Abrams, "Knowing the Maiden without Eyes: Reading the Sexual Reconstruction of the Jewish Mystic in a Zoharic Parable," *Da'at* 50–52 (2003): lix–lxxxiii; and further references in the following note.

227. Scholem, *On the Kabbalah and Its Symbolism*, 55–56; Talmage, "Apples of Gold," 316–18; Idel, *Kabbalah: New Perspectives*, 227–29; Tishby, *Wisdom of the Zohar*, 1084–85; David Stern, *Parables in Midrash: Narrative and Exegesis in Rabbinic Literature* (Cambridge, Mass.: Harvard University Press, 1991), 230–31; Yehuda Liebes, "Zohar and Eros" (Hebrew), *Alpayyim* 9 (1994): 87–98; and Wolfson, *Through a Speculum*, 384–87. On the representation of the female body as text, see Robert Scholes, *Semiotics and Interpretation* (New Haven, Conn.: Yale University Press, 1982), 127–41; and Shari Benstock, *Textualizing the Feminine: On the Limits of Genre* (Norman: University of Oklahoma Press, 1991).

228. For instance, see the commentary on "And Adam knew his wife Eve" (Gen. 4:1) in *Zohar Ḥadash*, 63c: "'And Adam'—this is the hidden, primordial Adam, engraved in the supernal, subtle engravings. 'Knew'—what he did not comprehended it before. He knew how to be face-to-face. When they gazed face-to-face for the sake of intercourse, it is written 'knew,' for he knew how to irrigate her, to inseminate her with seed, to produce offspring."

229. Wolfson, "Beautiful Maiden," 169–70, 185–87. On the twofold task of the mask to veil and to reveal, see the study "Die Maske: Verhüllung oder Offenbarung?" in Claas J. Bleeker, *The Sacred Bridge: Researches into the Nature and Structure of Religion* (Leiden: E. J. Brill, 1963), 236–49.

230. The point is captured in the Arabic *ta'bīr* ("interpretation") from *'ubūr* ("crossing over"). For the enlightened mystics, the "Folk of Allah," as opposed to the rationalist philosophers and theologians, the crossing over from exoteric to esoteric is not predicated on discarding the former; see William C. Chittick, *The Sufi Path of Knowledge: Ibn al-'Arabi's Cosmology* (Albany: State University of New York Press, 1998), 245; see also Henry Corbin, *Creative Imagination in the Sūfism of Ibn 'Arabī*, trans. Ralph Manheim (Princeton, N.J.: Princeton University Press, 1969), 28–29.

231. My analysis of the zoharic passage accords with the insights of Toshihiko Izutsu, *Creation and the Timeless Order of Things: Essays in Islamic Mystical Philosophy*, foreword by William C. Chittick (Ashland, Ore.: White Cloud Press, 1994), 40–41, regarding the metaphorical understanding of the Sufi use of the word *nūr* ("light"). Izutsu begins the argument by following an Aristotelian interpretation of metaphor as a word with a "double role," "pointing at the same time to two different meanings [A and B], the first being its literal or conventional meaning and the second its nonconventional or figurative meaning" (40). Having established that, he proposes *nūr* in the Sufi context as an example of metaphor, inasmuch as the term refers concurrently to physical and spiritual light. Izutsu proceeds to show how the Sufi hermeneutic reverses the relationship between literal and metaphorical—the real, the supreme metaphysical reality, is the light seen with the "eye of spiritual vision" (*'ayn al-basīrah*), whereas physical light is merely a figure of speech. It follows that the term *nūr* "functions as an *immediate sign* for the spiritual light and as a *mediate sign* for the physical" (41; emphasis in original). Finally, it would be instructive to explore in more detail the connotation of the term *remiza* in the zoharic context and the use of *ramz* in Islamic esotericism to denote "symbolic speech," that is, speaking through parable or allusion. For discussion of this technical terminology, see Johann Christoph Bürgel, "'Symbols and Hints': Some Considerations concerning the Meaning of Ibn Ṭufayl's *Ḥayy ibn Yaqẓān*," in *The World of Ibn Ṭufayl: Interdisci-*

plinary Perspectives on Ḥayy ibn Yaqẓān, ed. Lawrence I. Conrad (Leiden: E. J. Brill, 1996), 117–22; Dmitri Gutas, *Avicenna and the Aristotelian Tradition: Introduction to Reading Avicenna's Philosophical Works* (Leiden: E. J. Brill, 1988), 299–307; and Peter Heath, *Allegory and Philosophy in Avicenna (Ibn Sīnā) with a Translation of the Book of the Prophet Muhammad's Ascent to Heaven* (Philadelphia: University of Pennsylvania Press, 1992), 151–55.

232. Consider the comment of Erich Neumann, *The Origins and History of Consciousness*, trans. R. F. C. Hull, foreword by Carl G. Jung (Princeton, N.J.: Princeton University Press, 1954), 53: "The 'bridal veil' must be understood in this sense, as the symbol of *kedesha*, the harlot. She is 'unknown,' i.e., anonymous. To be 'unveiled' means to be naked, but this is only another form of anonymity. Always the goddess, the transpersonal, is the real and operative factor." Neumann insightfully grasps that the unveiling of the harlot is not a form of exposure but another masquerade, not a disclosure of her name but an ascription of anonymity. But why is this so? How can we conceive of unveiling as masking? That which is real—whose face we seek to expose and whose name we seek to disclose—is the goddess, the transpersonal that is forever beyond the confines of any particular manifestation. To translate Neumann's language into a kabbalistic idiom, every gradation is a mask by which that which has no face appears, the transpersonal, Ein Sof, that which is beyond any and all representation and hence may be considered the catalyst for the multifaceted imaginary representations, the drawing of verbal icons—visual signs—in the poetic imagination of the contemplative kabbalist.

233. The paradox is captured in the Zen maxim, "Face to face a thousand miles away" (Victor Sōgen Hori, *Zen Sand: The Book of Capping Phrases for Kōan Practice* [Honolulu: University of Hawai'i Press, 2003], 43), read in correlation with a second dictum, "When you're face to face, it's hard to hide" (147).

234. On the nexus of woman, text, veil, poetry, and the elusive nature of (un)truth, see Tova Rosen, *Unveiling Eve: Reading Gender in Medieval Hebrew Literature* (Philadelphia: University of Pennsylvania Press, 2003), 64–82.

235. See Fatima Mernissi, *Beyond the Veil: Male-Female Dynamics in Modern Muslim Society*, rev. ed. (Bloomington: Indiana University Press, 1987); Fatima Mernissi, *The Veil and the Male Elite: A Feminist Interpretation of Women's Rights in Islam*, trans. Mary Jo Lakeland (Reading, Mass.: Addison-Wesley, 1991), 85–101; Anne-Emmanuelle Berger, "The Newly Veiled Woman: Irigaray, Specularity, and the Islamic Veil," *Diacritics* 28 (1993): 93–119; Homa Hoodfar, "The Veil in Their Minds and on Our Heads: Veiling Practices and Muslim Women," in *Women, Gender, Religion: A Reader*, ed. Elizabeth A. Castelli with Rosamond C. Rodman (New York: Palgrave, 2001), 420–46; Juliette Minces, *La femme voilée l'Islam au féminin* (Paris: Calmann-Lévy, 1990); Anwar Hekmat, *Women and the Koran: The Status of Women in Islam* (Amherst, N.Y.: Prometheus Books, 1997), 181–213. For a similar phenomenon in the case of Jewish women, see Yedida K. Stillman, " 'Cover Her Face': Jewish Women and Veiling in Islamic Civilisation," in *Israel and Ishmael: Studies in Muslim-Jewish Relations*, ed. Tudor Parfitt (New York: St. Martin's Press, 2000), 13–31. On the connection of the veil and scopic desire in contemporary texts, see Peter Hitchcock, "The Eye and the Other: The Gaze and the Look in Egyptian Feminist Fiction," in *The Politics of (M)Othering: Womanhood, Identity, and Resistance in African Literature*, ed. Obioma Nnaemeka (London: Routledge, 1997), 69–81.

236. Alexander D. Knysh, *Islamic Mysticism: A Short History* (Leiden: E. J. Brill, 2000), 311–14.

237. It is worth noting in this context the use of the image of garbing on the part of kabbalists to denote the emanative process, a theme they connect with the midrashic dictum in *Genesis Rabbah* 3:4 (linked exegetically to Ps. 104:2) that God created the primordial light by donning a garment and shining forth the brilliance of his splendor. See, for instance, the remark of Ezra ben

Solomon of Gerona in *Perush Shir ha-Shirim*, in *Kitvei Ramban*, 2 vols., ed. Ḥayyim D. Chavel (Jerusalem: Mosad ha-Rav Kook, 1964), 2:493, that the word *salmah* ("cloak") denotes "the summoning of the emanation of wisdom that encompasses everything" (*hazmanat hamshakhat ha-ḥokhmah ha-sovevet et ha-kol*). The rabbinic image of God wrapping himself with the garment signifies that "he received the splendor from this effluence and the light verily sparkled." In his letter to Abraham ben Isaac, the cantor of Gerona, published by Scholem, "New Document," 157–58, Ezra employs very similar language to depict the emanative process, the "splendor of wisdom, which is his garment" (*zohar ha-ḥokhmah she-hu levusho*). The same interpretation is attributed to Isaac the Blind, referred to by the honorific title "our master, the pious one" (*rabbenu he-ḥasid*) by Azriel of Gerona, *Commentary on Talmudic Aggadoth*, 110–11. For analysis of this theme and its exegetical trajectory, see Altmann, *Studies*, 128–39.

238. In light of the qur'ānic emphasis on the removal of the veil on the day of reckoning, it is of interest to consider the remark in Swartz, *Medieval Critique of Anthropomorphism*, 277: "I heard the following tradition [from 'Abd al-Wahhāb b. al-Mubārak] in which Sahl b. Saʿd reports that the Prophet said: '[On the day of judgment] God will be concealed by seventy thousand veils of light and darkness. No one will hear even the slightest sound from [behind?] those veils else he would perish.'"

239. Hossein Ziai, *Knowledge and Illumination* (Atlanta: Scholars Press, 1990), 155–66; Hossein Ziai, "Ḥāfeẓ, Lisān al-Ghayb of Persian Poetic Wisdom," in *Gott ist schön und Er liebt die Schönheit: Festschrift für Annemarie Schimmel zum 7. April 1992*, ed. Alma Giese and J. Christoph Bürgel (Bern: Peter Lang, 1994), 463. On the Sufi notion of the time-atom severed from past and future, see Louis Massignon, "Time in Islamic Thought," in *Man and Time: Papers from the Eranos Yearbooks*, ed. Joseph Campbell (Princeton, N.J.: Princeton University Press, 1957), 110–11; Gerhard Böwering, "Ideas of Time in Persian Sufism," in *Classical Persian Sufism from Its Origins to Rumi (700–1300)*, ed. Leonard Lewisohn, vol. 1 of *The Heritage of Sufism* (Oxford: Oneworld, 1999), 223–25. I have discussed the matter elsewhere (Elliot R. Wolfson, *Alef, Mem, Tau: Kabbalistic Musings on Time, Truth, and Death* [Berkeley: University of California Press, 2006], chap. 2) and thus will not repeat all of the intricate details related to this rudimentary Sufi notion. Let me simply state that the atomistic conception of time is the temporal correlate to the ontological paradox of *fanā'* and *baqā'* the identity of perishing and abiding. To grasp the mystical ideal of passing away and enduring in the oneness of what is, one must take hold of the mystery of time disclosed in the moment that endures in its elapsing. Consider Ibn 'Arabī's explication of the qur'ānic verse "Everything will perish except his own face" (28:88) in his *Futūḥāt al-makkiyya*, cited in Chittick, *Self-Disclosure*, 156: "The pronoun that modifies 'face' goes back to 'thing' and it also goes back to the Real. You accord with that in which you stand, for you are the companion of a [present] moment [*waqt*]"; see Franz Rosenthal, "Ibn 'Arabī between 'Philosophy' and 'Mysticism,'" *Oriens* 31 (1988): 29.

240. Michael Sells, *Early Islamic Mysticism: Sufi, Qur'an, Miraj, Poetic and Theological Writings* (New York: Paulist Press, 1996), 284.

241. Izutsu, *Creation and the Timeless Order*, 11–13, 76–77; Sells, *Early Islamic Mysticism*, 43–45; Binyamin Abrahamov, *Divine Love in Islamic Mysticism: The Teachings of Al-Ghazāli and Al-Dabbāgh* (New York: RoutledgeCurzon, 2003), 27, 61–66.

242. Margaret Smith, *Rābiʿa the Mystic and Her Fellow-Saints in Islam* (Cambridge: Cambridge University Press, 1928), 121; Abrahamov, *Divine Love*, 27.

243. Sells, *Early Islamic Mysticism*, 155.

244 For discussion of the different facets of Rābiʿa's asceticism, see Smith, *Rābiʿa*, 40–52, and her account of the celibate lifestyle of other women saints in Islam, 195–205.

245. On depictions of Mary in the Qur'ān and subsequent Islamic tradition, see James Robson, "Stories of Jesus and Mary," *Muslim World* 40 (1950): 236–43; Jane I. Smith and Yvonne Y. Haddad, "The Virgin Mary in Islamic Tradition and Commentary," *Muslim World* 79 (1989): 161–87; Neal Robinson, "Jesus and Mary in the Qur'ān: Some Neglected Affinities," *Religion* 20 (1990): 161–75; Neal Robinson, *Christ in Islam and Christianity* (Albany: State University of New York Press, 1991), 4–7, 45; Ludwig Hagemann and Ernst Pulsfort, *Maria, die Mutter Jesu, in Bibel und Koran* (Würzburg: Echter, 1992); Mahmoud Ayoub, *The Qur'an and Its Interpreters*, 2 vols. (Albany: State University of New York Press, 1984), 2:93–107, 22–135; Schimmel, *Mystical Dimensions*, 429; Annemarie Schimmel, "Jesus and Mary as Poetical Images in Rūmi's Verse," in *Christian-Muslim Encounters*, ed. Yvonne Y. Haddad and Wadi Z. Haddad (Gainesville: University Press of Florida, 1995), 143–57; Aliah Schleifer, *Mary the Blessed Virgin of Islam* (Louisville, Ky.: Fons Vitae, 1997); Oddbjørn Leirvik, *Images of Jesus Christ in Islam: Introduction, Survey of Research, Issues of Dialogue* (Uppsala: Swedish Institute of Missionary Research, 1999), 23–27; Ralph W. J. Austin, "The Sophianic Feminine in the Work of Ibn 'Arabī and Rumi," *The Heritage of Sufism:* vol. 2: *The Legacy of Medieval Persian Sufism (1150–1500)*, ed. Leonard Lewisohn (Oxford: Oneworld, 1999), 243–44; David Marshall, "Christianity in the Qur'ān," in *Islamic Interpretations of Christianity*, ed. Lloyd Ridgeon (New York: St. Martin's Press, 2001), 4–7, 11–18; Ahmad Z. M. Hammad, *Mary, the Chosen Woman: The Mother of Jesus in the Quran: An Interlinear Commentary on Surat Maryam* (Bridgeview: Quranic Literacy Institute, 2001). It is worth mentioning in this connection that the affirmation of the Virgin Birth in Islamic tradition was utilized by medieval Christian polemicists, for example, Peter the Venerable, to bolster the claim that Jews are worse than Muslims; on this point, see Anna Sapir Abulafia, "The Intellectual and Spiritual Quest for Christ and Central Medieval Persecution of Jews," in *Religious Violence between Christians and Jews: Medieval Roots, Modern Perspectives*, ed. Anna Sapir Abulafia (Basingstoke: Palgrave, 2002), 63. On the reverence for Mary in contemporary Sufi teaching, see, for instance, Sheikh Muzaffer Ozak al-Jerrahi, *Blessed Virgin Mary*, trans. Muhtar Holland, foreword, introduction, and afterword by Nur al-Jerrahi (Westport, Conn.: Pir, 1991).

246. Smith, *Rābi'a*, 21.

247. In Q 3:35–36, Maryam is identified as the daughter of 'Imrān, and in 19:28 she is referred to as the "sister of Aaron," indicating that there was a conflation of Miriam of the Old Testament, the daughter of Amran and sister of Moses and Aaron (Num. 26:59), and Mary of the New Testament, the wife of Joseph and mother of Jesus. The confusion was noted from a relatively early period by Christians as a polemical strategy to underscore misrepresentations of the New Testament in the Qur'ān, although it is possible that the conflation in its inception was not a distortion but reflects a typological interpretation, perhaps traceable to some branch of Syrian Christianity, that linked Miriam and Mary; see Robinson, *Christ in Islam*, 9, 18–19, and Ayoub, *Qur'an and Its Interpreters*, 2:88–92; Martin Bauschke, *Jesus im Koran* (Cologne: Böhlau, 2001), 13–33.

248. In Q 4:156, the people of the book (*ahl al-kitāb*), which in this context refers exclusively to the Jews and not to Jews and Christians (for a thorough discussion of this appellation, see Heribert Busse, *Islam, Judaism, and Christianity: The Theological and Historical Affiliations* (Princeton, N.J.: Markus Wiener, 1998), 29–62, and see below, n. 275), are said to be punished for various reasons, including "their disbelief and their imputing to Mary a great falsehood." The nature of the falsehood is not specified, but it is likely that there is an allusion here to one of the disparaging ways that Jews cast Mary in order to discredit the Christian narrative, for example, dismissing the belief in the virginal conception by identifying the father of Jesus as a Roman soldier, implying thereby that Mary was guilty of adultery, or depicting Jesus as *ben niddah*, literally "son of a menstruant," a title that not only challenges the alleged virginity of Mary but also suggests that Jesus was conceived

while she was menstruating, an accusation that implies her failure to observe traditional Jewish purity laws. For select references to these themes, see Elliot R. Wolfson, "Re/membering the Covenant: Memory, Forgetfulness, and the Construction of History in the Zohar," in *Jewish History and Jewish Memory: Yerushalmi Festschrift*, ed. Elisheva Carlebach, John Efron, and David S. Myers (Hanover, N.H.: University of New England Press, 1998), 234n23 and 236n39. Along with the sources mentioned there, see as well Yaacov Deutsch, "New Evidence of Early Versions of *Toldot Yeshu*" (Hebrew), *Tarbiz* 69 (2000): 177–97, esp. 182. Deutsch raises the possibility that the designation *ben niddah* is a later interpolation dating from the fifteenth century, with the earlier texts emphasizing that Jesus was the offspring of an adulterous act. The insinuation of sexual immorality on the part of Mary is also implied in Q 19:28. It is of interest to consider in this connection the exegesis of Q 19:16–17 that links the retreat of Mary behind the curtain to her purifying herself from menstrual impurity; see Muḥammad Ibn 'Abd Allāh Kisā'i, *Tales of the Prophets (Qiṣaṣ al-anbiyā')*, trans. Wheeler M. Thackston (Chicago: Great Books of the Islamic World, 1997), 328; Brannon M. Wheeler, *Moses in the Quran and Islamic Exegesis* (London: RoutledgeCurzon, 2002), 77–79, 120. Finally, it is worth recalling the comment in Q 33:53 about the proper etiquette of requesting something from a woman who is situated "before a screen."

249. Jesus, or as he is referred to in the Qur'ān, 'Īsā ibn Maryam or simply ibn Maryam, is identified as a prophet (*nabī*), servant ('*abd*), messenger (*rasūl*), word (*kalima*), spirit (*rūḥ*), and the anointed one (*al-masīḥ*), but there is a categorical rejection of identifying him as the son of God or as a member of the Trinity; see Q 9:30, where Jews and Christians are both condemned for identifying a human figure as the son of God, for the former, 'Uzair (that is, Ezra), and for the latter, Jesus. For a representative list of studies dedicated to the portrayals of Jesus in Islam, see Geoffrey Parrinder, *Jesus in the Qur'an* (London: Faber and Faber, 1965); Don Wismer, *The Islamic Jesus: An Annotated Bibliography of Sources in English and French* (New York: Garland, 1977); Heikki Räisänen, "The Portrait of Jesus in the Qur'ān: Reflections of a Biblical Scholar," *Muslim World* 70 (1980): 122–33; Javad Nurbakhsh, *Jesus in the Eyes of the Sufis*, trans. Terry Graham, Leonard Lewisohn, and Hamid Mashkuri (London: Khaniqahi-Nimatullahi Publications, 1983); Busse, *Islam, Judaism, and Christianity*, 113–37; Muḥammad 'Ata ur-Raḥim, *Jesus: Prophet of Islam* (Elmhurst: Tahrike Tarsile Qur'an, 1991); Robinson, *Christ in Islam*; Reinhard Leuze, *Christentum und Islam* (Tübingen: J. C. B. Mohr, 1994), 56–71; Kenneth Cragg, *Jesus and the Muslim: An Exploration*; Kate Zebiri, "Contemporary Muslim Understanding of the Miracle of Jesus," *Muslim World* 90 (2000): 71–90; Leirvik, *Images of Jesus Christ*; Bauschke, *Jesus im Koran*. On the question of the divinity of Christ from the Muslim perspective, see also Abdelilah Ljamai, *Ibn Ḥazm et la polémique Islamo-Chrétienne dans l'histoire de l'Islam* (Leiden: Brill, 2003), 103–9.

250. See as well Q 5:116–17, where worship of Jesus or Mary is steadfastly rejected. On the possibility that the presentation of Christian faith in the relevant qur'ānic verses reflects some heterodox interpretation, for example, identifying the Trinity as God, Jesus, and Mary (who is sometimes referred to as "Theotokos," the God-bearer), see Hugh Goddard, *Muslim Perceptions of Christianity* (London: Grey Seal, 1996), 14–15. Needless to say, the question of the representations of Jesus and Mary in Islamic scripture, tradition, and commentaries is a vast and complex subject that has been discussed by several notable scholars. The view I have expressed is based solely on qur'ānic verses and hence does not deal adequately with the phenomenon of Islamic Christology. In addition to the relevant scholarly discussions mentioned in nn. 245 and 249, see Mahmud Mustafa Ayoub, "Jesus the Son of God: A Study of the Terms *Ibn* and *Walad* in the Qur'an and *Tafsīr* Tradition," in *Christian-Muslim Encounters*, ed. Yvonne Y. Haddad and Wadi Z. Haddad (Gainesville: University Press of Florida, 1995), 65–81.

251. Cragg, *Jesus and the Muslim*, 32.

252. Leirvik, *Images of Jesus Christ*, 96. Schimmel, "Jesus and Mary," 143–45, emphasizes the importance of the portrayal of Jesus as the ideal ascetic in Sufi sources.

253. On the impact of the figure of Virgin Mary on the formation of the narrative accounts of Rābiʿa, see Julian Baldick, "The Legend of Rābiʿa of Basra: Christian Antecedents, Muslim Counterparts," *Religion* 20 (1990): 233–47. Relevant to this orientation is Rūmī's comparison of the body to Mary and the spirit to Jesus, as noted by Lloyd V. J. Ridgeon, *Crescents on the Cross: Islamic Visions of Christianity* (Oxford: Oxford University Press, 2001), 38–39.

254. ʿAbd al-Karim Ibn Hawazin Qushayrī, *Principles of Sufism*, trans. B. R. von Schlegell (Berkeley: Mizan Press, 1992), 143.

255. Schimmel, *Mystical Dimensions*, 167–78.

256. Ibid., 112; Knysh, *Islamic Mysticism*, 71–72.

257. The paradox is poetically captured by al-Junayd, as cited in Sells, *Early Islamic Mysticism*, 254–55: "My annihilation is my abiding. From the reality of my annihilation, he annihilated me from both my abiding and my annihilation. I was, upon the reality of annihilation, without being or annihilation, through my abiding and annihilation, for the existence (*wujūd*) of annihilation in abiding, for the existence of my other is my annihilation. . . . He abides in your abiding, that is, the unity of the affirmer of unity abides through the abiding of the one who is one, even as the affirmer of unity passes away. Then you are you. You lacked yourself, and then you came to abide insofar as you passed away." See also 260: "He annihilated my construction just as he constructed me originally in the condition of my annihilation."

258. Ibid., 255. Compare the formulation of al-Qushayrī translated by Sells, *Early Islamic Mysticism*, 120: "Whoever is seized by the sovereign power of reality, to the point that he no longer witnesses any vision, vestige, trace, or ruin of the others, is said to have passed away from creatures and to endure through the real."

259. Ibid., 223.

260. Ibid., 121. On the Sufi ideal of extinction in and unity with God, see Helmut Ritter, *The Ocean of the Soul: Men, the World, and God in the Stories of Farīd al-Dīn ʿAṭṭār*, trans. John O'Kane with Bernd Radtke (Leiden: Brill, 2003), 593–614.

261. Böwering, "Ideas of Time," 223–25.

262. Reynold A. Nicholson, *Kashf al-Maḥjūb: The Oldest Persian Treatise on Sufism* (London: Luzac, 1936), 250. On the distinction between the "veil of covering" (*ḥijāb-i raynī*), which can never be removed, and the "veil of clouding" (*ḥijāb-i ghaynī*), which is removable, see Nicholson, *Kashf al-Maḥjūb*, 4–5, 391; William C. Chittick, "Paradox of the Veil in Sufism," in *Rending the Veil: Concealment and Secrecy in the History of Religions*, ed. Elliot R. Wolfson (New York: Seven Bridges Press, 1999), 65–67.

263. Nicholson, *Kashf al-Maḥjūb*, 274.

264. Ibid., 22.

265. Ibid., 149; see also 325. On the use of the image of being hidden behind the veil to denote ignorance, see Moezzi, *Divine Guide*, 166n197.

266. Nicholson, *Kashf al-Maḥjūb*, 374. The Sufi terms *qabd* and *basṭ* are reminiscent of two pairs of terms in Lurianic kabbalah, *hitpashṭut* and *histalqut* (expansion and withdrawal), and *gadlut* and *qaṭnut* (augmentation and diminution). Both pairs denote states of the theogonic myth, but they also apply psychologically to the consciousness of individuals. Although the later is more commonly associated with the metamorphosis of Lurianic theosophy in Hasidism, a careful reading of the sixteenth- and seventeenth-century kabbalistic sources yields no sound reason to separate the ontological and psychological. Kabbalists affirm a consubstantiality of divine and human, and hence to contemplate the one is to contemplate the other, an idea that I developed on the basis of the essay by my teacher, Alexander Altmann (see Wolfson, *Language, Eros, Being*, chap. 1, n. 302).

If that insight is properly heeded, there is no conceptual basis for the distinction between the theo-sophical and psychological when one considers the phenomenological orientation of medieval kabbalists.

267. Nicholson, *Kashf al-Mahjūb*, 414.

268. Chittick, *Self-Disclosure*, 106–8. One of the most elaborate accounts of the revelatory experience of unveiling (*kashf*) is found in *Ḥikmat al-ishrāq*, the "Wisdom of Illumination," by the twelfth-century Persian mystic, Suhrawardī. I cannot possibly do justice to Suhrawardī's complex blending of eastern spirituality and Neoplatonic philosophy in this note. Let me simply remark that, in accord with the latter, he affirms the possibility of the soul separating from the body and ascending mentally to the higher realm, where it contemplates by way of "unveiling and intuition" the intelligible lights without veils linked to the hindrance of corporeality, culminating in a pure vision of the Light of Lights, the formless and imageless source of all being, the "true King" who "possesses the essence of everything but whose essence is possessed by none."; see Shihābuddīn Yaḥya Suhrawardī, *The Philosophy of Illumination: A New Critical Edition of the Text of Ḥikmat al-ishrāq with English Translation, Notes, Commentary, and Introduction by John Walbridge and Hossein Ziai* (Provo, Utah: Brigham Young University Press, 2000), 96; Mehdi Amin Razavi, *Suhrawardi and the School of Illumination* (Surrey: Curzon, 1997), 87–92.

269. I note, parenthetically, as Fritz Meier has pointed out in *Essays on Islamic Piety and Mysticism* (trans. John O'Kane [Leiden: E. J. Brill, 1999]), 400–420, esp. 408–9, as early as the ninth century the practice of veiling the face could also symbolize the mystery of sanctity, that is, he who veiled his face was thought to be the incarnation of the hidden and impenetrable light of the divine. Like Moses, according to Hebrew scriptures (Exod. 34:33–35), the holy man in Islam had to veil his face so that the radiance of his countenance would not harm others. (See also Wolfson, *Language, Eros, Being*, chap. 3, n. 153.) On the use of this theme in later Islamic exegesis, see Wheeler, *Moses in the Quran*, 32.

270. On the creed that God spoke directly to Moses in Muslim faith, see Swartz, *Medieval Critique of Anthropomorphism*, 276n480.

271. Jalal al-Din Rūmī, *The Mathnawī of Jalālu'ddīn Rūmī*, trans. Reynold A. Nicholson (London: Luzac, 1968), 5:233–34 (hereafter Nicholson, *Mathnawī*).

272. Babylonian Talmud, Yevamot 49b.

273. Sells, *Early Islamic Mysticism*, 80.

274. Abū Bakr al-Kalābādhī, *The Doctrine of the Sūfīs (Kitāb al-Taʿarruf li-madhhab ahl al-taṣawwuf)*, trans. Arthur J. Arberry (Cambridge: Cambridge University Press, 1935), 117.

275. See above, n. 248.

276. For other accounts of the sin of the golden calf, see Q 7:138–40, 148–53, 20:83–98; Uri Rubin, *Between Bible and Qur'ān: The Children of Israel and the Islamic Self-Image* (Princeton, N.J.: Darwin Press, 1999), 100–113; Uri Rubin, "Traditions in Transformation: The Ark of the Covenant and the Golden Calf in Biblical and Islamic Historiography," *Oriens* 36 (2001): 196–214, esp. 201–9. The depiction of Jews as idolaters and promoters of anthropomorphic-corporealist views of God, in part supported by the scriptural narrative regarding the golden calf, continued to be a major ploy in the medieval Islamic polemic against Judaism; see Hawting, *Idea of Idolatry*, 75–85. For an attenuated reading of the golden calf episode that challenges a rigid distinction between idolatry and true worship, see the analysis of Ibn ʿArabī's exegesis in Ronald L. Nettler, *Sufi Metaphysics and Qur'ānic Prophets: Ibn ʿArabī's Thought and Method in Fuṣūṣ al-Ḥikam* (Cambridge: Islamic Texts Society, 2003), 64–66.

277. See Wolfson, *Language, Eros, Being*, chap. 3, n. 89.

278. Nicholson, *Mathnawī*, 1:1435–36. I note the similarity of the imagery used by Rūmī and the language of Joseph Gikatilla (for reference see Wolfson, *Language, Eros, Being,* chap. 7, n. 246).

279. Ibid., 1:3146. On the polished mirror as a symbol of the "purified heart of the lover" that facilitates the "mysterious union" of the lover and beloved in Sufism, see Schimmel, "Mawlānā Rūmī: Yesterday, Today, and Tomorrow," in *Poetry and Mysticism in Islam: The Heritage of Rūmī,* ed. Amin Banani, Richard Hovannisian, and Georges Sabagh (Cambridge: Cambridge University Press, 1994), 17. On the emptying of all images from the heart and Rumi's poetics of silence, see Fatemeh Keshavarz, *Reading Mystical Lyric: The Case of Jalal al-Din Rumi* (Columbia: University of South Carolina Press, 1998), 49–71.

280. Chittick, *Self-Disclosure,* xxi–xxii; Chittick, *Sufi Path of Knowledge,* 68–76; William C. Chittick, *Imaginal Worlds: Ibn al-'Arabī and the Problem of Religious Diversity* (Albany: State University of New York Press, 1994), 23–29; see also Nicholson, *Studies in Islamic Mysticism,* 140; Nettler, *Sufi Metaphysics,* 7–11, 18–22, 80–88, 116–22.

281. Muḥyīddīn Ibn 'Arabī, *The Bezels of Wisdom,* trans. and introduction by Ralph W. J. Austin, preface by Titus Burckhardt (New York: Paulist Press, 1980), 74–75.

282. Schimmel, *Mystical Dimensions,* 268. On the narrowing of the ontic gap between God, world, and soul in Sufi mysticism, see the wealth of material translated and analyzed by Ritter, *Ocean of the Soul,* 615–36.

283. See Wolfson, *Language, Eros, Being,* chap. 1, n. 270. It is of interest to recall the conjecture by Seyyed Hossein Nasr, *Sufi Essays* (Albany: State University of New York Press, 1973), 159–63, that the derivation of the "unicity of nature" from the "unity of the Divine principle" affirmed by masters of Islamic gnosis, the presumption that unity (*al-tawḥīd*) "pervades all things and all forms of knowledge," is indebted to a basic axiom of Eastern science expressed in Chinese and Japanese traditions in terms of the unity of the ten thousand things in the one substance of the whole. Nasr suggests, moreover, that just as Islam geographically "covers the middle belt of the world, intellectually and spiritually it occupies a position half way between the mental climate of the Occident and the intellectual climate of the Indian and Far Eastern worlds" (160).

284. Several interesting traditions concerning the veil are cited in the section on the symbols of the throne and footstool in Anton M. Heinen, *Islamic Cosmology: A Study of as-Suyūtī's al-Hay'a as-sanīya fī l-hay'a as-sunnīya, with Critical Edition, Translation, and Commentary* (Wiesbaden: Franz Steiner, 1982), 133–34.

285. Ghazālī, *The Niche of Lights: A Parallel English-Arabic Text,* trans. David Buchman (Provo, Utah: Brigham Young University Press, 1998), 44.

286. Ibid., 51. The boldness of al-Ghazālī's text is attested by the fact that some considered it a heretical affirmation of multiplicity within the divine. See Jim Colville, *Two Andalusian Philosophers: The Story of Hayy ibn Yaqzan by Abu Bakr Muhammad ibn Tufayl and The Definitive Statement by Abu'l Walid Muhammad ibn Rushd* (London: Kegan Paul International, 1999), 9, 69n17.

287. Ghazālī, *Niche of Lights,* 52; see Majid Fakhry, *A History of Islamic Philosophy,* 2nd ed. (New York: Columbia University Press, 1983), 248–49. A similar depiction is given by Ibn Ṭufayl in his account of the third and final type of mimesis that ends in a vision of the One wherein the self as an autonomous being vanishes; see Aaron W. Hughes, *The Texture of the Divine: Imagination in Medieval Islamic and Jewish Thought* (Bloomington: Indiana University Press, 2004), 101.

288. Heinen, *Islamic Cosmology,* 133.

289. Sells, *Early Islamic Mysticism,* 291.

290. Chittick, "Paradox of the Veil," 83.

291. Chittick, *Self-Disclosure,* 110; Chittick, "Paradox of the Veil," 74.

292. Chittick, *Self-Disclosure*, 129; Chittick, "Paradox of the Veil," 81–82.

293. Chittick, *Self-Disclosure*, 156; Chittick, "Paradox of the Veil," 74–75.

294. Chittick, *Self-Disclosure*, 105, 107–8, 113, 115, 156.

295. Muḥyīddīn Ibn al-ʿArabī, *Divine Governance of the Human Kingdom, At-Tadbīrāt al-ilāhiyyah fī iṣlāḥ al-mamlakat al-insāniyyah*, trans. Shaykh tosun Bayrak al-Jerrahi al-Halveti (Louisville, Ky.: Fons Vitae, 1997), 239. For a detailed rationalist interpretation of Q 28:88, see Abrahamov, *Anthropomorphism*, 98–109.

296. Ibn al-ʿArabī, *Divine Governance*, 239.

297. Chittick, *Sufi Path of Knowledge*, 230. The Sufi wisdom brings to mind the poem of enlightenment composed by the Zen master Tōzan Ryōkai after having caught a glimpse of his reflection in the water, cited in Keizan Jōkin and Jiyu Kennett, *The Denkōroku, or The Record of the Transmission of the Light*, trans. Hubert Nearman, 2nd ed. (Mount Shasta, Calif.: Shasta Abbey Press. 2001), 209: "Truly I should not seek for the TRUTH from others / For then it will be far from me; / Now I am going alone, / Everywhere I am able to meet HIM. / HE is ME now, / I am not HIM; / When we understand this, / We are instantaneously with the TRUTH."

298. On the identity of veil and face, see the relevant texts cited and analyzed in Chittick, *Self-Disclosure*, 128–35.

299. A similar claim is made for Buddhist phenomenology by Steven William Laycock, *Mind as Mirror and the Mirroring of Mind: Buddhist Reflections on Western Phenomenology* (Albany: State University of New York Press, 1994), 49–50. This comparison is worthy of further reflection, but this is not the appropriate context; perhaps one day I shall return to it.

300. Cited in Ziai, "Ḥāfeẓ, Lisān al-Ghayb," 466: "There is no veil blinding the lover's vision of the beloved, / Thou art thyself the veil Ḥāfeẓ! Remove thyself from the midst." Maria Subtelny graciously provided me with an alternative rendering of this passage, which has helped me refine my exposition: "Between [*miyān*] the lover and the beloved there is no barrier [*ḥāyil*] / You yourself are the veil [*ḥijāb*] of selfhood, Ḥāfeẓ, remove yourself from this midst [*miyān*]."

301. Daryush Shayegan, "The Visionary Typography of Ḥāfīẓ," in *The Green Sea of Heaven: Fifty Ghazals from the Dīwān of Ḥāfīẓ*, trans. Elizabeth T. Gray (Ashland, Ore.: White Cloud Press, 1995), 17. See also Michael Glünz, "The Poet's Heart: A Polyfunctional Object in the Poetic System of the Ghazal," in *Intoxication Earthly and Heavenly: Seven Studies on the Poet Hafiz of Shiraz*, ed. Michael Glünz and J. Christoph Bürgel (Bern: Peter Lang, 1991), 53–68; my thanks to Maria Subtelny for drawing my attention to this study.

302. The medium for visualization is most often designated as the veil, mirror, or heart of the visionary, but in the Persian tradition, it is also associated with the world-revealing cup of Jamshīd. See, for instance, Shihābuddīn Yaḥya Suhrawardī, *The Philosophical Allegories and Mystical Treatises*, trans. Wheeler M. Thackson (Costa Mesa: Mazda, 1999), 81; Ḥāfiẓ, *Fifty Poems*, no. 11 p. 94, no. 15, p. 97; Glünz, "Poet's Heart," 54 and 62. In the poetry of Ḥāfiẓ, the cup of the mythical king seems often conflated with the cup of wine whence the visionary enjoys the ecstasy of intoxication. See, for instance, Ḥāfiẓ, *Fifty Poems of Ḥāfiẓ*, no. 16, p. 100, no. 46, p. 129. In mystical and philosophical works, moreover, the cup is applied allegorically to the Active Intellect, identified as well as the Holy Spirit and the archangel Gabriel; see Ziai, "Ḥāfez, Lisān al-Ghayb," 454n16 and 465; Ritter, *Ocean of the Soul*, 602–3.

303. Ziai, "Ḥāfez, Lisān al-Ghayb," 467–69.

304. Ḥāfiz, *The Gift: Poems by Ḥāfiz the Great Sufi Master*, trans. Daniel Ladinsky (New York: Penguin Compass, 1999), 148.

305. This is reminiscent of the wisdom of the "gateless gate" (*wu-wen kuan*)—the title of a work by the Chinese master Wu-men Hui-hai (1183–1269)—articulated in the Zen Buddhist tradi-

tion: Only after having passed through the gate does one know that there is no gate through which to pass.

306. *Zohar*, 1:161b. The language of annihilation, *avaddon*, is derived from Job 28:22, where the word personifies a force of destruction, and hence it is paired with *mawet*, the personification of death. In scriptural context, these forces say of the wisdom hidden from all living beings (Job 28:20–21) that they have heard about it (*be-ozneinu shama'nu shim'ah*), evidently an inferior form of discernment. God alone comprehends its way and knows its place and thus employs it as the means of creation, a measuring by the way of wisdom, culminating in the instruction to man that wisdom is the fear of the Lord and understanding the shunning of evil (Job 28:23–28). The zoharic author obviously interprets *avaddon* in his own kabbalistic way, using the term to demarcate the mystical passing away into the attribute of the divine that is no/thing that is everything, the emptiness that is full, the fullness that is empty. I have thus taken the liberty to compare this to the Sufi *fanā' al-fanā'*, the passing of passing. I should note, in passing, that in the continuation of the zoharic text (3:161b–162a), *avaddon* and *mawet* are applied respectively to the male and female powers of the demonic, Samael and his female cohort, the "primordial snake" (*naḥash qadma'ah*), the "woman of harlotry" (*eshet zenunim*), whose "feet descend down to death" (Prov. 5:5). In the fifth chapter of *Alef, Mem, Tau*, I exegete this turn on the path, which leads the mystic hermeneut, the *maskil*, in emulation of Jacob, "to draw near truth, the signet of the holy king," *le'itqarva ba-emet ḥotama de-malka qaddisha* (*Zohar*, 1:162a).

307. The identification of the heart and throne is a crucial dimension of Sufi piety and is well attested in medieval Jewish philosophic, poetic, and mystical works; see E. Wolfson, *Through a Speculum*, 178–80, in addition to which many more examples could be adduced as illustration of the motif.

308. My translation is based on the Hebrew text published in Moshe Idel, *Le Porte della Giustizia, Sa'are Ṣedeq* (Milan: Adelphi, 2001), 482; the Italian translation by Maurizio Mottolese appears on 424. See also *Sha'arei Sedeq: Be'ur Sefer Yeṣirah*, ed. Yosef E. Parush (Jerusalem: Sha'ar ha-Shamayim, 1989), 27. For alternative English renderings, see Scholem, *Major Trends*, 155; Idel, *Mystical Experience*, 108.

309. The breakdown of the inside-outside polarity is also expressed by Abulafia and the author of *Sha'arei Sedeq* (traceable to earlier figures—for example, Abraham Ibn Ezra) with respect to the source of prophetic speech: the divine word is conceived of as originating in the human heart, but the human heart does naught but reflect back the luster and timbre of the divine word; see Scholem, *Major Trends*, 141–42; Gershom Scholem, "Eine kabbalistische Erklärung der Prophetie als Selbstbegegnung," *Monatsschrift für Geschichte und Wissenschaft des Judentums* 74 (1930): 285–90. Some of the pertinent sources are cited and analyzed by Idel, *Mystical Experience*, 84–85, 89–91. It is relevant here to recall as well the discussion of *ek-stasis* in Martin Buber, *Ecstatic Confessions*, ed. Paul Mendes-Flohr, trans. Esther Cameron (San Francisco: Harper and Row, 1985), 2–3, 7, 8. Buber insightfully articulated the view that ecstasy is the turning inward that entails projection outward, indeed, because it is an experience (*Erlebnis*) of the "most inward" it is placed the "furthest outward," an experience of I cast as an experience of God; see Paul R. Mendes-Flohr, *From Mysticism to Dialogue: Martin Buber's Transformation of German Social Thought* (Detroit: Wayne State University Press, 1989), 62–66; Elliot R. Wolfson, "The Problem of Unity in the Thought of Martin Buber," *Journal of the History of Philosophy* 27 (1989): 423–44, esp. 424–28.

310. Heinrich Zimmer, "On the Significance of the Indian Tantric Yoga," in *Spiritual Disciplines: Papers from the Eranos Yearbook*, ed. Joseph Campbell (Princeton, N.J.: Princeton University Press, 1985), 13. The affinity between Yoga and Abulafian kabbalah, indeed the bold claim that prophetic kabbalah is, in truth, a "Judaized version" of Indian yogic practice, was proffered by

Scholem, *Major Trends*, 139, 144. Idel, *Mystical Experience*, 14, 24, notes other interesting similarities between the meditational practice of Abulafia and Yoga techniques of breathing; see, however, Idel's more cautionary attitude, 39–40.

311. My formulation is indebted to Richard E. Aquila, "Self as Matter and Form: Some Reflections on Kant's View of the Soul," in *Figuring the Self: Subject, Absolute, and Others in Classical German Philosophy*, ed. David E. Klemm and Günter Zöller (Albany: State University of New York Press, 1997), 31–54, esp. 44.

312. I translate from the text transcribed by Scholem, "Eine kabbalistische Erklärung," 287: "The enlightened sage [*he-ḥakham ha-maskil*], his honor, R. Nathan, blessed be his memory, said: Know that the perfection of the secret of prophecy for the prophet is when suddenly he sees the image of himself standing before him, and he forgets himself and it disappears from him, and he sees his image before him speaking to him and informing him of future events. Concerning this secret the sages, blessed be their memory, said [*Genesis Rabbah* 27:1, 255–56] 'Great is the power of the prophets for they compare the form to its creator.'" For an alternative English translation, see Scholem, *Major Trends*, 142. A version of the text was published in *Shoshan Sodot* (Korets, 1784), 69b, noted and cited by Idel, *Mystical Experience*, 91–92. According to the interpretation of the aggadic dictum transmitted in the name of R. Nathan, disciple of Abulafia and teacher of Isaac of Acre (see Idel, *Mystical Experience*, 91–92; Moshe Idel, *Studies in Ecstatic Kabbalah* [Albany: State University of New York Press, 1988], 73–89, 98n18, 149n42, 151nn61–62), the peak of prophecy consists of the spontaneous dissolution of the distinction between inside and outside: the form that the prophet sees communicating information about the future of his own image. It is worth comparing this feature of prophetic kabbalah to the description of the final stage of the mystical ideal set forth by Ibn Sīnā cited by Ibn Ṭufayl, *Story of Hayy ibn Yaqzān*, in Colville, *Two Andalusian Philosophers*, 4–5: "His deepest being becomes like a flawless mirror facing the truth.... At this level, he sees the truth and he sees his own soul—as it is seeing—and looks from one to the other. He then loses all consciousness of himself, seeing only paradise, and there achieves union."

313. Idel, *Le Porte della Giustizia*, 245–50.

314. It is likely that implied here is the identification of Torah and the Active Intellect, a central idea in Abulafian kabbalah. If this surmise is correct, then the symbol of *malbush* applies as well to the Active Intellect. A similar notion is expressed by Isaac Ibn Latif, *Sha'ar ha-Shamayim* (MS Vatican ebr. 335), fol. 28a, in his description of the Active Intellect, based in part on the depiction of Maimonides, *Mishneh Torah*, Yesodei ha-Torah 2:7: "Perhaps this tenth intellect is called '[the man] clothed in linen' [*levush ha-baddim*] (Dan. 12:6) on account of the fact that it clothes [*malbush*] form in matter and matter in form."

315. Abulafia, *Oṣar Eden Ganuz*, fol. 66b (printed ed., 132).

316. On the tension between the apophatic and kataphatic in Abulafia's treatises, see Wolfson, *Abraham Abulafia*, 152–77.

317. Maimonides, *Guide*, I:26, 56.

318. Abraham Abulafia, *Or ha-Sekhel* (MS Vatican, Biblioteca Apostolica 233), fol. 71b (printed ed., Jerusalem 2001, 70).

319. Abulafia, *Or ha-Sekhel*, fol. 72b (printed ed., 69).

320. Idel, *Language, Torah, Hermeneutics*, 34–38, 79, 163n33.

321. Here I take issue with Scholem's assessment in *Major Trends*, 139, of Abulafia's use of the "theory of prophecy" derived from medieval philosophical sources. For an elaboration of the difference in approach between Scholem and myself with regard to the relationship between philosophy and kabbalah, see Elliot R. Wolfson, "Hebraic and Hellenic Conceptions of Wisdom in *Sefer ha-Bahir*," *Poetics Today* 19 (1998): 151–56. For further references, see above, n. 56.

322. Scholem, *Major Trends*, 141. The staying power of this conception is reflected in a comment of the sixteenth-century homilist in Padua, Menaḥem ben Moses Rabba, *Beit Moʻed*, (Venice, 1605) 155a, interpreting the aggadic tradition attributed to R. Simai (Babylonian Talmud, Shabbat 88a) that when Israel responded to Moses "all that the Lord shall speak we shall do and we shall listen" (Exod. 24:7), "600,000 ministering angels affixed on each and every Israelite two crowns, one for 'we shall do' and one for 'we shall listen'": "This teaches us that Torah brings forth the potentiality of man to complete actuality until he is like an angel of the Lord, which is the Active Intellect [*sekhel ha-poʻel*]. And the proof that Israel acquired perfection [*sheleimut*] by means of Torah is that they became the Active Intellect to the point that even their matter was transformed into the intellectual [*maskil*], as if the two parts were one alone. . . . Thus they put 'we shall do' first, which is comparable to matter, to 'we shall listen,' which is comparable to intellect, and as a consequence they were like the angels in complete actuality."

323. Abulafia, *Or ha-Sekhel*, fol. 75a (printed ed., 72).

324. Here I have followed the reading preserved in the manuscript; the printed version reads *ṣiyyurit gashmit*, which should be translated as "corporeal image" (see next note for references).

325. Abulafia, *Ḥayyei ha-Olam ha-Ba* (MS Oxford, Bodleian Library 1582), fols. 4a–b (printed ed., Jerusalem, 2001, 48–49).

326. Wolfson, *Through a Speculum*, 160–81, esp. 166–67.

327. Abulafia, *Ḥayyei ha-Olam ha-Ba*, fols. 4b–5a (printed ed., 49).

328. Abulafia, *Sitrei Torah*, fol. 135b (printed ed., 73).

329. On the name YHWA, see Wolfson, *Through a Speculum*, 252n264.

330. Corbin, *Creative Imagination*, 22, 33, *passim*; see 27, where Corbin remarks that the "dominant" aspect of Shiʻite thought is "the idea of the Theophany in Human form, the divine anthropomorphosis which fills the gulf left open by abstract monotheism . . . the manifestation of the unknowable God in the angelic form of the celestial anthropos." This axiom of Islamic esotericism resonates with the figure of *Christos Angelos* in the angelomorphic Christology that has been traced to Jewish Christians in the formative period known in scholarly parlance as Christian origins; see Henry Corbin, *Le paradoxe du monothéisme* (Paris: Éditions de l'Herne, 1981), 83–96.

331. Corbin, *Creative Imagination*, 63. On the holy spirit and the anthropomorphic manifestation of the angel, see Corbin, *Paradoxe du monothéisme*, 50–63, 143–50. On Ibn Sīnā's *al-ḥikma al-mashriqīya*, see Gutas, *Avicenna and the Aristotelian Tradition*, 115–30; Dimitri Gutas, "Ibn Ṭufayl on Ibn Sīnā's Eastern Philosophy," *Oriens* 34 (1994): 222–41.

332. Corbin, *Creative Imagination*, 35, cites the exegesis of Jacob's contest with the angel (Gen. 32:25– 29) by the "Jewish mystic Joseph ben Judah," i.e., Joseph ben Judah Ibn Aqnin, as an example of the soul's quest for union with the Active Intellect, personified as the angel in the form of an anthropos. Corbin then makes the following remark: "A whole series of Jewish speculative mystics found the same symbolism in the *Song of Songs*, where the Beloved plays the role of the active Intelligence, while the heroine is the thinking human soul." In a manner far more astute than many scholars of medieval Jewish mysticism, Corbin insightfully discerned that the philosophical interpretation of the Song as a figurative account of the conjunction of the human and Active Intellect may be demarcated as a form of speculative mysticism.

333. Henry Corbin, *Avicenna and the Visionary Recital*, trans. Willard R. Trask (New York: Bollingen Foundation, 1960), 8; for more extensive discussion of the process of individuation and angelic epiphany, see 77–93.

334. Ibid., 19–20.

335. Abulafia, *Ḥayyei ha-Olam ha-Ba*, fol. 3b (printed ed., 47).

336. Scholem, *Major Trends*, 140; Idel, *Mystical Experience*, 116–19.

337. Abulafia, *Ḥayyei ha-Olam ha-Ba*, fol. 12a (printed ed., 63).

338. Abulafia, *Sitrei Torah*, fol. 155b (printed ed., pp. 139–140).

339. *Sefer Yeṣirah* 2:2. For further references to this motif in Abulafia's writings, see E. Wolfson, *Abraham Abulafia*, 141n127.

340. Wolfson, "Anthropomorphic Imagery," 155–58.

341. See Wolfson, *Through a Speculum*, 245n235.

342. A scriptural locution that appears in 1 Sam. 24:6, 10, 26:9, 11,16, 23; 2 Sam. 1:14, 16, 19:22; Lam. 4:20.

343. Gen. 21:17, 31:11; Exod. 14:19; Judg. 13:6, 9; 1 Sam. 29:9; 2 Sam. 14:17, 20, 19:28.

344. I propose that, for Abulafia, the title *sar ha-panim* signifies that Metatron is the angel within whom opposites cohere, a coherence—note that I speak of "coherence," not "coincidence" or "confluence"—that marks the unity of the divine vis-à-vis the world, the mystery of providence (*hanhagah*), which is related soterically to the mystical name of seventy-two letters, identified as the "thick cloud" (*av anan*) within and through which the divine was revealed to the Israelites at Sinai according to Exodus 19:9—the consonants of the word *av* have the numerical value of seventy-two. This is one of the principle secrets disclosed in Abulafia, *Ḥayyei ha-Olam ha-Ba*, fols. 3b–4a (printed ed., 47). The secret is implied in the grammatical oddity that the plural form *panim* ("faces") is the word for the singular "face." The two-faced nature of Metatron is expressed through various images scattered about in Abulafia's voluminous corpus: he is the secret of the Tree of Knowledge that comprises good and evil; Abulafia, *Oṣar Eden Ganuz*, fol. 64b; printed ed., p. 128); he bears the attributes of mercy and judgment; he is the balance that mediates between the side of merit, *kaf zekhut*, and the side of debt, *kaf ḥovah* (Abulafia, *Or ha-Sekhel*, fol. 185b; printed ed., p. 82); he appears as *na'ar* and *zaqen*, youth and elder—a symbolic configuration adduced exegetically from the verse "I was young and now I am old" (*na'ar hayyiti gam zaqanti*; Ps. 37:25) and instantiated in the image of the "spiritual mentor" who is visualized either as a young or as an old man (Scholem, *Major Trends*, 139–40; Idel, *Mystical Experience*, 117–18); it is worthwhile to underscore the comparative gesture on Scholem's part in his identifying the path laid out by Abulafia to be "a Judaized version of that ancient spiritual technique which has found its classical expression in the practices of the Indian mystics who follow the system known as *Yoga*," an insight embellished by Idel, *Mystical Experience*, 25–26. It behooves me to note that Idel's criticism of Scholem's referring to Abulafia's path as "magic" rather than "technique" (41) obviously needs to be modified in light of the aforecited comment. Beyond the ostensibly pedantic scholarly quibble over terminology, it is conceptually erroneous and misleading to present Scholem's discussion of Abulafia as if he did not appreciate the fact that the primary intent of the meditational path was internal transformation rather than external alteration); he is the first and last of the ten separate intellects or, alternatively expressed, the head and tail of the sefirotic edifice, *Keter* and *Malkhut*, the front and back (*panim we-aḥor*), the warp and woof (*sheti wa-erev*), also related respectively to the two names Israel and Jacob, *yisra'el* decoded as *lero'shi* ("to my head") and *ya'aqov* as *aqevi* ("my heel") (Abulafia, *Or ha-Sekhel*, fol. 97b; printed ed., p. 94); a conception doubtlessly suggested to Abulafia by the depiction of the *sefirot* in *Sefer Yeṣirah*, "the end is fixed in their beginning and their beginning in their end"; Wolfson, *Abraham Abulafia*, 83n264.

345. Babylonian Talmud, Sanhedrin 38b.

346. There is still much to be elicited from Hugo Odeberg's exhaustive philological and textual presentation of conceptions of Metatron in various genre of exoteric and esoteric Jewish texts in Hugo Odeberg, ed., *Enoch, or The Hebrew Book of Enoch* (Cambridge: Cambridge University Press, 1928), 79–146.

347. On the interposition of speech in between imagination and intellect, see Abraham Abulafia, *Ḥayyei ha-Nefesh* (MS Munich, Bayerische Staatsbibliothek 408), fol. 91a–b (printed ed., Jerusalem, 2001, 158), and discussion in Idel, "Abulafia's Secrets," 304–6.

348. Abulafia utilizes a common saying in medieval Hebrew texts, *ke-shemo ken hu*, that is, the name of a thing instructs one about the nature of the thing that is so named, which is based on a larger assumption regarding the homology of language and being.

349. On the nexus between imagination (*dimyon*), daemon, *mediyun* (medium) and the political (*medini*), see Idel, *Language, Torah, Hermeneutics*, 56–67. Idel cites the same passage from *Oṣar Eden Ganuz* (see below, n. 351), but offers a slightly different interpretation than my own.

350. See above, n. 116.

351. Abulafia, *Osar Eden Ganuz*, fols. 60a–b (printed ed., 120–21; discrepancies between my rendering and the published text can be accounted for by the fact that I translated from the manuscript).

352. I have found an interesting conceptual analogy in an account of the visionary meditation according to the Nyingmapa school of Tibetan Buddhism in the teachings of Dzogchen expounded by Garab Dorje. The relevant text occurs in the commentary to the third statement of "The Last Testament of Garab Dorje," in Garab Dorje, *The Golden Letters: The Three Statements of Garab Dorje, the First Teacher of Dzogchen, Together with a Commentary by Dza Patrul Rinpoche Entitled "The Special Teaching of the Wise and Glorious King,"* trans. John Myrdhin Reynolds (Ithaca, N.Y.: Snow Lion Publications, 1996), 164, but before I cite this passage, it would be helpful to the reader to summarize briefly the "secret of self-liberation" laid out in the first statement. The state of "immediate intrinsic Awareness" (*Rigpa*), the "Primordial Base or Dharmakaya" (130), is attained as a result of the Son (*bu*), symbolic of "knowledge or cognition (*ye-shes*) of the vision or phenomena directly," searching for and encountering the Mother (*ma*), "its source or origin." The Son's visionary encounter with the Mother, which is described both as the "immediate pure presence" (130) and as "emptiness" (132), occasions the process of self-liberation, that is, "the vision is self liberated by means of the vision, like melted butter dissolving into butter. . . . The Awareness itself is self-liberated by means of Awareness; just like water dissolving into water. When searching for the unique state (of Rigpa), one encounters only one's own unique state. That is to say, one's own nature (Rigpa) simply encounters itself. . . . If that is the case, then when one recognizes one's essence, everything is brought together in a single moment within which a cognition is present that does not go beyond the knowledge of that singular unique essence (which is Rigpa). This is like a man and woman who are in love and who meet together secretly in solitude in order to make love" (131–32). For discussion of this theme, see Donatella Rossi, *The Philosophical View of the Great Perfection in the Tibetan Bon Religion* (Ithaca, N.Y.: Snow Lion, 1999), 61–64, and references to other scholarly treatments at 61n184. The shift from the image of mother and son to man and woman is instructive and shares a basic similarity with the symbolic presentation of different phases of the unitive experience in kabbalistic tradition, but this is not the place to enter into detail on this matter. (For a discussion of some of the relevant issues, see the section titled "Spiritual Eroticism, Ascetic Renunciation, and the Eschatological Re/turn" in Wolfson, *Language, Eros, Being,* chap. 8, as well as my studies cited in chap. 8, n. 224.) What is significant to emphasize is the self-liberation of the Son through the visualization process that results in the overcoming of ontic difference, a return to the emptiness of the Mother, portrayed as butter dissolving into butter or water into water. Now we can appreciate the comment on the description of the "realization of the Body of Light" (*'od lus*) in the third statement: "And having such a concrete experience with respect to the state of liberation, one's confidence becomes like the experience of space dissolving into space. . . . In this unique state of immediate Awareness, everything is liberated into this single

understanding of the state of immediate intrinsic Awareness. This is like taking fire from fire, or like transferring water into water, or like adding melted butter to butter. Thus the Mother (the Primordial State) and her Son (knowledge) become united. Because one's own Mother, as the origin or source, is just itself (and nothing else, existing in its own state of existence, and this brings emptiness), one can say that emptiness itself is liberated by means of emptiness. Thus, one individual's presence of Awareness dissolves (at the time of the realization of the Body of Light) and becomes integrated into the vision itself" (134–35). Commenting on this statement, especially the opening part, and applying it to anyone seeking enlightenment, Reynolds writes, "When a Siddha, like the master Garab Dorje, attains the Body of Light, it appears as if the material body dissolves into the vast space of the sky, or else dissolves into pure radiant energy, the lights of the rainbow. Matter is transformed into energy, and this radiant energy remains the vehicle of awareness. . . . The Siddha, however, does not really ascend in a physical sense to some extraterrestrial heaven world—but simply returns to the center of his or her being, the Primordial State. The Siddha lives in the condition of the mirror, rather than in the reflections, the world illusion" (164). For an in-depth philosophical analysis, see Herbert V. Guenther, *Matrix of Mystery: Scientific and Humanistic Aspects of rDzogs-Chen Thought* (Boulder, Colo.: Shambhala, 1984); Herbert V. Guenther, *From Reductionism to Creativity: rDzogs-chen and the New Sciences of Mind* (Boston: Shambhala, 1989). I do not think it frivolous to compare the account in the prophetic kabbalah to this description: the visualization that is bestowed on one who attains the unitive experience with the divine intellect as a consequence of following the path of meditation entails seeing an external image of that reality as a projection of the internal; the mind, therefore, may be likened to a mirror empty of all form so that which is formless may assume form in the form that has been rendered formless by donning the luminous, angelic body.

353. See Corbin's depiction of the imaginal world, *'ālam al-mithāl*, in *Paradoxe du monothéisme*, 120: "le monde où se spiritualisent les corps et où se corporalisent les Espirits."

354. For a more literal understanding of "unveiling" in kabbalistic hermeneutics, see Rojtman, *Black Fire on White Fire*, 84–85. Rojtman cites a passage from Gikatilla that ostensibly presents a different model from zoharic literature, which affirms the act of disrobing or unveiling and the consequent seeing of the naked body or exposed face. However, see my comments on Gikatilla's text in "Occultation of the Feminine and the Body of Secrecy in Medieval Kabbalah," in *Rending the Veil: Concealment and Secrecy in the History of Religions*, ed. Elliot R. Wolfson (New York: Seven Bridges Press, 1999), 116n8, and chap. 7, nn. 246–47.

355. *Zohar Ḥadash*, 73b; Liebes, *Sections of the Zohar Lexicon Language, Eros, Being*, 230.

356. Mishnah, Ḥagigah 1:8;Tosefta, Shabbat 2:10; Babylonian Talmud, Berakhot 63a, Shabbat 32a, Ḥagigah 11b; Ḥullin 60b, Keritut 5a; *Sifra de-vei Rav*, Qedoshim 1:1, 86a; *Leviticus Rabbah* 24:5, 557; *Numbers Rabbah* 13:15; *Avot de-Rabbi Natan*, version A, chap. 27, 84. On occasion we find in rabbinic literature the expression *gufei halakhot*, literally "bodies of the laws," which is more or less synonymous with *gufei torah*; see Mishnah, Avot 3:18; Tosefta, Eruvin 11:24, Ḥagigah 1:9; *Avot de-Rabbi Natan*, version A, chap. 27, 84.

357. The zoharic formulation is also based on metaphorical depictions of letters as the body and vowels as the soul that are widespread in medieval Hebrew texts; see Liebes, *Sections of the Zohar Lexicon*, 174–76.

358. Wolfson, "Occultation," 124–35.

359. Jacob Katz, *Exclusiveness and Tolerance: Studies in Jewish-Gentile Relations in Medieval and Modern Times* (Oxford: Oxford University Press, 1961), 22–23.

360. Liebes, *Sections of the Zohar Lexicon*, 173–74, already suggested that the use of the term *gufa* ("body") to refer to Torah in some zoharic texts might reflect the influence of the Christian

idea of *corpus mysticum*. On the phenomenological use of the term "docetic" to demarcate the image of the body that is real, an interpretative stance that is commensurate with my own, see Natalie Depraz, "Phénoménologie et docétisme: L'apparaître charnel," in *La gnose, une question philosophique: Pour une phénoménologie de l'invisible*, ed. Natalie Depraz and Jean-François Marquet (Paris: Éditions du Cerf, 2000), 87–105.

361. Liebes, *Studies in the Zohar*, 103–10.

362. The reference is to the commentary by Naḥmanides on Deut. 27:26. See Moses ben Naḥman, *Perushei ha-Torah le-R. Mosheh be Naḥman*, 2 vols., ed. Ḥayyim D. Chavel (Jerusalem: Mosad ha-Rav Kook, 1959–60), 2:472. The earlier rabbinic source cited by Naḥmanides as a basis for the custom to lift the Torah scroll is *Massekhet Soferim*, ed. Michael Higger (New York: Debe Rabbanan, 1937), 14:8, 261–62.

363. Joseph of Hamadan, "A Critical Edition of the *Sefer Ṭa'amey ha-Miẓwoth* (Book of Reasons of the Commandments) Attributed to Isaac Ibn Farḥi. Section I—Positive Commandments with Introduction and Notes," Menachem Meier (PhD diss., Brandeis University, 1974), 58.

364. Moshe Idel, "Torah: Between Presence and Representation of the Divine in Jewish Mysticism," in *Representation in Religion: Studies in Honor of Moshe Barasch*, ed. Jan Assmann and Albert I. Baumgarten (Leiden: E. J. Brill, 2001), 197–236; Idel, *Absorbing Perfections*, 69–74, 76.

365. Joseph of Hamadan, *Sefer Tashak*, xx.

366. Ibid., 13.

367. Ibid., 72.

368. Wolfson, "Ontology," 138–40.

369. *Zohar*, 3:73a.

370. Liebes, *Sections of the Zohar Lexicon*, 400–1; Tishby, *Wisdom of the Zohar*, 1086; Tishby, *Studies in Kabbalah*, 941–60; Beracha Sack, *The Kabbalah of Rabbi Moshe Cordovero* (Hebrew) (Jerusalem: Bialik Institute, 1995), 103–9; Moshe Idel, "Two Remarks on R. Yair ben Sabbatai's Sefer Ḥerev Piffiyot" (Hebrew), *Qiryat Sefer* 53 (1979): 213–14; Idel, *Absorbing Perfections*, 20, 99–101, 118–119, 349, 497n 49.

371. A similar esoteric explanation for the obligation incumbent upon every male Jew to write a Torah scroll, which represents the "shape" of God, is offered by the anonymous author of *Sefer ha-Yiḥud*, a kabbalistic treatise, more or less, from the period of the *Zohar*. For citation of the relevant passage, see Moshe Idel, "The Concept of Torah in Hekhalot Literature and Its Metamorphosis in Kabbalah" (Hebrew), *Jerusalem Studies in Jewish Thought* 1 (1981): 62–64; Idel, "Infinities," 145; Idel, *Absorbing Perfections*, 70.

372. Joseph of Hamadan, "Critical Edition of the *Sefer Ṭa'amey ha-Miẓwoth*," 78–80.

373. See, for example, *Zohar*, 3:170a; Tishby, *Wisdom of the Zohar*, 764–65.

374. Bezalel Safran, "Rabbi Azriel and Naḥmanides: Two Views of the Fall of Man," in *Rabbi Moses Naḥmanides (Ramban): Exploration in His Religious and Literary Virtuosity*," ed. Isadore Twersky (Cambridge, Mass.: Harvard University Press, 1983), 75–106.

375. Idel, *Kabbalah: New Perspectives*, 184–85; Elliot R. Wolfson, "Mystical Rationalization of the Commandments in *Sefer ha-Rimmon*," *Hebrew Union College Annual* 59 (1988): 231–35.

376. The kabbalistic representation of Torah as body is supported by the idea that the 248 positive commandments correspond to the 248 limbs, and the 365 negative commandments, to the 365 sinews. This formulation is a modification of the tradition attributed to R. Simlai (Babylonian Talmud, Makkot 23b), according to which the 248 positive commandments correspond to the limbs and the 365 negative commandments to the days of the year; see Scholem, *On the Kabbalah and Its Symbolism*, 128. It is worth noting, however, that the 248 limbs and 365 sinews are mentioned in Targum Pseudo-Jonathan to Genesis 1:27 as an explication of the "divine image" with

which Adam was created; see Wolfson, "Mystical Rationalization," 231n78. Concerning Simlai's dictum and particularly its impact on select medieval Jewish philosophers, see Arthur Hyman, "Rabbi Simlai's Saying and Belief concerning God," in *Perspectives on Jewish Thought and Mysticism,* ed. Alfred L. Ivry, Elliot R. Wolfson, and Alan Arkush (Amsterdam: Harwood Academic, 1998), 49–62.

377. Stephen D. Benin, *The Footprints of God: Divine Accommodation in Jewish and Christian Thought* (Albany: State University of New York Press, 1993), 147–62.

378. It is also possible to explain this matter in terms of the distinction between spiritual and corporeal substance, a Neoplatonic motif that was known by kabbalists in Provence and Northern Spain. If we adopt this hermeneutical framework, we could say that for kabbalists the mystery of incarnation entails the transformation of the former into the latter, a transformation facilitated by the mystical conversion of the latter into the former. See discussion of a similar theme in Mohamed A. Alibhai, "The Transformation of Spiritual Substance into Bodily Substance in Isma'ili Neoplatonism," in *Neoplatonism and Islamic Thought,* ed. Parviz Morewedge (Albany: State University of New York Press, 1992), 167–77.

379. On the use of poetry as a literary model to articulate an incarnational language from within a Christological framework, see Kathleen Norris, "A Word Made Flesh: Incarnational Language and the Writer," in *The Incarnation: An Interdisciplinary Symposium on the Incarnation of the Son of God,* ed. Stephen T. Davis, Daniel Kendall, and Gerald O'Collins (Oxford: Oxford University Press, 2002), 303–12.

380. The point was well grasped in the lecture "The Kabbalah," by Jorge Luis Borges, in *Seven Nights,* trans. Eliot Weinberger, intro. Alastair Reid (New York: New Directions, 1984), 95–98: "The diverse, and occasionally contradictory, teachings grouped under the name of the Kabbalah derive from a concept alien to the Western mind, that of the sacred book. . . . The idea is this: the Pentateuch, the Torah, is a sacred book. An infinite intelligence has condescended to the human task of producing a book. The Holy Spirit has condescended to literature which is as incredible as imagining that God condescended to become a man." For extended discussion of the kabbalistic influence on Borges, see Saúl Sosnowski, *Borges y la Cabala: La búsqueda del verbo* (Buenos Aires: Pardés Ediciones, 1986).

381. Focusing primarily on passages in the *oeuvre* of Ezra of Gerona, Moshe Idel, "Some Remarks on Ritual and Mysticism in Geronese Kabbalah," *Journal of Jewish Thought and Philosophy* 3 (1993): 111–30, has argued that we need to consider the kabbalistic approach to ritual without being burdened by a negative assessment of rabbinic halakhah as demythologized legalism, on one hand, and by an overemphasis on a symbolic narrative of a gnostic nature, on the other. I am in general agreement with this contention, but I would argue that in the final analysis, the spiritualized understanding of ritual cannot be separated from the theosophic orientation and its implicit theurgy. Using anthropological terminology that Idel himself summons, one could counter that the sensory and ideological poles of ritual should be examined in a manner that avoids polarization, that is, the efficacy of the performance of a commandment cannot be entertained without assuming an underlying symbolic-mythic complex that explains the dynamics of the world order. For Ezra to claim that one is immersed in the divine light as a consequence of fulfilling the ritual is dependent on a certain presupposition regarding the mechanics of being, which is connected in turn to a particular theosophy and its accompanying symbolism. To be sure, Idel himself ("Some Remarks," 120–21) asserts that the somatic experience of being enveloped by the light of the commandments is related to Ezra's theosophic conception of the divine attributes "arranged in an anthropomorphic order." Nevertheless, he concludes, Ezra "attempted to convey his understand-

ing of the effect of the commandments in terms that are not symbolic but strive to point to the efficacy of the ritual in terms understandable to his contemporaries." Even if the matter of intentionality (*kawwanah*) is not stated explicitly, it is valid to assume that Ezra would have presumed that the experience of conjunction is not possible if one is not cognizant of the technicalities of the theosophic drama. Indeed, his imparting the wisdom of kabbalah is intended to provide the informational data necessary for one to cultivate the proper intention.

382. *Kitvei Ramban*, 2:497. Some of the passages from Ezra have been cited previously by Daniel C. Matt, "The Mystic and the *Miẓwot*," in *Jewish Spirituality from the Bible through the Middle Ages*, ed. Arthur Green (New York: Crossroad, 1986), 378, but in this study all translations are my own. For a more recent discussion of the role of ritual practice in Ezra's kabbalah, including a critical edition and translation of the section of his *Perush Shir ha-Shirim* that deals extensively with the commandments, see Yacov M. Travis, "Kabbalistic Foundations of Jewish Spiritual Practice: Rabbi Ezra of Gerona on the Kabbalistic Meaning of the Mizvot" (PhD diss., Brandeis University, 2002). I thank the author for providing me with a copy of his work. The passage I cite occurs on p. 4 of the Hebrew section and the author's independent translation on p. 175 of the English section.

383. For explication of this theme, see Moshe Idel, "In the Light of Life: A Study of Kabbalistic Eschatology," in *Sanctity of Life and Martyrdom: Studies in Memory of Amir Yekutiel* (Hebrew), ed. Isaiah M. Gafni and Aviezer Ravitzky (Jerusalem: Zalman Shazar Center for Jewish History, 1992), 192–98; Idel, "Some Remarks," 118–19.

384. *Kitvei Ramban*, 2:528–29. Ezra alludes in this passage to the aggadic tradition transmitted in the name of R. Sheila that two ministering angels (*mal'akhei ha-sharet*) accompany a person (Babylonian Talmud, Ta'anit 11a). The full intent of the kabbalistic embellishment of the rabbinic teaching is made clear in Azriel of Gerona's explication of R. Sheila's dictum in his *Commentary on Talmudic Aggadoth*, 32–33.

385. Mopsik, *Grands textes*, 116–19. According to Mopsik's interpretation of the text of Ezra, the "theosophic signification" is secondary to the primary emphasis on the "identity between the concrete rite and the divine reality" (117). Pedaya, *Vision and Speech*, 150n27, similarly argues that mystical conjunction and theurgy should not be seen in a causal manner but rather as two aspects of the one prophetic experience of ecstasy. Though my work is not cited by her in this context, I too have emphasized the need to view the theurgical and mystical as two facets of a phenomenon that I have designated as ecstatic; see Elliot R. Wolfson, "Forms of Visionary Ascent as Ecstatic Experience in the Zoharic Literature," in *Gershom Scholem's Major Trends in Jewish Mysticism 50 Years After: Proceedings of the Sixth International Conference on the History of Jewish Mysticism*, ed. Peter Schäfer and Joseph Dan (Tübingen: J. C. B. Mohr, 1993), 209–35, esp. 219–21, and Wolfson, *Through a Speculum*, 374, "It is necessary to reintegrate the theurgical and mystical elements of the religious experience of the kabbalist, for it makes no sense to speak of effecting the nature of God if one is not experiencing God in some immediate and direct sense." The point was made forcefully in the dissertation by Brody, "Human Hands," 249–50: "The theurgic efficacy of a ritual act is profoundly intertwined with the Kabbalist's attainment of mystical adhesion, howsoever that might be conceived"; and the summary account on 396: "Careful analysis of many of our sources has consequently indicated that the transformative and theurgic sides of Kabbalistic experience and practice are all but inseparably interlinked. Contemporary scholarly literature has been far too facile in its differentiation between the 'mystical' and the 'theurgic' aspects of spiritual praxis, as if they represented two distinct foci of Kabbalistic interest and endeavor. On the contrary, they represent the two sides of a unified spiritual enterprise." On the interface of theurgic activity and mystical union as two stages of unification, see also Goldberg, "Mystical Union," 7–12, 83n31.

386. From here until the end of this sentence is lacking in the printed text; my translation is based on MS Oxford, Bodleian 1947, fol. 26b.

387. That is, "righteousness" is a technical term for *Malkhut* or *Shekhinah*, and hence the force of Ezra's exegesis of the verse "his righteousness lasts forever" (Ps. 112:9) is that the last of the emanations acts as a magnet to draw the disembodied soul back into the divine realm.

388. Mishnah, Avot 5:2; *Avot de-Rabbi Natan*, version A, chap. 25, 81.

389. The kabbalists utilize the rabbinic distinction between the "speculum that shines" and the "speculum that does not shine" (Babylonian Talmud, Yevamot 49b) to characterize respectively the sixth and tenth emanations, the masculine *Tif'eret* and the feminine *Malkhut*.

390. Mishnah, Avot 1:3.

391. *Liqquṭei Shikheḥah u-Fe'ah*, 17b–18a. The concluding phrase "it is not so" is a translation of the version in MS Oxford, Bodleian 1947, fol. 27a, *eino khen*. The printed text here reads *setumim*, which means "closed," an obvious corruption.

392. *Kitvei Ramban*, 2:538.

393. See above, n. 376.

394. Note the variant reading in MS Vatican 211, fol. 24b, *yihyeh ha-guf we-ha-neshamah shawin* ("the body and soul will be equal").

395. This is the reading in the printed text by Chavel as well as the *editio princeps* (Altona 1764, 16a), but note the variant *binyan elohi* in MS Leiden, Warner 32, fol. 23a, cited and discussed by Scholem, *On the Kabbalah and Its Symbolism*, 44–45. In the German version of this essay included in Gershom Scholem, *Zur Kabbalah und ihrer Symbolik* (Zurich: Rhein, 1960), 65, the reading is *binyan elohi*, as we find in the English translation. However, in the Hebrew edition, Gershom Scholem, *Pirqei Yesod be-Havanat ha-Qabbalah u-Semaleha*, trans. Joseph Ben-Shlomo (Jerusalem: Bialik Institute, 1977), 47, the expression is transcribed as *binyan eloha*. Idel, "Concept of Torah," 49n81, follows this emendation. The reading *binyan elohi* is confirmed in the manuscript version of Ezra's commentary transcribed in Tishby, *Mishnat ha-Zohar*, 2 vols. (Jerusalem: Bialik Institute, 1975), 2:366; for English translation, see Tishby, *Wisdom of the Zohar*, 1080.

396. On the identification of Torah as the name of God, see the statement from Ezra's *Perush ha-Aggadot* in *Liqquṭei Shikheḥah u-Fe'ah*, 19b, cited in Tishby, *Wisdom of the Zohar*, 1080.

397. *Kitvei Ramban*, 2:548.

398. See, for instance, Scholem, "Name of God," 165; and Scholem, *On the Kabbalah and Its Symbolism*, 35–36.

399. The original text is transcribed in Scholem, *Pirqei Yesod*, 196. For an alternative translation and analysis, see Gershom Scholem, *On the Mystical Shape of the Godhead: Basic Concepts in the Kabbalah*, trans. Ralph Manheim (New York: Schocken Books, 1969), 68–71.

400. It is of interest to compare the kabbalistic *guf ruḥani* to the depiction of the spirit (*al-rūḥ*) as a "subtle body" (*jismī laṭīf*) in Nicholson, *Kashf al-Maḥjūb*, 262; see also the account of al-Ghazālī's view regarding resurrection of the body in Ibn Rushd, *Averroës' Tahafut al-Tahafut*, 362: "it must be assumed that what arises from the dead is simulacra of these earthly bodies, not these bodies themselves, for that which has perished does not return individually and a thing can only return as an image of that which has perished, not as a being identical with what has perished." On the pneumatic or astral body, composed of air or fire, see Plotinus, *Enneads* III.5.6. On the daemonic body composed of fire, see Iamblichus, *De mysteriis*, trans. Emma C. Clarke, John M. Dillon, and Jackson P. Hershbell (Atlanta: Society of Biblical Literature, 2003), 12:246–47. The language in the *Tahafut al-Tahafut* by Averroës bears an evocative similarity to terminology employed by thirteenth-century kabbalists, attested especially in the zoharic compilation; see Scholem, *On the Mystical Shape*, 260–72. For a detailed analysis of al-Ghazālī's mystical eschatology, see Timothy J. Gianotti,

Al-Ghazālī's Unspeakable Doctrine of the Soul: Unveiling the Esoteric Psychology and Eschatology of the Ihya' (Leiden: Brill, 2001).

401. This is based on a rabbinic exegesis of Genesis 3:21; see *Genesis Rabbah* 20:12, 196–97; Gary A. Anderson, "The Garments of Skin in Apocryhphal Narrative and Biblical Commentary," in *Studies in Ancient Midrash*, ed. James L. Kugel (Cambridge, Mass.: Harvard University Press, 2001), 101–43; Gary A. Anderson, *The Genesis of Perfection: Adam and Eve in Jewish and Christian Imagination* (Louisville: Westminster John Knox Press, 2001), 117–34; see also S. N. Lambden, "From Fig Leaves to Fingernails: Some Notes on the Garments of Adam and Eve in the Hebrew Bible and Select Early Postbiblical Jewish Writings," in *A Walk in the Garden: Biblical, Iconographical, and Literary Images of Eden*, ed. Philip Morris and Deborah Sawyer (Sheffield: JSOT Press, 1992), 74–90; Stephen D. Ricks, "The Garment of Adam in Jewish, Muslim, and Christian Tradition," in *Judaism and Islam: Boundaries, Communication, and Interaction: Essays in Honor of William M. Brinner*, ed. Benjamin. H. Hary, John L. Hayes, and Fred Astren (Leiden: Brill, 2000), 203–25.

402. For this useful terminology I am indebted to Avraham Elqayam, "Between Referentialism and Performativism: Two Approaches in Understanding the Kabbalistic Symbol" (Hebrew), *Da'at* 24 (1990): 5–40.

403. To understand the wordplay in Azriel's comment, one must bear in mind that the custom among pious Jews is to refer to God as *ha-shem*, which literally means "the name," an honorific title that alludes to the Tetragrammaton, the most sacred divine name. As Tishby remarks in Azriel of Gerona, *Commentary on Talmudic Aggadoth*, 37n9 (in the name of Scholem), the source for this formulation is the older Heikhalot literature. See also Scholem, *On the Kabbalah and Its Symbolism*, 44.

404. Azriel is here interpreting a rabbinic passage that deals with the placing of dust on a Torah scroll (Babylonian Talmud, Ta'anit 16a).

405. Based on Ps. 19:8.

406. Azriel of Gerona, *Commentary on Talmudic Aggadoth*, 37. On the equation of Torah and the name, compare Azriel, *Perush ha-Tefillah*, MS Oxford-Bodleian 1938, fol. 206a: "'The Torah of the Lord is his delight' (Ps. 1:2), for this is the knowledge of his name [*yedi'at shemo*]"; see Gabrielle Sed-Rajna, *Commentaire sur la liturgie quotidienne, introduction, traduction annotée et glossaire des termes techniques* (Leiden: E. J. Brill, 1974), 46; Azriel of Gerona, *Perush ha-Tefillah: A Critical Edition of MS Ferrera 1*, ed. Martel Gavarin (MA thesis, Hebrew University, 1984), 11.

407. This usage is attested in *Zohar*, 3:152a, where, in the schematization of four levels of meaning, the commandments are referred to as "bodies of Torah" beneath the garments, which are the scriptural narratives. Liebes, *Studies in Zohar*, 181n133, concludes that in this zoharic passage those involved with practical commandments are accorded a lower status than those engaged in kabbalah. While there is surely a hierarchical delineation of the four levels at work here, I would be loath to express matters in the way suggested by Liebes. Just as garment, body, soul, and soul of souls coalesce to form an organic unity in which no layer is dispensable, so the stories, laws, mystical secrets, and messianic mysteries cohere together in one textual organism; see also Liebes, *Sections of the Zohar Lexicon*, 173.

408. Here it seems that Azriel is using the expression *gufei torah* both in the traditional sense to denote the fundamentals of Torah and in the kabbalistic sense as the corporeal form of Torah, which is the incarnation of God or the embodiment of the name.

409. Azriel of Gerona, *Commentary on Talmudic Aggadoth*, 37–39. In his *Perush ha-Tefillah*, fol. 206a, Azriel writes that one must be engaged in observing the commandments "to extend his imaginings and all his thoughts in the reasons for the law [*ta'amei torah*] for there is an abundance of holiness [*tosefet qiddush*] in them" (Sed-Rajna, *Commentaire*, 45).

410. *Kitvei Ramban*, 1:203.

411. *Sefer Yeṣirah*, 6:4. The slight variations probably do not reflect an alternative text in the possession of Naḥmanides but rather the fact that he was recalling the passage from memory, as was the custom of Jewish learning in the Middle Ages.

412. Moses ben Naḥman, *Perushei ha-Torah*, 1:494 (ad Exod. 30:19).

413. *Kitvei Ramban*, 2:513, slightly emended according to MS Vatican 211, fol. 26a.

414. Moses ben Naḥman, *Perushei ha-Torah*, 2:115–116 (ad Lev. 19:2); Safran, "Rabbi Azriel and Naḥmanides," 82–106; Chayim Henoch, *Ramban: Philosopher and Kabbalist: On the Basis of His Exegesis to the Mitzvoth* (Northvale, N.J.: Jason Aronson, 1998), 98–100; and the detailed analysis of asceticism and the transformation of the body in Jonathan Feldman, "The Power of the Soul over the Body: Corporeal Transformation and Attitudes towards the Body in the Thought of Naḥmanides" (PhD diss., New York University, 1999). On the modified asceticism of Naḥmanides, which includes codifying sexual restraint as part of the command to be holy, see Feldman's discussion, 106–22.

415. Moses ben Naḥman, *Perushei ha-Torah*, 2:395 (ad Deut. 11:22); see the pertinent comments of Scholem, *Messianic Idea*, 204–5.

416. Moses ben Naḥman, *Perushei ha-Torah*, 2:100 (ad Lev. 18:4).

417. Naḥmanides distinguishes between the righteous (*ṣaddiq*) and the pious (*ḥasid*): The former cleaves to *shem ha-meyuḥad*, the Tetragrammaton, presumably a reference to *Tif'eret*, the sixth emanation, and the latter to *shem ha-nikhbad*, the epithet Adonai, which is linked symbolically to *Shekhinah*; see Safran, "Rabbi Azriel and Naḥmanides," 83–85, 102n101; Idel, *Kabbalah: New Perspectives*, 46; Elliot R. Wolfson, "'By Way of Truth': Aspects of Naḥmanides' Kabbalistic Hermeneutic," *AJS Review* 14 (1989): 151–53 and sources cited on 152n141.

418. Moses ben Naḥman, *Perushei ha-Torah*, 1:275–76 (ad Gn 49:33).

419. See Elliot R. Wolfson, "The Secret of the Garment in Naḥmanides," *Da'at* 24 (1990): xl. For extended discussion of the eschatological motif of the "rabbinic garment," see Gershom Scholem, "The Paradise Garb of Souls and the Origin of the Concept of Ḥaluqa de-Rabbanan" (Hebrew) *Tarbiẓ* 24 (1955): 290–306; and Scholem, *On the Mystical Shape*, 264–65.

420. Moses ben Naḥman, *Perushei ha-Torah*, 1:6–7. For a parallel, albeit in a considerably different terminological register, see the sermon of Naḥmanides, *Torat ha-Shem Teminah*, in *Kitvei Ramban*, 1:167–68. The view I have expressed here is a modification of my remarks concerning the relationship of the exoteric and esoteric understanding of the text as hermeneutically elaborated by Naḥmanides in E. Wolfson, "By Way of Truth," 117n44. For a different understanding of the two readings proffered by Naḥmanides, see Scholem, *On the Kabbalah and Its Symbolism*, 38–39; Scholem, "Name of God," 77–79; Idel, "Concept of Torah," 52–55; Idel, *Absorbing Perfections*, 322. On the aggadic image of the primordial Torah being inscripted as black fire upon white fire in Jewish mystical hermeneutics, see Scholem, *On the Kabbalah and Its Symbolism*, 48–49; Idel, "Concept of Torah," 43–45; Idel, *Absorbing Perfections*, 45–69.

421. Wolfson, "Secret of the Garment," xli–xlii; Wolfson, *Through a Speculum*, 63–64. On the glorious angel in Naḥmanidean kabbalah, see the text translated by Scholem, *On the Mystical Shape*, 171. For discussion of this motif in thirteenth-century kabbalistic literature, see Scholem, *Origins*, 184–87, 214–16; Scholem, *On the Mystical Shape*, 186–87. On the centrality of this theme as an ancient trope of Jewish esotericism, see Wolfson, *Through a Speculum*, 184n247, 216, 224–28, 255–63, 310n147, 312–13, and the summary account offered by Moshe Idel, *Messianic Mystics* (New Haven, Conn.: Yale University Press, 1998), 85.

422. Moses ben Naḥman, *Perushei ha-Torah*, 2:395 (ad Deut. 11:22).

423. *Kitvei Ramban*, 2:303.

424. Ibid., 2:304–5.

425. Babylonian Talmud, Yoma 75b.

426. Moses ben Naḥman, *Perushei ha-Torah*, 1:365 (ad Exod. 16:6). For a parallel explanation in *Sha'ar ha Gemul*, see *Kitvei Ramban*, 2:305.

427. Babylonian Talmud, Berakhot 17a.

428. Moses ben Naḥman, *Perushei ha-Torah*, 1:365 (ad Exod. 16:6). For discussion of the manna and bodily transformation in Naḥmanides, see Feldman, "Power of the Soul," 195–210.

429. Wolfson, *Through a Speculum*, 361–63 (the passage from Naḥmanides is cited on 361n122); Elliot R. Wolfson, "Coronation of the Sabbath Bride: Kabbalistic Myth and the Ritual of Androgynisation," *Journal of Jewish Thought and Philosophy* 6 (1997): 335–42.

430. *Kitvei Ramban*, 1:304.

431. Ira Chernus, *Mysticism in Rabbinic Judaism: Studies in the History of Midrash* (Berlin: Walter de Gruyter, 1982), 83–86; E. Wolfson, *Through a Speculum*, 42–43.

432. Samuel Krauss, *The Jewish-Christian Controversy: From the Earliest Times to 1789*, vol. 1: *History*, ed. and rev. William Horbury (Tübingen: J. C. B. Mohr, 1995), 70, 229, 238.

433. Feldman, "Power of the Soul," 197n2, raises the issue of a contemporary Christian influence on Naḥmanides. In his opinion, however, this possibility should not be overemphasized, given the earlier rabbinic sources whence Naḥmanides derived his ideas. I would be less hesitant to stress the Christological affinities, as the likelihood of older sources influencing Naḥmanides does not preempt or preclude contemporary analogues. On the appropriation of the Christian symbol of the consecrated Host in a Jewish context, inspired in part by kabbalistic imagery, see the illuminating study by Michael Batterman, "Bread of Affliction, Emblem of Power: The Passover Matzah in Haggadah Manuscripts from Christian Spain," in *Imagining the Self, Imagining the Other: Visual Representation and Jewish-Christian Dynamics in the Middle Ages and Early Modern Period*, ed. Eva Frojmovic (Leiden: Brill, 2002), 53–89. For representative discussions of the variegated symbolism pertaining to the mystery of the Eucharist, see Piero Camporesi, "The Consecrated Host: A Wondrous Excess," in *Fragments for a History of the Human Body, Part One*, ed. Michel Feher with Ramona Naddaff and Nadia Tazi (New York: Zone, 1989), 221–37; Power, *Eucharistic Mystery*; Bynum, *Resurrection of the Body*, 156–99.

434. For a representative study of this theme in Islamic thought, with special emphasis on Isma'ili Neoplatonism, see Alibhai, "Transformation of Spiritual Substance," 167–77.

435. Michael Camille, "Image and the Self: Unwriting Late Medieval Bodies," in *Framing Medieval Bodies*, ed. Sarah Kay and Miri Rubin (Manchester: Manchester University Press, 1994), 62–99, esp. 74–77; see also Willemien Otten, "The Parallelism of Nature and Scripture: Reflections on Eriugena's Incarnational Exegesis," in *Iohannes Scottus Eriugena: The Bible and Hermeneutics: Proceedings of the Ninth International Colloquium of the Society for the Promotion of Eriugenian Studies Held at Leuven and Louvain-la-Neuve June 7–10, 1995*, ed. Gerd Van Riel, Carlos Steel, and James McEvoy (Leuven: University Press, 1996), 81–102.

436. Idel, "Some Remarks," 120–21, compares Ezra's description of the one who fulfills the commandments being encompassed by light and donning the pure and holy body to the Christian notion of the aura that encircles the body of Christ, known as the *mandorla*. In my opinion, this is a very evocative suggestion that is corroborated by the independent approach I have taken. Mention here should also be made of Sendor's observation, "Emergence," 1:154–64, that the discussion of the unity of the divine in early Provençal kabbalists such as Isaac the Blind and his nephew Asher ben David should be seen as responding to the apparent polytheism implied by the Neoplatonist doctrine of the primordial causes of John Scotus Eriugena. On the charge of the doctrinal

similarity of kabbalah and Christianity leveled at kabbalists by opponents in the thirteenth century and the possible impact this may have had on Isaac, see Sendor, "Emergence," 1:164–67.

437. *Zohar*, 2:60b, 87a, 90b, 3:13b, 19a, 21a, 35b–36a, 73a, 89b, 98b, 159a, 265b, 298b; Scholem, *On the Kabbalah and Its Symbolism*, 44; Idel, "Concept of Torah," 58–73; Tishby, *Wisdom of the Zohar*, 284, 293–94, 1086; Mopsik, *Grands textes*, 278–80; and Elliot R. Wolfson, "The Mystical Significance of Torah-Study in German Pietism," *Jewish Quarterly Review* 84 (1993): 59–60.

438. *Zohar*, 2:60b.

439. For discussion of these associations and citation of some relevant sources, see Wolfson, "Mystical Rationalization," 224–25 and the accompanying notes.

440. *Zohar*, 2:90b.

441. *Zohar*, 3:89b. In my judgment, the full force of the claim made in numerous zoharic passages and corroborated from the words of other kabbalists from this period is that the incarnation of the divine in the Torah scroll is to be understood ontologically. Consider, by way of contrast, the assessment in Paul Rorem, *Biblical and Liturgical Symbols within the Pseudo-Dionysian Synthesis* (Toronto: Pontifical Institute of Mediaeval Studies, 1984), 66: "For Dionysius, the divine procession 'down' to the scriptures and the liturgy is not an ontological bestowal of being, as in some Neoplatonists, but more a matter of revelation and manifestation. In itself, the divine is absolutely transcendent and unknowable." In the kabbalistic sources with which I am engaged, I see no justification in distinguishing between the *substantial presence* of God in the letters of the text and his disclosure.

442. Regarding this theme, see Wolfson, "Mystical Significance," 69–72; Elliot R. Wolfson, "Gender and Heresy in the Study of Kabbalah" (Hebrew), *Kabbalah: Journal for the Study of Jewish Mystical Texts* 6 (2001): 252n107; and Wolfson, "Before Alef," 146–50.

443. See Elliot R. Wolfson, *Along the Path: Studies in Kabbalistic Myth, Symbolism, and Hermeneutics* (Albany: State University of New York Press, 1995), 242n114.

444. On the symbolic background for this symbolism, see Elliot R. Wolfson, "Images of God's Feet: Some Observations on the Divine Body in Judaism," in *People of the Body: Jews and Judaism from an Embodied Perspective*, ed. Howard Eilberg-Schwartz (Albany: State University of New York Press, 1992), 143–81.

445. For references, see Wolfson, *Abraham Abulafia*, 154n28.

446. The orthography of the letter was also the subject of midrashic interpretation. For a sampling of sources, see Wolfson, "Before Alef," 154n33.

447. *Gagin*, literally, "roofs," but one of the connotations of this term attested already in rabbinic literature is the orthographic line that is part of the letter (see, for example, Babylonian Talmud, Shabbat 104b).

448. *Zohar*, 3:36a.

449. Liebes, *Sections of the Zohar Lexicon*, 401, suggests that heaven, earth, and the divine mediating between them, symbolized by the three lines of the *beit*, may correspond to *Binah* and *Malkhut* with *Tif'eret* in the middle, an interpretation found in the traditional commentary on *Zohar* by Shalom Buzaglo, *Miqdash Melekh ha-Shalem*, 5 vols. (Jerusalem: Makhon Benei Yissarchar, 1995–2000), 3:60. Implied in this approach is the belief that the opinion attributed to R. Eleazar reiterates and supports the view of R. Judah. I am doubtful of this suggestion, as it seems that zoharic hermeneutics is predicated on positing an exoteric interpretation followed by an esoteric, though I am not alleging that these two levels are in any absolute sense independent from one another.

450. The mystery of the threefold unity is linked to the orthography of *alef* in *Zohar*, 3:193b: "The image [*diyoqna*] of *alef* consists of three sides, the beginning of the supernal mystery of pri-

mordial Adam, for the image of *alef* is composed of two arms, one from here and the other from here, and the body in the middle, and all is one mystery, it is the mystery of unity, and therefore *alef* has the numerical value of one." A similar decoding of the shape of *alef* appears in *Sha'rei Ṣedeq*, 18–19; Idel, *Le Porte della Giustizia*, 473–74.

451. I have argued that an older mythopoeic complex extractable from the bahiric text posits a primal triad depicted imaginally as father, son, and daughter. The father regains the unity with the daughter through the agency of the son—that is, the daughter is given in matrimony to the son; brother weds sister. In some passages, the son represents the male potency, the phallic channel that connects father and daughter; see Wolfson, *Along the Path*, 63–88; Wolfson, "Before Alef."

452. Liebes, *Sections of the Zohar Lexicon*, 400. Curiously, when Liebes mentions the part of the zoharic passage that I have investigated, referring to the three lines that make up the letter *beit*, the beginning of Torah and the totality of the name, he makes no mention of the Christological element. On the threefold unity in the "mystery of the voice" (*raza de-qol*), i.e., *Tif'eret*, which comprises water, fire, and air (the central *sefirot* of *Ḥesed, Din,* and *Raḥamim*), discerned through the "vision of the holy spirit" (*ḥezyona de-ruaḥ qudsha*), linked exegetically to the three names of God mentioned in the *Shema* (Dt 6:4), see *Zohar*, 2:43b, and parallel in Moses de León, *Sheqel ha-Qodesh*, 103–6; Liebes, *Studies in Zohar*, 140–45; Wolfson, *Through a Speculum*, 380–83.

453. Liebes, *Studies in Zohar*, 66–67; Wolfson, "Re/membering the Covenant." For a relatively early attempt at a critical assessment of the affinities between kabbalah and Christianity, especially esoteric strands of the latter, see Adolphe Franck, *Die Kabbala, oder die Religions-Philosophie der Hebräer*, trans. Adolf Jellinek (Leipzing: Heinrich Hunger, 1844), 249–60.

454. Liebes, *Studies in Zohar*, 139–61. Recently, Schäfer and Green have independently adopted a similar strategy to explain the kabbalistic fascination with the feminine image of *Shekhinah* in light of the augmented Marian imagery in Christian piety during the twelfth and thirteenth centuries. On my own conjecture that a critical passage in *Sefer ha-Bahir* should be decoded as a polemic against the Christian myth of the virgin birth of the Messiah, deplorably ignored by both Schäfer and Green, see Wolfson, *Along the Path*, 83–86. If my surmise is correct, it would support the orientation of Schäfer and Green, who have both looked to Christian portrayals of Mary in order to explain one possible and too often neglected channel of influence on the early kabbalists.

455. Liebes, *Studies in Zohar*, 41–43, 79, 171n65, 174n90, 180n126, 191n209.

456. *Zohar*, 2:162b.

457. Babylonian Talmud, Berakhot 55a, and see Scholem, *On the Kabbalah and Its Symbolism*, 166–67; Wolfson, *Along the Path*, 159n23.

458. For an exemplary study of this theme, see David Lyle Jeffrey, *People of the Book: Christian Identity and Literary Culture* (Grand Rapids, Mich.: Eerdmans, 1996). On the attempt to forge a nexus between interpretation and incarnation, see Alla Bozarth-Campbell, *The Word's Body: An Incarnational Aesthetic of Interpretation* (Tuscaloosa: University of Alabama Press, 1979). See also a discussion of the metaphorical conjunction between *corpus* and *verba* in Augustine by Gellrich, *Idea of the Book*, 116–22. According to this insightful analysis, Augustine draws a parallel between his own writing and the incarnational Word that became flesh so that saving words could be spoken and written. In short, Augustine's *verba* became the *corpus* to explain God's *Verbum*. For further elucidation of these points, see Calvin L. Troup, *Temporality, Eternity, and Wisdom: The Rhetoric of Augustine's Confessions* (Columbia: University of South Carolina Press, 1999), 82–116.

459. Anna Sapir Abulafia, "Jewish Carnality in Twelfth-Century Renaissance Thought," in *Christianity and Judaism: Papers Read at the 1991 Summer Meeting and the 1992 Winter Meeting of the Ecclesiastical History Society*, ed. Diana Wood (Oxford: Blackwell, 1992), 59–75.

6. Semantic Differences; or, "Judaism"/"Christianity"

Daniel Boyarin

This essay previously appeared in *The Ways That Never Parted: Jews and Christians in Late Antiquity and the Early Middle Ages*, ed. Adam H. Becker and Annette Y. Reed (Tübingen: Mohr Siebeck, 2003), 65–87. The author wishes to thank Erich Gruen and Chana Kronfeld for their help in thinking through the issues in this paper, especially Professor Gruen, who has been instrumental in saving me from several lamentable errors (perhaps not as many as he would have liked).

1. Diarmaid MacCulloch, "Solitaries in Community," *Times Literary Supplement* 5107 (February 16, 2001): 10.

2. Steven D. Fraade, "Ascetical Aspects of Ancient Judaism," in *Jewish Spirituality from the Bible through the Middle Ages*, ed. Arthur Green, a volume in *World Spirituality: An Encyclopedic History of the Religious Quest* (New York: Crossroad, 1986).

3. Jacob Neusner, *The Three Stages in the Formation of Judaism* (Chico, Calif.: Scholars Press, 1985), 77; Rosemary Radford Ruether, "Judaism and Christianity: Two Fourth-Century Religions," *Sciences Religieuses/Studies in Religion* 2 (1972): 1–10; James William Parkes, *The Conflict of the Church and the Synagogue: A Study in the Origins of Antisemitism* (Cleveland: World; Jewish Publication Society of America, 1961), 153; Günter Stemberger, *Jews and Christians in the Holy Land: Palestine in the Fourth Century* (Edinburgh: T & T Clark, 1999), 1.

4. David Chidester, *Savage Systems: Colonialism and Comparative Religion in Southern Africa* (Charlottesville: University Press of Virginia, 1996), 260.

5. Homi K. Bhabha, *The Location of Culture* (London: Routledge, 1994), 38–39; see also Chidester, *Savage Systems*, xv.

6. "I shall therefore say that, where only a single subject (such and such an individual) is concerned, the existence of the ideas of his belief is material in that *his ideas are his material actions inserted into material practices governed by material rituals which are themselves defined by the material ideological apparatus from which derive the ideas of that subject*"; Louis Althusser, "Ideology and Ideological State Apparatuses (Notes Toward an Investigation)," in *Mapping Ideology*, ed. Slavoj Žižek (London: Verso, 1994), 127; emphasis in original.

7. For a very useful presentation of the notion of language as practice, see Pierre Bourdieu, *Outline of a Theory of Practice* (Cambridge: Cambridge University Press, 1977), 96–97.

8. Shaye J. D. Cohen, "Ioudaios: 'Judaean' and 'Jew' in Susanna, First Maccabees, and Second Maccabees," in *Geschichte—Tradition—Reflexion: Festschrift für Martin Hengel zum 70. Geburtstag*, ed. H. Cancik, H. Lichtenberger, and P. Schafer (Tübingen: Mohr Siebeck, 1996), 1:211–20.

9. Throughout my work, I shall be using the terms "B.C." and "A.D." instead of the customary "B.C.E." and "C.E." The latter seem to me hardly an improvement (from the perspective of Jews) on the older B.C. and A.D., since the term *Common Era* is just as imperialistic as the traditional usage. The virtue of B.C. and A.D. (imitating the French manner) is that it simply names the era without making a judgment, theological or cultural, about it; see Jonathan A. Goldstein, trans. and ed., *II Maccabees: A New Translation with Introduction and Commentary*; *The Anchor Bible* 41a (New York: Doubleday, 1983), 192.

10. Ibid.

11. See also Jonathan M. Hall, *Ethnic Identity in Greek Antiquity* (Cambridge: Cambridge University Press, 1997), 46–47.

12. Goldstein, *II Maccabees*, 230, is careful to remind us that *Hellenismos* is not necessarily attested in this meaning but that it is the "implied" antonym of *Medismos*.

13. Goldstein's own evidence and argument, therefore, militate against his translation of the term as "the Jewish religion"; *II Maccabees*, 300. Admittedly, 14:38 (on Razis) seems to lean a bit more in that direction but can also easily be explained as referring to loyalty to the cause of the Jews and fealty to their traditional ways, and not the religion "Judaism." For a similar conclusion, see also Cohen, "Ioudaios," 219: "Thus Ioudaismos should be translated not 'Judaism'—'religion' is not the focus of the term—but 'Jewishness' (Judaeaness?). . . . It is a conflict between 'Judaism,' the ways of the Ioudaioi, and the 'Hellenism,' the ways of the Greeks."

14. Similar, but not identical, as there was no formal citizenship in "Israel," and, presumably, one could be both a member of Israel and a citizen of a polis. I would be thus hard put to describe what happened to Paul as a conversion in the religious sense, pace Alan F. Segal, *Paul the Convert: The Apostolate and Apostasy of Saul the Pharisee* (New Haven, Conn.: Yale University Press, 1990).

15. Although it is much earlier, the following example discussed by Cohen is instructive. The earliest evidence we have for a "Greek Jew" is an inscription by a certain "Moschos," from the third century B.C.; David M. Lewis, "The First Greek Jew," *Jewish Social Studies* 2 (1957): 264-66. The extraordinary thing about this Moschos is that, although he is identified in the inscription as an *Ioudaios*, his "religion" is clearly that of the Greek gods. He may be a Greek Jew from our historical perspective, but from his own he is just an *Ioudaios* and not a Greek (for that is how he identifies himself), whatever his religious practice, thus anticipating Paul's usage in which Greek and Jew are identities as incompatible as man and woman; see Shaye J. D. Cohen, *The Beginnings of Jewishness: Boundaries, Varieties, Uncertainties* (Berkeley: University of California Press, 1998), 97-98; see also 134-35, where the point is made that one could not be both Greek and Jew because these were competing cultural identities, not genealogical ones, which makes sense but still surely does not lead to the conclusion that they were religions, as Cohen himself argues; compare Cohen, "Ioudaios," 219. Paul, in seeking to break down this boundary in Christ, certainly does not mean that followers of Jesus will be both Greeks and Jews religiously; see Hans Dieter Betz, "Christianity as Religion: Paul's Attempt at Definition in Romans," *Journal of Religion* 71 (1991): 315-44, and the discussion in Birger Pearson, "The Emergence of the Christian Religion," in *The Emergence of the Christian Religion: Essays on Early Christianity* (Harrisburg, Pa.: Trinity Press International, 1997), 15.

16. Felix Scheidweiler, ed. and trans., "The Gospel of Nicodemus, Acts of Pilate and Christ's Descent Into Hell," in *New Testament Apocrypha*, ed. Wilhelm Schneemelcher and R. M. Wilson; English edition ed. Edgar Hennecke (Philadelphia: Westminster, 1991), 1:508; See also Cohen, *Beginnings of Jewishness*, 159-60, and the correct reference there, in n. 68.

17. Cohen, *Beginnings of Jewishness*, 160.

18. However, it must not be thought that these ethnic groups themselves just existed. They are also constructed identity formations that arise in particular historical circumstances. For discussion of the construction of Israel as "ethnicity" in antiquity, see Regina M. Schwartz, *The Curse of Cain: The Violent Legacy of Monotheism* (Chicago: University of Chicago Press, 1997), and Liana Pardes, *The Biography of Ancient Israel: National Narratives in the Bible* (Berkeley: University of California Press, 2000). For ancient Greece and its ethnicities, see Hall, *Ethnic Identity*.

19. This goes further, then, than the approach of Jonathan Z. Smith, who took us pretty far indeed when he wrote, "All three [Gnosticism, Judaism, Apocalypticism] have most usually been treated as reified, substantive nouns (indeed, as proper names); I would like to reduce each to the status of qualifying adjectives. There is no essence of Gnosticism, Judaism or Apocalypticism. Rather there is a shifting cluster of attributes which, for a particular purpose and in terms of a given document, makes one or another of these labels appropriate"; Smith, *Map Is Not Territory: Studies in the History of Religions* (Chicago: University of Chicago Press, 1993), x. Smith's approach already makes it virtually impossible to speak of Judaism or even of Judaisms; I suggest, further, that these

labels function only as signifiers within a signifying system in which they are differentiated from others semiotically. Thus we have to determine the synchronic structure of the semantic field at any given time and place. For the period under question in this research, until there is "Christianity" in the semiotic system as something that is not Judaism, then there cannot be "Judaism" either.

20. Wilfred Cantwell Smith, *The Meaning and End of Religion* (London: SPCK, 1978); Talal Asad, *Genealogies of Religion: Discipline and Reasons of Power in Christianity and Islam* (Baltimore: Johns Hopkins University Press, 1993).

21. Seth Schwartz, *Imperialism and Jewish Society from 200 B.C.E. to 640 C.E.* (Princeton, N.J.: Princeton University Press, 2001), 179.

22. For a similar argument with respect to the emergence of sexuality as such a discrete category, see David M. Halperin, "How to Do the History of Male Homosexuality," *GLQ: A Journal of Lesbian and Gay Studies* 6, no. 1 (2000): 87-123.

23. Maurice Sachot, "Comment le christianisme est-il devenu religio?" *Revue des sciences religieuses* 59 (1985): 95-118; Sachot, "'Religio/Superstitio': Historique d'une subversion et d'un retournement," *Revue d'histoire des religions* 208, no. 4 (1991): 355-94. See also Eric Laupot, "Tacitus' Fragment 2: The Anti-Roman Movement of the Christiani and the Nazoreans," *Vigiliae Christianae (VigChr)* 54, no. 3 (2000): 233-47, who argues that the word "*religio*" has been substituted for an original "*superstitio*" in a Tacitean fragment reproduced in Sulpicius Severus's *Chronicles*. See also the interesting formulation of Frend: "After circaA.D. 100 there was less of a tendency for Christians to claim to be Israel and more of a tendency to contrast Christianity and Judaism as separate religions. Christianity claimed to be heir to the universalist claims of Judaism. 'Catholic' or 'universal' was applied to the church for the first time. One can recognize the transition in Ignatius' letters"; W. H. C. Frend, *The Rise of Christianity* (Philadelphia: Fortress, 1984), 124.

24. Seth Schwartz, *Imperialism and Jewish Society*, 179.

25. Bhabha, *Location of Culture*, 110-11.

26. Seth Schwartz, *Imperialism and Jewish Society*, 184.

27. For a fine discussion of the problems of this formulation of the historical issue, see Judith Lieu, "'The Parting of the Ways': Theological Construct or Historical Reality?" *SAT* 56 (1994): 101-19.

28. David Brakke, "'Outside the Places, Within the Truth': Athanasius of Alexandria and the Localization of the Holy," in *Pilgrimage and Holy Space in Late Antique Egypt (and Its Mediterranean Neighbors)*, ed. David Frankfurter (Leiden: Brill, in press); see also Brakke, "Jewish Flesh and Christian Spirit in Athanasius of Alexandria," *Journal of Early Christian Studies (JECS)* 9, no. 4 (2001): 453-81.

29. It should be emphasized that wave theory is the historical or diachronic complement of dialect geography. For discussion of the latter and the fuzzy boundaries that it indicates between dialects, see William Labov, "The Boundaries of Words and Their Meanings," in *New Ways of Analyzing Variation in English*, ed. Charles-James N. Bailey and Roger W. Shuy (Washington, D.C.: Georgetown University Press, 1973), 344-47.

30. Mary Louise Pratt, *Imperial Eyes: Travel Writing and Transculturation* (London: Routledge, 1992).

31. For other versions of the problematization of "pure precolonial" selves as projected by certain versions of postcolonial analyses, see Ania Loomba, Colonialism/Postcolonialism (London: Routledge, 1998), 181-82; see, too, "Bhabha's notion of 'hybridity' implies that the colonial space involves the interaction of two originally 'pure' cultures (the British/European and the native) that are only rendered ambivalent once they are brought into direct contact with each other"; Richard King, *Orientalism and Religion: Postcolonial Theory, India and the Mystic East* (London: Routledge, 1999), 204. While I am somewhat doubtful as to whether this critique is prop-

erly applied to Bhabha, it does seem relevant to me in considering the postcolonial model for reading Judaism and Christianity in antiquity, which are surely always already hybridized with respect to each other, as it were.

32. Robert Young, *Colonial Desire: Hybridity in Theory, Culture, and Race* (London: Routledge, 1995), 65.

33. The perspective outlined in Daniel Boyarin, *Border Lines: The Invention of Heresy and the Emergence of Christianity and Judaism* (Philadelphia: University of Pennsylvania Press, 2004), is generally similar to that of Mary Beard, John A North, and S. R. F. Price, *Religions of Rome* (Cambridge: Cambridge University Press, 1998), 307–12.

34. Hall, *Ethnic Identity*.

35. To be sure, he is careful to ascribe this version of wave theory to a single scholar, W. F. Wyatt; see Hall, *Ethnic Identity*, 166.

36. Labov, "Boundaries of Words," 347.

37. Hall, *Ethnic Identity*, 111.

38. "What an ethnic group does is actively and consciously to select certain artefacts from within the overall material cultural repertoire which then act as emblemic indicia of ethnic boundaries. In the words of Catherine Morgan, 'ethnic behaviour affects only those categories of artefact selected to carry social or political meaning under particular circumstances, rather than the totality of a society's material culture'"; Hall, *Ethnic Identity*, 135. In this case, religious ideas and practices are the equivalent of artifacts. One example of this point is the identification of "modalism" and its opposite as a variation within Judaeo-Christian theology that was eventually chosen to be among the most significant of indicia for Christian and Jewish separate religious identity.

39. It was Jack Miles who originally suggested to me that the conflict over the law animated every page of the New Testament and that, therefore, "rejection" of the law could not be made part of an "intensional" definition of Christianity over and against Judaism.

40. For this distinction, see Althusser, "Ideology."

41. Beard, North, and Price, *Religions*, 249.

42. This is partially anticipated by Beard et al., who cite R. Needham, "Polythetic Classification: Convergence and Consequences," *Man*, n.s. 10 (1975): 349–69.

43. Chana Kronfeld, *On the Margins of Modernism: Decentering Literary Dynamics* (Berkeley: University of California Press, 1996), 28. I wish specifically to thank Prof. Kronfeld for suggesting this direction, which has proved very fruitful for me, and for much else.

44. Just in case my formulation has not done so already, I wish to make absolutely clear that the distinction that I am drawing here is not between "folk" and "scientific" modes of classification but between the classifications of groups, people, and the things that people do and the classifications of nonhuman objects. These are related cognitive tasks, of course, but also significantly different; see also Robert D. Baird, *Category Formation and the History of Religions* (The Hague: Mouton, 1971).

45. Kronfeld, *On the Margins of Modernism*, 27.

46. Albert I. Baumgarten, "Literary Evidence for Jewish Christianity in the Galilee," in *The Galilee in Late Antiquity*, ed. Lee I. Levine (New York: Jewish Theological Seminary of America, 1992), 39–50.

47. For the general perspective, see Alan F. Segal, *The Other Judaisms of Late Antiquity* (Atlanta: Scholars Press, 1987).

48. Kronfeld, *On the Margins of Modernism*, 29. For an interesting use of family-resemblance semantics (without mentioning it explicitly) in an important problem in late antique religious

history, see Nathaniel Deutsch, *Guardians of the Gate: Angelic Vice Regency in Late Antiquity* (Leiden: Brill, 1999), 14.

49. For a good general introduction to this theory, see George Lakoff, *Women, Fire, and Dangerous Things: What Categories Reveal about the Mind* (Chicago: University of Chicago Press, 1987), 12–58.

50. Kronfeld, *On the Margins of Modernism*, 29.

51. Lakoff, *Women, Fire, and Dangerous Things*, 44–45.

52. The situation of law-observing "Jewish Christians" in Justin's *Dialogue* would be a case in point. "People of the Land," in Rabbinic parlance, is another.

53. As Kronfeld remarks, "turkey" is the best example of bird on Thanksgiving.

54. Kronfeld, *On the Margins of Modernism*, 30.

55. Lakoff, *Women, Fire, and Dangerous Things*, 45.

56. Another riveting analogy comes to the fore; Kronfeld writes, "My investigations of Hebrew and Yiddish modernist poetry have consistently presented a fascinating paradox: that although many modernists defined very clearly their poetic principles (typically formulated in rather strong terms by group manifestoes or individual aesthetic credos), the best examples—or prototypes—that came to represent these trends (individual poets or even individual works) are often quite atypical of or only marginally consistent with the principles of the group" (*On the Margins of Modernism*, 31), to which one might compare, I think, a paradox uncovered by Shaye Cohen, who shows that the prototypical converts to Judaism (from "paganism") in the Talmud do not follow the explicit rules laid down for conversion; Cohen, "The Conversion of Antoninus," in *The Talmud Yerushalmi and Graeco-Roman Culture*, ed. Peter Schafer (Tübingen: Mohr Siebeck, 1998), 167 and passim. Cohen could have made, I think, further progress in analyzing this paradox (to which he basically merely points) by considering comments such as the following: "Focusing on these modernist prototypes tends to foreground one or two highly salient poetic features which fulfill or match some particular (artistic, linguistic, ideological, or social) need. In each case, there are specific reasons, which need to be reconstructed and analyzed, why a particular feature came to be perceived as exemplary within the particular conditions for the creation and reception of a particular brand of modernism at a particular historical and cultural juncture. This contextually motivated salience raising creates, among other things, a series of 'deviant prototypes,' artistic paragons and exemplary texts that do not centrally belong to any trend but have nevertheless come to represent it" (Kronfeld, *On the Margins of Modernism*, 31–32).

57. Jerome, *Correspondence*, ed. Isidorus Hilberg (Vienna: Verlag der Osterreichischen Akademie der Wissenschaften, 1996), 55:381–82.

58. One of the interesting phenomena about religious categories is the ways that subgroups will mutually deny each other's' salience or centrality as members of the group. We might think that "Pharisee" is a Jew if anyone is a Jew (just as an integer is a number if anything is a number), but it seems that (in the Talmud's account) there were others who would have denied that claim, because by believing in the resurrection of the dead, Pharisees were rendering themselves less Jewish than others. Interestingly, this feature—believing in resurrection of the dead—is taken as absolutely necessary for being a Jew by some non-Christian Jews and for being a Christian by some Christians and denied by some of both. In other words, we have a doubly complicated system here, for, while a group such as the Fox Indians (example from Lakoff, *Women, Fire, and Dangerous Things*, 23–24) may have complicated rules for determining who is an "uncle," with graded salience of prototypicality in the category, in our case there are, in effect, competing groups claiming the right to be called "uncle" or not or to be "better" uncles than others. The semantic situation remains, nevertheless, the same. It is fascinating that one of the characteristic claims of heresiologists is that

they are "Christians" while others are hyphenated in some way, e.g., Valentinian Christians; in other words, that the claim is that "we" are the prototype itself. Similarly, the rabbis use the term "heretics," "kinds" [QTft], in my view, to imply that "we" are the prototype of Jew, while they, by being "kinds" of Jews, are less salient, less centrally members of the category. This kind of semantics gives us tools for understanding the complexity of the discourses of religious categorization.

59. J. L. Austin, *Philosophical Papers* (Oxford: Oxford University Press, 1961), 72.

60. Note the contrast between this account and Lakoff's statement that "we even have a folk model of what categories themselves are, and this folk model has evolved into the classical theory of categorization. Part of the problem that prototype theory now has, and will face in the future, is that it goes beyond our folk understanding of categorization. And much of what has given the classical theory its appeal over the centuries is that it meshes with our folk theory and seems like simple common sense"; *Women, Fire, and Dangerous Things*, 118. I am suggesting that, for the categories Jew and Christian, it is distinctly possible that for centuries "folk models" worked more like prototype or experiential real categories, while it was the work of certain "experts" to attempt to impose "traditional" or "objective" categorization upon them. For something like this claim, working, however, out of a somewhat different theoretical model, see Galit Hasan-Rokem, "Narratives in Dialogue: A Folk Literary Perspective on Interreligious Contacts in the Holy Land in Rabbinic Literature of Late Antiquity," in *Sharing the Sacred: Religious Contacts and Conflicts in the Holy Land First-Fifteenth Centuries CE*, ed. Guy Stroumsa and Arieh Kofsky (Jerusalem: Yad Ben Zvi, 1998), 109–29.

61. Boyarin, *Border Lines*.

7. The Name *God* in Blanchot

Jean-Luc Nancy

First published in French in *Le magazine littéraire* 424, special issue *Maurice Blanchot* (October 2003); the English translation first appeared in Jean-Luc Nancy, *Dis-Enclosure: The Deconstruction of Christianity*, trans. Bettina Bergo, Gabriel Malenfant, and Michael B. Smith (New York: Fordham University Press, 2008), 86–88.

1. Maurice Blanchot, *The Infinite Conversation*, trans. Susan Hanson (Minneapolis: University of Minnesota Press, 1992).

2. See Maurice Blanchot, *Thomas the Obscure*, trans. Robert Lamberton, in *The Station Hill Blanchot Reader* (Barrytown, N.Y.: Station Hill Press, 1999); Maurice Blanchot, *The Writing of the Disaster*, trans. Ann Smock (Lincoln: University of Nebraska Press, 1995); and Maurice Blanchot, *Le dernier à parler* (Montpellier: Fata Morgana, 1984).

8. Humanism's Cry: On Infinity in Religion, and Absence in Atheism— A Conversation with Blanchot and Nancy

Laurens ten Kate

Some parts of this text have been published earlier, though in a very different context and formulation, in Dutch: "De schreeuw van het humanisme: Om-schrijvingen van mens en God bij Blanchot, onder verwijzing naar Foucault," in *Maurice Blanchot: De stem en het schrift—Drie opstellen over de esthetische distantie in de vertelling, het humanisme en de toekomst van het boek*, ed. Arthur Cools (Zoetermeer: Klement, 2012), 105–32.

1. See, e.g., the influential handbook of comparative religious studies by Ninian Smart, *The World's Religions* (Cambridge: Cambridge University Press, 1998), 10: "In order to grasp the meanings and values of the plural cultures of today's world, we need to know something of the worldviews which underlie them."

2. I borrow these expressions from Peter Sloterdijk's work, esp. his trilogy *Sphären*, 3 vols. (Frankfurt am Main: Suhrkamp, 1998, 1999, 2004), and his *Du musst dein Leben ändern* (Frankfurt am Main: Suhrkamp, 2009).

3. See the first book in the Future of the Religious Past collection, Hent de Vries, ed., *Religion: Beyond a Concept* (New York: Fordham University Press, 2008), esp. the editor's introduction, "Why Still 'Religion?,'" 1–98, in which Blanchot's tentative question, one might say, is worked out in detail.

4. Maurice Blanchot, *The Writing of the Disaster*, trans. Ann Smock (Lincoln: University of Nebraska Press, 1995), 64.

5. See Karl Jaspers's ambitious study *The Origin and Goal of History*, trans. Michael Bullock (New York: Routledge, 2010; originally 1949), esp. pt. 1, chap. 2, in which Jaspers sketches a decisive "axial" shift in cultural history between 800 and 200 B.C.E., during which man broke with the world of myth, polytheism, the givenness of nature, and fate in favor of a self-emancipatory path toward human individualism, creativity, and responsibility, rapid technological progress, science, and knowledge, philosophy as the art of free thinking, new political structures resisting theocratic and tyrannic power, and the emergence of religions that turn God into an abstract, distant, moral principle (like monotheism, Confucianism, and Buddhism). Jaspers extends this axial shift beyond Western history as such, to Persia, India, and China. See on this also my "To World or not to World: An Axial Genealogy of Secular Life," in S. Latre, W. van Herck, G. Vanheeswijk (eds.), *Radical Secularization?: An Inquiry into the Religious Roots of Secular Culture* (New York: Bloomsbury, 2015), 270–30.

6. Blanchot, *Writing of the Disaster*, 64.

7. See also my "Intimate Distance: Rethinking the Unthought God in Christianity—On Jean-Luc Nancy's Deconstruction of Christianity, Compared and Confronted with the 'Theological Turn' in Phenomenology," *Sophia* 47 (2008): 327–43, esp. 327–28.

8. Blanchot, *Writing of the Disaster*, 64.

9. Ibid.

10. Ibid., 65.

11. See, e.g., Maurice Blanchot, "On Nietzsche's Side," in *The Work of Fire*, trans. Charlotte Mandell (Stanford, Calif.: Stanford University Press, 1995), 291: "In no way can the idea of the Death of God be the expression of a definitive knowledge, or the outline of a stable proposition. Anyone who wants to draw certainty from it, some 'There is no God' in the dogmatic sense of banal atheism, cunningly deflects away from complacency and calm. 'God is dead' is an enigma, an affirmation ambiguous because of its religious origin."

12. Maurice Blanchot, *The Infinite Conversation*, trans. Susan Hanson (Minneapolis: University of Minnesota Press, 1993), 246–63.

13. Jean-Luc Nancy, "The Name *God* in Blanchot," trans. Michael B. Smith, in *Dis-Enclosure: The Deconstruction of Christianity*, trans. Bettina Bergo, Gabriel Malenfant, and Michael B. Smith (New York: Fordham University Press, 2008), 85.

14. Nancy plays with both meanings of the French *fin*, just as Derrida has done in his "The Ends of Man" ("Les fins de l'homme"), in *Margins of Philosophy*, trans. Alan Bass (Chicago: University of Chicago Press, 1982).

15. See, e.g., Nancy, *L'impératif catégorique* (Paris: Flammarion, 1983); Nancy, *The Inoperative Community*, ed. Peter Connor, trans. Peter Connor et al. (Minneapolis: University of Minnesota Press, 1990); Nancy, *A Finite Thinking*, trans. Simon Sparks et al. (Stanford, Calif.: Stanford University Press, 2003); and Nancy, *Dis-Enclosure*.

16. This distinction was first introduced by Henri Birault in his *Heidegger et l'expérience de la pensée* (Paris: Gallimard, 1978).

17. See Nancy, "Postface," in Martin Crowley, *L'homme sans: Politiques de la finitude* (Fécamp: Lignes, 2009), 181–84.

18. Ibid., 181; my trans.

19. Ibid., 181–82.

20. In this treatment of infinity the well-known Hegelian distinction between "good" and "bad" infinity clearly resonates. Ian James lucidly formulates this resonance in "Incarnation and Infinity," in *Re-treating Religion: Deconstructing Christianity with Jean-Luc Nancy*, ed. Alena Alexandrova, Ignaas Devisch, Laurens ten Kate, and Aukje van Rooden (New York: Fordham University Press, 2012), 258. Nancy clearly distinguishes between "good" and "bad" conceptions of infinity as thought by Hegel. In *Hegel: The Restlessness of the Negative*, trans. Jason Smith and Steven Miller (Minneapolis: University of Minnesota Press, 2002), Nancy invokes this distinction explicitly: "An infinite process does not go on 'to infinity,' as if to the always postponed term of a progression (Hegel calls this 'bad infinity'): it is the instability of every finite determination, the bearing away of presence and of the given in the movement of presentation and the gift" (12). "Bad" infinity, then, would imply the infinity of a progression or unending expansion: It would be a continuation of finite space into infinity without limit or end. "Good" infinity is actual and, as it were, already traversing or folded into the finite.

21. One of the prime missions of humanism in, for instance, the late Roman era (the stoic "self-technologies" that Michel Foucault studied in his later work) or in the Renaissance, was to strive for true humanity (*humanitas*) as an "end" to be reached by study, dialogue, moral impeccability, art, knowledge, etc. Still, in this striving one can also read a different meaning of humanism.

22. Nancy, "Postface," 182. Further on, Nancy proposes to Crowley that "his *homme sans* is *homme sens*" (183).

23. Nancy, *Dis-Enclosure*, 1.

24. Ibid.

25. Ibid, 10; my emphasis.

26. Ibid.

27. Ibid., 176n12.

28. Ibid., 86–87.

29. See Nancy, *Adoration: The Deconstruction of Christianity II*, trans. John McKeane (New York: Fordham University Press, 2013).

30. Nancy, "On Dis-enclosure and Its Gesture, Adoration: A Concluding Dialogue with Jean-Luc Nancy," in *Re-treating Religion*, 311.

31. Nancy, "Prayer Demythified," in *Dis-Enclosure*, 136.

32. See Émile Benveniste, *Le vocabulaire des institutions indo-européennes*, vol. 2, *Pouvoir, droit, religion* (Paris: Minuit, 1969), 265.

33. Jacques Derrida, "Faith and Knowledge: The Two Sources of 'Religion' at the Limits of Reason Alone," trans. Samuel Weber, in *Acts of Religion*, ed. Gil Anidjar (New York: Routledge, 2002), 73.

34. Ibid.

35. Blanchot, *Infinite Conversation*, 247.

36. Ibid., 263.

37. Due to its length, the text was divided over two issues of *La Nouvelle Revue Française*, no. 178, pp. 586–604, and no. 179, pp. 812–21 (October–November 1967).

38. In the next chapter of *The Infinite Conversation*, Blanchot's reservations regarding the idea of a humanist future are formulated even more explicitly. "On a Change of Epoch: The Exigency of Return" (264–81) rephrases the problem of the future as a concept and experience of the "hope" with which "Atheism and Writing" ends and is devoted to exploring what Blanchot, with Nietzsche, calls a "love of the ignorance of the future" (271; trans. modified). This love is, according to Blanchot, the kernel of Nietzsche's theory of the Eternal Return and indicates a form of humanism that coincides neither with a belief in man and progression nor with relativism and conservatism.

39. Blanchot, *Infinite Conversation*, 248.

40. Ibid.

41. Georges Bataille, superscription above the first edition of *Madame Edwarda* (1941) cited by Blanchot, ibid., 248.

42. Blanchot, *Infinite Conversation*, 250.

43. See also on this play Nancy, *Hegel*, 5: "This world, the realm of the finite, shelters and reveals in itself the infinite work of negativity, that is, the restlessness of sense (or of the 'concept,' as Hegel names it): restlessness of conceiving-itself, grasping-itself, and relating-itself-to-self—in German, *begreifen*." See also, on the important notions of negation and negativity in Blanchot and Hegel, Françoise Collin, *Maurice Blanchot et la question de l'écriture* (Paris: Gallimard, 1971), esp. pt. 2, chap. 4; Annelies Schulte-Nordholt, *Maurice Blanchot: L'écriture comme expérience du dehors* (Geneva: Droz, 1995), esp. chap. 2; and John Gregg, *Maurice Blanchot and the Literature of Transgression* (Princeton, N.J.: Princeton University Press, 1994), esp. chap. 1.

44. For Nancy, this entanglement of outside and inside (the world) is a recurring theme in his "deconstruction of Christianity." If it is correct that the outside is not a "second world" but an "alienation" in the world—humans lose themselves by unloosing themselves in the world from the world—then this Christian structure is repeated by modern man: Stepping out, "absolving" himself, he claims absolute status in the world and over the world. See also Laurens ten Kate, "Outside In, Inside Out: Notes on the Retreating God in Nancy's Deconstruction of Christianity," in *Bijdragen: International Journal in Philosophy and Theology* 69, no. 3 (2008): 305–20. Maybe we encounter here the fundamental philosophical basis for the "theological origins of modernity," as analyzed by Michael Allen Gillespie in his book of that title (Chicago: University of Chicago Press, 2008), esp. chap. 3, "Humanism and the Apotheosis of Man," in which the author describes the factual historical evidence for the indebtedness of the Renaissance humanists to Christianity. The structure sketched here applies in different forms to the other monotheisms, too, as well as to, e.g., Zoroastrianism and Buddhism. Jaspers's entire axial spectrum should be involved in this analysis.

45. See Charles Taylor, *A Secular Age* (Cambridge, Mass.: Harvard University Press, 2007), esp. chap. 15.

46. Blanchot, *Infinite Conversation*, 247.

47. Ibid., 247, 248.

48. Ibid., 251.

49. Ibid., 247–48.

50. Ibid., 248.

51. Ibid.

52. Nancy, *Dis-Enclosure*, 85.

53. It is no coincidence that Nancy devotes two chapters to Blanchot in *Dis-Enclosure*: "On the Name *God* in Blanchot" and "Blanchot's Resurrection."

54. For an extensive volume of critical studies on the possibilities for a deconstructive rethinking of the axial religions, esp. the monotheistic traditions, see Alexandrova et al., *Re-treating Religion*, a result of research carried out in close collaboration with Nancy.

55. Blanchot, *Infinite Conversation*, 253.

56. Ibid., 252.

57. Ibid.

58. Ibid., 253.

59. Nancy, *Dis-Enclosure*, 86.

60. Blanchot, *Infinite Conversation*, 262.

61. Nancy, *Dis-Enclosure*, 88.

62. Gilles Deleuze, *Difference and Repetition*, trans. Paul Patton (New York: Columbia University Press, 1995).

63. Blanchot, *Infinite Conversation*, 249.

64. Ibid., 247. I refer once more to Crowley's *L'homme sans* for a formulation of this new humanism (or is it antihumanism? or is the opposition no longer valid here?) of a "man-without."

65. Blanchot, *Infinite Conversation*, 249.

66. Ibid., xii.

67. Ibid., 262.

9. Intuition, Interpellation, Insight: Elements of a Theory of Conversion

Nils F. Schott

1. Paul, First Letter to the Corinthians; Bernd Ulmer, "Konversionserzählungen als rekonstruktive Gattung," *Zeitschrift für Soziologie* 17, no. 1 (February 1988): 19–33; Jean-Louis Chrétien, *The Call and the Response*, trans. Anne A. Davenport (New York: Fordham University Press, 2004), chap. 1; Jean-Luc Marion, *Being Given: Toward a Phenomenology of Givenness*, trans. Jeffrey Kosky (Stanford, Calif.: Stanford University Press, 2002), 329–35. On the notion of the call in Paul, see Nils F. Schott, "Love and the Stick—The Worldly Aspects of the Call in the First Letter to the Corinthians," in *Paul and the Philosophers*, ed. Ward Blanton and Hent de Vries (New York: Fordham University Press, 2013), 310–26.

2. Hent de Vries, "Instances: Temporal Modes from Augustine to Derrida and Lyotard," in *Augustine and Postmodernism: Confessions and Circumfession*, ed. John D. Caputo and Michael J. Scanlon (Bloomington: Indiana University Press, 2005), 68–87.

3. Henry Pinard de la Boullaye, "Conversion," in *Dictionnaire de spiritualité, ascétique et mystique, doctrines et histoire*, ed. M. Viller, F. Cavallera, J. de Guibert, and C. Baumgartner (Paris: Beauchesne, 1932–), 1:2224 and 1:2225. Even more than eighty years later, the literature on the topic of conversion remains with the spectrum de la Boullaye sets out. For an overview of recent literature and trends in conversion studies, see Lewis R. Rambo, "Conversion Studies, Pastoral Counseling, and Cultural Studies: Engaging and Embracing a New Paradigm," *Pastoral Psychology* 59, no. 4 (2010): 433–45, and Detlef Pollack, "Überlegungen zum Begriff und Phänomen der Konversion aus religionssoziologischer Perspektive," in *Konversion und Konfession in der Frühen Neuzeit*, ed. Ute Lotz-Heumann, Jan-Friedrich Mißfelder, and Matthias Pohlig (Gütersloh: Gütersloher Verlagshaus, 2007). The emphasis on the sociology of religion in these surveys is no accident: the wide conception

of conversion calls for a study of all manifestations of conversion, and, among the social sciences, the perspective of sociology (with its emphasis on empirical study and its focus on Western societies) is most attuned to such a concept, despite the conscious turn away from an exclusive focus on the Christian tradition, a turn made explicit by the use of *Konversion* instead of *Bekehrung*. There is, of course, a wealth of studies in other disciplines, especially anthropology, but they too tend to place themselves on either a micro- or a macro-level of observation and interpretation that can be situated on the spectrum between "new orientation" and "total transformation" (see the article by Rambo just cited).

4. For a helpful overview—and an admirable attempt at a rigorous definition—see Armen Avanessian and Anke Hennig, *Metanoia oder: Wie Lesen die Welt verändert* (Zurich: Diaphanes, 2013).

5. Augustinus Aurelius, Bishop of Hippo, *The First Catechetical Instruction*, trans. Joseph P. Christopher (1926; rev. ed. Westminster: Newman, 1946), here 5.9.25; trans. modified.

6. Although drawing on other works, especially the *Essai sur les données immédiates de la conscience* and *Matière et mémoire*, this exposition of Bergson's notion relies mainly on chaps. 2 and 4 of his 1938 collection of essays *La pensée et le mouvant*, 15th ed. (Paris: Press Universitaires de France, 2003); all translations of this work are my own. For Bergson's notion of intuition, see *La pensée et le mouvant*, 4.102–3. As will quickly become clear, the methodological role Bergson assigns to intuition has much in common with what I claim for conversion. However, it is equally important to point out that they are not the same and that I do not assert any relation stronger than analogy between certain aspects of Bergsonian intuition and certain aspects of conversion as it emerges from conversion narratives—as attractive as that might be, especially in the light of Bergson's own "conversion"; see Philippe Soulez and Fréderic Worms, *Bergson* (Paris: Flammarion, 1997).

7. Bergson, *La pensée et le mouvant*, 2.25–27.

8. Ibid., 2.7, 29, 30, 31.

9. Plato, *Apology*, 31c–d and 40a.

10. Bergson, *La pensée et le mouvant*, 2.31; 4.119–21, 132, 137, and 142. One unexpected parallel can be found in the repeated—and mutually contradictory—narratives of Saul's conversion on the road to Damascus in Acts 9, 22, and 26. The contradictions among the three versions, together with the elements they share (sensual deprivation accompanying an intervention experienced as divine interpellation and a waiting period or deferral), indicate both the uniqueness of the experience and the need to narrate it.

11. Bergson, *La pensée et le mouvant*, 4.142.

12. Ibid., 4.132.

13. Louis Althusser, "Idéologies et appareils idéologiques d'état: Notes pour une recherche," *La Pensée*, no. 151 (June 1970) : 3–38; all translations are my own.

14. Ibid., 3.

15. Ibid., 27.

16. Ibid., 30; Althussser's emphasis.

17. Ibid., 31.

18. Ibid., 31–32; Althusser's emphasis.

19. Ibid., 22–24.

20. Ibid., 32.

21. Ibid., 33 and 36.

22. The broad sense of "conversion" discussed above integrates this newly established continuity into the very experience and concept of conversion.

23. This reorganization must be undertaken, because otherwise the new perspective that gives meaning to our lives is closed down or at least obscured again.

24. On this point and for the discussion that follows, compare de Vries, "Instances."

25. Augustinus Aurelius, Bishop of Hippo, *Confessions*, trans. Maria Boulding (New York: New City Press, 1997), 8.1.2.186. Note, however, that book 8 is not an account of a single afternoon. Rather, it narrates not just the space of time that precedes the experience but also the immediate narrative precedents. It is a story of stories that is not fully captured if it is described in terms of the events of an afternoon alone—and, as Jens Nörregaard points out, it cannot be captured in a single work; Nörregaard, *Augustins Bekehrung*, trans. A. Spelmeyer (Tübingen: Mohr Siebeck, 1923).

26. Augustine, *Confessions* 8.12.29.206-7.

27. For Augustine's conversion, see Marion, *In the Self's Place: The Approach of Saint Augustine*, trans. Jeffrey L. Kosky (Stanford, Calif.: Stanford University Press, 2012); Jean-François Lyotard, *The Confessions of Augustine*, trans. Richard Beardsworth (Stanford, Calif.: Stanford University Press, 2000); and Caputo and Scanlon, eds., *Augustine and Postmodernism*.

28. Ulmer, "Konversionserzählungen," 31–32. For a contemporary example, see the story of Pawel in Dan Bilefsky, "Changing Face in Poland: Skinhead Puts on Skullcap," *New York Times*, February 28, 2010, A6, http://www.nytimes.com/2010/02/28/world/europe/28poland.html.

29. For an articulation of crisis (in the conventional sense of a period of "disorientation") as a "stage" of conversion, see Lewis R. Rambo and Steven C. Baumann, "Psychology of Conversion and Spiritual Transformation," *Pastoral Psychology*, online first (May 2, 2011), http://www.springerlink.com.

30. Thus, for example, the fashioning of a new life that has Saul become Paul goes along with an almost complete absence, in Paul's letters, of allusions to his preconversion life. Conversely, the completion of the garden narrative in book 8 of the *Confessions* also marks the end of the biographical narrative. The new life calls for a completely different way of telling the story, and after preparatory work in books 9 and 10, Augustine begins a new story that commences with the creation of the world and, maybe more importantly, the creation of time.

31. This definition also echoes Aristotle's definition of time as the "number of motion in respect of 'before' and 'after'"; *Physics*, 4.11.219b1.

32. On the idea of retrospection, see David Yamane, "Narrative and Religious Experience," *Sociology of Religion* 61, no. 2 (2000): 171–89; on retrospection as a central concept in Bergson's thought, see Vladimir Jankélévitch, *Henri Bergson*, ed. Alexandre Lefebvre and Nils F. Schott (Durham, NC: Duke University Press, 2015), esp. 11–22.

33. This may serve to explain the wider notion of conversion as transformation and process with which I began: if conversion is understood to bring about a change but cannot be isolated from this change, it must be identical with it.

34. In the Western philosophical tradition, the problem is first articulated in its contradiction by Aristotle, which leads him to articulate time as an attribute of change (*Physics*, 4.11.219b2–220a26); compare de Vries on Lyotard, "Instances," 85. Bergson makes a similar point more forcefully: the instant is not just an attribute; it is a postexperiential abstraction that might well serve to describe phenomena in the outside world but does nothing to describe how creation, the new, is possible; see Bergson, *La pensée et le mouvant*, 2.30.

35. This is the temporal articulation of Ulmer's "intermediate area" ("Konversionserzählungen," 32) and an apt reminder of Bergson's description of intuition as capturing a temporality beyond the spatializing tripartition into past, present, and future.

36. The term "in abeyance" is Elizabeth Rottenberg's felicitous translation of Derrida's *en instance*; see Derrida, *Demeure: Fiction and Testimony*, preceded by Maurice Blanchot, *The Instant*

of My Death, trans. Elizabeth Rottenberg (Stanford, Calif.: Stanford University Press, 2000), 13–108, esp. 46. If it weren't such an ugly word, one could call this *anarchronicity*: there is no first time because time is not born of time. It derives from the opening provided by the present and endures because it remains undetermined—in abeyance, always already deferred; compare de Vries, "Instances," 79 and 84.

37. Indeed, only such openness makes it possible for there to be temporality; compare Gilles Deleuze, *Cinema 1: The Movement-Image*, trans. Hugh Tomlinson and Barbara Habberjam (Minneapolis: University of Minnesota Press, 1986), 219n15. It is not to be understood as a set of possibilities, which would predetermine the future yet again. However, as Bergson and Heidegger, to whose work Deleuze refers in this note, are careful to acknowledge, the openness of temporality quickly degenerates, in everyday life, into the uniformity of chronological time.

38. Another horizon we could add here is death; see Martin Heidegger, *Being and Time*, trans. John Macquarrie and Edward Robinson (New York: Harper and Row, 1962), §§46–53, 279–311. What they all share is that they are both ungraspable (absolute) and certain. The double relation to two horizons has been articulated as "messianic time"; see Giorgio Agamben, *The Time That Remains: A Commentary on the Letter to the Romans*, trans. Patricia Dailey (Stanford, Calif.: Stanford University Press, 2005), 59–87. This, of course, requires a suspension of our usual way of knowing: the return of the son of man who is the son of God and is dead is a contradiction not resolvable in the time of the world.

39. This identification presents itself in a number of conceptual moves, of which only a few can be mentioned here: the slide from no-where (and thus no-when) to now-here; the slide from now to eternity as a "standing now"; the definition of eternity as the omnitemporality of the "always already"; and, finally, the overcoming of any distinction between now and eternity in the intuitive vision; see Deleuze on Samuel Butler's *Erewhon* in *Différence et répétition* (Paris: PUF, 1968), 3; Leo Elders, *The Philosophical Theology of St. Thomas Aquinas* (Leiden: Brill, 1990), 177–78, esp. n. 30; Althusser, "Idéologies et appareils idéologiques d'état," 23 (although the term "omnitemporality" is my own); Bergson, *La pensée et le mouvant*, 4.142; and, once again, de Vries, "Instances."

10. Allowed and Forbidden Words: Canon and Censorship in *Grundbegriffe*, Critical Terms, and Encyclopedias: Confessions of a Person Involved

Christoph Auffarth

1. For the linguistic turn, see Jürgen Trabant, "Zur Einführung: Vom linguistic turn der Geschichte zum historical turn der Linguistik," in *Sprache der Geschichte*, ed. Trabant (Munich, 2005), vii–xxii. I thank for linguistic competences Helen Tartar and Ilinca Tanaseanu-Döbler and Marvin Döbler.

2. H. Wilhelm Krüger, "Ähnlichkeiten und Analogien—Diachronische Bemerkungen zur Entstehung des Wittgensteinschen Begriffs der Familienähnlichkeit," in *Wittgenstein Studies* 2 (1994), published electronically at http://sammelpunkt.philo.at:8080/423/1/08-2-94.TXT.

3. Typoskript 213, S. 70.

4. Rudolf Eisler, *Wörterbuch der philosophischen Begriffe, historisch-quellenmäßig bearbeitet* (Berlin: Mittler, 1900; new ed., 3 vols., 1927–30).

5. Hans Jörg Sandkühler, "'Eine lange Odyssee': Joachim Ritter, Ernst Cassirer und die Philosophie im 'Dritten Reich,'" in *Dialektik: Zeitschrift für Kulturphilosophie* 1 (2006): 139–79; also online

at http://www.philosophie.uni-bremen.de/fileadmin/mediapool/philosophie/CV/Ritter-Cassirer _2006.pdf.

6. Brunner and Schmitt were answering Karl Mannheim (one of the liberals); see Cancik, *Handbuch religionswissenschaftlicher Grundbegriffe* (*HrwG*) 1, 23, and, with much further evidence, Otto Gerhard Oexle, "Begriffsgeschichte: Eine noch nicht begriffene Geschichte," *Philosophisches Jahrbuch* 116 (2009): 381–400.

7. Otto Brunner, *Land und Herrschaft* (Vienna: Rohrer, 1943); Otto Brunner, *Land and Lordship: Structures of Governance in Medieval Austria* (Philadelphia: University of Pennsylvania Press, 1992).

8. During the Second World War, German scholars showed their commitment to the military mission in the form of lectures given in front of officers, e.g., about the goals of the war; see Karen Schönwälder, *Historiker und Politik: Geschichtswissenschaft im Nationalsozialismus* (Frankfurt am Main: Campus, 1992); Frank-Rutger Hausmann, *Deutsche Geisteswissenschaft im Zweiten Weltkrieg: Die "Aktion Ritterbusch" 1940–1945*, 2nd ed. (Dresden, 2003).

9. Otto Gerhard Oexle, "Sozialgeschichte—Begriffsgeschichte—Wissenschaftsgeschichte: Anmerkungen zum Werk Otto Brunners," *Vierteljahrschrift für Sozial-und Wirtschaftsgeschichte* 71 (1982): 305–41; see also Gadi Algazi, *Herrengewalt und Gewalt der Herren im Späten Mittelalter: Herrschaft, Gegenseitigkeit und Sprachgebrauch* (Frankfurt am Main, 1996); Gadi Algazi, "'Konkrete Ordnung' und die Sprache der Zeit," in *Geschichtsschreibung als Legitimationswissenschaft 1918–1945*, ed. Peter Schöttler (Frankfurt am Main, 1997), 166–203; Hans-Henning Kortüm, "'Wissenschaft im Doppelpaß'? Carl Schmitt, Otto Brunner und die Konstruktion der Fehde," *Historische Zeitschrift* 282 (2006): 585–61.

10. Oexle, "Begriffsgeschichte," 384–85.

11. Karl Mannheim, *Das konservative Denken* (1927), 453.

12. Lucian Hölscher, *Öffentlichkeit und Geheimnis: Eine begriffsgeschichtliche Untersuchung zur Entstehung der Öffentlichkeit in der frühen Neuzeit* (Stuttgart: Klett-Cotta, 1979).

13. Christof Dipper, "Die 'Geschichtliche Grundbegriffe': Von der Begriffsgeschichte zur Theorie der historischen Zeiten," *Historische Zeitschrift* 270 (1999): 289.

14. Dirk van Laak, *Gespräche in der Sicherheit des Schweigens: Carl Schmitt in der politischen Geistesgeschichte der frühen Bundesrepublik*, 2nd ed. (Berlin, 2002).

15. *Encyclopedia of Religion*, ed. Mircea Eliade, 16 vols. (1987–93). A second edition is expanded rather than revised, ed. Lindsay Jones, 15 vols. (2005).

16. *Metzler Lexikon Religion*, ed. Christoph Auffarth, Jutta Bernard, and Hubert Mohr, 4 vols. (Stuttgart, 1999–2002). The editors are students of the editors of the *HrwG*. This work has been edited for the English-speaking world by Kocku von Stuckrad as *The Brill Dictionary of Religion* (Leiden: Brill, 2006).

17. Jonathan Z. Smith, "Religion, Religions, Religious," in *Critical Terms for Religious Studies*, ed. Mark C. Taylor (Chicago: University of Chicago Press, 1998), 269–84. In his *Imagining Religion: From Babylon to Jonestown* (Chicago: University of Chicago Press, 1982), xi, Jonathan Smith writes, "While there is a staggering amount of data, phenomena, of human experiences and expressions that might be characterized in one culture or another, by one criterion or another, as religion— *there is no data for religion*. Religion is solely the creation of the scholar's study. It is created for the scholar's analytic purposes by his imaginative acts of comparison and generalization. Religion has no independent existence apart from the academy." His statement is rebutted by Gustavo Benavides in "There Is Data for Religion," in *Journal of the American Academy of Religion* 71 (2003): 895–903. Smith's saying is quoted on a homepage of humanist atheism, http://atheism.about.com/od/religiondefinition/a/definition.htm, in order to prove that there is no religion at all.

18. Christoph Auffarth and Hubert Mohr, "Religion," *MLR* 3 (2000): 160–72. Martin Riese-brodt pleads for a "commmonsense" definition—football is not a religion; Buddhist meditation is religious though there is no god in it; Riesebrodt, *Cultus und Heilsversprechen: Eine Theorie der Religionen* (Munich, 2007).

19. Dario Sabbatucci asserts this in "Kultur und Religion," in *Handbuch religionswissenschaft-licher Grundbegriffe* (*HrwG*) 1 (1988): 43–58.

20. Catherine Bell, "Belief: A Classical Lacuna and Disciplinary 'Problem,'" in *Introducing Religion: Essays in Honor of Jonathan Z. Smith*, ed. Willi Braun and Russell T. McCutcheon (London: Equinox 2008), 85–99. Both in the 1986 edition of the *Encyclopedia of Religion*, ed. Mircea Eliade, 16 vols. (New York: Macmillan) and in the 2nd edition, ed. Lindsay Jones, 15 vols. (2005), one is directed from "Belief" to "Doubt and Belief" (2nd ed., 4:2423–27), which restricts the lemma to "the philosophical discussion of the interrelations of doubt and belief in the Western tradition." The second entry the reader is directed to is "Faith."

21. Christoph Auffarth, "Sind heilige Stätten transportabel? Axis Mundi und soziales Gedächt-nis," in *Noch eine Chance für die Religionsphänomenologie?*, ed. Axel Michaels and Fritz Stolz (Bern, 2001), 235–57.

22. Jaroslav Pelikan, "Faith," *ER*, 2nd ed., 2954–59; he calls the quotation "probably the best-known definition" of faith.

23. Christoph Auffarth, "Theologie als Religionskritik in der Europäischen Religionsges-chichte," *Zeitschrift für Religionswissenschaft* 15 (2007): 5–27 and *Einführung*, 1–4.

24. Auffarth, Bernard, and Mohr, eds., *Metzler Lexikon Religion*. See note 16 above.

25. Auffarth, "Religiosität/Glaube," *Metzler Lexikon Religion*, 3:188–96.

26. Lucian Hölscher, ed., *Das Jenseits: Facetten eines religiösen Begriffs in der Neuzeit* (Göttin-gen: Wallstein 2007); Hölscher, ed., *Baupläne der sichtbaren Kirche: Sprachliche Konzepte religiöser Vergemeinschaftung in Europa* (Göttingen: Wallstein 2007); Hölscher and Michael Geyer, eds., *Die Gegenwart Gottes in der modernen Gesellschaft: Transzendenz und religiöse Vergemeinschaftung in Deutschland* (Göttingen: Wallstein, 2006); Hölscher, *Semantik der Leere: Grenzfragen der Ges-chichtswissenschaft* (Göttingen: Wallstein, 2009).

27. Lucian Hölscher, "Strukturwandlungen religiöser Semantik in Deutschland seit der Aufklärung," in *Europäische Religionsgeschichte: Konzepte, Entwicklungspfade und Vermittlungs-formen eines doppelten Pluralismus*, ed. Hans Kippenberg et al. (Göttingen, 2009), 723–46; Lucian Hölscher, "Semantic Structures of Religious Change in Modern Germany," in *The Decline of Chris-tendom in Western Europe 1750–2000*, ed. Hugh McLeod and Werner Ustor (Cambridge: Cam-bridge University Press, 2003), 184–200; Lucian Hölscher, "Religion im Wandel: Von Begriffen des religiösen Wandels zum Wandel religiöser Begriffe," in *Religion als Thema der Theologie: Ges-chichte, Standpunkte und Perspektiven theologischer Religionskritik und Religionsbegründung*, ed. Wilhelm Gräb (Gütersloh: Kaiser, 1999), 45–62.

28. Lucian Hölscher, *Die Entdeckung der Zukunft* (Frankfurt am Main: S. Fischer. 1999). See Christoph Auffarth, "Mittelalterliche Eschatologie" (PhD diss., University of Groningen, 1996), 139–66; expanded version: Christoph Auffarth, *Irdische Wege und Himmlischer Lohn* (Göttingen, 2002), 210–52; see also Lucian Hölscher, "The History of the Future: The Emergence and Decline of a Temporal Concept in European History," *History of Concepts Newsletter*, no. 5 (2002): 10–15.

29. Compare the American "endism debate" (e.g., Richard Sennett, *The Fall of Public Man* [New York: Knopf, 1977]), which was resolved by the end of Communism in 1989, hailed by Francis Fukuyama as the end of history.

30. Reinhart Koselleck, "Fortschritt und Niedergang—Nachtrag zur Geschichte zweier Begriffe," in *Begriffsgeschichten: Studien zur Semantik und Pragmatik der politischen und sozialen*

Sprache (Frankfurt am Main: Suhrkamp, 2006); Hartmut Zinser, ed., *Der Untergang von Religionen* (Berlin: Reimer, 1986).

31. The concept was propagated by Anton de Lagarde and his followers around 1878. They advocated a specific national religion with the Brother Grimms' *Deutsche Sagen* as Bible. The key word is "the second reformation."

32. Christoph Markschies, *Warum hat das Christentum in der Antike überlebt? Ein Beitrag zum Gespräch zwischen Kirchengeschichte und systematischer Theologie* (Leipzig: EVA, 2004).

33. One thinks, of course, of Edward Gibbon's *The History of the Decline and Fall of the Roman Empire* (London, 1776–88); see also Wolf-Friedrich Schäufele, *"Defecit ecclesia": Studien zur Verfallsidee in der Kirchengeschichtsanschauung des Mittelalter* (Mainz: von Zabern, 2006); Rodney Stark, *The Rise of Mormonism* (New York: Columbia University Press, 2005); Rodney Stark, *The Rise of Christianity: A Sociologist Reconsiders History* (Princeton: Princeton University Press, 1996); the Harper Paperback Edition of 1997 is more explicit: *The Rise of Christianity: How the Obscure, Marginal Jesus Movement Became the Dominant Religious Force in the Western World in a Few Centuries*. Jan Bremmer's valedictory lecture is an excellent discussion of these concepts: *The Rise of Christianity Through the Eyes of Gibbon, Harnack and Rodney Stark*, 2nd ed. (Groningen: Barkhuis 2010).

34. In the article "Fortschritt" in GGB, Christian Meier constructs a prehistory of "progress" before 1800 and in antiquity as *Könnens-Bewusstsein*.

35. Christoph Auffarth, "'Weltreligion' als ein Leitbegriff der Religionswissenschaft im Imperialismus," in *Mission und Macht im Wandel politischer Orientierungen: Europäische Missionsgesellschaften in politischen Spannungsfeldern in Afrika und Asien zwischen 1800 und 1945*, ed. Ulrich van der Heyden and Holger Stoecker (Stuttgart: Steiner, 2005), 17–36.

36. *Encyclopaedia Britannica*, 9th ed., 20:358–71; see also Jan Bremmer, "Methodologische en terminologische notities bij de opkomst vande godsdienstgeschiednis in de achttiende en negentiende eeuw," *Nederlands Theologisch Tijdschrift* 57 (2003): 317; Anton van der Lem, ed., *Religie in de academische Arena: Leven en werk von C. P. Tiele* (Leiden, 2002), and Arie Molendijk, "CPT en de Godsdienstwetenschap," in *Geloof en onderzoek: Uit het leven en werk van C. P. Tiele 1830–1902*, ed. E. H. Cossee and H. D. Tjalsma (Rotterdam, 2002), 23–40.

37. The lectures of Vivekananda to the World Parliament of Religion can be found in Swami Vivekananda, *Wege des Yoga: Reden und Schriften*, ed. and intro. Martin Kämpchen (Frankfurt, 2009) (Complete Works, Calcutta 2003, 1–26).

38. Harnack's claim here is based on Hegel's notion that the church had integrated the best of all heresies, so that the suppression of those heresies resulted from the action of the world spirit. This idea was sharply contested by, for instance, Nikolaus von Lenau (quoted by Karl Marx in the preface of *Capital*), who attributed such violence to an action of the anti-Spirit. See Christoph Auffarth, "Das Ende der Katharer im Konzept einer Europäischen Religionsgeschichte," in *Religion im kulturellen Diskurs—Religion in Cultural Discourse: Festschrift für Hans G. Kippenberg zu seinem 65. Geburtstag*, ed. Kocku von Stuckrad and Brigitte Luchesi (Berlin, 2004), 291–305.

39. Kurt Rudolph, "Synkretismus: Vom theologischen Scheltwort zum religionswissenschaftlichen Begriff," in *Humanitas Religiosa: Festschrift Haralds Biezais* (Stockholm, 1979), 194–212; repr. in Rudolph, *Geschichte und Probleme der Religionswissenschaft* (Leiden, 1992), 193–215. For uses of Hegel's notion of synthesis, see Christoph Auffarth, "Die Dschagga-Neger 'aufgehoben' zwischen Kolonialherrn und Missionar: Ein religionswissenschaftliches Ausstellungsprojekt zu Mission und Kolonialismus in Tanganjika um 1900," in *Religion und Museum: Zur visuellen Repräsentation von Religion/en im öffentlichen Raum*, ed. Peter J. Bräunlein (Bielefeld, 2004), 223–39.

40. Harnack, *Mission und Ausbreitung* 1904, 4th ed., 1924. The same question was recently raised by Christoph Markschies in *Warum überlebte das Christentum in der antiken Welt?*

41. Peter Burke, *Kultureller Austausch* (Frankfurt am Main, 2000); see Christoph Auffarth, "Weltreligion und Globalisierung: Chicago 1893—Edinburgh 1910—Chicago 1993," *Zeitschrift für Mission und Religionswissenschaft* 94 (2010): 42–57.

11. God Lisped: Divine Accommodation and Cracks in Calvin's Scriptural Voice

Ernst van den Hemel

1. Thomas More and Martin Luther, *A Translation of St. Thomas More's Responsio Ad Lutherum* (Washington, D.C.: Catholic University of America Press, 1962).

2. James Simpson, in *Burning to Read: English Fundamentalism and Its Reformation Opponents,* focuses largely on the rise of fundamentalist readings during the English Reformation. With remarkable erudition, Simpson succeeds in placing the texts of Tyndale and others in the context of sixteenth-century textuality; see also Brian Cummings, Unfortunately, both of these books focus largely on English religious texts.

3. Simpson, *Burning to Read*, 142.

4. Brian Cummings, *The Literary Culture of the Reformation: Grammar and Grace* (Oxford: Oxford University Press, 2002), 5.

5. Ibid., 29.

6. John Calvin, *Institutes of the Christian Religion*, 1.1.3, 39.

7. Ibid., 1.13.1, 110.

8. Edward A. Dowey, *The Knowledge of God in Calvin's Theology* (Grand Rapids, Mich.: W. B. Eerdmans, 1994), 6.

9. E. David Willis, "Rhetoric and Responsibility in Calvin's Theology," in *The Context of Contemporary Theology*, ed. Alexander J. McKelway and E. David Willis (Atlanta: John Knox Press, 1974), 4; quoted in Jon Balserak, *Divinity Compromised: A Study of Divine Accommodation in the Thought of John Calvin* (Dordrecht: Springer, 2006), 4.

10. Ford Lewis Battles, "God Was Accommodating Himself to Human Capacity," *Interpretation: A Journal of Bible and Theology* 31 (1977): 20.

11. Balserak, *Divinity Compromised*, 9.

12. Ibid., 196.

13. Ibid., 190.

14. Ibid.

15. Ibid., 190–91.

16. Cicero, *De Oratore* (Cambridge, Mass.: Harvard University Press, 1967), 2.38, p. 158.

17. Augustine, *Confessions*, trans. R. S. Pine-Coffin (London: Penguin Classics, 1961), 6.5, p. 117; this theme is discussed in more detail in Augustine, *De Doctrina Christiana*, trans. R. H. Green (Oxford: Oxford University Press, 1995).

18. Ibid., 12.29, p. 307.

19. Ibid., 12.31, p. 308.

20. Ibid., 13.24, p. 335.

21. Alister E. McGrath, *The Christian Theology Reader* (Oxford: Wiley-Blackwell, 2006), 87.

22. Augustine, "De Vera Religione," in *Augustine: Earlier Writings*, trans. John H. S. Burleigh (Louisville: Westminster John Knox Press, 2006), 235.

23. Augustine, *Confessions*, 3.7, p. 63.

24. For a detailed analysis of the role of accommodation in the theology of Augustine, see chap. 4, "The Times May Change but Not the Faith," in Stephen D. Benin, *The Footprints of God: Divine Accommodation in Jewish and Christian Thought* (Albany: State University of New York Press, 1993), 93–126.

25. Augustine, "Contra Faustum Manicheum," in *Opera Omnia CAG Electronic Edition* (Charlottesville, Va.: Intelex Corporation, n.d.), 19, 16; 3:512–13, http://library.nlx.com/xtf/view? docId=augustine_la/augustine_la.00.xml;chunk.id=div.augustine_la.pmpreface.1;toc.depth=1;toc .id=div.augustine_la.pmpreface.1;brand=default&fragment_id=; cited in Benin, *Footprints of God*, 107.

26. Origen, "Contra Celsum," in *Ante-Nicene Fathers*, ed. Philip Schaff, Alexander Roberts, and James Donaldson 4 (Grand Rapids, Mich.: W. B. Eerdmans , 1885), chap. 49, 4:520.

27. Ibid., chap. 71, 4:529.

28. Balserak, in *Divinity Compromised*, states that Chrysostom is the theologian who uses the concept of accommodation most frequently, surpassed only by Calvin.

29. John Chrysostom, quoted in Benin, *Footprints of God*, 61.

30. Ibid., 63.

31. Ibid., 68.

32. Calvin, *Institutes of the Christian Religion*, 1.8.1, 75.

33. Ibid., 1.8.2, 75–76.

34. Ibid., 1.8.3, 76.

35. Ibid., 1.8.5, 77.

36. Glenn S. Sunshine and Martin L. Klauber, "Jean Alphonse Turrettini on Accommodation and Biblical Error: Calvinist or Socinian?" *Calvin Theological Journal* 25 (1990): 27.

37. Calvin, *Commentary on the First Book of Moses Called Genesis*, trans. John King (Grand Rapids, Mich.: Christian Classics Ethereal Library, 1999), 1:41.

38. Calvin, *Institutes of the Christian Religion*, 1.14.3, 143.

39. Calvin, *Commentary on the First Book of Moses Called Genesis*, 1:41.

40. Indeed, Michael Heyd, in "Un role nouveau pour la science," argues that Turrettini used the notion of accommodation to separate religion and science.

41. Jean Alphonse Turrettini, *Joh. Alphonsi Turretini Dilucidationes Philosophico-Theologi-co-Dogmatico-Moralis Quam Revelatae Demonstrantur. . . : Acc I. Orationes . . . Ii: Commercium Epistolicum Inter Regem Borussiae Frideric I. et Pastores Genevenses de Syncretismo Protestantium*, 1748, 2.5.20; cited in Sunshine and Klauber, "Jean Alphonse Turrettini on Accommodation and Biblical Error," 23.

42. François Wendel, *Calvin*, 358.

43. Ibid., 359.

44. Calvin, *Commentaries on the Twelve Minor Prophets*, trans. John Owen (Grand Rapids, Mich.: Christian Classics Ethereal Library, 1999), 3:75.

45. Calvin, *Institutes of the Christian Religion*, 1.17.13, 195–96.

46. Ibid., 2.12.5, 405.

47. Balserak, *Divinity Compromised*, 154.

48. Commenting on Micah 6:3, "O my people, what have I done unto thee?," Calvin states, "Here God, in the first place, offers to give a reason, if he was accused of any thing. It seems indeed unbecoming the character of God, that he should be thus ready as one guilty to clear himself: but this is said by way of concession; for the Prophet could not otherwise express, that nothing that deserved blame could be found in God. It is a personification, by which a character; not his own, is

ascribed to God. It ought not therefore to appear inconsistent, that the Lord stands forth here, and is prepared to hear any accusation the people might have, that he might give an answer, *My people! what have I done?* By using this kind expression, my people, he renders double their wickedness; for God here descends from his own elevation, and not only addresses his people, in a paternal manner, but stands as it were on the opposite side, and is prepared, if the people had anything to say, to give answer to it, so that they might mutually discuss the question, as it is usually done by friends"; Calvin, *Commentaries on the Twelve Minor Prophets*, 3:224.

49. Calvin, *Institutes of the Christian Religion*, 2.15.2–3, 435.

50. Helm, *John Calvin's Ideas*, 196.

51. Ibid., 208.

52. "Epistle to the Reader," in Calvin, *Institutes of the Christian Religion*, 25.

53. Calvin, *Institutes of the Christian Religion*, 1.14.11, 149.

54. Calvin, *Commentaries on the First Twenty Chapters of the Book of the Prophet Ezekiel*, trans. Thomas Meyers (Grand Rapids, Mich.: Christian Classics Ethereal Library, 1999), 138.

55. Balserak, *Divinity Compromised*, 55.

56. Calvin, *Commentary on the First Book of Moses Called Genesis*, 1:36.

57. Calvin, *Institutes of the Christian Religion*, 1.14.22, 157.

58. Balserak, *Divinity Compromised*, 150.

59. Calvin, *Institutes of the Christian Religion*, 1.15.3, 162.

60. Calvin, *Commentary on the First Book of Moses Called Genesis*, 1:36.

61. Balserak, *Divinity Compromised*, 150.

12. Rethinking the Implicit: Fragments of the Project on Aggada and Halakhah in Walter Benjamin

Sergey Dolgopolski

This project was initiated in part by a reading of Deleuze' s *Le pli*, which turned the concept of the implicit from one of the most general and self-evident logical concepts to the very specific one, related to the notion of a very specific conceptual formation (Gilles Deleuze, *Le pli: Leibniz et le baroque* [Paris: Editions de minuit, 1988]), and of Lyotard's *Emma* (Jean-François Lyotard, "Emma," *Nouvelle revue de psychoanalyse* 9, numéro spécial "Excitationen" [Special numbered supplement] [1989]: 43–70), which emphasized the trend to consider *implicit* as something that actually exists, is "ready-made," and is just waiting for time to be "excitated,"— i.e., to be brought, as it were, from basement to kitchen, from shelf to table, from storage to window, from implicit to explicit. In this essay I try to say that there are cases, when bringing from the darkness of the storage to the light of window, that modify things drastically or even destroy them, making the very bringing problematic.

1. Thus, in Bilaik's approach, Aggada seems to be included in this wide category of substantial literary form. Compare it with Bialik's definition of Aggada in "Le Knusah Shel Ha-Aggada": "The Hebrew written Aggada is a fundamental literary form, which dominated several hundreds of years in the world of folk and personal liberal creativity of the Israeli nation." The term *form* is further defined by Bialik in terms of *subject*, shape and *style*; see C. N. Bilaik, *Kol kitvei Ch.N Bialik* (Tel Aviv, 1962), 220.

2. Franz Brentano, *The Theory of Categories*, trans. Roderick M. Chisholm and Norbert Guterman (The Hague and Boston, 1981), 169–70ff.

3. Within the project of *language*, the *implicit* could not be the same as the *indirect*. It is Brentano's critique of this project that allows us to try to think about the implicit in terms of what is being thought of *in obliquo*.

4. Brentano, *Theory of Categories*, 169.

5. Ibid.

6. Thinking *in obliquo* is therefore a state or an act that is irrelevant to any classification in terms of actual existence or nonexistence.

7. If the grammatical importance of *Sein* (being as opposed to nonbeing, or in this context, existence as opposed to nonexistence) is complicated by Brentano and thereby displaced from its central position in grammar, Brentano's results can be applied to expressions that are not subject to grammatical rulings of *Sein*. This includes the texts of the Talmud, which organizes expressions around legal topics and speakers who rule or discuss rulings about them, rather than confining the narration to predications describing (or even prescribing) allegedly existent matters of fact. In Brentano's terms the Talmud treats determinations in the Mishnah as relative determinations, because, in the Talmud, the speakers presume the Mishnahic sages had something thought of "indirectly." For instance, the speakers in the Talmud, or later interpreters of it, discover a mental disposition wherein this or that utterance in the Mishnah takes place. It is the indirect character of this determination that makes Talmud an experience of discovery and invention rather than an explanation and commentary.

8. Worth noting is that medieval scholars of the rabbinic tradition used the form of tractate to think about that tradition and interpreted its corpus as a set of "tractates."

9. An affinity of Max Kadushin's and Walter Benjamin's approaches is worth highlighting here. The former, in his "conceptual" approach to rabbinic exegetical tradition of Midrash, shows a similar line of thinking: what Kadushin calls "concept-values" organize what he denotes as "rabbinic mind." Neither are fully present there as explicitly fully defined or locally definable concepts; see Kadushin, *The Rabbinic Mind* (New York: Bloch, 1972); Kadushin, *A conceptual approach to the Mekilta* (New York: J. David for the Jewish Theological Seminary of America), 1969.

10. This treatment of "Predications" is similar to Brentano's critique of using grammatical notion predication for thinking about either thinking or existence.

11. Walter Benjamin, *Illuminations*, trans. Harry Zohn (New York: Schocken, 1978), l44–45.

12. Walter Benjamin to Gershom Sholem, August 11, 1934.

13. Bilaik, "Halakhah ve-Aggada," *Kol kitvei Ch. N Bilaik* (Tel Aviv, 1962), 228.

14. Benjamin, *Illuminations*, 143–44.

15. Ibid., 144.

16. Ibid.

17. Franz Kafka, *Parables and Paradoxes*, trans. (New York, 1958), 11.

18. Noteworthy, such a failure is not a mistake. The latter can be corrected on the way to one's goal. The former, if corrected, produces no effect at all.

19. Jill Robbins, "Kafka's Parables," in *Midrash and Literature*, ed. Geoffrey H. Hartman and Sanford Budick (New Haven, Conn.: Yale University Press, 1986), 265–84.

20. Ibid., 265–84.

21. Neither is the implicit of the utterance "bring your son to a burnt offering" a case of a gap between signifier and signified. Through miss-taking it, the utterance reveals itself as standing outside of signification. Instead, it relates to signification only indirectly. In Brentano's terms "bring your son to burnt offering" is a relative determination, therefore it includes what he calls "thinking of" obliquely. The implicitness of the utterance was not clarified at the beginning of the story, and even in the end it was pointed out in, still being kept "in obliquo." There are two major

points preventing one from reducing the implicit to the positive terms of a gap between the signifier and signified. One comes from Benjamin's perspective, the other from Brentano's. According to the former, mistake is productive only because it is never known in advance as mistake. In this process, time is of the essence. The time of miss-taking is, however, not controllable from any subject position. Neither a subject (a character) positioned in the beginning of the story nor the already wise subject at the end can survey the time of mistake. At the end of the story the mistake is already understood as mistake and thus is no longer productive. Looking backward from the end-point of the story, the character, Abraham, realizes he committed a mistake. This realization makes the mistake neutral, which it was not in the real moment of the beginning. Now, at the end of the story, Abraham is the same subject as before, but he can never take the same subject position he had in the beginning. He can no longer commit any mistaken interpretation of the divine command, nor can he commit interpretation at all, because the productive ambivalence of that command is now fully articulated and thereby totally lost. At the end of the story its subject, Abraham, is the same, but he can never repeat his movement from the beginning to end, even if the story does it as many times as readers choose to follow it again and again. Yet, this is only because the time of the story is not the time of its reading. As Benjamin has it, the characters lose "in parable," but win "in reality." The time of the story has no subject to go through it unchanged. At least it does not have a self-identical, atom-like subject to live through, control, or know the story from the beginning to end, or even from the end to beginning. Abraham at the end cannot understand, explain, or interpret Abraham in the beginning. Rather the story, and in particular, mistake-making, has its own time, and this time is neither reversible, nor is it traceable back. The time of miss-taking, in other words, is not the time scanned by any self-identical subject. Rather, time is a machine, a device that makes miss-taking both possible and productive, with no unified subject to control the machine. The very setup of that time-machine (if I can recycle the term) is what makes the mistake ambivalent (that is, carrying a possibility of not being a mistake) in the beginning of the story and not at all possible in its end. In yet other words, Benjamin's position would be that every miss-*take* contains an element of irreversible *taking* on the unconceivable. The *taking* in the miss-*take* is irreversible, happens in time uncontrolled, and approaches the unconceivable without ever being able to reveal it. The unconceivable utterance of G-d thus remains unconceivable even at the end of the story, and its meaning stays as implicit as it was in the beginning. The only difference is that toward the end of the story, both Abraham and the readers know that they deal with an implicit that cannot be conceived in any full explication, yet with which Abraham nevertheless had to deal.

Benjamin's and Brentano's are two symmetrically opposite ways to approach the implicit. Benjamin begins from the implicit and argues for its independent existence, which makes it irreducible to any explication or interpretation. In contrast, Brentano begins from the multiplicity of mutually exclusive interpretations, one at a time, and from there arrives to thinking of the non-explicability of the implicit, without any claims about its existence or nonexistence. In more detail, from Benjamin's standpoint, the utterance "bring [Isaac] to sacrifice" proves to be unconceivable and in that similar to *ideas*. The unconceivable remains implicit and therefore resists grasping. What gives the implicit power to remain implicit despite all attempts at explication? What else if not the power of its existence, as opposed to nonexistence? To remain implicit, the implicit therefore must exist. Conversely, either existence or nonexistence of the implicit is irrelevant for Brentano. For him the implicit is what is thought of, not what either exists or not. Therefore he begins from multiple explications or interpretations. You cannot directly think of the divine utterance "bring your son to burnt offering" in bypass of at least one of its competing interpretations. From that point of view, sticking to one of these senses at a time (either "slaughter" or "bring to the altar") makes Abraham destined to miss-take. Through that experience of miss-taking, by the end of the story, Abraham and readers think of the utterance as exceeding any of its interpretations, and therefore think of it as implicit—again, no matter existent or not.

What it means, however, is that in either Brentano's or Benjamin's views, the only way of speaking about the implicit in terms of signifier and signified would be defining the implicit as a gap between a signified ("slaughter") and another signified ("bring to the altar"). Both signified would then have the same signifier: the divine utterance. However, shared signifier cannot explain the glaring gap as opposed to a simple difference between the signified. This is why the linguistic theory of signification, or for that matter the project of language as an object of linguistics, provides no sufficient reading.

Can one overcome this limitation of purely linguistic approach to reading the story? Even beyond the narrower scope of linguistics, the terms of a gap between signifier and another signifier belong to Lacan's theory psychoanalysis, which still is considerably dependent on the model of language as the object of linguistics. However, in Lacan's theory of psychoanalysis the subject position plays more prominent role than it does in pure linguistics. The gap therefore can be discovered from a specific subject position, that of the analyst, thereupon it becomes noticeable from another subject position, that of the patient. The latter, of course, does not assume the position of the analyst, but rather gets access to the gap by means of the patience relationship to the analyst, which in most cases is that of transference. Is Abraham the analyst and the reader or even G-d's patient? That suggestion does not help. The machinery of miss-taking neither requires disclosing nor dismisses transference. Rather, its mode of work is closer to Freud's topology of evident and hidden content of dream than it is to Lacan's reformulation of Freud's theory in linguistic terms of signification and of gaps between signifiers.

22. TB Gittin 43b.

23. Ibid.

24. In the original there is a slight difference between Raba Bar Rav Huna's logical conclusion and Raba's citation of it, which shows Raba's attempt to use it for his own current discourse, where the expression "has not any [approved] betrothal" is used rather than "is not betrothed." Raba does it because he uses it as a symmetric analogy for a man who is half-a-slave, who semantically cannot "*be betrothed," he only can "*have approved or non-approved betrothal."

25. Isaiah 3:6.

26. Here Rava Bar Rav Huna speaks, slightly changing the "thesaurus" of his utterance: in his first analogical inference he used "is/is not [legally] betrothed"; now he uses thesaurus of "has/has not [legally approved] betrothal." Cited by Raba, the conclusion uses the second "thesaurus," which fits better to the Raba's task of making an analogy between a male half-slave betrothing a woman (free or not) and a female half-slave to be betrothed.

27. Rashi's medieval commentary *ad locum* explains the structure of miss-taking as follows: "This ruin"—with these words "The Bible says 'This ruin is in your hands' applies to the people of Jerusalem who lost their access to learning Torah, and they were asking their fellows [all Torah questions] saying, 'You have your garment, let you be our officer and let this ruin be under your hands,' meaning they tell us the hidden things which are hard to explain, for they are like your garment [which you miraculously have when we do not] you have an intimate knowledge of the Torah, because the garment is own intimately by its owner, so you tell us those hidden things and let you be our teacher, and this ruin, that is the matters of Torah, will be under your hand, because no one can hold the words of Torah without failing in them. That is, a man cannot understand the truth of the words of the [oral] Torah until he will fail by teaching them with mistake, and he is corrected, and he accepts and understands. [Thus Rava Bar Rav Huna said to Rav Hisda] They are under your hands, Oh Rav Hisda, and I failed." This explanation lets the readers decide whether

Rava Bar Rav Huna was ironic or not. Or else, it assumes, following the larger framework of the Talmud, that he was certainly ironic, both based on the explanation ("What was the reason etc.") and on a general tactic of failing proofs in the sequence.

28. Haiyim Zalman Dimitrovski, "Al Derekh Ha-Pilpul," in *Salo Wittmayer Baron: Jubilee Volume on the Occasion of His Eightieth Birthday*, Hebrew Section (1975), 111–83. Daniel Boyarin, *Sephardi Speculation: A Study in Methods of Talmudic Interpretation* (Jerusalem: Ben Zvi Institute, 1989); Sergey Dolgopolski, *What Is Talmud? The Art of Disagreement* (New York: Fordham University Press, 2009).

29. Walter Benjamin, *Illuminations*, ed. and intro. Hannah Arendt; trans. Harry Zohn (New York: Schocken, 1986), 111–40.

30. Ibid., 9.

31. Ibid., 111–12.

32. Ibid., 122.

33. The terms *Aggada* and *Halakhah* serve for Benjamin also as a marker for the tradition of a specific prose-form that he contrasts with the Western tradition of the prose-form, such as parable, which has perhaps implicit, but surely explicable "face value" doctrine behind it. In the perspective of Benjamin, the Talmud is similar to Aggada without any implied Halakhah—that is, the Talmudic story proves not to belong to the Western prose-form: it does not have any implicit but explicable "doctrine," even if medieval and modern interpreters of Talmud as a source of Halakhah constantly attempt to reach to such explication.

13. What Cannot Be Said: Apophasis and the Discourse of Love

Jean-Luc Marion

NOTE: This article originally appeared in translation in *Proceedings of the American Catholic Philosophical Association* 76 (2002): 39–56. It has been reprinted in *The Visible and the Revealed*, trans. Christina M. Gschwandtner et al. (New York: Fordham University Press, 2008), 101–19.

1. 1 Cor. 2:9, quoting Isa. 64:4: "From ages past no one has heard, no ear has perceived, no eye has seen any God besides you, who works for those who wait for him."

2. René Descartes, *Meditations*, Fifth Replies, *Oeuvres de Descartes*, ed. Charles Adams and Paul Tannery (Paris: Vrin, CNRS, 1964–79), 7:368, 2–4.

3. John Chrysostom, *On the Incomprehensible Nature of God* (Washington, D.C.: Catholic University of America Press, 1984).

4. Immanuel Kant, *Immanuel Kant's Critique of Pure Reason*, trans. Norman Kemp Smith (London: Macmillan, 1964), A761, B789.

5. Ludwig Wittgenstein, *Tractatus Logico-philosophicus* (London: Routledge, 1922), 7.

6. Martin Heidegger, "Protocole à un séminaire sur la conférence *Zeit und Sein*," *Questions* IV, ed. Jean Beaufret (Paris: Gallimard, 1976), 83; the German version can be found in *Zur Sache des Denkens* (Tübingen: Max Niemeyer, 1969), 51. Cf.: "It must remain an open question whether the nature of Western languages is in itself marked with the exclusive brand of metaphysics . . . or whether these languages offer other possibilities of utterance—and that means at the same time of a *telling silence*" (Martin Heidegger, *Identity and Difference*, trans. Joan Stambaugh [New York: Harper and Row, 1969], 73).

7. Wittgenstein, *Tractatus Logico-philosophicus*, 6.522 (see also 6.432 and 6.44).

8. Jacques Derrida, "How to Avoid Speaking," trans. Ken Frieden, in *Languages of the Unsayable: The Play of Negativity in Literature and Literary Theory*, ed. Sanford Budick and Wolfgang Iser (New York: Columbia University Press, 1989), 3–70; Derrida, *Given Time: I. Counterfeit Money*, trans. Peggy Kamuf (Chicago: University of Chicago Press, 1991); and Derrida, *Sauf le nom*, trans. John P. Leavey Jr., in Derrida, *On the Name*, ed. Thomas Dutoit (Stanford, Calif.: Stanford University Press, 1998), 35–85, in which Derrida discusses Jean-Luc Marion, *The Idol and Distance: Five Studies*, trans. Thomas A. Carlson (New York: Fordham University Press, 2001); Marion, *God without Being*, trans. Thomas A. Carlson (Chicago: University of Chicago Press, 1991), and Marion, *Reduction and Givenness: Investigations of Husserl, Heidegger, and Phenomenology*, trans. Thomas A. Carlson (Evanston, Ill.: Northwestern University Press, 1998).

9. Derrida, *Sauf le nom*, 70.

10. John Scotus Eriugena, *De Divisione Naturae*, I.14, Patrologia Latina 122, col. 462.

11. Aristotle, *On Interpretation*, 4.17a4.

12. See my response to Derrida in Marion, "In the Name: How to Avoid Speaking of 'Negative Theology,'" in *God, the Gift, and Postmodernism*, ed. John D. Caputo and Michael Scanlon (Bloomington: Indiana University Press, 1999), 20–42, and then in Marion, *In Excess: Studies of Saturated Phenomena*, trans. Robyn Horner and Vincent Berraud (New York: Fordham University Press, 2002), chap. 6, "In the Name: How to Avoid Speaking of It," esp. sec. 2, 134–42.

13. Stendhal, *La Chartreuse de Parme*, chap. 28.

14. Edmund Husserl, *Logische Untersuchungen*, 2 vols. (Halle: Max Niemeyer, 1922), 1:26, esp. 2:82ff.

15. J. L. Austin, *How to Do Things with Words* (Cambridge, Mass.: Harvard University Press, 1962), 109.

16. Ibid, 121: "Thus we distinguish the locutionary act (and within it the phonetic, the phatic, and the rhetic acts) which has a *meaning* [from] the illocutionary act which has a certain *force* in saying something."

17. Michel de Montaigne, *Essais*, I.28, ed. P. Villey (Paris : V. L. Saulnier, 1965), 1:189.

18. Austin, *How to Do Things with Words*, 15.

19. Stanley Cavell, "La passion," in the collective work modestly titled *Quelle philosophie pour le XXIe siècle? L'organon du nouveau siècle* (Paris: Pompidou Center, 2001), 373; the English original can be found as "Performative and Passionate Utterance," in Cavell, *Philosophy the Day after Tomorrow* (Cambridge, Mass.: Harvard University Press, 2005), 181; further citations will be to the English version. Cavell's discussion of Austin's conditions has been helpful for my own analysis.

20. Austin and Searle should not be confused on this point. Austin classifies "to promise" among the commissives (*How to Do Things with Words*, 157), mentions insincerity (18, 40), and has not a single word to say about "to love." J. R. Searle, *Speech Acts: An Essay in the Philosophy of Language* (Cambridge: Cambridge University Press, 1969), 57–62, gives a thorough analysis of the illocutionary act "to promise" (including the promise without sincerity) but without making the slightest allusion to "I love you."

21. Austin, *How to Do Things with Words*, 109. In this sense, it remains a performative (110).

22. Searle, *Speech Acts*, 25.

23. Cavell, "Performative and Passionate Utterance," 173.

24. Roland Barthes hesitates on this point; sometimes, he is confused: "this word [I-love-you] is always *true* (it has no other referent than its offering of itself: it is a performative)"; sometimes, he sees things correctly, though not without imprecision: "The atopia of love, what is proper to it and allows it to escape from all theses, is that *in the last instance* we can speak of it only according to *a*

strict allocutionary determination; in the discourse on love there is always a person to whom one speaks, even if this person takes the form of a ghost or a creature from the future. No one wants to talk about love, if it is not *for* someone" (Roland Barthes, *A Lover's Discourse: Fragments*, trans. Richard Howard [New York: Hill and Wang, 1978], trans. modified for this context). Or rather, no one wants to speak *about* love, if not to someone who is *loved*, for one can very well speak *about* love without love, and without a loved one.

25. Austin, *How to Do Things with Words*, 101 (my emphasis).

26. Cavell, "Performative and Passionate Utterance," 180.

27. Austin, *How to Do Things with Words*, 122 and 119.

28. Cavell, "Performative and Passionate Utterance," 180; cf. Austin: "The 'I' that accomplishes the action does thus come essentially into the picture" (*How to Do Things with Words*, 61).

29. Austin, *How to Do Things with Words*, 119.

30. Cavell, "Performative and Passionate Utterance."

31. Descartes mentions this in *Passions de l'âme*, §82, in *Oeuvres de Descartes*, 11:388–89.

32. Barthes's opinion could not be more misplaced: "Once the first avowal has been made, '*I love you*' has no meaning whatsoever; it merely repeats in an enigmatic mode—so blank does it appear—the old message (which may not have been transmitted in these words). I repeat it though it may no longer have any relevance; it leaves language behind, it rambles, where?" (Barthes, *Lover's Discourse*, 175; trans. modified). It does not ramble, since it repeats, and it does not repeat in a void, since it thereby maintains the lover's discourse, despite the apophasis that apophasis inevitably provokes. It is only this repetition that gives time to the lover's discourse, its only possible time, possibly precisely despite the impossibility that the present inflicts upon it.

33. Alphonse de Lamartine, "Le poète mourant," in *Les Nouvelles Méditations* (Paris: U. Canel, 1823), 125–26.

14. Givenness and the Basic Problems of Phenomenology

Tarek R. Dika

Since this essay was written, I, together with W. Chris Hackett, conducted an interview with Jean-Luc Marion at his home in Paris. I refer the reader to the interview, which can be found in *Quiet Powers of the Possible: Interviews in Contemporary French Phenomenology* (New York: Fordham University Press, 2015), where Marion raises a number of salient points that I could not fully address here.

1. Immanuel Kant, *Critique of Pure Reason*, trans. Paul Guyer and Allen Wood (Cambridge: Cambridge University Press, 1998), A575/B603–A579/B607.

2. Immanuel Kant, *Critique of Practical Reason*, trans. Mary J. Gregor (Cambridge: Cambridge University Press, 1996), 239–41.

3. Immanuel Kant, *Religion within the Boundaries of Mere Reason*, trans. Thomas M. Greene (Chicago: Open Court, 1934), 11.

4. See, e.g., Jean-Luc Marion, "Metaphysics and Phenomenology: A Relief for Theology," trans. Thomas A. Carlson, in *Religion: Beyond a Concept*, ed. Hent de Vries (New York: Fordham University Press, 2008), 290: "Phenomenology goes unambiguously beyond metaphysics in the strict sense that it gets rid of any *a priori* principle in order to admit givenness, which is originary precisely insofar as it is a posteriori for the one who receives it. Phenomenology goes beyond metaphysics insofar as it gives up the transcendental project in order to allow the development of a

finally radical empiricism—finally radical because it is no longer limited to sensible intuition but admits all originarily giving intuition." The essay originally appeared in *Critical Inquiry* 20 (Summer 1994); the quote is from p. 582.

5. See François-David Sebbah, *Testing the Limit: Derrida, Henry, Levinas, and the Phenomenological Tradition*, trans. Stephen Barker (Stanford, Calif.: Stanford University Press, 2012), 4: "To be interested in the practice of excess is thus, precisely, to be interested in the practice of the *limit*, the limit through whose transgression alone excess can be what it is. In fact, in the case of phenomenology, the legitimate limit—the limit as legitimizing norm—is the limit of the domain of what appears *as* it appears, the limit of the *given*."

6. See Michel Henry, "Quatre principes de la phénoménologie," *Revue de métaphysique et de moral*, no. 1 (1991): 3–25; Jean Greisch, "L'hermeneutique dans la 'phénoménologie comme telle': Trois questions à propos *Réduction et Donation*," *Revue de Métaphysique et de Morale* 96, no.1 (1991): 43–63; Natalie Dépraz, "Gibt es eine Gebung des Unendlichen?" in *Perspektiven der Philosophie*, ed. Rudolph Berlinger (Amsterdam: Rodopi, 1997), 111–55; Jean Grondin, "La tension de le donation ultime et de la pensée herméneutique de l'application chez Jean-Luc Marion," *Dialogue* 38, no. 3 (1999): 547–59; Dépraz, review of Jean-Luc Marion, *Étant donné*, *Revue de Métaphysique et de Morale*, no. 4 (October–December 2000), 564–68; Beatrice Han, "Transcendence and the Hermeneutic Circle: Some Thoughts on Marion and Heidegger," in *Transcendence in Philosophy and Religion*, ed. James Faulconer (Bloomington: Indiana University Press, 2003); Kevin Hart, ed., *Counter-Experiences: Reading Jean-Luc Marion* (Notre Dame, Ind.: University of Notre Dame Press, 2007); Jocelyn Benoist, *L'idée de phénoménologie* (Paris: Beauchesne, 2001); Benoist, "L'écart plutôt que l'excédent," *Philosophie* 78 (2003): 77–93; Emmanuel Falque, "Phénoménologie de l'extraordinaire," *Philosophie* 78 (2003): 52–76; Ruud Welton, "Saturation and Disappointment: Marion according to Husserl," *Tijdschrift voor Filosofie en Theologie* 65, no. 1 (2004): 79–96; Shane Mackinlay, *Interpreting Excess: Jean-Luc Marion, Saturated Phenomena, and Hermeneutics* (New York: Fordham University Press, 2010); Joeri Schrijvers, *Ontotheological Turnings? The Decentering of the Modern Subject in Recent French Phenomenology* (Albany: State University of New York Press, 2011).

7. See Jean-Yves Lacoste, "Penser à Dieu en l'aimant: Philosophie et théologie de J. L. Marion," *Archives de Philosophie* 50 (1987): 245–70; Dominique Janicaud et al., *Phenomenology and the "Theological Turn": The French Debate* (New York: Fordham University Press, 2000); Jeffrey L. Kosky, "Philosophy of Religion and Return to Phenomenology in Jean-Luc Marion: From *God without Being* to *Being Given*," *American Catholic Philosophical Quarterly* 78, no. 4 (2004): 629–47; Dominique Janicaud, *Phenomenology "Wide Open": After the French Debate*," trans. Charles N. Cabral (New York: Fordham University Press, 2005).

8. Jean-Luc Marion, *Being Given: Toward a Phenomenology of Givenness*, trans. Jeffrey L. Kosky (Stanford, Calif.: Stanford University Press, 2002), 197. Marion develops the concept of the saturated phenomenon in *Being Given*, §§19–24, and in *In Excess: Studies of Saturated Phenomena*, trans. Robyn Horner and Vincent Berraud (New York: Fordham University Press, 2002).

9. Marion compares saturated phenomena to Kant's concept of aesthetic ideas in *Being Given*, §20, 198: "in the case of the aesthetic idea, 'the representation of the imagination . . . occasions much thinking [*viel zu denken veranlasst*] though without it being possible for any determinate thought, i.e., concept, to be adequate to it [*adäquat sein kann*].' The excess of intuition over every concept makes it such that 'no language fully attains or makes intelligible' the aesthetic idea; in short, it prevents the aesthetic idea from making an object visible"; see Immanuel Kant, *Critique of the Power of Judgment*, trans. Paul Guyer and Eric Matthews (Cambridge: Cambridge University Press, 2000), §42, 192.

10. See Marion, *Being Given*, §§3 and 23.

11. See nn. 6–7, above.

12. See Marion, *Being Given*, §20, 196–99; §28, 294–96.

13. See n. 5, above.

14. See Jean-Luc Marion, *Reduction and Givenness: Investigations of Husserl, Heidegger, and Phenomenology*, trans. Thomas A. Carlson (Evanston, Ill.: Northwestern University Press, 1998), §1, 4–40; *Being Given*, bk. 2 and §28, 294–96.

15. See "On the Gift: A Discussion between Jacques Derrida and Jean-Luc Marion," moderated by Richard Kearney, in *God, the Gift, and Postmodernism*, ed. John D. Caputo and Michael J. Scanlon (Bloomington: Indiana University Press, 1999), 54–78. On 71, Derrida, disagreeing with Marion, states: "The excess, the structure, in which I am interested, is not an excess of intuition." I examine the nature of this disagreement in §4 of this chapter.

16. See Jacques Derrida, "Différance," in *Margins of Philosophy*, trans. Alan Bass (Chicago: University of Chicago Press, 1982), 1–28.

17. See Marion, *Being Given*, §28, 294–96.

18. Martin Heidegger, *Being and Time*, trans. John Macquarrie and Edward Robinson (New York: Harper and Row, 1962), §7, 51; cf. Marion, *Being Given*, §1, 8.

19. Derrida, "Différance," 23.

20. Jacques Derrida, *Of Grammatology*, trans. Gayatri Chakravorty Spivak (Baltimore: Johns Hopkins University Press, 1997), 65.

21. See Marion, *Reduction and Givenness*, 34: "Nothing precedes givenness, which is modulated in all the modes of the phenomenon, whatever they might be. More 'broadened' than intuition, more autonomous than signification, givenness gives the phenomenon through itself because it falls thoroughly to givenness to deal the thing in person."

22. Edmund Husserl, "Phenomenology," trans. Richard E. Palmer, in *The Essential Husserl* (Bloomington: Indiana University Press, 1999), 328–29.

23. Husserl refers to the fact that the intentional relatedness of consciousness to its object "resides in the meaning of all expressions in the vernacular languages" that relate to conscious experience as always being *of* something or other. Ibid., 323.

24. Ibid., 324.

25. See Edmund Husserl, *Crisis of the European Sciences and Transcendental Phenomenology: An Introduction to Phenomenological Philosophy*, trans. David Carr (Evanston, Ill.: Northwestern University Press, 1970), §48.

26. Ibid., §46; cf. Edmund Husserl, *Collected Works*, vol. 8, *The Idea of Phenomenology*, trans. L. Hardy (Dordrecht: Kluwer, 2010), 68: "The task is this: to track down [*nachzugehen*], within the framework [*Rahmens*] of pure evidence or self-givenness, *all correlations and forms of givenness*, and to elucidate them through analysis."

27. See Edmund Husserl, *Logical Investigations*, trans. J. N. Findlay (New York: Routledge, 1970), I, §2, 168: "Meanings inspired only by remote, confused, inauthentic intuitions—if by any intuitions at all—are not enough: we must go back to the 'things themselves.' We desire to render self-evident in fully-fledged intuitions that what is here given in actually performed abstractions is what the word-meanings in our expression of the law really and truly stand for." See Marvin Farber, *The Foundation of Phenomenology: Edmund Husserl and the Quest for a Rigorous Science of Philosophy* (Albany: State University of New York Press, 1967), 218: "The 'phenomenology' represented by the *Logical Investigations* makes use of immanent intuition alone, and does not pass beyond the sphere of the intuitively given. That is the meaning of the precept 'Back to the things themselves': it meant the appeal to intuitive givenness."

28. Edmund Husserl, *Ideas Pertaining to a Pure Phenomenology and Phenomenological Philosophy, I: General Introduction to a Pure Phenomenology*, trans. Fred Kersten (Dordrecht: Kluwer, 1982), §24, 44.

29. See ibid., §§32–34, §§56–62; cf. Martin Heidegger, *History of the Concept of Time: Prolegomena*, trans. Theodore Kisiel (Bloomington: Indiana University Press, 1985), §10b. It should not come as a surprise that Heidegger, suspending the methodological requirements of Husserlian phenomenology, determines the being of *Dasein*, not according to essence (as opposed to fact and existence), but rather according to facticity, existence, and mineness (*Jemeinigkeit*). The suspension of the eidetic reduction permits Heidegger to identify *Dasein* with *Jemeinigkeit*. For Husserl, such an identification cannot be made: there remains a gap between the "I" and the "me," the latter belonging to the domain of a constituted psychology, the former to pure, transcendental phenomenology. I discuss this below. See Heidegger, *Being and Time*, §9, §12, and §43; see also Husserl, "Phenomenology."

30. Husserl, *Idea of Phenomenology*, 66.

31. Husserl, *Ideas* I, §33, 63: "Important motives which have their ground in epistemological requirements [*Motive*] justify us in referring to 'pure' consciousness . . . also as *transcendental consciousness*, and the operation through which it is acquired as *transcendental epoché*"; cf. Edmund Husserl, *Cartesian Meditations: An Introduction to Phenomenology*, trans. Dorion Cairns (Dordrecht: Kluwer, 1960).

32. Heidegger, *History of the Concept of Time*, §11, 102.

33. Ibid., §11a, 103; see Husserl, *Ideas* I, §77.

34. Heidegger, *History of the Concept of Time*, §11b, 104.

35. Ibid.

36. Husserl, *Ideas* I, §49, 110. Marion describes the difference between Husserl's and Descartes's formulations in *Reduction and Givenness*, 82–83: "Husserl . . . modifies Descartes's formula: he omits *alia* in '*alia re*' and accepts *res* only between quotation marks: '*nulla "re*.'" Why? Obviously because *alia* (*res*) would imply that consciousness was itself and first a *res*; but Husserl undertakes here precisely to oppose consciousness to *realitas*; therefore, in defiance of any philological probity, he must modify what, in the quotation from Descartes, would implicitly extend *realitas* to the *res cogitans*, in order to retain from it only the application of substantiality to the ego."

37. Husserl, *Ideas* I, §49, 112.

38. Heidegger, *History of the Concept of Time*, §11c, 105.

39. Ibid., 106.

40. Ibid., §11d, 106.

41. See Husserl, *Ideas* I, §§1–17 ("Fact and Essence").

42. See ibid., §34 ("The Essence of Consciousness as Theme of Inquiry"); see also §§1–17.

43. Heidegger, *History of the Concept of Time*, §11d, 106.

44. Ibid., §13d, 124: "the kind of being of the acts is left undetermined."

45. Ibid., §11d, 107.

46. Heidegger, *Being and Time*, §6, 46.

47. See Descartes, AT IXB, 24–32; AT VII, §194, 12.

48. Heidegger, *History of the Concept of Time*, §12, 110.

49. Heidegger, *Basic Problems of Phenomenology*, §20, 281–82; cf. Aristotle, *Posterior Analytics*, in *The Complete Works of Aristotle*, ed. Jonathan Barnes (Princeton, N.J.: Princeton University Press, 1991), 1:71a–71b: "All teaching and all intellectual learning come about from already existing knowledge. This is evident if we consider it in every case; for the mathematical sciences are acquired

in this fashion, and so is each of the other arts. . . . It is necessary to be aware of things in two ways: of some things it is necessary to believe already that they are, of some one must grasp what the thing said is, and of others both—e.g., of the fact that everything is either affirmed or denied truly, one must believe that it is; of the triangle, that it signifies *this*; and of the unit both (both what it signifies and that it is). For each of these is not equally clear to us. . . . Before the induction, or before getting a deduction, you should perhaps be said to understand in a way—but in another way not. . . . But nothing, I think, prevents one from in a sense understanding and in a sense being ignorant of what one is learning; for what is absurd is not that you should know in some sense what you are learning, but that you should know it in this sense, i.e., in the way and sense in which you are learning it."

50. Heidegger, *Basic Problems of Phenomenology*, §5, 21; cf. Marion, *Reduction and Givenness*, 64–65.

51. "All ontologies . . . fall under the blow of the reduction and disappear therein"; Husserl, *Ideas Pertaining to a Pure Phenomenology and to a Phenomenological Philosophy*, III: *Phenomenology and the Foundation of the Sciences*, §14.

52. Marion, *Being Given*, §4, 39.

53. Ibid., §3, 38.

54. Marion, *Reduction and Givenness*, 203.

55. Marion, *Being Given*, §1, 14.

56. Ibid., §1, 15 (trans. modified).

57. Ibid., §1, 18; see Husserl, *Idea of Phenomenology*, 45.

58. Marion, *Being Given*, §1, 16.

59. Ibid., §2, 26.

60. Ibid., §3, 38.

61. Husserl, *Logical Investigations*, VI, §40, 774.

62. Ibid., 775.

63. Ibid.

64. Ibid., 784–85.

65. Marion, *Reduction and Givenness*, 11.

66. Husserl, *Logical Investigations*, II, VI, §40, 785.

67. Marion, *Reduction and Givenness*, 15.

68. Ibid., 19.

69. Cited in ibid., 36; see also Heidegger, *Four Seminars*, trans. Andrew Mitchell and François Raffoul (Bloomington: Indiana University Press, 2003), 67.

70. Husserl, *Logical Investigations*, VI, §63, 824.

71. Marion, *Reduction and Givenness*, 30.

72. Ibid., 20.

73. Jacques Derrida, *Speech and Phenomena*, trans. David B. Allison (Evanston, Ill.: Northwestern University Press, 1973), 93.

74. See Husserl, *Logical Investigations*, I, §11, 285–86: "If 'possibility' or 'truth' is lacking, an assertion's intention can only be carried out symbolically: it cannot derive any 'fullness' from intuition or from the categorial functions performed on the latter, in which fullness its value for knowledge consists. It then lacks, as one says, a 'true,' a 'genuine' meaning"; see also Derrida, *Speech and Phenomena*, 8: "being interested in language only within the compass of rationality, determining the logos from logic, Husserl had, in the most traditional manner, determined the essence of language by taking the logical as its telos or norm. That this telos is that of being as presence is what we

here wish to suggest." See also ibid., 97–98: "the theme of full 'presence,' the intuitionistic impera-tive, and the project of knowledge continue to command—at a distance, we said—the whole of the description. Husserl describes, and in one and the same movement effaces, the emancipation of speech as nonknowing. The originality of meaning as an aim is limited by the telos of vision. To be radical, the difference that separates intention from intuition would nonetheless have to be *pro-visional*." For Marion's response to these remarks, see *Reduction and Givenness*, 25–26.

75. Marion, *Reduction and Givenness*, 25–26.

76. Ibid., 29.

77. Ibid., 22–29.

78. Ibid., 22.

79. Ibid., 29.

80. Ibid., 32.

81. Ibid., 34.

82. Ibid., 33.

83. Ibid., 34.

84. Husserl, *Logical Investigations*, VI, §63, 824.

85. See ibid., §21: "signitive intentions are in themselves '*empty*,' and . . . 'are in *need* of fullness.' In the transition from a signitive intention to the corresponding intuition, we experience no mere increase, as in the change from a pale image or a mere sketch to a fully alive painting. The signitive intention is rather lacking in every sort of fullness: the intuitive presentation first brings fullness to it and, through identification, into it. A signitive intention merely points to its object, an intuitive intention gives it 'presence,' in the pregnant sense of the word, it imports something of the fullness of the object itself. . . . A signitive presentation . . . is 'in reality' no 'presentation,' in it nothing of the object comes to life. The ideal of complete fullness is, accordingly, the fullness of the object itself." It does not appear to me that Marion's reading of the quotation marks surrounding "true" and "genuine" in *Logical Investigations*, I, I, §11 (see n. 92 above)—according to which Husserl is char-acterizing, not his own position, but rather that of "natural consciousness"—holds here. On the contrary, what these quotation marks indicate is an attempt to say "metaphorically" what Husserl is struggling to say "literally."

86. Marion, *Being Given*, §3, 31–32: "What obscure authority imposes that all that is and all that gives itself be subsumed under the object and its objectness? . . . and what is the significance, in the case of the phenomenon, of the 'privilege of *primordial objectness* [*Urgegenständlichkeit*]' . . . ? . . . For in the end what motivates the phenomenon that appears only insofar as it gives itself to always admit objectness as its originary horizon? Why would this phenomenal horizon not open, starting with, for example, the very givenness that gives appearing to it?"; see also Jacques Derrida, *Introduction to Husserl's* Origin of Geometry, trans. John P. Leavey Jr. (Lincoln: University of Nebraska Press, 1989), 64: "The sense of sense in general is here determined as *object* . . . [this] is very much in accord with the initial direction of phenomenology: the object in general is the final category of everything that can appear, i.e., that can be for a pure consciousness in general. Objects in general join all regions to consciousness, the *Ur-Region*."

87. Marion, *Being Given*, §20, 197.

88. Ibid.

89. Ibid., §§21–25, 199–247; see also Kant, *Critique of Pure Reason*, B188/A149–B273/A226.

90. Marion, *Being Given*, §22, 213.

91. Ibid., §24, 235–36.

92. Ibid., §3, 27.

93. See nn. 20–21, above.

94. This should be carefully distinguished from *universality*. Givenness can be universal with respect to everything we call "given" (everything, according to Marion); to every phenomenon there may belong a "mode of givenness" without it being necessary that givenness itself be unconditioned by anything else.

95. Marion, *Being Given*, §5, 55.

96. Derrida, "Différance," 8.

97. Marion, *Being Given*, §28, 294–95.

98. Ibid., 295.

99. Ibid.

100. Ibid., 296.

101. Ibid., §20, 197: "unconditioned and irreducible phenomena . . . become thinkable and possible only if a finally nonfinite intuition could secure their givenness. . . . To the limited possibility of phenomenality, shouldn't we . . . oppose a finally unconditionally possible phenomenality, whose scope would not be the result of the finitude of the conditions of experience?"

102. Ibid., §23, 225.

103. Ibid., §22, 213.

104. Ibid., §20, 191: "The equality that Husserl officially maintains between intuition and intention in fact remains inaccessible to him. Intuition is (almost) always (partially) lacking to intention, as fulfillment is lacking to signification. In other words, intention and signification surpass intuition and fulfillment"; see ibid., §21, 209: "Either the phenomenon receives an intuition that exceeds the frame set by the concept and signification that aim at and foresee it."

105. Ibid., §23, 222: "The different types of phenomena can be defined as different variations of auto-manifestation (showing itself in and from itself) according to the degree of givenness (giving itself in and from itself)."

106. Ibid.

107. Ibid.

108. Ibid.

109. Ibid.

110. Ibid.

111. Ibid., 223: "The intention thus keeps mastery over the manifestation, and givenness is cut to the size of objectification."

112. Derrida, "Différance," 10.

113. Ibid., 11.

114. See Marion, *Being Given*, §22, 221.

115. See Husserl, *Logical Investigations* I, §8, 279–80: "Shall one say that in soliloquy one speaks to oneself, and employs words as signs, i.e., as indications, of one's own inner experiences? I cannot think such a view acceptable. . . . In a monologue words can perform no function of indicating the existence of mental acts, since such an indication would there be quite purposeless. For the acts in question are themselves experienced by us at that very moment."

116. See Derrida, *Speech and Phenomena*, 66: "The fact that nonpresence and otherness are internal to presence strikes at the very root of the argument for the uselessness of signs in the self-relation"; see also *Of Grammatology*, 47: "The general structure of the unmotivated trace connects within the same possibility, and they cannot be separated except by abstraction, the structure of the relationship with the other, the movement of temporalization, and language as writing."

117. Jean-Luc Marion, *The Reason of the Gift*, trans. Stephen E. Lewis (Charlottesville: University of Virginia Press, 2011), 34.

15. Prayer: Addressing the Name

Karmen MacKendrick

This essay first appeared as chapter 4 of Karmen MacKendrick, *Divine Enticement: Theological Seductions* (New York: Fordham University Press, 2013), 141–68.

1. Jean-Luc Nancy, "Of Divine Places," trans. Michael Holland, in *The Inoperative Community*, ed. Peter Connor (Minneapolis: University of Minnesota Press, 1991), 121.

2. Augustine, *Confessions*, trans. Henry Chadwick (Oxford: Oxford University Press, 1991), 10.6.

3. Jill Robbins writes, "Solitary prayer does not have that opening function. The collectivity that opens the ultimate meaning of prayer is itself conceived as a keeping open or a holding open of the possibility of community. It is more of an interrogation than an assertion. . . . Collective prayer is a room with windows. This figure of opening is prolonged when Levinas states, 'God is close to whoever invokes him [a virtual citation from Psalm 145], but the invocation presupposes an opening [*une ouverture*]'"; Robbins, "Who Prays? Levinas on Irremissible Responsibility," in *The Phenomenology of Prayer*, ed. Bruce Ellis Benson and Norman Wirzba (New York: Fordham University Press, 2005), 39. Robbins cites for the quotation Emmanuel Levinas, *Difficult Freedom: Essays on Judaism*, trans. Seán Hand (Baltimore: Johns Hopkins University Press, 1997), 270.

4. Nancy, "Of Divine Places," 117.

5. Ibid.

6. Friedrich Hölderlin, "Heimkunft / Homecoming," in *Friedrich Hölderlin: Selected Poems and Fragments*, trans. Michael Hamburger (New York: Penguin Books, 1994), 164–65.

7. Nancy, "Of Divine Places," 118.

8. Ibid., 121.

9. Maurice Blanchot, *The Space of Literature*, trans. Ann Smock (Lincoln: University of Nebraska Press, 1989), 72. The exchange can be found in Gustav Janouch, *Conversations with Kafka*, trans. Goronwy Rees (New York: New Directions, 1971), 47. Interestingly, Kafka also sees prayer in human interaction: "the relationship to one's fellow man is the relationship of prayer." Kafka, *Blue Octavo Notebooks*, 51, cited in Beth Hawkins, *Reluctant Theologians: Kafka, Celan, Jabès* (New York: Fordham University Press, 2003), 102.

10. Paul Celan, *Collected Prose*, trans. Rosemarie Waldrop (Riverdale-on-Hudson, N.Y.: Sheepmeadow Press, 1986), 34–35.

11. Merold Westphal, "Prayer as the Posture of the Decentered Self," in *The Phenomenology of Prayer*, 30.

12. Celan, *Collected Prose*, 49.

13. M. B. Pranger, *Eternity's Ennui: Temporality, Perseverance and Voice in Augustine and Western Literature* (Leiden: Brill, 2010), 45.

14. "Late have I loved you, beauty so old and so new: late have I loved you" (Augustine, *Confessions*, 10.27.38).

15. Blanchot, *The Infinite Conversation*, trans. Susan Hanson (Minneapolis: University of Minnesota Press, 1993), 20.

16. Ibid., 18.

17. "Speech affirms the abyss that there is between 'myself' and '*autrui*,' and it passes over the impassible, but without abolishing it or reducing it. Moreover, without this infinite distance, without this abysmal separation there would be no speech, so it is accurate to say that all veritable speech recalls the separation by that it speaks" (ibid., 63).

18. Ibid., 65.

19. Roland Barthes, *The Pleasure of the Text*, trans. Richard Miller (New York: Hill and Wang, 1975), 5.

20. Ibid., 6.

21. Jean-Luc Nancy, *Dis-Enclosure: The Deconstruction of Christianity*, trans. Bettina Bergo, Gabriel Malenfant, and Michael B. Smith (New York: Fordham University Press, 2008), 118.

22. Westphal, "Prayer as the Posture of the Decentered Self," 17.

23. More completely, "For the illocutionary act implicit in Samuel's prayerful speech act is the presentation of himself to God as a listener, and that is easier said than done. It is a performative, to be sure, but one that can scarcely be said to be performed more than to a certain degree" (ibid., 19).

24. Ibid., 17.

25. Pranger, *Eternity's Ennui*, 294.

26. Kevin Hart, "God and the Sublime," in *God Out of Place*, ed. Yves de Maeseneer (Utrecht: Ars Disputandi, 2005), 35–36.

27. Friedrich Hölderlin, "Patmos," in *Friedrich Hölderlin: Selected Poems and Fragments*, 230–31.

28. Jean-Luc Nancy, *The Birth to Presence*, trans. Brian Holmes et al. (Stanford, Calif.: Stanford University Press, 1993), 318.

29. Ann Smock, in conversation with Jean-Luc Nancy, in Nancy, *Birth to Presence*, 311.

30. Nancy, "Of Divine Places," 115, 119.

31. Nancy and Smock, in Nancy, *Birth to Presence*, 315.

32. Ibid., 314.

33. James R. Mensch, "Prayer as Kenosis," in *Phenomenology of Prayer*, 63–72. On the other hand, Kevin Hart argues that "God opens a space wherein love can be ventured, and the first step is always his" (Kevin Hart, "The Experience of the Kingdom of God," in *The Experience of God: A Postmodern Response*, ed. Kevin Hart and Barbara Wall [New York: Fordham University Press, 2005], 80). While enjoying the elegance of Hart's sentiment, I would be inclined to problematize agency, especially one-sided agency, somewhat more.

34. Nancy and Smock, in Nancy, *Birth to Presence*, 310.

35. Oliver Davies, "Soundings: Towards a Theological Poetics of Silence," in *Silence and the Word: Negative Theology and Incarnation*, ed. Oliver Davies and Denys Turner (Cambridge: Cambridge University Press, 2002), 211.

36. Virginia Burrus, "Praying Is Joying: Musings on Love in Evagrius Ponticus," in *Toward a Theology of Eros*, ed. Virginia Burrus and Catherine Keller (New York: Fordham University Press, 2006), 199.

37. Davies, "Soundings," 216. The quotation is from Jacques Derrida, "How to Avoid Speaking: Denials," in *Languages of the Unsayable: The Play of Negativity in Literature and Literary Theory*, ed. Sanford Budick and Wolfgang Iser (New York: Columbia University Press, 1989), 62.

38. My argument here is greatly influenced by Pranger's arguments about prayer and language in *Eternity's Ennui*.

39. Jacques Derrida, "*Sauf le nom*," trans. John P. Leavey Jr., in *On the Name*, ed. Thomas Dutoit (Stanford, Calif.: Stanford University Press, 1995), 38.

40. Jean-Louis Chrétien, *The Ark of Speech*, trans. Andrew Brown (London: Routledge, 2003), 93.

41. Blanchot, *Infinite Conversation*, 25.

42. "The center allows finding and turning, but the center is not to be found" (ibid., 26).

43. Augustine, *Confessions*, 10.26.37.

44. M. B. Pranger, "The Unfathomability of Sincerity: On the Seriousness of Augustine's *Confessions*," in *Actas do Congresso International As Confissoes de santo Agostinho 1600 Anos Depois:*

Presenca e Actualidade (Lisbon: Universidade Catolica Editora, 2002), 209: "We have to leave behind the autobiographical genre in its descriptive guise . . . and focus on the autobiographical promise, not as 'certitude' in the shape of 'reflex action'—never to be heard of again—but as performative. Inside the account of events or the story . . . the promise has really to be promised, it has to be sustained as such. // Let us assume then that in the *Confessions* the concept of conversion as promise holds the centre of the stage."

45. Ibid.: "the first thing that strikes us if we look at the conversion from the viewpoint of a promise is Augustine's self-confessed inability to keep it."

46. This is a point made at length by Nancy in "Shattered Love," in *The Inoperative Community*, ed. Peter Connor (Minneapolis: University of Minnesota Press, 1991), 82–109. I have previously taken it up in considering love and forgiveness in Karmen MacKendrick, *Fragmentation and Memory: Meditations on Christian Doctrine* (New York: Fordham University Press, 2008).

47. Kevin Hart, "Paul and the Reduction," interview with Lee Cole, *Journal of Philosophy and Scripture*, undated; accessed at http://www.philosophyandscripture.org/Issue2-2/Hart/hart.html.

48. Pranger, "Unfathomability of Sincerity," 213.

49. "All we can do to trace what really happened is to analyse the nature of the voices that have come together in the moment of conversion and to search for the way in which they are made to sound simultaneously" (ibid., 223).

50. Hart, "God and the Sublime," 35–36.

51. Pranger, "Unfathomability of Sincerity," especially but not exclusively 218, 223–24.

52. Ibid., 227.

53. Blanchot, *Infinite Conversation*, 65.

54. Pranger, "Unfathomability of Sincerity," 224.

55. Westphal, "Prayer as the Posture of the Decentered Self," 20.

56. Mark Cauchi, "The Infinite Supplicant: On a Limit and a Prayer," in *Phenomenology of Prayer*, 227.

57. See Augustine, Sermon 30 on the New Testament (Matt. 17:19), trans. R. G. MacMullen, in *Nicene and Post-Nicene Fathers*, series 1, vol. 6, ed. Philip Schaff (Buffalo, N.Y.: Christian Literature, 1888), online edition by Kevin Knight, 2009; accessed at http://www.newadvent.org/fathers/160330 .htm.

58. Chrétien, *Ark of Speech*, 75.

59. Jean-Luc Nancy, *Listening*, trans. Charlotte Mandell (New York: Fordham University Press, 2007), 13.

60. Jean-Louis Chrétien, *The Unforgettable and the Unhoped For*, trans. Jeffrey Bloechl (New York: Fordham University Press, 2002), 122.

61. William Franke, "Edmond Jabès or the Endless Self-Emptying of Language in the Name of God," *Literature and Theology* 22, no. 1 (2008): 115–16. Franke cites Edmond Jabès, *La mémoire des mots: Comment je lis Paul Celan* (Chitillon-sous-Bagneux: Fourbis, 1990), 9.

62. Franke, "Edmond Jabès or the Endless Self-Emptying of Language," 115–16. Franke adds in a footnote, "I explore the relationship between Jabès and Celan in 'The Singular and the Other at the Limits of Language in the Post-Holocaust Poetry of Edmond Jabès and Paul Celan,' *New Literary History* 36, no. 4 (2005): 621–38."

63. Nancy, *Listening*, 30.

64. Ibid., 41.

65. Nancy and Smock, in *Birth to Presence*, 311.

66. "On this account, we should say . . . that music (or even sound in general) is not exactly a phenomenon; that is to say, it does not stem from a logic of manifestation. It stems from a different

logic, which would have to be called evocation, but in this precise sense: while manifestation brings presence to light, evocation summons (convokes, invokes) presence to itself" (Nancy, *Listening*, 20).

67. On the nondiscursive function of praise, particularly in relation to eternity, see Karmen MacKendrick, "The Temporality of Praise," in *Relocating Praise: Literary Modalities and Rhetorical Contexts*, ed. Alice den Otter (Toronto: Canadian Scholars Press, 2000), 19–32.

68. "For he who desires, even if his tongue is silent, sings from his heart; and he who has no desire, whatever the cry with which he strikes men's ears, is mute for God" (Augustine, Ennaratio in Psalmos, 86.1, cited in Chrétien, *Ark of Speech*, 47).

69. Of Psalm 37:14, cited in Carol Harrison, *Beauty and Revelation in the Thought of St. Augustine* (Oxford: Oxford University Press, 1992), 259.

70. *Der cherubinische Wandersmann*, accessed at http://www.mscperu.org/deutsch/cherub/cheru401.htm.

71. Derrida, "*Sauf le nom*," 56.

72. See Pierre Klossowski: "In giving itself over to God, the soul knows that God gives himself over to the soul" (Klossowski, *Sade My Neighbor*, trans. Alphonso Lingis [Evanston, Ill.: Northwestern University Press, 1991], 115).

73. Denys Turner, "How Not to Pray," in Turner, *Faith Seeking* (London: SCM Press, 2002), 98.

74. Nancy, *Dis-Enclosure*, 137.

75. Ibid., 136.

76. Augustine, *Ad Simplicianum*, 1.2.21, translated and cited in Pranger, *Eternity's Ennui*, 339, available as "To Simplician: On Various Questions," in *Augustine: Earlier Writings*, ed. John H. S. Burleigh (Philadelphia: Westminster Press, 1953), 370–406, and online at http://www.romancatholicism.org/jansenism/augustine-simplician.htm.

77. Michael Purcell, "When God Hides His Face: The Inexperience of God," in *Experience of God*, 113.

78. Ibid., 114, 120–21.

79. Ibid., 126–29.

80. Ibid., 115. In this claim, Purcell interestingly echoes the thought of Franz Rosenzweig on the possibility of false messiahs. Rosenzweig writes that "The false Messiah . . . is the changing form of the enduring hope." Barbara E. Galli, *Franz Rosenzweig and Juhuda Halevi: Translating, Translations, and Translators* (Montreal: McGill-Queen's University Press, 1995), 259, cited in Elliot R. Wolfson, *Open Secret: Postmessianic Messianism and the Mystical Revision of Menaḥem Mendel Schneerson* (New York: Columbia University Press, 2009), 266.

81. Matt. 27:46 and Mark 15:34, cited in Kevin L. Hughes, "Schools for Scandal: A Response to Michael Purcell," in *Experience of God*, 132.

82. Hughes, "Schools for Scandal," 131.

83. Ibid., 133.

84. Ibid., 133–34.

85. Ibid., 135.

86. Rainer Maria Rilke, "The Olive Garden," in *New Poems* [1907], trans. Edward Snow (New York: North Point Press, 1984), 39; ellipsis in original.

87. Ibid., 39–41.

88. Celan, *Collected Prose*, 54–55; first ellipsis original.

89. Ibid., 50: "'Attention,' if you allow me a quote from Malebranche via Walter Benjamin's essay on Kafka, 'attention is the natural prayer of the soul.'" I have not attempted to track down the

nested references, which are not provided; see Simone Weil, "Absolutely Unmixed Attention Is Prayer," in *Gravity and Grace*, trans. Emma Crawford and Mario van der Ruhr (New York: Routledge, 2007), 117.

90. Among Christian traditions, this aspect of prayer is perhaps most pronounced in hesychasm, with its sometimes elaborate prescriptions of breathing, posture, and words connected in meditative prayer. Hesychasm is particularly associated with Orthodox Christianity.

91. Nancy, *Listening*, 7.

92. Ibid., 65.

93. Ibid., 42.

94. Jean-Louis Chrétien, "The Wounded Word," in *Phenomenology and the "Theological Turn": The French Debate*, by Dominique Janicaud et al. (New York: Fordham University Press, 2000), 149–50.

95. Chrétien, *Unforgettable and the Unhoped For*, 127.

96. Chrétien, "Wounded Word," 175.

97. Ibid., 174.

98. Nancy, *Dis-Enclosure*, 6.

99. Nancy, *Listening*, 67.

100. Jean-Louis Chrétien, *The Call and the Response*, trans. Anne Davenport (New York: Fordham University Press, 2004), 69.

101. "To be listening is always to be on the edge of meaning, or in an edgy meaning of extremity, and as if the sound were precisely nothing else than this edge, this fringe, this margin" (Nancy, *Listening*, 7).

102. Following, again, Pranger, "Unfathomability of Sincerity."

103. I borrow the term "in-finition" from Anne O'Byrne, who has used it in relation to Nancy in "Body Singular Plural," delivered at the International Association for Philosophy and Literature, 2004.

104. Blanchot, *Infinite Conversation*, 40.

105. Nancy, "Of Divine Places," 124.

106. Alexandre Kojève, *Introduction to the Reading of Hegel: Lectures on the Phenomenology of Spirit*, assembled by Raymond Queneau, ed. Alan Bloom, trans. James H. Nichols Jr. (Ithaca, N.Y.: Cornell University Press, 1980), 3.

107. Muriel Barbery, *The Elegance of the Hedgehog*, trans. Alison Anderson (New York: Europa Editions, 2008), 44. I am grateful to David Macallum, S.J., for bringing this text to my attention.

108. Ibid., 44, 43.

109. Elliot R. Wolfson, "Assaulting the Border: Kabbalistic Traces in the Margins of Derrida," *Journal of the American Academy of Religion* 70, no. 3 (2002): 506.

110. Ibid.

111. Patricia Cox Miller, "'Words with an Alien Voice': Gnostics, Scripture, and Canon," *Journal of the American Academy of Religion* 57, no. 3 (1989): 460, citing *Tripartite Tractate*, 65.39–66.5. Miller notes, "This use of the Greek word *ichnos*, "trace," is closely paralleled by Plotinus' understanding of the term, precisely in the context of theological language."

112. Burrus, "Praying Is Joying," 200, citing Nancy, "Of Divine Places," 119.

113. Barbery, *Elegance of the Hedgehog*, 43.

114. Nancy, *Dis-Enclosure*, 49.

115. Louis Mackey, *Peregrinations of the Word: Essays in Medieval Philosophy* (Ann Arbor: University of Michigan Press, 1997), 18–19.

16. A Quarrel with God: Cavell on Wittgenstein and Hegel

Asja Szafraniec

1. Stanley Cavell, *The Claim of Reason: Wittgenstein, Skepticism, Morality, and Tragedy* (New York: Oxford University Press, 1999), 416.

2. Ibid., 4.

3. Stanley Cavell, *Themes Out of School: Effects and Causes* (Chicago: University of Chicago Press, 1988), 32.

4. Stephen Mulhall, *Inheritance and Originality: Wittgenstein, Heidegger, Kierkegaard* (Oxford: Oxford University Press, 2001), 9.

5. Ludwig Wittgenstein, "Aspect and Image," in *The Wittgenstein Reader*, ed. Anthony Kenny (Oxford: Blackwell, 2006), 185.

6. Stanley Cavell, *Must We Mean What We Say?* (Cambridge: Cambridge University Press, 2002), 296.

7. Cavell, *Claim of Reason*, 470.

8. Ibid., 245.

9. Ibid., 265.

10. Ibid., 366.

11. Stanley Cavell, *The World Viewed: Reflections on the Ontology of Film* (Cambridge, Mass.: Harvard University Press, 1979), 93.

12. Cavell is not concerned with the validity of Hegel's thought in itself, but only with the value of certain of its insights to the extent they are relevant for Cavell's own set of problems.

13. Conceiving of Christianity in terms of the necessary inexpressibility of the human subject is not an option for Cavell.

14. For Cavell, failure to see aspects, or the lack of the ability to draw right connections, leads to the condition he describes as "soul blindness."

15. Cavell, *Claim of Reason*, 368 (my emphasis and insertion). If we consider that Wittgenstein relates "seeing connections" with "perspicuous representation" (*Philosophical Investigations*, para. 122), it becomes clear that Cavell aligns here Hegelian spirit with Wittgenstein's "perspicuous representation."

16. "When Kierkegaard finds the modern philosopher (in particular Hegel) supposing that he can traverse the infinite distance to God by erecting a very high and long system, he remarks that "philosophy rests not upon a mistaken presupposition but upon a comic presupposition" (Cavell, *Themes Out of School*, 231).

17. Stanley Cavell, *Disowning Knowledge in Seven Plays of Shakespeare* (Cambridge: Cambridge University Press, 2003), 64.

18. Cavell, *Claim of Reason*, 341.

19. Ibid., 468.

20. Ibid.

21. G. W. F. Hegel, *Introduction to the Philosophy of History*, trans. Leo Rauch (Indianapolis: Hackett, 1988), 36; my emphasis.

22. Cavell, *Must We Mean What We Say?*, 296.

23. Cavell, *Claim of Reason*, 476.

24. Ibid., 352.

25. Ibid., 366. For Cavell to call Christianity a myth is to disqualify it only in a certain sense. We must keep in mind that (1) our language contains whole mythologies and (2) Cavell attributes

the telling of mythologies not only to such thinkers as Hegel but also to Cavell's heroes of thought, such as Blake, Thoreau, Nietzsche, and Wittgenstein (the part on seeing aspects). Science can also take the form of mythology. Mythology presents us with an explanatory model that can be replicated from case to case without the need for individual intervention (again, "without my agreements"). Myth is an expression of a fantasy. Thus Wittgenstein's statement that "the human body is the best picture of the human soul" is a mythological expression.

Yet Cavell explicitly mentions Hegel's enterprise as being directed against myth ("it may be the ambition of an ambitious philosophy to unmask a field of myth. This can mean various things. . . . It can mean what Hegel did when he tried telling the entire myth of the soul, . . . by inventing a speech that he could call philosophy and in which he could tell the soul's story as part of God's" [ibid.]). We might ask how Cavell can see this as dealing with myth rather than engaging in it. Hegel "invented a speech," which is to say, he did not concede his meaning to factors external to him. Hegel's story is only a myth when it is taken as an explanatory model, repeated and taken for granted by others.

26. "Ordinary language philosophy remains an esoteric practice" (Cavell, *Themes Out of School*, 34).

27. "One fate of a genuine modern author is exactly his indirectness" (Cavell, *Must We Mean What We Say?*, 178).

28. Cavell, *Disowning Knowledge*, 95.

29. Cavell, *Claim of Reason*, 181.

30. Ibid., 183.

31. Ibid., 192.

32. Ibid., 368.

33. "It does not matter whether Charles actually returns. Which is to say, it will not affect how she lives now. Or rather, as she says more precisely: she will live in a way that is not incompatible with their recovering each other." Stanley Cavell, *Cities of Words: Pedagogical Letters on a Register of the Moral Life* (Cambridge, Mass.: Harvard University Press, 2004), 438.

34. Cavell, *Claim of Reason*, 369.

35. Ibid.

36. Ludwig Wittgenstein, *Philosophical Investigations*, para. 219 (Oxford: Blackwell, 2003), 72; Cavell, *Claim of Reason*, 365.

37. Cavell, *Claim of Reason*, 366.

38. Ibid., 483.

39. Cavell, *Must We Mean What We Say?*, 296.

40. Ibid.

41. Cavell, *Disowning Knowledge*, 95.

42. We might ask here whether we are to conceive "god" as equivalent to the general human form of mindedness, i.e., whether the silent space of the shared criteria we cannot touch but to which we are addressing ourselves, which we are hoping our words will satisfy, is the same thing.

43. Henry David Thoreau, *A Week on the Concord and Merrimack Rivers, Walden, the Maine Woods, Cape Cod* (New York: Penguin, 1985), 400. Cavell discusses this issue in *The Senses of Walden* (Chicago: University of Chicago Press, 1992), 111.

44. Charles Taylor, *A Secular Age* (Cambridge, Mass.: Harvard University Press, 2007), 637.

45. Stanley Cavell, *Pursuits of Happiness: The Hollywood Comedy of Remarriage* (Cambridge, Mass.: Harvard University Press, 2003), 256.

46. Ibid., 259.

17. Thinking about the Secular Body, Pain, and Liberal Politics
Talal Asad

This article is a slightly revised version of a response to statements on secularism by Charles Hirschkind and Matthew Scherer that appeared in a special issue of *Cultural Anthropology* 26, no. 4 (2011). Their interesting questions provoked me into thinking further about secularism and the secular, for which I am grateful. I wish to thank Hussein Agrama, Gil Anidjar, and Abou Farman Farmaian for their comments on an early draft.

1. Charles Taylor, *A Secular Age* (Cambridge, Mass.: Harvard University Press, 2007).

2. Berney Goodman, *When the Body Speaks Its Mind: A Psychiatrist Probes the Mysteries of Hypochondria and Munchausen's Syndrome* (New York: Putnam, 1994).

3. Edward Royle, *Victorian Infidels: The Origins of the British Secularist Movement, 1791–1866* (Manchester: Manchester University Press, 1974); see also Edward Royle, *Radicals, Secularists and Republicans: Popular Freethought in Britain, 1866–1915* (Manchester: Manchester University Press, 1980).

4. This is elegantly shown in Brian Dillon's *The Hypochondriacs: Nine Tormented Lives* (New York: Faber and Faber, 2010).

5. Winnifred Fallers Sullivan, *The Impossibility of Religious Freedom* (Princeton, N.J.: Princeton University Press, 2005).

6. Timothy Gorringe, *God's Just Vengeance* (Cambridge: Cambridge University Press, 1996), 224.

7. S. Agrell, "It's Wrong to Fund Private Religious Schools," http://www.theglobeandmail .com/servlet/story/RTGAM.20070917.wlibs0917/BNStory/ontarioelection2007/; accessed December 8, 2008.

8. Sam Harris, *The End of Faith* (New York: Norton, 2004), 12.

9. Henry Maine, *Ancient Law: Its Connection with the Early History of Society and Its Relation to Modern Ideas* (1861; Oxford: Oxford University Press, 1950).

10. Abou Ali Farman Farmaian, "Secular Immortal" (PhD diss., Anthropology Department, Graduate Center of the City University of New York, 2011).

11. John Donne, *The Complete Poetry and Selected Prose of John Donne*, ed. Charles M. Coffin (New York: Modern Library, 1952), 428–29.

12. Richard Tuck, *The Rights of War and Peace* (Oxford: Oxford University Press, 1999).

13. Ramie Targoff, *John Donne: Body and Soul* (Chicago: University of Chicago Press, 2008), 22.

14. Ray Monk, *Ludwig Wittgenstein: The Duty of Genius* (London: Penguin, 1991), 185.

15. Ibid., 374.

16. Ibid., 585.

17. Ludwig Wittgenstein, *Philosophical Investigations* (Oxford: Blackwell, 1953), II.iv.

18. Patricia Meyer Spacks, *Privacy: Concealing the Eighteenth-Century Self* (Chicago: University of Chicago Press, 2003), 11–12.

19. Michel Foucault, *Folie et Déraison: Histoire de la folie à l'âge classique* (Paris: Gallimard, 1972), 381.

20. Michel Foucault, *The Order of Things* (New York: Vintage, 1973), 277–78.

21. James Alan Fox and Marianne W. Zawitz, *Statistics on Homicide Trends in the U.S.* (Washington, D.C.: Bureau of Justice, n.d.).

22. Ignacio Ramonet, "Violences mâles," *Le Monde diplomatique*, June 2004. Ramonet points out that according to the statistical evidence such violence is as common in well-to-do families as among the poor.

23. Karen Halttunen, "Humanitarianism and the Pornography of Pain in Anglo-American Culture," *American Historical Review* 100, no. 2 (1995): 318, italics in original.

24. Ibid., 315; see also Halttunen's book *Murder Most Foul: The Killer in the American Gothic Imagination* (Cambridge, Mass.: Harvard University Press, 1998).

25. I myself have mistakenly confused the two in Talal Asad, *Formations of the Secular: Christianity, Islam, Modernity* (Stanford, Calif.: Stanford University Press, 2003).

26. Gilles Deleuze and Leopold von Sacher-Masoch, *Masochism* (New York: Zone Books, 1991), 20–21.

27. Ibid., 22.

28. Bhrigupati Singh, who is writing a book on Indian concepts of sovereignty, has reminded me that Deleuze, in *A Thousand Plateaus*, draws the idea of the contract/force couple from Georges Dumezil's account of Indo-European concepts of sovereignty, *Mitra-Varuna*.

29. See Phyllis Mack, *Heart Religion in the British Enlightenment* (Cambridge: Cambridge University Press, 2008).

30. Quoted in R. S. Crane, "Suggestions Toward a Genealogy of the 'Man of Feeling,'" *ELH: A Journal of English Literary History* 1, no. 3 (1934): 205.

31. For a useful survey of the efflorescence of violent films in American cinema, see Gabrielle Murray, "Representations of the Body in Pain and the Cinema Experience in Torture-Porn," in *Jump Cut: A Review of Contemporary Media*, no. 50 (Spring 2008); see also Noel Carroll, *The Philosophy of Horror or Paradoxes of the Heart* (New York: Routledge, 1990).

32. See Stanley Hauerwas and Romand Coles, *Christianity, Democracy, and the Radical Ordinary* (Eugene, Ore.: Cascade Books, 2008), which describes some of these attitudes by distinguishing what the authors call radical democracy from liberal democracy.

33. See James Q. Whitman, *Harsh Justice: Criminal Punishment and the Widening Divide between America and Europe* (New York: Oxford University Press), 203.

34. See esp. Gil Anidjar, "We Have Never Been Jewish: An Essay in Asymmetric Hematology," in *Jewish Blood: Metaphor and Reality in Jewish History, Culture, and Religion*, ed. Mitchell Hart (New York: Routledge, 2009).

18. The Rise of Literal-Mindedness

Peter Burke

This essay was previously published in *Common Knowledge* 2, no. 2 (1993): 108–21. In *Common Knowledge* 1, no. 2, Jacques Le Goff, J. G. A. Pocock, Quentin Skinner, and Clifford Geertz called for papers that would "uncover" or "construct" a commonality between Annales and Cambridge historiography (Call for Papers VII). This article is a response. The author wishes to express his thanks to Natalie Zemon Davis and Keith Thomas for encouraging him to discuss the subject of this essay in more detail and to the audiences of the paper that this essay is based on—audiences at the Davis Center, Princeton University; the University of Nijmegen; and the Department of Anthropology, University of Cambridge—for their questions and comments.

1. For earlier accounts of the shift, see Peter Burke, "The Repudiation of Ritual in Early-Modern Europe," in *Historical Anthropology of Early Modern Italy* (Cambridge: Cambridge University Press, 1987), and Peter Burke, "Historians, Anthropologists and Symbols," in *Culture Through Time*, ed. E. Ohnuki-Tierney (Stanford, Calif.: Stanford University Press, 1990), 268–83. On the problematic concept of mentalities, see Peter Burke, "Strengths and Weaknesses of the History of Mentalities," *History of European Ideas* 7 (1986): 439–51.

2. Cf. Timothy J. Reiss, *The Discourse of Modernism* (Ithaca, N.Y.: Cornell University Press, 1982).

3. Johan Huizinga, *The Waning of the Middle Ages* (1919; abbreviated English trans. by F. Hopman, London: Edward Arnold, 1924), chap. 15; a similar contrast is made by Lévi-Strauss.

4. Jurij Lotman, "The Poetics of Everyday Behaviour in Eighteenth-Century Russia," in *The Semiotics of Russian Culture*, ed. A. Shukman (Ann Arbor: University of Michigan Press, 1984), 231–56.

5. Ernst Kantorowicz, *The King's Two Bodies* (Princeton, N.J.: Princeton University Press, 1957); Marjorie Nicolson, *The Breaking of the Circle* (Evanston, Ill.: Northwestern University Press, 1950); Michel Foucault, *Les Mots et Les Choses* (Paris: Gallimard, 1966); Hans Blumenberg, *Die Lesbarkeit der Welt* (Frankfurt am Main: Suhrkampf, 1981).

6. Clifford Geertz, *Negara* (Princeton, N.J.: Princeton University Press, 1980), 135; see Peter Burke, "Repudiation of Ritual."

7. Jean Pépin, *Mythe et allégorie* (Paris: Aubier, 1958).

8. Brian Stock, *The Implications of Literacy* (Princeton, N.J.: Princeton University Press, 1983); Sheila Delaney, *Medieval Literary Politics* (Manchester: Manchester University Press, 1990).

9. Jeremy Bentham, *Theory of Fictions*, ed. C. K. Ogden (London: Routledge and Kegan Paul, 1932), and, on Bentham, Kenneth Burke, *A Grammar of Motives* (1945; Berkeley: University of California Press, 1969), 284–85; and Kenneth Burke, *A Rhetoric of Motives* (1950; Berkeley: University of California Press, 1969), 90–101.

10. On this problematic concept, see George M. Marsden, "Fundamentalism," in *Encyclopaedia of American Religious Experience* (New York: Scribner's, 1988), 2:947–62.

11. R. O. Crummey, *The Old Believers and the World of Antichrist* (Madison: University of Wisconsin Press, 1970), chap. 1.

12. Norman Knox, *The Word "Irony" and Its Context, 1500–1755* (Durham, N.C.: Duke University Press, 1961).

13. A violent example from Warsaw in 1664 is reported in Jan Pasek, *Memoirs of the Polish Baroque*, trans. Catherine S. Leach (Berkeley: University of California Press, 1976), 173.

14. A. G. Dickens, *Lollards and Protestants in the Diocese of York* (London: Oxford University Press, 1959).

15. The first use recorded in the *Oxford English Dictionary* dates from 1869.

16. Claude Lefort, *Machiavel: Le travail de l'oeuvre* (Paris: Gallimard, 1972), 199.

17. Among the most important studies of medieval hermeneutics are P. Synave, "La doctrine de St.Thomas Aquin sur le sens littéral des écritures," *Revue Biblique* 35 (1926): 40–65; Ceslaus Spicq, *Esquisse d'une histoire de L'exégèse latine au moyen age* (Paris: Vrin, 1944); M. D. Chenu, *La théologie au 12e siècle* (Paris: Vrin, 1957), esp. 159–90; Henri de Lubac, *Exégèse médiévale: Les quatre sens de l'écriture*, 4 vols. (Paris: Aubier, 1959–64).

18. J. B. Payne, "Toward the Hermeneutics of Erasmus," in *Scrinium Erasmianum*, ed. J. Coppens (Leiden: Brill, 1969), 2:13–49; Jerry Bentley, *Humanists and Holy Writ* (Princeton, N.J.: Princeton University Press, 1983); Gerhard Ebeling, *Evangelische Evangelienauslegung: Ein Untersuchung zu Luthers Hermeneutiek* (1942; Darmstadt: Wissenschaftliche Buchhandlung, 1969); Friedrich Beisser, *Claritas scipturae bei Martin Luther* (Göttingen: Vandenhoeck and Ruprecht, 1966).

19. Erasmus, *Ratio perveniendi ad veram theologiam* (Basel: Froben, 1520).

20. Richard Hooker, *Laws of Ecclesiastical Polity* (London: Dent, 1908), 1.14.3 (1:217).

21. *Oxford English Dictionary*, s.v. "context."

22. George N. Conklin, *Biblical Criticism and Heresy in Milton* (New York: King's Crown Press, 1949); John Locke, *The Reasonableness of Christianity* (London: Awnsham and Churchill,

1695), 2–3; compare Locke, *A Paraphrase and Notes on the Epistles of St. Paul*, ed. A. W. Wainwright (Oxford: Clarendon Press, 1987), 103–16.

23. John Toland, *Christianity Not Mysterious* (London: Buckley, 1696), 115.

24. Martin Luther, *Werke* (Weimar: Bohiau, 1883–1980), 16:69.

25. Susan Brigden, *London and the Reformation* (Oxford: Oxford University Press, 1989), 91–92, 307–8.

26. Perkin Walker, *The Decline of Hell* (London: Routledge and Kegan Paul, 1964).

27. Jean Delumeau, *Une histoire de paradis* (Paris: Fayard, 1992), esp. 181–227.

28. Guido Morpurgo-Tagliabue, *I processi di Galileo e l'epistemologia* (Milan: Comunità, 1963); Richard J. Blackwell, *Galileo, Bellarmine, and the Bible* (Notre Dame, Ind.: University of Notre Dame Press, 1991).

29. Hooker, *Laws*, 3.10.7, 3.10.9 (1:331, 355).

30. David Freeberg, *The Power of Images* (Chicago: University of Chicago Press, 1989); Serge Gruzinski, *La guerre des images* (Paris: Fayard, 1989).

31. Giovanni Andrea Gilio, *Due dialoghi* (Camerino: Gioioso, 1564), 30–33.

32. José de Siguenza, *La fundación del monasterio de el Escorial* (1605; Madrid: Turner, 1988), 262; trans. in Jonathan Brown, *The Golden Age of Painting in Spain* (New Haven, Conn.: Yale University Press, 1991), 63.

33. Terisio Pignatti, *Paolo Veronese: Convito in casa di Lévi* (Venice: Arsenale, 1986), 9–13.

34. Victor Baroni, *La Contre-Réforme devant la Bible* (1943; Geneva: Siatkin, 1986).

35. Jacques Bossuet, *Histoire des variations des églises Protestantes* (Paris: Veuve Cramoisy, 1688); Pierre Jurieu, *Accomplissement des prophéties* (Rotterdam: Archer, 1686).

36. Claude de Vert, "Lettre," in his *Explication des cérémonies de la Messe* (1703–13; Farnborough: Gregg, 1970), 4:347–82.

37. Ibid., 1:303, 2:xlvii.

38. Ibid., 2:xxviiiff.

39. Ibid., 4:50.

40. Ibid., 1:287, 294.

41. De Vert, "Lettre," 1:213n.

42. Henry Phillips, *The Theatre and Its Critics in Seventeenth-Century France* (Oxford: Oxford University Press, 1980), esp. 72–86.

43. Pierre Lebrun, *Discours*, new ed. (Paris: Veuve de Laulne, 1731), 189.

44. Pierre Lebrun, *Explication littérale, historique et dogmatique des prières et des cérémonies de la Messe* (1726; Farnborough: Gregg, 1970); l:xv, xviii–xix.

45. See J. Lebrun, "Sens et portée du retour aux origines dans l'oeuvre de Richard Simon," *17e siècle* 33 (1981): 185–98.

46. Ibid., 1:xxii–xxiii, xxxvii.

47. Lebrun, *Explication littérale*, 1:xxii–xxiii.

48. Ibid., 1:xxiii–xxvii.

49. Paul Ricoeur, "Structure et herméneutique," *Esprit* 31 (1963): 596–627, with reply by Lévi-Strauss.

19. From *Star Wars* to Jediism: The Emergence of Fiction-based Religion

Markus Altena Davidsen

An earlier version of this article was published in Danish as "Fiktionsbaseret religion: Fra *Star Wars* til jediisme," *Religionsvidenskabeligt Tidsskrift* 55 (2010): 3–21.

1. Jediism has received some scholarly attention, but earlier studies have focused on the "Jedi Census Phenomenon" of 2001 (see the section "'Jedi' as Religious Self-identification" in this essay) rather than on organized Jediism; see Adam Possamai, "Alternative Spiritualities, New Religious Movements and Jediism in Australia," *Australian Religion Studies Review* 16, no. 2 (2003): 69–86; Possamai, *Religion and Popular Culture: A Hyper-real Testament* (Brussels: P.I.E.–Peter Lang, 2005), 72–76; Jennifer Porter, "'I Am a Jedi': *Star Wars* Fandom, Religious Belief and the 2001 Census," in *Finding the Force of the "Star Wars" Franchise: Fans, Merchandise and Critics*, ed. Matthew Wilhelm Kapell and John Shelton Lawrence (New York: Peter Lang, 2006), 95–112. Readers might want to compare the present essay with Debra McCormick's treatment of Jediism in "The Sanctification of *Star Wars*: From Fans to Followers," in *Handbook of Hyper-real Religions*, ed. Adam Possamai (Leiden: Brill, 2012), 165–84; see also Markus Davidsen, "Jediism: A Convergence of *Star Wars* Fan Culture and Salad Bar Spirituality," *De Filosoof* 51 (2011): 24.

2. Bruce defines religion as "beliefs, actions and institutions which assume the existence of supernatural entities with powers of action, or impersonal powers or processes possessed of moral purpose"; see Steve Bruce, "Defining Religion: A Practical Response," *International Review of Sociology: Revue Internationale de Sociologie* 21, no. 1 (2011): 112.

3. Adam Possamai speaks about "hyper-real religions," with reference to Jean Baudrillard's concept of the hyper-real. For Possamai, new religions based on fiction are "hyper-real" because they attribute the status of reality to a virtual that usurps the empirically real. So far as I can see, hyper-reality in this sense is a common feature of all religions. I therefore prefer the more descriptive term *fiction-based religion*; cf. Possamai, *Religion and Popular Culture*, and Adam Possamai, "Yoda Goes to Glastonbury: An Introduction to Hyper-real Religions," in *Handbook of Hyper-real Religions*, ed. Adam Possamai (Leiden: Brill, 2012), 1–21.

4. This understanding of fiction as being dependent on the author's intention of (partial) nonreference follows Dorrit Cohn, *The Distinction of Fiction* (Baltimore: Johns Hopkins University Press, 1999), 12.

5. See Carole M. Cusack, *Invented Religions: Imagination, Fiction and Faith* (Farnham, UK: Ashgate, 2010), 53–82.

6. Anton Szandor LaVey, *The Satanic Rituals: Companion to The Satanic Bible* (New York: Avon, 1972), 173–201. On chaos magicians and Lovecraft, see Wouter Hanegraaff, "Fiction in the Desert of the Real: Lovecraft's Cthulhu Mythos," *Aries* 7 (2007): 105.

7. See Markus Altena Davidsen, "The Spiritual Milieu Based on J. R. R. Tolkien's Literary Mythology," in *Handbook of Hyper-real Religions*, ed. Adam Possamai (Leiden: Brill, 2012), 185–204.

8. See Danielle Kirby, "From Pulp Fiction to Revealed Text: A Study of the Role of the Text in the Otherkin Community," in *Exploring Religion and the Sacred in the Media Age*, ed. Christopher Deacy and Elisabeth Arweck (Farnham, UK: Ashgate, 2009), 141–54; Kirby, "Alternative Worlds: Metaphysical Questing and Virtual Community Amongst the Otherkin," in *Handbook of Hyper-real Religions*, ed. Adam Possamai (Leiden: Brill, 2012), 129–40; Joseph Laycock, "'We Are Spirits of Another Sort': Ontological Rebellion and Religious Dimensions," *Nova Religio: The Journal of Alternative and Emergent Religions* 15, no. 3 (2012): 65–90. Many new religious movements that are not, strictly speaking, fiction-based are still inspired by trends in fictional literature. This is especially clear in the well-documented influence of fantasy literature on all strands of the neo-pagan movement (witchcraft, heathenry, the goddess movement, etc.); see, e.g., Graham Harvey, "Discworld and Otherworld: The Imaginative Use of Fantasy Literature among Pagans," in *Popular Spiritualities: The Politics of Contemporary Enchantment*, ed. Lynne Hume and Kathleen McPhillips (Aldershot: Ashgate 2006), 41–52. For more examples of new religions inspired by or based on fiction, see Adam Possamai, ed., *Handbook of Hyper-real Religions* (Leiden: Brill, 2012).

9. The corpus of *Star Wars* texts (films, novels, computer games, etc.) is enormous, but the core is the six "canonical" movies, which were all written and produced (but not all directed) by George Lucas. The six movies comprise two relatively independent trilogies. The storyline in the second, "prequel" trilogy takes place before the events in the "original" trilogy. In order of production, the canonical movies are: *Star Wars Episode IV: A New Hope* (1977), *Star Wars Episode V: The Empire Strikes Back* (1980), *Star Wars Episode VI: Return of the Jedi* (1983), *Star Wars Episode I: The Phantom Menace* (1999), *Star Wars Episode II: Attack of the Clones* (2002), and *Star Wars Episode III: Revenge of the Sith* (2005).

10. George Lucas, *Star Wars Episode IV: A New Hope*, Lucasfilm, Ltd., 1977.

11. Dust, personal e-mail, May 22, 2008; translated from Danish.

12. The active, "poaching" character of fandom, as opposed to earlier stereotypes of fans as passive consumers, has been acknowledged since Henry Jenkins, *Textual Poachers: Television Fans and Participatory Culture* (New York: Routledge, 1992). The playful aspect of fan cultures in general is emphasized in fan research, especially by scholars who are themselves fans; see, e.g., Matt Hills, *Fan Cultures* (London: Routledge, 2002), chap. 4.

13. Will Brooker, *Using the Force: Creativity, Community and "Star Wars" Fans* (New York: Continuum, 2002), 6.

14. The ten most common self-identifications were Christian, Islam, Atheist, Agnostic, Buddhist, Hindu, Jewish, Spiritual, Sikh, and Jedi. In the category "Christian" were included the following self-identifications: Catholic, Protestant, Episcopalian, Presbyterian, Methodist, LDS, and Mormon; William Wan, "Soul-searching on Facebook," *Washington Post*, August 30, 2009, available at http://www.washingtonpost.com; accessed September 2, 2012.

15. Porter, "I Am a Jedi," 96–98.

16. Jedi Church: Census, http://www.jedichurch.org. In the menu "Learn," choose "News/Videos." Choose the news item "NZ Census Capitulates—Jedi Stats for New Zealand 2006 Census"; accessed September 2, 2012.

17. Agence France-Presse, "Jedi Census Ploy a Success," *The Australian IT*, August 28, 2002, cited in Possamai, *Religion and Popular Culture*, 72–73.

18. George Lucas's inspiration by Joseph Campbell, especially *The Hero with a Thousand Faces*, is an issue unto itself; see John Shelton Lawrence, "Joseph Campbell, George Lucas, and the Monomyth," in *Finding the Force of the "Star Wars" Franchise: Fans, Merchandise and Critics*, ed. Matthew Wilhelm Kapell and John Shelton Lawrence (New York: Peter Lang, 2006), 21–33.

19. Steven Hart, *A Galactic Gasbag*, 2002, http://www.salon.com/2002/04/10/lucas_5/; accessed September 2, 2012.

20. Bill Moyers, "Of Myth and Men: A Conversation Between Bill Moyers and George Lucas about the Meaning of the Force and the True Theology of *Star Wars*," *Time*, April 26, 1999.

21. Ibid.

22. Ibid.

23. This section draws on the articles "Force," "The Light Side," "The Dark Side," "Jedi Code," and "Jedi Order" from *Wookieepedia*, the *Star Wars* wikia. *Wookieepedia*, http://www.starwars.wikia.com; accessed March 5, 2009.

24. *Wookieepedia*, "Jedi Code"; accessed March 5, 2009.

25. I follow the standard practice in the study of social groups on the Internet of quoting anonymously from discussion forums, though with full reference to homepages; see, e.g., Storm A. King, "Researching Internet Communities: Proposed Ethical Guidelines for Reporting of the Results," *Information Society* 12, no. 2 (1996): 119–27. However, I do quote with full reference to sections of forums with an official character, such as the group's FAQ.

26. Temple of the Jedi Order: Doctrine, http://www.templeofthejediorder.org/home/doctrine; accessed September 2, 2012.

27. Jedi Sanctuary: Fan club, http://www.jedisanctuary.org/articles/index.php?page=not-a-fan-club; accessed May 2008; no longer available.

28. Jedi Church: Doctrine, http://www.jedichurch.org/jedi-doctrine.html; accessed September 2, 2012.

29. Temple of the Jedi Order: Main, http://www.templeofthejediorder.org; accessed February 3, 2010; the quote is no longer available.

30. Ibid.; accessed September 2, 2012.

31. Jedi Church: Doctrine.

32. Jediism Way: Welcome, http://www.thejediismway.org/index.php/topic,1.0.html; accessed February 3, 2010; no longer available.

33. The forum was located at Jedi Sanctuary, http://www.jedisanctuary.org; accessed April 2008; no longer available.

34. Ibid.

35. Force Academy: Force, http://www.forceacademy.com/theforce_menu.htm; accessed February 3, 2010; no longer available; Ashla Knights: Force, http://www.ashlaknights.net, subpage "So you want to be a Jedi"; accessed June 9, 2009; no longer available; and Jedi Sanctuary: Force, http://www.jedisanctuary.org/pages/force/origin-of-force.htm; accessed February 3, 2010; no longer available.

36. Jedi Foundation: FAQ, http://www.jediacademyonline.com/faq.html; accessed September 3, 2012.

37. Jedi Foundation: Main, http://www.jediacademyonline.com; accessed June 9, 2009; the quote is no longer available.

38. Jediism Way: About, http://www.thejediismway.org/index.php/topic,35.0.html; accessed February 3, 2010; no longer available.

39. Temple of the Jedi Order: Main; accessed February 3, 2010; quote no longer available.

40. Jedi Church: Doctrine.

41. Jediism Way: Welcome.

42. Jedi Foundation: FAQ.

43. Jedi Sanctuary: Campbell, http://www.jedisanctuary.org/pages/philo/joseph-campbell.htm; accessed February 3, 2010; no longer available.

44. Ashla Knights: Force; Force Academy: Force.

45. Jedi Church: Doctrine.

46. Temple of the Jedi Order: Doctrine.

47. Ibid.

48. Jediism Way: About.

49. Jedi Sanctuary: Welcome, http://www.jedisanctuary.org/pages/about/welcome.htm; accessed February 3, 2010; no longer available.

50. Ashla Knights: Practice, http://www.ashlaknights.net. Choose "Academy" in the top menu and then "Practice of Ashla" in the right menu; accessed February 3, 2010.

51. Jedi Foundation: Main; accessed June 9, 2009; the quote is no longer available.

52. Jedi Foundation: Circle, http://www.jediacademyonline.com/jcircle.html; accessed September 3, 2012.

53. Jedi Sanctuary: Teachings, http://www.jedisanctuary.org/pages/teachings/teachings-from-starwars-p2.htm; accessed February 3, 2010; no longer available.

54. Temple of the Jedi Order: Doctrine.

55. Ibid.

56. Ibid.

57. The forum is located at Temple of the Jedi Order, http://www.templeofthejediorder.org; accessed April 2008.

58. Temple of the Jedi Order: Clergy, http://www.templeofthejediorder.org. In the forum section "Committees," choose the section "Ceremonies and Rituals" and then the thread "Clergy Ceremonies and Rituals Committee"; accessed February 3, 2010.

59. On *Star Wars* as religion, see John C. Lyden, *Film as Religion: Myths, Morals, and Rituals* (New York: New York University Press, 2003), 216–25. On *Star Wars* fandom as religion, see John C. Lyden, "Whose Film Is It, Anyway? Canonicity and Authority in *Star Wars* Fandom," *Journal of the American Academy of Religion* 80, no. 3 (2012): 775–86. Lyden's identification of *Star Wars* fandom as religion continues a tradition initiated by Michael Jindra; see Jindra, "Star Trek Fandom as a Religious Phenomenon," *Sociology of Religion* 55, no. 1 (1994): 27–51.

60. See, e.g., Christopher Partridge, *The Re-enchantment of the West: Alternative Spiritualities, Sacralization, Popular Culture and Occulture*, vol. 1 (London: T. & T. Clark, 2004), chap. 6.

20. The Words of the Martyr: Media, Martyrdom, and the Construction of a Community

Pieter Nanninga

1. Some of the websites announcing the release of the video and offering links to online storage sites included: http://www.alboraq.info/showthread.php?t=51850; www.al-faloja.info/vb/showthread.php?t=25136; http://www.al-yemen.org/vb/showthread.php?t=266588; www.clearinghouse .infovlad.net/showthread.php?t=14976; http://hafsallah.multiply.com/journal/item/199; http://www .mu7ahideen.wordpress.com/2008/07/11/as-sahab-media-jihad-dan-kesyahidan/; and http://www .unitethemuslims.com/?p=2467. Since July 2008 some of these websites have shut down entirely, and by now probably all video files have been removed from the storage sites. I own a copy of the video *Jihad and Martyrdom*.

2. Cf. Ariel Merari, "Social, Organizational and Psychological Factors in Suicide Terrorism," in *Root Causes of Terrorism: Myths, Reality and Ways Forward*, ed. Tore Bjørgo (London: Routledge, 2005), 80; Assaf Moghadam, "Palestinian Suicide Terrorism in the Second Intifada: Motivations and Organizational Aspects," *Studies in Conflict and Terrorism* 26 (2003): 85; Ami Pedahzur, *Suicide Terrorism* (Cambridge: Polity Press, 2005), 178–79.

3. Cf. Robert A. Pape, *Dying to Win: The Strategic Logic of Suicide Terrorism* (New York: Random House, 2005), 81–82; Pedahzur, *Suicide Terrorism*, 179.

4. Probably, his attack took place on June 28, 2007; see CBS News, "New Al Sahab video in Honor of Slain Al Qaeda Commander," July 9, 2008, at http://www.cbsnews.com/blogs/2008/07/08/ monitor/entry4240518.shtml; ISAF News Release, "Suicide Bomber Kills 1 Afghan Civilian in Paktika," June 28, 2007, at http://www.nato.int/isaf/docu/pressreleases/2007/06-june/pr070628-487.html.

5. Martha Crenshaw, "The Logic of Terrorism: Terrorist Behavior as a Product of Strategic Choice," in *Origins of Terrorism: Psychologies, Ideologies, Theologies, State of Mind*, ed. Walter Reich (Washington, D.C.: Woodrow Wilson Center Press, 1998), 7–24.

6. Pedahzur, *Suicide Terrorism*, 27.

7. Pape, *Dying to Win*, 4. This goal of national liberation is true even for al-Qaeda, Pape claims, because this organization can be considered an "alliance of national liberation movements," fighting a common imperial threat; ibid., 104.

8. Mia M. Bloom, "Palestinian Suicide Bombing: Public Support, Market Share and Outbidding," *Political Science Quarterly* 119 (2004): 61–88; Bloom, *Dying to Kill: The Allure of Suicide Terror* (New York: Columbia University Press, 2005).

9. Bruce Hoffman and Gordon H. McCormick, "Terrorism, Signaling, and Suicide Attack," *Studies in Conflict and Terrorism* 27 (2004): 243–81.

10. Assaf Moghadam, "Terrorism, Occupation, and the Globalization of Martyrdom: A Critique of *Dying to Win*," *Studies in Conflict and Terrorism* 29 (2008): 707–29; Moghadam, *The Globalization of Martyrdom: Al Qaeda, Salafi Jihad, and the Diffusion of Suicide Attacks* (Baltimore: John Hopkins University Press, 2008); Moghadam, "Motives for Martyrdom: Al-Qaeda, Salafi Jihad, and the Spread of Suicide Attacks," *International Security* 33 (2009): 46–78.

11. Mohammed M. Hafez, *Suicide Bombers in Iraq: The Strategy and Ideology of Martyrdom* (Washington, D.C.: United States Institute of Peace Press, 2007), 226.

12. See, for the distinction between instrumental and expressive aspects of violence, David Riches, "The Phenomenon of Violence," in *The Anthropology of Violence*, ed. David Riches (Oxford: Blackwell, 1986), 1–27, esp. 4–5; Anton Blok, "The Meaning of 'Senseless' Violence," in *Honour and Violence* (Cambridge: Polity Press, 2001), 103–14; Ingo W. Schröder and Bettina E. Schmidt, "Introduction: Violent Imaginaries and Violent Practices," in *Anthropology of Violence and Conflict*, ed. Schmidt and Schröder (London: Routledge, 2001), 1–24, esp. 3–6.

13. Jeffrey C. Alexander, "Cultural Pragmatics: Social Performance Between Ritual and Strategy," *Sociological Theory* 22 (2004): 529. See also, for the concept of "performance" and the recent field of performance studies, Erving Goffman, *The Presentation of Self in Everyday Life* (Edinburgh: University of Edinburgh, 1956); Richard Schechner, *Performance Theory* (New York: Routledge, 2003); Jeffrey C. Alexander, Bernhard Giesen, and Jason L. Mast, eds., *Social Performance: Symbolic Action, Cultural Pragmatics, and Ritual* (Cambridge: Cambridge University Press, 2006); Richard Schechner, *Performance Studies: An Introduction* (London: Routledge, 2006).

14. Clifford Geertz, "Deep Play: Notes on the Balinese Cockfight," in *The Interpretation of Cultures* (New York, 1973), 448.

15. Cf. Mark Juergensmeyer, *Terror in the Mind of God: The Global Rise of Religious Violence* (Berkeley: University of California Press, 2003), 220.

16. Several studies about religion and violence have argued along these lines; see, among others, R. Scott Appleby, *The Ambivalence of the Sacred: Religion, Violence, and Reconciliation* (Lanham: Rowman and Littlefield, 2000); Juergensmeyer, *Terror in the Mind of God*; Malise Ruthven, *A Fury for God: The Islamist Attack on America* (London: Granta Books, 2002); Bruce Lincoln, *Holy Terrors: Thinking about Religion after September 11* (Chicago: University of Chicago Press, 2006); James W. Jones, *Blood That Cries Out from the Earth: The Psychology of Religious Terrorism* (Oxford: Oxford University Press, 2008); Hans Kippenberg, *Gewalt als Gottesdienst: Religionskriege im Zeitalter der Globalisierung* (Munich: Beck, 2008); Charles Selengut, *Sacred Fury: Understanding Religious Violence* (Lanham: Rowman and Littlefield, 2008); Mark Juergensmeyer, "Symbolic Violence: Religion and Empowerment," in *Powers: Religion as a Social and Spiritual Force*, ed. Meerten B. ter Borg and Jan Willem van Henten (New York: Fordham University Press, 2010), 39–50.

17. David Cook, *Martyrdom in Islam* (Cambridge: Cambridge University Press, 2007), 1–2.

18. See Juergensmeyer, *Terror in the Mind of God*, 128.

19. Olivier Roy, *Globalised Islam: The Search for a New Ummah* (London: Hurst, 2004), 55–57; Faisal Devji, *Landscapes of the Jihad: Militancy, Morality, Modernity* (London: Hurst, 2005), 84–86, 110, and 160–61; Moghadam, *The Globalization of Martyrdom*, 252; Marc Sageman, *Leaderless Jihad: Terror Networks in the Twenty-first Century* (Philadelphia: University of Pennsylvania Press, 2008).

20. The letter of July 9, 2005, was found during a "counterterrorism operation" in Iraq and published in a translated version on October 11, 2005, at http://www.dni.gov/press_releases/letter_in_english.pdf.

21. Al-Sahab is thought to operate out of the Afghan-Pakistani border area, possibly using minivans as mobile studios, as was indicated by a supposed cameraman who was interviewed by ABC News in June 2003; see Kathy Gannon, "Cameraman Sheds Light on al-Qaeda Videos," *Washington Post*, June 25, 2006. Furthermore, it is known that some of al-Qaeda's high-ranking operatives were attached to the organization, among which were Ayman al-Zawahiri, Khaled Shaykh Mohammed, and the American convert Adam Gadahn, alias Azzam al-Amriki. Khalid Shaykh Mohammed should have been media operations director under Ayman al-Zawahiri, as he himself declared at Guantánamo Bay; see "Verbatim Transcript of Combatant Status Review Tribunal Hearing for ISN 10024," March 10, 2007. See, about Adam Gadahn, Annette Stark, "Peace, Love, Death Metal," *Los Angeles City Beat*, September 9, 2004; Stark, "Threats, Lies, and Videotape," *Los Angeles City Beat*, November 4, 2004; Raffi Khatchadourian, "Azzam the American: The Making of an al-Qaeda Homegrown," *New Yorker*, January 22, 2007. Some other short descriptions of al-Sahab are provided in Jarret M. Brachman, *Global Jihadism: Theory and Practice* (London: Routledge, 2009), 131–33; Hanna Rogan, "Al-Qaeda's Online Media Strategies: From *Abu Reuter* to *Irhabi 007*," Norwegian Defence Research Establishment report, December 1, 2007, 48–56; Craig Whitlock, "Hearts and Minds: Power of 'the Clouds': Al-Qaeda's Growing Online Offensive," *Washington Post*, June 24, 2008.

22. "Those who believe and emigrate and strive [*jahadu*] in the cause of God with their goods and their lives are far greater in rank in the sight of God. These are the winners" (9:20). "God has purchased from the believers their persons and their goods; for them (in return) is the garden (of Paradise). They fight in God's path, and slay and are slain. It is a promise in truth which is binding on Him in the Torah, Evangel and the Quran. And who is truer to his covenant than God? Rejoice then in the bargain that you have made, for that is the superior triumph" (9:111).

23. The content analysis results deal only with the middle part of the video, i.e., Abu al-Hasan's biography and the general history of the mujahidin (from 4:44 until 35:31), after which the description of his suicide attack follows. I have excluded Abu al-Hasan's conversion story (5:46–9:18), in which it is impossible to distinguish between Abu al-Hasan's individual history and the general history of al-Qaeda, as well as Abu al-Hasan's "last will" (28:24–30:11), in which he addresses the umma and his fellow mujahidin without speaking about his biography or al-Qaeda's history. In total this part lasts 25:28 minutes, of which 34 percent is presented by Abu al-Hasan, 31 percent by the narrator, 24 percent by his three colleagues, and 11 percent by several other people.

24. Farhad Khosrokhavar, *Suicide Bombers: Allah's New Martyrs*, trans. David Macey (London: Pluto Press, 2005), 153.

25. See, about the concept of deterritorialization, Roy, *Globalised Islam*, 304–8.

26. Cf. Devji, *Landscapes of the Jihad*, 20–26.

27. See, for examples of the employment of "Western" ideas by movements resisting Western culture, Ian Buruma and Avishai Margalit, *Occidentalism: The West in the Eyes of Its Enemies* (New York: Penguin, 2004).

28. See Ian R. Edgar, "The Inspirational Night Dream in the Motivation and Justification of Jihad," *Nova Religio* 11 (2007): 59–76.

29. Don DeLillo, *Mao II* (New York: Viking, 1991), 157.

21. Militant Religiopolitical Rhetoric: How Abraham Kuyper Mobilized His Constituency

Arie L. Molendijk

1. Ron Suskind, "Without a Doubt: Faith, Certainty, and the Presidency of George W. Bush," *New York Times Magazine*, October 17, 2004.

2. Arie L. Molendijk, "Versäulung in den Niederlanden: Begriff, Theorie, *lieu de mémoire*," in *Religion und Gesellschaft: Europa im 20. Jahrhundert*, ed. Friedrich Wilhelm Graf and Klaus Große Kracht (Cologne: Böhlau Verlag, 2007), 307–27.

3. On Kuyper, see C. H. W. van den Berg, "Kuyper, Abraham," in *Biografisch Lexicon voor de geschiedenis van het Nederlandse protestantisme*, 6 vols. (Kampen: J. H. Kok, 1978–2006), 4:276–83; Adriaan Breukelaar, "Kuyper, Abraham," in *Biographisches-Bibliographisches Kirchenlexikon*, ed. F. W. Bautz and T. Bautz (n.p., 1992), 4:846–51; Jeroen Koch, *Abraham Kuyper: Een biografie* (Amsterdam: Boom, 2006); Henk te Velde, *Stijlen van leiderschap: Persoon en politiek van Thorbecke tot Den Uyl* (Amsterdam: Wereldbibliotheek, 2002); and Arie L. Molendijk, "Neo-Calvinist Culture Protestantism: Abraham Kuyper's Stone Lectures," *Church History and Religious Culture* 88 (2008): 235–50. Cf. Cornelis van der Kooi and Jan de Bruijn, eds., *Kuyper Reconsidered: Aspects of His Life and Work* (Amsterdam: VU University Press, 1999), and Luis E. Lugo, ed., *Religion, Pluralism, and Public Life: Abraham Kuyper's Legacy for the Twenty-First Century* (Grand Rapids, Mich.: Eerdmans, 2000). See also Peter S. Heslam, *Creating a Christian Worldview: Abraham Kuyper's Lectures on Calvinism* (Grand Rapids, Mich.: Eerdmans, 1998), James D. Bratt, ed., *Abraham Kuyper: A Centennial Reader* (Grand Rapids, Mich.: Eerdmans, 1998), and James D. Bratt, *Abraham Kuyper: Modern Calvinist, Christian Democrat* (Grand Rapids, Mich.: Eerdmans, 2013).

4. Jan Romein, "Abraham Kuyper: De klokkenist der kleine luyden," in *Erflaters van onze beschaving: Nederlandse gestalten uit zes eeuwen (1938–1940)*, 7th ed., edited by Jan Romein and Annie Romein (Amsterdam: Querido-Wereldbibliotheek, 1959), 749.

5. H. Bavinck, "Feestrede" (Eulogy), in *Gedenkboek opgedragen door het feestcomite aan Prof. Dr. Kuyper, bij zijn vijf en twintigjarig jubileum als hoofdredacteur van "De Standaard" (1872—1 april—1897)* (Amsterdam: G. J. C. Herdes, 1897), 46; translated in John Bolt, *A Free Church, A Holy Nation: Abraham Kuyper's American Public Theology* (Grand Rapids, Mich.: Eerdmans, 2001), 66.

6. Albert Venn Dicey to his wife, October 23, 1898, quoted in Robert S. Rait, ed., *Memorials of Albert Venn Dicey: Being Chiefly Letters and Diaries* (London: Macmillan, 1925), 154. The reference is to the Spanish-American War of 1898.

7. A. Kuyper, *Calvinism: Six Stone-Lectures* (New York: Höveker & Wormser, 1899), 143–45. Kuyper "improved" upon the translation that was made by his hosts in Princeton, much to their detriment. Here and throughout I have made some minor corrections in the English text.

8. Bolt, *A Free Church, A Holy Nation*, xviii (emphasis in the original).

9. Ibid., 43 (emphasis in the original).

10. Jacobus van Weringh, *Het maatschappijbeeld van Abraham Kuyper* (Assen: Van Gorcum, 1967).

11. Kuyper, *Confidentially* (1873), in *Abraham Kuyper*, ed. Bratt, 53.

12. Kuyper, "Modernism: A Fata Morgana in the Christian Domain," in *Abraham Kuyper*, ed. Bratt, 123.

13. Kuyper, *Calvinism*, 191.

14. Ibid., 202–3.

15. Ibid., 201–2.

16. Kuyper, "Our Instinctive Life" (1908), in *Abraham Kuyper*, ed. Bratt, 260.

17. Ibid.

18. Cf. Jan de Bruijn, *Abraham Kuyper: Een Beeldbiografie* (Amsterdam: Bert Bakker, 2008), 228–29.

19. Quoted in Bolt, *A Free Church, A Holy Nation*, 67.

20. Ibid., 64.

21. Ibid., 66.

22. Ibid., 67.

23. Kuyper, "Our Instinctive Life," in *Abraham Kuyper*, ed. Bratt, 264, referring to Gustave le Bon, *La psychologie des foules* (Paris, 1895).

24. Quoted in Bolt, *A Free Church, A Holy Nation*, 67 (my emphasis).

25. Ibid., 67.

26. Ibid., 70.

27. Kuyper, "Modernism: A Fata Morgana in the Christian Domain, " in *Abraham Kuyper*, ed. Bratt, 87–124; Kuyper, "Uniformity: The Curse of Modern Life," in *Abraham Kuyper*, ed. Bratt, 19–44.

28. Quoted in Bolt, *A Free Church, A Holy Nation*, 70.

29. Arie L. Molendijk, "'A Squeezed Out Lemon Peel': Abraham Kuyper on Modernism," in *Modernism in the Low Countries*, ed. Leo Kenis and Ernestine van der Wall (Leuven: Peeters, 2013), 189–203.

30. Quoted in Bolt, *A Free Church, A Holy Nation*, 75.

31. Ibid., 64.

32. J. C. Rullmann, *Kuyper-Bibliografie*, 3 vols. (The Hague: J. Bootsma, 1923–40), 1:127; P. J. Hoedemaker, in *De Vereeniging: Christelijke Stemmen* 26 (1871): 233–44.

33. Bavinck, Eulogy, quoted in Bolt, *A Free Church, A Holy Nation*, 65–66.

34. I use the term *Calvinist* here only to refer to Kuyper's constituency; other terms such as *antirevolutionary* could be used as well.

35. Van Weringh, *Het maatschappijbeeld van Abraham Kuyper*, 75–85.

36. Ibid., 85.

37. Kuyper, "The Blurring of the Boundaries," in *Abraham Kuyper*, ed. Bratt, 363–402.

38. Ibid., 378.

39. Ibid., 397.

40. Ibid. (emphasis in the original).

41. Kuyper, *Calvinism*, 274.

42. For an analysis, see Molendijk, "Neo-Calvinist Culture Protestantism."

43. Van Weringh, *Het maatschappijbeeld*, 104.

44. Ibid., 130.

45. Kuyper, *Calvinism*, 122.

46. Ibid., 246.

47. Kuyper, "Evolution" (1899), in *Abraham Kuyper*, ed. Bratt, 439.

48. Koch, *Abraham Kuyper*.

49. Kuyper, "Our Instinctive Life," in *Abraham Kuyper*, ed. Bratt, 276–77.

50. Kuyper, "Sphere Souvereignty" (1880), in *Abraham Kuyper*, ed. Bratt, 488.

51. Van Weringh, *Het maatschappijbeeld*, 85.

52. Koch, *Abraham Kuyper*.

53. This article is based on an earlier version published as "'Mine': The Rhetorics of Abraham Kuyper," in *Journal for the History of Modern Theology / Zeitschrift für Neuere Theologiegeschichte* 15 (2008): 248-62. This version is much improved by the careful reading and helpful suggestions of Helen Tartar, who suddenly passed away during the preparations of the volume. I have vivid memories of her presence during the many conferences of the program of the "Future of the Religious Past." It is hard to accept that we had our last conversation at the AAR Conference in Baltimore in November 2013.

22. Thinking through Religious Nationalism

Roger Friedland and Kenneth B. Moss

The authors thank Alexander Kaye, Akhmad Sahal, and especially Yakir Englander for their comments on various drafts and their generous readiness to share work in progress. Thanks too to Hent de Vries and the other participants at the seminar discussion on "Intersections of Religion and Nation" at the Johns Hopkins University Department of History Futures Seminar, December 3, 2010, for their comments. Of course, these readers are not responsible for any of the authors' claims.

1. Talal Asad, "Religion, Nation-State, Secularism," in *Nation and Religion: Perspectives on Europe and Asia*, ed. Peter van der Veer and Hartmut Lehmann (Princeton, N.J.: Princeton University Press, 1999), 186.

2. Ibid., 191.

3. For nationhood as event, see Rogers Brubaker, "Myths and Misconceptions in the Study of Nationalism," in *The State of the Nation*, ed. J. Hall (Cambridge: Cambridge University Press, 1998), 272-306; "Ethnicity without Groups," *Archives européennes de sociologie* 43, no. 2 (2002): 163-89. For nationalism as a contingent identity, see Craig Calhoun, *Nationalism* (Minneapolis: University of Minnesota Press, 1998). For the view that it is a diffused institutional form, see John Meyer, J. Boli, G. Thomas, and F. Ramirez, "World Society and the Nation-State," *American Journal of Sociology* 103, no. 1 (1997): 144-81.

4. On the character of this move in the works of Hans Kohn and Carlton Hayes, see William R. Hutchison, Introduction to *Many Are Chosen: Divine Election and Western Nationalism*, ed. William R. Hutchison and Hartmut Lehmann (Minneapolis: Fortress Press, 1994), 5-6.

5. Anthony D. Smith, *The Ethnic Origins of Nations* (Oxford: Blackwell, 1986).

6. Ibid.; E. J. Hobsbawm, *Nations and Nationalism since 1780: Programme, Myth, Reality* (Cambridge: Cambridge University Press, 1990); Ernest Gellner, *Nations and Nationalism* (Oxford: Blackwell, 1983); Benedict Anderson, *Imagined Communities* (London: Verso, 1983).

7. William Hutchison makes the telling point that the 1990 *Encyclopedia of Nationalism* "includes substantial entries for such relationships as 'Music and Nationalism' and 'Language and Nationalism,' but none for 'Religion and Nationalism'"; Hutchison, "Introduction," 6n6.

8. Benedict Anderson, "The Goodness of Nations," in van der Veer and Lehmann, *Nation and Religion*.

9. Philip Gorski, "'The Mosaic Moment': An Early Modernist Critique of Modernist Theories of Nationalism," *American Journal of Sociology* 105, no. 5 (2000): 1428-68; Philip Gorski, *The Disci-*

plinary Revolution: Calvinism and the Rise of the State in Early Modern Europe (Chicago: University of Chicago Press, 2003).

10. Rogers Brubaker, "Religion and Nationalism: Four Approaches," *Nations and Nationalism* 18, no. 1 (2012): 20; first published online November 3, 2011.

11. Ibid., 12.

12. Giovanni Borradori, *Philosophy in a Time of Terror: Dialogues with Jürgen Habermas and Jacques Derrida* (Chicago: University of Chicago Press, 2003), 33.

13. It might be argued, for instance, that they stand in some tension with genealogically oriented work by those historians of nationalism who stress its roots in religion (though, as Asad shows with particular power, the genealogical identification of a phenomenon's religious ancestors is not in itself a proof of religion's continued *presence* in any particular cultural institution, including secularism). More directly, one way to decide how fully we should agree with the claim that nationalism depends on the secular would be to carefully assess and judge what each of these scholars means by the secular and secularism.

14. Benedict Anderson, *Imagined Communities* (London: Verso, 2006), 6.

15. Carl Schmitt, *The Concept of the Political* (Chicago: University of Chicago Press, 1996), 49; see also Andrew Norris, "Carl Schmitt on Friends, Enemies, and the Political," *Telos* 112 (1998): 68–88.

16. Rogers Brubaker, "Ethnicity without Groups," *Archives Européennes de Sociologie* 43, no. 2 (2002): 168.

17. Philip Gorski, "Nation-ization Struggles: A Bourdieusian Theory of Nationalism," unpublished manuscript (New Haven, Conn.: Department of Sociology, Yale University, 2005).

18. Charles Tilly, *The Formation of National States in Western Europe* (Princeton, N.J.: Princeton University Press, 1975); Anthony Giddens, *Nation-State and Violence* (Cambridge: Polity Press, 1985); Michael Mann, *The Sources of Social Power* (Cambridge: Cambridge University Press, 1986); but see Philip Gorski, "Premodern Nationalism: An Oxymoron? The Evidence from England," in *Sage Handbook of Nationalism*, ed. G. Delanty and K. Kumar (New York: Russell Sage, 2006).

19. Craig Calhoun, *Nationalism* (Minneapolis: University of Minnesota Press, 1998); Anthony Smith, *National Identity* (London: Penguin, 1991).

20. Rogers Brubaker, "Myths and Misconceptions in the Study of Nationalism," in *The State of the Nation*, ed. John Hall (Cambridge: Cambridge University Press, 1998), 272–306.

21. Brubaker has criticized Friedland's understanding of nationalism as a state-centered form of collective subject formation; see Rogers Brubaker, "Religion and Nationalism: Four Approaches," paper presented at the Nation/Religion Conference, University of Konstanz, 2006, published in *Nations and Nationalism* 18, no. 1 (2012). "Where," Brubaker asks, "is 'the nation' in this definition?" "Not all state-centered collective subject formation," he writes, "centrally involves 'the nation'; and not all projects involving 'the nation' are state-centered." The first is undoubtedly correct: States are integral to the formation of many kinds of corporate groups and authorized collective subjects, whether armies, status groups, professions, or associations of all sorts. However, the second claim may be disputed. Brubaker argues that Friedland's definition is "underinclusive" because it neglects nationalist projects that are not state-centric, but rather "centered on an imagined national community that does not correspond with the boundaries of a state." However, as is clear in Brubaker's own typology of nationalisms, nations are always subjects and objects of state action, both seeking and sought by states; Brubaker, "Myths and Misconceptions." But, as he shows, they need not be both. As Brubaker points out, states may promote the formation and protection of nations or nationals without those nations becoming subjects—as in the case of the Soviet Union, which institutionalized national identities as ascribed administrative and political categories while suppressing actual

nationalisms; or states like that of interwar and Nazi Germany or Russia today, which promoted or promote the interests and identities of their nonresident nationals; Brubaker, "Myths and Misconceptions," 277, 286–87. Although Brubaker's warnings regarding an image of nation formation that is too state-centric are well taken, it can still be maintained that there is no national project that does not imply a state as target, objective, protector, guarantee, or expression. This appears to be Brubaker's own understanding: Nationalist politics, he argues, emerge based on a "perceived lack of congruence between" the "imagined community of the nation and the territorial organization of the state"; Brubaker, "Religion and Nationalism," 19.

22. Charles Taylor, "The Meaning of Secularism," *Hedgehog Review* (Fall 2010): 5.

23. Anderson, *Imagined Communities* (2006); Ramaswamy Sumathi, "Visualising India's Geobody: Globes, Maps, Bodyscapes," *Contributions to Indian Sociology* 36 (2002): 151 –89.

24. Max Weber, *Economy and Society: An Outline of Interpretive Sociology*, ed. Guenther Roth and Claus Wittich, trans. Ephraim Fischoff et al. (Berkeley: University of California Press, 1978), 368.

25. Ibid., 925.

26. Ibid., 398.

27. Giddens, *Nation-State and Violence*, 1985.

28. Max Weber, "Religious Rejections of the World and Their Directions," in *From Max Weber*, ed. Hans Gerth and C. Wright Mills (New York: Oxford University Press, 1958), 348.

29. Niklas Luhmann, *Love: A Sketch* (Cambridge: Polity, 2010).

30. Weber, "Religious Rejections," 333.

31. Roger Friedland, "The Institutional Logic of Religious Nationalism: Sex, Violence and the Ends of History," *Politics, Religion and Ideology* 12, no. 1 (2011): 1–24.

32. Weber, "Religious Rejections," 328–29; Weber, *Economy and Society*, 923; Robert N. Bellah, "Max Weber and World-Denying Love: A Look at the Historical Sociology of Religion," *Journal of the American Academy of Religion* 67 (1999): 277–304.

33. Weber, "Religious Rejections," 333.

34. Ibid., 335.

35. Ibid.

36. Ibid., 336.

37. That same impersonal love was laid out by Augustine well before Calvin; see Hannah Arendt, *Love and Saint Augustine* (Chicago: University of Chicago Press, 1996). On the particularism of grace and the depersonalization of love in "Puritan brotherliness," see M. Symonds and J. Pudsey, "The Forms of Brotherly Love in Max Weber's Sociology of Religion," *Sociological Theory* 24 (2006): 133–49.

38. Max Weber, "The Social Psychology of the World Religions," in *From Max Weber*, ed. Hans Gerth and C. Wright Mills (New York: Oxford University Press, 1958), 267–301; Philip Gorski, "Religious Nationalism: A Neo-Weberian Approach," presented at the Religion and Nation Conference, University of Konstanz, Germany, July 2007.

39. Brubaker, "Religion and Nationalism: Four Approaches," 22.

40. Stein Rokkan, "Dimensions of State-Formation and Nation Building: A Possible Paradigm for Research in Variations Within Europe," in *The Formation of National States in Western Europe*, ed. Charles Tilly (Princeton, N.J.: Princeton University Press, 1975), 562–600.

41. Brubaker, "Religion and Nationalism."

42. Robert E. Alvis, *Religion and the Rise of Nationalism: A Profile of an East-Central European City* (Syracuse, N.Y.: Syracuse University Press, 2005).

43. Ibid., xvii.

44. Ibid., 29.

45. Ibid.

46. Ibid., 91.

47. Ibid., 94ff.; quote on 98.

48. Ibid., 102.

49. Edward Aspinall, *Islam and the Nation: Separatist Rebellion in Aceh, Indonesia* (Stanford, Calif.: Stanford University Press, 2009).

50. Ibid., esp. 11–13, 33–34, 199ff.

51. Ibid., 98ff.

52. Ates Altinordu, "The Politicization of Religion: Political Catholicism and Political Islam in Comparative Perspective," *Politics and Society* 34, no. 4 (2010): 517–51.

53. Much historical scholarship on Zionism that has elaborated and debated this point; see among the more recent syntheses Yosef Salmon, "Meshihiut ve-normalizatsiah ba-mahshavah ha-tsionit ha-hilonit," "Dat ve-hiloniut bi-tnuah ha-leumit ha-tsionit," and "'Hadesh yameinu ke-kedem'—mitos tsioni," all repr. in Salmon, *Im ta'iru ve-im te'oreru: Ortodoksiyah bi-metsare ha-leumiyut* (Jerusalem: Merkaz Zalman Shazar le-toldot Yisrael, 2006), chaps. 13–15. It bears noting that, although Zionism considered as a single, broad movement did make liberal use of religious motifs, the movement was in fact a congeries of many different movements with dramatically different ideologies whose adherents related to traditional myths of the Land of Israel in radically different ways, used them to highly varying degrees, and accorded them varying weight in relation to other dimensions of Zionist thought (e.g., Zionism as an deeply untraditional political analysis regarding the dire situation of Jewry in the modern world and the possibility of Jewish political response; twentieth-century Zionism's robust socialist tradition). A useful introduction is Gideon Shimoni, *The Zionist Ideology* (Hanover, N.H.: Brandeis University Press, 1995).

54. Salmon, *Im ta'iru ve-im te'oreru*, 27–28 and chaps. 8–9; Ehud Luz, *Parallels Meet: Religion and Nationalism in the Early Zionist Movement (1882–1904)* (Philadelphia: Jewish Publication Society, 1988).

55. Aviezer Ravitsky, *Messianism, Zionism, and Jewish Religious Radicalism* (Chicago: University of Chicago Press, 1996), chap. 2.

56. Shimoni, *Zionist Ideology*, 44.

57. These included at least three main streams: the mystical-pietistic and charismatic movement of Hasidism, born in the Polish-Ukrainian lands in the late eighteenth century and today a robust and internally variegated global Jewish subculture unto itself; "Lithuanian" or yeshiva Judaism centered around the sacralization of prolonged male study of Talmud and its associated texts; and a combative "Hungarian ultra-orthodoxy" that fused various aspects of all of these with a precocious and eschatologically suffused revulsion against any and all forms of Jewish cultural modernism; in addition, a traditionalist Jewish community that concatenated elements of all three (as well as traditionalist elements of Middle Eastern Jewish background) also took shape in Palestine in the course of the nineteenth century. In light of their ideological convergence around conscious antimodernism and the forms of cooperation this has bred over the course of the twentieth century, these antimodern traditionalist streams may be said to constitute a single camp in Jewish public life with regard to a wide range of important political-theological (and practical) issues; see, among other key studies, Ravitsky, *Messianism, Zionism, and Jewish Religious Radicalism*; Menahem Friedman, *Hevrah ve-dat: Ha-ortodoksiyah ha-lo tsionit be-eretz yisrael* (Jerusalem: Yad ben Zvi, 1977); and Salmon, *Im ta'iru ve-im te'oreru*, chap. 2.

58. Meaning, broadly, "God-fearing."

59. In that sense, what probably needs explaining is less eventual traditionalist opposition to yet another anti-traditional challenge than the two decades of flirtation that preceded it; see Salmon, *Im ta'iru*, chaps. 8–9. We return to this retrospectively surprising openness to Zionism and to its possible future implications below.

60. Michael Silber, "Paamei lev ha-iyvri be-erets Hagar," in *Me'ah shanot tsionut datit*, ed. Avi Sagi and Dov Shvarts (Ramat Gan: Bar-Ilan, 2003), 1:244.

61. Ibid.

62. Ibid., 247.

63. Ibid., 231, 234–39.

64. Alexander Kaye, "The Legal Constructivism of Eliezer Goldman" (presented at the UCLA Center for Jewish Studies Symposium "Rethinking the History of Jewish Nationalism," January 2011); used by permission of author.

65. Ravitsky, *Messianism, Zionism, and Jewish Religious Radicalism*, 155.

66. Nissim Leon, *Harediyut rakah: Hithadshut datit ba-yahadut ha-mizrahit* (Jerusalem: Yad Yitshak Ben-Tsvi, 2010), 47.

67. Ravitsky, *Messianism, Zionism, and Jewish Religious Radicalism*, 163.

68. A core concept in haredi political culture meaning that haredi Jews ought to follow the opinions of religious leaders on all matters including political decisions and ideological outlook; see Lawrence Kaplan, "Daas Torah: A Modern Conception of Rabbinic Authority," in *Rabbinic Authority and Personal Autonomy*, ed. Moshe Z. Sokol (Northvale, N.J.: Jason Aronson, 1992), 1–60.

69. Kaplan, "Daas Torah," 53. Note that Kaplan is not suggesting that this multiplicity of opinions in leadership will destabilize haredi Judaism in the sense that it will destabilize relations of authority and intellectual submission. Rather, the destabilization (our term rather than his) that we may posit is that of haredi Judaism's neutralizing stance relative to the complex of land, peoplehood, and sovereignty within Israel and the occupied territories.

70. Talal Asad, *On Suicide Bombing* (New York: Columbia University Press, 2007).

71. Ibid., 91, 16.

72. Ibid., 85–88.

73. Ibid. 88.

74. Ibid. 62.

75. Ibid. 36.

76. Ibid. 29.

77. Ibid. 3.

78. Ibid. 42.

79. Ibid., 63–64; Talal Asad, *Formations of the Secular: Christianity, Islam, Modernity* (Stanford, Calif.: Stanford University Press, 2003), 11–12.

80. Ibid., 63.

81. Ibid., 68–69.

82. Ibid., 24.

83. Asad, *On Suicide Bombing*, 24.

84. Ibid., 42.

85. Ibid., 45.

86. Ibid., 50.

87. Ibid., 116.

88. Ibid., 49.

89. Ibid., 50, 52.

90. Lawrence Wright, *The Looming Tower: Al-Qaeda and the Road to 9/11* (New York: Knopf, 2006), 219.

91. Thomas Sizgorich, "Sanctified Violence: Monotheist Militancy as the Tie That Bound Christian Rome and Islam," *Journal of the American Academy of Religion* 77 (2007): 895 –921.

92. Asad, *On Suicide Bombing*, 11.

93. Ibid., 102.

94. Ibid., 37.

95. Ibid., 64.

96. Ibid., 59, 63, 91.

97. To make this last point clear, Michel Foucault, for example, pointed to the way in which the discursive grammar of classical Greece sought to subjectify heterosexual male citizens, in which self-disciplined passion and erotically asymmetrical relations between adult male citizens and hairless adolescents on the threshold of manhood was a vehicle for virtuous socialization; Foucault, *History of Sexuality* (1990). As Plato's trajectory makes clear, the profusion of homoerotic bonds beyond conventions of age and asymmetry led him later in his life to condemn the homoerotic bonds upon which he had once lavished praise as a boon to the promotion of solidarity and honor in defense of the polis.

98. Asad, *On Suicide Bombing*, 2, 47.

99. Assaf Moghadam, "Motives for Martyrdom: Al Qaida, Salafi Jihad, and the Spread of Suicide Attacks," *International Security* 33 (2008): 46–78, esp. 77.

100. Nathan French, "The 'I' of the Decider: The Role of Intention (Niyya) and the Shaping of Subjectivity in Classical and Contemporary Martyrdom Discussions" (presented at the American Academy of Religions, San Francisco, Fall 2011).

101. If religious communities use the state to serve their private needs, indeed to represent the nonreligious interests of their communities, this is not religious nationalism, even if the collectivities mobilized are "diacritically" marked by religious attributes.

102. Gorski, *Disciplinary Revolution*; Gorski, "'Mosaic Moment,'" 1428–68.

103. Roger Friedland and Richard Hecht, *To Rule Jerusalem* (Cambridge: Cambridge University Press, 1996); Gorski, *Disciplinary Revolution*; Gorski, "'Mosaic Moment.'"

104. Asad, *On Suicide Bombing*, 87; see also Bruce Lincoln, *Holy Terrors: Thinking About Religion after September 11* (Chicago: University of Chicago Press, 2003).

105. Roxanne Euben, *Enemy in the Mirror* (Princeton, N.J.: Princeton University Press, 1999); James P. Piscatori, *Islam in a World of Nation-States* (Cambridge: Cambridge University Press, 1986); Qutb, *Milestones*.

106. Giles Kepel, *Jihad: The Trail of Political Islam* (Cambridge, Mass.: Harvard University Press, 2002), 39.

107. Mehdi Khalaji, "Apocalyptic Politics: On the Rationality of Iranian Policy," *Policy Focus* no. 79 (Washington, D.C.: Washington Institute for Near East Policy, 2008), 16.

108. Roger Friedland, "The Constitution of Religious Political Violence: Institution, Culture and Power," in *The Oxford Handbook of Cultural Sociology*, ed. Jeffrey C. Alexander, Ronald Jacobs, and Philip Smith (New York: Oxford University Press, 2011); Roger Friedland, "The Institutional Logic of Religious Nationalism: Sex, Violence and the Ends of History," *Politics, Religion and Ideology* 12, no. 1 (2011): 1–24.

109. Giorgio Agamben, *Homo Sacer* (Stanford, Calif.: Stanford University Press, 1998), 112.

110. Ibid., 128–29.

111. Hannah Arendt, *The Human Condition* (Chicago: University of Chicago Press, 1958).

112. Gorski, "'Mosaic Moment'"; Thomas Hobbes, *Leviathan*, ed. C. B. Macpherson (New York: Penguin, 1985).

113. Roger Friedland, "L'eros del Sovrano," *Reset* 111 (2009): 63–68.

114. Qutb, *Milestones*, 1990.

115. Ibid., 66.

116. Ibid., 74.

117. Melinda Cooper, "Orientalism in the Mirror: The Sexual Politics of Anti-Imperialism," *Theory, Culture and Society* 25, no. 6 (2008): 25–49; Roger Friedland, "Money, Sex and God: The Erotic Logic of Religious Natioalism," *Sociological Theory* 20 (2000): 381–424.

118. Janet Afary, *Sexual Politics in Modern Iran* (New York: Cambridge University Press, 2009); Saba Mahmood, *The Politics of Piety: The Islamic Revival and the Feminist Subject* (Princeton, N.J.: Princeton University Press, 2005).

119. Hany ElWaziry, "Brotherhood Sheikh to Run for President," Almasri/Alyoum, English ed., May 30, 2011, http://www.almasryalyoum.com/en/node/455693.

120. According to the Pew Center surveys in 2003, Muslim respondents do not see democracy as a colonizing Western form. The same countries where majorities support the proposition that Islam should play a large or larger role in their societies are also major supporters of democratic government in their home countries; Pew Research Center 2003. Commitment to the public relevance of Islamic values is not inconsistent with support for democracy. Bin Laden, of course, represented the quintessential neofundamentalist. Those who supported bin Laden should hate the West's universalizing of political freedom. Pew asked respondents if they had confidence in bin Laden to "do the right thing." Those Islamic countries in which a sizable proportion had "a lot" or "some" confidence in bin Laden also had sizable majorities who believed that democracy was not simply a Western way of doing things and could work in their countries. But what about those Muslims who themselves supported bin Laden's variant of radical Islam? The Pew Center kindly ran cross-tabulations for Friedland with the question about support for bin Laden, and only for Muslim respondents. Reanalyzing 2003 survey data on Muslim support for democracy and for al-Qaeda's jihadism, precisely a form of radical Islam with restrictive views of gender relations, majorities—often overwhelmingly ones—of respondents in Jordan, Kuwait, Lebanon, Morocco, Lebanon, Pakistan, Palestine, and Turkey, showed that those who supported bin Laden's actions also believed that their country could and should have a democratic future. When Friedland received the printouts and reported his interpretation, the Pew project director's first response was that he must have misread the data. Crosstabulations provided to the author by Nicole Speulda, project director, Pew Research Center for the People and the Press, September 20, 2004.

121. Ronald F. Inglehart and Pippa Norris, "The True Clash of Civilizations," *Foreign Policy*, no. 135 (2003): 62 –70, esp. 67.

122. Qutb, *Milestones*, 83; Sayyid Qutb, *In The Shade of the Quran*, vol. 2, Surah 3 (Leicester: Islamic Foundation, 2000), 189.

123. Qutb, *Milestones*, 85–86.

124. Sizgorich, "Sanctified Violence," 895–921, 909; Thomas Sizgorich, "Do Prophets Come with a Sword?"*American Historical Review* 112 (2009): 993–1015.

125. Sizgorich, "Do Prophets Come with a Sword?" 911.

126. Nazih N. M. Ayubi, *Political Islam: Religion and Politics in the Arab World* (London: Routledge, 1991); Fatima Mernissi, *Beyond the Veil: Male-Female Dynamics in Modern Muslim Society*, rev. ed. (Bloomington: Indiana University Press, 1987), 39; Mahmood, *Politics of Piety*.

127. Stefania Pandolfo, *Impasse of the Angels: Scenes from a Moroccan Space of Memory* (Chicago: University of Chicago Press, 1997); Mark N. Swanson, "A Study of Twentieth-Century Com-

mentary on Surat al-Nur (24): 27–33," *Muslim World* 74 (1984): 187–203; Olivier Roy, *Globalized Islam: The Search for a New Ummah* (New York: Columbia University Press, 2004), 277. One of Pandolfo's Moroccan informants informs her that just as seduction by a woman sets a man on fire, so, too, "the society itself is on fire! Fitna of riches, fitna of children, fitna of invasion, razing, and war, fitna of blood, fitna of women.... It is all fitna, one fitna, and it has no cure! Fitnas comes in different forms, but the sovereign fitna, the Sultan of fitnas, is the fitna of love!"; Stefania Pandolfo, *Impasse of the Angels*, 98.

128. Roxanne Euben, "Killing (for) Politics: Jihad, Martyrdom and Political Action," *Political Theory* 30, no. 1 (2002): 4–35.

129. Euben, *Enemy in the Mirror*, 73–74.

130. Mahmood, *Politics of Piety*, 110–11.

131. Martin Riesebrodt, *Pious Passions: The Emergence of Modern Fundamentalism in the United States and Iran* (Berkeley: University of California Press, 1993), 145.

132. Qutb, *Milestones*, 83.

133. Pat Robertson, *The New World Order* (Dallas: New Word, 1991), 237.

134. The Islamic regulation of family life has, in fact, been the core of Islamic law during this century. "Throughout this century," writes Humphreys, "the sections on women, the family, and personal morality have been the most vital and living elements of the Shari'a, and in the courts of most countries they are the only parts of it still enforced" (R. Stephen Humphreys, *Between Memory and Desire: The Middle East in a Troubled Age* [Berkeley: University of California Press, 1999], 212).

135. Riesebrodt, *Pious Passions*.

136. Mahmood, *Politics of Piety*; Afary, *Sexual Politics in Iran*.

137. Talal Asad, *Genealogies of Religion: Discipline and Reasons of Power in Christianity and Islam* (Baltimore: Johns Hopkins University Press, 1993); Asad, *Formations of the Secular*.

138. Asad, *Formations of the Secular*, 192–93.

139. Qutb, *Milestones*, 86–88.

140. Caleb Elfenbein, "Differentiation and Islam: Colonialism, Sayyid Qutb, and Religious Transformation in Modern Egypt" (PhD diss., University of California Santa Barbara, 2008), 217.

141. Hamas, *The Covenant of the Islamic Resistance Movement* (New Haven, Conn.: Avalon Project, Yale University Law School, 1988).

142. Susan Friend Harding, *The Book of Jerry Falwell: Fundamentalist Language and Politics* (Princeton, N.J.: Princeton University Press, 2000), 244. Similar phenomena are visible in the contemporary Jewish world: a forthcoming study by Avi Sagi and Yakir Englander demonstrates parallel developments regarding the body, the nation, and the divine within contemporary religious Zionism.

143. Hans Blumenberg, *The Legitimacy of the Modern Age*, trans. Robert M. Wallace (Cambridge, Mass.: MIT Press, 1983), 214–15.

144. Freud writes, "The almighty and just God, and kindly Nature, appear to us as grand sublimations of father and mother, or rather as revivals and restorations of the young child's ideas of them" (Sigmund Freud, *Leonardo da Vinci and a Memory of His Childhood* [New York: W. W. Norton, 1989], 83).

145. Richard Koenigberg, "The Human Body Becomes a Body Politic," available at website on *The Psychoanalysis of Culture, Ideology and History*, http://www.psych-culture.com/docs/rk-human body.html.

146. Friedland, "Money, Sex and God."

147. Brubaker, "Religion and Nationalism," 18.

148. Ibid.

149. This has a certain kinship to the relationship between romantic love and sexuality. Luhmann argues that romantic love should not be understood as a legitimation for sexual pleasure, but that sexuality anchors love; it functions as a way to overcome the contradictions of the operation of the love code that depend on particular forms of intersubjective communication. "Sexuality forces one into a non-dissociable mode of involvement. It bars the way to withdrawal into 'pure love,' which distances the lover not only from themselves but also from the self that the other sees and desires, and therefore, also from the self by whom the other feels themselves seen and desired" (Luhmann, *Love*, 59). One might look to the exercise of coercive authority through the nation-state as a kind of practical supplement to the internal limits of religious codes. Just as the passioning of love depends on sexual practice, so might the politicization of religion through the instrumentation of the nation-state lead to its nationalization.

150. Berna Turam, *Between Islam and the State* (Stanford, Calif.: Stanford University Press, 2007); Hakan Yavuz, *Secularism and Muslim Democracy in Turkey* (Cambridge: Cambridge University Press, 2009).

151. Friedland and Hecht, *To Rule Jerusalem*; Nachman Ben-Yehuda, *Theocratic Democracy: The Social Construction of Religious and Secular Extremism* (New York: Oxford University Press, 2010), 203–9.

152. Blumenberg, *Legitimacy of the Modern Age*, 89–91.

153. Rival religious groups—traditional Southern Protestants versus liberals in America, liberal German Protestants versus Catholics in Germany—may also promote a religious nationalism in their interreligious struggles; Gorski, "Religious Nationalism."

154. Asad, *Formations of the Secular*.

155. Gorski, *Disciplinary Revolution*.

156. Mark C. Taylor, *After God* (Chicago: University of Chicago, 2007), 48–83; Louis Dupré, *Passage to Modernity: An Essay in the Hermeneutics of Nature and Culture* (New Haven, Conn.: Yale University Press, 1993).

157. Taylor, *After God*, 62.

158. Dupré, *Passage*.

159. D. M. McMahon, *Enemies of Enlightenment: The French Counter-Enlightenment and the Making of Modernity, 1778–1830* (New York: Oxford University Press, 2001).

160. Talal Asad, "Reading a Modern Classic: W. C. Smith's 'The Meaning and End of Religion,'" *History of Religions* 40 (2001): 205–22; Elfenbein, *Differentiation and Islam*.

161. Mahmood, *Politics of Piety*; Saba Mahmood, "Secularism, Hermeneutics, and Empire: The Politics of Islamic Reformation," *Public Culture* 18 (2006): 323–47. One might make the same kind of argument for cultural models of self-formation generally. Eva Illouz has shown how the linguistically centered therapeutic model of communication was institutionalized in therapy, insurance, personnel management, internet dating and medical diagnosis. The inner logic of mental health involves narrating past sufferings (Eva Illouz, *Cold Intimacies: The Making of Emotional Capitalism* [London: Polity, 2007]). Arguably, this has also been refracted in the politics of recognition, reconciliation, and memorialization in a number of political domains.

162. Asad, *Formations of the Secular*, 197.

163. Ibn Taymiyyah, cited in L. Gardet, "Dīn," in *Encyclopaedia of Islam*, ed. P. Bearman, T. Bianquis, C. E. Bosworth, E. van Donzel, and W. P. Heinrichs, 2nd ed. (Amsterdam: Brill, 2009), available at Brill Online, University of California Santa Barbara CDL, as http://www.brillonline.nl/subscriber/entry?entry=islam_COM-0168. Friedland thanks Nathan French for providing this source and the premodern political senses of both *umma* and *din*.

164. Andrew March, "Taking People As They Are: Islam As a 'Realistic Utopia' in the Political Theory of Sayyid Qutb," *American Political Science Review* 104 (2010): 189–207, esp. 203.

165. Nachman Ben-Yehuda, *Theocratic Democracy*, 17–18.

166. Ravitsky, *Messianism, Zionism, and Jewish Religious Radicalism*, chap. 2. For one widely reported instance in recent years, see Anshel Pfeffer, "Neturei Karta Welcomes Ahmadinejad," *Ha-aretz*, September 25, 2007, at *Haaretz.com*; accessed September 26, 2011.

167. Leon, *Harediut*; Nurit Stadler, *Yeshiva Fundamentalism: Piety, Gender, and Resistance in the Ultra-Orthodox World* (New York: New York University Press, 2009); Kimmy Caplan, *Be-sod ha-siah ha-haredi* (Jerusalem: Merkaz Zalman Shazar, 2007).

168. Stadler, *Yeshiva Fundamentalism*, 103–11.

169. We are indebted to Dr. Englander, a scholar of contemporary haredi and religious-Zionist Judaism, for his generous but sharp-eyed critique of an earlier version of these concluding thoughts and for his concrete suggestions (and countersuggestions) regarding haredi Jewry's (Jewries'?) relationship to Zionism and nationalism. The section that follows is much enriched by his arguments, but of course he in no way bears responsibility for its claims.

170. Shahar Ilan, *Haredim be-'e.m.: Ha-taktsivim, ha-hishtamtut u-remisat ha-hok* (Jerusalem: Keter, 2000); Ben-Yehuda, *Theocratic Democracy*, 202–3.

171. Thus, one study based on several bodies of data collected in the 1990s found that 70 percent of *haredim* showed intolerant attitudes toward Arab fellow-citizens as opposed to 34 perent of their nonharedi counterparts; Ilan, *Haredim be-'e.m.*, 59, citing Yohanan Peres and Efraim Yaar-Yuchtman, *Bein haskamah le-mahloket* (Jerusalem: Ha-Makhon ha-yisraeli le-demokratyah, 1998). A similar picture emerges from an unlooked-for haredi response to a 2002 public controversy over whether the ultra-nationalist and personally observant political activist Baruch Marzel should be denied the right to run for the Knesset (parliament) on a secular nationalist slate, on the grounds of his belonging previously to an ultra-right party, the *Kach* party, that had been declared illegal in 1988 due to its overt racism. As the sociologist Nachman Ben-Yehuda reports, "Lo and behold, the *Haredi* weekly *Hashavua* published in mid December 2002 a very large and positive review devoted to Baruch Marzel. It was highly unusual for a *Haredi* newspaper to devote any space to support a candidate for a non-Haredi party. Moreover, because whatever is published in that newspaper must clear haredi censorship, the implication is that this was not just a mistake of some free-spirited editor. Judging from a poll among the Haredi community in early December 2002, one can easily learn that Marzel enjoyed very significant popularity"; Ben-Yehuda, *Theocratic Democracy*, 203.

172. Ilan, *Haredim be-'e.m.*, 59, citing Peres and Yaar-Yuchtman, *Bein haskamah le-mahloket*.

173. Leon, *Harediut*, 50–51.

174. Yair Ettinger and Nir Hasson, "Shas Becomes the First Ultra-Orthodox Party to Join WZO," *Ha-aretz*, January 19, 2010, at *Haaretz.com*; accessed September 12, 2012.

175. Ibid.

176. Ravitsky, *Messianism, Zionism, and Jewish Religious Radicalism*, 200.

177. Ibid., chap. 5.

178. Ibid., 174.

179. Ibid., 200.

180. Here we might note the general tendency within early twentieth-century haredi circles to attack precisely this analogizing and normalizing element in Zionism. In a further wrinkle, even as the mainstream of haredi leaders anathematized the secular nationalist and secular Zionist argument that Jews are like other nations and/or should strive to be so, some haredi thinkers (albeit maverick ones) insisted that Jews *were* of course a *Volk*, but that the content of their nationhood

was unique and incomparable precisely in that it was wholly constituted by their unique receiving of a divine law intended only for them. On Breuer, see Matthias Morgenstern, *From Frankfurt to Jerusalem* (Leiden: Brill, 2002); on Birnbaum, see Nathan Birnbaum, *Gots Folk* (Berlin: Welt-Verlag, 1921), and the forthcoming study of Jess Olson. Our thanks to Akhmad Sahal for his stimulating thoughts on Breuer and nationalism.

181. Both citations drawn from Mendl Piekarz, *Hasidut Polin ben shte ha-milhamot u-ve-gezerot 1939–1945 ("ha-Shoah")* (Jerusalem: Mosad Bialik, 1997), 246.

182. Stadler, *Yeshiva Fundamentalism*, 107; Ilan, *Haredim be'e.m.*, 36.

183. Brubaker, "Religion and Nationalism," 22.

Contributors

Talal Asad was born in Saudi Arabia and educated in Britain. He now teaches anthropology at the Graduate Center of the City University of New York.

Jan Assmann is an emeritus professor of Egyptology at Heidelberg University and an honorary professor of cultural studies at the University of Constance. Among his recent publications in English are *Cultural Memory and Early Civilization* (2011), *Of God and Gods: Egypt, Israel, and the Rise of Monotheism* (2008), and *Religion and Cultural Memory: Ten Studies* (2006).

Christoph Auffarth is a professor of the study of religion (Religionswissenschaft) at Bremen University. His research focuses on early Greek religion in the context of the East. His PhD at Tübingen was on sacred kingship, creation, and asylum in the *Odyssey*; and his Habilitation was on polis-religion. He also holds a PhD in theology at Rijksuniversiteit Groningen on the eschatology of the crusaders in the Middle Ages. He edited the four volumes of *Metzler Lexikon Religion* (1999–2002; the English edition is the *Brill Dictionary of Religion,* ed. Kocku von Stuckrad 2006). His current research is on the religion of the Third Reich.

Loriliai Biernacki is an associate professor and the director of graduate studies in religious studies at the University of Colorado at Boulder. Her research interests include Hinduism, ethics, gender, and the interface between religion and science. Her first book, *Renowned Goddess of Desire: Women, Sex and Speech in Tantra* (Oxford, 2007), won the Kayden Award in 2008. She is coeditor of *God's Body: Panentheism across the World's Religious Traditions* (Oxford, 2013). She is currently working on a study and translation of a Sanskrit philosophical text by the eleventh-century Indian philosopher Abhinavagupta that addresses ideas of the body and the body-mind interface.

591

Jacqueline Borsje is a professor of medieval Irish culture and religion at the University of Ulster and a senior lecturer in the Cultural History of Christianity at the University of Amsterdam. Her research projects include words of power, cosmology, and mythology, fate, Christianization, evil, and monsters.

Daniel Boyarin is the Taubman Professor of Talmudic Culture in the Departments of Near Eastern Studies and Rhetoric at the University of California, Berkeley. Among his recent books are *The Jewish Gospels: The Story of the Jewish Christ* (2012), *Socrates and the Fat Rabbis* (2009), and *Border Lines: The Partition of Judaeo-Christianity* (2004).

Peter Burke was educated by the Jesuits and at St. John's College and St. Antony's College, Oxford. Burke was one of the first junior lecturers to be appointed at the University of Sussex, where he remained for seventeen years (1962–79), before moving to Cambridge, where he became a professor of Cultural History. He retired in 2004 but remains a Fellow of Emmanuel College and is also a Fellow of the British Academy, member of the Academia Europea, and PhD (honoris causa) from the universities of Lund, Copenhagen, Bucharest, and Zurich.

Markus Altena Davidsen is an assistant professor of religion at the Leiden Centre for the Study of Religion. He studied comparative religion at the University of Aarhus and wrote his MA thesis on Jediism. In 2014 Davidsen completed his PhD dissertation at Leiden University on new religious movements that base themselves on the fantasy works of J. R. R. Tolkien.

Tarek R. Dika is a postdoctoral fellow at the University of Michigan Society of Fellows and Assistant Professor of Comparative Literature at the University of Michigan. He is coeditor, with W. Chris Hackett, of *Quiet Powers of the Possible: Interviews in Contemporary French Phenomenology* (Fordham University Press, 2015).

Sergey Dolgopolski is an associate professor in the Department of Comparative Literature and the Institute of Jewish Thought and Heritage at the State University of New York at Buffalo. His recent books are *What Is Talmud? The Art of Disagreement* (Fordham University Press, 2009), and *The Open Past: Subjectivity and Remembering in the Talmud* (Fordham University Press, 2013). His research is at the intersection of rabbinic and philosophical thought.

Roger Friedland is a professor of religious studies and sociology at the University of California, Santa Barbara, and a visiting professor of Media, Culture, and Communication at New York University. Friedland is working on the institutional logics of love with John

Mohr, on the relation of religion and intimate life in Muslim-majority countries with Janet Afary, and on the status of the object in institutional logics with Diane-Laure Arjalies.

Ernst van den Hemel is a postdoctoral research fellow at the Center for the Humanties of Universiteit Utrecht. He completed his PhD at the University of Amsterdam as part of the project titled the Future of the Religious Past. His current research focuses on the postsecular and national identity. He teaches at the department of Religious Studies, Utrecht University. Van den Hemel is the secretary of the Foresight Committee Theology of Religious Studies of the Royal Dutch Academy of Sciences.

Laurens ten Kate holds degrees in theology and philosophy. His dissertation on Bataille's modern theory of the "sacred" (1994) was presented to the Catholic Theological University, Utrecht, where he taught philosophy of culture for several years. He publishes in the fields of Christian history and theology, art and literary theory, philosophy of culture, and religious studies. In 2001 he published *Flight of the Gods: Philosophical Perspectives on Negative Theology* in collaboration with Ilse N. Bulhof. Recently, he published as coordinating editor *Re-treating Religion: Deconstructing Christianity* with Jean-Luc Nancy (2012).

Ten Kate was acquiring editor of philosophy at Boom Publishers, Amsterdam, and senior researcher at the Faculty of Theology of the Free University of Amsterdam. He is currently an associate professor in the philosophy of religion and theology at the University of Humanities, Utrecht. He also teaches at the International School of Philosophy in Leusden, the Netherlands.

Michael Lambek is a professor of anthropology and the Canada Research Chair at the University of Toronto Scarborough. He has edited *Ordinary Ethics* and *A Companion to the Anthropology of Religion*, among many other works.

Karmen MacKendrick is a professor of philosophy and an associate chair of the McDevitt Center for Creativity and Innovation at Le Moyne College. Her work in philosophical theology is entangled with several other disciplines, particularly those involved with words, with flesh, or with the pleasures to be taken in both. These preoccupations appear in several books, most recently *Divine Enticement: Theological Seductions* (Fordham University Press, 2013).

Jean-Luc Marion is a professor of philosophy at the University of Paris-Sorbonne Paris IV and the John Nuveen Professor at the Divinity School and a professor in the Committee on Social Thought and the Department of Philosophy at the University of Chicago. Among his recent books to appear in English translation are *On the Ego and on God:*

Further Cartesian Questions (2007), *The Erotic Phenomenon* (2007), *Prolegomena to Charity* (2002), and *Being Given: Toward a Phenomenology of Givenness* (2002).

Arie L. Molendijk is a professor of the history of Christianity and philosophy at the University of Groningen. He has extensively published in the history of ideas, in particular on nineteenth- and twentieth-century theology, religious studies, and philosophy. Presently he is working on a book about one the most ambitious editorial projects of late Victorian Britain, Max Müller's huge edition of the *Sacred Books of the East* (50 vols., 1879–1910).

Kenneth B. Moss is the Felix Posen Associate Professor of Modern Jewish History at Johns Hopkins University. His book *Jewish Renaissance in the Russian Revolution* (Harvard University Press, 2009) examines the question of the autonomy of culture in Jewish nationalist praxis. He is currently researching Zionist and Jewish diasporist political thought in the 1930s.

Jean-Luc Nancy is the Distinguished Professor of Philosophy at the University Marc Bloch, Strasbourg. His many recent publications in English include *The Pleasure in Drawing* (2013), *Adoration: The Deconstruction of Christianity II* (2012), *The Truth of Democracy* (2010), and *Dis-Enclosure: The Deconstruction of Christiantiy* (2008).

Pieter Nanninga is a lecturer in the Department of Middle Eastern Studies at the University of Groningen, where he teaches on Islam and the modern Middle East. His research focuses on the jihadist movement, particularly on jihadist violence and the media. In 2014 he completed his PhD on jihadist suicide attacks and al-Sahab's martyrdom videos.

Nils F. Schott is the James M. Motley Postdoctoral Fellow in the Humanities at Johns Hopkins University. The author of *The Conversion of Knowledge*, he is the co-editor, with Hent de Vries, of *Love and Forgiveness for a More Just World* (Columbia University Press, 2015) as well as translator and co-editor, with Alexandre Lefebvre, of Vladimir Jankélévitch's *Henri Bergson*.

Asja Szafraniec teaches at Amsterdam University College. She is the author of *Beckett, Derrida, and the Event of Literature* (Stanford University Press, 2007), and of articles on the relation between continental and ordinary language philosophy, on the question of the specificity of the nature of philosophical discourse, and on the relation between philosophy and various forms of literary experiment. Her current research on the work of Stanley Cavell focuses on contemporary philosophy's response to the questions of skepticism, faith, and religion.

Elliot R. Wolfson holds the Marsha and Jay Glazer Endowed Chair in Jewish Studies in the Department of Religious Studies, University of California, Santa Barbara. His recent books include *Giving beyond the Gift: Apophasis and Overcoming Theomania* (2014), *A Dream Interpreted within a Dream: Oneiropoiesis and the Prism of Imagination* (2011), and *Open Secret: Postmessianic Messianism and the Mystical Revision of Menahem Mendel Schneerson* (2009).

The Future of the Religious Past
Hent de Vries, *General Editor*

Hent de Vries (ed.),
Religion: Beyond a Concept

Meerten B. ter Borg and Jan Willem van Henten (eds.),
Powers: Religion as a Social and Spiritual Force

Dick Houtman and Birgit Meyer (eds.),
Things: Religion and the Question of Materiality

Ernst van den Hemel and Asja Szafraniec (eds.),
Words: Religious Language Matters